Follow the Money

DUNCAN CAMPBELL-SMITH

Follow the Money

*The Audit Commission,
Public Money and the Management
of Public Services, 1983–2008*

ALLEN LANE
an imprint of
PENGUIN BOOKS

ALLEN LANE

Published by the Penguin Group
Penguin Books Ltd, 80 Strand, London WC2R ORL, England
Penguin Group (USA) Inc., 375 Hudson Street, New York, New York 10014, USA
Penguin Group (Canada), 90 Eglinton Avenue East, Suite 700, Toronto, Ontario, Canada M4P 2Y3
(a division of Pearson Penguin Canada Inc.)
Penguin Ireland, 25 St Stephen's Green, Dublin 2, Ireland
(a division of Penguin Books Ltd)
Penguin Group (Australia), 250 Camberwell Road, Camberwell, Victoria 3124, Australia
(a division of Pearson Australia Group Pty Ltd)
Penguin Books India Pvt Ltd, 11 Community Centre, Panchsheel Park, New Delhi – 110 017, India
Penguin Group (NZ), 67 Apollo Drive, Rosedale, North Shore 0632, New Zealand
(a division of Pearson New Zealand Ltd)
Penguin Books (South Africa) (Pty) Ltd, 24 Sturdee Avenue, Rosebank, Johannesburg 2196, South Africa

Penguin Books Ltd, Registered Offices: 80 Strand, London WC2R ORL, England

www.penguin.com

First published 2008
1

Copyright © Duncan Campbell-Smith, 2008

Set in 10.5/14 pt PostScript Linotype Sabon
Typeset by Rowland Phototypesetting Ltd, Bury St Edmunds, Suffolk
Printed in England by Clays Ltd, St Ives plc

ISBN: 978-1-846-14068-6

www.greenpenguin.co.uk

Contents

CONTENTS

CONTENTS

CONTENTS

Illustrations

1. Senior auditors gathered at a District Audit Service dinner in March 1938
2. Michael Heseltine, newly installed as secretary of state in May 1979 (Hulton Archive/Getty Images)
3. The first chairman of the Audit Commission, John Read (Hemming Group Ltd)
4. The front page of the *Local Government Chronicle*, 31 March 1983 (Adam Smith)
5. John Banham behind his desk as the first controller of the Commission (Hemming Group Ltd)
6. A cartoon depicting the changing face of public audit, before and after 1983 (Claire Blackman)
7. A typically ingenious chart, on the cost to local councils of brown envelopes (Audit Commission)
8. How the first controller depicted the forces giving rise to an urban underclass (Audit Commission)
9. David Cooksey, chairman of the Commission from 1986 to 1995 (Audit Commission)
10. Howard Davies, controller of the Commission from 1987 to 1992 (Hemming Group Ltd)
11. Leaders of the so-called Loony Left on the streets of Liverpool, March 1984 (*Liverpool Echo*)
12. Cliff Nicholson, deputy controller and operations director from 1983 to 1991
13. Peter Brokenshire, the acting controller of the Commission for the second half of 1992

ILLUSTRATIONS

14. Andrew Foster, who became controller in 1993 and served for ten years (Audit Commission)
15. A scoop for the *Guardian* on a Commission report into the police, October 1995 (*Guardian*)
16. The building at 1 Vincent Square occupied by the Commission until 2004 (Duncan Campbell-Smith)
17. Shirley Porter announces her appeal against charges of wilful misconduct (Philip Wolmuth)
18. The Westminster auditor, John Magill, outside the High Court in March 1997 (PA Photos)
19. The third chairman, Roger Brooke, with Andrew Foster at 1 Vincent Square (Hemming Group Ltd)
20. Hilary Armstrong, Labour's minister for local government from 1997 to 2001 (Hemming Group Ltd)
21. Helena Shovelton, who joined the Commission in 1995 and chaired it for three years from 1998 to 2001 (bill@MackenziePhoto)
22. Wendy Thomson, who set up the Commission's inspectorate between 1999 and 2001 (Audit Commission)
23. Nick Raynsford, minister for local and regional government from 2001 to 2005 (Getty Images)
24. Adrienne Fresko, who was acting chair for almost a year from December 2001 (Audit Commission)
25. A cartoon of Paul Kirby, creator of the Comprehensive Performance Assessment (James Parker)
26. James Strachan, chairman from the end of 2002 to the start of 2006 (Mark Wohlwender/Hemming Group Ltd)
27. Michael Lyons, deputy chairman under Strachan and acting chair in 2006 (Mark Wohlwender/Hemming Group Ltd)
28. Steve Bundred, holder of the retitled chief executive role since September 2003 (Audit Commission)
29. A selection of the Commission's reports since its earliest days (Audit Commission)
30. Michael O'Higgins, the chairman of the Commission since September 2006 (Mark Wohlwender/Hemming Group Ltd)
31. Millbank Tower, home to the Audit Commission since August 2004 (PA Pictures)

Foreword

Why isn't it better? That is the question which sooner or later hits every student of British government between the eyes with the force of a well-swung halibut. Here is one of the oldest and best-established parliamentary democracies in the world, comparatively rich and stable, whose state and municipal bureaucracy has been the subject of waves of reforms from Victorian times to the present day, led by bright, well-educated, diligent and uncorrupted public servants ... yet the prisons are more often than not overcrowded and dangerous, the public housing is too meagre and squalid to accommodate decently those who need it, the schools struggle to attain standards expected across the rest of Europe, and the National Health Service – that recipient of vast public affection and vaster still tax-levied income – cannot satisfy demand. Whose fault is this?

At Westminster, covered daily by a special squad of full-time journalists, the elected political classes blame each other and recommend new legislation to improve things. The public is sold a model of the world in which the NHS, for example, would be a gleaming national success story were it not for the callous and ignorant high-handedness of market-obsessed Conservatives or, alternatively, the sentimental Stalinism of unreformed socialists. 'Government' is reduced to a hatchet-duel of received opinions in the House of Commons, where success is measured by votes won and bills passed, not by the daily reality of well-administered services in distant suburbs. And much the same happens at local level, except that there the relative lack of power and accountability has produced such apathy that any reporting is meagre.

In recent years most reform-minded observers have concluded that the essence of the problem is an over-centralized, over-interventionist state apparatus, and that the best way of improving public services is radically to devolve power back to the very same boroughs, counties, hospital areas and schools from whence it was sucked during the twentieth century. Only then, perhaps, might we see again the practical transformations in education, town planning, hospital building and amenities that the Victorians of Chamberlain's Birmingham or the Edwardians of LCC-dominated London came to take for granted. After more than a decade of New Labour government, and after the centralizing changes of the Conservative administrations of Margaret Thatcher and John Major, this is the mood of the times. It is heard from David Cameron's opposition and it echoes inside Whitehall, too. Right at the end of this monumental and revelatory history, Duncan Campbell-Smith launches the Audit Commission in the same direction.

Yet his book is in itself another kind of answer to that question – why isn't it better? He plunges deep in tracing the recent history of that greater part of the job of government which is rarely talked about at Westminster and barely mentioned in the media, yet which is utterly essential to well-organized modern life. What happens after the legislation has passed, the dust has settled and the politicians have moved on? How do you actually make a council, or a health authority, improve in the hundred small ways which, to the rest of us, may make the difference between a successful minor operation and a life-threatening infection, or living in a clean housing estate as opposed to a dangerous, damp-infested modern slum? After the crisp-sounding headlines and the rousing political prose, where are the levers, inducements, measurements and encouragement that translate aspiration into achievement, in offices, streets, police stations and so on? In short, after you've spoken, how do you do? Here we find the seven-eighths of the iceberg that doesn't gleam brightly but tends to sink the ship.

There are titanic tales in this book, ranging from the struggle to bring to account the 'Loony Left' councils of the 1980s and Shirley Porter's Westminster regime, selling off cemeteries for pennies and attempting to use housing policy as a form of gerrymandering, through to the fascinating (and new to me) story of how apolitical auditors, aghast at the proposed poll tax, tried to rescue Margaret

Thatcher from herself, and failed. Some of the individual episodes recounted here are less familiar today but were potentially devastating in their time, notably the rescue of Hammersmith council from its incredibly dangerous entanglements with the global derivatives markets. In these pages, you will find some very well-known characters, from Michael Heseltine, the true originator of the Audit Commission, to Michael Lyons, now chairman of the BBC Trust and recently inquirer-in-chief for Gordon Brown. Alongside them is a range of strong characters running the Audit Commission itself, from the outspoken and publicity-minded John Banham, through the politically well-connected, colourful and radical Howard Davies, to later characters, less colourful but highly effective, such as Andrew Foster. This being, in essence, an institutional history, there is plenty of office politics too, culminating in what the author calls the Audit Commission's 'annus horribilis' and the emergence in 2000 of inspectors to work in parallel with time-honoured auditors.

But the essence of the story of the Commission is really a 25-year debate about the meaning of audit, and how to achieve better government for the country. It takes us from the early days of painstaking box-ticking and column-counting by the copperplate nib-wielding accountants of old, to the growing idea that audit should involve looking at the effectiveness of systems and policies. If this seems obvious now, it was much resented in the early days of the Audit Commission and, as Duncan Campbell-Smith points out, has made councils subject to far more invasive and independent appraisals than most companies listed on the stock market would tolerate. The difference between councils and companies, to quote perhaps the best epigram in this book, is that 'Private businesses do something with a view to making money; but public bodies spend money with a view to doing something.' As the meaning of audit widened, individuals from some distinctly non-municipal backgrounds – and especially from the McKinsey culture – spread their influence and the range of the Audit Commission grew apace. On the way, plenty of mistakes were made and there were moments when the future of the Commission seemed to hang by a thread. Yet, enjoying (if that is the word) a higher profile than its central-government sister, the National Audit Office, the Commission established itself as one of the most trusted and enthusiastically exploited weapons in the armoury of intelligent ministers.

This caused problems, of course. Under New Labour, the command-and-control enthusiasms of ministers embroiled the Audit Commission in what became a mind-dazzlingly complex array of targets. This culminated in the 'Best Value' comedy, when inspectors were scurrying round the country measuring ludicrously small things at inordinate length – everything from pest-control services to public toilets in Scarborough. As a caricature of an overweening centre which had become deluded into thinking it could run everything, this takes some beating.

But this is much more than a morality tale for localists. Not only did the Commission survive the excesses imposed by its political masters, and thrive, but it built up an impressive range of real achievements to look back on. This is not just a story about budgets, waste, the law, or the behaviour of freeloading councillors in Doncaster. It is also about the attempt to use numbers and comparisons to improve the lives of everyone from rough sleepers and victims of crime to prosperous but frightened heart-attack victims. Duncan Campbell-Smith has shone a light on a major part of the story of modern British governance that has been almost completely ignored by political writers. By its nature, it is not a light, easy read but this is an important subject, not an easy one. Thanks to this painstaking, comprehensive account, nobody will ever again be able to answer that question – 'Why isn't it better?' – without addressing the achievements and failures of the Audit Commission.

Andrew Marr

Sources and Acknowledgements

I would first of all like to thank the present chief executive of the Audit Commission, Steve Bundred, and his colleagues on the Board of the Commission for committing themselves to an authorized history without seeking to exercise editorial control. Their support gave me access to a wide pool of interviewees, including many past and present employees of the Commission whose personal recollections comprised an essential source for the book. I talked, in several cases more than once, to seventy people over the course of nine months. The interviews, most of them lasting a full couple of hours and a good few rather longer than that, were conducted under the Chatham House rule and produced a rich trawl of detailed memories. Relying heavily upon such material has not been without its dangers, of course. But I hope readers will feel the outcome is a balanced account, corroborated and amplified wherever possible from other primary and secondary sources. Direct quotes from the interviews are generally introduced with 'He/she recalled . . .', and have all been agreed with those responsible for them.

I am extremely grateful to the following interviewees, for their time and patience: Hilary Armstrong, John Banham, Mike Barnes, Jeremy Beecham, Mollie Bickerstaff, Greg Birdseye, Jonty Boyce, Peter Brokenshire, Roger Brooke, Sandy Bruce-Lockhart, Steve Bundred, Bill Butler, Tony Child, Bob Chilton, David Cooksey, Michael Dallas, Gareth Davies, Howard Davies, Ruth Davison, Doug Edmonds, Derek Elliott, Martin Evans, Steve Evans, Charlie Fisher, Kate Flannery, Andrew Foster, Adrienne Fresko, Gill Green, Jenny Grey, Roger Hamilton, Terry Hanafin, Terry Heiser, David Henderson-Stewart, Noel Hepworth, Michael Heseltine, Chris Hurford, Roy Irwin, Roger

Jarman, Ian Kennedy, Peter Kimmance, Neil Kinghan, Paul Kirby, Tom Legg, Trish Longdon, Michael Lyons, John Magill, Mavis McDonald, Andy McKeon, Martin McNeill, Jim McWhirr, Cliff Nicholson, Michael O'Higgins, Jeremy Orme, Kash Pandya, David Prince, Nick Raynsford, Geoffrey Rendle, the late Roy Shaw, Helena Shovelton, Brian Skinner, Peter Smith, James Strachan, Peter Thomas, Wendy Thomson, Tony Travers, Ross Tristem, Chris White, Harry Wilkinson, Peter Wilkinson and Peter Yetzes. There are many other individuals who played a very significant part in the Commission's history and whose recollections would undoubtedly have been valuable: their omission is only a reflection of my own poor planning, for which I hope they will forgive me. It will also be apparent from this list that I have omitted all titles. So many of the people mentioned in this book acquired titles during the course of the story that appending them appropriately would have been tiresome for the reader and often distracting. I hope it will not cause any offence that I have therefore avoided the use of titles throughout.

Personal recollections have been especially important in the absence of any significant historical records within the Commission. It handles an astonishing volume of papers for an organization of its relatively modest size – in 2007 it had over 13 million electronic documents on its data network – and it retains an archive large enough today to fill 34,000 carton boxes. But most of their contents comprise audit records, held for legal purposes, and no index has been kept to other, non-audit documents. The result, anyway, is that most of the Commission's own confidential papers – aside from its Minutes Book, with a record of the Commission members' monthly meetings since February 1983 – have been impossible to trace and may no longer survive. In these circumstances, I am especially indebted to those interviewees who also lent me documents in their own safe keeping. Harry Wilkinson turned up for our interview session with a small suitcase of papers that included the earliest Board papers submitted by John Banham – with the first controller's initial blueprints for the detailed workings of the Commission – and a set of copies of the Commission's internal newsletter, *Audit News*, covering many of the months between 1983 and 1987. Helena Shovelton kindly made available three dozen files with all of the Board papers for the difficult years of her chairmanship from 1998 to 2001, as well as a number of national reports from a handsome collection that she has retained. Derek Elliott lent me various court filings and public interest reports from the 1990s, as well as papers on the battle against fraud that has been his passion for so many years. James Strachan provided copies of his past speeches and press articles that helped me track the changing direction of the Commission in 2003–05. Other miscellaneous papers were lent to me by Mike Barnes, Bill Butler, Adrienne Fresko, Jim McWhirr, Geoffrey Rendle and Peter Wilkinson. Above all, Howard Davies came up with a set of file notes relating to his meetings and discussions between February 1987 and July 1991, which were dictated by him on the same day or very shortly afterwards. This valuable and often entertaining collection of 128 individual items by the second controller of the Commission is referred to throughout as the Davies Papers.

Many past and present members or executives of the Commission were kind enough to read early drafts of the history, in whole or part, and all offered important amendments. I would like to thank the following for helping me well beyond the interview stage: John Banham, Mike Barnes, Steve Bundred, Bill Butler, Tony Child, Howard Davies, Derek Elliott, Kate Flannery, Andrew Foster, Roger Hamilton, Cliff Nicholson, David Prince, Helena Shovelton, James Strachan, Peter Thomas, Ross Tristem and Harry Wilkinson. Special thanks are due to Jonty Boyce, who clarified many points about the structure and operations of the National Health Service through the 1990s; Jeremy Orme, who took enormous trouble to clarify for me the singular nature of the auditor's role in the public sector; Peter Wilkinson, who in addition to sharing his own long experience of working at all levels of the Commission also read drafts of the book, correcting many errors and alerting me to important themes I had missed or misconstrued; and Martin McNeill, who read every chapter with meticulous care, pointing out structural and stylistic infelicities as well as factual errors with a forensic thoroughness.

Beyond the Commission itself, I must thank several other individuals for their help. John Magill, the former auditor to the Westminster City Council and scourge of those eventually found guilty at Westminster of abusing their political powers, read successive drafts of the book's passages on that episode and offered a series of amendments with an eye for detail that the years have done nothing to dim. The Commission's in-house solicitor from 1987 to 1995, Tony Child, also provided documents with key arguments and court rulings on the Westminster case – and on the Hammersmith and Fulham case, too – which were a huge help to me in navigating the complexities of the Commission's biggest legal battles. I am indebted to the former permanent secretary Mavis McDonald and the writer and academic Rudolf Klein for sparing the time to read and comment on a late draft. And in the later stages of my work on the book, Tony Travers and Malcolm Dean generously shared with me their reflections on the Commission's story to date and its overall impact on the public sector. For the views finally expressed in the book, of course, I alone bear full responsibility.

Several individuals assisted me in the course of their work for the Commission and I would like to thank all of them here. Supported by Bethan Waters, Stuart Reid in particular gave me invaluable support, especially in clearing the use of direct quotes with my interviewees and in preparing the appendices and illustrations. Charlie Fisher, Gareth Sully and Paul Dodd assisted with design work for the cover and illustrations. In the library at Nicholson House in Bristol, Ann Cox and Dawn Witherden helped me to retrieve many reports and papers, and Julie Robinson tracked down a large number of periodical articles on my behalf. Fiona Coton scheduled many of my interviews and coped with occasional pleas for help in averting word-processing disasters. The interview tapes were expertly transcribed by Nicki Brown and Cat Taylor, whose invariably cheery response to some ridiculous deadlines was always much appreciated, and I am also much indebted to Janet Tyrrell for her wonderfully patient copy-editing skills. I am very grateful to Stuart Proffitt at Penguin for his encouragement en route and editorial suggestions as the book neared its destination. Finally, it is no formality to say it would never have arrived without the support of my wife Anne-Catherine. This book is dedicated to her, and to our sons Henry, Charlie and Jimmy for their stoic acceptance of the fact that, for well over a year, there was a hermit in the house.

Abbreviations

ACC	Association of County Councils
ACiW	Audit Commission in Wales
ACMT	Audit Commission Management Team
ACPO	Association of Chief Police Officers
ADA	Assistant District Auditor
ADC	Association of District Councils
AHP	Acute Hospital Portfolio
ALA	Association of London Authorities
ALMO	Arm's-Length Management Organization
AMA	Association of Metropolitan Authorities
AVU	Added Value Unit
BRI	Bristol Royal Infirmary
BV(PP/R)	Best Value (Performance Plan/Review)
BVIS	Best Value Inspectorate Service
CAA	Comprehensive Area Assessment
CBI	Confederation of British Industry
CCT	Compulsory Competitive Tendering
CHAI	Commission for Healthcare Audit and Inspection
CHI	Commission for Health Improvement
CIA	Chief Inspector of Audit
CIPFA	Chartered Institute of Public Finance and Accountancy
COAP	Code of Audit Practice
CPA	Comprehensive Performance Assessment
CSCI	Commission for Social Care Inspection
DA	District Audit (or district auditor, according to context)

DAS	District Audit Service
DCLG	Department for Communities and Local Government (commonly shortened to CLG)
DDA	Deputy District Auditor
Defra	Department for Environment, Food and Rural Affairs
DETR	Department of the Environment, Transport and the Regions
DfES	Department for Education and Skills
DHA	District Health Authority
DHSS	Department of Health and Social Security
DLO	Direct Labour Organization
DoE	Department of the Environment
DoH	Department of Health
DTLR	Department for Transport, Local Government and the Regions
FB4	DHSS unit responsible for audit of the NHS prior to 1990
FMPR	*Financial Management and Policy Review*
FT	Foundation Trust
GLA	Greater London Authority
GLC	Greater London Council
HA	Housing Association
HC	Housing Corporation
HMIC	Her Majesty's Inspectorate of Constabulary
HMIP	Her Majesty's Inspectorate of Prisons
HR	Human Resources
ICAEW	Institute of Chartered Accountants in England and Wales
IDeA	Improvement and Development Agency
ILEA	Inner London Education Authority
INLOGOV	Institute of Local Government Studies
KPI	Key Performance Indicator
LA	Local Authority
LAMSAC	Local Authorities Management Services Advisory Committee
LEA	Local Education Authority

LGA	Local Government Association
LGC	*Local Government Chronicle*
LGCE	Local Government Commission for England
LGORU	Local Government Operational Research Unit
MAD	Management Arrangements Diagnostic
MSBU	Management Services Business Unit
NAO	National Audit Office
NFI	National Fraud Initiative
NHS	National Health Service
NICE	National Institute for Health and Clinical Excellence
ODPM	Office of the Deputy Prime Minister
Ofsted	Office for Standards in Education
OPSR	Office for Public Sector Reform
OR	Operational Research
PAC	Public Accounts Committee
PCT	Primary Care Trust
PFI	Private Finance Initiative
PI	Performance Indicator
PRS	Policy, Research and Studies
PSA	Public Service Agreement
PSR	Public Services Research
QA	Quality Assurance
QCR	Quality Control Review
RD	Regional Director
RICS	Royal Institute of Chartered Surveyors
ROSS	Refuse Operations System Simulation
SADA	Senior Assistant District Auditor
SOLACE	Society of Local Authority Chief Executives
SSA	Standard Spending Assessment
SSI	Social Services Inspectorate
VFM	Value for Money
WAG	Welsh Assembly Government

Introduction

In response to idle inquiries about the subject of this book, the author learned long before its completion that almost *any* answer including the word 'audit' or 'auditors' – or even, sad to say, the words 'council' or 'local government' – could generally be relied on to prompt a glazed eye and rapid change of topic. So why a whole book devoted to the Audit Commission? The case for an 'institutional biography' of such a little-understood body is easily summarized. It has pulled off some remarkable, yet mostly unremarked, feats over the past twenty-five years. Tracing the story of the Commission offers a revealing glimpse of Whitehall and town hall at work through a period of extraordinary changes. It is also the tale of a hybrid organization, set up to combine an innovative and highly creative culture on the one hand with a by-the-book quasi-regulatory culture on the other. That was never to be the recipe for a dull bureaucracy.

The Audit Commission has been a pioneer, in ways that seem almost to have been taken for granted in Britain even while being widely acclaimed overseas. It has also found itself at the centre of an often bitter controversy over the impact of an indisputable drift towards centralized government. Many commentators have blamed this greater centralization in Britain for a corrosion both of local democracy and of the integrity of the professional classes working in the public sector. Some among them have eyed the Commission as one of the arch-culprits. The reality that emerges in this book is much more complicated. Arguably the Commission has been guilty on occasions of acting naively. But to see it simply as a vehicle of centralization would be to stand the story on its head. The Commission was driven from the outset by a fierce belief in the need to lift the public sector's performance, not least to buttress it against the encroachments of central government. How this stance has shifted to and fro over the years, in response to increasingly directive government policies, is a key theme of the book.

The Commission was established a quarter of a century ago, during Margaret Thatcher's first administration, thanks entirely to the drive of one of the very few effective government ministers in recent times to have enjoyed a successful career in business, Michael Heseltine. He had learned from his business life that structures and processes can be as important as strategy and policy. It gave him a natural interest in the machinery of government – which always rather bored Margaret Thatcher, as it did Tony Blair later – and he was ready to take an inventive approach. As secretary of state at the Department of the Environment, he wanted to find new ways of opening up the public sector to the disciplines of the private market. In one of several initiatives to this end, he took up an esoteric branch of officialdom, staffed by 'district auditors' and essentially responsible for probity in the local government of England and Wales. Then he rewrote their rule-book, opened up their franchise to competitors from the private sector (whose access to date, while established since 1972, had in practice been problematic) and created a new body to preside over them. This was the Audit Commission, comprising sixteen non-executive commissioners drawn from across the political spectrum and both sides of the public/private divide.

Heseltine endowed the Commission with the political equivalent of three magic powers. First, it could turn its hand just like a private sector consultancy to any analysis of the public sector beyond Westminster that, in its own view, might further the cause of better management. Second, it could take the traditional notion of auditing and add one novel twist scarcely applied anywhere before 1983 (and even now untested anywhere in the private sector, though it is much discussed): public bodies within its franchise would be audited by genuinely autonomous auditors – appointed and coordinated by the Commission itself, and answerable only to the public and the courts rather than to their 'client' bodies in the field. And third, it could operate within Whitehall while remaining entirely outside the civil service, with an independent status that even included a licence to publish unsolicited critiques of the impact 'on economy, efficiency and effectiveness in the provision of local authority services' of any statute, or 'any directions or guidance given by a Minister of the Crown'.[1] The consequences of Heseltine's boldness soon outran anything anticipated by his colleagues in government or their officials. The impact on public life in Britain has been profound, and often quite surprising.

CONSULTANCY POWER

Take first its remit to roam as a consultant. Crucially, Heseltine in 1983 chose as the first executive head of the Commission (its 'controller') a successful alumnus of a private sector organization with a formidably disciplined approach to the analysis of managerial problems in any context – McKinsey. This was John Banham, and over the next four years he proved an inspired choice. Banham saw immediately the opportunity to shape a role for the Commission as a very special kind of management consultancy. By taking the existing field force of auditors, with all their local knowledge and networks, and harnessing it to a freshly recruited central staff, most of them with backgrounds in operational research, he built a Commission that functioned as a sort of McKinsey-plus in the public sector. And after his departure, a second ex-McKinsey man, Howard Davies, continued and refined the process for a further five years.*

Banham and Davies built a powerful business model that owed more than a little to the tool kit that both men had mastered during service with their previous employer. Data gathered from all over England and Wales would be used for robustly evidence-based analysis of any facet of local government. A national report on each topic would present arguments and conclusions based on comparative data from across the country, presented with state-of-the-art graphics to make even the most esoteric statistics accessible to all. Guides would

---

* Readers inclined to conspiracy theories will not be surprised to learn that the author himself once worked for McKinsey, too. But there is plenty of evidence to betray several conspiracies behind the Commission, led by various bodies from the Treasury and the National Coal Board to Merton College, Oxford.

then be prepared for use by auditors at a local level, enabling them to pursue improvements with the audited bodies under their charge, relating the local performance back to the national picture. Nothing quite like this had ever happened before in the public sector. By instilling quasi-commercial disciplines and positioning public services as goods in a quasi-marketplace with citizens as the end-purchasers, it caught the essence of what came to be known as New Public Management. The impact achieved by the Commission between 1983 and 1989 was sufficiently impressive for its role then to be extended into the NHS, much to the displeasure of officials within the Department of Health. This, perversely, was a fair measure of the way that it was by then starting to change the landscape of government.

Through twenty-five years, the Commission has issued more than 250 national reports. These have been at the forefront of a prodigious publishing programme that has also extended to a wide range of Occasional Papers, Police Papers, Management Papers and Hand-books, Executive Briefings and Bulletins (for a list of most of the titles, see Appendix 1). The early reports usually examined the management of specific tasks, some of them gloriously mundane like the purchase of council supplies or the collection of ratepayers' rubbish bins. By the end of the 1980s, many were exploring far more complex topics such as the management of the probation service or the handling of community care for elderly people. By the end of the 1990s, with many of the easiest targets gone and the bar pitched ever higher – not least because councils were responding to their recommendations – the reports were increasingly looking into systemic weaknesses im-peding the delivery of public services. There is probably much in the resulting bibliography that can still be read profitably today – and the publication of national reports remains a vital dimension of the Commission's activities.

Capturing the essence of these reports within the confines of a narrative history has been a challenge. It was never going to be possible to do their contents real justice: many responded to complex situ-ations, and the background alone would in most cases have required a long digression from the narrative. On the other hand, any proper appreciation of the Commission would be impossible without some grasp of what the best reports contained. With no claim to consistency, the text therefore refers fleetingly to many while lingering for longer on some of more intrinsic interest. These include, for example, reports on the state of the social services in 1986 (*Making a Reality of Community Care*), on the case in 1990 for a revolution in the use of day surgery for NHS patients (*A Short Cut to Better Services*), on the need in 1996 to rethink the basic strategy behind the deployment of police officers in the community (*Streetwise: Effective Police Patrol*) and evidence that same year of disturbing trends across the whole of the youth justice system (*Misspent Youth*). All report references are noted in their own index.

Over the years the Commission has managed to make a happy habit of publishing timely reports on topics of acute interest to politicians as well as professional interest groups, and many have had an enormous influence that is also an important part of the story. At the most obvious level, reports and papers from the Commission have helped to trigger direct changes in whatever unlit corner of the public sector they exposed to an unaccustomed light. Within a few years of the publication of *A Short Cut*, for example, some minor operations hitherto involving overnight stays in hospital were being routinely handled by the NHS as day-surgery cases. More broadly, a string of reports within one sector could help elicit a seminal change in working practices across the whole of that sector. By the early 1990s, it was already apparent that a succession of papers on the need for more professionalism in the running of local councils had made a telling impact on the way that local government in general conducted its affairs. By the end of the 1990s, ten years after a cagey start, many senior police officers and their counterparts in the Home Office were happy to acknowledge that they owed a similar debt to the Commission, for the work it had contributed to the modernization of the police service. (Another institution that was arguably changed in a radical fashion by the Commission, though it was most certainly never the subject of a Commission publication, was the National Audit Office. Set up in the same year as the Commission, but reporting directly to Parliament – its head, the comptroller and auditor-general, is an officer of the House of Commons – the NAO was given a broadly parallel remit for auditing the departments and agencies of *central* government. From the start, it too produced national reports – but their style and content in the 1980s were soon made to look almost Ruritanian by comparison with the Commission's and a rapid catch-up was required.)

Auditors and analysts, with sharp pencils and disarmingly basic questions, were at first no more welcome inside hospitals than in police stations. But close cooperation with the Royal Colleges and the leaders of the medical profession produced a small library of powerful reports in the decade after the NHS was added to the Commission's audit franchise in 1990. These helped to change attitudes within the NHS to dozens of topics, from the prevention of coronary heart disease to the management of beds, records and medicines. In 2002, the government transferred one of the Commission's central duties within the health sector, the preparation of national reports, to a new body. After years of steady expansion, it was a rare diminution of the Commission's franchise and marked another stage in the restructuring of public services that has been such a constant feature of life under New Labour since 1997. But, in recent years, the influence of the Commission in the health service has grown again, as attention has come to focus increasingly on standards of financial management within the NHS.

At the most general level, the Commission's approach could fairly be said to have contributed significantly to the way that the analysis and management of the public sector were brought into line with their counterparts in the business world. Of course this was a wider phenomenon. By the end of the 1980s, with new technology trans-forming the presentational arts, it was increasingly evident that a powerfully written national report could change people's views of the world. Privately funded think-tanks and publicly funded inspectorates sprouted up on all sides. It would be absurd to attribute their prolifera-tion to the Commission alone. But they first emerged in response to an appetite that the Commission's publications had undoubtedly done much to nurture. And by the time that Whitehall came to review ways of appraising its own performance, after 2005, the 'Comprehen-sive Performance Assessment' designed by the Commission for local government was openly acknowledged as a model for the appraisal of state departments. (The notion that they might be answerable to anyone other than their ministers and Parliament would have struck an odd note twenty years earlier – another sign of broad changes for which the Commission has arguably been a potent catalyst.)

AUDITING POWER

The second of the Commission's mould-breaking powers has enabled it to pull off the implementation of an auditing concept generally regarded until 1983 as an ideal too perfect for attainment. The principles of both public and private audit decree that the power to hire and fire auditors should be independent of the bodies – municipal or corporate – that are the subject of audit. The *private* sector has had difficulty achieving this, whether in Britain or anywhere else. No stock exchange, for example, has ever tried to impose external auditors on the companies whose shares are traded under its umbrella, though this would be a logical step. Instead, shareholders vote to appoint or dismiss auditors, who formally report to them. In practice, as anyone will know who has ever attended an annual general meeting of a large public company, the auditors are effectively selected for the job by directors of the company and their remuneration is overseen by those directors. In the public sector, similarly, there was not much emphasis before 1983 on the separateness of district auditors. Though their integrity was very widely respected, and seldom if ever seriously impugned, individual auditors often worked so closely with their audited bodies over so many years as to be almost part of the municipal family. Indeed, this was one of the features of the local government system that persuaded Michael Heseltine to go for a new and far more rigorous approach.

Hence Heseltine's enthusiasm for the Commission, and its statutory responsibility for the appointment of auditors. For twenty-five years, the Commission has called upon a pool of audit firms comprising a number of private sector partnerships as well as the legacy body of district auditors (which has always been a separate conceptual entity, though it was only between 1994 and 2002 that it was actually run as an arm's-length agency). In financial terms, the Commission has 'purchased' audits from this pool and has 'resold' the audits to audited bodies – building a mark-up into the process, by which it has generated the cash to pay for its national report work and other publications. In so doing, the Commission has taken the 'purchaser/provider' concept that was central to Margaret Thatcher's reforming agenda all through the 1980s, and fashioned a derivative version for the special circumstances of the world of public audit. And, in the process, it has assured the auditors under its aegis of a robust independence. (The auditors and the central institution are often collectively referred to in this book as 'the Commission', where it would be pedantic to keep distinguishing between them and the distinction is not pertinent. Most importantly, though, the auditors have acted always as individuals with their own statutory responsibilities – or as representatives of private firms with their own joint and several liabilities – and they are identified separately from the Commission where the context duly demands it.)

The conspicuous independence of its auditors from their audited bodies has many times underpinned the effectiveness of the Commission as a policeman of the public sector. Sometimes this role has pushed it into the limelight. It had to confront the leaders of the so-called Loony Left in the 1980s, taking a firm stand against them in Liverpool and Lambeth – but treading with great care thereafter, to pre-empt what might arguably have become a full-blown constitutional crisis between central and local government under Margaret Thatcher. It is legitimate to wonder – given the animus against it within the Thatcher cabinet – whether local government in its historical form would have survived such a crisis. How it might have ended for the Thatcher government itself, but for the Commission's involvement, is probably just as hard to say. (The Commission was given no real opportunity to pull off a second rescue over the poll tax, though it cannot be faulted for not trying.)

Again, later in the 1980s, the Commission and one of its appointed auditors had to deal with the potential financial implosion of a London borough council. Hammersmith and Fulham had entered into a complex web of financial contracts with the international banking community which at one point threatened to expose *each citizen* of the borough to a bill for several thousand pounds. Without the Commission on hand, to flush out the crisis in the first place and to provide critical legal assistance to the auditor tasked with steering it to a safe resolution, English local government might easily have been lured into a much more extensive engagement with the global derivatives markets in the 1990s that could have had calamitous consequences. And no history of the Commission would be complete without its own account of the scandal at Westminster City Council, where an appointed auditor (again from a private firm, ironically, as at Hammersmith) had to toil through much of the 1990s on an investigation into a blatant misuse of public power by the country's flagship Tory council under Shirley Porter. In all these cases, and many other less egregious episodes, the Commission came under intense and often hostile scrutiny from all those who would have preferred to see auditors in the public sector taking a less inconvenient line. It stood its ground, as did the auditors, and the campaign medals were earned.

It is not just their stubborn independence, though, that has marked out the Commission's auditors as a rare species over this quarter-century. In reorganizing the audit function under the direction of the Commission, Michael Heseltine wanted to shake up the district auditors because he was ambitious for them to do much more than watch over the probity of local authorities' accounts. He also envisaged a much expanded role for private firms. In the event, Heseltine found himself pushing on an open door – and there proved to be less scope than imagined for the private firms to sweep in as new brooms – because the district auditors themselves had been keen for many years to widen their own remit beyond the 'regularity' work of checking that the accounts complied with the law. That remit has gone on widening ever since.

Here another striking distinction needs to be flagged between the private and public sectors. Private businesses do something with a view to making money; but public bodies spend money with a view to doing something. The key measure of a private business's activities is the 'money' outcome and the key to this is a set of financial statements – hence the importance attached to all the conventions governing those statements, and to the question that must be answered by the auditor: do they give a 'true and fair' view of what has been going on? But the key measure of a public body's activities must focus on the substance of 'non-money' outputs: given the expenditure recorded on, say, social services or highway maintenance or public museums, has the audited body, in the words of the relevant statute, 'made proper arrangements for securing economy, efficiency and effectiveness in its use of resources'?[2] Hence the greater scope for stretching the public auditors' remit. Even in the policeman role, auditors can be required to go in pursuit of the 'three Es' as well as their regularity agenda. But the three Es have *always* been central to the 'value-for-money' (VFM) agenda that has defined their consultant role. And of course the pursuit of VFM has been a constant theme of the Commission's reports – which is why the business model devised by Banham and his colleagues, built round investigative studies, was such an ingenious response to the divergent statutory duties laid on the Commission at the outset.

Much ink has been spilled over the years on the relative importance of regularity work on the one hand and of VFM on the other. Commentaries from time to time on the performance of the Commission have regularly questioned the balance between the policeman and consultant roles, too, and even their ultimate compatibility. In practice, though – given the importance of the three Es to both – they have always overlapped. Straightening out dubious accounting practices and pointing the way towards a more efficient use of resources have been two sides of one coin from the start. And this has been the common currency of the public auditors' work. Few of them have found themselves featured in front-page stories, battling against adversaries like the Militant socialists of Liverpool, the financial non-wizards of Hammersmith or the gerrymanderers of Westminster. Most have beavered away unseen – combating, for example, the so-called 'creative accounting' phenomenon across local government in the later 1980s, or struggling to oversee the huge expansion of compulsory competitive tendering by councils from the late 1980s to the arrival of New Labour.

In both these episodes, auditors were called upon to exercise their judgement in ways that hardly answered to simple categorization as 'regularity' or 'VFM'. It was plain by the 1990s that, whatever the label placed on it, their work was entailing a steadily more sophisticated assessment of what the audited body was doing. Under Banham and Davies, the Commission almost made a virtue of baulking at any overtly prescriptive messages for individual local authorities. Comparative data from across the country and prescriptive suggestions for the sector as a whole were left on the table, for individual councils to take up or otherwise at their own discretion. (Whether or not they exercised this sensibly would be for their local electorates to decide.) After the arrival of John Major's Citizen's Charter, though, this approach began to look almost perversely abstemious. Government looked to the Commission to provide support for a concerted drive to improve public services.

Andrew Foster, a former public servant in the social services and the NHS, embraced this same objective wholeheartedly through his ten years from 1993 as the longest-serving controller of the Commission. Armed with ever more measures of performance, the auditors engaged with their audited bodies in new ways: league tables heralded a readiness to *evaluate* the performance of councils, relative to their peers across the country, against a set of centrally directed criteria. It was a trend that accelerated rapidly after 1997. In its third decade, the Commission was expected to do more than illuminate the facts as in the 1980s, or point to underlying patterns as in the 1990s. It had to join with government in devising ways to effect real change. (It was an evolution labelled 'sight–insight–foresight' by those fond of such rubrics.) As this suggests, New Labour's continuing quest for a quantum improvement in Britain's public services posed a huge challenge for the Commission and its auditors – inviting them into a relationship with government that posed delicate questions for the independence of the Commission from government, always a far subtler matter than the statute-protected independence of the auditors from the audited.

STANDING APART

This independence from government was the third of Heseltine's magic powers. There exists today a broad spectrum of 'independent' bodies at the apex of British public life. At one end of it are those, like Her Majesty's Inspectorate of Constabulary (HMIC) or HM Inspectorate of Prisons, led by a 'designated office-holder'. They sit within a department of state and their leaders must report via a permanent secretary to a government minister. They may generally be regarded as independent, but their leaders can be dismissed – as some have been, in recent years. Then there are those bodies operating outside ministerial departments, such as Ofsted, the education inspectorate. They are free of ministerial control, but they are nonetheless a part of the government machine and must function within government conventions. Much more truly independent are most 'non-departmental public bodies', such as the Healthcare Commission launched in 2004. But even they are subject to policy directives, and the government pays the piper. The Audit Commission, like the BBC, sits at the opposite end of the spectrum from HMIC.

The Commission is a public corporation, wholly separate from government. It is manned by part-time commissioners under the leadership of a chairman, and served by an executive comprised of employees excluded by statute from the civil service and led by the controller. While in recent years it has begun to receive some direct fees from government, it remains substantially self-funding: if all government fees fell away tomorrow, the Commission would simply shorten by a fraction its menu of services. But these would remain extensive, including (as they always have done) the preparation of reports assessing the impact of government policy on the audited bodies within its franchise. And if these reports proved a serious irritant to the government? As a final measure of its independence, the secretary of state in its sponsoring department is precluded by law from issuing specific directives to the Commission. A general directive would be permissible, provided that it were issued publicly – but in twenty-five years, this has never once happened.

Perhaps, then, the Commission has been such a tame and toothless critic that directives would have been superfluous? The record suggests otherwise. In its early years while John Banham was controller, driving ahead with the commissioners' (usually) full support, it asserted its independence – especially in lambasting the government for the counter-productive complexity of local government finances – with a vigour that almost certainly had officials running an eye over the statutory small print governing those directives. This did much to establish the credibility of the Commission with those in the local government world who had initially been quick to dismiss it as a tool of Thatcherism (though its second chairman, David Cooksey, was still being tagged as Maggie's Hammer in the later 1980s). But the Commission paid a high price: its criticism of civil servants, rather than their masters, alienated many officials whose day-to-day cooperation was a prerequisite if it was to exert any real influence in Whitehall.

Howard Davies, a former civil servant himself, restored a vital balance to the Commission's relationships with the large spending departments of state while at the same time continuing to strengthen its ties with audited bodies. By the time of his departure in 1992, the Commission had used its power to publish a series of influential 'Section 27' reports. These were the papers that examined the impact of government policy on the local government world, and were so called because it was Section 27 of the founding statute that spelt out the extent of the Commission's remit in this area. They threw a harsh light on Whitehall's stance towards a range of problems, from environmental health and homelessness to food safety and urban regeneration. It was a disappointment to the Commission that its Section 27 licence to criticize was withheld from the legislation extending its remit into the NHS. While this often seemed to make little difference to the subsequent scope of the Commission's health work, it probably buttressed a view within the health department that Commission recommendations on policy would be out of place – or 'unhelpful', as they say in Whitehall. Independence for the Commission in this context would too often amount to excommunication. Elsewhere in government, though, its reports were usually well received, despite their critical content. This reflected an important truth, illustrated by the Commission's story on many occasions: for it to remain both independent *and* effective within the Whitehall village required patient negotiation from day to day. Taking too independent a line would risk exclusion from decision-making circles, with officials fencing the Commission off their territory with signs marked 'Policy Makers Only'. Too deferential a line would risk entangling the Commission in government initiatives, for which it was all too likely to be expected to act as executor on the ground – a high-risk job at the best of times.

Between one line and the other was a narrow path, and it grew steadily harder to follow as central government became increasingly preoccupied with improving public services from the early 1990s onwards. Through his first three-year term as controller, to 1996, Andrew Foster stepped along it with great care and no little skill. But he was determined to expand the franchise of the Commission wherever opportunities arose. Given the progress of John Major's Citizen's Charter and the ambitions of New Labour to go much further in the same direction, they arose soon enough. By 1997 and the arrival of the Blair government, the Commission was busy adapting to partnership arrangements with other bodies and collecting new responsibilities that acknowledged its leadership status: it was at the forefront of one government initiative after another to lift the quality of public services. Once again, though, the Commission had to pay a high price: Labour ministers came to see it almost as an executive agency, ready to act at Labour's bidding. The timing made this doubly unfortunate, for the late 1990s were marked by government initiatives that were long on aspirations but short on detailed planning. When things went badly awry, as they did in 1999–2001, it almost amounted to nemesis for the Commission. Ministers opted for a sudden change of direction immediately after the June 2001 general election and it was far from certain they would take the Commission with them. Notwithstanding its statutory independence, it would only have taken a statute to abolish it. For Foster and many of his colleagues, this was an uncomfortable time, made more so by a host of internal difficulties.

The lessons learned from that bumpy passage into the new century were turned to advantage in the aftermath, first under Foster's own lead and then under that of his successors. Radical thinking about the future of regulation in local government led to new ideas in 2001–02 that revived confidence in the Commission while helping the re-elected Blair government to refine its goals. After the Foster era came a new regime in which the Commission's independence was starkly, and sometimes brutally, reasserted by a chairman, James Strachan, who briefly assumed what was effectively an executive role. A former investment banker, Strachan sought to impose a fresh tempo. With shrewd timing he pushed hard for a new and simpler approach to the general regulation of local government and public services. (Ironically, this of course distanced the Commission not just from government but from its own philosophy of earlier years.) A new controller with long experience of working in local government himself, Steve Bundred, helped confirm this change of tack by reappraising the nature of the Commission's work both in theory and in practice. It helped that one of his colleagues in the boardroom of the Commission was Michael Lyons, handling a broadly similar brief as the author of an independent review on the future of local government. By the time a sixth chairman, Michael O'Higgins, came aboard in 2006, the Commission seemed once again to be in the happy position of both accumulating new responsibilities *and* enjoying respect as an independent entity at one remove from government and beholden to no single department of state.

NARRATIVE THREADS

The Commission's story has been presented as a narrative on various counts. It is hoped these will make amends for a regular need, inevitably, to take liberties with the precise order of events. In the first place, a narrative was needed to lay down many of the facts as a matter of record. It seems unlikely they will be systematically recorded elsewhere. Politicians have little interest in management issues: it is a rare political memoir of the 1980s or 1990s that even mentions the Commission, let alone devotes a paragraph to it. Few management books, on the other hand, have much interest in it either. Even in academia, where New Public Management has hardly been a neglected topic, the Commission gets short shrift. (A respectable academic history of auditing in Britain, published in 2006, makes no mention of it whatever – though by size the Commission's own field force has ranked for many years among the top ten audit firms in the country.)[3] Nor would future historians have faced an easy task, reconstructing its story at a distance: the surviving archives from the early years are meagre indeed – while e-mails, over-zealous shredding and undated papers from project consultants will as usual have cast a deep shadow across the record since the mid-1990s. The Commission would have been left to flit like a ghost through any history of the public sector under Thatcher and her successors. Like Hamlet's father, an honest ghost; but unedifying, nonetheless.

A narrative structure was also required, to capture properly the intensity of life within the Commission's walls. It has been a place driven by forceful personalities – many of its executives took key positions elsewhere in public life after leaving the Commission – and the interplay between them has defined its changing nature over the years. This has applied as much to the boardroom as anywhere else. Commission members, meeting monthly since 1983, have had to preside over an organization with sometimes strikingly disparate aims. They have had to run their own audit force, for example, yet have had to appoint auditors on merit from a wide field of external competitors as well as in-house employees. They have had to monitor the Commission's activities as both consultant and policeman. And they have had to mediate between an often powerful executive body and those beyond the walls who have sometimes (*sotto voce*) had strong advice to impart. More than eighty individuals have served on the Commission to date, and almost all of them have contributed far above and beyond the call of a bare monthly meeting. Under six very different individuals in the chair, their conscientious efforts have done much to sustain a public body with a unique provenance but some not unfamiliar management challenges.

Its head office, in London's Vincent Square until 2004, was launched without the blessings of what is commonly referred to as 'a structured environment'. It was a loose organization, staffed much as though it were a private business by a few clever men and women who were left to recruit talent as and where they found it. But a shared intellectual excitement and a sense of being out ahead of the rest of the field helped engender a highly creative culture, far removed from the usual image of risk-averse public sector endeavour. As the Commission expanded, and its responsibilities multiplied, the need for more structure grew inexorably – not least, in order to manage the working relationship between Vincent Square and the auditors working for the Commission in the field. No assessment of the record from 1983 to 2008 could truthfully depict a chronicle of uninterrupted triumphs on the management front. The Commission has had its setbacks, like any other institution. It has probably had rather more than its fair share, for example, of personality clashes: perhaps they have come with the territory, given the kind of individuals attracted to working for it. Certainly they posed many difficulties from the early 1990s onwards, especially for Andrew Foster, who in ten years as the controller had to manage the passage of the Commission through a highly political environment.

It was not always apparent at the time, of course, that it would be a journey lasting as far as 2008 and beyond. New Labour's direction of the public services since 1997 has seen non-departmental public bodies coming and going with sometimes alarming speed. It has been an achievement of sorts for the Commission just to have survived this era in (almost) one piece. Here again a narrative structure seemed essential, if only to capture the drama of the fast footwork needed on many occasions.

Viewed as a business, the Commission grew rapidly in size between 1983 and 2008, both at the centre and in the field (see Appendix 5, for the years up to 2006). Its field force also went through four difficult reorganizations – getting relaunched in 1983; taking on the NHS and adjusting to a simpler hierarchy in 1989–90; being transformed from the District Audit Service of Victorian pedigree to plain DA in 1994–95; and being amalgamated with the Commission's own newly created Best Value inspectorate in 2002. Huge amounts of time had to be devoted by senior managers and Commission members alike to matters of pay-and-rations, pensions, recruitment practices, staff promotions and the like. And running in parallel with all this was the need to administer an often complex relationship with the several private sector accounting firms that were mandated to work alongside the Commission's own auditors in the field (see Appendix 6). A full portrait of this relationship alone could probably fill another (albeit rather shorter) book. The author hopes enough has been said about them to reflect the importance of the audit contracts that underpinned everything, without dwelling too long on details that would surely be of limited interest to the general reader. Would we be interested, after all, in a history of (say) the East India Company devoted at length to the terms of its trading contracts? It is surely the story of the nabobs and the maharajahs that is worth the telling, and so it is here – not least because of what their activities reveal about the political world in which they had to operate.

As a biography, this book is focused far more on the Life than the

Times; given the complexity of local government, let alone the NHS, it could hardly be otherwise. Readers looking for more of a general background will turn to authors such as Christopher Foster, himself once a Commission member, whose *British Government in Crisis* presents a devastating picture of the turmoil there has been at the centre since 1979; or Simon Jenkins, whose books on the relentless centralization of political life since 1979, *Accountable to None* and *Thatcher & Sons*, chart its impact on the public sector far more broadly.[4] But a detailed chronicle of the Commission does offer, in effect, an insider's view of some of the more notable episodes – from Margaret Thatcher's war against the councils in the 1980s to New Labour's false start on public service reforms in the late 1990s – while providing another perspective on perennial themes such as the management of Whitehall and the formulation of government policy. Those inclined to see Britain's public services, for instance, as the product of a deeply flawed political system – one that seeks to deliver a Nordic welfare model on the back of a US-style tax regime – may cite as evidence the Commission's long struggle to deliver better results on the ground. As an institution charged in part with ensuring the most economic and efficient use of money in public services, it has accomplished a great deal. Whether enough money has been available to make those services truly *effective* has always been another matter, rather harder for anyone to be sure of.

Nonetheless, as a regulator intent on protecting the public purse while spreading best practice through the public sector in countless ways, the Commission has become indispensable. Conceivably it could be *replaced* – but probably only by a different body fulfilling the same functions. It has become an integral part of the way that the public sector in Britain works. In the process of growing into this role, the Commission has been a force for change that many people over a quarter of a century have conspicuously felt proud of working for. Old labels have slipped away. 'District Audit Service' went in 1994. Its successor, 'District Audit', went in 2002. Today the head offices of the Commission sit in a post-modern tower on London's Embankment, so no one speaks any longer of 'Vincent Square', which for twenty-one years – *pace* all the auditors working in the field – was almost synonymous with the institution itself. And for many who worked there, as the author can attest from dozens of interviews, Vincent Square represented the happiest and most productive period of their working lives. Given their disproportionate impact on so many facets of public life, as recorded here, it might be wondered why the Audit Commission has remained such a singular experiment of its kind. But then, as the record also shows, there was always much about it that assured it of a unique status.

I

The Audit Trail to 1982

To look for the antecedents of the Audit Commission is to tug at a thread that weaves back through centuries of English history. A fair place to catch it first is the Poor Relief Act of 1601. Authorizing churchwardens and overseers to levy rates on their fellow parishioners, for the relief of the destitute, the Act was largely a reworking of earlier Elizabethan statutes. It went further, though, in a signal respect. Since the poor rates were compulsory, it acknowledged the need for someone to keep a check on the money – how much was levied and where it ended up. The task was assigned to justices of the peace.

This effectively handed supervision to the local gentry, an arrangement that survived for well over two centuries. It was a haphazard process that left plenty of room for abuse. By the 1830s, the sheer scale of the abuse kept a Royal Commission busy for three years and prompted a new approach. The Poor Law Amendment Act of 1834 set up an overall supervisory body, the Poor Law Commissioners, and boards of guardians at a local level to collect the parish rates and disburse them. These guardians were directed to ditch the justices of the peace in favour of 'paid officers with such qualifications as the said commissioners shall think necessary'.[1]

In the following year Parliament turned its attention to England's boroughs, passing a far-reaching Act for the Regulation of Municipal Corporations. (This was the milestone Act later adopted by Sidney and Beatrice Webb as the finishing line for their marathon nine-volume history of English local government published in 1906.) The Act included a detailed provision for each newly structured municipality to *elect* two auditors, to carry out various specific duties 'and generally to guard against any fraudulent or negligent misappropriation of the borough fund'. Still lacking, though, was the vital ingredient of *independence*. The boards of guardians were left to appoint, and the ratepayers were left to elect, their own auditors. Ten years later, unsurprisingly, not much had changed. Parliament decided to take a tougher line. In 1844 it split England and Wales into districts, and each was assigned an 'auditor of the district' – with statutory powers not just to rule on accounts, but to take remedial action where necessary. Thus was born the local government auditor. A District Auditors' Society emerged in 1846.

Searching for a precedent to help imbue the district auditor with due *gravitas*, the early Victorians had to dig deep into the history books. They seem finally to have modelled his powers largely on those of the royal auditors who ran England's medieval Exchequer. Hence one notable piece of terminology that was rescued from the days of sheriffs and pipe rolls: where an expense was claimed but found to be improper, it was countered with a 'disallowance'.*

The district auditor's brief expanded steadily through the nineteenth century, as the Victorians built their cities and set up a plethora of authorities to run them. Elected auditors retained a (usually ineffective) role in many borough town halls, and there was some nascent competition from a growing commercial accountancy profession by the late 1880s. But at each stage of the great Victorian municipal reforms – setting up boards to improve public health from 1848, local schools from 1870, roads and railways from 1878, and much else besides – it was invariably the district auditor to whom Parliament turned, to keep an eye on the money. By 1868 there were fifty or so 'DAs' in the land. The Poor Law Amendment Act of that year formally

---

* The Exchequer itself had disappeared in 1834 – though its name lived on in various guises, not least the title used by the head of the Treasury – so the borrowed term 'disallowance' caught an ancient tradition just as it was fading from view. One other ancient tradition, meanwhile, had literally gone out with a bang. The Exchequer had for centuries used wooden 'Tally Sticks' to keep a physical record of payments due and discharged. By 1834, a small mountain of Tally Sticks had been accumulated at Westminster. In October of that year, in an episode colourfully described by the young journalist Charles Dickens, 'these preposterous sticks' were used as firewood in the boilers at Westminster, rather too enthusiastically. The boilers exploded and burnt down the Houses of Parliament. As a waggish district auditor of the 1960s pointed out, it was the closest any accounting system ever came to setting the Thames on fire.

acknowledged the district auditor tag for the first time and, far more important, ruled that they would in future be civil servants, appointed exclusively by central government. They ran a 'District Audit Service' (DAS) which was fully kitted out for action, at Parliament's expense, under the District Auditors Act of 1879.

Remarkably, the DAS needed no further fundamental adjustment until the Local Government Act of 1972. Between the one Act and the other, through just short of a hundred years, the DAS evolved into a close-knit and extremely effective professional body. By the end of the nineteenth century, its audit franchise had been expanded to cover all new-born councils, big and small: county councils from 1888, and urban and rural district councils together with parish councils and parish meetings from 1894. Beginning with the creation of twenty-eight new metropolitan boroughs in 1899, the DAS thereafter steadily encroached on the territory of the municipal corporations' elected auditors. (The latter enjoyed an astonishingly long farewell. A High Court judge in 1906 denounced their audit system as 'quite illusory' and most of them fell in line with the rest of the council world after the comprehensive Local Government Act of 1933 – but twenty-one of them were still holding out against the DAS in 1972.)

The service pioneered new accounting rules and methodologies for the job. Its leaders in the twentieth century were penning textbooks by the 1920s that defined the practice of local government finance for decades. An internal reorganization after the First World War introduced competitive examinations at all levels. No doubt this marked a shift in the culture of the service, to a rather more rigorously disciplined approach. But there was never any suggestion that modernization was a response to lax working standards. As hand-written accounts gave way to punch-card accounting machines and these eventually to computers, nothing seems ever to have seriously smirched the reputation of the DAS as a watchdog of impeccable integrity – and its clout grew with the years.

Illegalities and fraud had always to be handed over to the courts; but the district auditor retained virtually all his initial statutory powers despite the ever-widening scope of the DAS franchise. And where a disallowed item of spending resulted in an improper loss – or, indeed, where the auditor simply came upon a loss that he believed should have been avoided – he could impose a 'surcharge' on those he held responsible. To be paid, of course, out of their own pockets. Until 1927, appeals against a disallowance or surcharge decision could be lodged with the appropriate government minister. From that year onwards, though, most appeals over any issue involving more than £500 could only be referred to the High Court. This marked a watershed. Local authorities, invited by a district auditor to desist from any accounting practice, needed in future to think hard about the possibility of court action before begging to differ. The power of the DAS rose accordingly.

And the benefits were generally plain to see. If serious graft and corruption were conspicuously absent from English public life in the mid-twentieth century, as compared anyway with most other industrialized countries, the district auditor could take a decent share of the credit. As that arbiter of public standards from the Welsh valleys, Aneurin Bevan, put it to the centenary dinner of the august District Auditors' Society in 1946: 'the [District] Auditor is one of the most important institutions of a civilized society. He introduces quantitative measurement into the qualitative enthusiasm of partisan politicians.'[2] Nicely put – but might some of his hosts have winced ever so slightly? To any senior auditor with long experience of the distinctions between allowable and disallowable expenditure, 'quantitative measurement' must have sounded faint praise.

THE NATURE OF THE AUDITOR'S ROLE

In fact, large parts of the district auditor's work in the post-war world were essentially judgemental – as they always had been. This was true not just because itemized figures could be variously construed. Apart from a signature on a certificate of audit completion, no formal opinion was required from the district auditor at the end of the audit process. But he was required to give a report to the audited body, in which the level of detail (if any) depended on the individual auditor's personal inclination. It was also the case that DAs were required to exert influence more broadly over the conduct of local authorities. As early as 1906, at another annual Society dinner, the minister responsible for local government was minuted as having 'dwelt at some length on the importance of using, not only the powers of disallowance, but also the great influence which the [district] auditors possess in restraining waste and extravagance, and always on the side of purity in local administration'.[3] The courts not infrequently made the same observation through the inter-war years.

What was already becoming clear to many, as the Attlee Labour government embarked on its great crusade to expand Britain's welfare state, was that encouraging purity in local administration could potentially be of significantly greater benefit to ratepayers than picking over audit details. And for the auditors themselves, it was certainly a lot more interesting. After all, it was fairly uncommon to find serious illegalities in public bodies' accounts. Fraud, however newsworthy from time to time, was even rarer. Waste and extravagance by local authorities, on the other hand, were a very different matter. It had always been a part of the district auditor's job to keep an eye on what was sometimes called the 'substance of spending', as well as on the detailed accounting record. Some senior members of the service began to argue now for special studies that could look into how different authorities tackled the same tasks. Inquiries about the 'substance of spending' turned into projects helping to ensure that authorities were getting the best possible value for their money. It was soon being called value-for-money work, or plain 'VFM'.

For a decade or so after the war, the bread-and-butter business of checking every record and ticking off the boxes continued to dominate the agenda. There was no shortage of this 'regularity work' as local authorities struggled to catch up on the years of war. More fundamentally, the DAS had also to adjust to new responsibilities in education, health, welfare, housing, transport, and so on. Wherever the Attlee government's reforms obliged local authorities to take on extra statutory duties, fresh audit requirements sprang up. Rather as had happened in the mid-Victorian era, a rapid expansion of the state meant a steadily wider franchise for the DAS. By the late 1950s, though, the competing demands of VFM and regularity work were starting to become apparent.

The advocates of VFM saw no reason why district auditors

shouldn't aspire to a much broader role, in effect auditing the management systems, policies and performance of local government. The problem, of course, was time. To take on this new brief, they would inevitably have to cut back on the painstaking hours devoted to regularity work. They could do this, it was suggested, by gradually introducing a much more formulaic, system-based approach to the standard auditing tasks. At the same time, local authorities would have to provide more by way of internal audit processes, which district auditors would monitor as a long stop.

This sparked a debate that gave the annual conferences of the DAS in the early 1960s plenty to chew on. The would-be innovators produced a stream of papers outlining how sophisticated management analyses – in many cases going well beyond anything contemplated by professional accountants in the private sector – could be used to deliver performance audits. The old-school regularity brigade fought back against the 'planned audit approach' as a dilution of traditional standards. While familiar procedures were to be abbreviated into tedious and inadequate routines, they argued, the new analytical stuff would take the district auditor into areas that were really nothing to do with him. There were those in local government who agreed. The wrangling within the DAS may have struck some as a Lilliputian clash between Big-Endians and Little-Endians. But the better-informed councillors and their officials knew better, and some of them began to prepare the trenches. The district auditor was there to audit the books, not to interfere in managerial matters that were none of his business.

In 1964, in his report for the year past, the chief inspector of audit noted that 'ever increasing importance is being attached to the service he [i.e. the district auditor] can provide in his review of management control generally in the interests of efficiency and economy of administration.'[4] He consistently supported the trend, and through the rest of the decade it gathered momentum inexorably. A paper presented to the DAS annual conference in 1966, rather abruptly entitled 'Reappraisal', set out the views of several senior auditors from Lancashire on how the new 'structured form of audit' could work and how it would free up a significant proportion of the auditor's time for those management reviews. Two years later, a report by one of the research panels that the DAS now liked to foster was devoted to 'Audit Review'. It formally acknowledged the split between regularity auditing on the one hand and management auditing on the other. The latter would be 'directed to examining the efficiency of management control and basically involving the auditor in finding out whether maximum value is obtained for money spent'.[5]

By the end of the 1960s, a new VFM-oriented consensus was broadly in place. Indeed, management auditing was already producing some significant savings for those local authorities that embraced it, not least in the daunting business of computerization. But there was a snag, and it was fundamental. If the DAS was now going to weigh into the management of local authorities, how long could it really hope to go on being seen as independent? After all, the district auditors were basically civil servants. What was to stop them gradually becoming the agents of central government, no less than the civil servants of a Whitehall department? It was a good question, which leading local government officers and some diehard auditors were asking with genuine concern (or in some cases, perhaps, just a keen eye for a plausible argument against management auditing altogether).

The answer provided in July 1970 by one of the most thoughtful chief inspectors in the history of the DAS, Stuart Collins, was prescient. He 'proposed to the Department of the Environment that the local government audit function should be made the responsibility of an independent body – "perhaps an audit commission appointed by the Minister with provision for nominations of some members of local authorities associations"'.[6] This may have been the first mention of an 'audit commission', but others had already begun to cite the need for some kind of overarching body with rather more status than the District Auditors' Society. Back in 1967, an influential paper called *The Audit of Management* by a future chief inspector, Peter Kimmance, had drawn attention to the logic of somehow being able to apply valid local findings, where appropriate, at a national level. The timing of the Collins proposal, though, gave it added force. By 1970 it was clear that a major reorganization of local government was fast approaching. Fewer, larger authorities were in prospect. This could open the way to more resources for *internal* auditing by local government, adding to the momentum of the DAS's evolution into a more sophisticated *external* auditor. If a commission could be presented as the natural outcome of this process, perhaps it was an idea whose time had come?

Alas, not quite. When the Heath government's Local Government Act appeared in 1972, it did indeed bring sweeping changes – but they didn't include the formation of an audit commission. The idea had been shelved. A blueprint had certainly been drawn up – and, indeed, used as the basis for an 'Accounts Commission' that was successfully launched in Scotland the following year – but the Department of the Environment (DoE) had dropped it in the face of stiff opposition to its wider plans. A separate audit body had threatened to be one more area of controversy that it could plainly do without.

The audit arena was not entirely overlooked, however. Arriving at the DoE in 1971 in just his second government job was a wealthy young Tory MP, widely seen already as a future cabinet minister – Michael Heseltine. He had firm views on local government (it cost too much) and he worried that, for too many councillors, the DAS was a soft touch. A close relationship between council and auditor was certainly a common feature of the DAS regime. ('Between audits it was . . . quite usual for treasurers to telephone the directing officer [of a DAS audit] often in the evenings at home for advice,' noted one post-war district auditor in a memoir of his working life.)[7] This was frankly taken as a compliment by many senior auditors; but it was just the kind of thing Heseltine suspected and blamed for a lack of cost-cutting zeal. He supported the introduction of an audit commission as a way of enabling private accounting firms to compete with the DAS. After the idea of a commission was dropped, he fought hard to retain this side-benefit. The 1972 legislation as a result included a provision giving local authorities the right to choose between using the DAS and hiring a private auditing firm.

This looked at first like a breakthrough for the private firms, whose leaders had been pressing for more access to the town-hall market for years. Now they would be able to compete over local authorities, just as they did over commercial businesses. But the firms were to be disappointed. Heseltine went on to another post, at the Department of Industry, before the Act was through. In his absence, DoE officials were not about to let the authorities ditch centrally appointed auditors with statutory powers in favour (or so they feared) of their own cosy private arrangements, lacking any common methodology. A comprehensive Code of Practice was drawn up and introduced in 1973: it effectively dictated a single approach to audits – later, a fundamental principle of the Audit Commission – and this inevitably made life considerably more complicated for the private firms. (Some changes were also made to the way in which a district auditor's statutory powers could be used. Instead of applying disallowances and surcharges directly, for example, he now needed in most cases to work through the courts. But the special status of the district auditor was little altered in practice.) The benefits of using private auditors soon proved illusory – for authorities and firms alike – and the DAS resumed its near-monopoly.

Then, in 1979, Heseltine was back. As Margaret Thatcher's first secretary of state for the environment, he wasn't short of ambitious objectives. It is safe to assume, though, that one item on his agenda had a special piquancy. As he admitted in his 1987 account of these years, 'I hoped that the [DoE] officials who had so deftly frustrated the minister's intentions [over the audit reform in 1972–73] felt some chagrin at finding me back at the department in 1979 and, worse, in charge of it. I did not intend to fail a second time.'[8]

NEW MOMENTUM AND A POLITICAL CHAMPION

This time around, moreover, background events looked a little more conducive to the kind of changes Heseltine had in mind. Between 1973 and 1979, two events in particular had given the idea of an Audit Commission fresh momentum. One was rather specific: the *Layfield Report* and its aftermath. The other was quite the opposite: a sea change in the Conservative Party's stance towards the local government sector.

The *Layfield Report* was triggered indirectly by the reorganization of 1972. Whatever its merits for the longer term, the immediate impact of the 1972 Act had been calamitous. In the spring of 1974, the freshly reshaped councils of England and Wales posted their rate demands for the year to come. The average figure was 30 per cent higher than in the year before. In some authorities, the increase was well over 100 per cent. (It was payment in advance for the splurge in council spending that culminated the following year in Anthony Crosland's famous rebuke: 'The party's over.') The resulting public outcry prompted calls for a royal commission. It was only five years, however, since the Redcliffe-Maud Commission had reported on the structures of local government. The DoE baulked at the idea of another full-blown commission on broadly the same topic. Instead, a committee of inquiry was set up, in the summer of 1974, under the auspices of the Association of Metropolitan Authorities. It was chaired by a leading QC, Frank Layfield. He was given a tight deadline that Crosland as environment secretary refused to extend, and a challenging brief: his committee had to restrict itself to financial matters, as if these could really be tackled in isolation.

Nonetheless, when it was published in May 1976, the *Layfield Report* ranged widely in its recommendations – and a chapter headed 'Value for Money' set out the most detailed prescription yet for a future Audit Commission (though this title was carefully avoided). The Report's proposals, especially for an innovative local income tax, fell mostly on stony ground. By the time Heseltine returned to the DoE, almost all of them had been quietly brushed aside. The civil service had no interest whatever in seeing its control over local government delegated to a genuinely independent body. Layfield's audit recommendations were discarded in favour of a thin-looking compromise called the Advisory Committee on Local Government Audit. This body struggled hopelessly for two years, then withered away.[9] The real value of the Report, though, was that it sifted through a great deal of evidence on the audit question and pulled together much of the thinking on VFM and its implications since the early 1960s. Once Heseltine made up his mind to go forward with an Audit Commission, by the end of 1979, he had a lucid blueprint to hand that had already been widely aired.

Since much of it eventually found its way into the relevant legislation, it is worth setting out the Layfield Committee's recommendations in some detail. It took as its main premise the view that

... the best way of promoting efficiency and securing value for money is through the dissemination of comprehensive but intelligible information on the methods employed by local authorities and the results they achieve.

The existing Code of Practice, it acknowledged, already pointed the district auditors in this direction. But current practice fell well short of delivering what was needed. The DAS was essentially a federation of locally organized teams, without much direction from above or coordination of their work in any systematic way. Even if they had the special skills for the broader job, which the Report politely questioned, district auditors were in no position to blow the whistle on anyone unless laws had actually been broken.

On the other hand, the Committee had no interest in trying to supplant the DAS with a new set of high-powered sleuths reporting directly to Whitehall. The costs would almost certainly exceed any likely savings, not least because local authorities might be less inclined to cooperate than to clam up when approached for data. No – to have any chance of succeeding, a fresh approach to 'efficiency auditing' would unquestionably have to enlist the skills and experience of the district auditors, 'in whose capabilities and judgement they [the local authorities] generally appear to have confidence'. What was therefore needed was a new reporting structure for the DAS and a new set of marching orders. The Committee had four main proposals:[10]

First, the audit service in England and Wales should be made completely independent of both government and local authorities and should have a hierarchy of its own. At its head we envisage an independent official with a similar status to that of the Comptroller and Auditor General who, as head of the Exchequer and Audit Department, is responsible for auditing the accounts of government departments.

Second, the head of audit should have the sole responsibility for assigning auditors to each local authority: ... [which] should no longer have a choice. He should also be responsible for the organisation of the audit service, for the training of auditors and for setting up any special efficiency units within the service which might be appropriate. We envisage that most auditors would be civil servants ... with the special skills needed for the discharge of their wider responsibilities. But private auditors would still have a role. The head of the audit service should be able to approve their employment by local authorities for general audit work where this seemed appropriate. Private practitioners might also be used to supplement the work of the audit for specialised purposes . . .

Third, the head of audit should make regular reports on issues of general interest or public concern relating to more than one authority. These reports should be available to the public. They should be concerned particularly with comparisons between the methods employed by local authorities and the results achieved . . .

Last, there should be a specially constituted higher institution to which the head of audit's reports would be submitted. Such an institution could be either a parliamentary committee . . . or the body could be one with representation drawn largely from local government . . .

Here was the gist of the future Audit Commission. It would be a big change, which the Committee readily conceded would mean more staff and more money. It was, though, 'one of the rare instances where expansion would be justified'. As already noted, those who had commissioned the Report did not agree. Nor did backbench MPs on either side of the House give it much support. Three parliamentary select committees between 1976 and 1979 endorsed the idea of folding the DAS into the Exchequer and Audit Department, in effect making local authorities directly accountable to Parliament via the comptroller and auditor-general. Not much independence there.

As it happened, the Exchequer and Audit Department was itself targeted for reform by the new Thatcher government. This added another dimension to the debate over local auditing. While Heseltine drew on the Layfield recommendations to build his case for an independent Commission, opponents of the idea proposed that local auditing be part of a new National Audit Office. Both sides, though, were adamant on one thing: the financial arrangements for local government had to be radically overhauled. Nothing less would do if the Conservative Party was going to respond robustly to the antics of the Loony Left in Britain's town halls.

This reflected the second, and much more general, development of recent years that by 1979 had brought auditing into the spotlight. Local government since the huge upheavals of 1972–74 had become something of a *bête noire* to many in the Conservative Party, and beyond it. There was a widespread conviction that local councils were out of control, and costing voters a fortune in the process. Certainly local authorities *were* spending more. They had accounted for 23.4 per cent of all public expenditure in the UK in 1950. This had risen to 31 per cent by the time the *Layfield Report* was published. Three years later, the dismay and anger over the 1974–75 rate increases (and those of the following year, too) were still reverberating.

In a sense this was a little unfair. Those increases, after all, had been tied to a one-off reorganization of a kind that was inevitably costly. And by 1979, council spending in real terms had actually been held level for three years. But if this put a brake on earlier trends, it did nothing to slow the political bandwagon now on the roll. Regular horror stories in the media about profligate individual councils played well for the Tories in the general election, and whetted the party's appetite for reform thereafter. One popular tabloid target was the borough council of Tower Hamlets (population: 150,000), where a department of 245 social workers went on strike for ten months in 1979–80 – without, it was widely alleged, anyone really noticing.

The new public mood certainly did not go unnoticed within the senior ranks of the DAS. The novel interest in local councils, albeit for unflattering reasons, strengthened a feeling that Layfield's radical ideas might soon be back on the agenda. Heseltine's return was unsurprisingly welcomed within the DAS as a pivotal opportunity.

Ever since 1973, a file had sat on the office shelves of the service marked 'Audit Commission'. First compiled on the basis of papers prepared that year to assist the Scots with their Accounts Commission, it had been updated through the intervening years by one of the service's most senior auditors, Cliff Nicholson. By 1979, Nicholson was the deputy chief inspector, reporting to Peter Kimmance. The two of them were convinced that the contents of the file held the answer to the future of local government auditing. They were intent on presenting the case to whoever was the new environment secretary after the general election. When it turned out to be Heseltine, they felt the time had come at last to finish what Stuart Collins had begun.

True, Heseltine's main motive in backing the Commission idea seven years earlier had been his determination to break the monopoly of the DAS and allow in the chartered accountancy firms. But this only provided a second motive: the DAS men needed to pre-empt any over-hasty moves with their own long-considered idea. It was also vital to impress upon the new minister as quickly as possible that a new institution would need to have a broad remit. Within a few weeks of the election, Nicholson wrote a single-page memo restating the case for a wide-ranging Audit Commission and managed to get it through to the new minister's private office.

Looking back, Heseltine had a recollection of including the formation of an Audit Commission among a list of priorities that he scribbled on the back of an envelope for his permanent secretary, on his first day back at the Department of the Environment.[11] But he had no detailed prescription in mind for how such a Commission might work. His priority remained, as ever, the opening up of local government audit to the private firms. They were lobbying hard to remind him of their virtues, and Heseltine was confident their admission to the sector could make a big difference. He had little interest in the auditing process *per se*, nor was he instinctively sympathetic to the notion of setting up any new body resembling another 1970s 'quango' (the fashionable acronym at the time for quasi-autonomous non-governmental organizations). As he later put it, 'when it came to quango-hunting, I was already up with the leaders'.[12] The potential of a Commission as a vehicle for shaking things up was obvious, though, and Nicholson's memo suggesting some urgent homework hit its mark with the new minister: 'he agreed immediately'.[13] Heseltine asked for all the issues to be fully considered and directed the three top men in the DAS – Peter Kimmance, Cliff Nicholson and a third senior auditor, Malcolm Langley – to go away and prepare a paper outlining the practical options.

They reported back to Heseltine a few months later. Two main concerns emerged clearly from their work. First, as anticipated years before, the DAS would struggle to make real headway with VFM studies so long as it was seen as a branch of the civil service. Second, its status as such was having a debilitating impact on the staffing of the service. Too many bright young auditors were picking up a tip-top training – and then skipping into other branches of the profession that offered more flexibility and a lot more money. The paper's strong recommendation was for the establishment of an independent Audit Commission.

By his own account, Heseltine accepted this and tried to push through an immediate reform, but ran foul of the Treasury. 'It was the only serious battle that I lost in those first six months of government. Incomprehensibly, it was resisted on behalf of the Treasury by Nigel Lawson (then financial secretary), who argued that he was waiting for some obscure report.'[14] Given time to reconsider, Heseltine appears to have come to a better understanding of what might be required of a Commission. Nicholson recalled: '[His] initial thinking was that you should have accounts with key features and key measurements in them which would make the extravagance of Labour authorities absolutely apparent . . . You didn't have to have studies or anything like that, it was all going to come out of the accounts.'[15] The paper from the DAS men made it clear that no amount of accounting wizardry would suffice. Audit was the key.

The paper also made clear the DAS was vehemently opposed to any extension of the role played by accounting firms from the private sector. This came as no surprise to Heseltine, and he stood his ground for some months. (Several years on, he recalled the 'terrible rows' he had had with Peter Kimmance.)[16] But the case for some hybrid arrangement was not hard to see and there would be time later to resolve this issue. Heseltine accepted that the key priority was to launch a process of reform. He started consulting with interested parties accordingly.

Politically, it was a shrewd move by Heseltine. He could see, as he put it later, that resolving the future of the whole audit issue was 'something that was in the mainstream of the government's economic policy'.[17] Indeed, what must have seemed a truly arcane subject to most people at the start of the decade, even in Whitehall, was now a topic fraught with implications for one of the hottest topics on the political agenda – how best to reconfigure the relationship between central and local government. Fixing the future of local government auditing had been a side-issue in 1971. Now it was an issue that an environment secretary could reasonably treat as a priority.

The Thatcher government's honeymoon period was an extraordinary time. Ministers, advisers and policy wonks vied with each other to catch the radical mood; and this applied to local government, as to other policy areas. While plenty of grand ideas went the rounds – and the minister for local government, Tom King, was at one point reported in the press as saying that an abolition of all domestic rates was under consideration[18] – cogent and practical proposals were at a premium. The idea of an Audit Commission, devoted to promoting the 'three Es' of economy, efficiency and effectiveness, could hardly have been better timed. It would be part of a wider campaign to impose a greater financial discipline on local government. Central-government grants were being cut in real terms. Compulsory competitive tendering (CCT) was introduced for the first time in 1980, for construction, maintenance and highways work. An Audit Commission would be another big step in the same direction. Heseltine was determined to wrest back control of what he later described, looking back from 1987, as 'a barely controllable free-wheeling employment machine which for year after year had been run largely for the benefit of the machine-minders'.[19]

Not surprisingly, the machine-minders gave the Audit Commission idea a rather chilly reception. All of the main local authority associations opposed it. Few elected members or professional officers could see much difference between the Commission and all the other stratagems being devised in Whitehall to nobble their spending plans. Indeed, there probably *was* no difference, as far as many in the government were concerned. Thatcher herself looked back with no doubts at all. '[Michael] took a whole battery of new powers in an attempt to deal with the problem ... [including] the Audit Commission, as well as beginning a general squeeze on the central government grant – all designed to hold down public spending and to give ratepayers an incentive to think twice before re-electing high-spending councils.'[20]

With or without thinking twice, though, ratepayers jumped the wrong way in both 1980 and 1981. Lower central grants produced higher rates, and local election results in those two years were disastrous for the Tories. Relations between central government and the local councils deteriorated alarmingly. There was no doubt by 1981 that Thatcher's period in office, if she managed to cling on to it, was going to feature a grim struggle between them. So why, given Heseltine's enthusiasm and the general mood among the Tories, was progress on legislating for an Audit Commission still proving so tortuous by the summer of 1981?

OVERCOMING THE FINAL OBSTACLES

The simple answer was that too few people in Whitehall shared Heseltine's enthusiasm. Senior officials at the DoE continued to view the whole idea in much the same light as the Layfield recommendations of a few years earlier. Many of the professional accounting bodies (albeit with the conspicuous exception of the Institute of Chartered Accountants in England and Wales) were no less opposed to it than the local government associations. There could hardly have been a broader nay lobby. Setting up an independent Commission looked to the officials like a recipe for trouble. They advised Heseltine against going ahead with it.[21] (One of the senior officials with responsibility for local government was Terry Heiser, who went on to become the permanent secretary of the department in 1985. Heiser recalled in 2006 that he and his colleagues had viewed the idea of a Commission with scepticism because the whole concept of VFM was still very unclear – and they had a healthy regard for the work done by the DAS, which they were anxious not to destabilize or demoralize.)[22]

The attitude within the Treasury was scarcely less hostile than it had been back in 1979. This would have surprised many in local government, who were quick to see the putative Commission as a cat's-paw of the Treasury. Not for the last time, they were misreading the situation. The Treasury had deep misgivings about the whole project. Bruised by the IMF crisis of 1976 and distinctly uncomfortable with the gap between the new 1979 government's rhetoric and its unsustainably high level of spending, the Treasury was going through a fundamental reassessment of its stance on public expenditure. It was not happy at the idea of ceding any serious control over local government to a supposedly independent body – especially not an independent body founded upon some most un-Treasury-like rhetoric. 'As laymen [Treasury officials] were sceptical of the language of investment analysis or value-for-money audit . . . The "three Es" of the new audit, economy, efficiency and effectiveness, were full of vagueness. Value for money might prove a Trojan horse, out of which would pour battalions of consultants supporting demands for money and undermining the fragile walls of spending control.'[23] The Audit

Commission, in other words, might go native. It might claim to be independent, but turn out to be a meddlesome apologist for the councils.

So the discussions dragged on. It was probably only the cogency of the Layfield proposals and Heseltine's determination that kept the process moving ahead at all. And it was Heseltine, finally, who forced the issue. He was more committed than ever to injecting higher standards of management into the conduct of local government, after his successful battles to set up urban development corporations in London's docklands and on Merseyside. He was utterly convinced now that an Audit Commission would be an invaluable catalyst for this. Indeed, he thought it would be sensible to let an Audit Commission loose in Whitehall, too. His colleagues soon stamped on that idea and he let it pass – but he was not going to be stonewalled again on the local government audit. Told of a growing problem over recruitment at the DAS, he seized on it as a pretext for arbitrarily appointing fourteen partners from commercial firms, as what he called 'additional district auditors'. A range of local authorities found themselves saddled with more or less exactly the arrangement they had been offered under the 1972 Act – and had opted to reject.

It was a controversial move, but helped to bring things to a head. Agreement was finally reached on legislation in July 1981 (the same month, as it happened, that serious riots erupted in the streets of Liverpool and South London, firing Heseltine with a fresh determination to break with the past and look for new solutions in local government). It was said that local government representatives had resigned themselves to a Commission as a lesser evil than being swept up into the National Audit Office, which had begun to look the most likely alternative. The Treasury, meanwhile, had won assurances that it would be able to second one or two of its own senior officials to the new body. That was usually enough of a safeguard against anything too adventurous. Provisions for an Audit Commission were set out as Part III of the Local Government Finance Bill of November 1981. They got off to a bumpy start: opposition to other parts of the Bill forced it to be dropped, and the Commission sections had to be reintroduced as Part III of the Local Government Finance No. 2 Bill the following month.

Looking back on the progress of the Bill seven months later, in what would be the last ever annual report by a chief inspector of audit, Peter Kimmance would give a good account of the lively arguments that accompanied its passage. He summed up:

The new arrangements have had their critics. Some have seen the changes as unnecessary. More specifically there have been criticisms that the Commission will not be truly independent but will be a creature of the secretary of state. The ending of the arrangements for local authorities to choose their own auditors has been strongly opposed. There has been opposition also to the Commission's carrying out comparative studies, to the auditor's duty in connection with value for money, to the inclusion of passenger transport executives in the new audit arrangements and to the exclusion of water authorities from them. These and many other aspects have been the subject of prolonged and extensive debates and discussions.[24]

Scrutiny of this second Bill dragged on for months and Heseltine even tried again to pre-empt the Commission by pushing for the appointment of another seventy or so of his 'additional district auditors'. The legal advice within his department was that he had no power to make these appointments – and any attempt to build on the previous year's start would be blocked in the courts. (Cliff Nicholson was actually meeting with Heseltine and his permanent secretary, George Mosely, when the legal advice was handed to them.)[25] In the event, battle was joined in the High Court but was soon overtaken by events, as were the assistant district auditors themselves: the Bill finally received the Royal Assent on 13 July 1982. The Audit Commission would have legal status from 21 January 1983 and would begin operations three months later.

In most essentials, the Act followed the lines laid down by Layfield. The Commission would be an independent body, with thirteen to seventeen Commission members appointed by the secretary of state after consultations and with a broad remit to take on the historical role of the DAS and some wider functions. It would assimilate all of the existing district auditors, shorn of their formal title (or at least, the term 'district auditor' would now drop out of the statute book). It would appoint its own chief officer, the controller of audit, subject to the secretary of state's approval, and it would be left to the

Commission to decide whether and how to take forward the structure of the DAS itself. It would be responsible for appointing auditors to all local authorities; to police, fire and port-health authorities; to drainage boards; to passenger transport executives; and to planning committees and probation, after-care and children's regional planning committees. To help with this extensive franchise, the Commission would (at last!) be able to appoint private firms at its own discretion.

The Commission would draw up a code of audit practice, which would need to be approved by Parliament and updated periodically. Its auditors would be charged with applying the code, and ensuring that all accounts were properly compiled and in accordance with the relevant statutes. They would also have to satisfy themselves 'that the body whose accounts are being audited has made proper arrangements for securing economy, efficiency and effectiveness in its use of resources'. And at the conclusion of an audit, in addition to signing off the certificate of completion on the accounts as traditionally required, the auditor would now have to render a full professional opinion on them. This would be a radical departure: until now, as noted, auditors had submitted a 'report' which in the great majority of cases simply noted there was 'nothing to report'.

This was a wide remit indeed. So how big a stick would the auditor be carrying? Aside from the statutory authority to see whatever documents and information he wanted (and to require people to attend on him in person, if necessary), the auditor was to have three critical powers. First, he could, in the innocuous-sounding words of the Act, 'make a report on any matter coming to his notice in the course of an audit' – and publish it. Second, and picking up on changes that had been made in 1972 to the historical rights to impose disallowances and surcharges, the auditor could apply to the courts to take equivalent measures on his behalf where he encountered any improper accounting item. Under this Section 19 of the Act, those responsible for spending money unlawfully could be required by the courts to repay it. And if they were council members, they could be disqualified too. And third, under Section 20, where an auditor decided that 'a loss has been incurred or deficiency caused by the wilful misconduct of any person', he could sign a certificate requiring repayment of the missing sum by that person within fourteen days, subject only to an appeal to the courts. Again, disqualification could also follow.

After the stick came a 'miscellaneous and supplementary' part of the Act that was devoted to, if not exactly carrots, at least activities that it was hoped local authorities might come to welcome and appreciate over time. These centred on the remit of the Commission itself, as distinct from the auditors working for it in the field. Taking its cue from the *Layfield Report*, Section 26 empowered the Commission to 'undertake or promote comparative and other studies designed to enable it to make recommendations for improving economy, efficiency and effectiveness in the provision of local authority services [and the services of other audited bodies] . . . and for improving the financial or other management of such bodies'. Going one better than Layfield, the Act also required the Commission to look upwards as well as downwards. Section 27 empowered it to focus other special studies on the impact of any statutory provisions – or, indeed, 'of any directions or guidance given by a Minister of the Crown'.

Finally, there was a wily addition from Heseltine himself. Back in 1972, some last-minute footwork in Whitehall had effectively smothered his attempt to open up the public sector audit market. Mindful of this, he made a pre-emptive move against any further attempt to keep control in official hands. At the last moment, he added a provision to the Act that 'the first controller of audit shall be appointed by the secretary of state who shall determine the terms and conditions on which he is to be employed by the Commission'. As he fully appreciated, it was the controller who would really dictate the fortunes of the new body, not its part-time chairman. He knew that the future responsibility for Commission appointments would in all probability lie effectively with the civil service, while the choice of future controllers would in practice fall to the chairman and his or her commissioner colleagues. Heseltine was determined to make sure that at least the inaugural controller would be an individual sharing his own broad objectives. As for the subsequent relationship between controllers and their chairmen, that would be for the appointed individuals to work out for themselves. (Predictably, how well they managed this over the years was to be an important influence on the Commission's working effectiveness.)

As to who the first controller would actually be, and who would chair the Commission, and who would sit on it, these were details – like a hundred other, more mundane practicalities – that had yet to be resolved. For despite the endless delays in legislating for the Commission, remarkably little had actually been done by July 1982 to prepare for its launch. Except, that is, within the DoE. Once it had become absolutely clear that the Audit Commission was going to happen, department officials had ditched all their post-Layfield reservations and thrown themselves into preparing for it with some enthusiasm, as is the way of Whitehall. They had worked up a provisional restructuring of the DAS, with some outline plans and budgets.

The headquarters of the DAS was in Bristol. (When the government had been urging all departments to move more civil servants out of London back in the mid-70s, Stuart Collins had picked Bristol because he was a keen yachtsman with a boat moored at Plymouth. It was a standing joke in the DAS that if he'd been a keen mountaineer, they'd have ended up in Cumbria.) The DoE officials scheduled a Friday in mid-August for a day-long presentation to the senior people in the service. They travelled down to Bristol, where they were met by a deputation led by Cliff Nicholson. But there was a surprise in store for both sides.

When the officials presented their proposals, the auditors were taken aback and turned them down flat. Nicholson told the men from the ministry their ideas were simply unworkable. More than that, they flew in the face of the radical thinking behind the whole concept. As he put it, speaking for all of his colleagues: 'This isn't why we supported the Commission!'[26] By lunchtime, the auditors had cut short the discussion and seen the DoE team off, on the train back to London. Heseltine would have been proud of them.

2

Getting Started, 1982–83

The Audit Commission posed quite a challenge for those officials at the environment department in the early autumn of 1982. The legislation gave them less than nine months to launch it. The statutory basis for the 139-year-old District Audit Service had been scrapped, so there was no scope to prevaricate over replacing it. They could expect little or no cooperation from the local authorities or the unions, both being targeted relentlessly by the government as the main culprits in public sector over-spending. They knew a sceptical Treasury was watching every move. They had no individuals lined up for the top jobs. And now they even had to deal with a bolshie bunch of auditors in Bristol.

Michael Heseltine, having personally set so much store by the Commission, was anxious to see it off to a flying start. Aware of the rather daunting task confronting his officials, and only too well aware that much would inevitably depend on the calibre of the initial sixteen commissioners assigned to it, he took a direct hand in finding them. No one had yet been approached to take on the chairmanship, so the field was wide open.

Looking for advice, he met for dinner in mid-September with one of the leading figures in London's local government politics. Roy Shaw had been a Labour councillor for over twenty-five years. He had become leader of Camden Council in 1975, a post he would no doubt still have held but for a left-wing coup orchestrated earlier in the year, in the wake of the 1982 local elections. (Camden had seen a replay, in effect, of the coup that had toppled Ken Livingstone's predecessor at the GLC the previous year.) Shaw was still on the council, though, and was vice-chairman of the Association of Metropolitan Authorities. After Heseltine had explained to him the goals of the

Commission, he put his hand in the air. Shaw recalled: 'I said to him, "I want to be on it!" Right, he said, you can be the first appointment, and he told his official to make a note of it.'[1]

As this suggests, Heseltine was less concerned with party allegiances than with attracting good, experienced people. The Commission members would be paid to work just one day a month, under a chairman paid for one day a week – so they would need to make every hour count. He also wanted to ensure the right mix of backgrounds (which the Act left entirely to the secretary of state's discretion). Clearly local government had to be strongly represented. Heseltine brought aboard four other politicians. Three of them were Tories – Peter Bowness, leader of Croydon Borough Council and chairman of the London Boroughs Association; Ian Coutts, a member of Norfolk County Council and chairman of the Association of County Councils' Finance Committee; and Ian McCallum, a member of Woking Borough Council and chairman of the Association of District Councils – but one of the politicians was a Labour councillor (and future Labour MP), John Gunnell, the leader of West Yorkshire Metropolitan County Council. There was one senior officer, Keith Bridge, who was chief executive of Humberside County Council. Heseltine appointed, too, the general secretary of the National Association of Local Government Officers (NALGO), Geoffrey Drain, to represent the principal union in the sector.

Another essential constituency was the accountancy profession. In addition to Peter Kimmance, the outgoing head of the DAS, Heseltine successfully trawled three of the most distinguished professionals in the country. Noel Hepworth was head of the Chartered Institute of Public Finance and Accountancy (CIPFA), and had been one of the accountants on the 1974–76 Layfield Committee; Ian Hay Davison was senior partner of Arthur Andersen and chairman of the Accounting Standards Committee; and Christopher Foster was a partner of Coopers & Lybrand and one of the foremost academics in the accounting field, with a chair at the London School of Economics.

This left Heseltine with a maximum of six further places on the Commission, and he used five of them. One went to the chairman of (pre-privatization) British Gas in Wales, Dudley Fisher, a public sector accountant. He was a native of Norfolk but had picked up a string of honorary positions in Wales since the 1950s, so his appointment dealt handily with the principality. Another went to Lawrie Barratt, the successful house builder and a loyal Tory party man who had been knighted the previous year. Far more intriguing were the remaining appointments. Heseltine went for three businessmen with strong accounting backgrounds. Kenneth Bond was deputy managing director of the mighty GEC plc and had been Arnold Weinstock's right-hand man there for more than thirty years. David Lees had just been appointed finance director of GKN plc and was seen by many as a rising young star within the industrial sector. And as the first chairman of the Commission, Heseltine selected John Read.

Read was a 47-year-old Yorkshireman whose appointment struck most observers as a nod to the safe-pair-of-hands school of management. Confirmation of his name came late in the day – it had still not been released when Shaw received his invitation letter in the middle of November 1982 – but this may have been at Read's own request: he took over the chairmanship that same month of a London-based freight-forwarding company, LEP Group plc. He was a chartered accountant and had been a partner of the accountancy firm Price Waterhouse for seventeen years until 1975, working first in the US and then in a succession of European countries. Since 1975, he had risen through the senior executive ranks of Unigate, the dairy products company, and had picked up four non-executive directorships.

The implication of these three appointments from the business sector seemed clear to at least one of the other thirteen new commissioners. Noel Hepworth recalled: 'I always felt one of the very strong motives, both explicit and implicit, was to move a lot more of the audit activity to the private sector. The appointments seemed to me to be a statement that "we want to privatize as much of the audit as we possibly can do".'[2] Some of those other commissioners, Heseltine knew, would themselves be in favour of a privatization strategy. One of the local government men, Ian Coutts from Norfolk, had been a Conservative parliamentary candidate and was a man of forthright views on public sector inefficiency. He did not disguise his distrust of the DAS and was a strong supporter of privatization. The decisive factor, though, would inevitably be the stance of whoever emerged as the first controller of the Commission.

Heseltine had insisted that the appointment of the first controller should be within the secretary of state's gift; but when the search began in earnest, that autumn, he had no one to propose. A brief went out to the head-hunters, Spencer Stuart, that they should cast their net widely. They sought guidance on the appointment from a good many people – including Peter Kimmance, the retiring chief inspector. He told them at all costs to avoid appointing an auditor, who would just get enmeshed in detail. 'Get a flash fellow who will break down the accountancy attitude!'[3] It was sound advice. They followed it, and came up surprisingly quickly with what turned out in many ways to be an inspired choice.

THE FIRST CONTROLLER MAKES HIS MARK

John Banham was a management consultant working for McKinsey & Co. He had joined the firm in 1969, when it was still very much a US-based business with overseas offices; and in 1980, at the age of 40, he had become one of the firm's earliest British directors (and certainly the youngest). Every successful McKinsey consultant in those days had to ascend a ladder that took them from associate to principal to director. You could safely say two things about any individual who had made it to the director level: they would be very shrewd operators, and they would be well on their way (by the standards of most salaried employees outside the City and Premier League football, anyway) to being very, very rich.

Banham's particular blend of cleverness looked absolutely ideal. A Cambridge graduate with a First in Natural Sciences, he had served briefly in the Foreign Office before spending five years in marketing and advertising during the 1960s. As a management consultant, he had spent an unusually large proportion of his time at McKinsey on assignments in the public sector, including a stint in Washington DC in 1973–75, working for the US government (in an office across the street from the Watergate-racked White House). And, more than most consultants, he had a gift for writing up complicated analyses in elegant, easily readable prose. Indeed, a report that he had written in 1975 with the Central Policy Review Staff on the future of the British car industry had even been published as a set book for A-level economics students. He went on to write, in 1977, a critical review for the Tory opposition about the reorganization of the NHS in 1974, in which he had been directly involved. It was called *Realizing the Promises of a National Health Service* and drew on his experience in Washington.

But would he want the job, and the pay-cut it would obviously entail? The answer was yes, on both counts. As it happened, by the autumn of 1982 Banham had begun looking for a future beyond his consulting career. He had grown up in a family with a strong sense of public service: his father was a surgeon in the NHS and his mother was one of the prime movers behind the establishment of Cornwall's social services. Politics looked the most likely next step. As a good West Country man, he was a Liberal Party member, and he had been approached by the Liberals in Plymouth as a possible parliamentary candidate to contest the Sutton constituency (against Alan Clark, who had held it for the Conservatives since 1974).

Banham was just preparing to travel on a train from his home near Newbury down to Plymouth for an adoption meeting, late in November, when he received the first telephone call from Spencer Stuart. The head-hunter must have been persuasive: Banham knew little about local government and less about auditing. (He would later describe Part III of the 1982 Local Government Finance Act as 'serious competition for mogadon'.) But he was sufficiently intrigued to agree immediately to a meeting with John Read. Within a matter of weeks, he had accepted an offer of the controller's job – at a salary roughly a third of his McKinsey remuneration.

Unfortunately, this still meant that he was going to be the highest-paid public servant in Britain. He had yet to meet Heseltine, and Banham himself suggested it might be sensible for him to explain in person to the secretary of state how his terms and conditions had been settled. There followed a memorable pre-Christmas encounter in Heseltine's office at the DoE. One potential difficulty was obvious. Banham went straight to the point: the secretary of state did realize, didn't he, that he was planning to appoint not a Conservative Party member but a paid-up Liberal? No problem, said Heseltine. Nor was there any problem bringing in someone from the private sector, on a rather higher than normal salary. Then the future controller of the Audit Commission set about explaining how directors at McKinsey were remunerated. 'There was a clatter of pencils round the table. All these civil servants couldn't believe what they were hearing.'[4]

Perhaps they were impressed, though, that Banham had learned enough from his youthful stint in the Foreign Office to break the awkward news in a face-to-face meeting. It was a promising sign, given the diplomatic skills that the new job would certainly require. No one doubted, though, that there would be a row in Parliament when the terms were disclosed. In the event, Banham's terms were derided by a few Labour backbenchers and became a popular topic of gossip in local government circles. (Even six months later, any appearance by Banham at a meeting of councillors could be guaranteed to excite speculation in the bar over how much he'd been paid at McKinsey: as Cliff Nicholson recalled, 'the figure varied, and went up and up at each meeting'.)[5] But the announcement otherwise passed without much ado.

To Heseltine, anyway, the terms were of little consequence. His discussion with Banham confirmed what he had hoped would be the case: in appointing a McKinsey director, they were effectively going to be seeding the McKinsey culture – then widely seen as a leading catalyst of best management practices – into the world of local government where McKinsey fees would be simply unthinkable. If the Commission under Banham managed to trigger changes in any way comparable to the impact that McKinsey was generally thought to have had elsewhere in Britain since the early 1960s, it would be a coup indeed.* It was a bold notion, and there had to be some possibility of

---

* McKinsey's high standing among ministers and officials rested not just on reports of the work that it had done for a long list of major UK companies, since setting up in London in 1959, but also on Whitehall's direct experience of studies that it had famously carried out for public sector bodies such as the BBC, the National Health Service and the Bank of England. The extent of its influence had been remarkable, as has been noted in an authoritative history of British management: 'Up to the early 1970s, this firm became a dominant force for change in British industry, significantly altering the image of consultancy in general and forcing through a series of structural reorganizations that were to have a significant effect on large-scale British business' (John F. Wilson and Andrew Thomson, *The Making of Modern Management – British Management in Historical Perspective*, Oxford University Press, 2006, p. 121).

a violent reaction. But if it worked, and the McKinsey way became the Commission's way, then Banham would be a bargain at almost any price.

Taking on the job at the beginning of January 1983, Banham avoided spelling out the mission quite so explicitly in public; but it always had the clarity of a John Grisham thriller in his own mind. 'Basically, I saw the Commission as being a kind of McKinsey, [with the added dimension that we would be] serving clients who just had no option but to retain us – and if they didn't do what we told them [to do], not very nice things might happen to them. So I set things up, in a sense, as though this was the firm . . .'[6] (McKinsey people always referred to their consultancy as 'the firm'.) Before setting anything up, though, he had to avoid letting the DAS down.

Banham had decided even before confirming his acceptance that, whatever the statutory changes in the 1982 Act, he would want the Audit Commission to retain the District Audit Service in both name and structure. Replacing either would make his job immeasurably harder. In the same spirit, he needed urgently to revive their sagging morale. As he would later explain to the commissioners: 'recruitment has been halted for almost 3 years; promotions were very limited last year; wage increases have been well below the rate of inflation.' The auditors had all been offered new contracts with the Commission. Nonetheless, they badly needed reassuring 'that they have good prospects of remaining valued contributors to a challenging and worthwhile job, both professionally and personally'.[7]

Certainly the atmosphere in the Bristol headquarters was miserable. Peter Kimmance had retired just before Christmas. As if to confirm how far the DAS was now in limbo, his deputy and obvious successor, Cliff Nicholson, had not been allowed to succeed him as chief inspector. The DoE had told Nicholson it didn't want to 'close any doors' for the new Commission. Nor, apparently, did it want to open any that might subsequently let him into the department. He had been made 'acting under secretary for audits'.

Whatever his title, Nicholson was now at the head of a field force of about 470, all formally seconded from the DoE. But did any of them have a future? When the senior men were invited to a meeting at the DoE for officials to introduce John Banham to them, it was a frosty occasion. They all assumed the DAS was about to be privatized. (It must have been a memorable moment: both Banham and Nicholson referred to the occasion in their speeches at Banham's farewell dinner in Bristol four years later.)[8] Rescuing the situation was going to take genuine leadership – and Banham provided it, in a way that many in the service never forgot. He called Nicholson and his de facto deputy, Ian Pickwell, and asked the two of them to set up a series of presentation meetings for him around the thirteen regional districts of the DAS. Every member of the service was to be given the chance to meet the first controller. And it all had to happen in the space of seven days.

Banham arrived in Bristol the next Friday. He addressed the headquarters staff and all of the local audit officers in the morning. Then he and Nicholson set off for a meeting in Cardiff that afternoon. The following Monday, they started in Newcastle . . . and so it went on, with two sessions a day for the rest of the week. The new boss provided few hard details, and perhaps indulged a taste for more hyperbole than his audiences were fully aware of. The impact, though, was unmistakable. Especially effective were a few powerful slides out of the McKinsey tool set that he used to convey the scope of his ambitions for the future. One of these was known inside the consultancy as the 'Seven Ss': it presented six balls in a circle labelled with the key aspects of any organization (structure, strategy, style, staff, skills and systems), all of them linked into a ball in the centre labelled 'shared values' (or, as Banham re-labelled it, 'vision'). He spoke so eloquently to this diagram, then and on many occasions later, that DAS men would refer admiringly if rather indelicately for years afterwards to the impact of Banham's Balls.

The DAS had always been a peculiarly secluded world, a fraternity of professional men who typically shunned contact even with their local Rotary Club in case membership should be seen as a constraint on their integrity. Few of them had ever come across a cosmopolitan figure like John Banham before. When he portrayed the future Audit Commission in ways that made it sound as though he was talking about one of McKinsey's most powerful corporate clients, they were hugely flattered. The tour restored morale and bought vital time for the Commission to sort out its assimilation of the DAS. It also provided plenty of opportunities for Banham to hear directly from the senior auditors how they believed the Commission should work.

Not that he was short of advice. Earlier in the month he had met again with Michael Heseltine and his senior officials, for a private briefing. Heseltine would be gone from the DoE by the end of January, to become defence secretary, but he and Banham seem to have got along well during their brief working partnership. Over the next few weeks Banham also met with a good many partners from the commercial accounting firms that were preparing to compete fiercely, as Heseltine had always intended, for audits in the local government sector.

By the middle of February, Banham was ready to set out his thoughts on a launch strategy in a couple of formal papers for the approval of the commissioners.[9] Compared with anything from the DoE the previous summer, they were positively Napoleonic in their scope and ambition. Sticking with his message to the DAS, he gave them a rigorous sprint round the Seven Ss. His vision of the new body entailed 'no overnight miracles'. But it would be a catalyst for profound changes, rigorously defining best practice in local government – on which there was already 'no shortage of studies' in the accounting world – and pushing to implement it as widely as possible. Strategically, they would exploit existing research, look for some quick wins and focus on the big numbers. Above all, it would be 'vital for the Commission to avoid any (mistaken) impression that it is a tool of central government; still less that it is beholden to any particular party'.

The report sketched out a sweeping three-year programme. With a 'buy' rather than 'make' philosophy, the Commission would have a lean structure, to which the DAS would be bolted on in due course. There would be as few management layers as possible: 'The Commission is not a paper machine, designed to keep Ministers out of trouble in Parliament; it exists to get things done through Local Authorities.' Four directors would report directly to Banham, covering Operations, Administration, Special Studies and Management Practice. It was assumed their head office would be in London. (The head of the Commission's embryonic computer operations at the time,

Chris Hurford, recalled seeing a different plan: 'I remember being shown a paper that Banham wrote on a plane to New York of his design for the Commission: it was going to be one man and a dog in London and everyone else would be in Bristol.'[10] But no such plan ever emerged publicly.) The information systems behind the four directors would be lavish, but in most other respects the Commission's style would be almost austere: 'There would be no tea ladies, etc.'

To the Commission members with a local government background, their new controller's no-nonsense prescriptions must have sounded jarringly unlike anything they had heard before in the public sector, and even a little alarming.

The Commission's staff and style must be characterized by a commitment to the achievement of results . . . In all communications (by telephone, letter and circular) the Commission's staff will need to be responsive, polite but firm, express themselves clearly in jargon-free, elegant English and concerned for results almost regardless of the personal effort involved.

The blueprint concluded with a series of monthly deadlines spelling out the priorities for the first year. Some of these were wildly optimistic. The 'smooth transfer of DAS staff' scheduled for completion by the end of April, for example, would drag on into the following year and have to endure being roughed up in Parliament before it was over. For the most part, though, Banham's 'painfully tight' timetable would be achieved with remarkable success.

This would owe a lot to his own leadership skills, his extraordinary energy and his flair for publicity – none of which was yet fully apparent to the commissioners, to judge from their reactions. They met for their first formal meeting on 25 February 1983, in a conference room rented from the Association of County Councils. The minutes record a high level of general support, as might have been expected. But there were hiccups, too.

Banham had no doubt about the need for effective public relations. It would be 'critical to the Commission's early success', like good legal advice, and would need to come from external specialists. Part of their job would be to help develop 'channels for communications directly to the public in a particular area via the media should this be necessary and appropriate'. All of the senior officers faced a stiff challenge in building relationships throughout the world of local government. 'For this reason alone, early appointment of a public relations adviser will be crucial.' By all means, agreed the commissioners, let there be 'a carefully balanced educational programme'. But the controller's action plan was 'in places provocative for external consumption' and he was invited to compile something shorter as a basis for press briefings. As for outside help, rather oddly, they would wait until they needed it less. 'The question of retaining a public relations consultant was held open until the Commission had more experience of dealing with the media.'

On the delicate matter of appropriate salary levels, Banham was typically forthright. 'Anyone joining the staff of the Commission from central or local government is making a risky career move: the organization does not exist; the Commission itself is (corporately) an unknown quantity; the controller is untried; the attitude of an incoming Labour administration [were the Thatcher government to fall] is uncertain.' The risk would need to be acknowledged with a salary premium, of perhaps 25 to 30 per cent. The commissioners agreed to this, but not without a distinct clearing of the throat. 'The fact that the market was now oversupplied with accountants needed to be borne in mind in fixing salaries; . . . service contracts, golden handshake provisions etc. were to be avoided . . .'

Nor did they seem very enthused with Banham's prescription for recruiting the top people. There was no time to waste on formalities, in his view. 'Executive search firms could prove an unnecessary expense; and advertising would inevitably take up administrative time that cannot be spared, result in a number of disappointed applicants and probably cause problems in local government circles over the proposed salary levels.' He should just be allowed to get on with it – collecting names from well-placed luminaries, interviewing them and passing them to the chairman for a final chat. The commissioners were careful to have the minutes note 'that all directorships should be advertised'. And for appointments from within the DAS, no fewer than four people (the controller, the chairman and two other Commission members) would have to be on an Appointments Committee.

Perhaps this was just for the record, though. The informality of its recruitment practices was in fact to remain a hallmark of the Commission for several years: it took full advantage of not being part of the civil service and subject to Whitehall's employment procedures. (It was from the early 1990s, in line with a general trend in the UK public sector, that its appointments started to be governed increasingly by a strict set of formal processes.) Key candidates, anyway, were already apparent to everyone for some of the top jobs in the first appointments round. Indeed, one of them, Cliff Nicholson, had been pushed hard at Banham in recent weeks as a deputy controller, when Banham had seemed to be questioning the need for this role at all. The deputy job had been offered by the DoE to Peter Kimmance before he retired; but he had turned it down, and no further progress had been made.[11] At the meeting on 25 February, the point was made again: 'The post of deputy controller was essential.' But by then Banham had accepted the idea with good grace, setting out a detailed job spec of his own for someone combining the post with the role of director of operations.

What he needed, in a nutshell, was a deputy who could take charge effectively of running the District Audit Service, while at the same time fitting into a head-office culture that would be very different indeed from anything the DAS was accustomed to. This would be a tough role. The service had not undergone some magical conversion with the passing of the 1982 Act. Its traditional values and attitudes were unchanged, for better and for worse. Its workload was going to be significantly expanded. Many of its auditors in the field would inevitably be suspicious of the new regime and nervous, too, about the impact of a bigger role for the private firms. For all these reasons, it needed to be led by someone whose experience and judgement as an auditor it genuinely respected – preferably, indeed, someone whose own career would reflect the rather ancient traditions of the service. And the same individual would meanwhile have to cope adroitly within the walls of the head office with the needs of a new controller, in a highly charged political environment. In short, he would need to be part Methuselah, part Machiavelli. It was the Commission's great good fortune – and Banham's – that in Cliff Nicholson they found the next best thing.

A MANAGEMENT TEAM TAKES SHAPE

For a start, though still only 51, Nicholson had a mop of white hair and a slightly stooping gait that certainly made him seem much older, and he had been in the DAS for longer than anyone else in the service could remember. He had worked his way up from the bottom to the top. Starting out in 1952 as a clerical officer with no accounting qualifications whatever, his career had included stints in some of the service's plum jobs.

As a field manager in Middlesbrough, he had run the audits for the Teesside and North Yorkshire region, which had meant six happy years (1966–72) with an unusually high level of autonomy from his seniors. He had run the DAS's training division in London very successfully for four years (1972–76) and after that had been district auditor for three years to the London metropolitan boroughs, always ranked as the top DA job in the country. By the time he was appointed Peter Kimmance's deputy in 1979, there were few people in Britain, if any, who knew more about the practice of local government auditing than Nicholson.

Just as important, though, he had had the opportunity during his long career to work on some unusual assignments. Seconded to the Ministry of Housing and Local Government for three years in 1963, he had worked on a review of local government reorganization under Richard Crossman, a politician whose impatience with the topic was glaringly obvious from the start. He had also helped to launch on its way the 1966–69 Redcliffe-Maud Commission on Local Government, submitting a well-received paper on the lessons of earlier reorganizations. (He turned down an offer of a long-term secondment to the Commission, judging his long-term career prospects in Whitehall to be less attractive than the opportunities ahead in the DAS.) And for twelve months during 1978–79, he had spent three days a week in Belfast, as the accountant on a judicial investigation into allegations that government money was somehow being funnelled into the IRA. The allegations were shown to be groundless. They did lead, however, to further allegations against the head of the Northern Ireland

Housing Executive. Nicholson led an investigation that resulted eventually in the chief architect's dismissal.[12]

Nicholson had learned a lot from all three episodes, and shown an aptitude for handling himself well in tricky political situations. He had a sharp mind and a steely resolve, once it was made up; but he was deceptively mild-mannered, and not a man to badger others less averse than himself to overstatement.

Banham left it to John Read to confirm the appointment early in March. Nicholson and his London-based de facto deputy, Ian Pickwell, were invited to meet the chairman at his corporate office at Sunlight Wharf in London's Docklands. It was not a searching interview. The three men spent most of it looking through the window at a Hanson Trust helicopter landing on a nearby rooftop pad. 'All right, then,' said Read, as the engine noise died away. 'You've got your jobs!'[13] Pickwell would have the title of associate controller and be responsible for the Commission's relations with the private firms. Nicholson would be director of operations and deputy controller. Pickwell would report to him, as would the new head of the DAS – an auditor called Bert Pyke – and a director of accounting practice, who would be appointed very shortly.

Nicholson and Pickwell were relieved to hear that they could remain in their old offices until the end of the month. Neither relished having to work out of the temporary base that had been provided in the basement of the DoE – recalled later by Banham as 'a ghastly office in the bowels of Marsham Street which was enough to depress anybody'.[14] But they came up and down to London for a string of meetings that, step by step, brought the Audit Commission to life. The DAS was brought aboard, in principle at least. Virtually all of its employees accepted a transfer to the Commission, subject to the negotiation by their union of satisfactory terms and conditions. To avoid putting any time pressure on this process, the DoE agreed that they should formally remain as secondees until 1 April 1984. The department would continue with the day-to-day administration of the DAS until then.

The finances, of course, were a different matter. An initial float of £2 million was to be settled on the Commission, to tide it through its first months. Otherwise, it had to be self-sustaining, with a budget approved in Whitehall. Its income would be derived mainly from the fees paid to it by local authorities and other bodies within its franchise, in exchange for the auditing of their accounts carried out by the DAS or by private firms acting on a mandate from the Commission. Since there was a legal requirement that their accounts be audited, the Commission's income could be broadly projected from one year to the next – though additional fees earned on VFM projects would add a slightly less predictable increment. The Commission as yet had no director of finance and administration – its first, a former assistant secretary from the Department of Health and Social Security (DHSS) called John Vaughan, would be appointed in May – so the controller and his deputy prepared the first numbers.

Annual income for the year to March 1983 had been just shy of £13 million. A little over £8 million had gone on staff costs. Another £2.2 million had been paid out for the audit work done by private firms, leaving a surplus after other costs of £1.7 million. For the 1983–84 budget, it was decided that the Commission should make no change to the basis of its fees – given that councils had already fixed their own 1983–84 budgets, to have done otherwise would hardly have got the new regime off to a rousing start – but the prospect of a sizeable increase in the volume of VFM project work fed through to a healthy 15 per cent jump in income, to £15 million. More use would be made of private firms, but start-up costs and higher staff costs would cut the surplus to £0.5 million. (In the event, the pay-out to the firms went *down* by nearly £0.5 million. Start-up costs proved heavier than expected; but with fee income more or less on budget, the surplus for the Commission's first year would still top £2 million.)

Between fixing the budget and ordering the Commission's first office stationery came a hundred pressing tasks that the first appointees handled as best they could in the remaining pre-launch weeks. Then on 1 April 1983, on what the 1982 Act had called 'the second appointed day', the Commission at last opened its doors for business, figuratively speaking at least.

In the event, Nicholson arrived that morning along with Ian Pickwell and Bert Pyke at a new permanent office that had been leased for the Commission by the DoE. It had a rather grand address – 1 Vincent Square, Westminster – on the corner of one of London's most elegant squares, conveniently close to both Whitehall and Marsham Street. The office itself was a little less grand. When a journalist at *Accountancy Age* mischievously reported that the Commission had taken possession of an office with 'acres of sunlight', John Banham sent off a cross note to the editor pointing out the number of square feet in an acre. In fact the office comprised 5,500 square feet, enough for about twenty-five people, on the first floor of a rather nondescript building. And disconcertingly, it had no furniture. Indeed, the carpets were still covered in plastic and the telephones had yet to be connected.[15]

Two others arrived in the office whom the ex-DAS men already knew – the official from the DoE who had led the preparatory work there and would be the Commission's first secretary, Richard Jones, and Patricia Church, who was to be Banham's personal assistant. Of Banham himself there was no sign at all, that first day. Midway through the morning, though, someone else turned up – a stranger to all of them, called Ross Tristem. Introductions were a little strained, which was perhaps not surprising. The late arrival was the new director, special studies. More to the point, though, he was also a Treasury secondee – and for all that his new colleagues knew, just a mole inserted rather blatantly into the Commission to report back on its progress.

'What the hell are we going to do?' said Tristem, once pleasantries had been briefly exchanged. 'We can't go home and there's nowhere to sit.' Someone suggested they find a local pub. It turned out to be an unorthodox but highly effective start to their relationships. 'By the end, we'd got to know each other a little bit. I think they were still very suspicious . . . but probably a bit less so given that I was prepared to drink three pints with them at lunchtime.'[16] Certainly, their new colleague didn't strike Nicholson and the others as a typical Treasury man, by any definition.

As they would appreciate soon enough, Tristem didn't conform to any type at all. He was a maverick. But he had the intellectual firepower and Whitehall pedigree that conformed exactly to Banham's notion of the ideal team leader for the Commission's future work on value-for-money projects. Banham had heard late in 1982 about the work that Tristem had been doing for two years at the Cabinet Office as the Treasury's representative on something called the Financial Management Initiative. In essence, he was responsible for applying rigorous VFM analysis to the output of the public expenditure programmes of several Whitehall departments. Banham was impressed by what he heard from people in the Treasury. He then remembered that by a curious chance Tristem was a good friend of his mother. (In the early 1970s she had been head of the Cornwall Area Health Authority and had turned to the Department of Health and Social Security (DHSS) in Whitehall for extra money to expand the Royal Cornwall Hospital at Treliske outside Truro. Instead they had seconded Tristem to work with her for one day a month on overhauling the hospital's operations. He helped her to design changes that paid for the expansion and much else besides. They remained close, and delivered conference papers together in subsequent years.) Within days of being offered the controller's job, Banham got his mother to arrange a meeting between them. Tristem knew nothing whatever about the putative Audit Commission beforehand. He walked away from the meeting completely sold on the idea. As he would often say later, 'Bloody good salesman, John!'[17]

It was an idea perfectly suited to a man of Tristem's background and temperament. After graduating in metal physics from Nottingham University in 1961, he had begun his career working on the Polaris programme at Aldermaston. When the Wilson government put a question mark over the future of the independent deterrent, he managed to have himself transferred to the Home Office. Here his gift for original thinking blossomed. In 1965 he took an M.Sc. Degree course at Warwick University in Operational Research (OR) and Business Studies, while setting up the country's regional crime squads and subsequently conducting a national review of their performance. (This led afterwards to a change in their modus operandi.) The research he did for this provided him with material that he then used as the basis for a Ph.D. thesis at Warwick.

Another change of government brought another move. Tristem's boss at the Home Office was poached after the 1970 election by the DHSS to set up an OR group there, reporting directly to the new health minister, Keith Joseph. Tristem followed after him. For five years he worked in the DHSS on a broad range of critical policy issues within the National Health Service, reporting more or less directly to Joseph across the heads of several policy administrators. (It was to be important later that his work at the DHSS brought him into contact with an OR group seconded to the DHSS from the National Coal Board, then regarded as being at the forefront of OR work in Britain.)

This seems to have cemented his reputation in Whitehall as a gifted outsider. If he'd lived in the Middle Ages, Tristem was the kind of thinker who would have started a radical sect and gone to the stake rather than trim his views. When he was appointed to the Treasury in 1976, as head of a new section called the General Analysis Division, the permanent secretary of the day, Douglas Wass (also an ex-OR man), told him he was to be 'the Treasury's conscience'.[18] This Tristem took to mean that he had a licence to think about all the things his Treasury colleagues might be overlooking. He concentrated on probing the systems that were in place for controlling public expenditure and looking at ways to improve on their effectiveness. His formal title by 1982 was 'deputy chief scientific officer and head of the policy analysis division'. Had he been asked after two years to supply a detailed job description for this role, the rubric 'economy, efficiency and effectiveness' would have fitted quite naturally into it.

Tristem asked his superiors in the Treasury and the Cabinet Office what they thought of the idea of him joining Banham at the Audit Commission. They were keen for him to do it. He was urged to take it as a secondment and get the best salary he could negotiate. 'Robin [Butler, a close colleague and clearly a man on the rise] said "yes, I've talked to top level about it and, yes, you go for this"' – which was encouraging, given Butler's seniority in the Treasury.[19] (He was soon to become principal private secretary to the prime minister. As permanent secretary to the Treasury from 1985 and cabinet secretary from 1988, Butler would remain a powerful contact for the Commission through the years ahead.)

Tristem and Nicholson had minds that were almost as different as their career backgrounds, but they got along well from the start. (In time, fortuitously, each would also prove to be an effective mediator in the other's relationship with Banham.) And in those first days, Nicholson was impressed that Tristem had already done his homework on the VFM story to date. In particular, Tristem showed himself

familiar with some work that the DAS had launched with Michael
Heseltine's backing in 1980–81. Authorized to spend some of the
service's surplus fee income on a few 'special studies', Kimmance and
Nicholson had commissioned research from private accountancy firms
and worked it up into VFM reports that were much more sophisticated than anything the DAS had attempted before. They had recently
been published internally for the benefit of the DAS, and Tristem had
read them carefully.

Alas, they were nowhere near the standard he intended to set for
the future: they were heavy on numbers, but lacked the analytical
rigour of an OR approach. On the other hand, they were definitely
good enough to provide the basis for some guidance notes, to help
DAS auditors in the field make at least a start on tackling the topics
they covered. Tristem saw the value of this immediately. If he could
deliver these notes in time for the next audit round, he would be able
to get his directorate off to a flying start. And since they ought not
to require a huge amount of work, he would have a precious nine
months' leeway in which to start work on his own first studies – and
time also to think through the best way of aligning a much expanded
VFM agenda with the core work of the Commission on regularity
auditing.

LAUNCHING THE FIRST AUDIT ROUND

Integrating the two work streams successfully would need a carefully
planned approach, given the demands of the DAS calendar. Each
local authority's books for the financial year 1982–83 (FY83) had
just closed on 31 March. According to normal practice, these accounts
would be audited by the DAS and signed off by the end of October.
(The Commission had been given exemption, though, from legal responsibility for the FY83 figures.) Then, from around the beginning
of November 1983, the audit would start on the 1983–84 (FY84)
accounts. The winter months of 1983–84 would offer opportunities
for the auditors to pursue VFM projects, alongside regularity checks
on systems and procedures. Then the books would close in March
on FY84, triggering a next round of deadlines for regularity work,

culminating in the completion of FY84's audits in October 1984. Thus ran the audit cycle.

Banham and Tristem together decided to build on this schedule by arranging for a series of VFM seminars to be run all over the country in November 1983. All senior auditors would be invited to attend, and would be taken through 'audit guides' on which they would then be able to draw in their field work over the winter. A handful of topics would be chosen for the FY84 audit round, which would be pursued across the whole country. This would maximize the impact of each individual guide, and would provide enough feedback to justify subsequent analysis of the results of the work. All being well, this approach would be adopted every year. And the pro forma VFM recipe had one further ingredient. Ahead of the November seminars each year, the Special Studies directorate would prepare the way with fully researched studies on all of the chosen topics. These studies would be published in dashing yellow covers, and would be 'written in crisp, clear language so as to be readily understandable by ratepayers and the media as well as more specialist audiences'.[20]

With these decisions, remarkably, Banham and Tristem set going a working model that was without precedent in British public life and that proved over many years to be extraordinarily powerful. The essence of the model was simple and threefold: first, a national study based on comparative data; second, publication of a national report, drawing upon the study to identify best-practice ideas; and third, a country-wide audit of existing local practice in the delivery of the respective public services, drawing upon the national picture in order to make suggestions for improvement. It was a model that cleverly squared all of the separate obligations placed on the Commission by the 1982 Act – while in no way marginalizing its responsibility for appointing independent auditors, either from the DAS itself or from the private sector, to audit the public sector bodies under its aegis. And by 'buying in' the audit services at one price and 're-selling' them at a mark-up, the Commission would generate the revenues needed to pay for the preparation of its national reports and audit guides at the centre. Since the scope of the regularity work changed relatively little from one year to the next, as noted already, revenue growth would largely depend upon how much VFM work the councils decided to ask for. But this would certainly not be made the target of a hard sell: the Commission would agree an overall level of fees with the local authority associations at the start of each year, and would leave it to auditors and their respective authorities to settle on individual contracts, up to the agreed total. As the efficacy of the VFM programme came to be appreciated, so the quantity of VFM work (and fees) would rise.* Thus were laid the foundations for an institution that it seems fair to say no one in the DoE had fully envisaged.

The model was set out for the commissioners by their controller within the very first month, though possibly they underestimated the media element. The minutes of their 28 April meeting noted approvingly: 'A library of case studies of best practice would be made available to all auditors, and the Audit Commission would work with relevant universities and the Local Government Training Board to set management standards.'[21] Banham struck a slightly different note, picked up in the DAS newsletter – the new studies directorate, he stressed, would be at pains 'to avoid the academic literature business'.

So much for the long-term plan. In the Commission's inaugural year, some short-cuts were going to be needed. Recruits had still to be found for the special studies team, and further discussions would be needed with the Commission members before the first topics could be agreed. There was no possibility of delivering finished studies by November. Hence the value of the reports that Tristem was inheriting from the Audit inspectorate. The DAS could go forward with these, while work was beginning on research programmes for the

---

* Reviewing the implementation of this model three years later, at an appearance in front of the House of Commons Public Accounts Committee, Banham would take some pride in the outcome: 'The fee levels which we negotiate every year with the local authority associations limit the amount of work that can be done since we have to break even taking one year with another . . . So I could say that the main constraint [on our fee income] is the authority's belief that audit represents good value. That is the way it ought to be. We have resisted the temptation to force more work down people's throats . . . Basically what we lay down at the centre is the rate per day; the number of days is for the local authority to agree with the auditor. I am pleased to be able to report to the Committee that in the four years that we have been operating this system I cannot think of one instance where the auditor and the local authority have been unable to agree on the number of days that is appropriate' (*Minutes of Evidence*, PAC Session, 8 December 1986, paras. 326–7).

first full home-grown studies. There was a legacy of four inspectorate reports. Tristem had to put up with a lot of ribaldry over the fact that the weightiest of them, *Securing Further Improvements in Refuse Collection*, was built around a model called the Refuse Operations System Simulation – or ROSS, for short.[22] The others focused on securing better value for the £1.5 billion net spending by local authorities on polytechnics and colleges of further education; on reducing the cost to local government of purchasing goods and services from outside suppliers; and on improving productivity in the police, by shifting more work from uniformed officers to civilians, who each cost roughly £6,000 less per annum.

To coordinate the writing of audit guides on the four inspectorate reports, Tristem turned to two senior auditors, John Hall and Jack Sprigg, who had been involved in the original commissioning. Their brief was to pull together a pack – it later came to be christened the Audit Commission Handbook – that could be distributed to the DAS at the time of the planned November seminars.

With that set in train, Tristem turned to the task of finding some kindred spirits for his special studies team. His very first appointments were made that summer of 1983 and showed Tristem's great value to John Banham as someone with strong networks in both Whitehall and the rarefied world of operational research. One new hire was a former colleague from the Treasury's OR unit, Bert Benham. Another was an experienced OR consultant, Dr Stephen (Steve) Evans, from the Local Government Operational Research Unit (LGORU) in Reading. (It was part of the Royal Institution of Public Administration.)

Benham and Evans would help Tristem to entrench the OR mindset at the Commission. But what exactly *was* OR? Originating from the Second World War – when teams of scientists analysed data in order to answer questions such as 'Where would our anti-aircraft guns be most effectively positioned?' or 'What would be the most efficient search pattern in hunting for a submarine?' – OR brought a highly disciplined analytical approach to the resolution of management problems, through a better understanding of neglected underlying data. There was no shortage of neglected underlying data in UK local government. The breadth of subject matter being prepared for the

November seminars gave a hint of the range of available targets. The challenge was to pick topics that would yield the best return.

Evans, a physics graduate like Tristem, had begun his OR career with a stint in the Department of Transport. Since then he had worked for ten years at LGORU and made a name for himself as an expert on transportation, and vehicle-fleet management in particular. That was a clue to one idea in Tristem's mind. But Banham wanted them to take their time making a careful selection of the studies for 1984. He also saw the political importance, in the early days, of being seen as open to others' suggestions. This produced some comically futile meetings. He, Tristem and Nicholson went together one fine spring morning to meet with the local government committee of the TUC. Round the table at the TUC's headquarters were assembled all the union leaders representing workers in the sector. Banham led off, explaining the Commission's basic approach and asking them if they had any study ideas. 'They couldn't think of anything we could possibly do that would be of any use whatsoever ... They all had their harangue ... how good they were and what a waste of time we were. We were laughing at the end of it, and so were they!'[23]

More surprisingly, perhaps, most meetings with local authority officers and members' associations proved almost as unproductive. This is not to say they were a waste of time – on the contrary. Banham launched himself and all his senior colleagues on a blitz of conference speeches and presentations over several months precisely because he saw the huge importance of establishing the Commission's reputation in the wider world of accounting and local government politics. (He was invariably the star of the show, dazzling the audience with his McKinsey-style slides. But all of the Commission's staff were in huge demand. In his monthly report to the members in June, Banham noted: 'We have committed ourselves to around 15 talks to worthwhile audiences over the next 4 months; and commitments are increasing at the rate of about five a week.')[24] But very rarely did any of these appearances lead to a specific request for a research study from the Commission. For all his marketing brilliance, Banham's message about the enormous potential of the Commission was going to take a while to sink in.

In one sense, though, it was the ideal outcome: the Commission effectively had a blank sheet of paper with which to start. Over the summer, study proposals were aired with the local authorities so that a final programme could be announced 'after consultations'. It was then shown to the relevant departments in Whitehall, and approved by the Commission's members. The programme finally emerged in October 1983. Four special studies were listed. They would tackle non-teaching costs in schools; social services for the elderly, children in care and the mentally handicapped; vehicle-fleet maintenance; and housing and property maintenance. Full, yellow-jacketed booklets on all four would be published to a schedule starting towards the end of 1984.

It was quite a commitment. Yet the in-house resources at Vincent Square were still extremely limited – even though Banham had tried to line up support for the studies work by hiring a former local authority chief executive, Peter Brokenshire, as 'director of management practice'. His contribution, Banham had told the members, would be to bring 'mathematical/computer expertise and the marketing flair to present the [studies'] conclusions and get things done'.[25] Until the studies were available, though, there was little Brokenshire could usefully do. Indeed, it was to be some time before Brokenshire managed to establish any clear role for himself. Inevitably, most of the heavy lifting for studies would have to be contracted out to the private accountancy firms. Any lack of interest on their part would therefore have been seriously embarrassing. Fortunately, by October 1983 the Commission's relations with the firms had been substantially ironed out, to their general satisfaction. Though not, perhaps, entirely as Heseltine had anticipated.

DECIDING ON THE PRIVATE FIRMS' SHARE

Since getting a foot in the door in 1972, the private firms had lobbied ceaselessly to have the local government market properly opened up to them. After all, it comprised hundreds of authorities that were the equivalent in size of their largest corporate clients. By chance there were now thirteen firms with at least some relevant experience, just as there were thirteen audit districts in England and Wales (including Metropolitan London). All of the firms had warmly applauded the Commission's arrival, even though it had long been clear that talk of the DAS being completely wound down was wide of the mark.

The Commission had *carte blanche* under the 1982 Act to appoint auditors as it saw fit. As noted already, Heseltine's choice of commissioners seemed (to some, at least) a clear indication that he was expecting to see perhaps a majority of audits transferred from the DAS to partners in the private firms. The latter were certainly staring expectantly at the audit pie by the spring of 1983, confident of a much larger slice. Both Heseltine and the firms must therefore have been surprised to discover, quite early in the process, that Read and Banham shared with Kenneth Bond and David Lees a deep scepticism about the ability of the private firms to handle the work.

In Banham's case, scepticism based on past experience seems to have been quickly corroborated by his own dealings with the firms on local government affairs. Writing to a newly appointed director in June, he commented: 'I have not, candidly, been especially impressed with what I have seen of the private firms – with one or two honourable exceptions.'[26] One of the members, Noel Hepworth, recalled his three businessmen colleagues on the Commission expressing similar views in quite forthright terms: 'I think they were basically saying, "we're under a lot of pressure to increase the proportion going to the private sector, but in practice . . ." – well, their comments implied that they didn't think this was a terribly good idea.'[27]

In short, they left it to Cliff Nicholson, assisted by Ian Pickwell, to measure out the pie. And these two approached the job as dispassionately as a couple of long-serving DAS men reasonably could have done. It had been obvious to both of them for quite a while that the firms would have to be given more, for the simple reason that the DAS could no longer cope on its own. There were 456 principal local authorities in England and Wales to be audited, plus more than 8,000 smaller entities including 250 drainage boards and 200 other local bodies such as police authorities and port-health authorities. The DAS had been 'seriously under strength' for a few years, as the Commission's first annual report would note in 1984 (when it ended its first full year with 492 staff, up from 474 in April 1983). Now it was being projected that additional VFM work would expand the man-days required for the annual audit round by perhaps 20–30 per cent.

For the accounts that had just closed in March, the commission was deploying the thirteen firms on work that made up about 15 per cent of the fee value of the local government market. The list of firms had in practice been decided by the audited bodies themselves. It was unlikely the Commission would make many changes to it, if any. But how much extra work should they be asked to take on in 1983–84? Nicholson agreed a set of broad parameters with Banham. He would have to ensure that each DAS district remained as an economically viable practice for the service; at the same time, each private firm should be given enough work to allow it to develop real expertise, preferably in reasonably concentrated areas so that individual partners could build good links with their local DAS counterparts. It was also agreed that there would be no question of 'forcing auditors down authorities' throats'.[28] On the contrary, any local preference for a change should be given a sympathetic hearing – especially where DAS resources had been depleted by recent staff losses.

The deputy controller set off on a round of discussions with authority officers (and sometimes members, too) all over the country. Two Commission members lent a hand with the work: Noel Hepworth brought a former finance director's experience to bear, and all of his influence as the current head of CIPFA, while Roy Shaw had probably been dealing with the DAS as a local council politician for longer than anyone else in the country. Both of them supported Nicholson's own hunch that, keen as the firms were to ramp up their involvement, relatively few of their partners would yet have the skills to handle the expanding VFM agenda.

With happy timing, Peter Kimmance at this point handed a report to the Commission about the performance in the field of the 'additional district auditors' appointed by Heseltine early in 1982. Kimmance and a retired senior partner from one of the leading firms, Coopers & Lybrand, had been mandated back then to produce a performance review after twelve months. Through the snowy January and February of 1983, they had visited all but one of them on the location of their audits. Kimmance told the Commission, 'it appeared that all the firms had carried out a good audit of the authorities' financial systems, but that there had been great difference[s] in the breadth and depth of their value for money audits ... [which] clearly represented a major culture change. Too many were re-inventing the wheel; their operations needed to be put on a more systematic basis.'[29]

This view strengthened Banham's case for more direction from the centre on all VFM work. It also confirmed Nicholson's inclination to go for audit reassignments that would bring private firms into authorities posing relatively lightweight VFM challenges, leaving the tougher nuts for the DAS. Nicholson handed over his list of proposed transfers in the middle of April. He envisaged reassigning approximately sixty authorities to private sector auditors. The bottom line would be roughly a 30 per cent share of the FY84 audit workload for the firms. Endless hours were then devoted to the list's implementation. (Conceivably, Heseltine would have chided the businessmen on the Commission for going native, in putting up with all this discussion. But he was gone now, and no one else at the DoE had his interest in the matter.) The Commission debated the selection criteria and pored over the authorities' responses. The firms were required to parade their virtues in beauty contests that lasted through most of May and June, with Banham himself joining Nicholson and Pickwell in a process pursued with some rigour. As the senior partner of one of the firms recalled, 'they gave us a very thorough going over'.[30] The accountancy profession hummed with gossip about the likely outcome all through the summer. The selected partners were introduced to their new clients through July. The signing of contracts lasted well into October.

And when all of this was over, with some transfers amended here and some objections accommodated there, the pie-slices ended up just as intended – with the firms taking a workload of 28 per cent. Four of them would have the lion's share, and the rest of the quota would be scattered more or less equally across the other nine.[31] The possibility was left open – if only to placate a disgruntled 'privatization' lobby – that the firms' share might rise to 40 per cent in FY85, if their performance and that of the DAS warranted it. In the event, the 70/30 split, as it was called, would remain little changed for the next twenty-five years. (For a summary of the private firms' share of the market through the whole period, see Appendix 6.)

The durability of the 70/30 arrangement was a tribute to Nicholson's diplomatic skills and the care with which the proposed list was sold into the field. With some help from Noel Hepworth, the number of seriously aggrieved authorities was kept within single figures. The private firms for their part acquiesced in the 70/30 split. The resulting arrangements were not ideal: several firms were left with client authorities scattered all over the country. (Thornton Baker, one of the smaller firms, found it had one audit in Cheshire, two in South Wales and one in Oxfordshire – rather curbing the profitability of an audit division based in Manchester.) But the overall scheme, and in particular the 30 per cent quota, was quietly accepted. Perhaps this was simply a tacit acknowledgement by the firms that, as yet, they lacked the in-house resources to do more. They had also been skilfully handled by the ever-attentive Ian Pickwell.

One of the prominent private partners involved from the earliest days was Michael Dallas, of Coopers & Lybrand, one of the four main firms engaged in the first round of 1983. Dallas had worked on local authority audits since 1979 and liaised closely with Pickwell on bringing the firms into line with the new regime's requirements. He felt the firms had plenty to teach the DAS on the purely accounting front, however much they might lag on the VFM business. Besides, the firms had their own reservations over the latter. Dallas recalled: 'John had very strong ideas about what he wanted. He wanted a lot of aggression from the auditors – with plenty of quantification on the prospective savings. The firms felt a little nervous about that.'[32]

There were some other aspects of working for the Commission that prompted misgivings, too – not least its tough line on fees. As noted already, the members decided that it would not be politic to ask local authorities to swallow any increase in FY84 for which they would not already have budgeted. This meant that, for the first phase of the FY84 audits, running from November 1983 until March 1984, fees were going to be pegged at some distinctly sub-market rates. After 1 April 1984, in a break with the past, fees would be calculated on the basis of time spent on the audit, rather than (as previously) the size of the authority being audited. And all authorities would be charged a new *per diem* rate, averaging out for an audit team (and weighted according to the contribution of its variously salaried DAS members) at £170. This, though, was not the rate that the private firms would be paid. In fairly ruthless fashion, the Commission made its own estimate of what the firms' charge-out rates would be for FY85 – and then applied a 30 per cent cut across the board. Even after allowing for a 10 per cent increment to cover costs, the weighted outcome came to a *per diem* rate of only £145. This was what the Commission proposed to pay them, while pocketing the £25 difference as a margin to help defray its central costs.[33]

Another dictate that caused some firms' partners to take a deep breath was a virtually complete ban on consulting work for any authority by the firm retained as its auditor. This was totally counter to the prevailing trend within the commercial sector, where consulting revenues from audit clients were rising at a brisk pace, and must have come as a disappointment to some senior partners. Having been a consultant himself for thirteen years, Banham was sensitive to their loss. He set out the arguments for and against a blanket ban at some length for the Commission.[34] It was impossible to deny that the prospect of consultancy work might affect an auditor's independence, he conceded. Nor could they seriously defer to the profession's own safeguards, 'if indeed they are in place at all'. Banning consultancy work therefore had to be one option. His own recommendation, though, was that they should allow the firms to take consulting contracts provided that the Commission was always notified at the bidding stage, and given a chance to stamp on any impropriety. Among the virtues of this approach was that it would avert the possibility of firms abandoning Commission work, 'since consulting contracts are often more lucrative and strategically important to firms than individual audits'.

The Commission wasn't having it. After a lengthy discussion at only their second monthly meeting, in April 1983, they opted for a general prohibition. The Commission's rules, said the chairman, needed to be as clear-cut and unambiguous as the rules governing standards of behaviour in local government itself. This was a brave decision by John Read – and was taken against the wishes of at least one Commission member, Ian Hay Davison, who was a former senior partner of the accountants Arthur Andersen. But it resulted in a prohibition that, many years later, was accepted as good governance practice throughout the UK corporate sector. In the meantime, it was strictly adhered to by the Commission. The minutes of the commissioners' meeting on 5 June 1986, for example, recorded a request from Kent County Council for permission to award an £80,000 contract to its auditor for some consultancy work on its police authority. The members turned it down.

No doubt Read took his strong line out of personal conviction. But it must also have seemed the only prudent course, following a row that had blown up in Parliament in March. Birmingham City Council had been attacked for paying consultancy fees to the private firm that was responsible for its audit. Questions were raised about the integrity of the new regime in local government auditing. For the members, struggling to establish their credibility and to control an ambitious and unconventional chief executive, this was a little alarming. One of the 1982 Act's few real strictures on them was that a Code of Practice needed to be drawn up as soon as possible and submitted to Parliament for its approval. It was no time to risk adopting any policy that could be misconstrued by mischievous MPs.

ESTABLISHING SOME FIRST AUDIT GUIDELINES

The first draft of this Code of Practice, received by the members two months prior to the Commission's April start, had itself posed rather a dilemma. Running to 150 pages, it was far too long to be used as a box for the parliamentary tick of approval. On the other hand, it was not a paragraph longer than it needed to be, if it was to satisfy the 1982 Act's requirements for a Code that covered the 'standards, procedures and techniques to be adopted by auditors'.

The draft had been compiled between March and September 1982, under Cliff Nicholson's supervision, by an auditor with long experience of working both for the DAS and for CIPFA. As the man responsible for CIPFA's audit activities, Mike Barnes had been the natural choice as principal draughtsman. He had started his career with the DAS in 1968 and in 1981 had been secretary to a joint DAS/

CIPFA group that, for the first time, had prepared a set of external audit standards for local government auditors. These standards had provided the bedrock for the new Code.

It was dauntingly comprehensive. The members pondered the idea of asking someone to write a layman's guide to it. Then better sense prevailed. The extensive technical content of the draft was siphoned off into a working guide for those in the field, and later appeared as an internal publication, *The Commission Auditor*. Then Noel Hepworth and the other senior accountants on the Commission set to work on a much abbreviated version, which emerged in April as a second draft that was only 10 per cent as long as the original. This was the document that went off to all the professional accountancy bodies and local government associations for their comments. Subsequent amendments were relatively minor. After no less than 350 copies of it had been distributed to interested MPs, the Code was duly approved by Parliament in November.

The published version of the Code ran to eighteen pages in a small yellow-covered booklet. For the most part, it was a lofty restatement in forty-five paragraphs of the philosophy behind the Audit Commission, as defined through all of the formative discussions since 1970. In one critical respect, though, it rammed home a feature of the 1982 Act that had perhaps been too little noted until now. Paragraph 21 ('Auditor's Opinion') stated innocuously enough 'that when he has concluded the audit, the auditor shall state his opinion on the statement of accounts . . . He should refer expressly in his opinion . . . [as to whether] the statement of accounts presents fairly the financial position of the authority.' A seven-page appendix then helpfully set out the implications of this, with pro forma letters that might be used by auditors in the field.

If the auditors needed a reminder of the deeper waters they were now swimming into, this was it. Historically, as we have seen, no such opinion had been required of the DAS officer. He had *not* been obliged, like his counterpart in the commercial sector, to lay his professional reputation on the line with every completed audit. Different individuals approached the audit task in a whole variety of ways, and handled different authorities in disparate ways, too. Now, all alike would be signing up to one standardized assertion. This needed their auditing techniques to be a lot more uniform – and probably, indeed, a great deal more robust all round.

In their private discussion together in January, Michael Heseltine had no doubt shared with Banham his own longstanding scepticism about the calibre of the DAS. Talking to the private firms during his first few months in the job, Banham had picked up plenty of unguarded comments from partners that left him suspecting the situation might be rather worse than even Heseltine had supposed. Whether or not as a direct consequence of discussions about the Code, meanwhile, technical queries from field auditors were piling up fast in Vincent Square by June. What he urgently needed, Banham realized, was 'someone who understood about accountancy, which I did not'[35] – someone who could take a forensic view of what the auditors were actually doing in their work, and ensure it was up to the mark. Perhaps it was a little surprising that someone answering to this description had not been brought aboard right at the start. In yet another stroke of good fortune, anyway, the right man now appeared out of the blue.

Harry Wilkinson was a sometimes disquietingly self-effacing accountant with a distinguished career behind him at the firm of Ernst & Whinney. By chance, like Tristem, he had a personal link to Banham: the two of them had been in the same house together at Charterhouse school. It was Banham's name on a letterhead that initially caught his eye when a contact in Whitehall suggested he give the Commission a call. There was no doubting Wilkinson's real appeal, though, to the commissioners and directors who interviewed him. A classics scholar at Oxford and a partner at E&W, he was a clever man with a real grasp of technical accounting issues that suggested he would cope well with the innovative aspects of being the director of 'accountancy practice'. (This was a misnomer, of course: he should have been titled director of 'auditing practice', but never was. His title was not so misleading, though, in so far as he went on to work extensively on local government accounting as well as the Commission's own auditing – see Chapter 7.)

Wilkinson's career had much in common with John Read's. Like the Commission's chairman, he had worked extensively in the US and several European countries. Aged 47 (the same age as Read, as it happened), he was managing partner of E&W's offices in Zurich, Geneva and Vienna. Wanting to live in England now that he had a young family, he saw the new post as the rare opportunity it was – and took a sizeable cut in his salary to land it. He couldn't start until September, but Banham was writing before the end of June with candid assessments of how much needed to be done. 'My impression . . . is that in the regularity field and in terms of documentation in particular there is some ground to be made up; and the service may also have fallen behind in its use of computers and word processors . . . In my view, the most immediate risk facing the Commission is that the District Audit Service will not prove up to the new challenges.'[36]

If Harry Wilkinson read this as rhetoric to fire him up for the job, he knew better by November. What he discovered in his first couple of months was disconcerting. Things began well enough. His first impression of Vincent Square was of 'lots of enthusiasm, not that much organization'.[37] He had felt a little intimidated by some effusive Banham profiles of his future colleagues, and was relieved to find that not all of them were mega-stars of the Treasury. Two of them joined his Account Practice directorate: Bill Miller as quality control manager and Mike Barnes, seasoned by all his exertions on the Code of Practice, as the general technical adviser. Wilkinson welcomed their down-to-earth approach, and it was agreed that he and Miller would set off immediately to visit some audit teams in the field, as they were finalizing their work on the FY83 audits. They visited nine DAS districts and three private firms.

His only previous experience of public sector work had been as a newly qualified accountant with E&W in the Liberian capital, Monrovia. Even allowing for this, though, Wilkinson was a little shocked by what he found. 'Likeable and conscientious people though they were, [the DAS officers] were not working to any sort of disciplines as far as I could see . . . Nobody was saying to them "this is what you've got to do on an audit", so they were choosing which areas to investigate, those that suited their book.'[38] The results could be bizarre. The first audit Wilkinson reviewed was of a county council in the Midlands. The DAS team had chosen to examine whether or not its pension fund had received the correct dividend income on its investments. They appeared not to have heard of dividend vouchers, however, and had spent several days looking up the annual reports of all the companies in the pension portfolio to collate their dividend-payment details. Another worthless exercise had seen the same team poring over details of the overtime pay for 'retained' (part-time) firemen. It was a minute detail in the overall scheme of the council's finances but again had absorbed days and days of effort. 'So you had an audit lasting 500 man-days or so, that produced neither any sort of assurance of anything, nor any particularly clever recommendations.' Wilkinson asked Bill Miller if they had stumbled by chance on a maverick audit. They had not. It was clearly all too typical. This was the Heseltine hunch, amply confirmed.

The new director of accountancy practice returned to his office, intent on producing some detailed guidelines on how regularity work should be done. Whereas the Code of Practice had been 'a sort of high-level statement of aspirations',[39] he would focus on the brass tacks of the audit business. A stream of memoranda followed – until someone in the DAS suggested it might be far more effective to put together a general manual. Wilkinson agreed with Miller and Barnes that this made sense, and they set to work against a 31 March 1984 deadline.

Wilkinson's experience that autumn helps explain why the Commission's newly fanfared ambitions were being received with some scepticism among the senior officers of the local government world. They knew their DAS of old. It would take more than a summer of high-tech presentations to persuade them the 'three Es' were much more than a slogan. Then again, if the 'three Es' *did* begin to stir any real change, this was all too likely to be seen in the town halls as proof that the Commission was simply a tool of the Thatcher government. So the Commission would be damned if it had an impact, and damned if it didn't.

Cliff Nicholson saw the credibility gap at first hand many times. He later recalled, for example, going with Banham in July 1983 to an all-day conference in Hammersmith of the London boroughs' treasurers. The controller enthused his audience with a lively presentation in the morning. But he announced at lunchtime that he had to go on to another engagement, which left Nicholson alone to observe the aftermath. 'Well, the afternoon was quite a different meeting. The treasurers were all chuckling at John's exaggerations in the morning session. They were very pleased that he was sounding off and getting blows in against the government – but they didn't actually believe him.'[40]

The scepticism endured, despite the fact that – as a message from the controller pointed out in the *Audit News* newsletter that October – senior staff from the Commission were giving 'between them, four or five talks a week to relevant audiences around the country'. The main purpose of Banham's message was to show that everything possible was being done 'to clear up questions and issues that could stand in the way of the DAS doing an outstanding job in the audit round about to begin'. It was headlined 'We are nearing the end of the beginning' – a fair way of characterizing the weeks leading up to the launch of the November 1983 seminars.

The main questions and issues standing in the Commission's way – would it be truly independent? could it win the confidence of the local government world? would its people in the field be able to cope? – would take rather longer to answer. But this could not detract from what had already been achieved. A formidable team of directors had been recruited to lead the Commission. A working partnership had been successfully forged with the private firms. And a full programme of special studies had been set on its way, starting with the audit guides and local authority profiles that were now ready for distribution. All of these achievements were on show in the Audit Guidance seminars that now followed in Ipswich, Sheffield, Chester and Cardiff. It was the first time that DAS auditors and partners from the private firms had sat down together to prepare for an audit round.

Each man received a copy of the first edition of the Audit Commission Handbook, *Improving Economy, Efficiency and Effectiveness in Local Government in England and Wales*. Actually a ring binder, every copy had a pro forma 'statistical profile' (providing a picture of Barset borough council, with apologies to Trollope); a lucid overview of what should be looked for in well-managed authorities with a graphic illustration (Banham's Balls, no less); a section on each of the four key areas for special examination over the winter of 1983–84; and an appendix with further summary notes on development control, school meals and leisure centres.

The seminars went off well – and there was much praise all round for the VFM handbook. Indeed, on the next occasion of a Commons debate over local government, the secretary of state for the environment – now Patrick Jenkin, who had been appointed in the autumn – described the handbook as 'one of the most powerful tools for efficiency ever put into the hands of local councillors'.[41] The subject of the Commons debate was the Rate Support Grant. The Commission would have plenty to say about this in 1984, eliciting a less upbeat response from Whitehall.

3

Declarations of Independence, 1983–85

As the front-line troops of the District Audit Service and the private firms marched away from those November seminars in 1983 to begin their assault on the FY84 audit, the Commission directors knew they had made a decent start. Their plans had made a good impression on the leading auditors. But would the Commission itself have the big guns to provide all the support that the new tactics for the DAS and private firms would require? With fewer than twenty people at the centre and revenues of just £15 million, it needed a leap of faith to imagine that the Commission would ever have much real impact on some £26 billion worth of yearly spending by local authorities.

Few outside Vincent Square were ready to make that leap. Certainly not the great majority of local government personnel, nor probably a majority of the district auditors themselves. In Whitehall, Heseltine had been gone from the DoE almost a year and no one else had emerged to champion the audit cause. The Labour Party assumed (like many others) that the Commission would one way or another be squeezing town-hall budgets on the government's behalf and duly promised to abolish it at the first opportunity. This looked some way off, following the Falklands War and the Tory landslide in the June 1983 election. But Labour's hostility reflected a widespread ambivalence about the Commission's agenda, and a general scepticism that it would last long. Searching for recruits to Vincent Square a few months later, Ross Tristem was turned down by at least one senior civil servant on the grounds that a move to the Commission was just too much of a career gamble.[1] Yet within a very few years, the Commission would be established as a formidable force in local government – with a media profile far beyond anything achieved before in the normally arcane world of councillors and their committees.

In fact, its mixed reception in 1983 is a first clue to this remarkable outcome. In a sense, the Commission could hardly have timed its arrival better. The historical tension between the two traditions of local and central rule has been described as 'one of the most serious fault-lines in contemporary British government'.[2] The line was hit by a series of Richter-scale tremors in the 1980s – culminating, of course, in the poll-tax debacle. This made local government politics into big news and engaged the attention of the politicians at Westminster as had rarely happened before in twentieth-century Britain. Press comment on the poll-tax crisis, when it came, would prompt far more references in the media to Wat Tyler and the Peasants' Revolt of 1381 than to any modern parallels – because there were none. Councillors had come into conflict with the law at Clay Cross in the 1970s, at Poplar in the 1920s and at Keighley in the 1870s. But none of these episodes came close in scale to the rate-capping crisis of the 1980s, let alone the poll tax. The Commission, straddling the local/central fault-line, had an attentive media audience from the start.

Things might have worked out differently. The war between Thatcher's cabinet and the councils could conceivably have left the Commission cowering in the crossfire. Ensuring that this did not happen, and enabling the Commission instead to step skilfully into the space left between the two sides, required real leadership. Even Banham's most fervent admirers never praised him as the soul of discretion – and his ebullience would cause some problems. But he was a genuine leader, and without him there would have been no Commission worth its name to take forward beyond the mid-80s. Everyone involved in the story, interviewed twenty years later, was agreed on that.

If Banham had perhaps underestimated the depth of the Thatcher cabinet's animosity towards local government when he started out in January 1983, he was well aware of it by November. The Tories' manifesto in the June election had marked another stage in their protracted struggle to curb 'overspending'. Superficially, it was the same struggle that had fired Heseltine's interest in the audit process back in 1979. Heseltine, though, had seen poor local government as essentially a management problem that needed fixing. He never shared the antipathy towards town-hall politics evident among Thatcher and those aspiring to be One of Us. Theirs was now the prevailing sentiment, and the gloves were off. Legislation was promised that would allow Whitehall to cap the level of rates charged by local authorities.

A White Paper on 'rate-capping' – largely the brainchild of Leon Brittan, the chief secretary to the Treasury between 1981 and 1983 – duly appeared in the autumn. The newly installed environment secretary, Patrick Jenkin, summarized the political motivation behind it in a notable speech that September. 'The government has a duty to heed the increasingly bitter complaints of our domestic and commercial ratepayers. There can be no room in our unitary state for unilateral declarations of independence by individual local authorities relying on claims of a local mandate.'[3]

The prospect of rate-capping seriously alarmed many people in local government, not all of them Labour supporters by any means. Commission directors and district auditors in the field encountered a rising level of concern over where things were headed. And if they came to a full-blown crisis, where would this leave the Commission and its supposed independence?

Put crudely, Banham persuaded John Read and the members that only one course was really open to them over the coming year. The Commission would have to embrace a twin-track strategy. It would draw on the VFM audits of the winter to produce some 'prototype' national studies of sufficient quality to reassure the Treasury and the DoE that the original objectives of the 1982 legislation were being met. They would be audit-progress reports, in effect, but would prefigure the full-blown special studies that would follow. (The statistical profiles of individual councils would supplement these reports.) At the same time, the Commission would persuade the local authorities of its genuine independence from Whitehall by producing – as Section 27 of the Act had intended – a searching critique of some aspect of government policy. Specifically, it would tackle the damaging consequences of the way in which local government was being part-funded by Whitehall.

THE AUDIT-PROGRESS REPORTS

In the event, three audit-progress reports appeared in March, July and August 1984.[4] They went a long way towards meeting the first goal, at least as far as the Treasury was concerned. All three drew on mountains of data, assembled in the first instance by the consultancy arms of some of the leading accountancy firms and other external agencies. A project team from Harry Wilkinson's old firm, Ernst & Whinney, delivered the material for *Bringing Council Tenants' Arrears Under Control*. Consultants from Deloitte, Haskins & Sells worked on *Reducing the Cost of Local Government Purchases*. The third report, *Securing Further Improvements in Refuse Collection*, drew heavily on a research project conducted by the Local Authorities Management Services Advisory Committee (LAMSAC) and field findings gathered together by consultants from Arthur Andersen. (Consultants from Arthur Young worked on a fourth report, *Obtaining Better Value from Further Education*, which was not published until June 1985.)

By the time that the firms' work emerged as Audit Commission reports, however, it had been transformed out of all recognition. This involved a process that the outside world would soon come to identify closely with the whole *raison d'être* of the Commission. First, Ross Tristem and his two-man special studies team worked long hours on the presentation of the analytical content and organized the first drafts. Then they handed their drafts to the controller – whose editing amounted to a virtual re-writing of all three. This rather remarkable fact was a tribute, first, to Banham's prodigious energy. The three finished reports together ran to a total of well over a hundred pages, excluding introductions, summaries and appendices. Even allowing for a generous sprinkling of tables and charts, this represented an awful lot of closely argued text. Much of the content was inevitably dry stuff. But Banham brought to it all the brilliance he had displayed back in 1975–76 in his report on the UK motor industry.

He brought more than his own facility with the pen, though. Banham was of course also a distinguished alumnus from one of the best academies in the world for learning the arts of presentation. He applied the McKinsey rule-book, and it showed. In later years, the use of charts would become a staple of corporate life in Britain, as it had already become in the US. When that happened, many of McKinsey's basic designs – with their clever use of pie, bar, column, curve and dot – found their way into general usage. In the mid-1980s, though, they were still a revelation to most audiences seeing them for the first time. Hence the impact of a typical McKinsey presentation, even before its core content was really digested. It was not a strength that had evolved by accident. McKinsey had employed talented people in its 'visual aids' department for years. Their department head, Gene Zelazny, even wrote a book called *Say it with Charts*.[5] The basic creed was: 'chart the data so that their most significant message is immediately evident'.[6] All this had long become second nature for Banham and he instilled it into everything that the Audit Commission produced. Its charts, like McKinsey's, were designed to offer a message you couldn't refuse.

The outcome, more than evident in these first three titles, amounted to a novel way of looking at local government. It would be wrong to suggest that rigorous analysis had no precedent, of course. Various university-linked bodies and independent entities such as the Local Government Operational Research Unit had been doing excellent research for some years. But they made no attempt to present their conclusions in the way that the Audit Commission did, and their impact on councils and the wider public had been relatively slight. The council activities that now featured in the Commission's first reports had been dissected and put under a microscope as rarely before. And the findings were presented with an eye to remedial action, as though the councils were businesses with ailing margins in need of urgent attention. It was all a far cry from the usual stuff of local government studies.

The contents, for a start, were crystal clear. The first report, *Tenants' Arrears*, led the way: it documented the Problem, set out the Underlying Causes and prescribed the Action Required. An executive summary captured the urgency of the topic in less than two pages. Over a million council tenants were in arrears, as of September 1983, owing a total of £240 million. Within the boroughs of Inner and Outer London, remarkably, almost half of all tenants were in arrears.

And that was just the first paragraph. The contents of these reports were also thoroughly down-to-earth. Indeed, Banham kicked off *Reducing the Cost of Local Government Purchases* almost theatrically with his own analysis of something utterly mundane, with an arresting conclusion.

The very first exhibit (McKinsey-speak for any graphic) illustrated the fact that local authorities all over the country were paying wildly different prices for the brown envelopes in which rate demands were sent out to every household each year. Some spent less than 45p on a packet of 100, while others spent up to £1 or more. There was no sensible correlation with the quantity purchased: it was just a measure of purchasing competence. Any reader inclined to dismiss this as trivial knew better within a couple of pages. The results of a painstaking survey revealed that a selected group of councils had spent £600,000 on envelopes over three months. If all of them had paid the prices achieved by the most successful 25 per cent in their class of council, then the aggregate saving would have been £78,000. The survey had applied the same analysis to *forty-six* other items, from pencils to paving slabs. The total savings came to £20 *million* – which, it was helpfully pointed out, was more than the annual cost of the Commission itself. And in so far as the survey's sample was representative of annual spending by *all* the local authorities in England and Wales, which the Commission believed it to be, the putative savings could total as much as £200 *million*. It was a classic piece of McKinsey analysis.

And the reports were designed to persuade. Strategic options, for example, were captured in 'logic trees' that presented the full range of possible courses – with all the rigour needed for them to be 'meesey' (another McKinsey favourite, meaning courses that were Mutually Exclusive and Collectively Exhaustive, hence the acronym MECE). Auditors, of course, had no coercive powers over the choice a council would make: they could only point members and officers to facts that would help convince them of the Commission's case. So each report came with a generous dollop of supporting evidence. Appendices heaved with statistics and explanatory models. The report on refuse collection carried a full explanation of the ROSS model that everyone associated with Tristem, for instance, containing a list of the seventeen basic methods for disposing of household rubbish (from 'kerbside bin' to 'backdoor sack – bin liner – pull out in advance').

These first three reports, heavily based as they were on field work over the winter of 1983–84, had a further significance: they attested to the rather important fact that district auditors all over the country had found the vast majority of local authorities surprisingly receptive to value-for-money (VFM) discussions. No fewer than 1,340 individual projects had been launched with a direct involvement for the DAS. The private firms took on another 465 of them. Almost half were related to the *Purchasing* and *Refuse Collection* studies. The rest dealt with the other topics that had been inherited by the Commission from the last days of the Audit Inspectorate – not just housing and further education, but also the management of leisure centres, the administration of planning controls, and the scope for using more civilians in the police force.

One evening late in the spring of 1984, Cliff Nicholson was sitting with the heads of the thirteen DAS districts in Vincent Square, preparing for a meeting the next day with the leading auditors from the private firms. (They had taken to meeting together every three or four months to review progress in the field.) There was some excitement in the office, because the Special Studies directorate was just completing its first compilation of all the estimated VFM savings that had been sent back to head office since November. The district auditors asked what all the fuss was about. They were impressed when they heard the answer.[7] In aggregate, the potential savings were estimated at well over £100 million a year. (By the time that FY84 was completed in the autumn of 1984, the actual figure, reported in the 1985 Annual Report, would be £140 million.) This came close to meeting the controller's McKinsey-derived objective. McKinsey always aimed to deliver annual benefits to a client worth ten times the level of its fees. Banham wanted local government to see the same return on the cost of the Commission's services.

The savings seemed to confirm that the Audit Guides had at the very least been heeded by the DAS itself. Meanwhile, the anecdotal evidence suggested that the statistical profiles were being well-received by councils – and requests for copies were being regularly received from Whitehall and Westminster, too. The Commission had now to decide the ground rules for distribution of its profiles. It was no light matter. One of the first profiles, done late in 1983, had been of Bristol. A young Scotsman in the Commission's post-room received a call from a journalist at the *Bristol Evening Post* and obligingly sent one off. It ended up all over the front page of the newspaper two days later. An embarrassed Commission announced that its future publications policy would be reviewed – but by February 1984 it was clear that withholding the profiles from the public was hardly a practical option. It decided from that point on to make them available 'to anybody with legitimate interest in the authority in question'.[8]

Did it cross some minds at this juncture that fears over the perceived status of the Commission and its links to Whitehall might have been overplayed? Perhaps the need to assert the independence of the Commission was not quite so acute after all. But if anyone thought this, there is no record of their saying so. For by April 1984 the controller was almost ready to deliver that first Section 27 report on the central funding of local government.

THE BLOCK GRANT REPORT

It had been a long time in the preparation. The original game plan was revised and agreed with the Commission members at their meeting in August 1983. Two studies would be published, one on 'the local effects [on the three Es] . . . induced by changes in the Rate Support Grant formula and settlement levels, and [the other on those induced] by the year end controls and capital expenditure allocations'. Members were warned they would be controversial, but were promised detailed terms of reference before any work was commissioned.[9]

Banham circulated the terms in time for the members' meeting in November. He was then informed that, before any work proceeded, 'consultations needed to take place with ministers, the comptroller and auditor general and the Local Authority Associations'.[10] The commissioners were unmistakably nervous. They agreed with Banham's strategy; but they had an acute sense of the risks it would involve. Banham said he would report back on his consultations the next month.

He never did – and the consultations were obviously a tortuous affair. More than twenty years later, Banham could still recall how they started.[11] He telephoned the DoE's then deputy permanent secretary, Terry Heiser, who was the official responsible for local government. After a friendly chat about the Commission's progress so far, Banham made a tactful start. 'Look, I think we're going to do one of these Section 27 studies', he said. 'Do you have any ideas on what you'd like us to study?' Terry Heiser responded very warily. He tried in vain to suggest that, since it was still early days for the Commission, there ought surely to be plenty of other more pressing priorities. But Banham insisted: 'I think we have to do it.'

Eventually Heiser said he would consult with colleagues, as Banham recalled it, 'to see what they would like the Commission to look at'. He came back a few days later with the answer. 'It would be very helpful if we would study the local careers service and the impact that ministers' decisions have had on that.' Banham thought immediately of what had happened to Lord Rothschild ten years earlier, after his appointment by Edward Heath to set up the Central Policy Review Staff. He too had invited Whitehall to suggest a first research topic. He'd been asked to investigate the relationship between civil servants commissioning external research and the experts who did it. It nearly finished off the CPRS before it started. 'No,' replied Banham. 'I think we'll look at the Rate Support Grant.'

And look at it they did. By around the end of April, a work programme led by Ross Tristem had produced a first draft of *The Impact on Local Authorities' Economy, Efficiency and Effectiveness of the Block Grant Distribution System* – that is to say, of the mechanism by which Whitehall decided upon the annual allocation of £8.6 billion in central government funds to local authorities. A series of revisions then accommodated substantial amendments from the members over the next three months. Draft copies were circulating widely by midsummer, to the members' dismay. (It was especially galling that a draft had found its way to the National Audit Office, which had just found a slightly odd pretext for issuing a qualification to the Commission's accounts for its first year. By construing the allocated overheads for a minor audit activity as too low, and proposing its own higher level, the NAO concluded that revenues from the activity had fallen short of covering its total costs by £22,000. It was a fair reflection of the irritation felt inside the NAO that the 1982 Act had set up the Audit Commission at all instead of putting local government audit where it thought it belonged – in the NAO.)

The final report was formally published on 30 August 1984. It ran to sixty-eight pages, and its eloquent prose lit up a subject that scarcely anyone outside the DoE even pretended to understand. For those with a professional interest, it documented many of the weaknesses in the current system with a rare clarity. For anyone else with even the slightest political interest in the subject, it made two things transparent. The notion that local rates in recent years had been driven ever higher by excessive council spending on local services was a hopeless oversimplification. But the government's cumulative efforts to use the distribution system as a means of combating those higher rates had made good management of council finances increasingly difficult – not to say, for some, next to impossible. Indeed, the uncertainty sown in the minds of councillors about future funding from Whitehall was itself seen to be a primary explanation for the higher rates. In other words, since its introduction in 1981–82, the Block Grant system – and a complete refinement of the pre-existing Rate Support Grant – had been more to blame than profligate spending! Councillors had been busy building up reserves against future setbacks, in what the report cheekily characterized as 'an entirely understandable response'.[12]

This was not Margaret Thatcher's analysis of the problem, to say the least. The boldness of the stance taken by the Commission prompted an editorial in *The Times* on the day after the report's publication: it was headlined 'Watchdog Bites Owner'.* Noting that the Commission had exercised its right to examine government policy for the first time 'with pretty devastating results', the leader praised

* The headline was fondly quoted by Commission insiders for years afterwards, linked to warm memories of a cartoon with the same title that was apparently bought from the artist and hung on the wall in Reception at Vincent Square (Tristem, interview). All efforts to trace the cartoon, though, have failed.

the lucidity of the report and endorsed its conclusions – right down to the bottom line that, in the end, rescuing the finances of local goverment would need a 'complete reversal of approach' by the Thatcher government and ultimately a strengthening of local government's representative character.[13] As this acknowledged, the sheer breadth of the Commission's critique was enough to turn heads in Whitehall. What made the report especially sensitive, though, was its extraordinary timing. It dropped on the DoE just as the department was inching its way to a radical break with the whole Block Grant system. How far the report helped the process along is not clear. The DoE's officials discussed it several times with Tristem's team before it was published and were not unsympathetic to its conclusions. But it was undeniably a blunderbuss that scattered shot rather too liberally for more fastidious Whitehall critics. Others were inclined to brush it off as a transparent bid for popularity with the local authorities. (The official view in a subsequent appraisal of the Commission's first three-year term was distinctly cool. 'The analytical quality . . . created some concern in the Department. Consideration of options for change in the study also seemed less than adequate.')[14]

Soon after its publication, anyway, Patrick Jenkin went with cabinet colleagues to Chequers for a Sunday meeting with the prime minister to discuss the forthcoming Tory Party conference. He told her during their discussions that he wanted to use his speech to announce a formal review of the whole subject of council rates and the Block Grant. (She insisted on a lower profile 'studies team' rather than a formal review, but finally agreed to his proposal.)[15] For both Jenkin and his deputy permanent secretary, it must have been a little disconcerting to see a hard-hitting report on council finances surfacing at this moment, over which they had next to no control. The best authority on these events – which were to lead directly to the germination of the poll tax – suggests their dilemma:

In considering an overhaul [of the Block Grant system], Terry Heiser's private view was that the existing controls on local government spending were unsustainable . . . [But at the same time] DoE officials were keenly aware of other political pressures influencing the Whitehall debate about local government. Patrick Jenkin was fighting for political survival.[16]

FRAYED RELATIONS IN WHITEHALL

Jenkin may well have felt that his predicament was perhaps not fully appreciated in Vincent Square. On 4 September, two days after his visit to Chequers, he summoned John Read to a private meeting. There is no record of what was said, other than a summary in the next commissioners' meeting. Jenkin (unsurprisingly) had not been much interested in discussing the finer points of the report – but had conceded to Read that there was a need for action on the Block Grant system. Read was also told that DoE officials were working on the subject already, though it is very unlikely he was told about the extent of their plans. He suggested to Jenkin that his officials might like to meet the Commission's team responsible for the report. In the event, the follow-up was rather less constructive. One of Heiser's officials attacked the report in an issue of the weekly *Municipal Journal*. The Commission was given no warning of the article, and Ross Tristem wrote a scathing reply that was published the following week. The exchange was unfortunate, but it was perhaps a measure of the impact that the report had made. Almost overnight, it had won national recognition for the Commission as an authoritative voice on local government issues. No one seriously disputed any of its findings. Indeed, when the National Audit Office produced its own report on the Block Grant almost a year later – judged by the DoE to be 'notably good' – its broad conclusions were very similar. Iterative targets and penalties had left the system hopelessly complicated, 'to the point of making its sophistication worthless'.[17]

Above all, the Commission's report had a dramatic impact, as intended, on councillors' perceptions of the new body. As the DoE would later concede: 'The Commission's document and the disputes it engendered undoubtedly impressed the local government world with the Commission's independence from, and willingness to criticise, central government.'[18] Even Labour leaders could see this was no mere cipher in awe of No. 10. The blind Labour leader of Sheffield City Council, a luminary of the radical left called David Blunkett, would later tell the story of how the report had been read to him on a train, making him laugh out loud to hear so many 'off-message' truths being spelt out so lucidly.[19]

Shortly after making his announcement at the Tory conference – that a working group was going to be assembled, with external advisers, to look at the future of local government funding – Jenkin evidently thought the time had come to spell out a few messages more clearly to the commissioners. He arranged to make a visit to Vincent Square on the first day of November, joining the members in the boardroom that afternoon. It was not a happy occasion. 'He read us a lecture on the virtues of setting objectives', recalled Banham. In the boardroom audience were some of Britain's most distinguished and successful business figures – men like GEC's fiercely autocratic Kenneth Bond, Ian Hay Davison, a tough operator who had just taken on the job of chief executive in the scandal-racked Lloyd's insurance market, and David Lees, who was about to become chief executive at the engineering group GKN. They did not take kindly to being patronized with a list of tasks that Jenkin thought appropriate. Banham was appalled. 'These guys had steam coming out of their ears, they were so cross . . . I only just got him out alive.'[20]

It is striking that Read informed his colleagues a month later, on 6 December, that he had decided not to serve beyond his three-year term, expiring in January 1986. But there is nothing on record to connect his decision with the Jenkin visit, and the December minutes referred only to 'the pressure of other commitments'. Under the circumstances, the wording of the Commission's 1984 Annual Report that the members sent off to the publishers in mid-November was measured indeed. It welcomed the government's plan for a review of local government funding, which could provide an opportunity to correct the 'serious weaknesses' in the present system, and it offered to help 'in any way compatible with the independence of the Commission and its auditors'.

But the call never came. The Commission's views were never sought. The DoE studies team began work in October, reporting to the two junior ministers at the department, Kenneth Baker and William Waldegrave. The idea of a poll tax surfaced before the end of the year and rose rapidly up the agenda early in 1985. When Banham with

Tristem's assistance sent off a three-page memorandum to the DoE explaining why he thought a poll tax would be uncollectable, no reply was ever received.[21] Others had the same experience. An analysis by CIPFA was published in May 1985 starkly identifying some of the predictable negative consequences of a poll tax, but it authors were not contacted by the DoE studies team until well after the key decisions had been made. As for council executives with direct experience of local government finance, they were not invited to contribute at any stage.[22]

The poll-tax team may have ignored it, but the Commission received plenty of attention from other DoE officials in the run-up to its second Section 27 report, *Capital Expenditure Controls in Local Government in England*. The department made 'a major investment' of time and effort to assist with it. Its retrospective verdict, in 1987, unsurprisingly thought the resulting report had 'embodied substantially better analysis'. But there was still plenty of concern over it, especially 'the degree to which it strayed into matters of policy'.[23] In fact the report, published in April 1985, carried on very much where the first one had left off. Not only were the present arrangements largely ineffectual and hugely wasteful, but recent government policy had (once again) greatly worsened matters. The overall lack of control over local spending 'has been exacerbated by the success of the government's policy of encouraging sales of assets, notably council houses, and by direct government initiatives'. Given Margaret Thatcher's personal backing for many of these initiatives, especially the sale of council houses, this was dangerous stuff.

Especially so for a secretary of state heavily beleaguered in his dealings with the so-called Loony Left. Relations between Jenkin and Banham began to deteriorate, and they rapidly worsened over the following months. Undoubtedly, part of their problem was the extent to which – rather to the Commission's surprise, as well as the DoE's – Banham had developed quite a public profile for himself over the previous eighteen months. His star had risen in the media as Jenkin's own had fallen.

It had been Banham's intention from the start to build good ties with the media, to win as broad a coverage as possible for the Commission's special studies. After a slightly wobbly start with some of the accountancy trade papers in his early months, he had had a successful first year. Since around the spring of 1984, though, he had become a good deal more ambitious. All management meetings were now attended by a newly appointed press officer, Mark Oaten, an astute operator with keen political antennae. And the controller spread his wings. He even made a first appearance on the BBC's flagship current-affairs programme, *Question Time* – though not until November 1984, because the commissioners had taken a dim view of the idea when the invitation had first arrived in April. They worried that 'personal views expressed, or prejudices revealed, by the controller might complicate their task'.[24] When he did finally appear on the programme, one of his fellow guests was Derek Hatton, the deputy leader of Liverpool City Council and a leader of the Loony Left. The commissioners' fears proved unfounded, and their controller was generally thought to have acquitted himself well despite some provocation. After the broadcast, the programme's director surprised Banham by telling him that he was 'about to become a national figure'.[25]

Banham's flair with the media and his public-speaking skills were of incalculable value to the Commission in terms of winning it a national following. Who would ever have supposed before 1983 that a body dedicated to auditing local government accounts could one day be featured regularly on Radio 4's *Today* programme or the *Nine O'Clock News*? Yet that is what happened, courtesy of Banham's skilful soundbites whenever the Commission published an important new study. He even became a regular on the *Jimmy Young Show*, the flagship programme of the BBC's Radio 2 station throughout the 1980s – which hugely impressed all the young auditors of the DAS (and their mothers).

On one occasion, a *Jimmy Young Show* producer rang Vincent Square to ask if Banham could do an interview later that morning. He had already left the office, however, and was being driven down to the London borough of Richmond. He was going there to spend the morning with a young senior assistant district auditor, Derek Elliott, who was conducting an audit of the council. Like so many others in the DAS, Elliott was wholly devoted to the controller ('I would have torn my arms off for John Banham') and completely in awe of him. He met Banham from his car as soon as he arrived, apologizing that he had to turn straight around and drive back to the BBC. But Banham just told Elliott to call the show and fix up for the interview to be done live over the telephone from the office where he was working. Then he went off to see the chief executive. Elliott was hugely impressed by such insouciance – and rather stunned to find himself, thirty minutes later, sitting opposite Banham at the desk while the controller chatted nonchalantly with Jimmy Young, and a few million Radio 2 listeners. 'I felt so proud, you know!'[26]

Over time, though, Banham grew more outspoken – and critics would accuse him of making speeches to different audiences that were sometimes less than wholly consistent. By 1985, he was also happy to give vent (sometimes recklessly so) to his frustration over aspects of working with central government, and it led to trouble on more than one occasion. Inevitably, the DoE took the brunt of his more colourful asides on Whitehall. Addressing a housing conference in June, he picked up again on the subject of capital controls, for example. 'If I were asked to design a system that would produce more waste and inefficiency to control capital expenditure, it is not immediately certain to me what additional complication I would build in.' It was wonderful stuff for the journalists, and widely quoted.[27] But it was not calculated to endear him to the DoE. Its planning was redolent, he told one audience, of East European socialist governments. As for the atmosphere at Marsham Street, the *Local Government Chronicle* reported him musing that 'it reeked of death and decay'.

Shortly afterwards, Cliff Nicholson happened to meet Terry Heiser, who had recently become permanent secretary at the DoE. Nicholson recalled Heiser asking him wryly, 'So what happened to the superdiplomat we thought we had appointed?'[28] Working relations between the department and the Commission soured badly. Banham and Tristem crossed swords repeatedly with Heiser, and there were heated exchanges over the validity of the Commission's statistics. Banham knew perfectly well the risks he was taking. So when the question of his reappointment to another three-year term arose, towards the end of June 1985, he was certainly taking nothing for granted. And at this point, out of the blue, he was approached for another job. The two men behind the Conservative Party's advertising campaigns, Charles and Maurice Saatchi, had enjoyed an astonishingly successful few years and were now planning to expand their agency into a much larger business empire. Banham was asked by Maurice Saatchi if he would like to head up an acquisition of the Arthur Andersen consulting firm.

He went to see Patrick Jenkin, and candidly explained the position.[29] He did not want to step down, he said. There was still much to be done. But on the other hand, he fully appreciated that he had made life very difficult for the minister and his officials – and if they wanted to see the back of him, then it would be a mutually convenient moment for them to make the break. Jenkin conceded the truth of his remarks as graciously as he could. Then, like Terry Heiser before him, he asked Banham for time to consult his colleagues. When the two men met again, Jenkin delivered a verdict entirely in keeping with his reputation as something of a mandarin *manqué*. 'All I can tell you is, we haven't decided definitely to fire you.' Banham stayed.

In truth, as Jenkin was tacitly acknowledging, any abrupt departure by Banham at this point would have been extremely awkward. The government's battle with its main antagonists in local government – in particular the GLC and the Liverpool and Lambeth councils – was delicately poised. The Commission and its district auditors still had a critical role to play. To see what this involved, and why parting with the controller at this point would not have been a good idea, we need to go back twelve months to the summer of 1984.

COUNTERING 'NON-COMPLIANCE'

With the passing in July 1984 of the Rates Act, the Tories had honoured their 1983 election promise to introduce rate-capping. Radical left-wing opposition to the initiative lifted the conflict over local government spending to a new level altogether.

Local government finances had grown steadily more convoluted since 1979. At its most basic, the economic model for every council involved drawing upon rents and the sale of services for some minor part of its income (usually around a fifth of it), and then deriving the bulk of it from one or the other of two sources: local rates and central government funding via the Rate Support Grant. When the Thatcher government had begun curbing the grant, councils unsurprisingly had compensated for the lost income by raising their rates. This had led to an acrimonious game of cat and mouse for three years that involved the government setting a series of expenditure targets and grant penalties – swept up in the Block Grant system – and councils (as described in the Commission's Block Grant report) pressing on with higher rates wherever possible to build up reserves for the future.

The striking innovation in the 1984 Rates Act was that it gave Whitehall the power to dictate the annual spending not just of local government as a whole, but *of individual authorities specifically*. In fact, the power to assert a general scheme was never used. Instead, eighteen authorities were singled out in July as egregious over-spenders – all of them had budgeted in the current 1984–85 year to spend more than 25 per cent over the government's assessed target – and the legislation was used to put a cap on their rates alone for the financial year 1985–86 starting the following April. Almost all the targeted authorities were Labour-controlled. They comprised the Greater London Council (GLC) and the Inner London Education Authority (ILEA), and sixteen other councils including seven of the twelve Inner London boroughs.[30]

Within the Commission, one name on the list attracted special attention. Labour-controlled Basildon had been the only council in the country, the prior November, to offer itself to the Commission as the subject of a special management profile. This had intrigued many in Vincent Square: Basildon, after all, was a town with its own special place in UK election mythology, having served as an accurate early indicator of the outcome of a string of general elections. Peter Brokenshire, the director of management practice who had joined the Commission straight from being the chief executive of Greenwich for six years, had spent weeks in Basildon with two colleagues preparing a report on its affairs.

In essence, the Basildon report in March 1984 had commended the council on much of its work. True, it was spending in excess of the government's target assessment – Patrick Jenkin took to describing it as Moscow-down-the-Thames – but this was largely attributable to the fact that it had had to take on various social services that ought properly to have been the responsibility of Essex County Council.

When they found themselves nonetheless rate-capped, Basildon's councillors naturally published Brokenshire's report and the media had a field day trumpeting his endorsement of their efficiency. The Commission members were not happy with the controller, the DoE was not amused, and Basildon stayed on the government's hit-list.[31]

The eighteen rate-capped authorities were joined by Liverpool City Council, which was not itself being rate-capped for 1985–86. Now effectively being run by the Militant Tendency faction of the extreme left, it had already won a victory of sorts by setting an illegal budget for 1984–85, and forcing Jenkin into a damaging compromise that had greatly weakened his position. All of the rebel Labour councils declared their defiance of the Rates Act by saying they would refuse to set any rate at all for 1985–86. This 'non-compliance' strategy was endorsed over the summer of 1984 by the Labour Party's National Executive Council. As Liverpool's support made clear, the strategy was about more than just desperate local difficulties. Cold-shouldered by the Labour Party at Westminster and disabled by the political eclipse of the trade unions (culminating in the defeat of the miners' strike in 1984–85), the hard left had been busy for years building municipal socialism as the way forward. The squeeze on public spending introduced by the Conservatives after 1979 triggered a crisis atmosphere that gave the extremists the upper hand. Suddenly important councils were being led by pocket demagogues – memorably tagged by one leading commentator as 'the bed-sit brigade'[32] – and several (such as Derek Hatton, Ted Knight and Ken Livingstone) were soon household names. They were only too ready for a political confrontation with the Thatcher government.

This was a new world for the officers of the DAS and the partners of the private firms, and most particularly for the district auditors who headed up its work in each of its thirteen districts. The individual at the head of the firing line was the Metropolitan DA, responsible for most of London's borough councils as well as the GLC and the ILEA. Newly appointed to the Met job in 1984 was Brian Skinner – a man who in many ways embodied the DAS. He had joined it in 1955 and worked his way up the ladder, rung by rung: from audit examiner to assistant district auditor (ADA), to senior assistant district auditor (SADA), to deputy district auditor (DDA) and hence to the top. On the way, he served in Surrey, South Wales and Kent before coming to London as DDA in 1979.

With this much experience behind him, Skinner was quick to sense a culture shift that began after 1979. As he recalled:

Back in the 1960s, if an auditor said to an authority, 'Look, you really shouldn't do that', then it was a bit like Dixon of Dock Green and they wouldn't do it. [Dixon was the avuncular desk sergeant in a BBC police series that ran from 1955 to 1976, holding sway over any number of villains by the force of his personality and his reputation in the neighbourhood.] There was really a sort of unwritten rule. The generality of authorities would obey the policeman and they would obey the auditor. But [by 1984] we were going through a period when councils were cocking a snook at authority. If an auditor said 'Look, you can't do that', there were some authorities that were quite capable of shrugging their shoulders and just doing it.[33]

Coping with this called for sensitivity. Even the most extreme councils were run from month to month by officers with whom the DA and his staff usually had a cordial professional relationship. The extremists' behaviour often put these officers – and, indeed, those of the council's elected members who did not espouse the radicals' agenda – in a deeply invidious position. (At one London council, Southwark, dissenting Labour members were sent white feathers in the post.) The DA invariably wanted to acknowledge their predicament, but had his own obligations too. 'It was a little like being on stage: they knew my role, and I knew theirs. It was a bit of a game – but a nasty game.'[34]

And a game requiring infinite patience, too, because the legal rules confronting every DA were anything but transparent. Most pertinently in light of the looming 'non-compliance' campaign, the law prescribed no exact date by which a borough council was required to set a rate. (Only the higher-tier authorities, which included the GLC and the ILEA, were given a statutory deadline – which was 10 March for 1985–86.) April 1st was usually treated as the latest possible date for the boroughs, but delays were not unprecedented. Any later date, though, implied at the very least a loss of interest on revenues that remained uncollected. If months went by, then losses would sooner or later start to mount. But the law made no attempt to define the schedule. It was accordingly for the DA to decide if and when losses were resulting from 'the wilful misconduct of any person'. Where this applied, he could hold them liable for any losses under Section 20 of the 1982 Act, and their only recourse would be to appeal through the courts.

No one in the DAS relished this prospect, but in the wake of the Rates Act it looked as though court battles might be unavoidable. To help prepare the DAS, Cliff Nicholson and Ian Pickwell arranged, in September 1984, a series of seminars on the Rates Act. Some modest comfort was drawn from what had just happened in Liverpool, which had taken a bellicose stand in March, setting a budget but no rate. The DA had bided his time until mid-May, when he had written to all the council members, asking if there was any reason why he should not issue certificates of misconduct against them. In June he had warned that he was about to take action under Section 20. And on 11 July, the council had backed down and set a legal rate. (The problem for Jenkin was that it had done so only after extracting a lot more money from the government via the DoE's urban programme aimed at rejuvenating run-down city districts.)

In Vincent Square, the Commission's response to these events in Liverpool set a pattern for what was to follow. Nicholson assumed overall responsibility for keeping the members informed. He presented a first 'Operations Review' in April 1984, and was asked to update it on a quarterly basis thereafter. In doing so, he regularly reminded members that they could expect to be kept informed of what their DAs were doing – they were, after all, employees – but had to remember that each DA was a legally independent authority whose status as such had to be respected meticulously. (Banham never asked Nicholson to attend Commission meetings as a matter of routine, and felt this decision was vindicated again by the measure of protection it gave his deputy now. Some of the individual members, strongly supportive of the Thatcher government, were impatient to see a much harder line taken against councils run by the hard left.

In the months that followed, its legal detachment from the district auditors suited the Commission in more ways than one. It had no interest in being cast by the media as the principal adversary of the Loony Left. On the contrary, this might have seriously compromised its credibility as a partner on VFM work even with the majority of councils who wanted no truck with the extremists. It would also have entailed a media-management problem that might easily have engulfed the Commission. Nicholson and Pickwell carefully distanced themselves from the auditors in public, and only off the record with well-trusted journalists would they risk any background briefing. (Ironically, this in itself marked a significant increase in press activity over anything the old Audit Inspectorate had ever known. Indeed, good links with a few key commentators survived as an important legacy of these years for the Commission.) But while they needed to be seen as detached from the minutiae of the crisis, the reality of course was different. From that autumn of 1984, the deputy controller and his small staff were spending as much as half their time assisting DAs in the field over the non-compliance campaign.

PRESSURES ON THE DISTRICT AUDITORS

The first priority was to dissuade the capped councils – and their Militant allies in Liverpool and elsewhere, too – from going into the 1985–86 financial year without setting a rate. It was heavy going, and not all of the DAs had the backbone for it. As Nicholson recalled: 'Some of them were way out of their depth: they'd never come across anything like this before. We really had to press the auditors – and there were a few who were very reluctant.'[35]

Running in parallel with this work was another, closely associated task. The Rates Act prompted many councils – especially the capped authorities but many others, too – to start looking much more actively for alternative cash sources that could supplement their rates. In this connection, the fact that local government's revenue and capital accounts were controlled separately by Whitehall was a godsend. To take only the most obvious consequence, a council could raise a significant amount of capital by selling properties and leasing them back – starting with the town hall. This was very often a false economy in the long run. But it could fund a lot of spending in the short run. (As the Commission's second Section 27 report put it, 'The present arrangements are a recipe for unproductive creative accounting.')[36]

Here again, much was left to the auditor's discretion. Section 19 of the 1982 Act empowered the auditor to lodge an appeal in the courts for repayment of a dodgy accounting item – but it had to be a spending item that was expressly 'contrary to law'. Successful creative accounting ruses were by definition *not* 'contrary to law': if they ended up being deemed illegal, they had plainly failed to be creative enough. The auditor was nonetheless obliged to submit reports to council members, telling them they were being imprudent and urging caution.

All this amounted to a formidable extra workload. There was the added complication for the DAS that most of it fell in London, where there were several boroughs threatening not to set a rate, including six that were rate-capped. It was far more than Brian Skinner could possibly cope with alone. When the thirteen DAs met for one of their regular conferences that autumn, there was a tense discussion about this. Traditionally, their proud independence precluded any sharing of work. It was the DA for Essex and East Anglia, Jim Lees, who stated the obvious solution to Skinner's predicament: 'Well, we've got to help him, haven't we?'[37] Whereupon DAs with little or no prior involvement were reassigned to help in the Met district, and the work went ahead.

Part of Skinner's difficulty was that in addition to the rate-setting crisis, he was faced with constant criticism over his handling of Ken Livingstone's GLC. The Tories had pledged in their 1983 election manifesto to scrap it. In the run-up to the Local Government Act of 1985 that legislated for this – and indeed for several months thereafter, until its lights went out on 31 March 1986 – Livingstone orchestrated a surprisingly popular campaign against abolition ('Say No to No Say'). It cost the best part of £10 million over two years, and Skinner was bombarded with letters for most of the period demanding to know why he, as the auditor, was not taking steps to halt such a blatant misappropriation of funds. Legal arguments, over whether the spending was improper or not, absorbed a huge amount of very expensive time devoted to the problem by several leading QCs. This was the real significance of the whole episode for Skinner. It exemplified the way in which local government in the mid-80s was infested with lawyers. 'Everything that anyone did was vouched for by a lawyer. The GLC's officers were first class. There would be a legal opinion from a leading silk that would say "you can do this". It was belt-and-braces stuff, and they were past masters at it.'[38] The pressure on Skinner himself, and on all his colleagues, can easily be imagined.

The notion that the auditors of the DAS were somehow falling short, by not lashing out more conspicuously at the hard left, was not confined over the winter of 1984–85 to apoplectic opponents of the GLC. Hardly a week passed without a media revelation of some new absurdity.[39] Haringey ruled that only Nicaraguan coffee could be served on its premises. Lambeth announced that the word 'family' was discriminatory and had been banned from its council literature. Brent appointed ninety anti-racism officers (and went on to suspend a respected local headmistress on bogus grounds of racial misconduct). Lewisham voted £64,000 for the gathering of public complaints about the police. Hackney twinned itself with East Germany, the USSR and Nicaragua. So where, Westminster politicians and their civil servants wanted to know, were the officers of the audit service, and what were they doing to roll back this tide of nonsense? The Commission's members were on the receiving end of much of this frustration, and they in turn pressed Banham and Nicholson for answers. Nicholson recalled: 'I had a lot of trouble with Commission meetings, particularly over rate-setting. Always the same refrain, you know – why aren't the auditors doing something?'[40]

In fact, they were steadily making progress. Under Section 15 (3) of the 1982 Act, an auditor could publish a report drawing the public's attention to any aspect of a local authority audit that he considered worthy of general interest. The authority was then obliged to convene a meeting to consider the report, and to advertise (within fourteen days of the meeting) its availability for inspection by local electors. Once the media began to take more interest in local government politics, this recourse offered the auditor a bigger stick. The audit for 1984–85 prompted fifty-four Public Interest Reports and there were eighty-nine for 1985–86. Most seriously of all, auditors could confront councillors with the possibility of disqualification and (under Section 20) surcharges that might leave them bankrupt. Those ambitious for a career at Westminster, which was closed to bankrupts, had a lot to lose. This applied, for example, to David Blunkett in Sheffield. He must have listened with special care, when he chaired a meeting that was addressed by John Banham in person. The controller visited the city – where he had family roots going back over a century – to spell out to the city council, in his own inimitable way, the dire consequences of failing to set a rate.

With three days to go before their 10 March deadline for the 1985–86 financial year, the GLC, the ILEA, South Yorkshire and Merseyside capitulated. Basildon and the other non-London boroughs followed suit. By late March, there remained only eleven authorities that had yet to set a rate. The start of the new financial year came and went, and still they hung on. Choosing his timing very carefully, Skinner announced early in May that he would move with surcharges and disqualifications against any borough that had not set its rate by the end of the month. Shortly after this, the Labour Party's National Executive withdrew its support for any councillors breaking the law.

This set the stage for the endgame – which Skinner handled with a skill that was much admired by his younger colleagues. One of these was Peter Yetzes, a computer buff who had joined the DAS in 1984 to set up and run a computer audit team in London and the south-east. Within a year or so, Yetzes was pioneering a role for the service as an IT consultancy. Some of his first clients included the same London boroughs that were making life so difficult for Skinner. On several occasions in 1985, Yetzes accompanied his DA to potentially confrontational meetings and came away marvelling at Skinner's diplomacy. He recalled: 'He had a manner and a way about him with councillors which I thought was brilliant. He never said too much: he always knew when to stop and leave them wanting more.'[41]

Ironically, the breakthrough contract for the IT consultancy came from Islington Council. Yetzes and his small computer-audit team were busy advising the council on a major IT strategy for the future, just as the rate-making crisis was coming to a head. Yetzes even persuaded the council's leader, Margaret Hodge, and several other members to attend a weekend retreat near Windsor to review the IT work. It must have been a curious occasion, given what was happening on the main stage. On 10 May, after a series of warning letters, Skinner sent a courtesy copy of a final Public Interest Report to Islington's chief executive, as a prelude to its formal despatch. In response, he was invited to Islington town hall for a meeting with

Hodge, her deputy and her two most senior officials. His visit proved to be one of the more eventful days in the life of the DAS for many a year.

He went by taxi, but was in for a shock.[42] As they drove down Upper Street from the Angel Islington, they found the road blocked by a huge crowd. 'The cabbie said, "I can't get up to the town hall, there's too many people!" So I walked up and there were literally thousands of people outside the hall, with refuse carts and vans and Ted Knight's battle bus, all going up and down the street sounding their horns.' ('Red Ted' Knight, the Labour leader of Lambeth Borough Council, was one of the Left's most outspoken opponents of rate-capping, and indeed of Thatcherism in all its guises.) Skinner met his deputy at the council treasurer's office, which was a short walk from the town hall. 'There I rang up the chief executive and said, "What's going on?" He said, "I don't know, we didn't organize it." Anyway, I said, "OK, I'm coming to see you" and we set off. All of a sudden a great cry went up, "There he is!" but we kept going.'

They made it into the town hall, where the councillors insisted the demonstrations outside were entirely spontaneous. The auditors accepted this with as much humour as they could muster. It was nice to know they were expected. But making their exit after the meeting was no joking matter. Skinner asked his hosts if there was some alternative to using the front door, where the crowd was eagerly awaiting his reappearance. No, they said, he had to use the front door. 'So I went back and stood there on the front steps and there was this mass of people shrieking at me.'

He and his deputy were jostled and kicked as they struggled to get down the street, with four or five policemen escorting them, but it was hopeless. Skinner asked a policeman if he could help them find a taxi. 'He said, "No sir, we've got to be impartial, but what we can do is get you back to the town hall!" So we went back, and a nice police officer there offered to smuggle us out in his car. He said, "You and your deputy get on the back seat and I'll cover you with coats." So that's what we did. Some people at the back gate flung it open and that's how we got out.'

On other occasions, the personal pressures on Brian Skinner were more sinister. He lived in Beckenham, a London borough that bordered on Lambeth, and used to shop at a Tesco store near his home that was actually inside the Lambeth boundaries. He stepped inside the store one evening to find a photograph of his face on a Western-style 'Wanted' poster. Under the photograph was the rhyme 'This is Mr Skinner / He wants your dinner' accompanied by the menacing words: 'If you see this man, act on sight!' The Commission had to seek police assistance in tracking down and destroying all copies of the poster.[43]

But tact and patience won their due rewards eventually. Islington backed down on the deadline, followed soon after by Southwark. One of the remaining few was Camden – where the Commission's own Roy Shaw was still on the council. He had to sit through some interminable late-night sittings early that June, but had a shrewd adviser: 'I got an agreement with Cliff Nicholson that he would tell me when I had to say "No, I'm not going any further." '[44] Fortunately for Shaw, this point was never reached. Things came to a head in the council chamber on 5 June – 'there was absolute chaos, all the Trots in London turned up!' – and at 3 a.m. a rate for Camden was finally agreed upon. Greenwich followed its example seven days later. That left just two authorities refusing to set a rate for 1985–86 – Lambeth and Liverpool.

Skinner and his counterpart in Liverpool, a DA called Tim McMahon, liaised closely over their next steps and shared the same lawyer, Anthony Scrivener QC. The cases were now the focus of intense media interest – as the Commission members were only too well aware. Nicholson and his team in Vincent Square were still struggling to assist the DAs with a mass of awkward questions arising from the late setting of rates. (Should any consequent additional costs be charged against the councillors? Were Public Interest Reports still called for, where late rates looked more than likely to mean deficit budgets?) But the deputy controller had also to stand shoulder to shoulder with Banham in fending off anxious inquiries from the members, and reminding them of their limited powers.

One thing they *could* do: the members were entitled, under Section 22 of the 1982 Act, to direct an auditor to carry out an extraordinary audit wherever they thought it appropriate. On 6 June, they duly requested extraordinary audits of the Lambeth and Liverpool councils.

It was little more than a gesture, though. Skinner and McMahon were by then already preparing to disqualify all of the individual councillors in Liverpool and in Lambeth, and to lay charges against them for the costs incurred by their failure to set a rate. Assuming the councillors appealed, the rest would be up to the courts.

On 6 September, the district auditors for Liverpool and Lambeth served 'certificates for the recovery of loss due to wilful misconduct' on the councillors of those two authorities, relating to their failure to set a rate for the 1985–86 financial year until 14 June and 3 July respectively. A surcharge of £106,103 was laid against fifty Liverpool councillors, or £2,165 each. Against thirty-one Lambeth councillors the surcharge was £126,947, or £3,967 each. Because the fines exceeded £2,000 per capita, all the councillors also faced disqualification.

It would be tedious to plot in detail the legal battles that ensued. The salient facts can be quickly told. The Lambeth and Liverpool councillors appealed in the High Court against the auditors' certificates. After hearings in January and February, both appeals were dismissed on 5 March 1986. The Lambeth councillors gave up the struggle, were disqualified on 2 April and accepted the Commission's terms in May for the payment by instalments of their surcharge and costs. (Their leader, 'Red Ted' Knight, reportedly went off to set up a café in the borough.) The Liverpool councillors took their case to the Court of Appeal, where it was dismissed on 31 July. They turned finally to the House of Lords, which delivered a unanimous 5–0 judgment in favour of the auditor on 12 March 1987. Derek Hatton and his colleagues – now reduced to forty-seven in all – were disqualified from office for five years and ordered to pay surcharges and costs totalling £333,000.

TRACKING DOWN
WILFUL MISCONDUCT

Much more intriguing is what happened over the *other* authorities that had also failed to set their rates for 1985–86 until after the start of the financial year – and it is worth jumping ahead here to see how this last chapter of the rate-capping story unfolded. There were seven

other late rate-setters: Camden, Islington, Hackney, Southwark, Sheffield and Greenwich – plus Tower Hamlets, which, like Liverpool,
had failed to set a rate on time though it was not itself rate-capped.
All of them had caved in earlier (though not much earlier) than
Liverpool and Lambeth, but all had nonetheless run up material
losses. The question was: were those losses consequent upon *wilful
misconduct*? If so, then their councillors were as much in the firing
line as those who were already heading for the High Court.

It was far from obvious to the Commission, in the autumn of 1985,
that much of a distinction could be drawn between the latter and
councillors from the renegade seven. True, the situation in Liverpool
had been especially confrontational: Labour's Militant activists had
pushed the city close to open violence. (A twentieth-anniversary article
in the *Local Government Chronicle* of 26 August 2004 would recall:
'In Liverpool, feelings had been running so high that in April 1984,
the MP for Liverpool Riverside, Bob Parry, warned that if troops
were sent in, they would be resisted and violence would ensue.') But
the atmosphere in Sheffield had been almost as intimidating for the
auditors, and there had been ugly episodes in many of the London
boroughs: demonstrators in Hackney, for example, had physically
barred councillors from entering the town hall for one meeting. By
early November, the Commission members were pressing hard to
know what their district auditors had in mind: 'Members asked that
the results of the auditors' investigations into any losses at Hackney
and other authorities as a result of delayed rate-making should be
reported at the next meeting.'[45]

And they went on pressing – until well into 1987. For more than
fifteen months, in fact, the members went on asking for definitive
answers, and failing to get them. Even in February 1987, after they
had been told that their Lordships had just finished hearing Liverpool's
appeal, the refrain remained the same: 'Members asked about the
position at other late rate-making authorities. The deputy controller
explained that auditors were still awaiting information from authorities, without which they could not proceed. Members expressed
their concern at the continuing delays.'[46] Virtually every month, Cliff
Nicholson would be summoned into the Commission members' meeting to present his update on the situation. Roy Shaw, as a Camden

councillor and therefore an interested party to the discussion, would have to step outside. The deputy controller would remind the members that the district auditors had to be trusted to handle the job. Everyone would reiterate their commitment to the principle that the auditors and their lawyers had of course to prepare their ground with the utmost care. But it would be agreed that the law could not be applied selectively. Then would follow yet another review of the obstacles to any immediate action.

Of these, there was an almost comical supply. Nothing could be done that might impugn the auditors' independence. Reports in the public interest could not be issued while the Lambeth and Liverpool actions were proceeding. Investigations into wilful misconduct could not be pursued while ratepayers' objections to a borough's accounts were still outstanding. Legal advice was needed on whether to pursue the seven boroughs simultaneously or in sequence. Special audits could not be requested until fresh auditors (at Islington and Hackney) had been appointed. No action could be taken until the councils' objections to the new auditors had been resolved.

And so on, interminably. Did some of the members begin to suspect a concealed agenda? Probably. Ian Coutts, the Tory accountant from Norfolk, vented exasperation with the process on more than one occasion. (In October 1986, for example, he 'expressed his concern that although the Commission had been assured at earlier meetings that investigations were continuing as fast as possible, the Commission were now being asked to accept that even more time was needed for auditors to form their view. The controller shared that concern . . .' As ever, a decision was promised before the next meeting.)[47] No one, though, was so naive as to articulate what that agenda might be – least of all the controller or his deputy.

Banham and Nicholson had in fact decided, probably well before the end of 1985, that having shown their valour in combat with Lambeth and Liverpool, discretion would be much the better ploy in dealing with the seven authorities. Without doubt, the auditors *could* have been pressed hard behind the scenes to bring these authorities to book, no less than Lambeth and Liverpool (with potentially dire consequences for some local politicians with ambitions one day to win election to Westminster). In the event, all the practical advice and assistance from Vincent Square would prod the auditors in the opposite direction.

Banham pushed them to find any excuse they could for not taking action. This could not be spelt out at the time – though Banham admitted it to his successor the following year – and lip-service needed paying to the clear legal obligations laid on the district auditors by the 1982 Act. But to Banham and Nicholson both, there always appeared to be a compelling rationale for masterly inaction. Prior to the March 1986 ruling in the High Court, they were actually quite nervous about the outcome of the Lambeth and Liverpool cases – the very first, after all, to be brought under Section 20 of the Act. The lawyers warned them that proving wilful misconduct might turn out to be trickier than supposed. In the short term, they needed to focus on preparing the Commission against the consequences of an unfavourable High Court ruling, rather than adding to their workload by opening new cases. Then, once the High Court had pronounced, it was suddenly a different world. Rate-capping did not go away. On the contrary, twelve councils were again capped for the 1986–87 year – including Liverpool, Lambeth and half a dozen of the usual culprits from among the Inner London boroughs. In place of non-compliance, however, the councils opted for a series of private negotiations with the DoE. This was the way things were now to be. The radicals had had their day, and lost. The high watermark of municipal socialism in Britain had come and gone.

In these circumstances, there seemed to Banham and Nicholson no point in pursuing further court actions. The law needed no further clarification. Financial recompense was hardly an issue: the councillors would have lacked the funding even to reimburse their legal costs. On the downside, though, further cases might just incur defeats on unforeseen technicalities – and would surely dash the lingering hopes, still clung to in Vincent Square, of persuading the Liverpool councillors to abandon their appeal to the Lords.

There also lurked, still, just a smidgeon of doubt in their minds about how their Lordships might rule. It was not unknown for their judgments to run counter to the consensus view at the Bar and to turn on a technicality. The gist of the Liverpool councillors' case seemed to be that the district auditor, in failing to remind them that they had the right to ask for a public hearing over a Section 20 charge, had fallen short of seeing that natural justice was done. Convening a public hearing in Liverpool early that summer would probably have led directly to a public riot, but no one could be sure how their Lordships would weigh this in the balance. So a defeat for the Commission could not be ruled out. It hardly seemed a prudent moment to launch seven actions in the lower courts, which a setback in the Lords would turn into a seven-headed Hydra for the government. As for what was in the Commission's best interest – Banham knew his own mind on that. 'I remember thinking to myself, all we'll do is compromise the Commission's reputation and independence, and our ability to work with councils in the future.'[48]

Unfortunately, hostile critics at Westminster (and indeed among the Commission members, too) saw this as the Commission's only genuine concern, and they were not impressed. Cliff Nicholson was well aware even by the early summer of 1985 that some believed the auditors were being intimidated. 'The feeling in central government departments was, "Well, here's a toothless wonder! It can't even make them set the rates!"'[49] In the immediate aftermath of the 1986 High Court victory, the same voices wanted to see the letter of the law applied rigorously. Tory MPs started pressing to see Public Interest Reports issued, with an eye to the impact this might have on the approaching May local elections. Pressure on the DAS to take action rose alarmingly and Nicholson persuaded Banham that they needed to take legal advice on their position.

A conference was arranged with one of the top names at the Bar – Bob Alexander QC, who was also at that time the chairman of the Bar Council. Alexander was no stranger to local government affairs, having defended Ken Livingstone's GLC in 1981 against critics of its Fares Fair Policy (unsuccessfully). Now he listened intently to a full account of the Commission's difficulties from its controller. Banham would reflect afterwards that Alexander could easily have booked himself a few years' worth of lucrative fees, by advising the Commission that the law left it no choice but to prosecute the miscreant councils, as Parliament had clearly intended. Instead, Alexander summed up the position rather differently, with the kind of Ciceronian summation for which he was famous at the Bar. Banham always remembered it word for word: 'I would far rather defend you against the charge of paying undue regard to the dictates of natural justice than prosecute on your behalf a useless case.'[50] In other words, Banham should stick to his guns. The Commission's critics were never remotely likely to take legal action against it for being excessively cautious and it should ignore them rather than embark on a perilous adventure in the courts.

Sheffield's David Blunkett, interviewed for a feature in *New Society* magazine in March 1986, took his opportunity to spell out a few of the perils. After some compliments to the Commission on its 'constructive' work in Sheffield – Blunkett was a different kind of political animal from the Derek Hattons and Ted Knights of the Loony Left – came this rush of sabre-rattling:

If they do take on the other six [authorities], why haven't they done so before? They do have discretion and it will look as if different standards are being used. So there would be consequences . . . for the future of the Commission itself. If it was seen to act in a highly political way as a tool of government, it would be hard [for it] to carry out its other roles. And if the Commission took on Sheffield and *lost*, that would blow open its achievements [*sic*] in Lambeth and Liverpool.[51]

Banham and Nicholson needed no persuading. Through the rest of 1986 and well into 1987, they sat patiently on their hands while even the most intransigent of councillors grasped the implications of the High Court ruling. In time, too, the merits of their approach won acceptance in Whitehall. Banham recalled: 'Basically, peace and good sense were breaking out, and there was no need to do anything.'[52] The Commission's auditors responded by quietly closing, one by one, their investigations into wilful misconduct – even the outcome in Sheffield was finally resolved, in June 1987. (As late as March, its district auditor, Alex Smith, had drafted two papers for the Commission – one justifying the issue of a 'wilful misconduct' certificate, the other not. On the basis of the first, he had sought a legal opinion and been advised to go ahead. He decided not to, nor to take any further legal advice.)[53] Losses due to late rate-setting were fudged in subsequent accounts and no further surcharges were ordered.

This broad outcome to the rate-capping saga certainly averted a crisis for the auditors of the DAS. They could scarcely have coped with a wider conflagration, on top of what was now being expected of them by their new masters in Vincent Square. Arguably it also rescued the Thatcher government from what might have become a full-blown constitutional crisis. It is easy to imagine how careless handling of the crisis might have led (as the poll tax would later lead) to a very different sequel – and to understand why, going back to the summer of 1985, Patrick Jenkin had declined to accept Banham's offer to resign.

True, some of the controller's speeches were deeply irritating; and he seemed content to be described by journalists as a loose cannon, generally the equivalent in Whitehall of being handed the Black Spot. But as Jenkin must have been well aware, his presence at the Commission assisted the government in two crucial ways. By 1985 he had already established it, and the DAS, as a genuinely independent body. This put the auditors rather than the DoE itself in the front line against the Loony Left, which was no small thing. (How might the Thatcher government's battle with the left-wing councils have developed, had the Commission been stillborn, leaving a ramshackle audit service to limp on?) And second, the strong following that Banham had built up in local government circles encouraged a good many Labour-controlled councils quietly to distance themselves from the non-compliance campaign. The Loony Left may in the end have marginalized itself, but other councils' respect for the Commission was helping to see the left on its way.

All this, however, was far from apparent at the time to Margaret Thatcher herself. And at the very moment that Banham's stand-off with Patrick Jenkin was being defused, an Exocet was homing in on the Commission from another direction (to use a metaphor much loved by the media at this post-Falklands time). Only one person in Vincent Square seems to have had sight of it, but it could easily have finished off the nascent Audit Commission altogether.

4

Under the Banham Banner, 1985–87

Around the beginning of June 1985, Ross Tristem received a call from an old Treasury colleague. Robin Butler had been Margaret Thatcher's principal private secretary since 1982. Could Tristem meet him for lunch? Expecting to have another discreet chat about developments in Vincent Square, as he'd had with various Treasury people over the past couple of years, Tristem was totally unprepared for the conversation that ensued. 'Margaret wants to get John out,' said Butler. She had been incensed, apparently, by Banham's attacks on the DoE. It was, her private secretary explained, an 'over-her-dead-body' situation.[1]

This concerned Butler greatly, because he knew from his own conversations with the Treasury that it was now more than happy with the Commission. Its officials had told him they valued the work it was doing, and certainly didn't want to see Banham dislodged. 'We've got to try and bridge this problem,' said Butler to Tristem. 'Why don't you take me through what you've been doing?' Tristem did so, and Butler was impressed. But how much potential savings did Tristem reckon that they had identified to date? This could be key, said Butler, because the annual spending round was not going well: the prime minister was having a terrible time trying to extract savings from her cabinet colleagues. None of them had yet been prepared to offer her anything like the sums she was looking for. Well, said Tristem, he couldn't be definitive about it, but it was a substantial sum of money – probably around £1 billion on a recurring basis, perhaps even a little more. 'Ah!' said Butler. 'Right. Leave it with me.' A few days later, he called Tristem back with a plan.

When Tristem approached Banham, he spared him the full

background. He simply explained that Butler wanted a meeting, to discuss all the savings that the Commission had so far identified. 'I think it's worthwhile,' was his advice. 'He's Margaret Thatcher's private secretary, after all!' But Banham needed no persuading. With characteristic enthusiasm, he prepared a barrelful of detailed slides that would graphically depict the findings of the special studies research, and the savings being identified by auditors in the field. He and Tristem took Butler through the presentation a week or so later. In pulling it together, Banham had been a little fortunate: the final draft of the Commission's 1985 Annual Report had been at hand in Vincent Square, with most of the figures that he needed on potential savings. And the timing was also felicitous in a deeper sense. For by the summer of 1985 the Special Studies directorate had really begun to flourish. Banham had a good story to tell – a better one, in some ways, than he could possibly have predicted only a year before.

TAKING STOCK OF SPECIAL STUDIES

Two milestones had been passed. One was the establishment of Tristem's operational research team; the other was a decision that the Commission should abandon the 'buying' of studies in favour of 'making' its own. Tristem's team had been scarcely more than a skeleton crew for the first half of 1984, comprising Bert Benham, Steve Evans – and one other individual, who had insisted when he joined in October 1983 that he be allowed to buy an expensive piece of kit for his own desk. This was David Henderson-Stewart, a former McKinsey consultant brought aboard by Banham, and the desk kit was an IBM personal computer. The extent of the Commission's output between March and August of 1984 – producing not only the three audit-progress reports but also the block grant study – belied the small size of this team, even with its PC. It was also a terrible stretch. Tristem needed more resources. Banham remained as sceptical as ever about the quality of the private firms' work, and Tristem easily persuaded him to approve the formation of a proper OR-based studies team.

The appointments were made in August and September of 1984.

Greg Birdseye, yet another physicist, had worked at the forefront of local government OR since 1972. James Kennedy was a chemist and was poached from the National Coal Board's OR staff. David Browning came from the DHSS, where he had worked under Tristem a few years earlier. John Gaughan was the fourth, who, sadly, would die only a few years later. All four were in their late thirties, and joined as project managers to coordinate the work being commissioned from the firms. One other person joined as a senior manager in the autumn. Doug Edmonds actually came over on a six-month secondment from the London Borough Council of Hillingdon, where he was head of corporate staff. But he had worked for twelve years on the NCB's OR staff from 1962 to 1974. The atmosphere in the Vincent Square office struck a chord.

When I left the Coal Board OR, I thought to myself, 'that's the last time I'm going to ever be able to work with such a universally bright set of people' – all Oxbridge graduates, that sort of thing. But coming to the Audit Commission was like returning to that world, except that they all had an extra ten years' experience. There was very much a 'new-organization' feeling of 'we can do it!' And the OR world was agog. Here was OR resurging in an area, local government, where it had never succeeded before. It was very exciting.[2]

By the end of October 1984, Tristem had a team that was too large for the Commission's first-floor office. They moved a little further round Vincent Square, relocating to rooms rented in the head-office building of LAMSAC. Then they went off to a hotel in Windsor to meet the district auditors for the first time, at the VFM seminars to prepare for the 1984–85 audit round.

The first batch of reports presented to the auditors at Windsor included the three audit-progress reports published earlier in the year, plus the first two home-grown titles instigated by the Commission itself. These comprised a report into vehicle-fleet management by councils and a report on the management of non-teaching costs in secondary schools. All went down well. (Steve Evans had supervised the work on vehicle-fleet management. He recalled: 'We told the auditors that we thought this was what VFM stood for!')[3] Behind the scenes, though, the report-production process was already prompting some second thoughts at the centre.

Banham had originally justified a 'buy' strategy on the grounds that the Commission needed to be 'as simple and lean as possible'[4] in order to keep overhead costs to a minimum. Outside consultants had accordingly been hired to help with all of the reports so far. But now these needed to be turned into action plans. Over the coming months – and here the Commission built significantly on the McKinsey model, by treating implementation as an integral part of the whole process – guides based on the reports would be used by auditors within individual authorities to pin down potential VFM opportunities. It followed from this, though, that to be really effective each national report required a significant after-sale service. The auditors would need to be enthused at initial training seminars. Their questions would have to be answered during the course of the audit. And their work on the outcome would need supervising for months thereafter. All of this assumed that the Commission's knowledge base, once accumulated, would remain in place. But where much of the core work on a study was done externally, it would inevitably pose a dilemma. Paying off the consultants after publication of the report would mean losing the knowledge base. Retaining them would be horribly expensive.

Just how expensive was soon clear. Consultants from Arthur Andersen were brought in during 1984 to handle a study that was published as the third home-grown title in February 1985. By the time it appeared, *Managing Social Services for the Elderly More Effectively* had already cost the Commission over £600,000. Since Tristem's total commissioning budget for a year's studies was only just over £1 million, this was unsustainable. 'It was quite clear to me that at the rate Arthur Andersen was spending our money, we weren't going to get many projects done. I told John we just couldn't afford to buy and not make.'[5]

Before Doug Edmonds turned his six-month secondment into a permanent transfer that March, Banham had reappraised the strategy and changed tack. He agreed with Tristem: they would do as much as possible in-house. This, however, would not involve the Commission turning its back on outside resources. Instead, the pro forma study team would in future comprise two Commission staffers, together with one acknowledged top expert in the field being researched, and one youngish high-flier from the DAS, or an auditor from the firms if they could release one. This was a neat solution. As well as making far better use of the available budget, it helped bring the Commission and the DAS closer together. From this point on, Cliff Nicholson was continually being badgered to release good auditors for study work – something he was actually always happy to do, though he also guarded with a jealous eye the right of the DAS to reclaim them.

Whether much of this background found its way into the presentation that Banham and Tristem laid out for Robin Butler may be doubted. Banham knew that it was hard numbers the prime minister's private secretary would be interested in, and he included plenty of them. They came in two varieties. The first comprised local authority 'profiles'. Their format was clever and well-suited to this kind of presentation. For any selected authority, a range of boxes was available under each of various headings – social services, or education, or highway maintenance, and so on. Each box contained three items: a cost category; a figure representing the average cost that was being achieved by a 'family' of comparable authorities across the country; and a figure for the cost achieved by the authority under scrutiny. (For each of the main local authority types – that is, shire counties and districts, metropolitan counties and districts, and London boroughs – there were seven different 'families' reflecting local geographies and socio-economic conditions.)

It made a lot of complex data look really quite straightforward. Curious to know about Islington's spending on residential services for the elderly? Turn to the Islington profile, select the Personal Services box and look for the Elderly Residential Services cost category. If it showed £50 per person for the 'family average' of comparable authorities over the latest reported year, and £85 for Islington, then you would see at a glance the relatively heavy scale of Islington's spending. Of course, there could be various reasons for the relative overspend. The Commission's profile went into some of these. It showed, for instance, the percentage of old people within the authority area who were in residential care. (But how far did an 'overspend' reflect a deliberate policy choice and how far did it betray incompetence? That was a question that numbers alone could never answer.)

The second variety of numbers in the presentation showed the potential savings that might be garnered in the wake of the

Commission's studies. Here was the real meat. More than 1,600 VFM audits conducted over the Commission's first winter of 1983–84 had generated potential savings (as has already been noted) that were valued by the Commission at £140 million a year. To this could be added another £200 million a year, if the potential savings on purchasing costs were to be fully realized. As for the second round of audits, launched through the winter of 1984–85 in coordination with the first three proper national reports – on vehicle-fleet management, secondary schools' non-teaching costs and care of the elderly – these had prompted over 1,000 projects promising savings not far short of £600 million.

Banham approached his meeting with Butler with all of his usual gusto – but even he must have been surprised by the response: Butler asked him to attend a full meeting of all the cabinet in No. 10 on 4 July, to give his presentation to the prime minister and her colleagues. Banham, delighted, agreed to do so – on condition that he would be able to offer exactly the same presentation to the shadow cabinet. He saw this as essential, to safeguard the Commission's independence, and the condition was accepted. (The meeting with the shadow cabinet took place later in July and was chaired by Neil Kinnock.)

The presentation at No. 10 was a highly unusual event. Banham, accompanied by John Read, was one of very few non-mandarin outsiders ever invited to address cabinet in this way, and he was almost certainly the first to give them a McKinsey-style slide show. He did not disappoint his sponsor – though neither did he miss the opportunity to make a few none too subtle political points. The July edition of the Commission's internal newsletter, *Audit News*, recorded:

What began as a 15 minute summary of the Commission's work developed into an hour-long question, answer and discussion session, with further education – as the flavour of the month – coming under most scrutiny ... John Banham reminded ministers that the majority of local authorities were, in the Commission's opinion, doing a good job, and that they compared very favourably with the rest of the public service [sic]. The controller emphasized that value improvements could not be achieved overnight – especially because capital investment was often required. He also stressed that it was for authorities to decide how the 'fruits' of their efforts were to be used; there must be positive incentives for them. The cabinet was also reminded of the Commission's views on the present grant distribution and capital control systems.

The July meeting of the Commission members happened to be that very afternoon. After Banham had presented his report as usual, John Read congratulated the controller on his morning's work. The minutes recorded: 'The presentation, which did not cover any particular local issues, had apparently impressed the prime minister and her colleagues; follow-up meetings, to discuss how the Commission's approach to value-for-money could be applied more widely in the public service, were now being arranged.'[6] Butler's stratagem had paid off handsomely. 'PM told how to save a billion' ran the headline in the *Sunday Times* that weekend.[7]

How the hard-pressed spending ministers around the cabinet table reacted to Banham's talk is not recorded, though it is probably safe to suppose that Michael Heseltine (assuming he was present) listened to it with some satisfaction. (As he recalled in 2007: 'I think the Commission did a lot of good work: they drew the curtains back and we were very lucky to have people of the calibre of John Banham. I've never doubted that.')[8] But by pointing the way to *annual* savings of well over £900 million, Banham had more than made amends with the prime minister for his outspoken speeches. Tristem recalled: 'It swayed the prime minister because it gave her a stick to beat the cabinet with. So John had got his reprieve, and the Commission now had the Treasury fully behind it.'[9]

Perhaps Margaret Thatcher saw in Banham a man with a real campaigning zeal. And that would surely have been a fair assessment. In a sense, campaigning was the essence of his whole approach: he had set himself at the head of a campaign to put the Commission on the map. And in so far as curbing local council spending by £900 million was one measure of his campaign objectives, he now had the prime minister's support. How long it might take to pin down savings on that scale was a question for another day. In the meantime, the campaign could roll. Banham had all the backing he needed.

HIGH MORALE IN VINCENT SQUARE

While Banham had won at least a respite with Margaret Thatcher, though, Patrick Jenkin was less fortunate. A government reshuffle early in September 1985 saw his departure from the cabinet. His successor at the Department of the Environment was Kenneth Baker, a politician of a very different hue. Baker was soon asking for a meeting with the Commission's members. His private secretary rang Vincent Square to arrange a visit, but Banham had a better idea. Recalling the Jenkin debacle, he suggested a different approach – which Baker followed up in style. 'Out came all these massive invitations embossed with the Royal Coat of Arms, from the Secretary of State for the Environment, and up we went to his offices in Marsham Street,' Banham recalled, of their meeting on 3 October. 'We all filed in there – and sure enough, just as I'd envisaged, there were the sandwiches curling at the edges, with the Yugoslav Riesling. Then along came Ken Baker, saying "Ladies and Gentlemen, I want you to know our Nation is grateful to you." And if he had then said, "and by the way, there's the window, now jump," we would all have hurtled out of the window.'[10]

Within a few weeks, Baker had persuaded Read to postpone his January departure for eight months – a rather important move, since nothing had yet been done to find a new chairman. At the same time, with Baker's approval, Banham was asked to serve a second term from April 1986. He accepted, though for two and a half years rather than a full three. It was an invitation few inside the DoE would have expected a little earlier in the year, and it certainly surprised one or two members of the Commission. But for those on Banham's staff, it was a boost to morale.

So what sort of working atmosphere had evolved at Vincent Square by the autumn of 1985? Any young auditor from the DAS, seconded to a special studies team from the Bristol office or one of the district auditors' offices, was in for a culture shock. Frank Ingram only arrived about eighteen months later, but his description of the experience for the house newsletter would have rung just as true in 1985: 'At first the absence of immediate pressure in Special Studies is both startling and disconcerting. No endless lists of reports to draft, meetings to attend, telephone calls to answer and no staff time budgets. Just an empty desk and some rather hazy terms of reference. But the pressure is there, of course.' Ingram's note was certainly not designed to deter others from following him. Vincent Square, he said, was an exciting place to work. 'The staff there are highly motivated and the place really does buzz. So if you get the opportunity of a secondment to Special Studies, while it may be something of a digression for those intent on a career in audit, I would urge you to accept it.'[11]

When he asked the way to Mr Nicholson's office, the reply came back: 'Sorry? Oh, you mean Cliff – yes.' Banham had told everyone from his first day 'just call me John', and that was the style in London. In the DAS, auditors still generally addressed each other by their surnames. Many DAS visitors to Vincent Square found the apparent informality – endorsed by some strikingly non-DoE paintings that hung on the walls, by the Australian artist Katie Clemson – rather a challenge. Whether in 1 Vincent Square itself or the LAMSAC building down the street, no one stood on hierarchy. The controller himself worked in a modest office and his door was always open. Banham's personal accessibility set the tone: people milled in and out of each other's offices for impromptu meetings at any hour of the day.

One factor behind many of the spontaneous gatherings was the paucity of computer resources, but a general enthusiasm to use them. David Henderson-Stewart had led the way with his IBM PC, using a Lotus Notes spreadsheet that was state-of-the-art for manipulating statistics. Some others had now acquired Olivetti and Compaq machines with Wordstar word-processing programmes. Peter Brokenshire, the management practice director, was especially keen to encourage their use. The Commission, after all, had come into being at the same time as the PC. It had no legacy of outdated hardware from the pre-PC era, which was shackling so many IT initiatives in other organizations. It was another opportunity for the Commission to lead the way. (It was also another sign of the gap between Vincent Square and the DAS. Each district office of the DAS had been given a PC in 1984, and these had been linked into a national network, largely at Brokenshire's instigation. Attitudes to this were mixed in the regional offices. The head of computer audit in Bristol,

Chris Hurford, later recalled that 'some of the district auditors felt it was all an extravagance and computing would never catch on'.[12] It was only seven years earlier, on joining the nascent computer team in 1978, that Hurford had parted company with a district auditor who forbade the use of electronic calculators in the office. He thought they made auditors lazy.)

Above all, there was a dynamism in Vincent Square that was unmistakable. Everyone who worked there sensed the Commission was genuinely a new departure in public sector administration. There was an air of *inquiry* about the place – and Banham epitomized it at the start of each morning, pausing for a brief catch-up with most of the people whose desks lined one or other route from the reception desk to his office. How far had they got with yesterday's figures? What would the next stage of their inquiry be? Did they see this morning's newspaper story? And had they thought of adding this or that category of data to their current review? Along with the questions came a constant stream of new ideas – some of them inspired, but a good many, inevitably, that were probably best forgotten. The snag was that all would need a response and might prompt days of work unless quickly intercepted. The interceptor-in-chief was Cliff Nicholson.

It was battle stations on the interception front every Monday morning. Banham and Nicholson shared the Commission's chauffeured car from Paddington Station to Vincent Square each week. (The deputy controller continued to live in Bristol until he retired, travelling up to London on Monday mornings and back on Friday evenings. Banham was living near Newbury, in Berkshire, commuting daily by train.) It was a regular ordeal for Nicholson. 'I used to hate those car journeys. John had had all weekend to think up ideas – most of which were quite impractical. I used to spend half an hour umming and aahing, from Paddington to the office, as far as possible knocking things down before they went any further.'[13]

Nicholson was *not* a deputy in search of extra jobs. On the contrary, his burden of work at this time was already exceptionally heavy. Not only was he having to spend many hours each week privately advising the district auditors on their next steps in the crisis over the late rate-setters, he was also working at full stretch to support his director of accounting practice with a radical reappraisal of the DAS's fundamental working practices. As Harry Wilkinson had discovered on his first foray into the town halls back in the autumn of 1983, the traditional way of conducting audits was relatively haphazard in comparison with what was now needed, to comply with the Code of Audit Practice. Here was a whole other dimension to the work of the Commission, far removed from the politics of rate-capping and national reports alike.

MODERNIZING THE REGULARITY AUDIT

On his return to Vincent Square after travelling round the DAS in 1983, the former Ernst & Whinney man with scarcely three months' experience of local government work had sat down to write what was (rather remarkably) the DAS's first definitive set of rules laying out the scope and objectives of an audit. Assisted by Bill Miller and Mike Barnes, he had finished it as planned in March 1984. The contents were painstakingly packaged by the team themselves into buff-coloured binders and posted off late one evening to beat an urgent deadline: several of the thirteen district auditors were keen to have them, before signing off finally on their 1983–84 audits and launching into the regularity work for 1984–85. Wilkinson and the chief inspector of audit (CIA), Bert Pyke, were themselves anxious to ensure that copies of the 'buff binder' went out to every individual 'section' in the DAS. (Reporting to the typical district auditor were four or five sections, each of them located in a different part of the DA's region and responsible for either a county and a number of district councils or a group of metropolitan authorities.) It was to be quickly adopted by them as the bible of the service, with revised and improved versions following in later years. Copies were *not* sent at this stage, however, to partners working in the private firms. The DAS still regarded the firms as competitors. They were expected to produce their own materials (and did so, eventually).

The following month, in April 1984, in a speech to the annual meeting of the District Auditors' Society, Wilkinson aired some of his impressions of the service after his first half-year in the job.[14] (On his copy of the speech he pencilled a cautionary note to himself: 'Temper criticism to be constructive.') Then he spelt out how the new approach would differ from the old. Every regularity audit would consist of three principal tasks. The balance sheet would need to be verified. A fundamental point, one might have supposed – but Wilkinson stressed to his audience that 'in order to ensure against material mis-statements we must know and audit what is in the major amounts in the balance sheet . . . we can no longer ignore [sic] addressing fixed assets'. The auditor's second main task would be to check on the integrity of all systems used for basic transactions – collecting the rates and paying the wages, most obviously, but also coordinating the wide range of other complex operations underpinning the finances of a local authority. Here again, Wilkinson was flagging an initiative that could surely have been taken at almost any point since the introduction of mainframe computers. But he adopted an emollient tone: 'For better or worse, we are into systems-based auditing because the Code of Practice says so.' And third, the auditor would be responsible for legality and probity issues, including investigating any objections to the accounts or questions about them raised by ratepayers. Procedures for detecting fraud and corruption would be especially pertinent in this context. Wilkinson tacitly deferred to his audience's experience on this front, though, and invited them to expand the buff folder in the months ahead with their 'practical advice'. Assuming a satisfactory resolution of all objections and completion of the systems review and balance sheet audit, the auditor could then sign off with a certificate that the audit had been completed and could give an unqualified opinion that the statement of accounts '*presents fairly* . . . the financial position of the authority'.

The single biggest change for every audit team, of course, would be the allocation of about 30 per cent of its time to non-regularity tasks. These would include evaluating the data for an authority's comparative profile; reviewing the management arrangements in place to tackle the VFM agenda; and setting in train VFM projects in line with the topics proposed in the current year's audit guides from Vincent Square, which were universally known, at Banham's behest, as the Commission's 'flavours'.

With this much more complicated agenda, every auditor would

have to adjust to some important changes in working methodology. Wilkinson wanted all working papers to be treated with a lot more respect than some he had seen in his first six months (the worst of which were 'frankly appalling'). He was also going to press for more accurate records to be kept of planned and actual time spent on individual audits – where the DAS unsurprisingly trailed far behind practice in the private sector and seemed to be slow in coming to terms with the potential of new technology. Time-keeping, though, was an issue that would not be resolved satisfactorily until well into the 1990s.*

Finally, at the conclusion of every audit, the authority's members would have to be handed not only the auditor's opinion, but also a 'management letter' specifying any matters raised by the auditor and discussed with council officers. The letter would also, in the words of the Code of Practice, 'summarize the benefits anticipated from implementation of agreed actions'. Importantly, the auditor would have to seek a meeting with the authority's members to discuss the letter with them.

There was one other topic discussed by Wilkinson that April day in 1984: 'quality assurance'. Handled prior to 1982 by the old training and standards arm of the DAS, the Audit Inspectorate, this would now be tackled differently. Following the completion of each year's audit round and prior to the launch of the next year's VFM projects, there would be an intense spate of reviews: at least one for each of the private firms, and one for the DAS in each of the thirteen districts.

---

*Developments on the time-keeping front provide a record of the DAS's move into the computer age. As of 1982, the service had no computers whatever. Payroll and administration were handled by the DoE. Civil service rules did not allow DAS secretaries to use word-processors, which were defined as mechanical aids only appropriate to lower pay grades. The DoE paid for a first PC to be installed in the Bristol office for training purposes (i.e. to understand how local authorities were using them) in March 1983. Written time reports were initially collated monthly by the thirteen district offices from their branches and posted to Bristol, where the papers were logged into the solitary PC. By the end of 1983, each district office had one PC and the time reports were put on floppy disks that were then posted to Bristol. By the end of 1984, audit teams had been given one PC each and were sending their time reports on floppy disks to the district offices, which had finally been connected to Bristol on a network. Each district office's PC had a 20 MB hard disk, which was thought likely to suffice for fifty years. (Chris Hurford, interview with the author.)

He would lead the team reviewing the firms' performances and Bill Miller would do the same for the DAS audits – assisted by representatives of two of the private firms (Coopers & Lybrand and Price Waterhouse). Every visitation by the so-called 'Quality Control Review' (QCR) would draw on discussions with the authority's officers as well as the paper record. It would look carefully to see that all the necessary ingredients of a rigorous audit had been properly planned. It would test how thoroughly the audit had been implemented, on both regularity and VFM work. And it would scrutinize the conclusions of the audit, including the management letter and any VFM project reports.

The evaluation of VFM projects would have to weigh the validity of any prospective savings. Wilkinson indicated that this would be left to a VFM specialist, and perhaps this was one aspect of the new regime on which he was happy to defer. As he would admit in an article that he wrote for the trade press the following year, the Commission 'recognises that the specification of potential savings is a very inexact science whose results must be used with a high degree of caution'.[15] There would be plenty more to say on this topic in due course.

So how did the auditors score, when Wilkinson handed over his first report card to the Commission a year later in April 1985?[16] In general, pretty well. The firms had perhaps outperformed on the regularity work (while occasionally overdoing it, especially with their scrutiny of current stocks). But the DAS had handled VFM work rather better. Wilkinson noted that the DAS had shown 'a most encouraging response to the changed direction of audits and an increasing professionalism'. He was also complimentary about the firms, but he had already made up his mind that there were too many of them, stretched too randomly across the country: 'Though all firms show, at this stage, a strong commitment to the work, there are differences in performance and there must be a case for a gradual shift towards fewer firms and more concentrated areas of local expertise.'

Presenting Wilkinson's findings to the Commission members, the controller drew one main conclusion above all: there were no grounds for any significant redistribution of audits, and certainly not for giving any larger share to the firms. (For those on the Commission who were familiar with the claims that had been made to Michael Heseltine by some of the firms' more aggressive marketing partners, it was all quite revealing.)[17] As Banham also reminded the members, an increased share for the firms was anyway going to be an inevitable consequence of the abolition of the GLC and of the metropolitan counties, both scheduled for 1986. Extra audit work in the troublesome London boroughs, where the firms were relatively prominent, would similarly be of benefit to them – as, too, would be the planned privatization of the municipal bus companies.

In the weeks that followed the completion of his report, Wilkinson and his Vincent Square team held a series of seminars with DAS officers around the country. In future, these would be a regular annual event, giving auditors a chance to hear the results of the quality assurance exercise and to chew over with the Commission team any key regularity issues that looked likely to pose problems in the audit year ahead, of which there was never any shortage. In addition to structural changes like the scrapping of the metropolitan counties, there was a stream of legislative changes through these years that impinged directly on regularity audits. The steady expansion of compulsory competitive tendering (CCT), for instance, led to a proliferation within every large council of direct labour organizations (and direct service organizations) that all needed to be separately audited.

Above all, there were the continuing difficulties for many auditors of just catching up with the new demands made on them since 1983 by the Code of Audit Practice – and one fundamental requirement in particular, as Wilkinson later recalled.

The big, big problem was *systems* auditing. You obviously couldn't audit every individual transaction, so you always had to look at the underlying systems – and you had to do that in a fairly structured manner, because it was going to take up quite a lot of your audit. But under the old regime, this had never happened. They might have chosen one system that they wanted to look at, but they had never systematically covered *all* of the major systems. That was what you now had to do, under the Code of Practice.[18]

It was not a change that happened overnight. In fact, despite the show of optimism in his formal reports to the Commission, Wilkinson was privately surprised at the slow pace of adjustment within the DAS. He began by hoping that auditors in the field would very largely push the process ahead for themselves, but found them waiting instead for the buff binder to be made ever more prescriptive. 'It took a long time to devise a fresh approach to the audit of systems.'

This was probably a fair measure of the calibre of the DAS at that time. Travelling around it in the course of his reviews, Wilkinson was well placed to judge this. He found its senior ranks often impressive: 'There were lots of very clever people there, auditors who were capable of reaching agreement with local authorities where I thought it might not be possible, on both legality and VFM issues.' On the other hand, as a former partner of a leading international firm, he was often struck by the distinctive age profile of DAS teams 'and this took years to change'. Even in middle-ranking jobs, many officers were in their fifties and had spent thirty years or more in the field – often working in sections that were remote from the district auditor, never mind the chief inspector. (The private firms, by contrast, mostly employed junior staff in the field: their auditors were rarely over 40 years old, unless they were partners in a supervisory role.) All this had its benefits, in terms of experience and the institutional memory of the DAS. But it was inevitably a case of old dogs and new tricks for some section teams. For all its evident strengths, no one would have described the DAS in its first couple of years under the Commission as a dynamic institution.

Still, progress *was* made. By the time that the second annual round of reviews was handed to the Commission members, in July 1986, Wilkinson was able to report that the regularity work done by the DAS 'had made great strides in the last two years'.[19] The typical authority audit was now being completed with far more thoroughness. There were no grounds, it was agreed again, for shifting a higher proportion of work to the private firms. Indeed, the members were assured by the controller that there was now 'evidence suggesting that the District Audit Service as a whole ranked No. 3 or 4 among the firms involved in local government audits'. This was a tribute both to the DAS and to Wilkinson's quiet professionalism, which by 1986 had begun to earn him a reputation as a highly accomplished technician – one might also say an accountant's accountant. Despite his self-effacing manner, Wilkinson's expertise had accordingly begun to land him on several committees at CIPFA.

Indeed, his CIPFA responsibilities came to involve a significant extension of his role around this time. Having effectively written most of the rule book on how the auditors of local government were to tackle their job, he now took the lead in writing a parallel code of practice on how the auditors' clients in local government, the accountants, should be doing theirs. This came about as the result of an initiative by the DoE. The public furore over creative accounting two or three years earlier had alerted the department afresh to the generally lamentable state of financial reporting in local government. Its first response was to pursue the idea of standardized accounting statements, which was set out in a 1984 consultation paper. Reactions to this paper were mixed – with the Commission among the critics – but the government ploughed on and issued another paper late in 1985. It again proposed that councils should, in essence, be held to a standard format of accounts by new legislation, akin to the Companies Act. There was some modest support for this from the accounting profession, including the Institute of Chartered Accountants. But the local authority associations, unsurprisingly in view of all the tensions over rate-capping, simply stonewalled the proposals. Nor was the Commission any more persuaded, second time around: its members agreed at their December 1985 meeting that 'while there was some merit to the proposals, . . . [they] were bureaucratic and unnecessary'.[20] This view was endorsed by CIPFA.

At this point, the DoE changed tack and adopted the only obvious alternative approach: it invited the local authority associations, working with CIPFA and the Commission, to come up with their own solution. But it insisted that more standardized accounts had to be the outcome, or legislation would ensue. Hence the formation, in the spring of 1986, of a working group to write a Code of Practice on Local Authority Accounting as the basis of financial reporting in local government. (In preparing it, the group was also asked to begin thinking about the implementation of the poll tax, which was unveiled to the world in a Green Paper, *Paying for Local Government*, in January 1986.) Published in July 1987, the code would eventually be credited by many in the profession with bringing UK public sector accounting properly into the twentieth century.

The prime mover behind the committee and the single biggest

contributor to the code was Harry Wilkinson. 'I wasn't doing it for the Audit Commission, but I took the initiative and did a huge amount of work on it. I couldn't be the name at the top – that had to be a local authority man – but I put in more time on it than anybody else. I did it wearing my CIPFA hat. I don't think the Commission knew what I was doing.'[21] For a few years starting early in 1986, in fact, Wilkinson simply seconded himself out to CIPFA for a large proportion of his time. The members agreed that the Commission 'should make its own proposals for improvement' and offer them to CIPFA and the local authority associations. But they showed no real understanding of what was at stake or of the commitment that Wilkinson would have to make to the task.[22]

It was a curious arrangement – not least in so far as it made Wilkinson, in a sense, both judge and jury for local government accounting. It also cast a revealing light on the nature of the Audit Commission and its whole management ethos. John Banham led from the front – with an obvious preference for taking on much of his role single-handedly, from writing study reports to handling the media and dealing with the Commission members – and as a leader he was dazzlingly effective. He inspired all his troops. Nonetheless, he had little real interest in managing them. The DAS was left almost entirely to Cliff Nicholson. And the other senior directors of the Commission, an eclectic mix of talents, were left free to shape their own franchises – with few constraints, but not much support either. It was all part of the unusual culture at 1 Vincent Square. So Harry Wilkinson went his own way, and others did the same. Ian Pickwell, for example, was originally appointed as associate controller to manage the private firms. While he was always ready to offer them affable advice, he made no effort to institute a formal reporting procedure for them. By 1986 he was spending much of his time helping Brian Skinner cope with the awkward squad among the Met district's London boroughs.

The same was true of Peter Brokenshire. It was originally expected by his colleagues in 1983 that, as director of management practice, he would take charge of ensuring that DAS auditors properly scrutinized the managerial aspects of local government – the relations between members and officers, the dissemination of information, and so on. But Brokenshire had difficulty developing this role. The

Commission's interaction with the DAS was too heavily monopolized by special studies on the one hand and regularity issues on the other. So he found his own way in a fresh direction. Based on his own personal experience in local government, Brokenshire always believed that a lack of basic management information was a fundamental problem for the sector. He was to devote much of his career with the Commission to promoting ways of disseminating information more efficiently – at first for use by councils themselves and later, in the 1990s, for use by the ratepayers who elected them. His first step down this road was to mastermind the production of a ring-bound manual for local authorities, with thematic chapters devoted to separate ser-vices and the broad indicators that might be used to monitor them. At the same time, and encouraged by the reception in local government circles for his detailed paper on Basildon Council, and another shortly afterwards on Wansdyke Council, he began to focus on studies of individual authorities, and how they were managed.

Several councils over the following two years approached their DAS auditor *requesting* a detailed external report on their manage-ment arrangements. They included the county councils of Cleveland, Norfolk and Northumberland and the district councils in Milton Keynes and Hambleton. The most intriguing request came from Liver-pool City Council, after the leadership there was wrested away from the Militant councillors led by Derek Hatton. Some of the reports were prepared by firms, not always to the liking of the Commission. (Members noted in March 1985 that the Norwich study by Deloittes 'was of poor quality with an absence of figures', and aired concern that reports were being sought by some authorities as part of their manoeuvring for a higher Block Grant.)[23]

All this represented a subtle but important shift in the definition of a key directorship, but it was never openly discussed at any meeting that colleagues could later recall. Management meetings were held in the very early days, at which the directors debated topics like the structure of the DAS, or indeed how auditors might best go about the evaluation of an authority's management practices. But this approach soon petered out. By the middle of 1984, as noted, management meetings were always attended by the press relations adviser, and no one was in any doubt about the real agenda: how were the latest special studies going, and how could they eventually be reported to the outside world – meaning the general news media as well as bodies like the Institute of Local Government – in ways that would maximize their impact. The strategy behind the questions was at least clear to all, and was compelling in many ways. The expansion of Ross Tristem's team delivered the resources to pursue it – and Tristem himself had never been in any doubt about the franchise he wanted to build.

Banham naturally saw the success of his presentation to the cabinet, in July 1985, as confirmation of the strategy. Studies that could win the attention of Margaret Thatcher and Jimmy Young alike would be the making of the Commission. He would throw all his formidable energies into producing and promoting a series of ambitious papers that would promise a significant improvement in the quality of local government in the UK. This of course would need a constructive response from central as well as local government. How far the Commission's campaigning tactics would be compatible with eliciting a supportive response from Whitehall was an interesting question.

RAISING THE BAR ON VALUE-FOR-MONEY WORK

The Commission's first yellow-jacketed publications back in 1984 had looked a little amateurish, with the font style and spacing of a rural parish magazine. With the publication in February 1985 of the report on social services for the elderly, largely the work of consultants Arthur Andersen, a new and much slicker style appeared. By the summer of 1985, when the report on further education finally appeared, the special studies had collected a nickname. To the district auditors and their teams, every addition to the *oeuvre* was another Yellow Peril.

There were not too many Yellow Perils in 1985. In fact, the sheer amount of work required for each study had (again) been a little underestimated. By now it was clear that most would need a year to eighteen months to reach completion. Since most of the people in the Special Studies directorate had been recruited only in the summer and autumn of 1984, there was insufficient time to prepare the full quota of reports ahead of the next audit round, kicking off in November 1985.

Four 'flavours' were chosen for the 1985-86 VFM programme. Two were based on topics that had already been given some attention, so the lack of a special study would in neither case be a problem. (Purchasing costs had been the subject of a published study in 1984, to which local government's response had been disappointing; and cash-flow issues were in part the focus of work done on the Block Grant and capital controls. Audit projects and questionnaires on the two topics provided the data for later reports: *Improving Cash Flow Management in Local Government* appeared in October 1986 and *Improving Supply Management in Local Authorities* appeared in March 1987.) The other two picked up where the very first study, on council tenants' rent arrears, had left off – tackling further dimensions of local government's involvement with property.

If broadly defined to cover council housing, municipal buildings and roads, then no aspect of any authority's activities was more important than property. Banham and Tristem realized that the Commission, in relying much more heavily on in-house resources, needed to focus on areas that all local authorities would see as vital. Education and social services also qualified under this heading – but property was top of the list. One flavour for 1985–86 could be given its own audit guide based on a full study: *Saving Energy in Local Government Buildings* had been under preparation for a year and was published in November 1985. A team under Steve Evans had collaborated with the energy efficiency office of the Department of Energy (which provided much of the funding for it) and eighteen authorities had participated in the work. It must have been a slightly daunting read for most auditors, with its 'kWh/sq.m./annum' measures of normalized performance. But it came up with a rule of thumb, recommending that one central staff person be dedicated to promoting energy efficiency for every £1 million of expenditure on energy. Applied consistently by the DAS, this eventually became the accepted norm for local government policy on energy management.

The other property-related flavour drew on research originally commissioned by the Audit Inspectorate in 1982 from consultants at the private firm Ernst & Whinney, and built on the rent-arrears report. E&W's work continued through 1984 and into 1985, piling up huge bills for the Commission – another reason why Tristem had little problem persuading Banham to bring more work in-house – but also amassing mountains of data on the management of council estates. As a new boy on Tristem's staff, Greg Birdseye was handed the job of turning the data into something that could be useful for auditors and their council clients. The E&W team had looked in great detail at how fifteen authorities, broadly representative of all local government, managed their estates. It was a big subject. There were almost 5 million council houses in England and Wales, equal to about a third of the country's entire housing stock. Leaving aside all the costs of design and maintenance – let alone the capital investment in building – the cost of just managing these council houses was the single most expensive service provided by many councils. Aggregate spending on it had also been rising appreciably faster than retail inflation since 1979. Birdseye was a project manager with no staff. But he produced a VFM handbook for auditors and an unpublished report on the E&W work, *Housing Supervision and Management*, that went beyond the Commission's report on rent arrears in a significant respect.

The rent-arrears study was classic audit territory. Our report broadened it to cover 15 different aspects of housing management: the administration of waiting lists, the provision of sheltered schemes for the elderly, the control of repairs expenditure and so on. It went beyond number-crunching into some of the more difficult management areas. That was where the value-for-money auditing came in – not just for economy, but the other 'E's as well.[24]

The two property flavours prompted more than 700 local VFM projects over that winter of 1985–86, and auditors reported back potential cost savings of nearly £100 million a year. This was half the total number of projects on all of the flavours, plus locally originated projects. (The prospective cost savings would eventually add up to an estimated £225 million a year.) While the auditors chased down the savings, John Banham took another look at *Housing Supervision*. What he saw in it was evidence not just of ill-spent millions but of a managerial failure with devastating social and political consequences. A much discussed book published the previous year – Alice Coleman's *Utopia on Trial: Vision and Reality in Planning Housing* – had examined the link between badly designed council housing and anti-social behaviour. Banham sensed an opportunity – an obligation, even – to alert the general public to a whole catalogue of dire council-housing problems. And since the appropriate response would have to include action by central government, as well as initiatives that the Commission could recommend at a local level, he sat down to write a report with a suitably polemical tone.

The result, *Managing the Crisis in Council Housing*, powerfully combined the fact-based analysis of the Commission's earlier, unpublished report with eloquent appeals for a fresh approach at every level. Less than a third of its 100 pages dealt with the specifics of improving housing management (above all, by redefining the role and accountability of the chief housing officer). Two further sections dwelt at length on the impoverished services blighting so many council estates, and on the poor controls hampering any better administration of their finances. It set out a good many proposed remedies at the local level and urged their adoption. 'But it would be naive,' it then observed, 'to suggest that these measures will be adequate to meet all the problems inherited from the past . . . In such circumstances proposing a managerial solution may be tantamount to suggesting a rearrangement of the deckchairs on the Titanic. More radical approaches may be required.'[25] A final section looked at some possibilities 'worthy of consideration by all concerned', from public–private partnership ideas to greater public funding for the most benighted authorities and even possible fiscal reforms. Any and all would be preferable, as the introduction to the report made clear, to Whitehall's meddling micromanagement of so many aspects of housing affairs, via controls that were themselves 'an important contributory cause of the present crisis . . .'.[26]

This was what Whitehall customarily described as 'trespassing'. Critics wishing to avoid any hint of a confrontation in public tut-tutted about the controller perhaps straying into policy territory, as though he had wandered unwittingly from the narrow paths of number-crunching. In reality, of course, Banham had struck out very deliberately and marked a new red route on his map. He had illustrated in some considerable style how difficult it would invariably be for the Commission to discuss local government's *effectiveness*, in whatever area, without raising questions over policy. And as long as he was controller, it was evidently not a demarcation that was going to prompt a huge amount of hand-wringing in Vincent Square.

Early in February 1986, while Banham was still putting the last touches to his report on council housing, Ross Tristem presented a paper to the members at their monthly meeting on the proposed VFM programme for the next three years. They pressed to know the likely timetable of future studies. Tristem had not prepared this: perhaps he had assumed they knew the scale of what was being planned for the year and would be content with that. In fact, a prodigious amount of work was under way: the following twelve months would see no less than six studies published by the Commission, starting with the *Housing Crisis* report in March. Council housing was the subject of another report, into maintenance, in November 1986. Other subjects included the management of secondary schools, the management of both cash flow and purchasing in local government, and (in a Section 27 study focused on the impact of government policy) the care of the mentally ill and the handicapped. All were going to be tackled by the Special Studies directorate in an investigative spirit that would not stop short of open prescriptions where these were felt to be appropriate.

This, and the sheer scale of the studies output, posed an obvious problem for a public body presided over by a Commission meeting one day a month. The surge of reports in 1986 posed even more of a challenge in so far as several of the members were new to the role. Four of the original appointees had retired in January – Lawrie Barratt, Kenneth Bond, Keith Bridge and Ian McCallum – and Ian Hay Davison had stepped down the previous August. Their successors were two businessmen, Harry Axton and Murray Stuart; Robert (Bob) Wall, a prominent local Tory politician from Bristol; John Barratt, who was about to wrap up thirteen years as chief executive of Cambridgeshire County Council; and Eric Meade, an accountant. So how did John Read and his colleagues, old and new, cope?

A SHIFTING CONTEXT

Read was regarded by the others as an intelligent and effective chairman. He had begun in 1983 by splitting the Commission up into a series of committees. This had not worked well, however, and was soon abandoned. For the most part, all of their activities were thereafter handled by the members sitting as one committee. They worked well together. Coming from a variety of backgrounds, they met at Vincent Square with often quite disparate views that some of them pushed robustly. But there seem to have been few if any private or political disagreements of any real importance, and certainly none that compromised the Commission's public reputation.

In general, the members were happy to be steered by the chairman – and he was steered by Banham. Too much so, indeed, for some members' liking. Harry Axton, briefing Banham's successor a year later, would complain that during his first months serving on the Commission in 1986, 'he had found it was an uninformed body which merely took note of what John Banham told it. He thought the whole organization under Banham "far too much of a one-man show".'[27] But the formal minutes of their monthly meetings nonetheless chronicled a positive and constructive rapport between the Commission's chairman, its members and their controller, though a triangular relationship not without its tensions. Banham always met with them alone, to present his own monthly report. This would typically range over the operating results of the Commission itself and any matters of pay-and-rations that needed to be aired. Cliff Nicholson would join them if an update was required on any DAS affairs, as was generally the case after April 1984. Other directors would attend as the agenda demanded. This sometimes happened for the presentation of a new study, but it was far from the rule. Banham's editorial ownership of almost all the studies generally extended to managing their safe passage past the members, too.

By 1986, special studies had come to assume an importance that went far beyond anything the members had been expecting in the first year or two of the Commission. The studies programme had been launched quite cautiously in 1984, with the controller stressing 'the importance that he attached to the detailed involvement of members during the report preparation process'.[28] And there were conventions to be respected. The Commission, for example, would always voice an 'overall view' when a public statement was required, rather than an 'agreed view' that might imply some degree of horse-trading round the table. Now, two years later, the programme had built an impressive momentum. Wide-ranging in their coverage, massively documented and often engagingly written, the studies were attracting huge attention. The Commission's members could take some of the credit for this. But while they had ultimate responsibility for the studies, how much power they really had over their content was another matter. In most cases, they were inevitably approving the publication of material they had had very little time to scrutinize properly. This was not without its risks.

It is probably fair to say that all who worked with him, while in awe of Banham's writing skills and presentational talents, were less struck by any meticulous regard on his part for the accuracy of every single detail. Sometimes he just got on with the story. For the cognoscenti of Vincent Square, saying that something could be found 'in John's evidence box' was, for a while, a proverbial reference to its non-existence. Tales would be told affectionately for years afterwards of this or that colourful flourish that had added a rhetorical, but strictly speaking fictional, element to a persuasive text that had to be edited out of the final version. And it was not unknown for Banham and Tristem to be found late at night in Vincent Square (or even, on at least one famous occasion, at the printer's) still arm-wrestling over each other's final, final amendments to a study.

By the same token, Commission members' comments were not always treated as holy writ. All reports were circulated in draft just ahead (and *only* just ahead) of the monthly meetings. Most went to a panel of three members for special consideration before reaching the meeting. Under a 'ten-day rule', members had to have at least that much time for scrutiny of every study's final version before it went off to the printer, and earlier drafts had often been discussed in a monthly meeting at considerable length. No redrafting was ever contemplated *en courant*, though: the controller, who had a dread of 'drafting by committee', gave assurances that appropriate amendments would be made, and usually they were. Alternatively, members could find, as Noel Hepworth did on one occasion, that a lengthy argument could lead to Banham conceding the need for a deletion and then re-inserting the deleted matter in a different section of the text. As Hepworth good-humouredly recalled: 'He had his own view, and one way or another, he would work his view back in.'[29] Greg Birdseye, early in his career at the Commission, sat with Banham to listen to Roy Shaw proposing a long series of proposed amendments to a study. After Shaw had gone, Birdseye volunteered to work up a fresh draft. 'Oh, I don't think we really need to, do we?' replied Banham disarmingly.[30]

Content was one thing, however; tone was quite another. There was a growing sense, as 1986 wore on, that Banham's stance towards Whitehall was causing at least some of the members acute discomfort. It was often a case of remarks made privately or unguarded comments in the media, openly criticizing officials rather than their political masters. (Some members with a public sector background put this down to a lack of familiarity with central government's ways, shared by Banham and his chairman alike.) But the problem extended to the written word, too.

In April, for example, the DoE circulated a consultation paper on controlling local government's capital expenditure. Banham penned an outspoken response that, *inter alia*, compared local authorities' performance on this score very favourably with the government's own record. The members asked him to redraft it, dropping the awkward comparison and generally toning down the language. The revised response went off to the DoE a week or so later without further discussion. When the members met again in May, they were evidently a little upset that the second draft had not been circulated, and made it clear they would have pressed for more changes. 'Reception of such papers [as Banham had sent in] by officials and their consequent advice to ministers would be likely to be more favourable if the paper could be written less abrasively, and with less overt criticism of present systems.'[31]

Overt criticism, though, was what Banham now believed was necessary, if the Commission was to make any impression on policy makers. His confidence in central government generally, and the DoE in particular, had taken a serious dip since that happy excursion to Downing Street and the subsequent presentation to the shadow cabinet, the previous summer. He had begun the controller's job in 1983 assuming that his main challenge would be winning support among local councillors. He made it his mission to get on terms with them – only to find himself far more impressed by the work they were doing than he had ever expected to be. He had underestimated local government.

Much worse, though, he had hopelessly underestimated the fundamental antipathy to local government among Margaret Thatcher and
her cabinet colleagues. The endless battles over the Block Grant,
rate-capping and now the proposed poll tax were bad enough. What
he found personally dispiriting was the lacklustre response that he
sensed among ministers and their most senior officials to so much that
the Commission itself was trying to do.

He made no secret of his disappointment. In a review of the
Commission's first three years that he wrote for its 1986 Report &
Accounts, published that July, Banham spelt out his frustration:

Given ... the turbulence of central–local government relations over the past
several years, it might have been expected that local authorities would react
defensively to implied criticisms from the Commission ... In fact, the Commission
has been greatly encouraged by the generally positive reaction of members and
officers to its work ... [On the other hand] it has sometimes seemed as though
the general reaction within Whitehall [to the Commission's studies] has been to
welcome the reports formally, adjust the planned expenditure in the service in
question downwards by the amount of the potential value improvements indicated
– and largely to ignore the steps identified as being necessary at the national level
before the potential improvements can be realised.

A feeble disclaimer followed, suggesting 'this apparent reaction
would be misleading' and claiming the Commission had been encouraged 'by the absence of any substantive challenge from departments to
any of its reports'. But the message was stark enough. As it suggested,
Banham had begun to contemplate a career move. Some on the Commission may have half suspected as much. (Noel Hepworth, for one,
had been a little sceptical about the announcement of the controller's
second term, the previous September. He recalled: 'I was surprised,
given the tension which had emerged between the DoE and the Commission – but I recall thinking he'd seen the writing on the wall and
he was going to get out.')[32] One trigger in Banham's own mind was
the work being done by a team under Ross Tristem on an important
new study. This was a Section 27 inquiry into society's treatment of
the mentally ill. Tristem, having worked on National Health Service
issues for five years in the 1970s, was even more than usually enthusiastic about this study, for reasons that were not hard to fathom.

Banham could see by the summer of 1986 that Tristem had an eye to extending the Commission's audit remit into the NHS.

This looked a logical development to Banham, too, but he had no illusions about the implications. 'I knew that it was going to be really important for the Commission to get involved with health care, and I realized that I would be seen as far too unsafe a pair of hands. For ministers, it would really just have been unthinkable. There was no way I could have taken the Commission into health.'[33] Indeed, it crossed his mind more than once that the Commission's wings might be about to be clipped even within its existing franchise. He knew he had made many enemies in the DoE, and worried that it might act soon to give private firms a much larger stake in local government audit. Above all, he also knew the department's ministers and many of its officials were confidently looking to John Read's successor as chairman, due to be installed over the summer, to keep him on a very much shorter rein. This grated badly. If the right offer came along, he was going to be in a receptive frame of mind.

CHANGES AT THE TOP

Candidates to succeed Read in the chairmanship had not been easy to find. He had only reluctantly agreed to postpone his departure until August 1986, and by May the DoE had drawn a blank with its initial list of names. Then Kenneth Baker himself had an idea. He had been the minister for information technology during a three-year stint at the Department of Trade and Industry up to 1984. One of the businessmen advising him in those years, in particular on the privatiz-ation of British Telecom, had been a venture capitalist called David Cooksey.

Cooksey had set up his own venture capital fund, Advent Venture Partners, in 1981. It specialized in information technology and tele-communications. He had also been the founding chairman of the British Venture Capital Association in 1983–84, so he had contacts in the Treasury, too. On his 46th birthday that May, he went along at Baker's invitation for a drink with the minister at the DoE. Hardly had Baker begun to broach the subject of the Audit Commission, when a call arrived from 10 Downing Street. Baker was summoned, and emerged an hour later as the new education secretary. So that was the end of Cooksey's first discussion about the chairmanship. But he was invited back to the DoE days later for a second chat, this time with Terry Heiser. The permanent secretary had to acknowledge it was not really a first-division job that was on the table – but if Cooksey took it and did well, he could expect a bigger plum thereafter. It was, perhaps, a curious way to have presented the job, given the Commission's achievements over the previous three years and its pivotal role in managing the rate-setting crisis.

Cooksey himself thought better of it than that. He was a little surprised to have been offered it, especially given that the Commission already included a few seasoned businessmen. He could see it was not the easiest of jobs: the Liverpool councillors had just appealed against their March defeat in the High Court and no one could be sure where that might lead. But he was intrigued: 'It fascinated me as an opportunity to look at how one could actually make government work better.'[34] Six weeks later he went in to see the new secretary of state for the environment, the chain-smoking Nicholas Ridley. Their discussion lasted for the better part of a full packet of twenty, and Cooksey accepted the job. He would take office on 1 September.

Whatever the private briefing he had collected from Ridley, it was obvious to all that the new chairman's relationship with Banham would inevitably be a little uneasy in the early stages. Cooksey had huge respect for what Banham had achieved, but was well aware that others had strong (and divergent) views about the way the Commission's profile had been built up. He must have pondered hard on how best to forge an effective working relationship with Banham, ahead of their first meeting at the start of September. He need not have worried. 'I arrived to meet John and the first thing he said to me was "By the way, I'm not going to be here for much longer."' The Confederation of British Industry (CBI) had invited him to become its next director-general – much to the private amazement, or so it was said, of Margaret Thatcher.[35] Banham had accepted, and would be leaving the Commission within six months, perhaps even fewer.

Nothing needed to be said about it by either of them at Cooksey's first monthly meeting, that September. The first priority was to see John Read properly thanked for his successful chairmanship. It falls to few chairmen of successful public bodies to receive no public recognition of any kind for their work; but so it was, sadly, for John Read. His name lived on within the Commission through the Read Award, given each year for the most valuable contribution to VFM work. (His successor would follow his example, creating the Cooksey Award in later years for the most valuable contribution to financial audit work.) But Read collected none of the usual rewards available for a job well done in the voluntary sector. If this signalled any reservations in Whitehall about his achievement, they were not shared by his colleagues on the Commission. They saw him off with congratulations all round.

But rumours of the CBI appointment soon surfaced in the press. Acknowledging them at the next meeting on 2 October 1986, Banham told the members he would be leaving – 'if the [CBI] post were offered and accepted' – at the end of the financial year, the following March.[36] His departure was officially confirmed a couple of weeks later. The changed circumstances came as a relief to everyone at Vincent Square, since tensions within the Commission itself were now well known to the staff. But it was nonetheless an eventful (and occasionally fraught) six months that followed.

A conference had been held in Milton Keynes in June, at which the Commission's senior executives had hosted a series of discussions with guests drawn from across Whitehall, Westminster, local government and the accounting professions. The sessions seemed to have gone off well: reflecting on them afterwards, Banham penned a Strategy Review paper that set out what he thought had been achieved since 1983, comparing the record with his original objectives as approved by the Commission members in February of that year.[37] His verdict was that they had 'been implemented in virtually every particular over the past three years'. Across most of the 'seven Ss' scoreboard, the prescription was broadly 'more of the same'. But the paper was held back from general circulation until David Cooksey had had a chance to review it. Only in November was it finally distributed – with an acknowledgement by Banham of the risks that he had felt compelled to run, and the emerging tensions among the members themselves. Now Banham set about managing expectations of his (as yet unknown) successor as controller:

There would be obvious risks in a policy of 'more of the same' . . . The tone of the Commission's publications may be seen as too shrill in sensitive policy-related areas, e.g. education and council housing. The medium might become the message, and the Commission come to be regarded as an embarrassing irritant to authorities and Ministers alike, rather than a stimulant to corrective action.

The final paragraph noted that the Commission's initial strategy in 1983 had been adopted without it consulting any other local government or accounting bodies – 'there seemed no point in doing so, since all had opposed the [Commission's] establishment'. However, 'times have changed' and therefore the paper was being sent to all interested parties. 'Comments should be addressed to the chairman . . .'

Cooksey himself did not wait until November before introducing fresh ways to the Commission. He insisted from the outset, for example, that all future monthly meetings should be attended by Cliff Nicholson in his capacity as deputy controller. And each would now be preceded in the morning by separate presentations: some would be made by district auditors or partners in private firms, others would feature project managers talking about their VFM work or Vincent Square managers addressing technical issues. (Mike Barnes, for example, made a presentation on the poll tax.) Relevant papers would be posted in advance for all of them. Cooksey also moved quickly in response to complaints from the new commissioners to tighten up the procedures for the Commission's scrutiny of draft reports. Panel reviews were to be instituted more rigorously; drafts were to be circulated further in advance of meetings; contentious points in every report were to be identified in a separate briefing note, to assist with members' preparations; and where amendments were agreed with the controller in a monthly meeting, the subsequent draft was to be re-circulated with a copy of the amendment attached to it.

In addition to study reports, there were two other sensitive matters for urgent discussion. One was the *Report of the Widdicombe Inquiry into the Conduct of Local Authority Business*. It had arrived in four volumes in June 1986 after a year of gathering evidence. The Commission had submitted a set of rather detailed recommendations of its own – drafted by a panel of three members, after a first draft by the controller had met with a mixed reception – and most of them had been ignored. The Commission now returned the compliment, rejecting the Widdicombe Committee's proposal that auditors' surcharge and disqualification powers should be transferred to the Commission itself. The members responded more positively, though, to a recommendation that the Commission should have an important new legal power. Where it expected a council to take unlawful action, it would be able to issue a prohibition order blocking it. Unless overturned in the High Court, the order would have the force of law. This, slightly amended, turned out to be the one significant legacy of the Widdicombe Inquiry: the Local Government Act of 1988 provided for prohibition powers, though it gave them to the auditors rather than the Commission itself.

The other matter needing a response was the government's Green Paper setting out the poll tax proposals, published in January 1986. Banham and the members had agreed together in May that their response to the Department of the Environment should be restricted to a technical commentary. (It was revealing, though, that an agenda paper from Banham had questioned the point of responding at all, 'given other priorities, the political nature of some of the proposals, and the lack of any indication that Government is interested in the Commission's views'.)[38] In October, Banham presented the members with a draft response that tackled the poll tax and the Widdicombe recommendations all in one, presenting the DoE with a set of modest reforms aimed at improving local accountability. Unsurprisingly, it fell foul of a lengthy discussion. A separate response on the poll tax was submitted the next month, and duly ignored.

A very much more substantial piece of work emerged from the Commission a few weeks later, which was certainly *not* ignored. This was the third Section 27 study, on which Tristem had been working hard for so long, with David Browning as his project manager. It dealt with the effects of government policy on the treatment of elderly people, the mentally ill and the handicapped in society.[39] (The DoE shared its responsibilities in this area with the DHSS, where officials were as yet less familiar than their DoE counterparts with the independence of the Commission – as would soon become apparent).

It had for many years been government policy to shift care of the most vulnerable in society away from NHS hospitals or residential homes run by local authorities and into non-residential 'care-settings', where services could be provided more effectively. This, it was widely agreed, would improve the quality of life for those affected while at the same time cutting NHS costs and providing much better value for the money spent. The problem, as the Commission's report spelt out in huge detail, was that the resources provided by the NHS and the authorities' homes were being run down relatively quickly, far outpacing the build-up of resources in society that were supposed to take the strain. The alternative to hospitals and homes was inevitably a more complex network of local support agencies and day-care services. On close inspection, these turned out to be burdened by what the report generously termed 'organizational fragmentation and confusion'. Whether at national, regional or local level, in fact, the network was in a terrible mess. As a result, too many of those discharged from the care of the state were either finding places in private residential homes – with serious financial implications, given their dependence on benefits – or else simply vanishing from the data. By 1986 there were 37,000 fewer mentally ill and handicapped people in institutions than ten years previously. It was widely feared that many were ending up homeless on the streets.

The Commission had no legal obligation to show its reports to interested parties ahead of publication – it was just one of the significant ways in which it differed from the National Audit Office, its counterpart in the world of central government – but in fact it generally did so. When the DHSS saw a draft of *Making a Reality of Community Care*, there was trouble. Some at the Commission believed the DHSS was intent on blocking its publication, and departmental representations were certainly made to the new chairman. But Cooksey won respect in Vincent Square for standing his ground – while at the same time managing to placate critics of the report in Whitehall. A DoE review acknowledged a few months later that the Commission had 'clearly made greater efforts [than with previous Section 27 reports] to minimize unnecessary disagreements'.[40] Following a page-by-page review of the report with senior DHSS officials – which saw no substantial changes, but some redrafting to amend its tone –

arrangements were made with the permanent secretary of the DHSS, Kenneth Stowe, for his department and the Commission to launch the report in December 1986 with a joint press conference. The report was widely noted in the media – and its main conclusions went unchallenged. This episode incidentally illustrated a remarkable feature of the Commission under John Banham. Whatever the risks that were sometimes taken with studies, it is striking that no material errors ever surfaced. Banham was justly proud of this. 'No one was ever able to point to any hole in any of our studies – though they were stuffed full of facts, and you can imagine the critical attitude of everyone out there. We were in the errors business, after all.'[41]

Commission members themselves never needed to be reminded of this. On the contrary, they fretted constantly about the dangers of a report getting something badly wrong. At their first discussion of *Making a Reality of Community Care*, in October, they had voiced again their disquiet over the short time allowed for a first reading of the draft. One of the problems they faced was the sheer length and density of many reports. This had already led to fresh thinking, several months earlier, about alternative ways of tackling some topics. Each study delved into a subject area in considerable depth. But some subjects, perhaps as the off-shoot of a study, looked likely to 'raise issues which appear to merit broader debate' without needing much extra data. It had been agreed that in such cases the answer would be an 'Occasional Paper'. These would run to twenty pages or less, and would be aimed at furthering 'wider discussions of important management issues affecting local government services'.

Occasional Paper No. 1 appeared in Cooksey's first month, September 1986. Researched and written by David Henderson-Stewart (and rewritten as usual by the controller), its title was self-explanatory: *Value for Money in the Fire Service: Some Strategic Issues to be Resolved*. It was prompted by the findings of local VFM work during the 1984–85 audit round, in which auditors had studied the accounts of thirty-six fire brigades (out of a total of fifty-four) in England and Wales. All the detailed comparisons of best and worst practice around the country, however, proved to be of far less interest than one big comparison that the author grasped by going to the Netherlands. What he saw there was that the Dutch employed relatively few professional firemen and paid them well, while relying overwhelmingly on volunteers to put out the occasional big fire. The British paid full-time wages, at a level that caused constant problems over pay and conditions, to large numbers of professional firemen who spent much of their time in the station fast asleep. This prompted Henderson-Stewart to work on a full set of international comparisons. They revealed that Britain's fire service was roughly twice as expensive as any of its continental European counterparts. He recalled: 'It wasn't particularly popular with the fire service, as you can imagine. But I think John quite liked it. He liked being a little bit controversial.'[42]

And controversial he remained until the end. Banham certainly didn't lose any of his appetite for the public stage in his last months at Vincent Square. Late in 1986, he suggested to Robert Sheldon, the chairman of the House of Commons' Public Accounts Committee (PAC), that it might be interesting for the committee to have him talk to them about the review of the Commission's work between 1983 and 1986, contained in its recently published 1985–86 Annual Report and Accounts. (Unlike the NAO, the Commission had no statutory obligation to appear before the PAC.) Sheldon agreed and an invitation was sent to Cooksey and Banham together. Before the session started, doubts were expressed by some PAC members and the lawyers about the propriety of the hearing. After some delay, it was decided to go ahead, but only as a one-off, with the Audit Commission chairman and controller taking questions 'on a courtesy basis'. Given a unique chance to grill the men from the Commission, however, most of the members wasted no time on courtesies and subjected Banham to a typically feisty PAC interrogation. Those members with careers behind them in local government had plainly found some of the 1983–86 review too critical of councils for their taste: Banham was roundly admonished for straying into policy matters, and for resorting to what were several times scathingly referred to as his 'headline-grabbing and evocative [sic]' tactics. This drew a spirited defence from Banham of the Commission's research findings in several areas and the way in which its conclusions had been presented. He was also at pains to point out how hugely impressed he had been – outside London, anyway – by the calibre of management in most local authorities: he was happy to wink at a reminder that he had compared it very favourably in public with the standards of management in central government, though on this occasion he stopped short of pursuing the comparison.* David Cooksey, meanwhile, took little part in the proceedings. 'Of course, I didn't get a word in edgeways . . . John said, "Fire away with your questions," and that was it.'[43]

The Labour MPs on the PAC might have been even more prickly over the comments in the 1983-86 review had they been able to see the draft of a forthcoming national report to which Banham referred during their session together. It was very much a pet project of his own, which he intended to see through to publication before his departure. He had been chipping away for more than a year at the text of a paper about the grave problems facing local government in London's inner boroughs. It would be his swan-song. This had not been his intention at the outset – but it was not inappropriate. Several of the studies published since 1983 were drawn upon for powerful evidence, adding to a slightly valedictory tone in Occasional Paper No. 2, *The Management of London's Authorities: Preventing the Breakdown of Services*. The notion of an ambitious review of the capital's problems had first surfaced in September 1985, when Banham had presented a proposal to the members at their monthly meeting. They had ruled out a Section 27 study, and urged the controller to shelve his plans for a comparison between London and the crisis in US cities. In his concluding remarks, Read had said, 'the review of the situation in Inner London should go ahead, but it should be an in-house document, not necessarily for publication'.[44]

* Not short enough, perhaps, for the comptroller and auditor-general of the NAO, Gordon Downey, who was present at the session. Having waved aside the reference to his past remarks with his usual charm ('I could be tempted, were you to ask me, to draw some comparisons with central government but you clearly would rather I did not'), Banham was invited to compare the Commission's overheads with those of the NAO. 'I would not dream of being so indiscreet,' he replied. 'We certainly have been more than impressed with his palatial accommodation but that is all I can say.' When Downey was asked, towards the close, for his views on the logic of a merger between the NAO and the Commission, he asserted they were rather different bodies – adding pointedly that neither had any detailed information on the other's operations, of the kind needed (say) to make a comparison between local and central government efficiency. 'Therefore, I would not dream of making such a comparison and I am not sure I would accept Mr Banham's ability to do so.' (*Minutes of Evidence*, PAC, 8 December 1986, paras. 303, 312 and 368.)

Sure enough, a year later, Banham had a coruscating paper ready for the printers (*Exhibit 1 – North America: a View of the Factors Causing an Urban 'Underclass'*). He also had a new chairman, however, and Cooksey took a less relaxed view than Read of content that had not been rigorously checked by the Commission members themselves. In fact, he went so far as to convene a meeting for himself and Banham with all the leaders (or in some cases chief executives) of the London authorities that featured in the paper. Cooksey recalled: 'I was insistent that we actually went through it line by line, and that we could justify everything that was written in it so that it could not be rubbished on publication.'[45] It did not come as a surprise to Ross Tristem and his colleagues – now newly re-installed with their own space in 1 Vincent Square – that this process prompted a lively discussion. The meeting with the authorities lasted five hours – and had to be reconvened later for a further five.

This, though, only confirmed again what had always been evident: the controller saw it as a key part of his role to preach the urgent need for reform. Sometimes the strength of the cause ran a little ahead of the evidence – though few substantial changes to draft reports were ever needed (and none followed in this case, either). It did nothing to alter the fact that his paper on the London authorities was a powerful polemic. A reader from Mars – to use one of his own favourite rhetorical devices – would have had no difficulty understanding how the Commission had risen to prominence so quickly since 1983.

It started with a graphic depiction of the social problems afflicting boroughs like Hackney and Southwark, a catalogue 'so serious as to be difficult to comprehend by those who have never lived in a rundown Inner City area'. These were the same problems, it pointed out, as those that had spawned the rise of an urban 'underclass' in US ghetto districts like New York's South Bronx and the Southside of Chicago. The analytical nub of the paper was its presentation of the costs of various services, as measured by previous studies, in the worst-afflicted group of Inner London boroughs. These were compared with the costs achieved in a second London group (also scarred by housing deprivation) and in a group of the eight most deprived Metropolitan boroughs (excluding Liverpool, for which the data were not available). In one instance after another, the same conclusion jumped out of all the numbers: the Inner London boroughs were spending far more money, to far less effect. 'The Commission believes that some large part of this difference is attributable to local management.'[46]

The paper suggested some of the reasons for this management breakdown. They included an alarmingly high rate of staff turnover, an encroachment by politically elected members on the role of paid executives, and a culture of 'management by members' that had resulted in a thick undergrowth of committees and sub-committees: it was not uncommon for a district auditor's complaint to be still 'circulating for review' two and a half years after its submission. Turning to the remedies, it set out 'the near-term steps that warrant urgent consideration by the authorities concerned, as well as government'. It was the contrast, though, between the 'illustrative' measures it recommended and the 'implied national strategy' that must have caught many an eye in Whitehall that January, as the battle-lines were being drawn up over the poll tax. Current strategy was described as 'Tight central control [over] rates, borrowing, capital spend, pay and conditions, [plus] privatisation'. The *required* strategy was summarized as, 'Make local government work [with measures to] strengthen local accountability, distinguish roles of members and officers, [provide] access to local sources of capital [and] reform grant system, [plus] partnerships with private sector.'[47]

As for the consequences of failure, Banham returned at the end to his starting point – the terrible warning available from North America:

To summarise, the Commission foresees very considerable problems in Inner London ... [and they could lead, unless tackled now, to a situation already evident in some US cities with] high welfare dependency and generation intervals of 15 years or less; youth unemployment of 70 per cent or more; extremely high crime rates, much of it drug-related; uneasy relations between the police and a disaffected and largely unemployable urban 'underclass' with no stake in the development of the society in which they live. This future cannot be allowed to happen.

The report closed with a Parthian shot from its author. 'The Commission', he wrote, 'has been heartened at the concern to see constructive action that is evident in some of the boroughs referred to in this paper.' By contrast, reforms urged on central government by the

Commission, of the Block Grant system and the control of capital spending, had got nowhere. 'No action has yet been taken on either front by government. The consequences are apparent to the most casual observer.'[48] Combative as ever, Banham had penned a hugely controversial paper (with the significance of London's savage Broadwater Farm riot of October 1985 still being hotly disputed in the background). Many Inner London councillors were enraged by it – so much so, indeed, that it may have been counter-productive, as some alleged. On the other hand, it alerted a wider audience to a grave social problem that had much to gain from more media attention. The paper was in this respect a fitting finale for its author.

Few readers early in 1987 could have doubted that the Commission was losing a controller whose personal contribution to its success was going to be hard to replace. But not, as it turned out, impossible. In fact, Banham himself had already seen to that. He had flown to Australia on a short speaking tour at the invitation of the Australian Institute of Public Administration just a couple of months earlier. It subsequently became a part of the Commission's folklore that Banham had written his entire paper on London boroughs on the plane coming home. This was a slight exaggeration – but he did come back with the kind of bright idea that still had Cliff Nicholson drawing a deep breath on most Monday mornings.

Howard Davies, one of Banham's younger colleagues during his last year at McKinsey in 1982, was a man with an uncanny knack of being in exactly the right place at the right time. He proved it, on the return leg of a McKinsey trip to New Zealand, by stopping off at the Gabba cricket ground in Brisbane on 14 November 1986. This allowed him to witness one of the most famous feats with the bat in the history of English cricket: Ian Botham's innings of 138 on the first day of the First Test in the 1986/7 Ashes series. And then he proved it a second time, by taking the same plane back to London as Banham a few days later. Spotting Banham on the flight, Davies went over and offered his congratulations on the CBI appointment. He asked who was taking over at the Audit Commission. 'Oh, we haven't sorted that out yet,' replied Banham airily. This was a matter for the Commission's chairman, in which he would play no formal part. There was a short pause, before he raised his eyebrows and prodded a lively finger at his former colleague. 'But ... why don't *you* do it? You'd be terrific!'[49]

Davies laughed politely and that was that. The next morning, though, Banham stepped round the door of Ross Tristem's office in Vincent Square with some news. 'I think I've just found my successor!' he said.[50] And indeed he had.

5

Straight Down the Line, 1987–89

Beginning his involvement with the Audit Commission at 35,000 feet nicely matched Howard Davies's track record as a high-flier. His Oxford college had awarded him its top history scholarship. Starting a (brief) career in the Foreign Office, he had picked up the most sought-after first foreign posting, as private secretary to the British ambassador in Paris. Switching from there to the Treasury, he had been granted a Harkness Fellowship in 1979 to go to Stanford Business School in California. And after quitting the Treasury in 1982 to work for McKinsey, he was seconded back into the Treasury three years later to work as a special adviser to the chancellor, Nigel Lawson.

In this capacity, he frequently accompanied Lawson to excellent lunches – one of which, in the summer of 1985, was hosted by the chairman of Advent Venture Partners. David Cooksey (as yet unconnected with the Commission) spent much of the lunch extolling the virtues of the UK venture capital industry. It was one of the great unsung successes, he suggested, of the Tory administration. The chancellor, by then one of the administration's most acclaimed successes, liked the idea so much that he decided to make UK venture capital his subject for the annual Stock Exchange lecture that he was due to give a couple of weeks later. He delegated the writing of the speech, as usual, to his special adviser. Since it needed to be done in a hurry, Davies arranged a joint drafting session with Cooksey. The two of them spent a day working on it together at Cooksey's offices in Buckingham Gate, with several follow-up conversations. They got to know each other in the process.

The next time they spoke together was shortly after Davies's return from Australia in the middle of November 1986. (He was back at

McKinsey by then, having left his job at the Treasury the previous March.) Davies had taken John Banham's advice, as they'd parted ways at Heathrow, that he should think seriously about the Audit Commission post. He telephoned Cooksey, who by now was chairing the Commission, to register his interest. Cooksey asked him to come over to Buckingham Gate for 'a sort of off-line conversation'. This ended with Davies's hat firmly in the ring. Cooksey was careful, though, to stress that the normal appointment process would naturally have to run its course.[1] It did so, with interviews all through January handled by a Commission panel made up of Cooksey himself, Harry Axton, Ian Coutts and Roy Shaw. There were several external candidates, including at least two under-secretaries from the DoE, and two internal candidates, Cliff Nicholson and Peter Brokenshire. But by February of 1997 Davies had got the job. Cooksey recalled: 'It was quite clear to the panel that Howard had an appeal and a skill set which was quite extraordinary.'

Banham's final weeks were not uneventful. There were papers to be launched and conferences to be addressed. His impending exit did not incline the departing controller to pull his punches any more than usual. (He told a joint seminar with CIPFA and Birmingham University's Institute of Local Government Studies (INLOGOV) in February that 'politics and management don't mix' – a popular refrain of his, after four years in Vincent Square. One of the next speakers was a black Labour councillor from Lambeth, Linda Bellos, who promptly told him his paper on the London boroughs had included 'racist' exhibits.)[2] Relations between Banham and Cooksey frayed a little towards the end. The chairman was frustrated that so little seemed to have been done to chase down the late rate-setters; Banham worried that Cooksey had not yet come to appreciate properly the legal niceties of the Commission's position. But nothing marred a generally affectionate send-off for the first controller. The district auditors gave him a farewell dinner in Bristol, at which Cliff Nicholson gave a memorably wicked speech incorporating several of Banham's favourite expressions. ('I'm telling you, baby . . . it's down to you . . . but we're in pretty good shape!') And the District Auditors' Society saw him off at a dinner for 200 people on the campus of Birmingham University in April.

One of several speakers at Birmingham congratulated Banham on being 'the youngest McKinsey director, the youngest director-general of the CBI and the oldest controller of the Audit Commission'. This went down well with an audience that was more than mindful of the youth of his successor. The McKinsey pedigree that Davies shared with Banham was noted, as too the oddity that both men had stepped from Oxbridge into the Foreign Office.* But it was the age gap between the first and second controller that really intrigued. Where Banham had been a 43-year-old director of McKinsey when he was appointed, Davies had not even been a partner of the firm and had only just turned 36.

His youth raised hackles at the Department of the Environment when his name was first proposed. Its officials appeared wary of the response they might draw from Nicholas Ridley, whose approval was required for the appointment. But they need not have worried: the secretary of state had had the new man's credentials carefully spelt out to him by the chancellor. For their part, the Commission members were not so much bothered by his youthfulness as slightly bemused. 'We were prepared for our first meeting with him by the chairman, who warned us about him looking a lot older than he actually was, with his white hair,' recalled Noel Hepworth.[3] And if there were any concerns that the new controller might lack the weight needed in the role, these were soon forgotten. Indeed, it was very quickly evident that Davies intended to assert a few home truths of his own from the outset. Having been a Whitehall official himself, Davies was going to be far more scrupulous than his predecessor over the choice of public targets for the Commission: directors and members alike were immediately alerted to the fact that he would not tolerate public

---

* Davies's brief career in the Foreign Office gave rise to a perceptive portrait of him many years later by his erstwhile boss in Paris, the former ambassador Nicholas Henderson. Describing Davies in his Paris days as someone 'radically minded and unsympathetic to conventional authority . . . [who] had the skills of an official without behaving like one', Henderson approved of his appointment to lead the Commission. 'The post might have been designed expressly for his training and talents which were making him very like the product of the École Nationale d'Administration . . . [He] brought to the task of inspection some of the qualities of both Scrooge and Sherlock Holmes.' (Nicholas Henderson, *Old Friends and Modern Instances*, published by Profile Books, 2000.)

criticism of civil servants. He was also going to be much keener on Hard Facts. Where these got in the way of a good story, the story would need to be amended. On both counts, Davies's first few months involved him in some fundamental repositioning.

Top of the agenda was the relationship with Whitehall. By chance, Davies's first day in the office, 16 March 1987, more or less coincided with the delivery of an eagerly awaited first draft of a Quinquennial Policy Review of the Commission by officials at the DoE. (It first arrived as a draft, for the Commission's comments. These did not go back to the DoE until June, according to the minutes of the monthly meeting for July, so finalization of the text was evidently a protracted process.) The 54-page report had been under preparation for six months, with the full cooperation of the Commission's staff. In general it amounted to a favourable verdict. In its five years, the new body had broadly fulfilled its original remit, though it was noted that a 30 per cent share of the audit market for private firms fell 'well short of the secretary of state's aspiration that the private sector involvement should increase to at least 50 per cent within the first two years'. The District Audit Service had been 'invigorated' – even if the action taken by its auditors over late rate-setting 'at times has appeared slow, immensely laborious, and concerned with technicalities' – and the Commission had run its own operations 'in a very effective way'. Standards had been raised in the audit of local government, and VFM work had made 'a substantial impact'.

But there was more. It was less a case of 'doing poorly, must try harder' than of 'doing surprisingly well, no need to try *quite* so hard'. The review went to considerable lengths to spell out what 'trying too hard' had involved. Its few references to Banham described him slightly waspishly not as the controller but as the 'spokesman' – a role 'well-suited to his personal style'. The department, it said, had always assumed that the Commission would feel a need to demonstrate its independence of central government, as it had done by seizing on the Block Grant issue. Officials had nonetheless been surprised.

It was not foreseen that the Commission or its spokesman would need or wish to maintain a continuing high level of criticism of the aspects of central government policy, even though proposals for legislation are now in train ... Though the stridency of comment from the Commission has now diminished, some wish for the Commission to go on proving [its independence of central government] still appears to persist.[4]

Nor was it just a bid for independence that had given rise to 'difficulties and criticisms', said the review.

The Commission has trespassed into matters of policy and this has been exacerbated by the high public profile taken by its spokesman. It has tried to cover too wide a range of VFM issues with the result that some of its work . . . has been described as superficial, unrealistic, ill-timed and unbalanced.[5]

The Section 27 studies came in for particular criticism.

The new controller was certainly not inclined to enter a debate with officials over whether or not his predecessor had paid too high a price either for establishing the Commission's independence or for putting it on the map. It was soon apparent to Davies, as it had long been to everyone else at Vincent Square, that these were two of John Banham's most important achievements. On the other hand, Davies showed immediately the value to the Commission of having a controller who was himself steeped in the ways of Whitehall. (His civil service training extended to the practice of dictating a note for his files on the content of all external meetings and discussions – leaving a detailed record that has survived for at least the first few years of his time in Vincent Square.) He arranged to meet with the two senior civil servants responsible for local government, Ken Ennals and David Heigham. They had 'a business-like but very friendly' lunch on 27 March and discussed 'all the major topics facing the Commission and the department' – including the review, which Davies cheekily suggested to the officials that they might like to consider publishing.[6] (Ennals and Heigham surprised him by agreeing 'there was case on this occasion for publication, perhaps of a slightly bowdlerised version if necessary'. In the event it appears not to have happened.)

In the afternoon he met their permanent secretary, Terry Heiser. This must have been a slightly more difficult meeting, given Heiser's poor relationship with his predecessor. It also transpired that Heiser wanted to explain his reservations about the whole concept of a value-for-money audit and his concern over the Commission's past tendency to trespass into policy areas. But again the outcome was entirely friendly. The permanent secretary thanked the controller for the invitation he had received to have dinner with the Commission's management team in May, and he specified a few issues on which the Commission's views would be most welcome in Marsham Street.[7]

While mending the Commission's fences with the civil service, Davies was also quick to strengthen his political bridges. He had lunched with Ridley's special adviser just before starting at the Commission. Ten days after his arrival, he sent David Cooksey and Cliff Nicholson a memo noting the main points of a conversation with the chancellor the previous evening. Davies noted in it Nigel Lawson's advice that 'we should do our best to improve relationships with [the] DoE'. Doubtless the message was not lost on his colleagues that their new controller had ready access to No. 11.[8]

The night after his conversation with the chancellor saw Davies appearing as a guest for the first time on the BBC's *Question Time* programme. Evidently, this controller like the last was going to have a ready eye for good media opportunities. In fact, there was plenty of continuity within Vincent Square. John Banham's secretary, Patricia Church, was appointed administration manager to run a central office that was now expanding steadily. But Davies was keen to retain the informal working atmosphere he found there. A few small changes actually pushed the non-hierarchical culture a little further. He dispensed with the chauffeur-driven car, for example, and urged colleagues to treat his office as though it were part of an open-floor plan.

Davies knew from private lunch conversations before his start date that the directors were hoping to see him introduce a more collaborative style of management, and he was keen to respond to this. By March 1987 Nicholson was already attending monthly meetings in his role as deputy controller, and Davies now brought other directors into the meetings where they could make a direct contribution. He also conferred with the directors on matters such as media tactics that had previously been settled without much discussion. And Vincent Square staffers enjoying an end-of-the-day beer in their local pub, the Royal Oak, even had to adjust to the sight of their controller buying his deputy a drink at the bar from time to time.

Davies also reached out to the DAS, taking every opportunity to show his interest in the history and traditions of the service. (There was plenty of that to absorb. On just his third day in the job, there was a reception at County Hall to celebrate the publication of *Watchdogs' Tales*, a collection of historical essays on the Commission spiced with many personal memoirs of life in the service. Davies went along to meet with a rare gathering of retired auditors – one of whom turned out to be a man who had joined the service in 1917!)[9] Introducing himself in the April 1987 issue of *Audit News* – 'those of you who are familiar with *Private Eye* can think of this as a message from Lord Gnome' – Davies made clear his intention that all areas of the Commission, including every office of the DAS, should remain 'interesting and fun places to work'. There would be no fun, though, where facts were ignored. Unfortunately, there soon arose an issue on this score that jarred with the spirit of an otherwise happy transition.

REAPPRAISING THE STORY AND THE SCORE SO FAR

Reading through the DoE's review, Davies came upon the striking assertion that 'it is estimated that some £350–400 million a year of improvements have been implemented to date'.[10] Not bad, for an audit operation that was still costing *in toto* only about £22 million a year (of which less than half was attributable to VFM work *per se*). The department had stopped short of endorsing roughly £1 billion as the valuation of total savings captured to date, but this higher figure was now being widely cited. And no wonder: it had been quoted in the previous year's annual report of the Commission as a figure based on savings that 'should ultimately be achievable'. True, the billion would only be landed 'if all the potential can be realised' – but this element of conditionality appeared to have seeped away over time.[11] Aware that some breakdown of the billion would have to be prepared within a couple of months for publication in the 1987 Annual Report, Davies asked to see how estimates had been compiled.

This prompted a few extremely uncomfortable meetings between the new controller and his senior staff. Some awkward truths emerged. The standard analysis of most VFM topics typically identified a small number of exemplary practitioners and a long tail of delinquent councils. This was legitimate and useful research. How far local circumstances would allow the laggards to lift their performance into line with the paragons was, of course, always going to be a moot point. The first snag with the £1 billion savings estimate was that it relied too much on assuming everyone would one day reach parity with the best. The second was that the resulting projections of *prospective future* savings had somehow been parlayed into *actual achieved* savings. There was room here for serious embarrassment. Davies decided that the Commission should pre-empt any challenge to its figures by adopting a new 'bottom-up' approach to the assessment of savings. Auditors across the country were asked to submit real numbers. The critical number would be the total of *'fulfilled'* savings that auditors could actually verify. The *'identified'* savings would be a locally derived number for the potential total. The notional total based on a rolling out of best practice across the whole of England and Wales would now be described only as *'target'* savings. The new labels produced a handy acronym: FIT. The Commission would pursue future VFM savings as, yes, a FITness programme.

The outcome was published in the 1987 Annual Report in July. It was too soon to present any figures for 1986–87. For the previous three financial years, identified savings stood at £492 million. Of these, just £80 million (or 16 per cent, representing a compound of 28 per cent, 13 per cent and 5 per cent respectively for the first, second and third year over the period) had so far been fulfilled. 'It is clear from auditors' reports,' commented the report a little flatly, 'that in many cases the balance of the identified saving will certainly be achieved over a period.'[12] This was very careful wording indeed.

Davies himself saw the whole exercise as 'a sort of conceptual write-off'.[13] Remarkably, given the scale of the write-off, it was effected without prompting much third-party comment – suggesting, perhaps, deeper reserves of public scepticism about the Commission's progress and its much-vaunted savings to date than was reflected in all the media headlines. Cliff Nicholson, looking back on this period, had no doubt such scepticism was widespread. (He recalled: 'We had got off to a rousing start but that would have faded. By 1987, I think that the Commission's reputation was more dependent on the quality of the work being produced by auditors on the ground than at the centre.')[14] Whatever the general perception, the Commission now played a cool hand. It presented the new approach as the evolution of a more mature methodology, based on hard statistics that were only now becoming available to it. Davies had finessed the dangers inherent in moving from the old savings numbers to the new.

But the new numbers, however calmly received, raised some fundamental questions for the future of the Commission. If local government was really responding to VFM audits as slowly as they indicated, what was the true impact of even the most brilliant special study? What kind of help would make the biggest contribution *in practice* to improving local government's performance? Might something more be needed now, to tackle the implementation gap? The new controller was well aware of the dilemma: 'in terms of what you did for an encore, it was quite challenging'.[15] To hear what auditors and their clients around the country thought the Commission should be doing, and to meet with as many of the district auditors and private firms' partners as possible, Davies set off on his travels. Usually accompanied by the chief inspector of audit – Les Stanford, who had succeeded Bert Pyke in the summer of 1985 – he visited most of the twelve audit districts (ADs) outside London within the next five months.

Typically a visit would include spending some time with a local audit section. (Davies found many working in odd nooks and crannies, like the lord mayor's housekeeper's apartment in the battlements of Manchester town hall.) Then a lunch with the senior auditor would be followed by a 'town-hall' session with all of the local office's staff. Davies would chair a McKinsey-style SWOT session – a discussion, that is, about the strengths, weaknesses, opportunities and threats inherent in the Commission's position – and would collect views on the relationship between the Commission and the DAS. And alongside the DAS office visits he arranged to meet with council leaders and officers, local authority associations, trade unionists and the press.

What he heard was cheering in at least one respect. The great majority of authorities were now reasonably well-disposed towards the Commission, however much they wanted to see its working practices amended. Among many hitherto hostile Labour-led councils, there was an obvious disaffection with the tactics of the left in 1985–

86: the disqualification of the Liverpool and Lambeth councillors had made a big impression. Indeed, some Labour-led councils' officers remained anxious about the potential for further serious trouble in Liverpool or the Inner London boroughs. (Davies himself, with one eye on the continuing problems in London boroughs like Southwark, was careful to correct those who assured him that surcharging for late rate-setting was a thing of the past.) But this only strengthened the inclination of the broad majority of councillors and officers to see closer cooperation with the Commission as a way of pulling back from the brink.

Hostility towards the Commission had not entirely disappeared. In a meeting with the Association of County Councils (ACC) in June, Davies and his chairman were rudely informed that the Commission was inept in virtually every aspect of its work, and should go back to the basics of its audit role. There ensued 'a lively and abusive exchange' between the Labour leader of Nottinghamshire and the Vincent Square controller.[16] But this was unusual. More typical was the friendly welcome extended to Davies by several city council leaders at an Association of Metropolitan Authorities conference in Oldham two months later (at which Michael Howard, the local government minister, 'was received very coolly indeed').[17]

External attitudes towards the Commission, then, had certainly changed for the better since 1983. But what of the views of people within the DAS itself? Here Davies encountered a surprising range of attitudes. He encountered some good anecdotes, too. In Bristol, for example, local auditors told him about a parish council at war with one of its parishioners. She had served as the council clerk, but had fallen out with her colleagues and then refused to hand over the council books. Court action resulted in her going to gaol and then on hunger strike. After her husband paid the fines to secure her release, she still would not part with the books. The case was now waiting to be heard in the High Court. The legal costs to the council had multiplied the parish rate several times over. Yet only one ratepayer in the parish had commented on this – and, in the meantime, the woman's husband had himself been elected to the council.[18]

More importantly, he found senior officers who were proud of what the Commission had done for the service since 1983 and enthusiastic about their links with Vincent Square. Will Werry, the head of Audit District 4 in Birmingham, was a good example: he even had two people on his staff, Joy Tight and David Reeson, whose time was divided between local audit work in the Midlands and assisting Ross Tristem with special studies at the centre. It was often the case that the more go-ahead auditors like Werry were also keen to see their franchise expanded. Many of the open discussions with their staff would end with the controller being asked why the Commission could not take on more audits elsewhere in the public sector – of the courts and prisons, for example, or the police, or the universities, or even (a favourite) the National Health Service.

Others were less well-disposed towards their visitor from London. Chris Hurford, still heading up the computerization of the DAS while also leading the computer-audit function, was hard at work around this time on upgrading the IT network linking all the offices together. He spent a good deal of time talking to all of the DAs and had no illusions about their views on Vincent Square. 'I would have said a half to two thirds of them resented the Commission.'[19] Unsurprisingly, several had therefore made little effort to counter the rise of an 'us' and 'them' barrier between the provincial offices and the centre. They accepted it as a natural sequel to the time-honoured legal independence of the district auditor. It also suited some audit teams, especially in the strongholds of the Loony Left, to keep their distance from the Commission. When Davies visited Sheffield early in June, the entire staff of Audit District 11 assembled at Trent Polytechnic for a 'town-hall' meeting that lasted all afternoon. He found them generally quite positive. 'All staff present, however, said that they claimed to work for the District Audit Service rather than the Audit Commission.'[20]

In just a few cases, the antipathy towards Vincent Square went a lot further. Davies was received politely enough in Wales, though his hosts had plenty of negative things to say on new-fangled ideas like the management letter. What Davies did not know was that the district auditor of Wales, confronted with a batch of brand-new clipboards bearing the Audit Commission logo, had recently ordered his staff to cover up the offending logo with snowpake before using the boards outside the building.[21]

At one level, such a diversity of attitudes within the service was of no great moment. Truculent Welsh auditors, like inter-district cricket matches, were part of a long tradition. Of far more concern to the new controller was the fact that the same diversity was apparent in the technical abilities of the DAS. Davies was very impressed by the standards he found in some places – like Middlesbrough, for instance, where a section run by John Sherring was setting a brisk pace: hiring excellent graduates, training its people well, pushing ahead with computer work and exploring ways of helping clients to make the very most of VFM audits. But he also found section heads and even one or two DAs who were disinclined to hire graduates in case they took on ideas above their station, leaned on CIPFA for all their training needs, took a Luddite view of computers and treated VFM work as an irritating distraction.

Here, of course, was the main constraint on the clever model that Banham and Ross Tristem had devised for the Commission at its outset. Davies emerged from his district visits convinced that the national report/guide/implementation/review procedure was still wholly viable: 'I think it had quite a long way to run.'[22] He was also confident by the summer of 1987 that the model was being driven intelligently from the centre: the key personnel assembled by Banham were in his view a good team. But putting a McKinsey office on top of an audit firm – which was the essence of the approach he had inherited – posed a fundamental dilemma.

You depended very heavily on your district auditors and audit managers. Some of them were phenomenally good and had councillors eating out of their hands. But others were hopeless and still basically living in the nineteenth century. The same was true of the firms. So the real problem was an unevenness of quality. We could control the quality of our work at the top quite well. What we couldn't control so well was the quality of the local delivery.[23]

Those who worked under Ross Tristem in the studies directorate were well aware of this reality. It was reflected, after all, in the variable quality of audit workshops around the country, which always depended on the calibre of the participants – and their attitude towards the Commission, too. (One of his team, Greg Birdseye, vividly recalled the difficulties that could sometimes be encountered, especially in Wales: 'I can remember going to do audit workshops and you'd get twenty-seven people all looking sullenly at you, resenting these eggheads from their ivory tower in London, coming down to Cardiff telling us how to do our audits . . .')[24] It was a weakness that would inevitably take some years to remedy properly, but Davies saw no reason to delay making immediate changes.

STRIKING A FRESH BALANCE
TO THE AGENDA

While retaining the basic study-to-report procedure, he proposed altering the modus operandi of the Commission in a number of ways that would complement the new approach being taken to VFM numbers. Staff from the centre, from the DAS and from the private firms would now be required to work together more closely. They might also be supported in due course by regional 'project officers' who would not be qualified as full auditors, but would be specially trained for VFM work and would benefit from specializing in it. Regular conferences would now be held with both the DAS and the firms in attendance. Much more would have to be done to enhance auditors' skill levels in the field. This would include improving the quality of their advice to councils. And VFM audits, like statistical profiles, would have to be applied with more sensitivity to the practical usage that could be made of them. In addition to these proposed adjustments to the Commission's way of working, there would have to be some reappraisal of how study targets were chosen. In particular, it would need to be decided whether Section 27 reports should look at future policy proposals, or wait until government policies had made their impact.

A fresh strategy had been awaited since the start of the year: Banham and Cooksey had both promised as much, at that conference with CIPFA and INLOGOV back in February, and it needed to be produced in the months ahead. (It would be part, as Cooksey had made clear in his wrap-up speech, of a veritable frenzy of bridge-building, with both central Whitehall departments *and* the DAS itself.)[25] Davies now fulfilled the promise with a paper called *The Way Ahead*. It was not finally published until September 1987, when copies were sent to all local authorities, but it was sent in draft to the Commission members in June – along with a first disclosure to the members of the delicate problem over past VFM savings. The next monthly meeting was on the afternoon of 2 July and Cooksey convened a 'pre-meeting' for that morning to review the papers.

They had clearly come as a shock to some of the members. Harry Axton, a property developer who drove a Bentley and was rather averse to castles in the air, thought that 'in making grand claims in the past the Commission had conned itself and other people . . . we have now found there was a difference between expectation and truth'. The Norfolk Tory Ian Coutts, who basically saw the Commission's work as an important contribution to the Thatcherite revolution, thought the VFM disclosure was 'appalling' and 'a very sad situation'. Christopher Foster, also an accountant and a distinguished academic, agreed they were 'in a grave situation'.[26]

Others were more phlegmatic, especially (and ironically) the Labour politicians. John Gunnell, the former leader of the West Yorkshire Metropolitan CC and always thoroughly down to earth, said he assumed most members had always warned outsiders that the Commission's grander claims needed to be taken with a pinch of salt. Plenty had been achieved and 'the Commission's packaging had shown flair'. Camden's Roy Shaw agreed. The important point to remember was that 'the structure of local authorities was a hundred years out of date', said the old Labour warhorse of London local politics, and the Commission had been leading by example. Clive Wilkinson, the leader of Birmingham City Council for ten years up to 1984 and newly arrived in February, questioned whether they needed to have a new strategy at all and saw 'the main task as one of consolidation'.

Davies must have welcomed this last comment. He agreed that consolidation was needed, and in one area above all others: regularity work. Indeed, while the implications of *The Way Ahead* for VFM work could be explored over the next several months, a declaration of intent on regularity was in his view needed with some urgency. He took this view for several reasons. It was, to begin with, a simple matter of political expediency. Many councils by 1987 were turning for extra cash to the dubious devices of creative accounting. It was a concern in Whitehall, as the DoE's review had noted, that the

Commission had so far shown 'an apparent inability to date to make any impact' on it.[27] Any egregious example of creative accounting that suggested laxity on the Commission's part might prove to be embarrassing. It might also lead to damaging press coverage. The Commission had drawn little overt criticism to date over creative accounting (or, indeed, the late rate-setting problems). But interest in the story was growing, even among the tabloids. Davies himself had been finding it increasingly difficult to avoid. 'It seems that whatever I say [to the press] about anything is treated as being about accounting techniques', he noted in May.[28]

A more substantial reason for wanting to reassert the importance of regularity work was the need to underscore the *raison d'être* of the District Audit Service. The reappraisal of VFM's actual impact over the first four years of the Commission inevitably raised questions about the future evolution of the auditors' role. Unless some clear answers were provided, as Davies told the members in July, he feared lasting damage to the morale of the service. Above all, though, was a conviction that grew in Davies's own mind during his early months. Regularity work and VFM auditing had been thought of since 1983 very largely as distinct tasks – probably inevitably, given all the attention lavished on the Yellow Perils. If this had helped foster an exaggeration of VFM's benefits, it had also entailed a risk that regularity would be underplayed. The result was a tension between VFM and regularity work. Some accepted this as unavoidable, given the Commission's dual brief to carve out a new audit role for itself *and* to ensure that district auditors discharged their traditional responsibilities. Others, usually lawyers, were more inclined to worry over the tension, pointing to the innate conflict between the duty of the Commission to coordinate the work of auditors across different districts and its responsibility under the 1982 Act for ensuring the continuing legal independence of every individual district auditor. Either way, as someone put it to Davies at one of his first meetings with the leaders of CIPFA, 'there would be a bit of a problem with an audit service that implied it wasn't really very interested in auditing'.[29]

He responded by looking hard at what had been achieved since 1983 and making clear what in his view needed to be done if the Commission was to build on it successfully. The answer was plain:

regularity and VFM had to be seen as inseparable. Auditors needed to think of them again as one process. Davies called it 'the integrated audit'. Where the process was successfully completed, the auditor's opinion and certificate could be read in conjunction with the management letter and the three together would give a balanced view of an authority's performance. To some extent, it was just a matter of 'back to basics': reports of the chief inspectors of audit in the late 1970s had spelt out the same message about regularity and VFM work being two sides of the same coin. The only difference was that the VFM agenda was now so very much more sophisticated. The high quality of the work produced by Ross Tristem and his team pointed to substantial improvements that could be made in the administration of local government. This delivered a fresh agenda each November. The priority now was to have an organization that could take the agenda forward as part of the regular audit cycle and persuade local authorities to act on it. Setting this in place would be Davies's first goal for the Commission – an objective he would recall as 'turning a campaign into a permanent piece of machinery'.[30]

He set out his objective in some detail in a speech on regularity to the Society of London Treasurers in mid-September. He showed how the integrated audit would build on 'structures of control' that were already rooted in audit law and the audit Code of Practice, and gave his audience plenty of anecdotal evidence that the Commission was well on its way to delivering a quality audit product. Then he cited three examples of VFM research that had been done for special studies, but that had disclosed anomalies subsequently pursued by auditors as part of their regularity examinations. As he commented on one: 'It would be interesting, if academic, to know whether the authority and the auditor considered this to be additional value-for-money days or additional regularity time.' In reality, that is to say, either category would have been appropriate. A very similar kind of observation had in fact been made in the annual report of the chief inspector of audit published ten years earlier: 'It is to be expected that normal day-to-day regularity work will reveal errors and omissions which have led to an authority either paying out more money than was due or failing to collect money due to them. The special investigations into value for money . . . sometimes reveal less costly means of providing the same service. Often these two aspects of the audit are blurred, one type of enquiry leading on to another' (para. 35). So, in at least one respect it was a case, by 1987, of *plus ça change*.

CRACKING DOWN ON CREATIVE ACCOUNTING

Curiously, Davies's September speech made no reference at all to creative accounting. Perhaps he sensed it was a phenomenon, like late rate-setting, that would prove to be short-lived. If so, he was right. As of September 1987, though, it would have been a brave prediction to make too explicitly.

Creative accounting was the sequel to the excessive rate increases of the early 1980s. In both cases, councils resorted to ever more desperate measures to sustain higher spending in the face of lower Whitehall funding; and the government responded with a succession of blocking measures that steadily closed out the councils' options. The courts in each instance settled the final outcome, but it was the district auditors of the DAS who were the arbiters of the process that needed playing out on the ground. The outcome of the battle over rates had hung in the balance from the 1984 Rates Act to the High Court ruling on Liverpool and Lambeth in 1986. Well before it was settled, as we have seen, many councils in search of extra cash had begun sharpening their pencils in the accounting department. The opportunities afforded by some wretchedly convoluted rules of revenue and capital accounting were simply too tempting to ignore.[31]

Deferred purchases were a favourite. Councillors could buy voter-friendly assets like swimming pools and leisure centres on terms that required no immediate payment but saddled future ratepayers with (enhanced) costs to be met several years later. Another popular practice curbed current expenditure: costs such as housing maintenance could be conveniently parked as an investment in the capital account rather than driven through the income statement as normal accounting practice required. Borrowing constraints, meanwhile, were easily circumvented: assets could be sold (or leased) to third parties for sizeable capital sums and then re-acquired on short leases. And if cash was temporarily surplus to requirements (in ways that might prompt a lower Block Grant in the following year), it could always be squirrelled away in 'advanced payment' deals that released revenues later and made a nonsense of Whitehall's year-by-year guidelines.

As the Commission's 1986 Annual Report noted, creative accounting became 'almost an industry'. (Perhaps this explains why the Confederation of British Industry put out a press release on creative accounting in the middle of April 1987. Their former controller's wish to speak out on the subject prompted some bemusement in Vincent Square.) While Harry Wilkinson toiled away on CIPFA's Code of Accounting Practice that was aimed at curbing the most egregious abuses, DAS auditors turned increasingly to Public Interest Reports (PIRs) as a way of alerting council members to what was being done in their name, often by a small minority of colleagues. In 1985–86 there were eighty-nine reports, up 65 per cent from the previous record of fifty-four set just the previous year. Another eighty-four PIRs followed in 1986–87, largely fuelled again by auditors' worries over a rising tide of dodgy accounting practices.

These were growing steadily more sophisticated. There was concern inside the Treasury, which was passed on to Davies, over the extent of 'hidden' borrowing by the councils: late in April 1987, Robin Butler attended a City lunch where the aggregate borrowing of local authorities was much discussed, and called Davies in for a long conversation about it.[32] At the DoE, the minister for local government, Michael Howard, fretted that his officials might not be fully up to the task of tracking the problem: he asked Cooksey and Davies privately whether they thought it might be a good idea to appoint a City expert as an adviser to the department. (Davies strongly advised against it.)

As everyone in Whitehall was well aware, there was a risk of repeating the cat-and-mouse games played over the Block Grant. This year's loopholes might be plugged, without closing the scope for next year's. By 1987, fresh legislation had been put in place to impede deferred purchases. But it was apparent that many councils were searching for alternatives – and there were plenty of investment bankers bearing helpful suggestions. Large authorities, like big public companies, carried multimillion-pound loan portfolios that could earn them revenues in the global market for financial derivatives. By taking, say, the fixed rate of interest on an existing loan and accepting an investment bank's offer to swap it for a floating rate of interest, a council could earn a small fee (or 'premium'). There could be legitimate reasons for selling 'interest-rate swaps' as a way of improving a portfolio's aggregate risk profile – or it could be done more aggressively with an eye to maximizing the premium income. More than a few councils were warming to the latter activity. Many of them received letters from their auditors over that summer, urging more caution. In August, the controller issued a general statement on interest-rate swaps to all local authorities. As he reported to the commissioners: 'The legal position was still not clear and remained under review.'[33]

At this point, and around the time that Howard Davies was preparing his speech on regularity for the London treasurers, Margaret Thatcher's newly re-elected government opted to raise the stakes significantly. In June 1987 the Tories had retained a majority of just over 100 seats in the Commons, and there was a fresh resolve in Whitehall to stem the tide of creative accounting once and for all. The CIPFA Code of Accounting Practice was published early in July and was given a positive reception in the media. It looked time for some fundamental changes to the way in which councils' accounting activities were monitored. In its 1986 Annual Report, the Commission itself had observed a little contentiously that nothing short of radical reforms to the Block Grant and capital expenditure rules (as it had advocated in 1984–85) would suffice to crack the problem. 'Nor does the solution lie in yet more rules to block the loopholes through which creative accounting operates.' In the event, on the contrary, just three more rules did the trick.

Two of them were enacted by the Local Government Act 1988 that came into force the following May. The less important one picked up a recommendation of the Widdicombe Committee Inquiry, as already noted. It gave auditors the power to issue a 'prohibition order' pre-empting any decision that they believed would lead to a breach of the law. Unless overturned in the courts, the order would itself have the force of law. This sledgehammer was eventually used to crack a few parish council nuts, but was otherwise shunned by auditors who never really saw it as their job to pre-empt councils' decisions. Far more important was a power given to auditors to apply for judicial review of any decision or failure to act by a client council 'which (in either case) it is reasonable to believe would have an effect on the accounts of that body'.[34] This seemed to auditors far more in keeping with their historical role as watchdogs, and was so broadly worded as to constitute an important addition to their armoury.

The judicial review option would soon prove a potent antidote to creative accounting. One of the fashionable creative ideas that arrived in 1988 was 'factoring' – an arrangement allowing a council to sell for cash today its title to capital receipts it anticipated collecting tomorrow. Half a dozen authorities launched short-lived factoring schemes during 1988 without consulting their auditors, but the first to persist with a major scheme in the face of written appeals to desist was the metropolitan borough of Wirral. This meant that it was once again the district auditor for Liverpool, Tim McMahon, who found himself in the firing line. No doubt he was relieved to reach his retirement in September. It was left to his successor, Jim Milstead, to pioneer the 'Section 25' judicial review. He applied to the High Court in November to have Wirral's factoring scheme declared unlawful. This took the steam out of factoring plans in local government even before the application was granted in 1989 – and Milstead's action turned out to be the high-water mark, in a sense, for creative accounting in general.*

What finally scotched it was the third and last of the government's rules, which arrived as part of the 1989 Local Government and Housing Act. Section 5 of the Act obliged local authorities to designate one of their executives other than the finance director as a 'monitoring

---

* In a piquant twist to the story, the Wirral councillors took the plunge on factoring without intending to part with any assets. They anticipated selling off council houses and a shopping centre to a total value of £20 million over four years. They paid £80,000 in banking and legal fees to concoct an elaborate scheme that was designed not to realize a discounted capital sum but simply to provide them in 1988–89 with a capital receipt which would have the effect of raising their expenditure ceiling for the year. They planned to spend £37 million and faced a ceiling of £31 million unless their capital receipts could be boosted in this way. They were given a favourable (though not unqualified) QC's opinion on their scheme. The district auditor, assisted and advised as ever by Cliff Nicholson and his staff in Vincent Square, thought it bogus on several counts. 'These arrangements are peculiar,' as Milstead noted mildly in his affidavit to the court.

officer', charged in effect with the duties of a whistleblower. (It was a post suggested by the Widdicombe Report in 1986, which envisaged the appointment of 'propriety officers'.) He or she would have to confer with the finance director where something appeared to be seriously fishy and send a formal report about it to all the members. This significant measure inaugurated a fresh departure in local authority governance – supervision by a new triumvirate of the finance director, the monitoring officer and the district auditor – which was followed by a further, dramatic decline in creative accounting's popularity.

Meanwhile, for the Commission itself, weathering the crisis over creative accounting entailed a significant legacy: for the first time, it had appointed its own in-house solicitor. Until 1983, the old DAS had always been able to call on its sponsoring department in Whitehall or the Treasury solicitor for legal advice. It was also the case that most senior people within the service were themselves legally qualified. Studying part-time for a law degree had traditionally been a route to promotion, and certainly most of the thirteen district auditors serving in 1987 were legally qualified. (Brian Skinner, for example, had trained as a barrister.) Nonetheless, it was an odd anomaly by the mid-80s that no one in Vincent Square could be called upon for a professional opinion on local government law, let alone audit law. District auditors were making delicate but weighty judgements about the prudence or otherwise of controversial policies being adopted in defiance of their possible long-term consequences. As a service, the DAS was inclined to believe that those consequences would prove to be expensive, but the verdict might be a long time coming. In the meantime, auditors had to tread warily and they did so with very little outside help. Solicitors were rarely consulted. A silk's formal opinion would occasionally be sought, but this was a daunting process that was reserved for only the most serious problems. The battle with Liverpool and Lambeth in 1986 prompted a fresh approach. A first step was the appointment of a City firm of solicitors, Clifford Turner, to advise the Commission. But it was soon clear that local government law was not the forte of a City firm. Peter Brokenshire had a better idea, and persuaded his colleagues to let him approach someone for whom it was meat and drink.

Tony Child had been working as the council solicitor at Greenwich borough since 1976. His first seven years there had coincided with Brokenshire's time as chief executive, so the two men knew each other well. In more recent years, Child had made himself known well beyond the borders of Greenwich, with some feisty actions against the Tory government. In 1984, he had successfully challenged a consultation process launched by the government with a view to curbing the payment of benefits to striking miners. In the spring of 1985, he had justified the late setting of a rate by Greenwich on the grounds that the council could properly wait for the result of a judicial review against the principle of rate-capping.* That review went against him – but he had had more success with a second review, in 1986, which had forced the government into retroactive legislation to legitimize rate-capping.

Some now muttered of poachers and gamekeepers when his move to the Commission was announced, but this was not how Child saw it. He had worked with his district auditor, Brian Skinner, on many VFM issues and taken an active interest in the work of the Commission. His old Greenwich boss offered him an opportunity to combine the role of an in-house lawyer with a place on the Management Practices team. This suited Child. He wanted to remain a lawyer rather than end up in a broader management position, which seemed his most likely destination at Greenwich. He had also quite enjoyed his first taste of the media limelight.

He arrived in Vincent Square at the beginning of February 1987. In his office was one small book-case, sporting a solitary legal tome. But Child soon perked up when a London audit team called on him for some urgent advice. (It was the start of a long case against creative

---

* In the event, he failed to have the date of the judicial review brought forward and pushed the council into setting a rate on the first Saturday of June 1985. 'We set the rate on a Saturday because the council meeting started at 7 p.m. on the Friday and was disrupted when protestors invaded the council chamber. Eventually it was adjourned at about 3 a.m., so we came back at 7 a.m. with no protesters and finally set the rate at noon. I rushed off to play wicket-keeper in a cricket match at Woodford Green – I just got there in time, took a catch in the second over and scored a fifty that day.' He scored less well in the judicial review that followed some weeks later: 'Some of the things which our politicians had said were not well received by the judge.' (Interview with the author.)

accounting in the borough of Haringey.) Word of the new man at the Commission spread quickly in the following months. 'As soon as people found out I was there, I'm afraid they formed an orderly queue. So I was very quickly engaged full-time on legal work and within a year had to take on an assistant.'[35] His legal career at the Commission, though, did not take off immediately. A few days after joining, Child's colleagues sent him to Coventry.

This was not a metaphorical rejection, but a way of involving him in the latest of the line of management studies into individual authorities that had begun with Basildon. Tony Child joined a small team comprising David Henderson-Stewart and outside consultants from the accountants Armitage & Norton, researching a study into 'Coventry City Council's central administrative organization, and the contribution that it makes to the council's public services'. By central organization was meant the members, the offices of the chief executive, the city treasurer and council secretary, the manpower services unit and the central computer departments. In Coventry, these together accounted for costs of about £9 million a year. Across England and Wales *in toto*, such central organizations were costing an estimated £2 billion a year. Peter Brokenshire's objective with the study was explicitly twofold: 'to identify changes in the activities of Coventry's central organization that would help it to adapt to its new [political and social] environment . . . and to develop the Audit Commission's own thinking about this subject in order to make a contribution to better management in local government'.[36]

The result in June was an impressive 63-page report, many sections of which came as a revelation – not to say a shock – to the leader and his colleagues on the council. Henderson-Stewart recalled how vividly the analysis stacked up: 'We just struck it lucky time after time.' In examining the IT department's operations, for example, they discovered that Coventry was by far the heaviest spender of thirty-five metropolitan districts that were surveyed. The report compared it in detail to Trafford, in Lancashire, a district approximately half Coventry's size. Trafford had a central computer budget of £1.6 million and employed a total IT staff of twenty-five people who wrote all of their own programmes. Coventry had a budget of £4 million, employed 108 people and purchased much of its applications software externally. 'I remember the leader was absolutely rocked by this.'[37] The impact in Coventry, however, was probably less important in the long run than its impact on the new controller in Vincent Square.

THE DILEMMA OVER CONSULTING

Having made clear in September the premium that he wanted to set upon regularity work and the integrated audit, Davies was ready by the autumn of 1987 to review with his team the strategic implications of *The Way Ahead*. Given the basic problem this paper had addressed – how best to go about closing the implementation gap between prospective and actual savings – one inescapable conclusion was that auditors in the field would need to spend more time looking at the management arrangements of their client councils. As Davies recalled: 'In most other environments, if you saw lots of malfunctions and lots of inefficiencies, you would say almost automatically, "well, this is all down to management". So why didn't we think along the same lines, in local government? Why had we not devoted much more thought to the management of local authorities, their structure and the kind of leadership they needed?'[38]

It was not easy, though, to see how best to go about it. Peter Brokenshire had struggled to build any substantial franchise for his Management Practices directorate by March 1987. But having worked so long inside local government himself, he was still convinced of the original rationale for tackling management issues. Even the modest work done on individual authorities during the Banham years had in his view proved the point. Within days of Davies's arrival at Vincent Square, Brokenshire tried to enlist his support for the idea of turning Management Practices into a separate consulting subsidiary. It would operate at arm's-length from the rest of the Commission, to get around the fears over a conflict of interest for auditors that had prompted the Commission members to rule against consulting in its very first year.

Davies was sympathetic to the idea – Audit Commission Associates was his suggested title for the business – and he seems to have entertained the possibility quite seriously: he floated it during a discussion that he and David Cooksey had with the environment secretary, Nich-olas Ridley, in April. (Ridley responded positively and thought that any conflicts of interest ought to be easily manageable.)[39] Nothing had come of the idea by June. The Coventry Council report – full of cogent analysis, seminal numbers and arresting charts – was therefore a timely reminder of how much the Commission, or a subsidiary of it, might be able to offer. And at the same time, around mid-1987, other councils were also showing signs of interest in the notion of engaging people from the Commission as quasi-consultants.

Remarkably, these prospective clients even included both Liverpool and Lambeth. Davies met on several occasions with the chief executive of Liverpool, a long-suffering officer called Michael Reddington, initially at his request, to talk about the possibility of a major review of the council's services and management arrangements. Reddington, according to Davies's note of their first meeting in April 1987, urgently wanted to launch the kind of strategic re-think that he thought might usefully have followed bankruptcy two years earlier. 'If it is not poss-ible for members, officers and the Audit Commission to tackle this at the moment [said Reddington] then there is no future for a local council in Liverpool and they might as well throw in the towel.'[40] And in September, at a meeting with Lambeth's chastened Labour members under their new leader, Linda Bellos, Davies and Brian Skinner found the heirs to Red Ted Knight almost as amenable.

Reaching agreement to launch contractual reviews in such highly politicized councils could be a time-consuming business. Liverpool City Council, for example, had reached an outline agreement for a review in May 1987, but the whole idea had been swept away by the volatile local politics of the city. (A contract was eventually clinched: a review was undertaken for the council in the spring and summer of 1988, which 'highlighted the severe problems and shortcomings of many of Liverpool's services. The report was accepted by the council and made public.')[41] The time and patience needed to deal with such problems was one reason why, in the end, Davies decided to drop the notion of consulting to individual councils. But there were at least three other, more fundamental negatives.

To start with, the difficulties of staffing a consultancy arm looked daunting – even if Davies were happy to part with some of the Commission's regular employees, which was far from the case. As Davies well understood, from his time at McKinsey, consulting could be an extraordinarily labour-intensive business. A huge amount of time had been invested in the Coventry report, but what good had it done the DAS in general? This pointed to the second worry in Davies's mind. One-off consulting assignments would hardly be in keeping with his determination to forge standardized lines of inquiry that could be widely adopted by field sections of the DAS. It would take optimism of an heroic kind to think other city councils would turn to a finished article like the Coventry report with an eye to their own improvement opportunities. Better, surely, to use talented managers such as David Henderson-Stewart on work like the national statistical profiles. These could generate benefits year after year across a wide front. This point was of particular relevance in the autumn of 1987, when the Commission was straining its resources to produce a first edition of *Performance Review in Local Government*, pulling together all its work on national and local statistical profiles.

But there was also a third concern, which went to the heart of what the Commission was about and raised issues that were to reverberate under Davies's successors. He felt an instinctive unease about taking the Commission – even via an arm's-length arrangement – into consultancy work that would tell individual councils what they *ought* to be doing, as opposed simply to describing what they *were* doing. The line between these two categories could occasionally be blurred *at the national level* that was addressed in special studies. Prescriptions, after all, were sometimes unavoidable as part of the process of setting out the conclusions from masses of comparative data. In dealing with value-for-money studies at a local level, it was a different matter.

From the start, Davies firmly believed that local democracy required authorities to make their own decisions on all matters of policy. The vital job of the Commission was to provide as much objective information as possible, via local audit work and comparisons with the national picture, so that those decisions could be properly informed.

We could illuminate the choices that previously had too often been obfuscated by local professional bodies and the barons of the municipal departments that employed them. The line we had to take with any council was: 'you should see the Commission's work as an interesting way of revealing what is actually going on in your authority'. If at the end of the day the council then said, 'yes, we're spending twice as much per capita on this service as any other authority in the country and we're happy with that, it's the right thing for us to be doing' – well then, fine. At that point, we rest our case, we put down our calculators and we go home.[42]

But sometimes, as this implies, the dialogue developed rather differently. Commission figures would reveal decisions that had been taken without any real awareness on the councillors' part. Thus, Davies recalled a memorable discussion with a leading Labour council in the north. 'I can see that you've obviously decided in this authority to be particularly generous on your children's services,' he told them. 'There are some unusually big numbers here, by national standards, that show you've clearly decided to make this a very high priority!' In fact, of course, they had decided nothing of the sort, as the Commission had suspected from the outset. The authority was saddled with an especially powerful director of social services. He had cornered a budget far larger in relative terms than any of the councillors had appreciated. In disclosing this kind of anomaly sensitively but objectively, the Commission could make a valuable contribution that auditors before 1983 had rarely if ever attempted.

Sceptics in the media often preferred a simpler view of the Commission. It was a stick with which Whitehall could beat local government around the head. To Davies, this was a basic misunderstanding of the Commission as it stood. If it went into the consulting business, however, it might all too easily come to be true. Even as an arm's-length operation, he finally concluded, a management-practices consultancy working under the aegis of the Commission would cross some wires that were better left safely apart.

On all three counts, the Coventry report looked a strategic cul-de-sac. This was never made explicit, and the Commission's annual reports continued to talk about the value of local reviews for another two years. But the Coventry report was never published and the Liverpool project was almost the last of its kind. It did help point, however, to a better way forward: Davies and Brokenshire, searching for an alternative approach to the management agenda that could promote it as an essential part of the integrated audit, came up with a new idea. The Commission would publish a series of Management Papers. These came to resemble the Occasional Papers launched in 1986. Slimmer and much more accessible than the special studies, they were designed as concise introductions to management issues of current relevance. They would include a useful discussion of recent developments, but would always be careful to set down plenty of checklists (the key success factors, the performance measures and so on) that would make them handy tools for auditors and council officers alike. They would be prescriptive as well as descriptive – but only in a generic sense. They would set out for councillors a view of how things worked in general across local government – leaving it to individual councils to apply the lessons at their own discretion.

THE FIRST AND SECOND MANAGEMENT PAPERS

The first paper was twelve pages long and could be read in less than half an hour – but it encompassed an enormous range of issues and set much of the agenda for the papers that were to follow. A longer first draft by David Henderson-Stewart was titled *The Well Ordered Council*. Its potential impact was immediately apparent to the controller and the chairman, and plans were laid for an ambitious launch. A shorter version was rechristened *The Competitive Council*. Davies rewrote much of the text with the kind of flair that Vincent Square staffers were accustomed to from their controllers. And it was decided to make publication of the paper into the keystone of a conference to mark the fifth anniversary of the Commission, on 29 March 1988.

The backdrop to the conference was encouraging. Davies and his chairman had both toiled extraordinarily hard over the previous twelve months to improve the Commission's relations with both central and local government. Davies in particular had completed a punishing schedule of trips around the country, meeting authorities and speaking at association conferences. Now there were signs that all this effort was paying off. Even Nicholas Ridley set aside his usual disdain for the whole world of local government to compliment David Cooksey on the progress that had been made. The two men had spent an hour and a half in conversation at the end of January. 'Ridley had said that there was a "green light" ahead of the Commission and he was very happy with the state of relationships between us and the department. He had also had echoes from the local authorities that we were getting along better with them, too, so had no criticisms to raise [on their behalf].'[43]

But the conference, when it arrived, threatened at first to be a disaster that might undo much of this good work. Held at the Queen Elizabeth II Conference Centre opposite Westminster Abbey, it got off to a horrible start. Hundreds of guests from local government, Whitehall and the private sector arrived shortly before a scheduled 9 a.m. beginning, only to find an officious security regime that took most of the first hour of the day to clear the entry queues. Ridley then opened the proceedings with a dismally graceless speech, fully in keeping with his notorious private views on local government. (At a meeting the following month with Sir Roy Griffiths, the deputy chairman of the NHS management board, Ridley would start their discussion by saying 'councils are run by people who have failed in their own businesses during the day and try to run other people's at night.')[44] Next up on the podium was a last-minute and distinctly lacklustre replacement for Labour's Jack Cunningham, whose absence was a big disappointment. Finally it was Davies's turn. As the setting for his first big presentation of the Commission to a general audience, he could hardly have faced a more hostile gathering.

'You have to imagine the immense scepticism with which this unknown youngster was anyway viewed by many of the local government people,' recalled Henderson-Stewart, who attended as part of the Commission's contingent. 'The mood was really quite mutinous as Howard got to his feet and I thought, "crikey, what's going to happen now?" Well, he was absolutely brilliant. Within two or three minutes he'd made a couple of good jokes and he had the whole place eating out of his hand. It was a very witty and clever speech.'[45]

And he had some good material. In effect, Davies took his audience through *The Competitive Council*. Starting with some dramatic statistics on the 1980–90 decade (with secondary school pupil numbers down 25 per cent and the number of over-85-year-olds up almost 50 per cent) he warned of dramatic shifts ahead in the landscape of local government. This was partly a matter of the Thatcher government's political agenda: new laws were pending to replace the rates by the poll tax, to privatize council houses, to restructure the educational system and to introduce compulsory competitive tendering across a wide range of council services. But it was also a reflection of deeper changes in society's attitude to local government. Yesterday's essentially passive ratepayers and client groups were fast learning to behave as customers. They expected ever improving standards in public services. To meet this challenge, councils would have to be much clearer about their criteria for future success, and how these criteria could be met. The Commission identified eight characteristics of the well-managed council (and it openly acknowledged there were shades here of *In Search of Excellence,* the business best-seller by Tom Peters and Robert Waterman, two former McKinsey consultants, that similarly listed the key attributes of winning companies). They included understanding the customers, setting clear objectives and responsibilities, and training and communicating effectively. Above all, both members and officers needed to think hard about their managerial roles. Endless committee meetings, with mixed objectives and a tediously legalistic approach to the agenda, had to be left behind.

Davies's speech, like the paper it launched, was littered with references to forthcoming titles in the same series. The Commission's reorientation around the management of local government was now in the public domain. It involved much more than just the publication of Management Papers (of which ten were to appear during Davies's time as the controller). It prompted the Commission, for example, to select audit flavours that set less store by simply cutting costs and more by helping councils to manage their operations. Thus, for the winter of 1987–88, the chosen topics were the care of the mentally handicapped, managing property and managing the maintenance of the roads. The flavours for 1988–89 took a similar line, in the realms of education administration, police efficiency and the consolidation by councils of their own direct labour organizations (DLOs) for the new era of competitive tendering.

Reactions to the fifth-anniversary conference were encouraging.

A special report on the Commission appeared in *The Times* on the day of the conference, built round soft interviews with Cooksey, Davies and Cliff Nicholson. (Davies's former ambassador in Paris, though, may not have enjoyed the interview with his former private secretary. Davies was quoted by *The Times* as saying that his job in the Foreign Office was 'the most fatuous occupation you could imagine. I thought the embassy was over-staffed, under-worked and occupied in almost entirely futile tasks.' Asked if there should be penalties for councillors who wasted public money, Davies thought not – 'and in any case, if there were, I'm sure you'd want to lock up the people responsible for the Concorde project before you locked up people in local authorities.')[46] Other media coverage the following morning was almost equally positive – as was the feedback from those in local government who sent in their reactions to Vincent Square.

Among those who responded positively were a good many chief executives. At one level, this was no surprise. *The Competitive Council* stressed the pivotal role of the chief executive in coordinating a council's political and managerial processes. 'The success of this [coordination] is one of the most crucial factors in the well-managed authority.' Naturally, the chief executives and their professional association, the Society of Local Authority Chief Executives (SOL-ACE), considered this a shrewd observation. Viewed in the context of local government's recent history, however, their response was more interesting. The chief executive in most councils had until comparatively recent times been known as the town clerk. The new title was generally (though not universally) adopted as part of the 1974 reorganization of local government. Some councils, such as Greenwich, had embraced the spirit of this change. They soon had genuinely influential officers at the helm, such as Peter Brokenshire had been. Even fourteen years later, though, many other 'chief executives' exerted no more authority than the old town clerks.

These unreconstructed councils were effectively run by the main service departments, whose chief officers related to the elected members in ways that varied widely according to local circumstances. It was hard to generalize, as ever with local government, but one feature was commonplace: the chief executive was still not in any position to control the chief officers, who remained accountable only to their respective committees. Indeed, in the most old-fashioned councils, the chief executive struggled to be seen as *primus inter pares* with the likes of the highways engineer, the social services director or the education officer. Where they needed to communicate with him, letters would as often as not be exchanged through the post. (It was 'him' rather than 'her' almost everywhere: the Commission found in 1988 that of more than 400 chief executives, all but four were men.)

But had not the Commission, in effect, endorsed this outdated approach? It had mostly dealt with the chief officers whose service departments were the natural focus of the VFM agenda. It had largely ignored the work of the chief executives who now were applauding *The Competitive Council*. Their reaction to the March conference prompted a re-think by Davies and Brokenshire. The message of their own paper, after all, was that successful councils would need chief executives more in line with private sector practice: executives with real authority, free of specific service responsibilities and empowered to get things done across all council departments. It had been assumed in 1974 that imposing a quasi-corporate structure on councils would be enough to effect this change. Managers would join local government from the private sector and bring their corporate ways with them. It had not happened. The pay was too low, the responsibilities too ill-defined and the prospective clout all too hypothetical. Only a tiny handful of chief executives by 1988 had anything other than a background in local government. Davies and Brokenshire decided the Commission could play a valuable role here, as a proxy in effect for those managers who had never turned up.

Most immediately, a start would be made by publishing a second Management Paper that would tackle head-on the role of the chief executive. Davies opted to write much of the paper himself – or, to be more precise, to re-draft an original version that would be prepared for the Commission externally. The work was taken on by an old friend of the controller, Martin McNeill, then a graduate student at the London Business School. Researched over the autumn, the result appeared in January 1989, and was entitled *More Equal than Others: the Chief Executive in Local Government*. The paper warned against identifying local government simply as a set of local services. These could always be hived off by Parliament or subjected to close control from Whitehall via hypothecated grants, an increasingly popular notion among Tory politicians at Westminster. Rather, the essence of local government should be seen as its responsibility 'for ensuring delivery of a range of public goods, trading off different demands against each other and against the willingness of the electorate to pay to see any of them satisfied'. In this allocation of resources, 'it is right that choices about the scale and balance of provision should be made locally, by people who are sensitive to local needs'. The survival of genuine local democracy demanded no less. (It is striking, with hindsight, how closely all this prefigured the notion of 'place-shaping' that would emerge eighteen years later, in a review of the future of local government by Michael Lyons – see Chapter 16.) But all of this presumed the existence of competent 'central processes' – ultimately controlled by elected members, but delivered from day to day by a full-blooded chief executive. And to avoid mistaking the nominal version for the real thing, the paper set out a clear job specification. Ten boxes laid out, almost as an audit guide, a series of questions that every authority ought to ask about its own chief executive. (Is his role clearly defined? Does he receive all the information he needs? Is he involved in the overall management of resources? Does he have the managerial skills required?) The answers would tell whether or not the incumbent could meet the Commission's test of a real chief executive: that he be 'both the authority's centre of continuity and its agent of change'.

Buried in the middle of the new paper was a reference to the fact that local government had become far more politicized, along party lines, in recent years. Independent councillors now comprised only 15 per cent of the total, down from almost 40 per cent in 1965. Where fully half of all councils had been non-aligned in 1965, now only 14 per cent were free of party control. Here was a potent source of trouble for many chief executives, often calling for some finely tuned political skills. One side-effect of the politicization went unremarked in the paper. The 1980s had in many places seen a steep drop in the collective experience of many elected councils. Old hands had drifted away, disaffected with the ever more confrontational climate; more factious members, attracted by it, had arrived with little or no understanding of local government. Without necessarily assisting the evolution of the chief executive's role, less supervision from the council chamber meant a de facto strengthening of some officers' powers.

This was especially true of those working in the financial department. Thus, in the 1986 local elections, of the forty Labour candidates who had been elected to the Inner London borough of Hammersmith and Fulham, only eleven had had any previous council experience at all.[47] This result had consolidated Labour's hold on the council but greatly weakened the council's hold on its more adventurous financial officers. Quite how potentially calamitous had been the consequences for the ratepayers of Hammersmith, the Commission was only just in the throes of establishing.

6

Closing the Swap Shop, 1988–91

The Hammersmith and Fulham swaps affair began like the plot of a Raymond Chandler thriller, with a telephone call to the controller's office in Vincent Square, late on a hot June afternoon in 1988. It was from a woman working for Goldman Sachs, the US investment bank. Davies asked his secretary to put the call through to Mike Barnes, who was head of technical support. Half an hour later, a sombre-looking Barnes appeared at Davies's door. 'I think you'd better talk to them', he said.[1]

Davies duly returned the call. The banker happily explained again the reason for it. She was an American, newly arrived in the London office. She worked on the swaps desk at Goldman and had been familiarizing herself with the book of the bank's existing positions. She'd been intrigued, she said, 'by this guy Hammersmith'. Finding him (she persisted with the joke) on the other side of several Goldman contracts, and not knowing the name, she had made some inquiries. 'And I find this guy's real big in the market. In fact, he's on the other side of everything. He's in for billions and *all on the same side* of the market! Anyway, I've asked about him and people have explained the Audit Commission is responsible for him. So I thought I'd call you up and let you know. This guy's exposure is *absolutely massive.*'

Davies made two more calls within the hour. The first was to the accountancy firm Deloitte, Haskins & Sells, where one of the partners, Tony Hazell, was assigned as the auditor to Hammersmith. Hazell said he had no idea what the lady from Goldman was talking about. Then Davies rang the chief executive of the council. He explained his concern. The chief executive tried to make light of the matter. He could confirm that Hammersmith was involved in the swaps market, he said, but didn't think it was much of a player. Davies knew better than to suppose that a bank like Goldman might have rung him on a whim. 'Would you mind just inquiring,' he persisted, 'and see what you think the position is?' It was early in the evening when the chief executive called back. Yes, he said, the council did indeed have a lot of swap positions – and the treasurer saw it as a nice little earner. 'I really wouldn't worry about this, Howard. Anyway, everybody knows that interest rates are going to fall.'

With this, of course, the clock struck thirteen. Davies responded accordingly: 'So I said, are you telling me all of your positions are geared to interest rates going down? He was. Right, I said, I'm sending in the auditor and I'm sending a team from here as well.'

While detailed figures would take months to unravel, it was clear within days that something extraordinary had been happening at Hammersmith. It was a borough with bank borrowings of £308 million as of 1 April 1988 and a capital expenditure budget of £44.6 million for 1988–89. Yet in the books of its treasury department was a 'capital markets fund account' recording literally hundreds of derivatives contracts signed with banks from all over the world. Just as Goldman had said, the capital amounts covered by these contracts ran into many billions of pounds.

Hammersmith town hall was an unlikely hotbed of financial rocket science. In fact, it was one of London's loonier left-wing councils. (After a lunch with Deloitte's audit team a year earlier, Howard Davies had noted: 'They are clearly now getting to grips with a difficult authority in Hammersmith and Fulham where they are not allowed to refer to 'members', because that is regarded as sexist terminology.')[2] It had apparently made a profit on its derivatives activities to date, which was unsurprising given that it had been collecting premiums on contracts with contingent liabilities that only lay in the future. But what might its exposure eventually be? And how would it be affected by any unforetold *rise* in interest rates?

SWAPS AND THE LEGAL OPTIONS

As Tony Hazell and his colleagues from Deloitte began grappling with the paperwork, the Audit Commission had to take stock of its own position. It had been concerned over the use of complex derivatives by local authorities since the earliest days of creative accounting: the minutes of the members' monthly meetings record a string of anxious references to the subject. Perhaps, with hindsight, it is surprising that more assertive action had not been taken by the Commission already. Now, all district auditors were asked to report back on how many of their client councils were currently active in the market. Back came the answer within days: 137 of them. The Commission had urged caution on several occasions, but nothing more. Clearly this was no longer enough.

There were just three basic options. Either derivatives trading was lawful. Or trades relating to the hedge of an underlying loan were lawful, but no others. Or all such trading was unlawful, and based on an erroneous reading of what the 1972 Local Government Act empowered councils to do in the financial markets. A joint legal opinion was urgently sought from a leading counsel, Roger Henderson QC, and a junior counsel, John Howell. What they handed to the Commission early in July, however, were three opinions. In one, both agreed that derivatives contracts were generally beyond the powers (*ultra vires*) of local authorities. The QC opined, separately, that hedging derivatives related to an underlying portfolio ('parallel contracts') could be legitimate. His junior advised, in a third opinion, that all derivatives were unlawful.

Davies and Cliff Nicholson, mindful of the sensible ways in which swaps could evidently be used to reduce a council's exposure to interest rate movements, opted for Henderson's opinion – the hybrid option. In a memo that went out on 13 July, they alerted the auditors to the legal advice that had been received. The only swaps to be accepted as legitimate, they advised, were those used to hedge individual loans – and even here, trading such swaps would be unlawful. Other derivatives were not to be accepted.

They had pondered hard over the Howell opinion. It had the attraction of being a simpler response, but was it really practical? It would have entailed a huge setback for the capital markets and the unwinding of hundreds of contracts all across local government. Davies could see no justification for that. On the contrary, he and Nicholson urged auditors to be pragmatic and use their common sense. 'Where authorities have engaged in swap transactions beyond the limited scope accepted as legitimate [but] the response is one of agreement to limit any future activity to hedging individual loans, there is no need to take action on previous activity. The transactions cannot be unravelled and the authorities should be discouraged from seeking to do so.'[3]

Back in Hammersmith town hall, Tony Hazell duly extracted a promise from the council that it would suspend swap transactions from 1 August. But its response to the auditor was curmudgeonly at best. The officer responsible for the capital markets fund account took exception to the joint opinion from the Commission's counsel, of which the council had been given a copy. It was 'too narrow and ignored cash and investment management considerations'.[4] The finance director warned that swap activities could only be halted 'temporarily' and would not preclude further selective trades as 'the most prudent response to the present uncertain position . . .'[5]

Over the following six months, Hammersmith compounded the managerial ineptitude that had already brought it to the brink of disaster. As an illustration of just how badly a local authority could be run, it might almost have been designed to accompany the first two of the Commission's Management Papers. Neither the leader of the council nor any of its elected members had any idea what was happening in their finance department. Indeed, in view of the massive potential exposure so rapidly accumulated, it was questionable whether even the finance officers really understood what they were doing. (The Commission's in-house lawyer, Tony Child, thought not.) None of them had sought any outside legal advice over derivatives, though they had been in the market since December 1983 and had been deep into speculative contracts since April 1987. The council's own director of legal services was not asked for his views until February 1989. Letters from the auditor to the chief executive generally drew replies from the finance director (or, just as often, his deputy). And all of them seemed to be in a collective state of denial over the time-bomb ticking in their treasury. It was not until the end of October that leading counsel was even instructed.

Anthony Scrivener QC's opinion for the council took six weeks to complete and was received a few days before Christmas 1988. Another three weeks elapsed before a copy of it was sent to the auditor. In a covering letter, the council officers explained why in their view the opinion allowed them 'a wider range of powers' than counsel to the Commission had deemed legitimate. Accordingly, and with breath-taking defiance in the circumstances, the letter said 'the council is considering what action it should take, if necessary, in conjunction with other local authorities'.[6]

By mid-January 1989, though, the Commission's patience was wearing very thin. Even more astonishing than Hammersmith's dila-tory handling of the crisis was the sheer financial scale of it, which by now was becoming horribly apparent. Back in April 1987, the council had been a party to deals with a notional principal sum of just £135 million. The equivalent figure for August 1988 was £4.2 billion. This guy Hammersmith, as the lady banker had put it, was accounting for a half of one per cent of the entire global market in derivatives! At one point, its contracts had represented roughly 10 per cent of the sterling sector of the market. Under an 'interim strategy' adopted from that August, the council had continued – true to the weasel words in their response to Tony Hazell – to strike fresh deals in the market. It seemed all too likely, though, that these were just digging the hole deeper. (Later records would show that, between April 1987 and April 1989, the council executed a staggering 613 deals, involving a notional principal sum of £6,208.5 million – equivalent to more than one contract for every working day, with an average principal sum of about £12 million.)[7] Meanwhile, there was one unambiguous change since August 1988. The level of sterling interest rates had almost doubled, from around 8 per cent to 15 per cent. As of February 1989, Hammersmith's treasury had lost its reckless one-way bet in spectacular style. By one estimate, the cost of closing out all of its derivative contracts was now around £300 million – or roughly an eye-popping £4,000 from every ratepayer in the borough.

The Commission had to tread extremely warily. It had no *direct* statutory responsibility for tackling Hammersmith's predicament.

That was down to the auditor. (The subtlety of this distinction, given the Commission's statutory responsibility for appointing all auditors and prescribing the code of practice that governed their fulfilment of their duties, would be a source of confusion to many third parties.) Nor was the Commission's advisory role entirely straightforward: Tony Child conferred closely with Cliff Nicholson but was formally engaged (in line with his usual practice) as solicitor to the auditor with the statutory burden. Yet of course it was the Commission that had to take the heat from the City. This mounted steadily through the autumn of 1988 as the banks grew increasingly exasperated over the auditor's failure to produce a clear-cut ruling. By early 1989 there existed a tense stand-off, which remarkably had still to be picked up by the media.

If Hammersmith's contracts were to be declared illegal, the banks would face substantial losses. Leading City law firms, led by Clifford Chance and Linklaters & Paines, put two arguments to the Commission. First, it was unconscionable that anyone could think of nullifying contracts freely entered into by the council. (Some colourful doomsday scenarios were lined up in support of this view.) And second, according to a precedent in the private sector, any legitimacy for parallel contracts – that is to say, contracts entered into as a hedge against market risks incurred on underlying borrowings by the council – would mean the openly speculative trades had been unlawful only because the council did too many of them or executed them for the wrong purpose. That would not preclude the banks from enforcing these latter contracts. (This was known as 'the *Rolled Steel* argument', a reference to the commercial precedent.)

This second line of argument from the banks proved counter-productive. Tony Child had been certain from the start that Hammersmith's capital markets fund had been unlawful: 'it was completely unrelated to treasury management in any way'.[8] But the banks' stance made him more acutely aware than ever of the different consequences that would flow, depending on whether it was the scale and nature of the transactions that made them unlawful or the fact that there was no power to trade like that at all. 'If there was no power, it protected authorities for the future. If we didn't win on the "no power" point, the banks were going to say: "You've got a pyrrhic victory and we can still enforce these deals."' Child himself did not accept the Rolled Steel argument – but he was determined to close the door on it, just in case.

Accordingly, at the end of January, he exercised his duty as solicitor to the auditor and bravely advised him that he should disregard Roger Henderson's advice on parallel contracts – which was still broadly espoused by the Commission itself – and be guided instead by the opinion written by John Howell, the junior counsel. In other words, the auditor should argue that *all* trading in derivatives was *ultra vires* for local authorities. And he should apply to the High Court for a Section 19 declaration by the judge to this effect – meaning that all of the capital markets fund's actions in 1987–88 and 1988–89 would be deemed illegal. Hazell accepted Child's advice.

There was now an awkward difference of view between the Commission on the one hand and its auditor on the other. Davies and Nicholson had no choice but to back the auditor in public, of course – and to hope that a way would turn up in due course of reconciling Child's uncompromising legal strategy with a practical agenda for cautious councils using swaps to hedge their loans books.

FROM COUNTING HOUSE TO COURTROOM

The controller and his deputy hosted a conference in Vincent Square late on the afternoon of 8 February 1989 that for the first time brought together all of the key players. For the council, the leader and some of his committee chairmen attended along with the finance officers and their external counsel, Anthony Scrivener. From Deloitte, Tony Hazell came with his main partner on the audit, Michael Roberts. Tony Child and his assistant, Judy Libovitch, sat alongside Mike Barnes and Harry Wilkinson. No record of the discussion survives but presumably, given Child's advice to Hazell, the full implications of the Howell opinion must have been spelt out. After so many months of investigation, some degree of consensus on the way forward might have been expected. There seems to have been none.

At least, though, the conference energized the members and officers of the council. A torrid schedule of meetings now ensued in the town hall. But while the auditor struggled to administer the last rites to all their fantasy finances, the members and officers spent most of the next two weeks vehemently reassuring themselves that all was well. Seemingly unaware of the enormity of its potential liabilities, the members and officers of the council continued to insist on the legality of its activities. 'Treasurers sought to reassure members that the potential exposure (which they feared at the time could be as high as £2.5 billion) was notional rather than real money. The clear impression given to elected representatives was that the authority had played the markets and won.'[9]

The capital markets fund was a corpse that wouldn't lie down. But several nails now went into the coffin in quick succession. News of the crisis finally broke in the media, with a scoop by the *Independent* newspaper on 25 February. Two days later, Tony Hazell issued a Public Interest Report warning that court action was imminent. And the morning after that, a letter was delivered to the council from the Department of the Environment. Hammersmith's finance director had written to Nicholas Ridley on the 24th asking him to sanction further trades in the capital markets and to indemnify councillors and officers against any penalties for handling them. Ridley declined to do so. This brought squawks of indignation from the council, but a white flag too. It issued a press release explaining that it wished to honour any and all payment obligations incumbent on the capital markets fund. 'However, further payment made in these circumstances without the sanction of the Secretary of State would render those authorising the payments liable to surcharge.'[10]

On 6 March, having had confirmation from the auditor that he was proceeding with a Section 19 application to the courts for all of the fund's activities since April 1987 to be declared *ultra vires*, the council passed a formal resolution to suspend all its capital market activities.

Thus far, the Audit Commission had handled the crisis with considerable skill. It had positioned itself (and accommodated a subtle repositioning) adroitly on the legal fundamentals of the case. It had complied with the procedural niceties of the situation since June 1988 with patience and sensitivity, while providing vital support and encouragement to the auditor. And it had coped well with the intermittent involvement of interested third parties. But it still had two vital contributions to make.

The first, in American football parlance, consisted of some defensive blocking. Once the full import of the auditor's position was clear, there was intense pressure on both Deloitte and the Commission to ditch the case, not least from other local authorities. If Hazell's Section 19 application was granted, it would of course put an end to derivatives trading by all councils, as the Commission itself was all too well aware. Existing contracts would need to be rescinded – and putative gains would have to be surrendered. Tony Child recalled: 'Many people in local government were saying "Back off, don't get involved! Hammersmith have dug this pit for themselves. Why should the rest of us suffer, if we've been doing it for perfectly proper reasons? And if some of us have made money out of it, why should we have to give it back?" '[11]

But of course it was the bankers who leaned hardest on the Commission. Doubtless their regard for the sanctity of contract would have prompted fierce opposition even had Hammersmith council been in line for a huge net windfall. The fact that it wasn't, and that the banks together stood to forfeit a net gain of several hundred million pounds, may just have added to their distress. Some of them took an extraordinarily aggressive stance towards the Commission. On one occasion, Davies was visited in Vincent Square by a senior executive who warned that his bank was considering legal action not just against the Commission, but against the controller in person, too.

The banks with the most to lose included two of the British clearers, Midland Bank and Barclays Bank, plus Security Pacific National Bank and Chemical Bank of the US and Mitsubishi Finance International, the City subsidiary of a Japanese bank. They formed a steering group to fight the action. And while their legal advisers prepared to contest it in the courts, the banks began to canvas for appropriate retrospective legislation in the ugly event that Hammersmith's trades were eventually to be declared *ultra vires*. They won support for this cause from the British Bankers' Association – and at first, too, from the Bank of England.

The Bank had been very concerned indeed for some time about the impact of the case on the markets, and had initially tried to persuade the Commission to back off. But the Bank official in charge of the brief was Eddie George, who had been Howard Davies's counterpart at the Bank when Davies was working in the Treasury. George, a future governor of the Bank and widely known as Steady Eddie for the sureness of his touch, contacted the controller and the two of them talked through the issues at some length. George quickly appreciated the Commission's dilemma: he was soon taking an active role in explaining its position to the banks, while looking for ways to resolve the problems he could see ahead.

Meanwhile, Davies and Nicholson stood their ground. The auditor was fully entitled to make up his own mind on the Hammersmith case. He had decided to take a more radical stance than the Commission itself on the law governing swaps. That was his prerogative. It in no way diminished the Commission's support for his action. Rumours swirled all through the DAS about the pressures on the controller. There was scurrilous talk of private investigators, paid by City financiers to dig up dirt on the controller and his team. Suspicious individuals were said to be loitering in the corners of Vincent Square. Meanwhile, more plausibly, the banks' PR people were working over-time to win support in the financial press. Would not success for the auditor, after all, be the end of an era for the City of London?

Faced with their overt opposition, Tony Child named the five lead banks as third party respondents in the district auditor's application. This allowed their interests to be represented in court. But it helped to concentrate minds in Hammersmith town hall, too. By the time the application was lodged, on 31 May, most of the councillors were more than happy to acknowledge the auditor as the prospective saviour he really was.

The banks were soon disabused of any notion that Whitehall might see their defeat as a blow to the City of London's reputation. When Davies and his chairman sat down to talk about the case with Ridley at the DoE, late in June 1989, he told them the Bank had tried this line with No. 11 – 'but the chancellor had responded "robustly" to these arguments'. Ridley himself thought retrospective legislation to validate selected trades was simply out of the question. He saw 'some advantages' if the banks ended up getting their come-uppance. In fact, it would be rough justice. 'The government had spent a lot of time and energy attempting to close off loopholes but the banks had persisted in doing business with local authorities contrary to the spirit and sometimes the letter of the legislation.'[12]

Tracking down the letter of the legislation and relating it specifically to what exactly Hammersmith council had been doing since 1987, was going to be a gruesomely complicated business. On this score, at least, the banks and their City lawyers must have supposed themselves at a significant advantage to any local government auditor. Surprisingly, the opposite proved true. This was the second of the Commission's vital contributions. In Tony Child, they fielded a solicitor with an unsurpassed knowledge of local government law *and* a readiness to immerse himself in the financial minutiae of the derivatives' market until he could describe its activities with a rare lucidity. As for his willingness to be his own man and to scrap hard against any odds, there was never much doubt about that.

Child, Hazell and their two assistants met together at the start of March to begin their work on the district auditor's affidavit. Child himself never went to Hammersmith (though he and Judy Libovitch did visit the City offices of the council's solicitor, Herbert Smith, to copy documents lodged there). Instead, with the help of innumerable shopping expeditions by the auditor, dozens of box files were brought from the town hall to the Commission's offices in Vincent Square. There, over the next eight weeks or so, Child and his assistant – together with Hazell's counsel, John Howell – pored over hundreds of contracts to reconstruct a detailed narrative of the key events in the case.

The crisis hinged, in common parlance, round Hammersmith's swaps – but in reality, of course, the capital markets fund had gorged itself on every dish in the derivatives diner. For days on end, the team at Vincent Square waded through the documentation for swaps and options, caps, floors and collars. They produced succinct illustrations of everything from simple straddles to exotic 'mandatory cash exercise strangle options'. And the end result was a 140-page affidavit that won the auditor's case a credibility and authority in the courtroom that none of the respondents ever matched.

UP THE LEGAL LADDER

Proceedings began in Crypt Court 2 of the Royal Courts on 1 October 1989, before Lord Justice Woolf and Mr Justice French. They lasted ten and a half days. Right at the outset, there was a clash of views between Hammersmith's lead counsel and the bench. The council, said Tony Scrivener, wished to argue *both* that parallel contracts could be lawful *and* that all swaps could be deemed *ultra vires*. Lord Justice Woolf thought this impermissible. It had to be one argument or the other. Scrivener refused to concede the point, though it was quite clear to Child that the lawyers at Herbert Smith were strongly committed to the *ultra vires* view.

Next morning (and thereafter), Scrivener failed to appear. Junior counsel stood to say that Hammersmith accepted all swaps were *ultra vires*. From that point on, the citing of the council as a respondent in the case was a pure technicality. The Commission continued to insist in public that it was a dispute between the auditor and his client council. But in truth it was essentially the Commission and its auditor versus the banks.

The High Court ruled for the auditor. Everything turned on its judgment on Section 111 (1) of the 1972 Local Government Act. This empowered local authorities to do anything 'which is calculated to facilitate, or is conducive or incidental to, the discharge of any of their functions'. The High Court decided that swaps did not facilitate a function, but rather the *consequence* of a function. They were therefore beyond the legitimate powers of a council.[13] The banks, not unreasonably pointing out that swaps had been undertaken by council treasurers for many years without anyone publicly impugning their legitimacy, turned to the Court of Appeal. The council, having flipped its case over in the High Court, now joined the auditor against the banks.

Privately, Davies and his colleagues had their own worries about the practical consequences of the High Court ruling. After all, it threatened precisely the problems that they had sought to duck at the outset in opting for the Henderson opinion. In December 1989, Davies went with the chairman, David Cooksey, to see Chris Patten, who had succeeded Nicholas Ridley at the DoE. The visit was not expressly arranged to talk about the swaps case. They covered a broad agenda of other matters – and Patten made it clear that he could say nothing about it while the appeal was pending. But inevitably the discussion turned to the Hammersmith case.

The permanent secretary, Terry Heiser, made it clear he was fiercely opposed to the idea of any retrospective legislation, as Ridley had been. All that Cooksey and Davies could do was point out the difficulties that might lie ahead. 'The chairman said that the Commission would on balance hope that the secretary of state might do something to allow councils who undertook debt-management type deals in the past in good faith to honour their obligations.' Patten said he noted this view.[14]

The appeal by the banks was heard in February 1990, and was presided over by the president of the Family Division. This expediency was reportedly forced on the Court of Appeal by the huge workload with which it was struggling at the time. The proceedings lasted just over fifteen days. On the day of the ruling, it was a measure of the intense interest in the case that something highly unusual happened. 'For the only time in my life, at a Court of Appeal judgment,' remembered Child, 'they locked the doors. So once you were in, you were not going to be let out again until all the details of the judgment had been delivered, in case it affected the markets.'[15]

The Appeal judges ruled, in effect, that wherever they enabled a council to manage the interest rate risk on its loan portfolio, swaps were facilitating a function and were therefore legitimate. Where they were traded in pursuit of a profit, they were not. In the case of Hammersmith specifically, contracts before the auditor's intervention should be seen as speculative and unlawful. Subsequent swaps could be seen as part of an attempt to reduce the council's portfolio risk and were therefore to be honoured. The media generally welcomed the judgment. In the *Financial Times*, the Lex Column observed: 'overseas financial institutions can feel more confident that City deals will not be sabotaged by arcane UK laws. The integrity of the markets has been preserved, without allowing the banks to escape the consequences of their foolishness in over-trading with Hammersmith and Fulham.'[16]

The banks themselves wasted no time in issuing writs to enforce payments of more than £3 million outstanding on the post-July 1988 contracts. The Appeal ruling meant there was no immediate need to invoke the Rolled Steel argument for these. However, there was little doubt in legal circles that the banks would in due course turn their attention to building a case for further payments. This was a widespread expectation for a good reason: many senior lawyers thought the Appeal Court's ruling had in several respects been rather bizarre. Indeed, it was considered so unsatisfactory that Cooksey was privately urged by many powerful figures at the Bar to ensure that matters did not rest there.[17] The final decision, as ever, had to lie with the auditor. But all eyes, inevitably, were on the Commission. How would it react?

It was a dilemma for the Commission. At their next monthly meeting, on 1 March, the members were told that Hazell was considering an appeal. In the meantime, the controller had turned back to Roger Henderson QC for further legal advice on the implications of the case. A conference with him would follow a week later. It was agreed that the chairman should subsequently call for a special meeting if he thought it appropriate – and David Cooksey had no doubt this was needed. And so, on the afternoon of 13 March 1990, for the first time since the Commission's launch in 1983, the members met for an extraordinary meeting. It was attended also by an independent solicitor – they were now well past the point where Tony Child could advise both the Commission and the auditor. The members fully appreciated that the Commission and the auditor were separate parties, and that the appeal decision was down to the auditor alone. It was Henderson's advice that Hazell's primary duty related to the ratepayers of Hammersmith and Fulham – but he was also entitled to take into consideration the effects of the case on local government generally, and on this score it was legitimate for the Commission to offer its own advice. But what should that advice be? It was a long discussion.

There was plenty to be said for the Appeal Court ruling. It had much in common, after all, with the original July 1988 opinion from Henderson 'which the Commission had consistently supported'. If accepting the ruling meant sacrificing the immediate interests of the Hammersmith community-charge payers in the wider interest of councils across the country – well, a case could certainly be made for doing just that. And they needed to acknowledge that any appeal to the House of Lords was always fraught with risk and the possibility of huge additional legal costs. Cooksey recalled: an unsuccessful appeal 'would have risked bankrupting the Commission but for our ability to put up our charges'.[18]

On the other hand, the Appeal ruling had plenty of disadvantages, too. It cast the definition of legitimate swaps much more widely than Henderson had done, which prompted some unease over the dodgy dealing that might arise in future. And, from a technical standpoint, there were several unclear aspects of the ruling that seemed likely to cause trouble even over Hammersmith. It was also a minor concern that the Appeal Court had reached a most unsatisfactory conclusion on costs, leaving the Commission with substantial expenses that members thought should be met from the ill-fated capital markets fund.

Reaching a decision proved a tortuous process. It was agreed that the auditor would not be criticized by the Commission if he chose not to appeal. Then it was agreed he would be fully supported if he did. But what should be the Commission's recommendation? Finally, and for the only time during his chairmanship, Cooksey decided that they would have to take a vote round the table. Even then, the outcome that was recorded in the minutes read like a truly Delphic utterance: 'on balance, the wider implications of the Court of Appeal judgment for local authority auditors and audit law generally were such as to suggest that an appeal to the House of Lords could be of value'.[19]

Tony Child's advice to the auditor was never made public but was almost certainly a great deal more forthright. There is no reason to suppose that he had changed his mind. He was ready to oppose the banks' writs. He was also ready to fight them in the ditches over applications of the *Rolled Steel* argument, which he feared might now regain some traction. But wouldn't it just be much simpler and therefore of greater assistance to local authorities everywhere if the House of Lords could be persuaded to back a blanket prohibition on swaps? Tony Hazell decided to appeal.

Whatever the verdict in the Lords, it was apparent that many local authorities were soon going to face some difficult meetings with their bankers. The Commission needed to be able to assist in this process, which meant some fence-mending of its own in the City might be no bad thing. Davies set up a string of meetings with the banks – and indeed with representatives from the Bank of England – through the early summer. 'Although it had not been possible to avoid the [Hammersmith] case going to the Lords, the meetings had helped to explain the Commission's position and had improved relationships with the banks,' as he later explained to the commissioners.[20]

By the autumn, the Commission was exploring with the British Bankers' Association how councils might best handle a post-verdict settlement. The BBA was optimistic enough to start work on an 'interest rate swaps code of practice' and asked for the Commission's comments on a first draft. Nothing was expected from the Lords much before the end of 1990 at the earliest.

Early on the evening of 31 October, the controller was the last person left in the office at Vincent Square. At about 7 p.m., the fax machine outside his door whirred into life. On the sheet of paper that slid gently into its in-tray was a letter addressed to the Commission solicitor. It was from the House of Lords Committee considering the Hammersmith and Fulham case. Their Lordships had provisionally decided, it said, to find against the banks on point 1A. In plain English, it had provisionally decided that councils had no power to engage in *any* swap transactions. Their Lordships had agreed with John Howell's opinion. Child had backed the winner. Davies put the letter in his pocket and went home. Next morning, he came in a little late, calculating that Tony Child and his assistant would arrive as punctually as usual. He stepped into Child's office and handed the two of them the letter. They read it together. Then, as Child recalled, 'we started jumping up and down in celebration'.[21]

Whether Davies actually jumped up and down with them is unrecorded. No doubt he felt mightily relieved that the court action was finally over. It had been a long haul since Mike Barnes had taken that first telephone call from Goldman Sachs in June 1988. And for all the reasons aired at the extraordinary meeting, it was a ruling he could welcome. Celebrations, though, were probably left to the lawyers. Davies would not have regarded a Lords ruling in favour of the Appeal Court as a disaster for the Commission. Nor did he see this ruling against the banks as a triumph. The truth was that he and

Nicholson had worked hard to insulate the Commission's credibility as an institution from the outcome of the legal action. A ruling in favour of the Appeal Court ought therefore to have been manageable. That was in many ways a better measure of their success over the past two and a half years than any specific ruling from the Lords. The Commission had properly fulfilled its role by stepping forward to halt an evident abuse of derivatives trading. How exactly such an abuse should be prevented from recurring in the future was a matter for the lawyers to decide. Davies, as ever with Nicholson's help, had held the ring for them to do so. He had shrewdly protected the reputation of the Commission throughout the process, and in so doing had greatly enhanced his own reputation as a cool head in a crisis.

He had also done local government a signal favour. For the Lords' ruling was not just a get-out-of-gaol card on existing derivatives-linked liabilities. It also marked a pre-emptive strike against the strong likelihood of a broader and more damaging crisis arising in the future. As the best detailed study of the episode concluded in 1998: 'For British local authorities, the House of Lords' ruling severely curtailed their capital markets activities, but effectively fireproofed them from the derivative debacles that came to be a recurring feature for US authorities, notably Orange County, during the 1990s.'[22]

By chance, the members were convening for their next monthly meeting on that same 1 November that had Child jumping in his office. It was business as usual in the boardroom. The provisional decision from the Lords went into the minutes simply as an event with some especially onerous housekeeping implications. 'Accounting Practice would consider what advice to give auditors to enable them to help local authorities in complying with the judgment. Discussions would take place with the banks and others to try to reach a constructive solution.' The threat posed by the court action had long since closed the capital markets to all local authorities. The unwinding of all their derivative trades, though, still seemed almost as daunting a task as it had appeared at the outset. Harry Wilkinson and the Accounting Practice directorate set to work almost immediately on the technical guidelines that would be needed by the auditors.

The formal judgment emerged from the House of Lords in January 1991. In addition to the ruling on the illegality of council activities in the swaps market, there was a welcome finding on the costs of the case. (Indeed, this proved rather a windfall. The court calculated a post-tax reimbursement based on gross costs in line with City fees. Because the Commission had relied so heavily on its own, rather less expensive in-house lawyers for most of the case, the final payout proved to be extremely generous: the income statement for 1991–92 showed costs of £31,000 and recoveries of £441,000.) But the judgment was by no means the last act of the drama. The great unravelling of contracts took several years to complete. The banks wrote off an estimated £600 million, though fears for the standing of the City of London proved to have been grossly overblown. The lawyers prospered as the banks and their former council clients squabbled over the restitution payments. The final curtain did not fall until May 1996, when the House of Lords ruled that such payments needed only to be accompanied by simple rather than compound interest.

As for the councils themselves, and their ratepayers, those facing sizeable losses on their trading books could count themselves fortunate indeed to see the losses cancelled – and there were a good few, though none in Hammersmith's league. Those confident of making a real return were less pleased to see their putative profits forgone, though few of them made much fuss. One exception was Westminster City Council, which sent its treasurer to appear before the House of Lords in 1990 and give evidence on behalf of the banks against the district auditor. Westminster's big day in the Lords, though, was yet to come.

7

A Credible Authority, 1988–91

Late in 1987, Howard Davies took a delegation from Vincent Square to meet with a group of the country's top police officers. The venue was a secluded country hotel and under discussion was the possibility that the Audit Commission might begin to look at how economy, efficiency and effectiveness were faring in the police service. It was not the first time the two sides had met. An agenda had already been agreed for a series of 'consultation meetings' and a special studies team under Ross Tristem and Steve Evans had had a chance to conduct some preliminary research. For this occasion, some initial findings had been worked up into an audit guide, as an illustration of how the Commission worked. The guide was presented during an afternoon session. Dinner was to follow, with two more sessions the next day.

There were four chief constables around the conference table, and they were impressed. The number-crunchers seemed to have un-earthed some quite surprising insights from all the data they had collected. As they broke for dinner, though, one officer expressed some disappointment over the slightly skimpy format involved in an audit guide. 'It's a pity you've only produced a guide,' said the chief constable of Greater Manchester, James Anderton. 'It would be useful as a national paper because you would get more exposure to all the police forces in the country *and* their authorities.'

Later that evening, Davies made an early exit from the bar. At breakfast the next morning, he presented Anderton with a 5,000-word draft report that he had written overnight on the basis of the analysis in the guide. Steve Evans recalled: 'Howard told him "that's what a national paper would look like. Those are roughly the sort of things it would say." Well, Jim Anderton was just gobsmacked that a chief executive would go away and write a draft like that!'[1]

The story nicely captures the extent of Davies's personal commitment to the output of the Special Studies directorate. Much of his first year as controller was taken up with other matters. But there was never much doubt that his real interest in the job lay in producing the Commission's national reports. Their intellectual integrity and incisiveness were of paramount importance to him from the start. He usually tried to take a slightly more detached stance than had his predecessor. He would attend a brainstorming session at the outset of a study when the lines of analysis were agreed, with the participation of outside experts; and he would join the 'progress review' (McKinsey parlance, again) half way through, when the team met together – often in a two-day retreat away from the office – to agree on the key messages emerging from their work. But the work itself and the drafting, he left to the team.

Nevertheless, any contrast with his predecessor could often be less striking than the similarities. Like John Banham, Davies was gifted 'at pen' (as auditors in the DAS used to say) and did a huge amount of rewriting. When it came to presenting a report, both men enjoyed public speaking and had no fear of the media. And for both, without doubt, ensuring that heads were turned by whatever was in the Commission's window was always of more personal interest than actually running the shop. In this respect, of course, Davies was much the more fortunate. He was not required to build the shop in the first place, as Banham had been. And he could look for support from a well-seasoned Commission and a chairman with at least half a year's experience in the job before he arrived.

Cooksey had in fact made a strong start by March 1987. He'd quickly won the respect of the other members of the Commission and was pulling together a good team. The 1986 recruits – Axton, Barratt, Meade, Stuart and Wall – had all proved their worth as conscientious contributors to the Commission's monthly deliberations. One of them, Harry Axton, had agreed to become deputy chairman, though it was rare indeed that Cooksey himself ever missed a monthly meeting. Two new commissioners had been appointed a couple of months before Davies arrived: a Tory peer, Elizabeth Anson, and the former Labour leader of Birmingham City Council, Clive Wilkinson. Of the sixteen original members appointed in 1983, nine were still on board. (These were Peter Bowness, Ian Coutts, Geoffrey Drain, Dudley Fisher, Christopher Foster, John Gunnell, Noel Hepworth, David Lees and Roy Shaw. The seven who had departed since 1983 were Lawrie Barratt, Kenneth Bond, Keith Bridge, Ian Hay Davison, Peter Kimmance, Ian McCallum and the first chairman, John Read.)

Davies recorded his own slight surprise, after the very first monthly meeting he attended, to find the dynamic of the group so positive. 'There was general unanimity of view on most topics and an extremely constructive and business-like atmosphere . . .' Even at this first meeting, though, Davies could not resist the chance to tease one or two members. 'There was one amusing moment when Birmingham was described as "the epicentre" of the country, to Clive Wilkinson's great pleasure. But I commented that I thought that the point about epicentres was that nothing happened there.' It must have taken the members more than a few meetings to get the measure of their second controller.[2]

In the years that followed, his own relationship with the chairman made a weighty contribution. Over time, Cooksey and Davies would in fact forge by far the most effective chairman–controller partnership in the first twenty-five years of the Commission's history. The relationship between the individuals in the two top seats was always of huge importance to the success of the institution; it could hardly be otherwise, given the sensitivity of Vincent Square's relations with Whitehall and government ministers. Their complementary skills, and the respect that each had for the other's contribution, helped Cooksey and Davies make a memorable success of it.

Cooksey recalled:

Howard and I had the most extraordinarily positive working relationship. I found that in meetings together we could get through an agenda in forty minutes that with anyone else would have taken two hours. We were able to concentrate on just what the key issues really were. But I have to say that, through all our time together at the Commission, I could never define what Howard's personal politics were. He was able to just stand back and press for what he believed was the best possible outcome. And there were some big issues around at that time.[3]

In fact there was only one issue on which they ever disagreed: Davies wanted to open a sub-office in Brussels, to have a voice in debates within the EU Commission. Cooksey decided this was significantly outside the Commission's remit and stamped on the idea.*

Many of the issues they faced together in 1987 sprang directly from the impact of fresh legislation. In the run-up to the June general election, the Tories put councillors on notice that the whole franchise of local government in England and Wales was in for a battering. Changes in the structure of education, reforms to housing benefit and a broad extension of the competitive contract tendering rules were just three of the items on a crowded agenda. Managing the consequences was going to be a mighty challenge.

This, of course, was the premise of *The Competitive Council*, launched at that 1988 anniversary conference, and the decision to focus on management processes. Special studies as well as Management Papers would be heavily influenced as a result. But local authorities were not the only organizations in need of better management. Nor were all of the Commission's primary concerns in 1987–92 triggered by legislative changes. There was another needy area of the public sector that had been included in the Commission's audit franchise ever since 1983, but nothing at all had been done to help it. This was just about to change when Davies arrived at Vincent Square, and led straight to that heroic piece of drafting in a hotel bedroom.

A SLOW START WITH THE POLICE

Someone who had always been keen to engage with the police was Ross Tristem. In his six years at the Home Office, from 1964 to 1970, the organization and management of police forces had been his main interest. The country's regional crime squads in 1986 were still structured and worked operationally along the lines that Tristem had

---

* Davies's thinking may have been a little premature, but Commission members would later have cause to reflect on the importance of a voice in Brussels. An EU Directive on auditor appointments in November 1996 threatened for a few months to drive a coach and horses through the Commission's 70/30 arrangements. It was eventually accommodated without serious upheaval.

designed for them in his doctoral thesis at Warwick University. His motives for re-engaging with them in 1986 were far from sentimental. As special studies director, Tristem had no doubt whatever that huge inefficiencies lurked within the police service. It was the most rigidly controlled environment in the public sector by far. Police officers of every rank, he knew, spent an inordinate amount of their time on clerical work and mundane duties. This pushed police costs far higher than they needed to be, and did nothing to help in the battle against crime.

Banham had never needed much persuading of this, but nor did he have any illusions about the difficulty of gaining access to the police for any study project. The Commission had of course been auditing the 'police authorities' that were part of local government, as the 1982 Act required. But the statutory power to engage in centrally coordinated VFM work had been ignored, for the simple reason that the senior officers of the service refused to countenance the idea. This had been enough to scotch it, given their political clout at Westminster – at least until the dust had settled on the miners' strike.

No doubt their opposition reflected a strong aversion in the police to anything 'not invented here'. Police officers of whatever seniority had all risen through the ranks, and assimilating external ideas had never been regarded as a traditional strength of the service. But their antipathy to the Commission probably also owed something to an acute sensitivity in the mid-80s over governance trends. The police service was not a national body, led from London. It comprised, in England and Wales, forty-three separate forces. Only one, the Metropolitan Police, reported to the home secretary. The rest operated within a tripartite structure. Individual forces were led by chief constables with their own powers and responsibilities; they were legally accountable to local police authorities, largely comprising elected councillors, which provided their financing (and were part of the Commission's audit franchise); and they were subject to controls exerted directly by the Home Office. The whole structure was watched over from the centre by a very powerful inspectorate, Her Majesty's Inspectorate of Constabulary (HMIC), based in the Home Office – but was intended to enshrine a devolvement of power to local forces.

In practice, the Home Office's growing control over the finances of the police was exerting a steadily greater degree of centralization, especially evident after the introduction of new funding rules in 1983. There was also a tense stand-off between many senior police officers and their own Inspectorate, which was seen increasingly as just an arm of the Home Office. The ad hoc adoption of national arrangements to combat the miners' strike in 1984–85 had only heightened suspicions that a *national* police force would emerge as one long-term consequence of that protracted crisis, leaving the police authorities stranded as toothless observers. This did not at first sight appear a propitious backdrop for any attempt by the Audit Commission to win new work from the police. Surely it would be seen as yet another agent of the centralizing tendency?

But Tristem could be very persistent. Banham had finally been persuaded by him in mid-1986 to make a formal approach. He went along with Peter Brokenshire to a meeting with officials and senior police officers. But it did not go well – 'they came away with a flea in their ear', recalled Tristem.[4] By the autumn of 1986, Tristem was ready to make another push and this time he offered to handle the initiative himself. He may have felt he personally had little to lose. He had recently been in discussions with the Treasury, who were pushing him either to return to his old Whitehall post, after a three-year secondment that had already been extended several months, or else to move permanently to the Commission. Within a few months, the news of Howard Davies's appointment would clinch his decision not to return. (Tristem recalled: 'I didn't know Howard from my Treasury days, though I had seen minutes with his name on them. As soon as I knew he was coming, I just went over to the Treasury and had lunch with people there that he'd worked with. They all said he was a very bright guy and that was good enough for me.') But as yet he was undecided and saw winning or losing work with the police as a way of helping him to make up his mind.

Despite the rebuff to the Commission's first approach, a further meeting was granted. Tristem went along to the Home Office with Cliff Nicholson for a round-table discussion with its officials and the top brass of the Inspectorate. It proved a memorable day. The two of them were shown up to a conference room, where they found twenty or so awaiting them on the home team. As they walked through the door, one of their hosts turned round and, seeing Tristem, exclaimed in surprise 'Good God, it's you!'[5] It was Stanley Bailey, the outgoing president of the Association of Chief Police Officers (ACPO) – and a former colleague of Tristem at the Home Office in the 1960s. Neither had had any idea that the other would be attending the meeting. Bailey and his successor as ACPO president, James Anderton – who were the chief constables respectively of Northumbria and Greater Manchester – were attending it as representatives of the police authorities around the country. Tristem recalled:

We shook hands and had a laugh about times past – and he introduced me to Jim Anderton. Then Bailey said: 'What are you trying to do?' So I told him what we were after and he said, 'I've got no problems with that.' Then I saw him take Jim Anderton over to the window and chat to him. I guessed what he was saying to him – 'We'll go with them, not the Inspectorate.' They obviously thought it was a case of divide and rule.

Once the meeting got under way, Tristem and Nicholson briefly set out their ideas on how they might be of assistance. They were proposing to do value-for-money projects, of a kind that might even help individual forces in their submissions to the Home Office for funding. (This was not such a fanciful idea: wherever new funds were provided for extra officers, the recipient force had to provide evidence of VFM gains for the following three years.) It was soon apparent, though, that the chief inspector of constabulary was fiercely opposed to any VFM role for the Commission. His response was uncompromising: the police service was a professional organization where there could be no room for rank amateurs. And besides, said the chief inspector, 'the police themselves won't agree to it!'

At which point, things turned sticky. 'Well, I'm afraid', said Tristem, 'that if we want to do it, we can. And there will be a *per diem* fine for anybody who doesn't cooperate, including people in the Home Office.' He turned to Nicholson for corroboration of this. 'That's right, isn't it, Cliff?'

'Yes', replied Nicholson. 'The 1982 Act clearly states our obligation to undertake value-for-money work on the police authorities as we think appropriate.'

The chief inspector was not impressed. Clearly looking for some support, he turned to the two most senior police officers at the table. 'How do you feel about this?' he asked them. 'I expect you're pretty anti all this as well, aren't you?'

'Basically, no', said Jim Anderton. 'I think we could do with people taking a look at us. In fact, I'll volunteer Manchester as one of the early authorities for a study!'

'Yes, and you can come to Northumbria as well', added Bailey, helpfully.

Or so, at least, Tristem remembered it. And from this jarring exchange, there followed a series of difficult negotiations that lasted some months. One by one, chief constables around the country followed the example of Bailey and Anderton. By April 1987, in his very first monthly report to the members as their controller, Howard Davies was able to report that 'virtually every police authority has offered to take part in the special study of the police, preliminary consultations on which are now in progress'.[6]

As talks progressed, though, it became clear the chief constables were none too keen on delegating the overview of any studies entirely to their more junior colleagues. Nor were they completely relaxed about working with local auditors: all projects would have to be closely supervised by the Commission itself. The members of the Commission for their part grew a little anxious over the prospect of too direct an arrangement between Vincent Square and the chief constables. They worried it might look like a consultancy deal, 'on a scale denied to the professional firms'.[7]

Agreement was finally reached in the autumn of 1987. A 'liaison group' was established, of four chief constables – including Jim Anderton but also David O'Dowd, chief constable of Northampton-shire and himself a future chief inspector of constabulary. The Commission put up a project team that would be fronted by the controller. Most of the team's work would be carried out under Ross Tristem or Steve Evans by that keenest of the Commission's new young recruits, Frank Ingram. It was the cautious beginning of one of the most fruitful relationships with a client organization that the Audit Commission achieved in its first quarter-century.

REINFORCING THE THIN BLUE LINE

The first steps were chosen with great care. Davies, like Tristem, never really doubted there would be plenty to do if they could ever win the confidence of senior officers. Indeed, even as early as June 1987 the controller was hearing from some of Tristem's staff about extraordinarily wasteful practices that were being unearthed in preliminary discussions. (One manager, John Potts, '[had] thought Manchester was a well-run police authority but was now having second thoughts . . . he already believes there is an awful lot for the Commission to get its teeth into'.)[8] But any hint of this conviction might have scuppered all their chances.

Instead, they launched those consultation meetings with the four chief constables that took them off to country hotels together. Study topics were proposed that could deliver quick gains without threatening anything too ambitious or encroaching on what senior officers would regard as operational territory. Eventually, a modest research programme was agreed that would examine six support services used by the police. This was completed by the autumn of 1988 and two 'Police Papers' were published in May and October of that year.

The first, *Administrative Support for Operational Police Officers*, looked at the use being made by the police of civilian support units. The value of civilian assistance was twofold. It could cut the time spent by highly trained policemen on basically clerical deskwork. Constables were spending 25 per cent of their duty hours on paperwork; sergeants and inspectors nearer 40 per cent of their time. And it could reduce the financial cost of the work very significantly. In broad terms, police officers were paid *three times* as much per annum as their closest counterparts in civilian employment. A substantial amount of work had already been done on this problem by the Home Office's Police Requirements Support Unit. The Commission's paper served up a powerful analysis of their findings. Local forces that had employed support units properly had benefited in quite dramatic ways. In twenty-one tightly written pages, the paper showed how other, less progressive forces might follow their example. Of course, it concluded diplomatically, 'it is necessary for each force to have due regard to local circumstances, particularly the geographical characteristics and management culture of the force. This is not, however, an alibi for inaction.' (Commission authors rarely resisted any temptation to use a figure of speech based on police terminology.)

The second paper was based much more on original research by the Commission's own team – indeed, in many ways, it was a model of its kind. *Improving the Performance of the Fingerprint Service* addressed a problem area that many senior officers felt uneasy about: they knew serious reforms were needed, but their local forces were as ever waiting on initiatives at a national level for which there never seemed to be sufficient supporting evidence. The Commission's paper offered plenty of this and attracted considerable attention in the media. (On the day of its publication, in a routine that would soon become familiar, the controller was interviewed first by the BBC's flagship early morning programmes on both radio and TV, and then by local radio stations from round the country later in the day.) Davies had no difficulty impressing interviewers with a startling headline fact. In 1987, there were over 2 million crimes committed, of a type (burglary, car theft and so on) where fingerprints might normally be deposited. In only 40,000 cases (i.e. less than 2 per cent) were offenders identified with the help of fingerprints. In each of these 40,000, the successful use of prints had had to surmount a long series of obstacles that had successfully stymied progress on the other 98 per cent of the crimes. The paper looked meticulously at each of these obstacles.

Some of its conclusions might have been predicted easily enough. Both arms of the fingerprint service – comprising the 'scenes of crime officers' (SOCOs) and the fingerprint experts, in charge of the searching and checking within thirty-three bureaux scattered across the country – were badly under-resourced. There was too little use being made of the latest technology. The coordination of the SOCOs and the bureaux left much to be desired. But other findings were more surprising. The disparity between the performances of different forces, for a start, was simply enormous. 'Raising performance to that of the best tenth of forces would almost double the existing number of identifications.' The variation in performance was similarly wide for the fingerprint bureaux themselves: 'Some bureaux obtain six times as many identifications per fingerprint officer as others.' In general, there was a serious imbalance between the effort put into *taking* fresh prints and the resources thrown at *managing* them effectively. 'In some forces less than 10 per cent of marks submitted are searched. In one force visited there was a four-year backlog of arrested persons' prints waiting to be classified and filed – its fingerprint collection is virtually useless.'[9]

The Commission team responded to these findings by offering the police a 'fingerprint diagnostic model'. This defined forty-nine key indicators of performance, starting with the number of crime scenes visited as a percentage of relevant offences. An ingenious schematic outline of the model illustrated how any force could use it as a guide to its own performance and the main areas 'in which opportunities for improvement may exist'. The paper concluded by suggesting all forces 'should liaise with their local auditor' to make use of the model in their region.

This was pushing the relationship with the police a little beyond the original understanding – but by now some of the most influential voices in ACPO could see the quality of the work on offer. Phase 2 of the research programme was waved ahead, to look at issues in the central management of forces, with an autumn 1989 deadline. The 1989 Annual Report noted with satisfaction that 'a close and collaborative relationship' had been built with the liaison group. Its four chief constables had met with the home team regularly 'and helped them with their enquiries'.

The joint sessions between them began to generate a close collaboration, not least between the chief constables and the controller. Many encounters were enjoyed on both sides. One of their early meetings caught the flavour of the relationship well. The chief constables were regaled with a Commission team's research into the costs of vehicle fleet maintenance. To illustrate the disparities encountered between forces, the annual cost of a standard two-litre patrol car was quoted for Forces A, B, C and D. The chief constables listened hard, as it was explained that Force B had costs that were ludicrously out of line with the other three, never mind the rest of the country. At this point, the chief constable of Manchester, Jim Anderton, caught the controller's eye. 'I expect, Howard, that it would be a mistake for me to ask who

Force B is?' The controller replied with due solemnity: 'Yes, Jim, it would be a *very serious mistake indeed* to ask that!'[10] (Returning to Manchester, Anderton discovered all his garage staff were effectively given every incentive by their bonus scheme to keep cars off rather than on the road. That was the end of the road for his vehicle fleet management director.)

Taking their lead from the top, rank-and-file officers were no longer so reluctant to meet with their local auditors. By the summer of 1990, the Commission's chairman was able to report proudly in the next Annual Report that 'the change in the perception of [the auditors'] work over the last two years is quite remarkable'. And the result was a series of Police Papers, aimed at steadily more ambitious targets. Three more dealt with support services, looking at the management of vehicle fleets, of police training and of police communications rooms. By the summer of 1990, the Commission was ready to weigh into heavier matters, with a critique (*Footing the Bill*) of the funding arrangements inherent in the current tripartite system whereby the Home Office and local government governed the police. Another financial paper (*Taking Care of the Coppers*) followed, analysing the various ways in which police forces raised some £70 million of miscellaneous income each year – and suggesting ways for them to lift this figure. (One way, said the paper, would be to charge realistically for sending officers to patrol league football matches. By undercharging for this, chief constables were effectively subsidizing the football league by well over £2 million a year.)

The final stage of the collaboration, under Davies's controllership, saw the publication of a handful of papers that explored the actual structure, financing and management of the police force in some depth. Impressed by the rigour of its methodologies and its scrupulous regard for hard evidence, the chief constables allowed the Commission a licence to roam that surprised many senior officers. One paper, *Effective Policing: Performance Review in Police Forces*, looked hard at the ways in which the police were judged on their effectiveness. This was an increasingly topical issue, given rising crime levels that many Tory politicians privately regarded as a bitter disappointment after the steep rise in police pay since 1979. While it acknowledged 'a danger of placing greater emphasis on matters which can be measured quantitatively than on those which can only be monitored qualitatively', the paper set out a detailed case for clearer and more standardized measures of performance. These measures would require more coordination from the centre. Nonetheless, the paper repeated concerns voiced in earlier work that the importance of local police authorities was being gradually eroded. It welcomed a forthcoming review of their role by the Association of Metropolitan Authorities and urged that members of the authorities should 'be to the fore in the development of new measures [of police performance] . . . Police authorities should also have a higher profile in representing their forces to their communities.'[11]

By this time, the quality of the Commission's work was as readily acknowledged by the Home Office as by the chief constables. Kenneth Baker was in charge of the Home Office from Margaret Thatcher's fall in November 1990 to the general election of 1992. His public position on the police was uncompromising. ('All my political life I have had a very simple attitude to the police – they deserve our full support.')[12] But he was more open to reform ideas than this would suggest.

He called Cooksey and Davies in for a meeting early in March 1991 to discuss the latest Police Paper, *Reviewing the Organisation of Provincial Police Forces* and its immediate predecessors. Evidently impressed with much of what he had read, Baker asked for the Commission's views on several key aspects of policy. The officials round his table, though keen to point out where suggested reforms were already in the pipeline, were not unreceptive. As Davies noted later, the chief inspector of constabulary, John Woodcock, 'said rather ruefully that the Inspectorate wished that they got as much publicity for their work as we did for ours'.[13]

Baker even asked his visitors if there were any other parts of his empire they would like to get involved with. Davies 'referred to the Met' – knowing of course that the Metropolitan police, reporting directly to the home secretary, was still an area jealously guarded by the National Audit Office. The home secretary 'said that his brief on this point said "resist". We had a couple of minutes bouncing backwards and forwards on the statutory position.' The Commission men got nowhere on that, but noted appreciatively that Baker's team stayed on after his departure, to chat further about what had been said. It was a much better reception than they had ever had at the Home Office before.

Two more Police Papers were published before Davies's departure. One looked at the use being made of traffic wardens. The other, *Pounds and Coppers*, argued for delegating more control away from the centre, so that financial management could be 'integrated with operational management at all levels in the police service'. Here the Commission was entering trickier territory. The tension between the chief constables and the Home Office, over what many of them saw as the creeping nationalization of the force, was still unresolved. The Commission's analysis helped fuel an intensification of the debate, but no clear decisions emerged before the 1992 election.

PREPARING FOR
COMPETITIVE TENDERING

Their success in gaining the confidence of the police and the Home Office, though, only flagged up once again what most senior ministers and their officials were by now quite happy to concede – and what its appointment as external auditor to the National Health Service (see Chapter 8) had already triumphantly confirmed. Though still less than a decade old, the Commission was without doubt a power in the land. Nicholas Ridley acknowledged this graciously in December 1988, visiting Vincent Square for lunch with the members and a wide-ranging discussion. He praised the Commission's work and stressed the value of its independence, 'even if this meant criticism of the government from time to time'. A year later and in the same job, Chris Patten put the same point slightly differently when Cooksey and Davies visited him in Marsham Street. The Commission, he told them, 'had a very high "street credibility" at the present time'.[14]

And no wonder. Scaling mountains of data in every direction, there seemed to be no aspect of local government that the Commission was not intent on conquering, from housing and highways to environmental health, education and the arts. Steve Evans, recalling his time as associate director of special studies, was especially fond of the mountaineering metaphor. He would compare the early years of the studies directorate under Banham with an exciting, makeshift expedition. 'We were like a two-person climb up the mountain. Move quickly, carry lightweight packs, don't lay down ropes, make a quick assault and get back down!' By the mid-1990s, things were very different. Study teams needed to consult much more with professional and client bodies, and to check on their delivery of key messages. 'So it became more like a big mountain expedition – laying down base camps, supply lines, ropes up the steep inclines and all the rest of it.'[15]

In between came the studies of the Davies era. It was a transitional period that could not last for long. But while it lasted, it made Vincent Square a remarkable place to work. By 1988, Sherpa Tristem generally had six research teams in action at any one time. Most had four members each. Two would be full-time Commission staffers, a project leader and a support analyst. The third would be a seconded auditor from the DAS (typically equivalent to principal level at the Treasury). The fourth would be an expert from the field under study – often someone ranked high in their own profession. Assisting them would be an 'advisory group' of senior figures, drawn from the relevant sectors – not uncommonly, the most distinguished men in their field. The Commission team would periodically present this group with its findings to date and suggestions for further work. After discussion together, the advisory group would offer its advice, which the team could act upon or not, as it thought appropriate.

With these resources, the Commission turned out its big national reports, Occasional Papers, Management Papers, Police Papers and a miscellaneous scattering of Working Papers. Some were only a dozen pages long; others – no longer Yellow Perils since *Improving Highways Agency Arrangements* in September 1987 but dressed austerely in snow-white covers – extended to seventy pages or more. Counting all of them equally, the Commission produced well over sixty titles (just four of them under Section 27) in the five and a half years from the start of 1987 to the middle of 1992. Their aggregate content represented a remarkable, not to say Himalayan, study of the public sector in England and Wales over the period.

Many of the papers took a microscope to the management of services for which councils were legally required after 1988 to invite competitive bids. This radical reform ensured a genuine need: there was nothing academic about the Commission's choice of studies. The compulsory competitive tendering (CCT) provisions of the Local Government Act 1988 followed the lines of the 1980 legislation that had applied to building works and highway maintenance. Now CCT also applied to a slew of other activities accounting for a substantial chunk of local government expenditure. (It covered street cleansing, ground maintenance, refuse collection, building cleaning, vehicle maintenance and catering. The maintenance of sports and recreation facilities was added subsequently.) Authorities had to put the work out to tender. If it had hitherto been done by in-house direct labour organizations (DLOs), the latter had to bid for it just like any rival in the private sector. At the very least, this would pose some complicated accounting problems for council finance departments and their auditors. Davies assembled a group of district auditors and leading partners from the firms to explore these. Michael Dallas of Coopers & Lybrand was delighted when Davies asked him to chair it. (This exemplified for Dallas the way in which working in the public sector brought his peers together, as rarely – if ever – happened in the commercial world. 'There was a feeling among the firms that we are all in this together – it was a very interesting market.')[16]

Some miscreant councils would turn a blind eye to CCT for years, despite the best endeavours of the DAS. But those councils intent on complying with the law offered the Commission a challenge that seemed almost tailor-made for the Special Studies directorate. Some of their most basic municipal activities had scarcely ever been subjected to rigorous analysis. Whether they wanted to go on running them competently via their own DLOs, or to cast a more knowledgeable eye over the claims of competing private sector contractors, councils needed to understand the managerial agenda far better than before. Could the Commission help them do so?

Vincent Square's philosophical commitment to competitive tendering had never been in doubt. Indeed, it had argued for much more of it well before the 1988 Act. In the dying days of the Banham era, Occasional Paper No. 3 had championed it in characteristically forthright terms. 'The Commission is aware of a wide range of strategies adopted by authorities to avoid tackling the problems of non-competitive in-house services ... [which] are, quite simply, destroying value to no good purpose.'[17] That paper identified savings worth about £500 million from more CCT in housing maintenance, vehicle management and refuse collection. Part of the Commission's response now was a substantial primer on the mechanics of CCT, *Preparing for Compulsory Competition*, which alerted councils to the many difficult questions it would raise. (When, for example, could they legitimately pull back from out-sourcing work hitherto done by a DLO, if the putative savings were outweighed by the prospective redundancy costs involved?) The primer also included a reminder to councils that the onus for stamping out 'anti-competitiveness' lay, above all, on them. True, auditors were now required to give written opinions on the profitability measures wheeled out by DLOs as part of the bidding process. Nonetheless, 'auditors are watchdogs, not bloodhounds, and should not be expected to seek out every conceivable anti-competitive practice'.[18]

So much for the generalities. By the time this 1988 paper appeared, the Special Studies directorate had already begun turning out a series of remarkably detailed reports on the underlying activities themselves. *Improving the Condition of Local Authority Roads* (1988) added to earlier work on the management of highways. *Competitive Management of Parks and Green Spaces* (1988) looked at the spending of around £800 million a year by local government on the *un*built environment. About half as much was being spent each year on sports amenities, and *Sport for Whom?* (1989) sought to clarify the proper role of local government in this arena. For all their detail, these were usually reports aimed primarily at 'those with responsibility for strategic issues – leaders of councils, committee chairmen, chief executives and chief officers'. The intensification of the CCT regime prompted the Commission to develop alongside them a line of companion papers – typically 70–80 pages long – written specifically for those with responsibility for managing these activities from day to day. These were christened Management Handbooks, and four were published in quick succession: *Improving Highway Maintenance* (1988), *Local Authority Property* (1988), *Building Maintenance DLOs* (1989) and *Local Authority Support for Sport* (1990). These were meaty texts, geared above all to the needs of hard-pressed council officers. Nor did the directorate restrict itself to looking at management activities covered by the CCT rules. While its high-ways team focused on such matters as the optimal number of times a year that drainage gulleys at the side of the road needed to be dredged, other researchers turned their minds to how council-funded museums and art galleries should be managed, or how local subsidies for entertainment and the arts should be handled.

External pressures, though, still determined the choice of topic. *The Road to Wigan Pier?* (1991) was the response, for example, to a registration scheme introduced by the Museum and Galleries Commission. With about 650 museums run by local government, and all of them needing to register by 1992 in order to be eligible for grants, a review of museum services was timely. It also tackled real issues: 'striking an appropriate balance between stewardship of the collection and presenting the results of that work to the public is not easy. [Where the balance is lost] some museums are worthy but dull.'*

ADJUSTING TO THE LOCAL MANAGEMENT OF SCHOOLS

But the most important external catalyst of Commission work in these years, aside from CCT, was the Education Reform Act of 1988. Education had been a sector of particular interest to the Commission from its earliest days. Indeed, an audit guide on school meals had been its very first publication, back in September 1983. (Based on work by the Audit Inspectorate, it had included some prescient obser-vations. 'Where authorities have changed from traditional two-course no-choice meals to cafeteria operations, there is much less waste and more choice for the children; but many children now eat sausages,

---

* Adopting the title of Orwell's novel for the report caused a certain amount of puzzlement. The point about the museum at Wigan, of course, was that it contained few if any original artifacts. Many museum professionals feared that under-funding of their sector was leading too many of their institutions in the same direction. Steve Evans recalled: 'Only two people understood the joke. Somebody said to us one day, "You must have a real committee of people devising the titles of your reports" and we said, "No, it's the controller."' (Steve Evans, interview.)

baked beans and chips, or a similar meal, every day. Many have questioned the long-term effects of this change in eating habits.')[19] For five years, concern over the failure of schools to adjust to the end of the baby-boom era had been a constant theme of the Commission's commentary on the sector, re both secondary and further education. (A progress report, *Surplus Capacity in Secondary Schools*, observed in August 1988 that local education authorities (LEAs) were still burdened with 24 per cent spare capacity.) The radical changes introduced in the 1988 Act, with which the Commission was broadly in sympathy, brought to the fore financial and budgeting issues on which councils needed more urgent guidance.

At the heart of the Act was a new obligation on LEAs to hand over to schools the management of their own budgets. The level of each school's funding would be calculated by a formula and passed over under an operational scheme to be devised by each council for its own area. Management of the school's budget would then be delegated to the school's governing body. Where parents voted for it in sufficient numbers, this delegation could be extended so far as to remove a school from LEA control altogether – schools could 'opt out' and be accorded the status of 'grant-maintained' institutions.

The impact on all local authorities was far-reaching. It was also virtually immediate: LEAs had to submit their operational schemes to the Department of Education and Science for approval by April 1989. The Commission produced an Occasional Paper in June 1988, *Delegation of Management Authority to Schools*, which itemized some of the huge adjustments that were needed. 'Any department which provides services to schools may have to redefine its relationship with them.' The Occasional Paper format, however, could hardly do justice to the complexity of the task ahead. Accordingly, in November, the Commission despatched *The Local Management of Schools: A Note to Local Education Authorities*, which was effectively an instant Management Handbook for LEA officers. It set out in 200 paragraphs over fifty-seven pages a comprehensive guide to next steps.

Powerful voices in Whitehall – including that of the chancellor, Nigel Lawson – had been in favour of cutting local government out of the education sector altogether. This had not happened, under the 1988 Act, but clearly local authorities had had their powers severely curtailed. Unsurprisingly, this did nothing for the morale of their education officers. There was an obvious danger, in the immediate aftermath of the legislation, that councils might neglect those tasks that were left to them.

To help counter this, the Commission produced a report in October 1989 on the role of LEA inspectors and advisers. *Assuring Quality in Education* was an important reminder that the increased autonomy of schools could only go so far. Teaching standards still required monitoring, which remained a responsibility of the authorities – though, as the report noted, 'the amount of observation of teaching by inspectors and advisers is uneven and in some LEAs disturbingly small'. The team behind the report was led by one of Vincent Square's most experienced study managers, Bert Benham, and it included no less than three external experts on temporary assignment to the Commission. Her Majesty's Inspectors of Education provided one of them, and the report was thus a precursor to future cooperation between the Commission and HM Inspectors.

A couple of months later, the Commission elaborated further on the ways in which LEAs could still regard themselves as vital guardians of the schools sector. *Losing an Empire, Finding a Role*, another Occasional Paper, looked mostly at the new role, but it also had things to say about the empire now lost – or needing to be lost.

A recent audit report at a large metropolitan LEA revealed the existence of 37 separate Education Committees holding a total of 265 meetings in one year at a cost, in attendance allowances alone, of £200,000 (or the equivalent of 15 teaching posts). This cannot be allowed to go on under the new arrangements.[20]

As the paper made clear, it was down to elected councillors to ensure that their officers adjusted properly to the new regime. Indeed, the education reforms in this respect duplicated the impact of CCT. Councils now had to operate in a world of more fixed contracts, more delegated operations and more cooperation with external partners.

And members needed to acknowledge that their own contribution to local government had to change accordingly. Howard Davies and Peter Brokenshire gave a lot of thought to this subject over the next several months. The result was a Management Paper in September 1990 entitled *We Can't Go on Meeting Like This: the Changing Role of Local Authority Members.* In effect, it made explicit what had been implied in many of the reports published since 1987. Councils were becoming far more complex organizations. Members therefore needed to streamline their committee structures and agendas, and to demand better information about the performance of services, both in-house and contracted. Only in this way would they be able to focus, as they had to, on 'policy, strategy and results' rather than on day-to-day operational details. The paper was widely noted when it appeared, and much cited in town halls well into the 1990s.

As, indeed, were most of the publications issuing from Vincent Square in these years. In theory, this might perhaps have raised a question mark over the structure established in 1983 as a result of the amalgamation of the Commission and the DAS. More than ever, the public image of the Commission was becoming heavily associated with its reports and papers. Did its control of the leading audit field force now strike outsiders as slightly anomalous? Journalists commented occasionally to this effect in interviews and profiles. But it certainly never bothered Cooksey or his controller. As Davies recalled:

I was quite happy with the slightly ambiguous relationship between an in-house DAS and the Commission. I felt the private firms never really cared about it, as long as they had open access to me and to the studies people, and as long as we managed the market fairly. I never heard anyone really complain about the asymmetry of our having the district auditors as employees. It was one of those things that didn't work in theory, but worked quite well in practice.[21]

WRESTLING WITH THE POLL TAX

And so to something that worked quite well in theory, but scarcely at all in practice. Of all the research projects in the Davies era that were linked to Thatcherite reforms, none was tied so specifically as the work done on the poll tax – or the community charge, as the government wanted everyone to call it.

The story of the Commission's involvement prior to 1987 can be briefly retold. Many members had had grave reservations about it, but Christopher Foster had been one of its early champions and had been co-opted as an 'assessor' to the working party set up at the DoE back in September 1984. Unsurprisingly, the Commission had deliberated for many months over how best to respond to the initial proposals, set out in a Green Paper in January 1986. CIPFA had already produced 'rudimentary but damning analyses' of some technical aspects of the putative tax the previous year.[22] It had been decided to stick to further technical commentary, and John Banham had accordingly sent off a confidential paper to the DoE in November 1986 – to which there seems to have been no response. By the time that Howard Davies came to begin the homework for his new job in earnest, in February 1987, the government was pushing ahead with plans to introduce the community charge even faster than the Green Paper had envisaged. Responses to the paper had been almost unanimously unfavourable within local government, but this had not deterred the latest environment secretary, Nicholas Ridley.

On his first day in office, Davies received a typically blunt appraisal from his Special Studies director. Tristem thought there was 'some point in the Commission developing its own point of view on paying for local government'. But the work would require expensive help from outside consultants, and he had no budget for it.[23] There were others who wanted the Commission to take a stand, too – including none other than the man now charged by Thatcher with chairing her manifesto committee for the approaching general election, John MacGregor. As chief secretary to the Treasury, he approached David Cooksey to ask if the Commission 'would be prepared to do more work on paying for local government and on strengthening local democracy'.

Davies noted: '[MacGregor] appears to be concerned about the implications of the Green Paper proposals and would like the tools with which to change the prime minister's mind.'[24] A week later, on 25 March, Davies was given a fuller picture of the Treasury's concern. He had a private meeting with the only member of the cabinet who had argued against the community charge – Nigel Lawson. The chancellor cautioned his former special adviser against saying anything in public on the subject before the 1987 election. The prime minister, he warned, had 'a blind spot' over it. Lawson thought some work by the Commission afterwards on the detailed implications of the community charge could, however, add a lot of value. But he did not expect its conclusions to differ radically from his own. 'If we came out with the view that [the community charge] should be phased in "over a period of, say, 100 years" that would be fine by him.'[25]

It was a prescient assessment, and advice that Davies and Cooksey were happy to follow. The controller, though, did take the opportunity of a private meeting with the head of the prime minister's policy unit, Brian Griffiths, on 30 March, to say that 'if there were any circumstances in which the Commission's intervention could be used to amend government thinking [on the charge], we could always be asked'.[26] He could scarcely have imagined how long it would take for his offer to be taken up.

In the aftermath of the election, Cooksey and Davies continued to hold back from any involvement. Perhaps they half expected the Treasury's opposition to prevail. It was soon clear this was not going to happen. The two of them had lunch with the new minister for local government, Michael Howard, in his first ministerial post, at the end of July 1987. It was the very day that Howard announced the timetable for the introduction of the community charge and they found him 'surprisingly optimistic'.[27] Three months later, after the 1987 Tory party conference, that timetable was accelerated. The notion of 'dual running', by which the new tax and the old rates system would have coexisted for a while, was ditched in the face of vociferous support in Blackpool for an abrupt end to the rates. Ridley introduced legislation for an overnight switch of regimes into the Commons that December.

Howard was generally given credit for averting a serious revolt within Tory ranks, and he certainly worked hard at his brief. The Commission controller, though, was not one of his converts to the cause. Davies noted after a meeting between them in February: '[Howard] asked me whether I was in favour of Clause 28 of the Local Government Bill. [This was the clause of the Bill outlawing support for homosexuality in local government and asserting that no authority should "promote the teaching in any maintained school of the acceptability of homosexuality as a pretended family relationship".] I said no. He then asked whether I was in favour of the community charge to which I also said no. He seemed to take it in good part.'[28]

The Bill was passed in the Commons by a comfortable majority in April 1988. A few days before the end of the Commons debate, Howard announced that local authorities would receive £25 million in 1988–89 to help them prepare for implementation of the charge. Some research into this had already been begun in Vincent Square. Now it was decided at the Commission that the time had come to publish a detailed exposition of exactly what the community charge would entail, for those who had to run it.

The resulting paper, *Managing the Implementation of Community Charge*, appeared in July as a 25-page guide for auditors. (The Bill received its royal assent on 29 July.) It stopped some way short of recommending a phased introduction over 100 years. But in most other respects, it sent a shot across the bows just as Lawson had imagined it would. The difficulties of moving from a system with 18 million ratepayers to a system with 37 million charge-payers were spelt out in gruesome detail. 'Register compilation is unlikely to be a simple task at any authority,' said the guide (para. 16), before elaborating on eleven specific and quite daunting problems. On top of these were other, more general problems like the adoption of fresh computer systems – which would be necessary in many places – and the communications challenge. 'Explaining the provisions [of the Act] to both new and existing payers will be no easy task . . . This process will be more difficult where an authority has already generated resistance by issuing anti-poll tax publicity' (para. 24).

The guide was scrupulously neutral in tone, but it could not quite avoid altogether any reference to the obvious superiority of the existing rates system. 'The problems of collection will go beyond those implicit in the volume [of payments] increases which are expected. The attempted evasion rate will certainly exceed current experience under rating, where it is virtually non-existent' (para. 36). To illustrate the scale of the management problem faced by councils, the report set down a chilling statistical comparison of the costs of the community charge and of rates in a typical metropolitan district. In the new world, for example, a metropolitan district council could expect to have to handle 50,000 court summonses a year, instead of the 14,000 required under the rates.

The guide, written primarily for the town halls, was widely read at

Westminster. (The *Guidelines for Development of Community Charge Software* that followed in December 1988 was probably scrutinized less avidly.) It prompted many MPs to wonder whether the whole idea was not utterly misconceived. Davies recalled:

They hadn't really understood the sheer scale of what was involved. The councils had not been very persuasive and effective in communicating just what a task it actually was. I think our papers were very influential. People looked at them and suddenly realised that the great joy of the rates, in administrative terms, was that it was hard to hide a house.[29]

Taxes tied to houses were simpler than taxes tied to (easy-to-hide) people. What was more, by charging for houses, you ducked all the problems of chasing after people to keep the system updated. Every ex-householder had the perfect incentive to ensure the registers were altered: they (or, more likely, their solicitor) wanted to pass the rates liability over to the purchaser. Thus, in large part, the information system administered itself. Such simplicity, now it was about to be abandoned, had a powerful appeal.

Gloom over the prospects for the charge only deepened through 1989, as the government tied itself in knots over a safety-net scheme that was supposed to alleviate the impact of the charge on the worst-affected councils. In effect, low-spending authorities found themselves having to watch subsidies being passed at their expense to high-spending authorities. And all over the country, councils drew up spending forecasts for the first year of the charge, 1990–91, that were far above the 'standard spending assessments' (SSAs) calculated in Whitehall as representative of their appropriate spending levels. As a result, the average community charge for the year emerged about £100 per capita higher than the government had intended.

By the time the charge was introduced on 1 April 1990, many of those around the prime minister feared a Tory debacle in the local elections on 3 May. The sense of a political crisis was heightened, of course, by the 'poll-tax riot' that broke out in Trafalgar Square on 31 March, with 374 policemen injured and 339 people arrested. Far from signalling an end to the debate, the launch of the charge therefore triggered a fresh wave of second thoughts and further intense discussion within Whitehall about ways to amend or reform it. The immediate objective was to find some way of ensuring lower charges in the second year. Margaret Thatcher herself was keen to enforce them via a broader (and perhaps even a universal) application of the rate-capping that had been such a feature of the previous decade. The critical difficulty was that the government's lawyers were advising, as Thatcher put it in her memoirs, 'that anything like the scale of capping I wanted to see was unlikely to be sustainable in the courts'. And she could not risk the possibility of defeat in the courts, which might entail a rejection of SSAs and the whole basis of the community charge.[30] In mid-April, two committees of ministers and senior officials were set up, involving both the DoE and the Treasury. 'These groups considered several options, including universal capping; a more generous rebate system; and the possibility of giving the Audit Commission . . . powers to limit council spending.'[31]

At the Commission itself, the controller was approached by Thatcher's private secretary, Charles Powell. Here at last, admittedly rather late in the day, was the request for help that Davies had invited back at the end of March 1987. Powell and others around the prime minister saw two ways in which, just possibly, the Commission's intervention might be used to speed along a change of heart on her part. It was plainly out of the question simply to suggest a major rethink. She would reject that out of hand as a surrender to the defeatists (or, much worse, to the mob). An unforeseen disclosure of horrendous administrative technicalities by the Commission's district auditors, on the other hand – well, that *might* provide the kind of pretext for reform that could ease her and the government off the hook. And if the Commission could also provide some cogent ideas for the content of that reform, given the unavailability of widespread capping, then so much the better.

Davies set to work on a paper. He was invited to present it at a Sunday lunch at Chequers with the prime minister and some of her close advisers on 6 May. There was every possibility of this turning out to be a tense occasion: it would follow three days after the local council elections that no one in government was expecting to be anything less than a disaster. Through the second half of April, the press had a field day with contradictory briefings from ministers and advisers about possible reforms. It was disclosed that Thatcher had set up a cabinet committee, which she was chairing herself, to decide the best way forward. 'Confusion immediately ensued.'[32] Ridley, who by now had moved from the DoE to be the trade and industry secretary, attacked the idea of any major reforms. His successor, Chris Patten, was hard at work on a reform agenda.

Then came the elections. Unfortunately for the advocates of a radical change of direction, the results were far from a disaster for the government. In fact, they turned out to offer something for everyone. The Tories picked up votes in Labour-held London boroughs with a high community charge. In Conservative-controlled areas outside London with similarly high charges, Labour did well. Happiest of all, though, was Kenneth Baker. He had spent much of the campaign escorting members of the media around the Tory boroughs of Wandsworth and Westminster, extolling their virtues as fiscally responsible flagship authorities. In the elections, the Tories had significantly boosted their majorities on both councils. Baker held up these results as proof of the poll-tax pudding. It was a PR coup that took many MPs at Westminster by surprise, and probably some cabinet ministers too.

Did this fatally undermine all efforts to persuade Thatcher that a major rescue operation was needed on local government financing? Perhaps. In her memoirs, she suggested the election result had shown 'the community charge was already transforming local government. There was the prospect that . . . local government elections could now be fought and won on genuinely local issues and the local record . . .'[33] But the planned lunch at Chequers still went ahead on 6 May. It was an unusually hot Bank Holiday weekend, and Howard Davies duly went along with his completed paper. In light of the calamitous outcome for the prime minister of her subsequent decision to soldier on with the community charge, Davies's paper and his note of the discussions with her that day are an intriguing record of a road not taken.[34]

His three-page brief, entitled 'Rehabilitating the Community Charge', wasted no space on the technical obstacles. These had been detailed already by the Commission, and seemed unlikely to be of much interest to the prime minister. He set out instead only a brief summary of the problem that he judged she would find acceptable.

The average charge was far too high. Councils, being rational, had done everything possible to muddy 'the waters of comparison' between them. The basis of calculating spending assessments (the SSA review) was poorly understood. Lifting the level of Whitehall grants was no guarantee of lower charges and might simply result in even higher spending. And the new system had been hobbled by 'the inevitable anomalies'. He had a package of three remedies, with a possible fourth for consideration.

First, the SSA review should be made transparent to the public, preferably with some adjudication by an independent commission. Second, instead of trying to cap councils, the government should compel them to hold a local referendum wherever they proposed to spend, say, 10 per cent in excess of the SSA. The ballot paper would carry the alternative spending proposals from the opposition, properly approved by the council treasurer, and no council could proceed without 'a clear majority on a decent turnout'. And third, the responsibility for collecting vehicle excise duty (VED) should be transferred from central to local government. Authorities would be allowed to raise rates and to levy differential rates on cars, for example by taxing them more in cities than in rural areas. 'There is an environmental case for higher taxation on cars . . . Some of the opprobrium attributable to higher rates . . . would be attracted to local councils.'

The optional fourth idea was that the government should arbitrarily exempt the 20 per cent of payers who were at present being awarded 80 per cent discounts. The theory that everyone should pay was fine; but in practice the outcome was a nonsense. On average, these payers were chipping in £6 each. It was costing £15 to collect this – and, of course, these payers would account for the lion's share of subsequent collection problems, court summonses, sensational tabloid stories and the rest.

According to figures calculated for Davies at the Commission, a combination of these measures could allow the average charge to be cut from £370 to £280. This would entail an additional cost to the Exchequer of just £1.5 billion, assuming a rise in VED from £100 per vehicle to £175. This was his 'poll-tax mitigation' package – and once lunch was over, Davies had the chance to present it in a meeting with just the prime minister and the head of her policy unit, Brian Griffiths.

The VED proposal was discussed at length, but it seemed clear to Davies by the end 'that they will not go in that direction in the long run'. Similarly, the idea of exempting the 20 per cent payers 'was not ruled out, out of hand', but raised fundamental difficulties, given the importance of universal payment to the whole rationale for the community charge from the outset. Thatcher responded with some enthusiasm, however, to the idea of making the SSA review more public by introducing an independent body to look at it. There was some talk 'about whether the Audit Commission could undertake this work' and it was agreed that the idea should be taken further. She seemed a little more ambivalent about the referenda suggestion, but Griffiths 'was highly enthusiastic and said that it could be attractive from an accountability and democracy point of view and would be good for the prime minister's image'.

After they rejoined the other lunch guests – Charles Powell, Gordon Reece, Brian Griffiths's wife and the prime minister's former parliamentary private secretary, Michael Alison – there was a short further discussion about the community charge, and the nuisance posed by its inclusion in the retail price index. But the afternoon soon drew to a close. Thatcher passed a copy of Davies's paper – an aide-memoire, she called it – to Powell and it was left that he and Griffiths would follow up with its author. (No one at any point mentioned Chris Patten or his (just appointed) junior minister, Michael Portillo, the two members of the government most directly responsible for the charge.) Davies did indeed receive a call on the Tuesday morning from officials at the DoE. To their evident dismay, they had been given instructions from Downing Street to start preparing a new raft of reform possibilities. Chris Patten, it seemed, had reacted positively to Davies's paper – Davies thought he saw it as 'actually quite a useful intervention' – and was happy for work to start immediately.

Within a month or so, however, the whole initiative was called off. At the end of June, Michael Portillo in effect pronounced the end of all the reform discussions when he spoke at the Association of District Councils' annual conference. By the middle of July, Chris Patten was unveiling detailed plans for the continuation of the flat-rate poll tax into 1991–92. So what had happened? Thatcher recalled the moment

in her memoirs. 'Throughout May and early June papers were produced and discussions between ministers and officials held . . . But
suddenly the whole basis of our discussions was changed by new legal
advice.' Contrary to earlier understandings, the government's lawyers
had suddenly come round to the view that widespread capping of
councils would after all be permissible under the existing law. Court
action later in June strengthened the advice by affirming that the SSA
system was an acceptable basis for the estimation by the government
of individual councils' spending needs.

In other words, the government was free to cap as many individual
councils as it wanted for 1991–92. Thatcher would have preferred to
continue exploring general powers. She had clearly also been thinking
hard about one of the ideas of 6 May.

I would have liked to combine this [universal capping] with the use of local
referenda, so that an authority which wanted to spend more than the limit set by
central government would have first to win the agreement of its electorate. This
would have done a good deal to defuse the accusation that new spending controls
would undermine local democracy.[35]

But all that, and any chance of a more transparent SSA process too,
now went by the board. The lawyers had opened up a pragmatic way
forward and she took it. Indeed, the best historical account of the
episode, published in 1994, was in no doubt that she embraced it
enthusiastically. The lawyers' advice 'was manna from heaven'. Some
concessions were made in the following weeks, in so far as additional
Whitehall grants were made available to assist poorer households in
1991–92. But there was no longer any question of major amendments
to the system. 'The prime minister had decided that the worst was
over . . . [and] it was just a question of sitting in the Downing Street
bunker and waiting for the shelling to stop.'[36]

In much the same spirit, the Audit Commission turned to helping
councils adjust to the new fiscal regime. David Cooksey, in his Chairman's Foreword to the 1990 Annual Report, warned of 'danger signs'
across the local government landscape – not least the jump in spending
budgeted for 1990–91 that was apparent at many councils. The work
of the Commission and its auditors, he suggested, was 'more important
now than at any stage since the Commission was established'.

Understandably enough, every audience addressed by the controller wanted to hear his views on the situation. Given his private reservations and the media's ravenous appetite for signs of any fresh revolt, it was a delicate time. Davies developed a nice line that usually saw him out of trouble. What an extraordinary phenomenon it was, he would say, this new tax! Why, the controversy around it had even managed to infect the language of political debate. Those who supported it insisted on calling it the 'community charge', while those opposed to it were equally stubborn about calling it the 'poll tax'. It was all deeply unfortunate. 'And that, ladies and gentlemen, is absolutely all that I propose to say about the poll tax!'

The Commission, anyway, had to deal with the situation as it found it – and its duty was to assist local government. Its previous short guide had addressed the challenge of inaugurating the community charge. Now it looked at the tasks involved in managing the charge – from registration and billing to benefits, collections and the recovery of payments in arrears. Guidelines were prepared for CIPFA by Harry Wilkinson on some of the more ticklish accounting issues. (Wilkinson recalled: 'There was a thing called the Collection Fund. I remember devising how this should work and writing a standard footnote . . . [which I then expounded by] giving seminars round the country. It was quite pleasing when you saw every authority collecting the poll tax was using your standard footnote – I found that quite satisfying in an anorakish type of way.')[37] Seminars were held for audit teams across all the districts. And the Commission produced a 36-page Occasional Paper which was to be the first of a series dedicated solely to the community charge.

Published in November 1990, *The Administration of the Community Charge* was a daunting read. But then, the demands being made of council officers all over the country were pretty daunting, too. The pages of the Occasional Paper gave a vivid glimpse of their travails. With gritty professionalism, most had established a register of charge-payers by December 1989, as required. This had been difficult enough. What was apparent by late 1990 was that every register was going to require constant updating. Based on evidence collected by the Commission for the January–August period of 1990, it looked likely that an average district authority could expect to have to change about a third of the entries each year. In London boroughs, the turnover rate would probably be closer to a half.

The complications attending the register – and every other aspect of the charge – were laid out with the usual exemplary graphics and 146 paragraphs of deadpan text. It was posted to councils all over England and Wales. And within days, doubtless while a good many had yet to be pulled from their envelopes, Thatcher was gone. Michael Heseltine returned as environment secretary in the new government formed by John Major at the end of November. On 5 December, Heseltine announced a full review of the community charge. The team asked to find a replacement for it was made up exclusively of DoE officials, though the Treasury kept a close watching brief. Within four months, the last rites had been administered and the charge replaced by a council tax, to be introduced in April 1993.

Nothing was asked of the Commission through this period. Its only contribution in the months after Thatcher's resignation consisted of occasional reminders to Whitehall of the heavy burden that was being placed on local authority treasurers by the breakneck speed of the council tax's introduction. The controller, though, may have allowed himself a wry smile in March, when the new chancellor unveiled his first budget. Norman Lamont stunned the Commons with a huge reduction in the poll tax for 1991–92. His reduction of £140 was not so far from the £90 proposed by Davies – though Lamont opted not for a hike in vehicle excise duty but an additional two and a half percentage points on VAT. Engineering a quantum drop in the poll tax was known in Whitehall as the Big Bertha option. The outcome of Lamont's budget for local authorities was indeed a bombshell: the 1991–92 community charge bills had been printed, and in many cases posted already. All had now to be reprinted. It was an appropriately messy ending to the whole sad saga.

SOMETHING STRANGE STIRS
IN WESTMINSTER

The size of its Tory majority in the local elections of May 1990 was not the only surprise sprung by Westminster City Council around this time. In fact, for those closely involved with the council and its colourful Tory leader, Shirley Porter, surprises had been almost a feature of Westminster local politics for a few years now. One person who could certainly attest to that was the council's auditor, John Magill.

Magill was a leading partner in Touche Ross, the private firm with the smallest share of the audit market in local government through the 1980s. Since Westminster had for decades been regarded in many ways as the premier council in England, it was an oddity that its audit should have fallen to a firm with no local authority clients in England or Wales before 1981. It was a plum dropped in its lap by Michael Heseltine in pre-Commission days. Westminster was one of the councils to which he arbitrarily assigned his 'additional district auditors' drawn from the private sector – and he gave it to Douglas Morpeth, a luminary of the accounting profession who happened also to be a figurehead partner at Touche Ross. Morpeth retired in 1986, and the plum passed to John Magill.

Magill was a busy man. Now 42 and a partner in the firm since 1975, he was a mainstay of Touche Ross's thriving privatization practice, advising the government on its sale of British Gas and of the water industry. He was about to become, in 1987, the head of his firm's national accounting and auditing department; and he also handled all of the firm's litigation. He had led Touche Ross's work in tendering for Audit Commission mandates since 1983. (He would know all about value-for-money issues, his colleagues had reckoned at the outset, since he had worked for three years in the firm's consultancy business.) But Touche Ross had picked up only a few additional audits since then, and the work was not a huge burden on Magill's time. Taking over personal direction of the glamorous Westminster job in 1986 was a feather in his cap and might, he hoped, open up more doors in the public sector. But otherwise it would not mark much of a change to his workload. Magill recalled: 'I went into what I perceived to be the simplest, cleanest, most straightforward audit that you could possibly imagine.'[38]

Surprise number one for the new Westminster auditor arrived within months of his taking over from Morpeth. He was presented by a group of opposition councillors with a statutory objection to the city council's accounts. It had been failing for years to levy any charge on local businesses for the collection of their commercial rubbish. When Magill looked into it, he found that Morpeth had actually agreed in 1981 that this was illegal and had twice tried to persuade Tory councillors to charge for this service. His first attempt had been rebuffed by the head of the committee responsible for the task, an ambitious and publicity-seeking councillor called Shirley Porter. Two years later, and newly installed as the leader of the council, Porter had rejected Morpeth's advice a second time.[39]

Many Commission auditors spent a lifetime in the field without ever encountering a statutory objection. Certainly Magill was poorly prepared to handle this one on his own: 'I had very, very little knowledge of local authority structures and regulations, frankly.'[40] The Commission came to his aid. Its genial associate controller, Ian Pickwell, was a qualified barrister and a fluent writer. He assisted Magill through the process of a public hearing – involving a dozen or so people one evening, in a small committee room of City Hall – and he helped him to write up a subsequent 'statement of reasons', supporting the final decision. Magill upheld the objection, and Porter's council backed down.

The next big surprise popped up in 1988. It involved Magill in a rerun of much the same process. Objections were received to the accounts; a public hearing needed to be held; and reasons needed to be stated publicly, in writing, for the auditor's eventual view. This time, though, the issue in contention attracted a great deal more public interest.

Once installed as leader in Westminster's City Hall in 1983, Shirley Porter had soon proved to be a very different kind of politician from the broad run of men and women who sat as councillors in English local government. She asserted her own control over the council in ways that drastically reduced the status of its professional officers while at the same time diminishing the accountability of the small clique of politicians around her. In the four years prior to her election as leader, a bare handful of senior officers retired; in the following four years, almost fifty first- and second-tier officials quit.[41] Porter ran the council's affairs with a sharp eye to the coverage she could win in the national media. And she set out to make Westminster a byword for the kind of ruthless efficiency that she construed as the essence of Thatcherism.

This involved a fierce crackdown on spending – which prompted a bizarre decision, in 1986, to sell off three north London cemeteries which were costing the council over £400,000 a year to maintain. The council persuaded itself that it was under no legal obligation to run cemeteries. These three brought in no revenues and were just, as Porter later put it to Magill, 'a liability to Westminster rate-payers'.[42] They were sold for 5 pence each, together with a handful of buildings and twelve acres of grazing land, in a deal valued altogether at 85 pence. (The pennies were netted off against a cheque for £70,000 which the council had to write out to the purchaser, in a final mad twist to the whole transaction, because vacant possession to a cemetery lodge had been promised in the contract and could not in the end be delivered.) Apparently jubilant at saving themselves the annual running costs, Porter and her colleagues seem not to have asked themselves why anyone would voluntarily take on such an open-ended financial burden.

The short answer, of course, was that the buyer – a shrewd north London property surveyor called Clive Lewis – had spotted the re-sale and rental value of the buildings included in the package. Sure enough, this value was soon realized to the tune of several hundred thousand pounds. The council had acted with extraordinary commercial naivety. But there was a longer answer, because the council had also shown astonishing ineptitude in drawing up the sale contract. Not entirely oblivious to the political risks posed by any neglect of the cemeteries, the council had included a covenant relating to their future upkeep. Unfortunately, the covenant was legally binding only on the immediate purchaser. Disastrously, it did not apply in the event of a re-sale. The re-sale duly followed, in 1987, in a deeply murky series of transactions linked to the prospect of future planning permission for the grazing land. Inevitably, the subsequent owners ignored the cemeteries themselves, where 200,000 graves 'would soon disappear beneath long grass, brambles and discarded syringes'.[43]

Shocked relatives and opposition councillors mobilized for action early in 1988. The story became a national scandal – one of the three cemeteries was located in East Finchley, Margaret Thatcher's constituency – and a series of objections were lodged with John Magill by May. To establish the facts, Magill delved into the murk and interviewed dozens of people over the summer. Then, once again with Ian Pickwell's help, he wrote a Public Interest Report that was published in November 1988. At this point, Pickwell's role was taken over by the Commission's new in-house solicitor, Tony Child. There was much to do. The level of interest in the case – and the stance taken towards public hearings by the courts during the legal battles over the Lambeth and Liverpool late rate-setting saga – left Magill no option but to press ahead with elaborate arrangements for a public hearing. It promised to be a lively affair. Porter's political opponents were determined to make the very most of the opportunity to embarrass her in front of the national media.

Understandably, Magill felt some nervousness in the days leading up to the event. (He was, after all, a commercial accountant, not a High Court judge.) Held on 19–21 July 1989 at County Hall, the old headquarters of the GLC, it lasted three days and played to a packed house. There was scarcely a precedent for any hearing over an objection being hijacked by a political protest in this way, but the proceedings passed off without a blip – leaving the auditor to begin his compilation of a scathing final report on the whole disastrous transaction. It was published in February 1990. He identified twenty unlawful actions, ascribing them to 'negligence and misconduct', but stopped short of surcharging any individual officers or councillors. (The sale was eventually reversed by the council in June 1992 – though the land and buildings were excluded from the re-purchase – and an annual contract was awarded for the maintenance of the cemeteries. Labour councillors estimated the episode's net cost to the council at £4.25 million.)

Magill and Child, though, would later remember the County Hall episode for more than just the crowds that milled around the hearing. At the end of the first day, a Wednesday, Tony Child was handed an

envelope addressed to the auditor. Inside, he and Magill found yet
another objection to Westminster's accounts. This one was based on
the Porter-led council's decision, since July 1987, to pursue a carefully
targeted programme of council-house sales that was allegedly aimed
at reducing the number of Labour-voting tenants in key council wards
and attracting (supposedly) Tory-voting home-owners in their place.
It was signed by twelve 'objectors', led by a Labour councillor, Neale
Coleman. And that night, BBC television's *Panorama* current affairs
programme – transferred to the Wednesday evening, though its regular
slot was a Monday evening – ran a devastating feature on the same
allegations. Two days later, for good measure, a further letter from
the objectors was handed to the auditor and his solicitor, identifying
the council's alleged policy explicitly as 'gerrymandering'.

Here was another nasty surprise for Magill. The cemeteries episode,
while hardly covering the council in glory, had made little difference
to his basic assumption that Westminster remained one of the best-run
authorities in England. Magill recalled: 'I thought the cemeteries
business was a bit of a one-off.'[44] But the latest allegations went to
the heart of the council's decision-making process. If it was true that
this had been distorted to confer benefits on the ruling political party
at the expense of Westminster's ratepayers, then the implications
could hardly be more serious. But *was* it true?

Magill and Child applied immediately to the BBC for access to the
documents that had been shown in the *Panorama* feature. Entitled
'Lady Porter – the pursuit of power', the documentary was the outcome of an intensive investigation by one of the programme's most
respected and senior reporters, John Ware. (His commentary had cut
straight to the chase. 'With a little help from Mrs Thatcher, Shirley
Porter is credited with cleaning up much of dirty London. But tonight's
Panorama discloses how she's spent millions of pounds of ratepayers'
money to try to keep her Tory council in power, a policy which may
be unlawful.')[45] Some difficult discussions ensued, and a meeting was
arranged between Howard Davies and the BBC's head of news and
current affairs, Ian Hargreaves. Davies explained the legal position
and the auditor's powers – and Hargreaves agreed the BBC would
assist Magill's inquiries. After all, a facsimile of the most critical paper
had been shown on television, so was in a sense published evidence

already. The documents were handed over early in September. Others requested from the council itself arrived a few weeks later. (Or at least, most of them did – the most critical were actually withheld, but it would be a long time yet before this was realized.) Davies had to stand by Magill in other ways, too. The leader of the Labour opposition on Westminster Council, Paul Dimoldenburg, pressed Davies hard to appoint a special auditor as a way of speeding up the investigation into the *Panorama* allegations. He was particularly incensed that Magill stuck to his plans for a family holiday in August. The controller expressed complete confidence in Magill and refused to intervene.

There then followed several months of tortuous negotiation with the council, as Magill struggled to have all of the relevant files in City Hall made available for his inquiries. The courts decreed half way through 1990 that the resolution of the objectors' case against Porter and her colleagues would be left to Magill – but this hardly seemed to make his progress any easier. Documentation presented by the council was, as he later complained, 'far from complete'.[46] But by December 1990, he and Tony Child were ready to begin a programme of formal interviews. And, as these interviews progressed, the biggest surprise of all began to dawn on Magill. He recalled:

Since 1986, I had been working with all the senior officers. I knew them all very well, including the managing director. I wouldn't say they were friends, but we were all on good terms, personally. The idea that these people, many of them leading figures in their own professional bodies, might not be straight was something that had never really crossed my mind.[47]

Alas, the sheer weight of evidence that now began to surface forced Magill to an unsavoury conclusion. He and Child were being seriously misled and worse, as they struggled to pursue their investigation.

Attempts were also being made to block their path completely. As the interviews proceeded through 1991, Howard Davies was contacted by officials at the DoE and told that Porter had been into the department to see Michael Heseltine. She had told him that the Commission was running a political campaign against her council, led personally by the controller, and had appealed to the secretary of state to call a halt to the whole process. The officials talked to Davies at some length, then briefed the minister. Heseltine subsequently made no attempt whatever to intervene.[48]

Considering the lengths to which the District Audit Service had gone in pursuing the miscreant Labour councillors of Lambeth and Liverpool, any suggestion that the Commission or its auditors in the field were inclined to throw in the towel at Tory Westminster would of course have been highly inflammatory. Nonetheless, the stakes in pursuing Porter were high for all concerned in Vincent Square.* David Cooksey and Howard Davies never flinched in their support for Magill's investigation, or their backing for Tony Child in his role as Magill's solicitor. But there would be little room for mistakes, in what was clearly set to be a very protracted business indeed.

ACCOUNTING FOR CAPITAL ASSETS

No one ever called on a secretary of state to complain about Harry Wilkinson. The famously diffident head of the Accountancy Practice directorate was never going to appear on television's *Question Time* or be invited to lunch at Chequers. Behind the scenes, however, Wilkinson in these years was a driving force behind one of the most important developments in local authority accounting for decades. One outcome was that every council in Britain had to compile another register. This one was almost as problematic as the community-charge register, and intellectually a great deal more challenging. Once assembled, though, it would prove rather more durable. It comprised a register of fixed assets – everything owned by the authority, from schools to scaffolding – with a note of each asset's current value. Its introduction was central to the fundamental reform of a tangled web known to treasurers across the land as capital accounting.

Wilkinson rightly received much credit for CIPFA's first Account-

---

* Towards the end of 1991, for example, someone in City Hall called the *Evening Standard* newspaper on a Friday afternoon with a tip-off that Davies was about to be fired. Through the weekend journalists contacted the Commission members one by one to try to substantiate the story – and one by one the members all telephoned the controller to alert him to the canard and to reassure him of their full support (Davies, interview).

ing Code of Practice when it was published in July 1987 – as did Cliff Nicholson, as usual a key player in the background. As the two of them were the first to admit, however, the code was seriously deficient in a critical respect. It had nothing new to say about a chapter of the accounting rules that had survived virtually unchanged since the first councils had opened their books at the end of the nineteenth century. For almost a hundred years, local authorities had kept track of their assets in a fashion that by the 1980s was looking frankly bizarre. The Companies Act had long required businesses to show all their fixed assets in the balance sheet. Elaborate accounting standards laid down how the value of any asset should be reduced over time, to reflect its declining economic value. Each periodic reduction in value had to be run as a depreciation charge through the profit and loss account. And where a business borrowed money to buy an asset, the capital transaction would be kept quite separate from the profit and loss account. Repayments prompted direct adjustments to the value of the loan shown on the balance sheet, but only the interest charges would show up as a charge against revenues.

None of this applied to local authorities. Assets held for generations were usually completely absent from the balance sheet. Recently acquired assets might be there, but their value in the accounts could vary wildly, depending on how their purchase had been financed. (Those bought out of cash reserves, as was happening increasingly often, might not be shown at all.) Capital transactions, meanwhile, were included in the profit and loss account: loan repayments could be charged against revenues, just like interest charges.

The consequences made a mockery of public sector accounting. It was a problem to which John Banham had alluded at the end of 1986, in drawing the attention of the Public Accounts Committee to the £10 billion backlog of maintenance work on the country's council housing: it had 'sneaked up on us without the accounting anywhere flagging that this is happening'.[49] As a report from CIPFA would later put it with disarming bluntness, there was a 'virtually complete absence of historical cost information about the assets held' by individual councils.[50] This generally ruled out any meaningful comparison between the accounts of different authorities. It also hampered the treasurer of any individual authority who wanted to assess the real efficiency of its various services: there was simply no way to quantify properly their separate usage of the council's underlying assets. This feature of local authority accounting was one of the most important ways in which it differed from chartered accounting for businesses. Yet as CIPFA noted, '[the] cost of fixed assets used in the provision of services is reflected in local authorities' revenue accounts in an inconsistent and almost arbitrary way'.[51]

In short, councils were not accounting for their assets. In so far as rigorous accounting practices must be a precondition of true accountability for public money, local government could not be held properly accountable. By the time Harry Wilkinson began his close involvement with CIPFA, the public sector branch of the accounting profession had been anguishing over all this for a decade. A review published in 1975 had proposed the introduction of depreciation charges. Another report in 1983 had argued the case for measuring the use of assets by individual services (or 'asset-rental accounting', as CIPFA described it). The debate, though, 'did not lead to action'.[52] As part of his work for the 1987 code, Wilkinson therefore began to devise his own solution to the capital accounting conundrum.

Nothing was included in the code, because Wilkinson came up with a technically brilliant model that most people thought at first would simply pose too many practical problems. As CIPFA later noted, 'it was not possible [in the code] to address and resolve the intractable problem in any meaningful way'. Instead, Wilkinson was asked to head a working party dedicated solely to refining his solution. On the day of the code's publication, a young recruit arrived at CIPFA as a technical manager and was co-opted on to the team. This was Martin Evans, who eleven years later would join the Audit Commission and follow in Wilkinson's footsteps as head of Accountancy Practice. With help from Evans and others at CIPFA, Wilkinson only needed a short time to finalize his ideas. His working party's report was published a couple of months later, in September 1987.

Evans recalled: 'Harry came up with some really good proposals about how we could nail it [capital accounting] once and for all in a pragmatic way, which would be capable of practical implementation.'[53] Essentially, his proposals opened up ways for a council to include meaningful values for its assets in its balance sheet. Realistic valuations would be recorded, and then steadily diminished by amounts that would appear as 'capital charges' in the revenue account and that would represent the economic usage of the assets as well as their depreciation. At the same time, capital financing transactions would in future be kept strictly separate from the revenue account, as in the private sector. Loan repayments would no longer be treated as costs.

CIPFA needed to mobilize support for Wilkinson's reform ideas across local government, which proved to be more difficult than expected. A 'steering group' initially made very heavy weather of it, between January 1989 and September 1990. A 'working group' then needed to begin the job anew early in the summer of 1991, again with active assistance from Wilkinson and Evans. (This helps to explain why fully six and a half years elapsed between the publication of the initial report on capital-asset accounting by Wilkinson's working party and the implementation of its proposals.) Aside from the tortuous politics surrounding the issue, though, there were two main snags. First, the proposed 'asset-rent' capital charges were notional and might seriously dilute the extent to which the revenue account echoed a council's cash position. This would have been unacceptable, since the bottom line of the account was used in the calculation of the council's local taxation needs. Wilkinson played a big part in resolving this by showing how the charges could be reversed out when the time came to use the revenue account for tax decisions.

And second, the capital charges would be based, in effect, on a percentage of the underlying assets' balance sheet values. Every authority would therefore need an accurate register of its assets, showing verifiable current values. For most treasurers, rather remarkably, this work needed to be undertaken *ab initio*. While Wilkinson and his colleagues finalized the accounting treatment for the valuation process, one of the Audit Commission's most respected district auditors was appointed as midwife-in-chief to the birth of all the new registers. This was Will Werry, who travelled extensively round the country and produced *Asset Registers: a Practical Guide* in October 1991, a paper that was highly valued over the next twelve months and beyond. Guidance notes were also issued by the Royal Institute of Chartered Surveyors (RICS). This was probably just as well, given a little technical difficulty that CIPFA's final report noted at the end: 'During our discussions it has emerged that valuers and accountants use the same terminology, but often with quite different meaning.'[54]

Martin Evans spent a lot of time on the road, too. He had been seconded to the Institute of Chartered Accountants in England and Wales (ICAEW) for much of the period since 1989, returning to CIPFA as its technical director in mid-1991 – not least, to help it win support for the capital-asset reform. 'I had to go round [the country] and be ritually slaughtered by treasurers. There was a lot of talk about deckchairs on the Titanic and all that sort of stuff. But we were absolutely committed to getting it accepted.'[55]

And accepted it was. Through the second half of 1992, implementation studies in Solihull and two other boroughs confirmed what many treasurers had actually already concluded: the practical obstacles were less serious than had at first been supposed. A fresh Accounting Code of Practice followed, to give effect to the new capital accounting regime from April 1994. It was estimated that local authorities would need about two years to complete the work on their registers, at a cost of perhaps £6 million. Harry Wilkinson made a final, critical contribution at this stage, thanks to the influence he was able to exert through the Commission on the auditors of the DAS.

Evans continued to bang the drum at CIPFA, but knew the successful adoption of capital accounting would depend heavily on the line taken by the auditors.

Harry established that line. It was 'provided you're taking the steps to get there, we won't be hard on you in the first year. We'll be fairly pragmatic – but we expect you to be there.' CIPFA knew it might not have succeeded, without Harry's practical approach. But nor would we have been able to do it without the intellectual foundations he laid down. So Harry's role should be written up in neon letters.[56]

There are two postscripts to the capital accounting story. Wilkinson's work helped foster a close bond between the Audit Commission and CIPFA that endured. During its first twenty-five years, the Commission was generally seen by all of the key professional accountancy associations as worth involving in important initiatives. But CIPFA drew three of its presidents from the Commission – Cliff

Nicholson, Chris Hurford and Mike Barnes – and this was a fair reflection of a special and lasting tie between the two bodies.

Wilkinson's work also resulted in a link between local government and the National Health Service. He wrote a number of papers for accounting journals in 1988, describing the principles of his capital accounting model. One of his attentive readers would appear to have been the finance director of the NHS. This was a partner of the accountancy firm KPMG, Sheila Masters, who was on secondment to the DHSS. She was able to drive through a thorough-going reform of capital accounting in the NHS over the next two years – and most professional accountants could see a close parallel between the practices she installed and the model Wilkinson had devised. By 1988–89, however, the influence of the Audit Commission on the NHS was about to pass well beyond the sphere of abstract accounting principles.

8

At the Cutting Edge, 1989–91

Government reshuffles bring surprises for some and disappointment for others. The reshuffle that followed Margaret Thatcher's third election victory on 11 June 1987 was no exception. And no one was more surprised by the outcome than John Moore, who had expected to be asked to continue as transport secretary and was astonished to find himself appointed instead as the new secretary of state for health.* Arriving at the dismal offices of the Department of Health and Social Security in the Elephant and Castle, Moore had to adjust rapidly to a considerably more stressful environment. It was a critical time for the National Health Service. Its total cost had risen by well over 30 per cent in real terms since 1979, yet public discontent with the service had become such a dominant item in the news that Labour had put health at the top of its daily briefings for the media through most of the election campaign.

Since the early 1980s, the government had signalled clearly enough its intention to think anew about some of the fundamental assumptions underlying the NHS – not least the way in which decision-making within the largest organization in Western Europe was

---

*It later emerged that the prime minister had actually intended to appoint Cecil Parkinson to health and John Moore to energy. At the last moment, however, Willie Whitelaw pointed out to her that this might in due course require Parkinson to stand up in the Commons and talk about increasing or reducing benefits for unmarried mothers – not a happy prospect, given that Parkinson had just spent four years as a backbencher in the wake of an extramarital affair that had left his ex-lover as a single mother. Jobs were swapped just in time, and Moore went to health instead. (Davies Papers, Nos 68 and 106.)

dominated by its doctors, and by local interests over which White-hall's control was sketchy at best. A fresh structure based on 191 district health authorities had been set up in 1982. A former managing director of a leading supermarket chain, Roy Griffiths, had been installed since 1983 as an adviser to the secretary of state. Hospital 'administrators' had been reborn as 'managers' and reinforced with a first modest influx of external recruits. Hospitals had been assigned de facto chief executives, known as general managers (though they still had no direct authority over doctors). Performance indicators had been introduced, to try to mitigate a crippling lack of managerial information.

Despite all this – or in some respects, as critics were quick to claim, because of it – the furore in the media over the failings of the NHS had raged on. It showed no signs of abating in the wake of the election. Once he had taken aboard his initial briefings, Moore resolved immediately to go on the offensive. The consequences of long hospital waiting lists were being paraded almost daily in the media. He wanted someone to look rigorously at their causes, and a dozen other basic inefficiencies of the NHS. Who better for the job, he decided, than the Audit Commission? Its 1986 report on the social services, *Making a Reality of Community Care* (see pages 146–7), had drawn plaudits from all sides over recent months. Media coverage of its work in local government was almost invariably positive. And it was now being run not by John Banham – viewed askance by DHSS officials – but by Moore's old Treasury colleague, Howard Davies, whose stock in Whitehall was rising fast.

Moore had been Lawson's financial secretary to the Treasury back in 1985–86 when Davies was working as the chancellor's special adviser. The two of them had got along well. (Along with Lawson's parliamentary private secretary, John Major, they had bonded as a kind of political triumvirate within the Treasury.) So it came as no surprise to Davies, a few weeks after the election, when he got a call from Moore asking him out to lunch. They met on 9 July at a res-taurant down the road from Vincent Square. It proved to be one of the more important lunches Davies enjoyed as controller. Moore asked him whether the Commission would be able to take on a series of studies into the management practices of the NHS. It took only a few moments for Davies to discover that the new health secretary knew very little about the Commission's standard modus operandi and nothing whatever about the existing arrangements for the audit of the NHS.

Once these had been explained to him, though, Moore was even keener than before to engage the services of the Commission. He jumped at the idea of appointing the DAS as auditors to the NHS. (He could see no reason, indeed, why it should not also audit the 90,000 staff in the benefit offices run by the DHSS.) By the end of the meal, the two men were discussing how the idea of an external NHS audit might be presented to district health authorities all over the country.[1] It would not be entirely accurate to say the controller was unprepared for this discussion: just in case it might prove useful, he had turned up at the restaurant with a copy of his latest marketing pitch for local government audiences.

In fact, Davies had already given plenty of thought to the notion of adding the NHS to the Commission's core franchise in local government. He had had little choice. Within his first few months as controller, the idea had several times been floated in discussion with him by colleagues in Vincent Square, auditors in the field and private sector accountants in the firms. (As we have seen, Ross Tristem had eyed the NHS audit covetously for years, but given up hope of winning it so long as John Banham was making waves in Whitehall – a conclusion Banham himself thought not unreasonable.) Davies knew, too, that extending the Commission's remit was a hot topic among policy wonks. Those inside the prime minister's policy unit at No. 10 were certainly thinking about it, and even Roy Griffiths at the DHSS had been quite happy to talk over the idea in a discussion with Davies just a couple of weeks before the 1987 election.[2]

After all, local government and the institutional framework of the NHS were just so similar that it was hard *not* to be struck by the potential for a shared audit service. Long gone, of course, were the days when most hospitals had been run by municipal corporations – or, indeed, as infirmaries attached to the local workhouse. In both categories, hospital operations had been a natural part of the district auditor's franchise – and helped explain why the old District Audit

Service had actually reported into the Ministry of Health until 1948.*

After the setting up of the NHS, sponsorship of the DAS had been switched elsewhere and the job of auditing hospitals – and indeed the rest of the health service – had passed to an internal taskforce at the health department. This was still the position forty years later. As Davies explained to Moore in the restaurant on that July day in 1987, for the most part the health service at a local level *had no external auditors*. Instead, a unit within the DHSS, universally known as 'FB4', watched over its finances. (Or most of them, anyway – a small fraction of the work was mandated out to private firms in much the same way as were some local government audits. The FB4 staff referred to their counterparts as 'privateers'.)

So how far did FB4 act as an effective proxy for an external auditor? It was hard for outsiders to judge precisely, since only the DHSS (and its own auditor, the National Audit Office) had regular access to its work. But many – not least within the Treasury – were convinced a better job could be done, and fancied the Commission to do it. Davies himself caught a flavour of this over a lunch he had attended in Birmingham just before the meeting with John Moore. His Birmingham hosts were local partners of the accountants Price Waterhouse. As usual, Davies made a note of their comments later that day.

They have one health authority at the moment and are bidding for ten more. But the proportion of VFM time is only around 10 per cent and they consider that the whole thing is extremely badly managed by the DHSS. They would welcome our taking it over . . . At present, they argued, the fees and days calculation at the NHS [is] completely chaotic and FB4 in the DHSS [is] generally hopeless.

The current finance director on the board of the NHS, Davies also noted, was a partner of Price Waterhouse on secondment.[3]

Feeble as FB4 might be, however, Davies had worked in Whitehall

---

* A Ministry of Health was first established as part of a broader reorganization after the Great War. The DAS had until then reported to a Local Government Board, but was made part of the Ministry of Health from 1919. Ministers of Health regularly appeared as guest speakers at the annual dinners of the DAS through the interwar years. The first to address them, in 1920, blazed the trail with admirable candour, admitting that 'personally I shrink from anything to do with accounts'. (R. U. Davies (ed.), *Watchdogs' Tales*, HMSO, 1986, p. 29.)

too long to have any illusions that a push for it to be displaced by the Commission could be taken on lightly. The secretary of state for health might be keen on the idea – but his officials were decidedly not. Nor were they hearing anything from their colleagues in the DoE that inclined them to give way gracefully. The Commission was fiercely independent, yet highly rated by the Treasury. This sounded like trouble. There was never any doubt that officials inside the DHSS would fight any move to open up the NHS to the Commission. This being the case, as Davies knew and Moore had to acknowledge, it could not happen unless fresh legislation provided a statutory basis for it. This did not preclude the Treasury from beginning serious contingency work on the idea, which proceeded through the autumn. But it did suggest a long slog was likely. The prime minister seemed to confirm as much herself: legislative reforms of the NHS would be on her *fourth*-term agenda, she implied in various comments to the press in December.

By then, Davies was pushing the idea to the back of his mind. The Commission's members were certainly not exerting any pressure on him: they had debated the idea in a desultory fashion over the summer, with mixed views on the desirability of such a fundamental expansion of the Commission's responsibilities. Also complicating matters was the fact that Moore had fallen ill with pneumonia in November. So why waste time and energy clutching at straws?

GAINING ACCESS TO THE NHS

He was in for a surprise, along with almost everyone else in Whitehall and Westminster. On the last Monday of January 1988, Margaret Thatcher appeared for an interview on the BBC's flagship current affairs programme, *Panorama*. It was certain from the outset that the NHS would figure prominently. A one-day strike of nurses was in the offing. Scarcely a day was passing without more shrill NHS headlines in the press. As everyone expected, the prime minister was duly pressed hard in the interview for an instant solution to the crisis. What no one expected was her answer. In a complete about-turn from her position the previous month, she announced that she was herself going to chair a fundamental review of the NHS, its current performance and possible alternatives to its current structure and financing. 'We shall consider all these things ... We shall come forward with proposals for consultations and if they meet what people want, we shall translate them into legislation.'[4]

This came as news to her private advisers, most of the cabinet and every official in the DHSS. Most were baffled, not to say appalled, by what seemed an uncharacteristic gaffe on her part. Her chancellor knew better. He had told her, over a private dinner at No. 11 'on a Sunday evening towards the end of January', that the pressures to spend more on the NHS were now 'almost impossible to resist'. But before any additional money was spent, he favoured 'some kind of review' to determine how best to ensure that it resulted in real value for patients. She had agreed. 'We decided that, because of the sensitivity, the enquiry would need to be small and entirely internal.'[5] Perhaps her enthusiasm for the review prompted an honest slip the next evening. Or perhaps, on reflection, she was ready for a less than entirely internal process – though in other respects, she appears to have gone along with Lawson's suggestions.

The consequences, anyway, were all too plain. Over the rest of the week – alongside their front-page coverage of the nurses' strike – the press made sure that expectations were firmly planted in the public's mind of a radical White Paper on the NHS. A cottage industry promptly sprang up in Whitehall, dedicated to finding something to put in it. The first step involved setting up the review body that the prime minister had just announced. It was launched on 28 January with herself as chairman and was unusually intimate. It had only four other members: the chancellor and John Major (now the chief secretary to the Treasury), along with John Moore from the DHSS and his junior minister, Tony Newton.

That same evening, Davies went to a drinks party at the Carlton Club and heard from a former McKinsey colleague within the Treasury that the prime minister 'had said that it was essential that there should be some quasi-independent external efficiency audit' of the NHS.[6] This did not necessarily mean she was thinking of the Audit Commission, but it was nonetheless encouraging. Davies responded by sending his ex-colleague a full paper on the Commission's working methodology, for him to circulate at his discretion. Davies knew the announcement of the review group would guarantee a seller's market in Whitehall for radical ideas – it could only be a matter of time before the notion of shoe-horning the Commission into the NHS attracted serious attention. Sure enough, two weeks later, Davies and Ross Tristem were summoned to the Treasury, for a secret meeting with John Major. It was not to be disclosed to DHSS officials, and Davies was asked not to discuss the subject with anyone at the Commission either. Discretion was still a key part of the whole process, since his brief as controller gave Davies no authority at all for any official talks of this kind.

The meeting at the Treasury began at 5 p.m. on Friday, 12 February. Tristem recalled:

John Major started off by saying, 'The Department of Health people say they've done everything they can already – there are no savings to be made and the pips are now squeaking.' I told him we'd just done an energy audit on local government and found huge savings, and I said, 'Have they done an energy audit in the NHS?' Major turned straight to the under-secretary at the table, Liz Singleton, and said, 'Ring them up and ask if they've done an energy audit!' So she got on the telephone while we went on talking. Then she came back and said, 'No, they haven't done an energy audit.' Major said, 'Right, that's it!' So we were off to a bright start.[7]

The meeting lasted an hour and a half. Major wanted to know *exactly* how the Commission handled its regularity work, how it coordinated the work of the DAS and the firms, how it pursued its VFM agenda and how its basic model could possibly be applied to the NHS. By 6.30 p.m., when he had to leave for a vote in the House of Commons, Major was half-persuaded but needed to hear more – so he asked them, much to Tristem's amazement, to take the next possible slot in his diary for a return visit. So back the two of them went on the following Tuesday, 16 February, and Major resumed his grilling for another hour. Finally, he closed his notebook and concluded the meeting. Davies recalled: 'In a rather solid sort of way, he just said, "You have persuaded me. I think this is a good idea. I think we should go for this."'[8]

Since John Moore's support could be taken as read, Major's conversion to the cause effectively set the review group's objective on the audit issue. The chancellor's view was never in doubt – and David Cooksey was invited to the Treasury around this date to talk over the Commission's prospective role with him. As Lawson put it in his memoirs: 'if improved value for money, in order to improve the service for patients, was the heart of the matter, then a high-calibre watchdog, as the Audit Commission had proved itself to be in the local government field, was, I felt, highly desirable.'[9]

The eventual outcome, though, was still far from certain. A huge battle ensued between Treasury and DHSS officials over the next few months on a wide range of options for the financing and structure of the NHS. When the horse-trading began over fundamental choices, there was no predicting what might happen to any of the peripheral issues, even one as important as audit. Tristem was on good terms with several of the Treasury individuals involved and participated in a good many of the bilateral discussions. It amused him that the DHSS officials appeared not to have grasped the degree of support for the Commission: 'We had a series of absolutely disastrous meetings with the DHSS, who put every obstacle they could in the way of this [audit proposal]. Their officials couldn't understand why they were losing every argument. They didn't realize the outcome was already set!'[10]

Perhaps. But Davies was working hard to sustain the pressure on ministers and their advisers. He went alone to meet John Moore at the end of March and again late in May 1988, to talk through several variations on the theme of a role for the Commission within the NHS. Moore also helped organize a dinner that was held in the boardroom of the Royal Horseguards Hotel on 20 April under the auspices of the Centre for Policy Studies. Several senior NHS managers together with various politicians and academics attended, and David Willetts, the CPS director (and another former Treasury man), chaired a discussion in which Davies was able to expound at length on the virtues of the Commission to an influential audience. Judging by the responses this drew, though, Davies was less than confident that the potential role of the Commission was yet properly understood. And at the end of the evening, as they were leaving the hotel, Moore suggested to him that they needed to have another meeting. As Davies noted later, he also wanted 'to have it outside the DHSS. He shook his head when referring to them [the DHSS officials] in the context of a role for the Audit Commission which was in itself bad news.'[11]

Davies was given more cheer by Roy Griffiths, who by now had been appointed deputy chairman of the NHS. He had recently submitted to the cabinet a formal paper responding to the Commission's *Making a Reality of Community Care* report. It made several proposals which involved a transfer of more responsibility to local authorities in this area. Ministers rejected this approach rather abruptly. Griffiths was deeply disappointed by their reaction – but it did nothing to diminish his respect for the Commission's work. Meeting him for lunch in June, Davies explained yet again how the Commission would audit the NHS. Griffiths departed saying it had been an extremely helpful discussion – 'and for the first time', noted Davies, 'I thought that it might become a reality'.[12]

Among the NHS executive directors and their DHSS counterparts, however, few reacted as positively as Griffiths. Most remained firmly opposed to any role whatever for the Commission. In one sense, their position was perhaps not unreasonable. As the finance director of the NHS, Sheila Masters, insisted throughout the negotiations, the health sector was different from local government. No one in Whitehall was charged with ultimate responsibility for the performance of councils. They had to answer to their local electors and were constitutionally independent of central government. Therefore it made sense to have a watchdog body keep an eye on them. But the NHS had no such autonomy. It was managed as a hierarchy, reporting into a central executive that was fully answerable for its performance to the health department. To share that responsibility would be to blur it. And every published national report would inevitably be seen as, in some sense, a criticism of the department. It would be better by far to have the Commission's reports produced privately, and handed over to the department with no publicity so that it could quietly get on with the job of pursuing whatever actions were needed.

Davies and Tristem argued otherwise. The Commission would not be *sharing* the NHS executive's power; it would be *complementing* it. Its role would be to provide another lever, to help improve the responsiveness of a hugely complex organization. A direct, hierarchical instruction from the centre might not always elicit the desired response. As an alternative approach, the Commission would offer valuable insights that (it could be hoped) the professionals of the NHS might heed on their merits. The chief executive of the NHS, Duncan Nichol, came round to this way of thinking in the end. Most of his senior colleagues and their DHSS counterparts did not. As Nigel Lawson recalled, the department 'took the view that it was perfectly capable of monitoring Health Service performance itself'.[13]

The permanent secretary of the department, anyway, was adamant. As the ultimate accounting officer for the NHS, he simply could not do his job in the face of an external auditor that did not report directly to him. Moore was strongly advised to have nothing to do with the idea. Still not properly recovered from the pneumonia that had laid him low seven months earlier, he warned Davies regretfully that they were facing a stand-off. And the same applied to the bigger issues being wrestled over by the DHSS and the Treasury. By the mid-summer of 1988, little real headway was being made on any of them.

Fortunately for the Commission, this was wholly unacceptable to Margaret Thatcher. She had taken personal ownership of the whole process: it had to succeed. She moved decisively in July to break the log-jam. The DHSS, freshly located since the start of the year in a recently completed building at the heart of Whitehall, was broken into two departments. Moore was left with Social Security – and a new Department of Health (DoH) was given its first secretary of state: the redoubtable Kenneth Clarke.

Clarke wasted no time before inviting the controller of the Commission and his chairman to visit him at the DoH. He tackled them in straightforward style. He had inherited this idea of an external audit. The Treasury wanted it. His officials were firmly saying 'No'. Could they talk him through the rationale for it? By the end of a lengthy discussion, Clarke appeared to be in favour of going ahead – and he was in fact to remain unwavering in his support for the principle of an external audit from this point onwards. It was entirely consistent with the approach he took to the whole reform initiative. With Clarke's forceful backing, and unrelenting pressure from the Treasury – who were especially adept, as Lawson put it, at 'the knocking down of nonsenses'[14] – the wider reform discussions began to resolve themselves through the autumn.

On the audit issue, an 'NHS/DoE Working Group' was set up. It made good progress on the practical details under a fully supportive senior official at the DoE, Derek Osborn. Progress was also greatly assisted by the enthusiasm of an influential adviser to the Conservative Party on NHS reform, a clever GP called Clive Froggatt. Widely regarded as a key architect of the 'purchaser–provider' NHS that eventually emerged, Froggatt was one of the hardest working and most crucial champions of the Commission's cause.*

By October, the breadth of support for the Commission was clear. At a Treasury dinner that month, John Major told Davies he thought the Commission's NHS arrangements would work out all right. 'There are a lot of powerful people batting for you.'[15] In fact, as the later drafts of a prospective White Paper began to circulate, some people close to the process worried that the Commission's potential was in danger of being overstated. A few months afterwards, Roy Griffiths would tell Davies that ministers had begun attaching 'high importance' to the audit function in these final stages. He worried that there might be 'unrealistic expectations about what could be achieved through the audit process'.[16] But Clarke gave Davies and Cooksey no reason to worry on this score. He met them early in December for a final sign-off on the audit provisions of the White Paper. His own expectations remained unchanged, and were much as agreed between the three of them at the outset. The proposed role for the Commission went into the White Paper, *Working for Patients*, that was published in January 1989.

It emerged a full eighteen months later as the National Health Service and Community Care Act of 1990. In essence, the responsibilities that had been laid on the Commission in 1982 *vis-à-vis* local authorities were now to apply also to health service bodies. The DAS would conduct NHS regularity audits and value-for-money work

---

* Froggatt would go on to act as a kind of guru on all NHS matters to a succession of health secretaries, from Kenneth Clarke to Virginia Bottomley and William Walde-grave. The tabloids later hailed him as 'the most politically powerful GP in Britain' – but savaged him in 1994 when he was arrested and given a suspended gaol sentence for faking heroin prescriptions. Though struck off the medical register in 1995, Frog-gatt later spoke on many platforms as a vocal critic of government policy on drug abuse.

under the supervision of the Commission in line with its existing practice. The statutory powers of individual auditors would be rather narrower – notably, with no application of Sections 19 or 20 of the 1982 Act – and the Commission itself would not carry over into the NHS its Section 27 power to review the impact of government legislation. (The latter dilution was especially a matter of regret to Davies, who considered Section 27 an important element in the Commission's independence from Whitehall.)[17] But in all other respects, the Commission would be expected to replicate its familiar approach exactly.

REORGANIZING FOR AN EXPANDED FRANCHISE

Kenneth Clarke more than once visited Vincent Square for informal discussions over the next few months, to discuss the Commission's progress. Within the Department of Health's new Whitehall headquarters at Richmond House, these visits may not have been regarded as wholly satisfactory, to judge by a conversation that Clarke and Davies had there at the end of February 1989. Davies noted: 'He has been advised to attend the Commission [monthly meeting] on April 6, but officials have suggested that he be accompanied by a large group of them to prevent indiscretions or difficulties. He will attend and I suggested that he should be accompanied by a private secretary plus one.'[18] Clarke accepted this suggestion and joined the members for lunch before the April meeting. The minutes of the meeting recorded: 'The secretary of state paid tribute to the work of the Commission and its auditors in local government and hoped that a similar independent approach could be applied in the audit of the National Health Service.'

The legislative timetable in the January 1989 White Paper gave the Commission about twenty months in which to prepare for its new franchise. The task was nonetheless daunting, once the full scale of it became apparent. There were some parallels with the position in the months prior to the launch of the Commission itself, in April 1983. But there was one huge difference. The DAS in 1983 had been a self-sufficient organization, quite capable of functioning in its old familiar ways even while being subjected to all the excitements of the Banham bombardment. By comparison, the FB4 unit of the old DHSS was a sorry-looking outfit. The White Paper proposed that it be transferred into the Commission. Once this was disclosed, the unit's reporting structure within the DoH was effectively dissolved. This posed an urgent problem. FB4 was a sizeable organization: it had almost 250 people in the field and its gross audit fees from the NHS exceeded £10 million a year. (This compared with around 550 in the field for the DAS, which was budgeting gross fees of £23.5 million for the year about to start in April 1989.) Planning for FB4's transfer needed to be agreed as quickly as possible. Ministerial authority was granted to the Commission to push on with the work immediately, rather than await passage of the Bill. Davies commissioned a quick external study of the best way forward, while some first contacts with FB4 itself were instigated by Cliff Nicholson and Brian Skinner – who had just arrived on the central staff of the Commission, to succeed Les Stanford as the chief inspector of audit (or 'director of audit' as the post was soon afterwards re-christened).

The whole transition got off to a shaky start. To begin with, the Commission staffers were shocked at the low morale and poor qualifications of the FB4 personnel. A bare handful of them had CIPFA credentials and some had no accounting qualifications at all. Whatever its failings, and there were plenty of them, the DAS was a professional culture with a strong *esprit de corps*. FB4 sometimes resembled a back office of an especially drab municipal finance department.

A second surprise for the Commission was the attitude of the senior DoH officials responsible for FB4. They seemed to assume that NHS audits would remain a distinct operation, managed by FB4 within whatever integrated field force emerged in the end. This resulted in a series of uneasy meetings. Once it was clear that FB4 would cease to exist, the health officials promptly began to offer attractive incentive packages to the best members of its staff to stay with the department. As a result, the average calibre of those transferring to the DAS fell some way short of the latter's existing standards. This disparity in skill levels – and some concern, too, about the evident potential for turf battles – encouraged the Commission's directors to go for a complete integration of the health and local government audits from the start. The study that Davies had commissioned externally, *Organizing for the 1990s*, arrived in March and reached the same conclusion.[19] It went a significant step further, though, in also recommending that the merged field force be structured along radically different lines from the old DAS. This was accepted, and preparations for the NHS audit thus led directly into a sweeping reform of the DAS's whole presence at a local level.

In place of the longstanding thirteen DAS districts, the future structure would comprise seven regions. Within each, a regional director with his own office would assume many of the heavier administrative responsibilities that had been an increasing burden on district auditors for some years. He would also be supported by a special adviser (NHS). Below the regional directors, a less hierarchical culture would be encouraged by doing away with deputy district auditors altogether: their role had been ambiguous for years. Immediately below the directors would be the district auditors, whose numbers would rise from 13 to 30 by 1990–91. The number of senior assistant district auditors (SADAs) would be doubled from 60 to 120.

Alongside these changes, the proportion of the NHS audits awarded to private firms would rise from the existing 12 per cent to roughly 30 per cent, in line with the quota for local government work. (The firms, needless to say, responded to this proposal with some enthusiasm, as soon as access to the enormous NHS market became a real prospect.) On this basis, the DAS still had to gear up to handle around 500 of the 700 principal audits within the NHS, on top of the 320 or so it was handling in local government. To manage the process as a discrete project – working alongside Brian Skinner's small staff and reporting to Cliff Nicholson – Davies turned again to his friend Martin McNeill, who was about to graduate that June from the London Business School. It was McNeill's LBS dissertation that had been adapted six months earlier for publication as the second Management Paper, *More Equal than Others*. Now he was happy to work again with the Management Practice directorate. He and Peter Brokenshire got along well – not least, perhaps, because McNeill had had some

direct experience of local government, having been a Labour councillor at Camden in 1978–82 – and he would contribute to further
Management Papers while handling the reorganization assignment.

The head of FB4 took immediate retirement, but McNeill worked
closely with two of his three deputies – the third, Ken Sneath, managed
FB4's special studies work – and they coordinated a massive round
of interviews. To pre-empt any impression of unfairness, all of the
DAS's existing staff were actually included in the interview process,
as well as FB4's staff. The formal position was that a job needed to
be found for every member of FB4 wishing to accept a transfer. In
practice, many opted to accept improved terms within the DoH –
including some who were only offered roles in the DAS that they
regarded as beneath them.

This gave rise to some acrimony, especially at the most senior levels.
The ostensible equivalent of a district auditor within FB4 was called
a 'statutory auditor'. The Commission hoped at the outset that a
significant number of the dozen or so statutory auditors might be
assimilated into its own enlarged corps of DAs. Despite its obvious
political attractions, however, this happy outcome simply could not
be engineered: two thirds of the statutory auditors either lacked the
requisite skills or sniffed at the prospect of a transfer. As one of them
candidly confessed to Cliff Nicholson at the time: 'No, I don't want
to come to you. I don't agree with any of this and I've got the Queen's
commission in my pocket – so what more could I want?'[20]

In the end, only around 110 of FB4's staff of 260 made the move
(and many of them struggled to make the grade in subsequent
years). This reduced the recruitment needs of the DAS to a slightly
more manageable level – but the drive to hire new auditors, together
with the additional training of its current staff, and the expansion
of computer and other support facilities, nonetheless posed a huge
administrative and technical challenge. Harry Wilkinson soon found
himself, for example, making regular trips to the headquarters of the
NHS at Quarry Bank in Leeds to take charge of seminars on future
accounting policies and practice. The service rose to the challenge
with remarkable success. Cooksey recalled: 'The DAS slipped into its
new NHS role in the oddest fashion – looking back, it was really
extraordinary how well it coped.'[21] In the face of considerable scepti-

cism within the DoH, it took over the NHS audit franchise in October 1990 with scarcely a blip. As for the Commission (as opposed to the auditors), it faced no substantive change in its working model: it had to continue in its role as the 'purchaser of audits', only adjusting to the hefty enlargement of its constituency.

Two other organizational innovations need to be mentioned here for the contribution they made to the outcome. The first, unrelated to the NHS, resulted from a paper for the Commission members by Cliff Nicholson in August 1988. The deputy controller had taken stock of all the additional audit tasks implied in the government's heavy legislative programme affecting local government. Unless DAS audit teams were granted additional days to complete these tasks, value-for-money work would inevitably be ditched to make time for them. Nicholson proposed that local authorities be told of the extra days, and costs, required – and the members backed him. His figures were presented at a conference with the AMA, the ACC and the ADC in September. It was a measure of the Commission's rapidly improving relations with all three that agreement was quickly forthcoming. (Some members of the associations still referred to David Cooksey as 'Maggie's Hammer', a nickname bestowed by the public sector unions, but their hostility was skin-deep.) The scheme governing any resort to additional time was introduced with the 1988–89 audit round – and the extras were henceforth known as 'Nicholson days'. Over the next three audit rounds, Nicholson days added 20 per cent to the local government workload handled by the Commission.

The other innovation, introducing 'special project officers', had been prefigured in *The Way Ahead* back in 1987. That paper had acknowledged that relying on fully qualified auditors to conduct all VFM work was not making the best of the service's resources. By introducing project officers (the 'special' tag soon disappeared) to handle non-audit work, costs could be reduced – and the resulting VFM work might also be improved, since each project officer could take on the same project many times over, acquiring more expertise that most auditors would have time to develop. In practice, few project officers had been recruited by 1989. Only Will Werry, the enterprising district auditor in Birmingham, had made much headway with the idea. But winning the NHS changed that. Training for VFM audits in the health sector was going to be far more intensive. Assigning fewer individuals to handle larger proportions of the work on each audit would pay even bigger premiums. Cliff Nicholson soon found himself being badgered by Ross Tristem to take on many more project officers. Tristem recalled: 'We had a bit of a battle about that at first, but I think in the end we agreed to try it on an experimental basis.'[22]

It was an issue that needed managing with care. Some auditors were happy to be told their VFM workload would be lightened, and were guilty in a few cases of treating newly recruited project officers with unwarranted disdain. But others regarded VFM audits as more interesting than their regularity work. They watched the influx of young project officers with some concern. And their numbers grew rapidly. Nicholson quickly acknowledged the benefits and within a few years of winning its NHS mandate, the DAS had hired more than seventy of them. Different skill levels were built into a hierarchy within each of the seven regions. The more senior of the project officers were skilled analysts, and were assigned some demanding roles. In due course, the private firms followed in the footsteps of the DAS, transferring young qualified accountants to the non-financial work. (Indeed, years later, the attractions of the VFM work in the health sector ended up prompting some to abandon their CIPFA training in favour of a career with the Commission's NHS project teams.) Within quite a short time-frame, both audits and special studies within the health sector would come to rely heavily on the contribution of project officers.

This was confirmation of the Commission's true priorities from the start. Unlike FB4, it was never going to be primarily concerned with checking out the financial accounts of the health sector. Its real interest always lay in the pursuit of economy, efficiency and effectiveness. This meant special studies, and all that went with them. Hence the Treasury's enthusiastic backing – and, of course, the bitter opposition of the DHSS. It also meant the Commission was pitching its ambitions awfully high. Nigel Lawson was acutely aware of the obstacles to any reform agenda for the NHS. He summarized them very eloquently a few years later. One formidable obstacle was simply the vast scale of the health service, but there was more to it. The NHS was the closest thing the English have to a religion, with those who practise in it regarding themselves as a priesthood. This made it quite extraordinarily difficult to reform. For a bunch of laymen . . . to presume to tell the priesthood that they must change their ways in any respect whatever was clearly intolerable.[23]

It was a point that others had made over the years. (Indeed, the founder of the NHS himself made it many times in public: addressing the Institute of Hospital Administrators in May 1950, for example, Aneurin Bevan told them: 'medical staffs produce an air of sacerdotalism in the hospital which is very intimidating for the secular mind. You have to stand up against it.')[24] But however familiar the refrain, it had lost none of its relevance. The Commission would have a challenge on its hands.

Kenneth Clarke talked to Davies about this in a private discussion at the end of February 1989. The secretary of state acknowledged that meaningful studies from the Commission would inevitably stray into the domain of 'medical audit' – that is to say, assessments of the relative effectiveness of alternative treatments. This was the preserve of the Royal Colleges, warned Clarke, though there were signs of them accepting the need for a more formal process. Davies noted afterwards: 'He thought many doctors would go for it as soon as they saw what was involved. The difficulty was that some of them, when they heard the words "value for money", heard "cost-cutting", so we would need to be particularly careful.'[25]

This advice was certainly heeded. The controller and his chairman started as they meant to continue, treading with great care through three initial tasks – clarifying the exact breadth of the Commission's NHS remit, finding the right people to take it on and picking suitable targets for the crucial first studies.

PREPARING FOR THE NHS MANDATE

The remit was quickly settled. Davies came away from that February meeting at the DoH confident that Clarke fully intended the Commission to go on with business as usual. The department was accustomed to a different approach by the National Audit Office (NAO).

This had involved a line-by-line scrutiny of every NAO report, but no scope for public comment by DoH officials following publication. Clarke agreed that the Commission should report on the NHS in its own way. It would choose its own subjects, engage with the DoH on an informal consultation basis and then proceed straight to publication – leaving officials free to sling brickbats if they saw occasion to do so. Otherwise, Clarke had had only two demands to make. The Commission should be wary at all times of 'going native'. And it should avoid laying down fresh macro-economic policies for the health service. Davies was happy to reassure him on both counts.[26]

A first detailed conversation with the chief executive of the NHS, Duncan Nichol, ended just as positively in April. He had been reading the early Management Papers published by the Commission. Was that the kind of work the Commission intended to pursue in the NHS? In due course, said Davies. This went down well: Nichol said 'he would favour such an approach and was attracted by the methodology and tone we had adopted'. Nichol also disclosed to Davies, in discussing the regular audit side of the equation, 'that he was aware of discussions and doubts in the Department [of Health] about our future work'.[27]

With broad backing for the Commission's intended approach, it was time to settle on the key appointments. Ross Tristem still had his own network of contacts in the health service from his five years at the DHSS back in the 1970s, and was keen as mustard to add the health brief to his existing role. Davies knew the Treasury would be comfortable seeing Tristem in charge of health studies. The appointment of the Commission's most experienced VFM director would also send a useful signal to NHS managers. But he decided health *and* local government would be too much for one director. After an initial period during which Tristem ran both and set up the NHS work, therefore, Davies split the Special Studies directorate into two. Tristem became the director of health studies, leaving a director of local government studies to be found in due course.

What the new Health Studies directorate then ideally needed, as a back-up for Tristem, was a clever doctor with an original mind, experience of working in the NHS, a good knowledge of public health matters and some acquaintance with financial analysis. It was a formidable wish list. As it happened, however, Davies had known the right man for the job all along. His name was Jonathan (Jonty) Boyce and he had been – like Martin McNeill – a close friend of the controller since university days. He too had recently finished a one-year management course at the London Business School. But he had begun his career with an Oxford First in Psychology, Philosophy and Physiology (PPP), which he had followed up with a degree in medicine, an M.Sc. in public health and a doctorate on the epidemiology of hip fractures. He was a Fellow of both the Royal College of Physicians and the Faculty of Public Health Medicine.

Always looking for a new challenge, Boyce had quickly tired of a stint in general practice. He had served as director of public health in Northampton for two years before his LBS course and had been working since the autumn of 1988 for a private health insurer in Tunbridge Wells. Ever since the spring of 1987, Davies had been talking to him from time to time about the Commission's work on issues such as community care for mentally handicapped adults. Late in 1988 he told Boyce of the impending extension of the Commission into health and asked if he would be interested in taking a pay-cut to join the team at Vincent Square. He wasn't, at that point – but by the time Davies returned to the idea in the early summer of 1989, Boyce was ready to change his mind.

To clinch matters, Davies invited him along to Vincent Square as a guest to hear the inaugural Audit Commission lecture in June. (Subsequently an annual event, this first one was being given by John Major.) There, Boyce met with several of the directors, with predictable consequences. 'I remember going along and meeting Harry Wilkinson and Ross Tristem and others at Vincent Square for the first time and thinking to myself: this is an interesting bunch of characters, this looks fun, this could be an exciting place to work.'[28] He went along to be interviewed by Tristem shortly afterwards, for the post of 'associate director, health studies'. Tristem warmed to him when Boyce started by saying he needed to make a clean breast of his business acumen. He had inherited a small business years ago and had sold it for £10,000. The business was called Filofax – later, of course, a cult brand of the 1970s. Tristem enjoyed that, and the two men hit it off immediately. At the end of the interview, characteristically,

Tristem simply announced, 'That's fine, when can you start?' Boyce went off to China for a month's holiday and started in August.*

Over the next few months, Tristem kept up the pace with a rapid series of new hires to staff his new directorate. Some, like Ian Jones and Paul Durham, were former Treasury colleagues. A few came directly from the DoH, like John Bailey, an economist, and Ken Sneath from its FB4 unit. Some came from academia, notably a research project manager from St Thomas's Hospital called Linda Jarrett. Others again were transferred from the local government side of the Commission – including the now highly experienced David Browning and one of the very few women at a senior level (and a talented cartoonist), Claire Blackman.

It was clear to Tristem from the start that they should adopt the basic business model used by the local government directorate. National studies based on comparative data would be at the core of their work. Each study would generate two products: a glossy report to help publicize the conclusions, and an audit guide ('a painting-by-numbers guide', as Davies used to describe it) to make use of the conclusions at a local level. Tristem appointed Ken Sneath and David Browning alongside Boyce as associate directors. All would have their own teams, and they would pursue separate studies concurrently.

Most of the arrangements for these executive teams had been made by the end of 1989 – but there still remained the question of new

---

* The fact that Boyce, McNeill and the controller had all been at Oxford together took a while to be picked up externally. But when Martin McNeill was finally appointed to the staff, which happened late in 1990, *Private Eye* noted that he had been best man at Davies's wedding in 1984 ('Out of audit' ran the headline) and other connections quickly surfaced. *Private Eye* ran another item in December 1990 saying its previous disclosure 'did not do justice to the generosity of [Davies's] patronage'. Its researchers had discovered that Davies, Boyce and McNeill – together with the present author – had all been contemporaries at Merton College. And, what was more, they had all been members of its wine society – 'and all but Davies were presidents of the society during their time at the college'. The Commission members discussed these revelations in January. In a special minute, it was recorded that the appointments of both McNeill and Boyce had – at the controller's request – involved the chairman and his deputy, though 'neither . . . were aware of the connections referred to in *Private Eye*'. It was agreed controls would be put in place to avoid 'this sort of situation in the future'. The members, though, 'emphasized that they had no reason to be dissatisfied with the performance of the individuals appointed to the posts referred to by *Private Eye*'.

appointments to the Commission itself. By the end of 1989, further departures had seen three more of the Commission's original members on their way. Christopher Foster, Geoffrey Drain and Dudley Fisher had retired in 1988. Of the six originals left, it was now agreed that three more – Ian Coutts, John Gunnell and David Lees – would step down in January 1990. Two members more recently appointed – John Barratt and Eric Meade – had meanwhile gone in 1989 and a third, Elizabeth Anson, would join the retiring members in January.

Five new members had been added to the Commission since 1987. Andrew Likierman was a professor of management accounting at London Business School and ran a small unit within the school dedicated to teaching and research on issues of public sector management. Eleanor James, another academic, taught at Aberystwyth University and added a Welsh viewpoint to the table, as Dudley Fisher had done. Tony Christopher of the Inland Revenue Staff Federation – chairman of the TUC for 1989 – took up the trade unionist's seat vacated by Geoffrey Drain. Alan Brown joined straight from retiring as chief executive of Oxfordshire County Council. And Jeremy Orme, a senior regulator with the Securities and Investments Board, brought with him the rectitude that might have been expected of a former managing partner of a leading City accountancy firm, Robson Rhodes, with more than a passing resemblance to the Duke of Wellington. All of these changes would soon leave the Commission with just thirteen members (including the chairman). Drafts of the NHS and Community Care Bill included a provision for the total number of members to be increased from seventeen to twenty – so by December 1989, the need to find some suitable new members was quite pressing.

Kenneth Clarke, however, was in no hurry. The chairman and controller went to see him in January 1990. They had intended to try to persuade him of the importance of appointing a distinguished clinician to the Commission. Instead, bafflingly, they found him reluctant to appoint anyone at all 'at this stage'.[29] But perhaps their entreaties at least encouraged his officials to speed up their search for health-related members. Two were appointed from managerial backgrounds in March 1990: Peter Wood, who was chairman of Huddersfield Health Authority, and Chris West, who was general manager of

Portsmouth and East Hampshire Health Authority and an executive highly rated by Clarke himself. (A third appointment was made the next month – of John Clout, the leader of North Yorkshire County Council – and this lifted the Commission by April 1990 back to sixteen members, including the chairman.) The Commission had to wait another six months for the appointment of a doctor – a Newcastle-based GP, Donald Irvine, who was chairman of the General Medical Council's Standards Committee. He would be joined, early in 1991, by the most senior figure in the country's nursing hierarchy, Jennifer Hunt, who was also a member of the Clinical Standards Advisory Group.

The main purpose of the visit to the DoH by Cooksey and Davies in January 1990, however, was nothing to do with appointments. They wanted to talk over the prospective costs of the NHS brief with the secretary of state. In particular, they were keen to win his approval for a relatively expensive programme of national studies that was already well under way. Davies noted that Clarke was 'in principle, sympathetic', though warily non-committal. The matter was set to one side, while Cliff Nicholson was delegated over the next couple of months to negotiate the size of the total capital float for the Commission's NHS work.

Nicholson found it heavy going. He was looking for a working balance of approximately £2.5 million, which equated to the float provided by the DoE in 1982, but officials in the Department of Health stonewalled for weeks. 'They'd lost the battle [against the Treasury], they'd lost the audit function and they weren't going to use any money [on us].' Eventually Nicholson went to Richmond House for a showdown meeting. It almost ended in disaster. 'I was making no progress at all – so I just sat back, pulled away from the table and said, "Oh, I'm going! I'm wasting my time here, I guess I'll have to speak to the chairman and get him to talk to Ken Clarke."' The discussion resumed, and the money was agreed. 'But they hated the idea that our chairman had got a direct line to their secretary of state.'[30]

Whether further discussions were ever held, with the secretary of state or anyone else, on the cost of special studies is unclear. But by early 1990 – several months before the NHS Bill was even enacted, and with a mischievous disregard for the niceties of DoH budgeting

– Ross Tristem's Health Studies directorate was already well embarked on its initial work programme. The subjects for the first three reports had indeed been chosen by the autumn of 1989, partly on the basis of consultations with outside parties and partly as a matter of personal inclination and serendipity.

When a shortlist of subjects had been shown as early as April 1989 to Roy Griffiths, he had responded well to most of them – except estate management, which he thought was already being looked at within the DoH. Duncan Nichol had been similarly enthusiastic about the list, again with the possible exception of estate management. Others had been less encouraging. There was no shortage of continuing advice from doctors that the Commission could best add value by looking into matters such as the clearance of bins and the regulation of heating. Nor did officials at the DoH make any effort to disguise their view that the Commission should stay away from value-for-money altogether. The exchanges between Vincent Square and Richmond House had verged on the ludicrous over the summer of 1989: every suggestion from the Commission prompted the rejoinder that work on *that* was already well in hand. Especially, of course, work on estate management.

Tristem was telephoned one morning in the early autumn of 1989 by an under-secretary at the DoH, who rather sheepishly passed on the outcome of a department-wide consultation on possible areas for a study. 'Well, I'm not going to put this on paper', a bemused Tristem heard him say, 'but we have got only one suggestion, and that is that you should look at the use of walking sticks in the NHS.'[31] This, of course, provided just the right opening (as in 1983–4) for Vincent Square to do precisely what it wanted. The Commission staff resolved to look at two areas with a strong clinical dimension, leaving a third to concentrate on something more purely administrative.

As a senior registrar at a regional health authority from 1981 to 1985, Jonty Boyce had developed a strong interest in day surgery. Discussions with various surgeons quickly established now that some of them still considered it a dangerous folly, while others saw it as a huge opportunity. So that was the first choice. John Bailey would manage it, with Boyce as the associate director in charge. (It was wryly noted that the NHS Management Executive, some of whose senior people were scarcely reconciled to the Commission's health mission, not long afterwards set up its own value-for-money unit – and as the subject of their first special study, chose . . . day surgery.) The choice of subject for the second study was prompted by David Cooksey. In his venture-capital world, the chairman had come across a remarkably successful entrepreneur called Jean Shanks, who ran her own private sector pathology service. She persuaded him that the NHS pathology laboratories were grossly inefficient – so that was obviously a suitable target for investigation, assigned to Paul Durham. It would be overseen by Browning, who was still busy with local government.

And the third study, naturally, would look at estate management. This would be directed by Doug Edmonds, who had had plenty of experience at discussing property portfolios with local councils. Management of the study was assigned to another newcomer – Geoffrey Rendle, who had arrived at Vincent Square in April 1989 expecting to work on local government, only to find himself pitched straight into working with FB4's researchers on the topics they were planning to finalize after transferring to the Commission. (He would continue to work on NHS studies until 2001.)

THE FIRST HEALTH STUDIES

Arriving in Vincent Square to take up his new role, Jonty Boyce found the atmosphere just as congenial and exciting as he had expected from his first impressions. He recalled:

There were about forty-five people in Vincent Square when I arrived. The office was very, very small – just the ground floor, which was partly devoted to reception areas and so on, and the first floor. So it was cramped. But it was also possible to get to know everybody very quickly. It was like being in a sort of academic common room, where people came in saying, 'Hey, look, I've got this wonderful bit of information' or 'What about this for an interesting graph?' People were talking all the time: the place was buzzing with ideas. And we were open to the outside world. We had people there on secondment, and others who popped in regularly to talk. So we were permeable and that was really important. It was a very open, fluid environment to work in.[32]

Though he kept it to himself at the time, however, Boyce still had plenty of misgivings on one score: he was worried that complicated measurements of clinical performance might just prove too difficult for his colleagues in the field. He knew from his own experience as a doctor that they would confront appalling obstacles in any search for useful data. And he wondered privately whether auditors with no medical background whatever would be able to cope. It was exciting to be at the cutting edge. But would they have sharp enough knives for the job? He was about to find out.

The initial hypothesis of the day-surgery project was that the NHS was missing a very big trick. A few District Health Authorities (DHAs) maintained 'day-case units' where beds were available for patients undergoing same-day surgery (not to be confused with 'out-patient' care, a quite separate category). These units were not for overnight stays: the ward closed at night. Clearly, they cost much less to run than normal wards. Yet in most hospitals, almost everyone receiving surgical treatment was being dealt with as an 'in-patient', staying in a hospital bed for at least one night and usually rather more. The case to be proved was that day surgery was being unjustly neglected – and that using it for all appropriate patients would yield significant savings for the NHS.

Boyce had his own circumstantial evidence for believing in this hypothesis. Working in Northampton, he had known of an eye surgeon at Kettering General Hospital in the mid-1980s who performed almost all of his cataract operations as day cases, sending his patients home within hours of their treatment. Most eye doctors thought him a madman, and some colleagues were incensed by his unprofessional behaviour, as they saw it. But there was no evidence whatever that his results were any worse, and Boyce suspected that he was on to something important.

At the start of the project, in September 1989, Boyce's team approached the Royal College of Surgeons for their advice. The College responded encouragingly, and its president recommended that they talk to a consultant general surgeon working in North Tees General Hospital called Brendan Devlin. An Irishman who had trained as an economist before turning to medicine, Devlin was fascinated by the challenge of clinical audit – that is, measuring the outcome of specific categories of treatment. They duly contacted him and Devlin came down to Vincent Square for a series of meetings with Boyce and his colleagues – John Bailey, Linda Jarrett and Claire Blackman. Together, they planned a research programme that would challenge the medical profession's reservations over day surgery in the most robust manner possible. They brought one crucial insight to the task at the outset. It was no use simply quantifying and comparing the number of day cases handled by different hospitals. This would deliver no compelling case for change: every hospital would point to factors making it unique. The essential requirement was to measure day-case numbers in relation to *individual types of operation*. Thus, two hospitals might be handling exactly the same number of day cases. Pointing out that the number was disappointingly low would have little impact. But if it could be shown that the cases comprised, say, 90 per cent hernias at the one hospital and 90 per cent cataracts at the other, then the onus would be on each hospital to explain its neglect of the category so actively undertaken by the other.

So far, so straightforward. There was just one problem. The data to quantify individual types of operation did not exist. Over the next nine months or so, the *basic data* had all to be pulled together – and this, in a sense, was the great unsung achievement of the Commission in its first health study. The more acknowledged feat was nonetheless well worth acclaiming. With its very first effort, the Commission vindicated the trust of those who had accepted its argument that rigorous research, cleverly analysed, could unearth opportunities for substantial improvements to the efficiency of the great NHS behemoth.

A project advisory group of eight senior figures from the NHS was drawn together around Brendan Devlin. (It included the new Commission member, Chris West.) With their assistance, Boyce's team identified a 'basket' of twenty common procedures that at least *some* surgeons in *some* hospitals were happy to treat as day cases. The first five of the twenty were inguinal hernia repairs, excisions of breast lumps, anal fissure excisions, varicose veins ligations and cystoscopies. (The term 'basket of procedures' – which the Commission team alighted on one day after reading in the financial pages of the press about a basket of currencies – would soon pass into common medical parlance and is still used in this context.) The team then needed to quantify, for each of the 220 or so hospitals around England and Wales, exactly how many patients were handled as day cases for each procedure in the basket. Every hospital had a computerized 'patient administration system' that in theory recorded this information. But Boyce knew it was hopelessly unreliable: he had quickly learned that in the course of his doctorate work on hip fractures. Procedures were regularly coded inconsistently or simply omitted. The only way to be sure of what operations had been done was to search the operating-theatre register of each hospital.

Today, every register is computerized; but not so in 1989–90. Each one comprised a huge book. Boyce recalled:

All the entries in each book were written by hand, by surgeons who very often used acronyms, abbreviations and their own different descriptions of the same thing. So we had to train our auditors to go through the theatre registers looking for the twenty basket procedures. Linda Jarrett and I went to Cambridge one day to do the first training session with twenty auditors. We took photocopied pages from theatre registers for them to practise on, and then – much to their amazement – we gave them an exam at the end of the day! Some we had to drop from the team because they weren't good enough.[33]

Once the auditors – or increasingly, the project officers – were set to this remarkable task, it was quickly realized that the project faced another maddening hurdle. Theatre registers made no mention of whether or not patients had stayed the night in hospital. Fortunately, the patient-administration systems, while useless for the details of operations, were at least reliable for information on accommodation. Once the full list of operations had been painstakingly compiled, the team turned to the hospitals' computer departments for lists of all admissions that could be correlated with the theatre data. It was a massive undertaking – but at the end of the process, the team had a data bank that eventually proved quite as revealing as they could possibly have hoped.

Attitudes to day surgery around the country varied astonishingly. For no less than seven of the twenty selected procedures – operations, for example, for the decompression of carpal tunnels, or the correction of bat ears – the extent of individual DHAs' dependence on day surgery varied from o to 100 per cent. The team's analysis ranged widely over the clinical, financial, administrative and manning implications of this level of disparity. The bottom-line conclusions were striking. Current hospital expenditure on day cases was amounting to only 2 per cent of the total spending on in-patients and day cases combined. If, instead, DHAs adopted a consistent approach to the twenty procedures in the Commission's basket, the NHS would be able to treat an additional 186,000 patients each year at no extra cost. If DHAs extended day surgery to all of the appropriate procedures (as identified by reference to international best practice and the recommendations of the Royal College of Surgeons), an additional 300,000 patients could be treated. Put another way, this would be equivalent to taking care of 34 per cent of the patients on NHS waiting lists in England and Wales.

The resulting seventy-page national report, *A Short Cut to Better Services*, did more than set out the analysis with the usual excellent graphics. It explored the reasons for the neglect of day surgery, from poor management of facilities and misplaced clinical reservations to simple prejudice and professional snobbery – and it set out suggested ways of overcoming these obstacles. All of these would be carefully simplified in the months ahead for an audit guide, to be used in the local audit round of 1991–92. For, as with the Commission's national reports on local government, the day-surgery report would be ensured a real impact only when the DAS auditors took its findings and used them as a framework for their own work in a local context.

The report was published in October 1990, just in time to celebrate the Commission's assumption of its NHS responsibilities under the Act passed in June. (The timing did not impress the National Audit Office, which had already qualified the Commission's 1989–90 accounts in view of 'unauthorized spending' on the health directorate ahead of the legislation.) The DoH unfortunately issued a press release on improved waiting-list figures the same day, which was an unhelpful distraction. But as the report circulated, acclaim for its contents grew steadily – and its long-term influence proved to be profound. To take just one dramatic instance of this: within the next ten to fifteen years, the proportion of cataract operations performed as day cases rose to virtually 100 per cent, just as Boyce's surgeon in Kettering had always argued it should. This was not wholly attributable to the day-surgery report, of course – but few surgeons would deny the report's influence was far-reaching. (A BBC television documentary on the NHS in February 2007 looked at the work of various hospital consultants – and pilloried one individual who, in the face of much tut-tutting from his colleagues, insisted on treating cataract cases as in-patients.)

Days after the publication of the report, Cooksey and Davies met Kenneth Clarke for an hour. He had taken the trouble to digest the main points of the report and told them he was pleased with it. Indeed, as Davies noted, he seemed 'notably more relaxed' about the Commission's new role. The significance of the first report's excellence had not been lost on him.[34] And if Clarke was relieved at the positive reception for the day-surgery report, so too were Tristem and his colleagues. Their approach had been vindicated. They had engaged at an early stage with the Royal College and other key professional associations. They had spread their research net widely to engage as many DHAs as possible. And they had effectively pre-empted any knee-jerk resistance from a proud profession by working throughout with a 'project advisory group' comprising some of the most distinguished clinicians in the field (and a few top managers as well).

The second and third health reports followed the same basic recipe. The examination of the pathology sector was entitled simply *The Pathology Services: a Management Review*. It delivered an extremely thorough analysis of the management of the sector, amply bearing out its initial hypothesis that 'the application of management techniques has lagged behind the science' of pathology. Its conclusions did not quite match the bravura of the day-surgery report, but posed plenty of awkward questions to be followed up in the audit round. Might it not be the case, for example, that the unit costs of individual tests could be significantly reduced if laboratories were prepared to pool their resources more intelligently?

Ken Clarke himself warned the Commission in October that it might have more difficulty with the medical profession over this second report. He was right – as the final report indicated, in a roundabout fashion. Paul Durham's study team encountered a deeply entrenched attachment to the notion that every large hospital needed its own laboratory. 'As a result, each district has one or more laboratories equipped and staffed to provide a near comprehensive service . . . This pattern has been reinforced by the policy of district self-sufficiency which has been pursued by most districts up to now' (para. 77). The result of this, in many laboratories, was a conspicuously low level of demand for less common investigations – with correspondingly higher unit costs. When the study team inquired as to the feasibility of outsourcing by one lab to another, this was widely rejected as out of the question. Transportation risks, time factors, the lack of close working relationships – for all sorts of reasons, it was inconceivable. Or, as the report amenably put it, 'It is argued that the separation of pathologists from the process of investigation could . . . cause difficulties' (para. 86). And this objection was raised in the context of cooperation between hospitals in neighbouring DHAs perhaps only 20 or 30 miles apart. The real problem, suspected the Commission, was that few if any of the DHAs had made any effort to see how others did it. This, of course, was precisely where the Commission had something valuable to offer. Davies recalled:

The gist of the response from many people was 'How on earth can your boring old auditors come in here and tell us anything about how to run our exciting pathology lab?' My answer was always: 'Of course our auditors don't know anything about how to run pathology labs – but they do know a lot about how *other people* run pathology labs. Isn't that something you might want to know about?'[35]

The study team opted accordingly to look into best practice in the United States. The contrast was stark. It emerged that hospitals in New York City were sending blood specimens by air courier to specialized labs all over the continent. Many, for example, were shipped by Fedex to its central sorting facility in Memphis, bundled up and down conveyor belts on to the next plane to the west coast and tested in Los Angeles in time for a result to be passed back to New York early the following day. The lesson for the NHS was obvious, but was resisted nonetheless. The Commission opted to play a long game. When the national report, *Pathology Services: a Management Review*, was published in January 1991 it included no inflammatory references to the US practice. The scope for reducing costs was explored with 'an illustrative example' (an old McKinsey ruse to avoid upsetting the client with actual but unpalatable data). It was noted, however, that 'The first step in the exploration of possible frameworks for inter-laboratory cooperation is the development of the costing approach outlined earlier' (para. 90). And the report provided a detailed basis for auditors in due course to begin comparing unit costs, and the potential for reducing them. As with day surgery, the report's influence stretched far into the future.

The day of the pathology report's publication most unfortunately coincided with the date of another event – the launch of Operation Desert Storm to liberate Kuwait from Saddam Hussein. While this killed any chances of media coverage for the report, it helped to make its publication that much more memorable. On the day before, one of the surgeons working with the Audit Commission's team received instructions to restrict his operating-theatre list to as few cases as possible over the coming days. He mentioned it to Ross Tristem, who guessed the reason immediately and walked around the desks at Vincent Square telling his staff that the Gulf offensive was about to begin. It was a fair bet, he suggested, that the Ministry of Defence was worried it would be flying home far more casualties than it would have theatres to operate on them. All this made a big impression on the younger managers in particular. Geoffrey Rendle recalled:

It reflected an atmosphere where the top man didn't mind going around giving out pieces of information from desk to desk. And there was the sense that the wider implications of our work mattered, too. So it felt like being in a very high-powered think-tank. It was one of the most stimulating environments I've ever worked in.[36]

The third of the initial three reports, *NHS Estate Management and Property Maintenance*, appeared two months later. This was more familiar territory for the Commission, and drew heavily on six pilot projects undertaken by FB4 in its last months. It juggled with some alarming numbers: the NHS in England owned a property portfolio with an estimated value of £24 billion, and 40 per cent of this estate was classified by District Health Authorities as 'in poor condition' and needing substantial remedial spending.

It was Geoffrey Rendle's first study, but held no mysteries for a man cast in the classic Audit Commission mould: Rendle was a Cambridge mathematician with a background in Operations Research. (He had worked for London Transport in the 1970s, where one of his jobs was to work out why London buses so often turn up three at a time.) He produced a report in March 1991 that drew attention to the complexity of estate management in the NHS, where the changing usage of buildings over time posed a greater challenge than was typically encountered in local government. One of its main conclusions was that health authorities were generally rather better than local councils at looking after their buildings. But there were still plenty of ways for them to do better. An audit guide set out for the DAS a lengthy menu of items that could be checked at a local level, in the 1991–92 audit round.

A DIFFERENT KIND OF CLIENT

It was clear by the summer of 1991 that the Commission's take-up of the NHS external audit had been an impressive success. The quality of the first three national reports had been widely acclaimed. The sheer quantity of the Commission's output was no less noted. In addition to the national reports, a series of Occasional Papers had been launched. The first two papers drew on the legacy of FB4's work on the provision of sterile services and the scope for energy savings in the NHS. A third paper in May 1991 set out the encouraging responses of patients to a questionnaire on day surgery. In parallel with the statistical profiles long since adopted in local government, profiles had begun to be developed for District Health Authorities. And a work programme had been announced for the next round of special studies: these would look at the management of hospital beds and of nursing resources.

The work on nursing, managed by Ian Jones, led to a report, *The Virtue of Patients*, and two handbooks on nursing. Jonty Boyce led the investigation into the management of beds, which produced one of the most forceful reports published by the Commission: *Lying in Wait: the Use of Medical Beds in Acute Hospitals*. Boyce recalled:

Many years later, I was with a team in some hospital somewhere and we went to one of the senior managers to introduce ourselves. He said, 'Oh yes, the Audit Commission', and got down from a shelf his copy of *Lying in Wait*. 'You lot were responsible for this', he said, 'and this was the most useful thing that anyone ever wrote about our job.' That was very pleasing.[37]

Meanwhile, inside the corridors of the DoH at Richmond House, reactions to all this were mixed, to say the least. Two months after the fall of Margaret Thatcher and the arrival of John Major's government, Cooksey and Davies paid their first visit to Kenneth Clarke's successor as health secretary, William Waldegrave. He was complimentary about the studies to date and fully supportive of the future work programme. Davies noted in a memo to colleagues on the meeting, 'He regarded with some glee the prospect of our taking on some of the traditional shibboleths of the nursing profession.'[38] So after all the bitterness of the 1988 battles over the health reforms White Paper, might a friendlier, more constructive relationship with the DoH be about to blossom? Possibly. But Davies spied the worm in the bud: 'It was clear that there were no current concerns about our work even though the department has not yet grasped the need to do something about what we say.'[39]

Indeed not, and senior officials showed no inclination to accept any such cap-in-hand stance. They insisted on the right to have a DoH representative at all meetings of the Commission's study advisory groups, but sent along only very junior nominees. (Boyce thought the day-surgery study caused them particular unease: 'They were deeply suspicious and didn't like it at all.')[40] They bridled at any suggestion by the NHS management executive that the Commission was ahead of the game – and appear to have moved quickly to limit what they saw as competition from Vincent Square, when they could. Under enabling legislation in the run-up to the transfer of the health-audit work, the Commission undertook some consultancy work, specially commissioned by the NHS executive board. It resulted in a sizeable study, managed by Boyce, which analysed supply chains throughout the health service. (It was a rare instance of a consultancy project by the Commission, and its legality was much debated at the outset. Davies brought in two former McKinsey colleagues, Deborah

Sandford and Andrew Elliott, to assist with it. A fee of £100,000 was paid.) A subsequent strategy review by the Commission reported that the study had been 'very well received'. As the review then noted, however: 'Unfortunately, the section enabling this work to be undertaken was repealed when the 1990 Act was passed.' There were to be no sequels.[41]

It might have been hoped that the DoH would gradually take a more relaxed view of the Commission's brief. The lesson from the DoE's experience in recent years had surely been that a collaborative approach could bring dividends. Enough trust and goodwill now existed in Marsham Street for quite critical Section 27 reports from the Commission to be, if not publicly applauded, at least received as serious contributions to future policy. *Urban Regeneration and Economic Development – the Local Government Dimension*, for example, had appeared in September 1989 with some harsh things to say about the government's various support programmes for deprived inner-city areas. '[They] are seen as a patchwork quilt of complexity and idiosyncrasy. They baffle local authorities and business alike. The rules of the game seem over-complex and sometimes capricious.'[42] This must have been uncomfortable reading for some in the DoE. But the 77-page report had been heavily researched and had constructive proposals to make. For example, it urged that more attention be given to best practice in the local implementation of development strategies, and identified several of the key steps that appeared to have yielded the best results to date. The Commission also announced that it would be following up its report with a guide for auditors, which could be useful to their discussions with the many local authorities that had embarked on economic development activities. The response from DoE officials was accordingly positive and conducive to a further exchange of ideas.

The health department saw no grounds for comfort here. Even though its officials had nothing to fear from Section 27 reports – since the Commission had had its authority to undertake such work specifically excluded under the 1990 Act – many of them nonetheless seemed wary from the start of the Commission's every move. Ross Tristem, himself a veteran of the department, attributed its sensitivity in part to the huge range of vested interests that jostled within it.

'There were the doctors, the nurses, the administrators in the regions, the central planning people, the economists, the architects and a dozen others. So whatever we did was bound to upset somebody in the department at the highest level.'[43]

More fundamental, perhaps, was the department's view of its responsibilities, which had prompted so much resistance to the Commission during the heated debates of 1988. Even forty years on, it seemed there was no escaping the 1948 rhetoric of Aneurin Bevan about the sound of a dropped bedpan in Tredegar reverberating around the Palace of Westminster. Put more prosaically, ministers of health and their officials would be answerable for the performance of the NHS down to the smallest detail. No sensible person ever endorsed this as a practical policy – but it was a convenient fiction for those intent on attacking the government. And since it could hardly be publicly refuted by health officials, they remained on their guard and ready to respond as though they did indeed have direct charge over everything that moved in the NHS. Hence an intractable problem. If the Audit Commission was critical of councils, the DoE could choose to treat it as an ally in the struggle for better local government. If the Commission was critical of hospitals, it was an entirely different matter. Even the mildest criticism of the NHS was liable to be seen by DoH officials as a direct affront to them and their ministers – reproaching them, as it were, for their mismanagement of that dropped bedpan. Here was a tension that only a healthy mutual respect between Richmond House and Vincent Square would reliably keep at bay.

9

Matters of Succession, 1991–93

The government formed by John Major at the end of November 1990 had little time to restore the Tories' electoral prospects. Constitutionally, Major had only eighteen months at the most before he would have to go to the country. Most commentators expected an election in 1991, and most expected a Tory defeat. The opinion polls seemed to confirm as much. Dead and buried until they promised in March to scrap the poll tax, the Tories then began a slow recovery – but never looked like overhauling Labour's lead in the polls. This was unsettling for everyone working at the Audit Commission. The Labour Party had put out a paper in May 1989 proposing its replacement by something to be called a Quality Commission. The details were sketchy, but councils would no longer be forced to use competitive tenders, and the Quality Commission would be an umbrella body for various agencies and inspectorates expected to act as a proxy for the disciplines of the marketplace. The Audit Commission would be swallowed up within it.

One of Labour's main spokesmen on local government, Jack Cunningham, had confirmed as much in a slightly bizarre fashion in July 1990. Invited to give the Commission's second annual Public Sector Management Lecture, he told his hosts about their after-life with as much charm as he could muster.[1] The Commission members agreed at their next monthly meeting that the annual lectures were worthwhile, but in 1991 'a non-political speaker would be invited'. Cliff Nicholson was asked to communicate to all staff 'the clear message that . . . under a future Labour government, the Audit Commission would become the "Quality Commission" mentioned in the Labour Party's recent policy document'.[2]

It must have intrigued many on the staff, though, that Cunningham had been invited to give the lecture in the first place. As this should have suggested, Howard Davies had not been neglecting his Labour contacts. In fact, the controller enjoyed quite a cordial relationship with both Cunningham and another of the party's strongest young contenders for future office, Jack Straw. And both men had made it clear in private that Labour's attitude to the future of the Commission was rather more ambivalent than its public position might suggest. They respected the authority of its national reports, and so (they said) did Neil Kinnock. The only strident advocate of 'abolition' was David Blunkett, a man with his own strong views on the Commission that were perhaps not entirely uncoloured by his past dealings with the Sheffield district auditor. Blunkett had left behind his days as leader of Sheffield City Council, having entered the Commons at the 1987 election as MP for Sheffield Brightside. As well as being on Labour's National Executive Council, he was also now their shadow spokesman on local government.

Attending carefully to Labour's preparations for government through 1991, every opportunity was taken to talk to key Labour figures about the Commission's work – and how useful its role could be in educating local authorities on new legislative requirements. It had helped to march compulsory competitive tendering (CCT) up the hill. It did not need spelling out too explicitly that it might be adept, too, at helping to march it back down again. Some progress was made, as a meeting in July confirmed. Davies went along with David Cooksey to the House of Commons to talk to Bryan Gould, a leading member of Kinnock's shadow cabinet. With them went the resident trade unionist on the Commission, Tony Christopher, who had accompanied Davies on earlier visits to see Gould (and who was also busy working his contacts within the TUC on the Commission's behalf). They were given a friendly hearing, and 'made a strong case for a future Labour government retaining a single Commission rather than establishing several new bodies'.[3]

Gould was non-committal on how exactly a Quality Commission would coexist with it, but was at pains to stress that there was no question of abolishing the Audit Commission. On the contrary, as Davies noted, he insisted that 'what was being discussed was an expansion of the existing role of the Commission, with powers to intervene when [a council's] service quality was seen to be poor and even to send in a management team to rectify it. They had considered the question of CCT and decided to remove the compulsory element, though they were in favour of getting the *best value* [italics added] for money . . .'[4] The phrase 'best value' had a future ahead of it.

The significance of Labour's changed attitude to the Commission is worth noting. Under Margaret Thatcher, the Tories had set out to rein back irresponsible spending by local government. The Audit Commission had been set up as a consequence. Opposed to Thatcher's spending cuts, Labour policy had duly repudiated the Commission. John Banham's Commission had then turned out, to an extent that few in government had anticipated, to be one of the primary catalysts for an infusion of private sector management techniques into the public sector. These had at first been aimed above all at cutting costs. But they had increasingly been targeted over the past five years or so – in a process heavily influenced by Howard Davies's Commission – at raising the standard of services in the public sector. Labour politicians, without formally jettisoning their hostility to the Commission, had been drawn willy-nilly into engaging with the consequences of its work. Now they were even ready to echo its talk of management and markets in the public sector. They had yet to reconcile their formal policy with this shift, but the adjustment had begun.

It was often messy. A few days before the July 1991 meeting at the Commons, BBC Radio's *Today* programme had asserted that Labour remained committed to scrapping the Commission. Gould confided to his visitors from Vincent Square that the Party had sent a formal complaint about this to the BBC. The error, he told them, 'was traceable to some mistaken comments made by David Blunkett who had "got it wrong" '.[5] Davies pointed out to Gould that neither he nor anyone else at Vincent Square had ever met Blunkett. This came as a surprise to Gould, who promised to fix a meeting. Blunkett's view of the Commission was to change completely over the next year or so. After the election had been fought and lost, he was made shadow secretary of state for health. Ross Tristem telephoned his office and invited him to come to Vincent Square for a pre-publication presentation about the next national report on the NHS. He accepted, and turned up with Dawn Primarolo, another young Labour MP who had entered Parliament in 1987. Blunkett was impressed and asked to be given another presentation the following month. Tristem recalled:

After that, he kept coming back! He came over quite frequently with Dawn Primarolo. One day, as we were walking down the corridor, he put his arm around me and said, 'I was against the Audit Commission when I first started, but I'm 100 per cent behind it now!' He saw it wasn't about knocking local government, it was about trying to improve services.[6]

As the year progressed, Davies grew quietly confident that the Commission would have a future under Labour. Neil Kinnock's team could plainly see the contribution it was making on the research front. They were also pragmatic enough, he thought, to acknowledge political realities. At a time when ditching CCT would inevitably entail some risk of a fresh Loony Left rumpus in the media, abolishing the Commission would surely be almost perverse. Indeed, scrapping it would be a double folly – not only inviting jibes about collusion with the Loony Left, but losing a precious source of private briefings about the clandestine activities out on the loonier fringes. These still represented a potentially key weakness for Labour in the coming election, as the shadow cabinet was nervously aware.

The designated manager of Labour's campaign was Jack Cunningham. He had regular meetings with Davies through these months, tapping him gratefully for information about what was going on in left-wing councils. Davies recalled: 'He made it clear on several occasions that the Commission would only be abolished over his dead body.'[7] This was not to say that it would be business as usual after the election. Davies thought it more than likely that changes might be made to the Commission's role within the NHS, as part of a much broader re-think of the reforms now pending in the wake of the June 1990 Act. But local government was another matter. 'The idea that Labour would devote scarce legislative time in the early years of their government to removing a bulwark against crazy council spending struck me as cloud cuckoo land.'[8]

Perhaps there was another reason, too, why the Commission was starting to look less like a red rag to the Labour bull. John Major had launched his own approach to local government, with plenty of distinctly unThatcherite rhetoric. In many respects, his agenda sounded much like Labour's. Not only was the poll tax to be scrapped. A quantum jump in the quality of local services was to be the new Holy Grail – and citizens as consumers of those services were to be active arbiters of their quality.

If the Major government's rhetoric had inadvertently been slipped into drafts of Labour's manifesto for the coming election, would anyone have noticed? ('People have a right to first-class services. We will develop customer contracts . . . Councils will have to carry out an annual survey of customer satisfaction . . . contracts of chief officers will be linked to quality targets . . .' ran Labour's final version.) Politicians in both parties were intent in 1991 on distancing themselves as far as possible from the bulldozing convictions that had led to the poll tax. Suddenly it was fashionable to talk about taxpayers (and even, for the first time, rail passengers) as *customers* – with rights, which needed protecting with the help of public charters.

Addressing the Conservative Council in March 1991, the prime minister unveiled his Citizen's Charter. It would be the bedrock, he suggested, of Tory domestic programmes for a decade to come. It was easy to deride the Citizen's Charter, and few columnists in the media resisted any temptation to do so. Largely unremarked, however, was the fundamental bearing it had upon the role of the Audit Commission. Here the impact of the Citizen's Charter was subtle but highly significant.

THE COMMISSION AND THE CITIZEN'S CHARTER

The gist of the idea was simple enough. As John Major put it in his March address, 'all must know where they stand and what they have a right to expect'. The political novelty of the Citizen's Charter was the extent of its reach into the most mundane areas of everyday life. This put local authorities – along with central government, the NHS and the public utilities – at the centre of attention. For all of them, standards of service would be spelt out in detail; subsequent performance would be monitored; and shortcomings would be redressed. All of which was predicated on the assumption that lavish quantities of relevant data would always be forthcoming. But where was this data to be found? It did not take long for the Commission to get the call.

And as John Major appreciated better than most, the well-regarded mavericks of Vincent Square were not just heroic collectors of statistics. Almost two years earlier, in June 1989, Major had used the inaugural Audit Commission lecture to deliver an intriguing plea for public sector reform. As he put it in his memoirs: 'I argued that we needed to improve [the public sector's] use of resources; measure its performance more rigorously; and make services act more responsively towards their users.'[9] This was a far cry from the standard fare that might have been expected from a Treasury minister, but perhaps not quite such a cry in the wilderness as some would later claim. A policy document published by the Cabinet Office in 1988, entitled *Service to the Public*, had set out a similar agenda for reform. 'The process to be adopted was to define aims and objectives, to secure information to assess whether aims had been achieved and to set out clearly defined methods of evaluation.'[10]

Aware of the Cabinet Office paper and encouraged by Major's endorsement of it in his June lecture, Peter Brokenshire and his colleagues went on to produce a Management Paper (No. 5 in the series) that turned out to be a significant harbinger of things to come. It appeared in December 1989 and was called *Managing Services Effectively: Performance Review*. In effect, it carried on where Major had left off.

It is often hard to measure performance in the public service [*sic*], especially in terms of quality and effectiveness. However it is wrong to over-state the difficulties . . . Quality and effectiveness can be monitored in various ways, including feedback from users, and more (and better) inspection.

The key was to identify 'performance indicators' for any given service, which would cut through superfluous statistics and provide the critical numbers worth setting against a meaningful yardstick. The resulting comparison would be a useful measure of that service.

The paper set out the four ingredients of 'performance' – cost, resources, outputs and outcomes – and drew on secondary education and council housing to help define them and show how performance indicators (PIs) could be used to monitor them. Thus, in education, the ingredients would include teachers' salaries (a cost), school premises (a resource), pupil numbers by age cohort (an output) and exam results or destination of school-leavers (an outcome). PIs could track all four ingredients – plus the take-up of the respective service by the target population, the equivalent of sales in the private sector and an equally important indicator of quality. These PIs together would deliver a performance review based on facts, where anecdote and personal impressions had previously ruled the roost.

Pulse-quickening stuff, for most politicians, this was not. But it built logically on the management truths that the Commission had been demonstrating persuasively since 1983 – and it appealed strongly to John Major. Within a few months of his arrival in 10 Downing Street, there was little doubt the Commission would be closely involved in his Charter project. All that remained to be settled was what exactly it would *do*. This was far from clear at a seminar on the Charter that was chaired by Major early in June 1991, nor did a White Paper issued the following month advance matters very far. By September, David Cooksey and his controller were paying regular visits to the DoE in Marsham Street in a bid to clarify their role.

Through the autumn of 1991, various papers were presented at the monthly meetings of the Commission members. The cost of coordinating any Charter-related activities was evidently a serious concern. Amendments were considered to the Code of Audit Practice, with plans laid for a consultation paper. Some plans were even unravelled, to avoid pre-empting the outcome of Charter legislation. A scheduled paper on the police, looking at accountability, was cancelled. The foundation work would be used instead as a basis for talking to the police about the Citizen's Charter. But by mid-November, when the Commission members assembled at a country hotel in Sonning-on-Thames for their annual weekend retreat, the question on the agenda was still: 'How do we take forward the Citizen's Charter initiative?' The answer by the Sunday afternoon was clear enough: we ask the controller to go away and prepare a business plan setting out all the options. Davies duly came back to them in December, and confirmed what was already apparent to the media. The Major government was looking to the Commission to develop a range of performance indicators, much as its own 1989 Management Paper had proposed, and to devise ways in which these might be used by the DAS to assess the *relative* merits of individual councils. Davies suggested, and the members agreed, that a temporary unit should be set up in Vincent Square with its own budget to develop these PIs. It was minuted at the monthly meeting that he would report back on the results in April.

Privately, however, the controller himself had some misgivings about the role this seemed to envisage for the Commission. He had hinted as much, in a paper he had written back in June 1991 that perhaps deserved a closer reading than some had given it. *How Effective is the Audit Commission?* was prompted by the members: they wanted a useful brief to fortify the case for retaining the Commission after the election. It served this purpose handsomely, explaining how the Commission went about its job and why it could fairly be seen as meeting an important need. National reports – on housing the homeless, for example, and on highways maintenance – had demonstrably made a positive contribution to government policy on the one hand and attitudes towards standard practice in local government on the other. Perhaps even more crucially, the audit guides generated by the reports were making a real difference at ground level. The bare numbers were impressive. A total of 82 studies over eight years had led to 4,682 local studies; and these had so far enabled local authorities, 'acting on auditors' advice', to achieve annually recurring savings of £662 million (out of identified savings opportunities of £1.3 billion a year). And the value of the audit guides extended, in a sense, well beyond what was quantifiable. 'Armed with the guide, the auditor can review even complex areas of activity in quite a short space of time . . . The technique also ensures that auditors can tell their council or hospital how its performance compares with others. That is something which many public sector managers are anxious to learn' (paras 31–2).

So much for the achievements to date. None could doubt the Commission's success as a self-standing institution (which, incidentally, had drawn 1,859 applications in 1990 for 67 graduate trainee positions). But what of its future? With Labour pressing its Quality Commission from one side and John Major pushing his Citizen's Charter from the other, Davies had a few cautionary notes to sound

in a last section on 'Moving ahead'. He welcomed the growing importance for the Commission of joint projects with other types of audit
and inspection. These included the department of HM Chief Inspector
of Schools and HM Inspectorate of Constabulary; good progress
was also being made towards joint working with the Social Services
Inspectorate. However – and here Labour's Quality Commission
architects were surely being addressed directly – this did not amount
to an argument for making a goulash of them all. 'The Commission's
distinctive contribution is to bring an independent perspective (independent of the authority and of any professional group) to the debate
. . . So it would be wrong to think that its work could be merged with
that of the professional inspectorates' (para. 73, § vii).

As for the Citizen's Charter – it was nowhere mentioned by name,
but its implications were clearly a concern. Aware of the prime minister's enthusiasm for performance indicators and his vision of league
tables for local authorities, Davies appeared to have two main worries.
The first centred on the question of publicity for council data. The
Commission itself had no choice but to act in the public domain.

But individual authorities are protected by the need to clear references to their
own performance with them before publication . . . Whilst that provision remains,
it is not open to the Commission to publish league tables of internal management
costs and efficiencies which identify individual councils. (para. 70)

Thus, in-depth VFM reports remained confidential to the authority
involved. Of course, the key conclusions would be made public in the
management letter. 'This is an essential feature of the auditor's public
role. Accountability to the public cannot be satisfied by secret assurances.' Where no statutory constraints applied, there was certainly
scope for more publicity: 'open comparisons of performance from
one place to another stimulate management interest and promote
improvements' (para. 71). But any steps in this direction had to be
taken with due regard for 'the response from those under audit'.
Performance indicators could be tracked as *confidential* data, and still
be a potent tool of management. It was all a matter of striking the
right balance.

This led on to the controller's second worry, which went to the
heart of the matter – how best to align the Commission behind the

Citizen's Charter without compromising the integrity of its own audit-based approach? Davies had always argued consistently that it was the Commission's job in local government to 'illuminate the choices' faced by elected representatives. He had therefore been wary of anything that smacked of awarding prizes for relative performance. Its work lay in investigation, not adjudication. But where to draw the line? Back in 1987, he had decided that consultancy work fell on the wrong side of it. The same would obviously apply to any invitation from Whitehall to put the Commission's name to a government initiative with no scope for independent audit. (An egregious example of this came along exactly a year after the paper on effectiveness was published. The DfES asked the Commission to join it in publishing school league tables 'under its direction', over which the Commission would have no rights of independent audit whatever. The members declined the invitation.)[11] But on which side of the line might publicly paraded performance indicators and league tables fall?

It could hardly be disputed that the Commission would have a role to play: it had advocated PIs in the first place and was now the vital source, after all, for much of the critical data. Davies made a careful distinction, though, between providing the data and making political use of it. 'The Commission is most likely to be effective in promoting customer-oriented service delivery where it can provide tools *for use by those responsible* [italics added]' (para. 73, § ii). To underline the suggestion that *those responsible* might not include the Commission, he stressed that some uses made of the data might well involve a rather different mindset from the Commission's – in particular where customer satisfaction was concerned.

There is a suspicion that some of those who argue for greater focus on undefined 'quality of service' do so simply to generate a case for more resources. That might be a legitimate tactic. But the Commission's focus is not on campaigning, rather on getting the best out of whatever resources are devoted to the service in question. So 'quality' measures are not useful if they do not lead to practical action. (para. 73, § iv)

None of this, however, was to deny that the political climate was changing. By the early 1990s, attitudes in Westminster towards local government were clearly undergoing a subtle but fundamental shift.

As it was rather unsympathetically described at the end of the decade, with the clarity of hindsight, in a book co-authored by five academics at the London School of Economics:

Ruling colonies in the Empire was replaced by regulation of Britain's internal colonies – its counties, towns and cities. Central government was now regulating not only how local authorities should carry out their functions (process controls) but also in many cases the level and nature of the services they should provide (output controls) . . . [So] central government pursued a strategy of increasing regulation, mixing heightened oversight with new elements of competition.[12]

This was not, of course, how those engaged in promoting it saw the shift. They tended, like John Major, to emphasize instead the great importance of listening to the views of the end-users of public services.

As it happened, the executive team in Vincent Square had begun moving in this direction of its own accord, before the Citizen's Charter surfaced. It was a development encapsulated in the appointment of Bob Chilton to succeed Ross Tristem as head of the Local Government Studies directorate. When he saw the Commission's advertisement in the *Guardian*, Bob Chilton was working as the chief executive of the Medway Towns authority. It was a slightly unlikely position for someone of his strong academic background. He had gained a Ph.D. at Cambridge in 1972 with his work on London's housing market and had done a brief stint as an academic at South Bank Polytechnic, prior to the Medway job. But he had also worked his way up the local government ladder via several London boroughs in the 1970s and had been London's youngest director of housing, at Kensington and Chelsea in the early 1980s. Arriving in Vincent Square late in 1989, Chilton brought exactly the right mix of down-to-earth experience and intellectual firepower that made him a natural for the Commission. Indeed, he had applied back in 1983, and been undone (he suspected) by a rather too forthright approach to an interview with John Banham. He was elated to get Tristem's old job in 1989.

Chilton inherited a heavy workload of studies, not least two important projects on environmental health. During the course of 1990, though, he began to make his influence felt. By 1991, it was evident that local government studies under his guidance were going to move beyond the approach of earlier years – in important ways that were fully in keeping with the spirit of the Citizen's Charter. He was intent on defining the focus of each study rather less narrowly than was typically the hallmark of the Operational Research approach. Chilton saw the OR stance as well suited to the kind of work done in the 1980s – tackling specific problems, with a view to enhancing efficiency through analytical insights – but it typically left each study in a silo of its own, and focused almost exclusively on the provider's viewpoint. He wanted to break with the past in both respects. Chilton thought the Commission should look at broad issues, and he saw most problems as leading back (often quite directly) to the overarching question of how authorities were organizing themselves to deliver services effectively. In other words, reappraising management arrangements would be integral to most solutions with any chance of making a practical difference. (There was scope here, of course, for a scrap over turf rights between Chilton's area and the Management Practice directorate – but with Peter Brokenshire now approaching retirement, it was not a problem.)

At the same time, Chilton wanted his studies directorate to shift its focus towards the end-user. The OR question – 'How do we provide this better?' – had not lost its relevance. But it had to be weighed increasingly against the question 'How are people experiencing this service?' Now head of the Health Studies directorate, Ross Tristem had no argument with any of this. He could see the logic of Chilton's approach – and was anyway moving in the same direction himself, within the health-studies context. Few attempts had ever been made before the 1990 NHS Act to mobilize the views of patients in a coherent way. It had generally been axiomatic that the doctors knew best. Tristem was alert to the opportunity this offered, in the new climate. Where new ideas encountered scepticism from the doctors, patients' views might be a potent catalyst of change. Eight months after the publication of the national report on day surgery, the Commission released its third NHS Occasional Paper, *Measuring Quality: the Patient's View of Day Surgery*.

In short, Howard Davies needed no persuading that the customer-service dimension warranted more attention in the public sector – and he was content to see the Commission's own directors evolving a less technocratic, less producer-driven philosophy. He was even intrigued to see how John Major's government would fare with its promotion of the customer dimension as the Tories' Big Idea. What he was *not* yet wholly comfortable about embracing was the idea that the Commission might become the government's partner in mobilizing the Citizen's Charter and all that it looked like entailing. (It might be legitimate, too, to wonder who else shared his discomfort. Michael Heseltine, attending a meeting of the Commission members in November 1991, told them that '[if he had a criticism] . . . it was that the Commission does not have enough enemies'.)[13]

Davies's reservations made no apparent difference to the passage of the Local Government Act that emerged in March 1992, to provide for the Citizen's Charter. It took care of the publicity constraints noted by Davies in his June paper, however, and authorized the Commission to give:

such directions as it thinks fit for requiring relevant bodies to publish such information relating to their activities in any financial year as will . . . facilitate the making of appropriate comparisons (by reference to the criteria of cost, economy, efficiency and effectiveness) between

(a) the standards of performance achieved by different relevant bodies in that financial year; and

(b) the standards of performance achieved by such bodies in different financial years.[14]

The 1990 NHS Act had expanded the Commission's franchise. This 1992 Act extended the nature of its basic role. By the time of its enactment, though, John Major had at last called a general election. It would fall on 9 April. A new Labour government's plans would eclipse the Charter soon enough – or so the Commission's controller, like most other observers, assumed.

A SURPRISING PROLOGUE TO THE 1992 GENERAL ELECTION

Labour's growing assertiveness in the run-up to the election caused some friction with the Commission, involving both councillors and shadow ministers. The party's election manifesto – contrary to popular belief, then and since – made no reference to the Audit Commission. But it did refer to both a Health Quality Commission and an Education Standards Commission. No one could be sure how the various bodies would be expected to relate to each other. Whatever the private assurances given by insiders like Jack Cunningham, there seemed every likelihood of a difficult transition period just around the corner.

At a meeting with the Association of London Authorities (ALA) at the beginning of February 1992, Cooksey and Davies were surprised to find themselves attacked by Margaret Hodge, now in her tenth year as Islington's Labour leader. The Commission's overheads, she asserted, had risen steadily as the productivity of its staff had declined. She agreed afterwards with Cooksey to send her evidence to the Commission for it to provide a response. But as Cooksey complained to the Commission members later, 'She had not done so and instead the ALA had issued the data in a press release a few days after the meeting.'[15] The release suggested the Commission had become 'rather bloated' with a rise in staff numbers at Vincent Square that was 'disproportionate'. The thrust of the ALA's argument was that the Commission was racking up surpluses from its council audits which it was then squandering on central studies 'which do not produce any income'. A series of dubious percentages were cited, and the ALA challenged the Commission 'to take a long hard look at these figures'.

Davies did so and replied with a paper – *How Efficient is the Audit Commission?* – put out in March. He tackled the figures head-on – scathingly correcting most of them and explaining the ALA's errors. As for its central charge, it betrayed a 'fundamental misunderstanding'. Davies summarized the financial arrangements governing the Commission's work, reminding the ALA that no power had ever existed for it to charge directly for its central studies.

This point is, of course, well understood by the main local authority associations and by all individual authorities. No individual authority, over the last eight years, has ever demonstrated any misunderstanding of this point which is fundamental to the way in which the Commission operates.

But then, no authority in eight years had been able to anticipate the imminent arrival of a Labour government, either. The spat soon fizzled out – though Margaret Hodge followed it up a year later in an article in *The Times* on the Commission's tenth anniversary, repeating her allegations and complaining that the Commission 'bristles when questioned on these matters'.[16]

With just a couple of weeks to go in the election campaign, Vincent Square received a visit from its most consistent Labour adversary – Robin Cook. Shadow health minister since 1989, he had opposed extending the Commission's franchise into the NHS. He had several times been invited to the Commission, to discuss its approach to health issues, but had always previously declined to come. David Cooksey recalled:

I can remember the impossibility of trying to brief Robin Cook on the health-service issues. It was absolutely appalling. We fixed appointment after appointment to see him every time we produced a paper on the health service. Never once did he turn up for a single meeting.[17]

Now, at last, he did come – alone, and rather frosty. Davies received him in his own office, and they were joined there by Ross Tristem and Jonty Boyce. With his party on the brink of power at long last, Cook said he had come to ask for a brief to be prepared, for delivery on his first day inside the health department. How, he wanted to know, could he set about measuring the effectiveness of the NHS? Asking for its assistance, though, did not stop a combative Cook launching into some last rites for the Commission. 'It was a very uncomfortable meeting', recalled Jonty Boyce. 'Labour thought they were going to win, and Cook was quite vicious really. He said to us, "we are going to get rid of you!" '[18] Nevertheless Ross Tristem, diligent as ever, prepared a draft for Cook within days and sent it to the controller for his comments.

Then, just two days before the election, the controller trumped even Cook's appearance with some news of his own. He assembled all the Vincent Square staff outside his office, and announced his resignation. He would be leaving in June.

This came as a huge shock to everyone at the Commission – with the sole exception of the chairman. David Cooksey had been privy to Davies's secret from an early stage, for the simple reason that, as a member of the council of the Confederation of British Industry, he had been *au fait* with recent deliberations within the CBI over the choice of a new director-general – and this was the job for which Davies was leaving the Commission. John Banham had handed in his notice as its director-general back in November. (Much to the astonishment of senior officials at the DoE, Michael Heseltine had invited Banham to chair a new review body looking into the structure and boundaries of local authorities across the country. This was the Local Government Commission for England (LGCE), which had just been set up by the same Act that launched the Citizen's Charter.) Davies, for the second time in his career, had lined himself up as Banham's successor – and had got the job.

Inevitably, it was supposed by many that the prospect of a Labour victory lay behind his decision. This was only half true. Certainly he expected Labour to win. But there was no question of jumping, rather than waiting to be pushed by a vengeful Labour government (though even Davies must have wondered in the last days of the campaign how Labour's conflicting views would play out in the end). It was rather that, as Davies had told close friends, running the CBI under a Labour government looked an even bigger challenge than running the Commission.

Whatever his motive, Davies's resignation left the staff in Vincent Square stunned. As they headed home on the evening before the election, they now had two reasons to suppose that things would never be the same. Geoffrey Rendle recalled: 'I remember saying goodbye to Jonty Boyce, and he said to me, "See you tomorrow in the new world." I don't think we had any particular expectations of what a Labour government would do. But we were not expecting the current arrangements to survive.'[19]

The morning after the election, Ross Tristem was sitting at his desk reading about Major's sensational victory at the polls when a large brown envelope arrived on his desk. 'I opened it up and out fell all these shredded bits of paper – with a note from Howard. It said, "Here's what I think of your NHS paper for the Labour Party!" '[20]

STRIKING OUT IN A NEW DIRECTION

Labour's defeat came as a monumental relief to the whole team at Vincent Square – not least the chairman. Given the general expectation of a Labour victory, David Cooksey had been content to let Davies break the news of his exit after the election: there had seemed little point in starting the search for a successor any sooner. (In fact, Davies only broke the news before election day because of pressure from the CBI, who were concerned about the risk of a press leak.) And had Labour won, the uncertainty over the Commission's future might have hung over the search process for months. Now, it could begin in earnest. It was nonetheless awkward to be starting it so late. There was no possibility of finding the next controller by June – unless, of course, they promoted someone internally.

There was just one candidate in this category, but a good one – Peter Brokenshire. Since losing out to Davies in 1987, Brokenshire had settled into a generally happy and productive role as head of a Management Practice directorate that had flourished in recent years. David Henderson-Stewart's brilliance with numbers had given it real momentum. Several younger additions to the team – among them Alan Watson, Dermot O'Donovan, Martin McNeill and (unusually, straight from the army) Peter Wilkinson – had helped Brokenshire to build a strong team. Its quality was evident in a dozen or so Management Papers that had appeared since those two first titles, *The Competitive Council* and *More Equal than Others*, in 1988. Several were widely acclaimed – especially the 1990 paper on the changing role of the 21,000 local councillors in England and Wales, *We Can't Go on Meeting Like This* – and were to be quoted approvingly for years afterwards.

Especially notable, perhaps, was a rather unconventional audit guide addressing Brokenshire's long-held conviction that the basic management of many local authorities still urgently needed pulling into the twentieth century. Finalized in 1990, it was called simply *Management Arrangements*. It acknowledged that DAS auditors faced a challenge, in tackling any council over the way in which it ran itself: 'while some have undertaken work in this area, many more have been hesitant to begin, because the work demands rather different skills to other audit work'. Stressing that it was nevertheless a critical part of their role, the guide provided auditors with a step-by-step 'management arrangements diagnostic' – soon to be known to all auditors as the MAD – with which any council could be thoroughly reviewed. How to plan the review, and how to engage with the council in making any subsequent changes actually happen, were then spelt out in a suitably methodical fashion – all complete with handy checklists and a nicely illustrated graphic ('Beware the swamp' calibrated the steps between 'very firm ground' and 'very, very marshy' for anyone trying to influence a council, with an elegantly drawn alligator sitting in the corner of the matrix).

Brokenshire's role, though, went well beyond overseeing the production of written papers. He drew on his wide network of contacts throughout local government to ensure that each paper was actively championed among the professionals to whom its message was addressed. 'One obviously had to try and get people on board. So I spent a lot of time just going around talking to chief executives and using their help to pick people all around the country who could give us a few hours of their time.'[21]

The results rarely captured the media's attention. The soft benefits of better management practice were rather harder to chronicle than the quantifiable savings targeted by the classic special studies. It often involved some patient selling of the Audit Commission's role over many meetings, to chief executives who were not always easily persuaded of its relevance. (One notable sceptic was the chief executive of Gloucestershire County Council, Michael Bichard, who later became a distinguished Whitehall permanent secretary. Brokenshire recalled: 'I remember going to a meeting with him and presenting all our stuff – and he said: "This is all very well, but chief executives should be doing this rather than the Audit Commission." So I said: "Yes, I agree with that. But they haven't been, have they?" ')[22] But for this very reason, it was also work that spread the influence of the Commission in a lasting fashion. As he steered it along, Brokenshire grew into a sort of elder statesman role at Vincent Square.

This was especially evident after the retirement in August 1991 of the man credited with this role over most of the previous ten years.

Cliff Nicholson had finally stepped down at the end of a tough twelve months, steering through the absorption of the NHS audit and serving as president of CIPFA. It was a fitting conclusion to an extraordinary career for the clerical officer who had joined the DAS in 1952 with no accounting qualifications. David Cooksey's tribute in the 1992 Annual Report was no more than the truth:

His contribution ... cannot be overstated. He provided the essential thread of continuity between the old and the new and ensured that the best traditions of District Audit were maintained and developed within the new structure. No one has done more to ensure the Commission's success.

Nicholson's retirement, however, had also accentuated a faint suspicion among the Commission members that the day-to-day management of the place had taken on a slightly Heath-Robinson complexion. After the resignation of its original finance and administration director, John Vaughan, in the wake of a reorganization of the management team in 1987, no direct successor had been appointed. The controller had himself taken on oversight of personnel issues, aided by a strong personnel officer in Bristol, Terry Wright, and Nicholson had assumed the responsibility for finance.

Now, both Davies and Nicholson would be gone. The hiatus this left behind was made all the more conspicuous by the fact that no one else could possibly succeed Nicholson as deputy controller. His had always been an *ad hominem* position, fashioned to take advantage of Nicholson's standing within the DAS and his knowledge of the basic issues that would confront the development of the new Commission. Whoever succeeded Davies would have no choice but to re-examine the way the ten-year-old Commission went about its business. The members had a sense of this. It would be misleading to suggest they fretted greatly about it: for the most part, they took the executive activities of the Commission for granted. It was, in a sense, all back-stage business to them. The metaphor is only a slight exaggeration. For most of the members, each of their monthly meetings felt in many ways like a staged preview at which, like friends of the director, they were invited to offer helpful last-minute criticisms before the curtain went up for the public on this or that national report. How the rude mechanicals were organized behind the scenes was not usually of much concern. But from time to time it attracted their attention. And by April 1992 it was definitely on their minds.

They knew the internal management agenda had not been their controller's first priority. Murray Stuart, who had succeeded Harry Axton as the deputy chairman in February 1991, was especially exercised about this. A tough-minded Scottish businessman – he had just become chairman of Scottish Power, the utility group – Stuart was adamant that there had to be a much tighter grip on the management of the Commission itself. One implication, Stuart argued, was that central services should report to someone at the most senior level, based full-time in Vincent Square. Davies had assigned responsibility for all central management services to Martin McNeill, who had finally joined the staff late in 1990. McNeill had actually made a substantial impact on the financial management of the Commission. But he was still only an associate director and worked out of the office in Bristol. (This was no longer the old city-centre office occupied since the 1970s, though: the Commission had just relocated to fresh premises in the business district adjacent to Bristol's Parkway railway station. Its new home was aptly christened Nicholson House.)

And Stuart's assessment also implied a case for broader change. Accepting this, David Cooksey tacitly acknowledged the need for a change of style at the very top. Davies had exerted a remarkable hold over the place, by leading from the front in many ways – and by the sheer force of his personality. But this meant he would be no easier to replicate than Nicholson. To be effective, his successor would surely need to be someone with a much more structured approach. They would also need to have had experience of managing a large organization – for this is what the Audit Commission was now fast becoming (see Appendix 5). It had trebled its income since 1984-85, from £20 million to £63 million, and more or less doubled the size of its central staff, to 148. The staff of the DAS itself had numbered little more than 300 people in 1983. This had grown to 955 by 1991-92, and was still expanding steadily as new recruits came aboard to help cope with the new NHS work.

To Cooksey and his colleagues, it all amounted to a clear case for breaking with the past and finding an external candidate who could lead the Commission into a different era. Cooksey recalled: 'I think it was felt very strongly by the members that we needed somebody from outside [as Davies's successor] to get this managerial change made, otherwise the change wouldn't happen.'[23] So just short of a decade after the first call, out went a third call to the head-hunters, Spencer Stuart, to launch the search for a new controller. And this time around, the job spec was a little different. 'What we wanted was somebody who'd actually concentrate on delivering the service, as opposed to [advocating] huge policy shifts or persuading the government to do this, that or the other . . . We wanted a really solid managerial type.'[24]

Peter Brokenshire not only accepted this decision with characteristic grace, but agreed to serve as acting controller from Davies's departure in June until the end of 1992 while continuing to fill his substantial role as director of management practice. (There was a rumour at the time that he was planning to join John Banham as an executive member of the Local Government Commission for England, which would have been a great deal less convenient. He did in fact join it later, but only as a board member.) By the end of the year, it was agreed, the new appointee would be safely installed and Brokenshire would be able to take up a well-earned retirement. And well-earned it certainly proved to be. As Brokenshire recalled: 'By December, I was absolutely shattered.'[25]

A STRESSFUL INTERREGNUM

The burden he carried over those months had little to do with managing the Commission itself: it was in the nature of an interregnum that not much could really be changed, though Brokenshire set out plenty of ideas for his successor. Nor was he overly stretched by the special studies that appeared after April 1992. These were certainly substantial – they included two major reports each on housing, community care and the education of children with special needs – but most of the work on them had been completed before Davies finally departed in June. What really weighed on Brokenshire was the Citizen's Charter. The new government included a minister for the Citizen's Charter, with a place in the cabinet. The first was William Waldegrave. Within weeks, a formal direction was made to the Commission for a wide-ranging set of performance indicators to be published by the end of the year (and updated at the end of each subsequent year). Local authorities would be given three months to put in place the systems that would collect the data during 1993–94 – for publication in the press by the end of 1994. It was envisaged that the same regime would be extended to cover health bodies in due course.

It was perhaps a lucky break for the Commission that Brokenshire was still around to take on this assignment. As the principal author of the *Performance Review* paper in December 1989, he had a strong personal interest in the Citizen's Charter. And he was much less exercised than Davies over the possibility that enacting its provisions might in future take the Commission across that invisible line into adjudication. This aspect of the work was not lost on the Commission members. They were now well aware of the subtler implications of the Charter which Davies had flagged up in 1991. A new addition to the Commission since February was Tony Travers, an academic at the London School of Economics and a leading authority on local government. He recalled:

I think there was a definite realization that this was a departure and that the Commission was now being used by the government to implement policy. We were collectively very much aware in discussions about the Charter that the Commission was being pulled towards acting much more in the future as the government's agent. But the Commission didn't know how to say no.[26]

Neither did the members and their acting controller have any illusions about the scale of the task involved in complying with the Charter legislation. Peter Brokenshire put David Henderson-Stewart in charge of a small team comprising three managers from the Management Practice directorate. They included Peter Wilkinson, who had joined the Commission in May 1990 after serving for twenty years in the army. Wilkinson had done two tours of duty with the Royal Artillery in Northern Ireland, which left him with a colourful choice of similes for the rest of his career. Recalling later the brief handed over to the Commission by the Citizen's Charter Unit, Wilkinson thought it 'worse than a ticking package in a Belfast pub'.[27]

They toiled for months on a collection of PIs that might somehow convert a sweeping political aspiration into a set of quantitative measures, applicable in the public sector. It had never been done before, and the team trawled widely for constructive ideas. Wilkinson even travelled to Washington DC at one point, to talk to progressive Democrats in the Clinton camp about their ideas on the assessment of public services. Most of the work was a lot less glamorous – heavy going, indeed. But the team injected plenty of arithmetical rigour – Henderson-Stewart's leadership saw to that – and managed also to focus increasingly (as more than one prominent figure from local government urged) on outcomes as they would be perceived by a Charter-fired citizenry.

When the citizens caught their first glimpse of the draft package, reactions were as often as not ribald. The *Local Government Chronicle* ran a cartoon of a road sign welcoming motorists to 'Stats-womped', a district council boasting a list of fatuous indicators ('our office staff are the twelfth most helpful in Britain'). At the Association of Metropolitan Authorities' annual conference, a speaker invited delegates to consider the few indicators designed by the Commission for social services departments. He had them rolling in the aisles when he disclosed the first one: a measure of the time taken to provide an elderly person with a bath board. No joking matter for plenty of elderly people, as the Citizens' Advice Bureau could attest – but hardly the usual stuff of national directives in any sector. Brokenshire and Wilkinson had to make six presentations of the package to public audiences around the country that autumn, starting with the Civic Centre in Newcastle. Launching off with a spirited 'Good morning, Fellow Citizens' generally kept outright ridicule at bay, but it was often a close call.

Late in the process, in November 1992, the Commission members held the first of what would turn out to be a series of annual away-day retreats at the Runnymede Hotel in Egham, Surrey. (It would be hard to overstate the intensity with which Commission members approached regular off-site discussions during these years. Travers recalled: 'The Commission was privately obsessed with questions about its own role and its accountability.')[28] Their discussions together, guided by papers prepared for them by Brokenshire, provided an opportunity to acknowledge the Charter's impact explicitly, and where the new focus on quality in public services was leading.

There was no disagreement with Brokenshire's summary of the position.

Much of the quality work [involved in the Charter] could be regarded as outside the Commission's regulatory remit which it exercises through its appointed auditors, but perhaps can be seen more as a facilitating role. This work is nevertheless becoming regarded as an integral part of the Commission's central functions and further demonstrates the balancing act the Commission has successfully adopted ... [Given agreement at the retreat] the present positioning of the Commission in its various roles of regulator, enabler and facilitator is accepted as being about right.[29]

The Charter team's work finally culminated in a paper, *Charting a Course*, that went out to Commission members ahead of their monthly meeting at the beginning of December 1992. At the meeting, it was agreed only minor amendments to the paper were needed. It was then to be sent out to all local authorities, in line with the Commission's statutory duty. This statutory duty, it was also agreed, would be brought to the public's attention via publication in the national press of a summary version of the formal direction provided by the government. Plainly, the members were only too conscious of the ambivalence with which the wider world was watching their activity on the Charter.

Watching their activity at the meeting, meanwhile, was a newcomer to the Commission – and the man who would take over as controller in January 1993. Cooksey had announced the appointment of Andrew Foster at the monthly meeting in September. For Brokenshire, it was a chance to cross paths again with someone he had hired thirteen years earlier as a member of his executive team at Greenwich. For most of the members, it was a first opportunity to meet someone whose credentials for the top slot seemed almost too good to be true. Spencer Stuart had come up with a shortlist early in the summer. Cooksey and his deputy, assisted by a third Commission member, Bob Wall, had settled on their choice by the end of June – but there had been one slight snag. Andrew Foster was deputy chief executive of the NHS inside the Department of Health, and a man fancied by some to become its next head after the current incumbent, Duncan Nichol. The Audit Commission had poached its audit arm.

How might the DoH react to the Commission pinching one of its senior men?

From Cooksey's perspective, it was a complication worth accepting as part of a real coup for the Commission. Two leaders out of the Oxbridge–McKinsey mould had served it well through the Thatcher years. Going for a third was certainly one option. But the weather at Westminster was changing. The new preoccupation with charters and citizen consumers hugely added to the attractions of a candidate steeped in the very different culture of delivering services within the public sector. Foster would bring this experience to bear, as well as all the management skills honed in a successful climb up the ladder of a large organization. The fact that this organization happened to be the health service struck Cooksey and his colleagues, given all the difficulties between the Commission and the Department of Health, as decidedly a bonus. In time, they could surely look to him to heal the rift between the two institutions.

They would be appointing someone who had begun his career as a 1960s social worker, armed with a sociology degree and a post-graduate diploma in Applied Social Studies from the London School of Economics. Foster had worked his way up the social services departments of two London boroughs by 1979, in which year he was appointed director of social services at Greenwich Borough Council. At 32, and reporting to Peter Brokenshire, Foster was the youngest social services director in the country. He was hugely ambitious and shared with Brokenshire an impatience with ineptitude in the public sector. He had an almost vocational commitment to improving social services (influenced, no doubt, by his father, who had been a conscientious objector in the war and was a deeply religious man). But he combined this with a passion for organizational efficiency. At a time when social workers were too often the butt of jokes about profligacy and waste, this often made him unpopular with his peers. It did not hamper his career.

The next step up, after three years at Greenwich, was a move out of London. He was appointed as director of social services for North Yorkshire County Council. This new position carried responsibility for a population three times the size of Greenwich, and took Foster for the first time into a role that was more strategic than operational.

He thrived, and five years later, in 1987, was made chief executive of the Yorkshire Regional Health Authority. This was one of the larger RHAs in the country, with seventeen District Health Authorities, each built around a big hospital. Having cut his teeth in North Yorkshire on a £30 million budget with a staff of 5,000, Foster was now running a budget of £2 billion with a staff of 70,000.

It was a difficult time for the NHS: Margaret Thatcher's promised reforms were soon hanging over it like a Damoclean sword. A sense of foreboding among the doctors did nothing to lessen the long-cherished prejudice of the medical profession as a whole against managers from a social services background. In this tricky environment, Foster proved himself a tough operator. By 1990, his superiors in the health service had picked him out as the kind of strategic manager that was in short supply. He was brought down to Richmond House with a Grade 2 civil service job, as deputy to Duncan Nichol on the NHS executive and effectively its chief operating officer. There, Foster had been watching the delicate feuding between Health Department officials and the Audit Commission for two years by the time the call came from Spencer Stuart. He anguished over his final decision for a weekend or two, but accepted Cooksey's offer. He was then sworn to secrecy while the Commission's chairman worked out how best to broach the subject of his transfer with the Health Department.

How its officials responded is unrecorded. The secretary of state, Virginia Bottomley, was incensed. It was said that she had her eye on Foster as a future permanent secretary for the department. Having tried in vain to persuade Cooksey to change his mind, she insisted that Foster work out his full six months' notice period. Hence the December timing of Foster's first appearance in Vincent Square. What this prologue would portend for the Commission's relationship with the DoH remained to be seen.

A THIRD CONTROLLER TAKES
THE HELM

If the enforced delay had tested his patience, there was never any suggestion from the freshly installed controller of a whirlwind first hundred days. That was not the new man's style. Instead, he launched himself into an elaborate programme of exploratory meetings over the next several weeks. He started with the Commission members themselves, and the executive team around him. A district auditor seconded as an 'associate controller' to Vincent Square since 1991, Brian Willmor, helped with this induction. Then Foster worked his way around the seven regions of the DAS, talking to district auditors but also reaching well beyond them to tap his own extensive network of personal contacts within local government and the NHS.

At least one initiative, though, could not be delayed. Foster arrived at Vincent Square knowing full well that structures and procedures were not its main strengths. All the same, he appeared to find his new environment even more ascetic than he had anticipated. One of the stalwarts of the two studies directorates, Steve Evans, recalled: 'My guess is that he was slightly taken aback at the absence of support in various areas. For a start, the chief executive's office was physically pretty small. The support staff for the chief executive was small, too, and our systems in many areas were totally unconsolidated. I think it all came as rather a shock to him.'[30]

Foster decided immediately to appoint a second associate controller – someone who could serve him as a kind of chief of staff. (Willmor, who returned to the DAS late in 1993, had been tasked by Davies with bringing first-hand knowledge of the audit field to the Commission's monthly meetings.) Expecting to make an external appointment, he was surprised to receive applications from a handful of insiders. One came from Peter Wilkinson. Now aged 39, Wilkinson had proved his mettle on the Citizen's Charter work, acting as Brokenshire's assistant. At the same time, he had been on the staff less than three years – a good part of which had been spent on secondment to a health authority in Portsmouth, where he had been sent to devise an NHS version of the Management Arrangements Diagnostic. He was therefore still a relative newcomer to Vincent Square, and his military background inevitably marked him out as a manager with a rather different take on life from many of his older colleagues. Indeed, Wilkinson had contemplated leaving after his first few months at Vincent Square, so alien was the culture he found there. (He recalled: 'People had a great deal of freedom to get on and do things, but there wasn't necessarily much linkage between what different individuals ended up doing. Someone said to me in the early days, "to be successful here, you need to be able to survive naked with a pen-knife on Dartmoor".')[31] Foster sensed in his early days that he would want to forge a fresh team around himself in due course. He appointed Wilkinson as a clear step in that direction.

The first task that the two of them tackled together was the preparation of a broad initial strategy document. It emerged in March, entitled *Adding Value*. Much of its content was unremarkable and bore more than a passing resemblance to the admonitions of Foster's predecessor back in 1987. Regularity and probity work needed re-emphasis; auditors should work with more heed to the needs of local authorities; major reports should be revisited to follow up on opportunities that might have emerged since the original study; and so on. Probably more telling than its content, though, was the way in which the paper was pulled together. In most essentials, it had been agreed by the Commission members at their Egham retreat the previous November. At his first monthly meeting as their controller, in January 1993, Foster undertook to repackage the members' findings before the next meeting as a 'public consultation paper'. In the interim, no fewer than six staff groups were set up as review bodies. Further consultations with people in local government and the health service followed during February. Bits of the emerging draft were rewritten to accommodate changes from the members (though they agreed in February that it 'was faithful to their discussions at the away-day') and comments from one or two consultants whom the new controller retained as private advisers. Then the final version was printed in time for a conference to celebrate the tenth anniversary of the Commission on 5 March.

Good use was made of it, too. The strategy was launched 'for public consultation' – with responses to be collected by the controller's office for a further three months, and summarized for the members in June. It was used as the basis of Vincent Square's first conscious marketing effort, with slim *Adding Value* brochures posted widely to advertise the virtues of the Commission to its various audiences. And it was taken as the cue for the first management conference of its kind, at which district auditors and their senior managers from the field gathered alongside directors and associate directors from the centre: about seventy of the top staff participated in a two-day session, to chew over the implications of the newly articulated strategy.

The conference was chiefly notable for a lively discussion – redolent, perhaps, of debates in pre-1982 days – about the significance to the auditors of their responsibility for value-for-money work. One of the more senior district auditors in the DAS, Frank Kerkham, pointed out in forceful terms that too little attention was paid by the world at large to the ways in which *public* audit differed profoundly from its counterpart in the private sector. Indeed, there was no *real* counterpart, in so far as private sector auditors had no obligation to conduct VFM work. Nor did the latter have anything like the genuine independence that accrued to public auditors by virtue of their independent appointment process, and their entitlement to publish reports on any negative findings in the public interest. These were good reasons to trumpet the unique nature of the role played by DAS auditors, Kerkham insisted.

His colleagues agreed. Peter Wilkinson was tasked with drafting a first statement of the 'Principles of Public Audit' (PoPA) which would enshrine these three critical differences, centred on independence, VFM and Public Interest Reports. They were set down eloquently in the chairman's statement at the head of the 1993 Annual Report which appeared a few months later. (Just for good measure, it also cited an old chestnut from the lips of Nye Bevan that auditors were still fond of quoting: 'The district auditor is unique – another expression of the British genius for government.')[32] A few years later, they were adopted with little change as the principles underpinning the Public Audit Forum, a body set up at the government's instigation in 1996 to promote consultation between the NAO, the Commission and its counterparts in Scotland and Northern Ireland.

The whole process involved in the publication of *Adding Value*, and the PoPA that followed it, flagged the arrival of a controller who worked in very different ways from his two predecessors. The district auditors of old would not have marked his card as 'good with pen'. Nor was he ever likely to descend on Vincent Square of a Monday morning with a slate of weekend ideas pulled from nowhere. But if the Commission members were looking for someone to involve all his colleagues in the management process, elicit views effectively across a wide front and shape them into a consensus that he would then promote tirelessly and persuasively, then they had found their man. Suddenly meetings of the Commission's top management actually consisted of discussions about the management of the Commission – which came as rather a welcome novelty to most of the directors. Harry Wilkinson recalled: 'The meetings were in very sharp, positive contrast to what had gone before. Andrew was inclusive, and would go around the table asking all of us what we thought.'[33]

How this newly consensual approach might feed back into the content of the Commission's policies was a question for the longer term. The fact that a section of the *Adding Value* strategy document paper was subtitled 'The Citizens' Perspective', though, did not suggest that supporting the Citizen's Charter was going to pose a huge dilemma. In one of his first press interviews, Foster told the *Local Government Chronicle* that his initial review of the Commission had suggested to him it might have a broader role as 'a guardian of quality public services ... [He said] its Citizen's Charter work and a new commitment to include quality in all aspects of its work meant the Commission could have a different image in five years' time. "Are we going to become the consumer affairs body on the public services over the next five years? I think that's a potential image", he said.'[34]

What concerned the staff directors rather more urgently was what the new controller's approach to Vincent Square would mean for their own personal futures. What would he do with a team, and a team structure, that in many respects had scarcely changed since 1983? While it was obvious quite quickly what the eventual answer would be, spelling it out took a while. While he was soon anxious to strengthen what he saw as its managerial weaknesses, Foster respected the intellectual strengths of the team he had inherited. He tackled his change agenda with characteristic care. The first step was to alter the organizational structure, and this he did in September. Management services were reassigned to a new 'director of resources' in Vincent Square. And Harry Wilkinson's role was divided into two new positions. A 'director of audit support' would handle the technical side of audit and accounting. The old Management Practice directorate's activities would also be swept into audit support. A 'director of purchasing' would take charge of coordinating the assignment of audits to the DAS and the private firms, prescribing their fees and monitoring their performance. (The actual assignment would remain as always the preserve of the Commission members themselves, advised by their own appointments panel and, of course, the executive team that would now be led by the new purchasing director.)

This signalled quite an upheaval: what was often described by managers themselves as the vaguely anarchic spirit of Vincent Square since 1983 was now to be superseded. The immediate outcome, however, was in practice less clear-cut. Harry Wilkinson, for example, lost his department but retained his title, and devoted himself for the next couple of years to 'a lot of technical issues rather than all the nitty gritty' before his mandatory retirement in 1996.[35] The new resources director – Bill Ogley, formerly the finance director of Hertfordshire County Council – arrived in the autumn of 1993, but Martin McNeill remained in his Bristol office until the spring of 1994. Still, the eventual outcome was clear enough: the old guard, assembled by John Banham and retained by Howard Davies, was on its way out. Inevitably, perhaps, the parting had its problems. Foster was a conscientious public sector servant, not a connoisseur of corporate coups. Those like Ross Tristem and David Henderson-Stewart who had thrived in earlier times found the new, more structured environment a less happy place to be – but they stayed on into 1994 or 1995, with all of the predictable consequences. Peter Wilkinson recalled: 'it wasn't an easy period at all'.[36]

There was one item on his change agenda, however, that the new controller ticked off in short order. He took note of the Commission members' discussions at their Egham retreat, looked hard at his own findings over his first five months and agreed his decision with Cooksey and the members in June 1993: the District Audit Service would be detached and run at arm's length from the Commission 'on an agency basis'. The decision was announced that month as part of a Management Action Plan. The search for a chief executive started immediately, as of course did speculation within the DAS and beyond over what the news might really portend. Diehards in the service shook their heads over Foster's evident failure to understand the delicate ties between the DAS and Vincent Square. A full spin-off for the service could only be a matter of time. As Foster recalled: 'I was the Butcher of Kabul.'[37]

Supporters of the move, on the other hand, generally viewed it as the essential precondition for any effective modernization of what the auditors themselves would sometimes self-deprecatingly refer to as 'The Brown Cardigan Brigade' – the rank and file of the 139-year-old DAS who appeared to have clung on to some antediluvian attitudes (and sartorial standards) since 1983, almost in defiance of the radical transformation of local government spurred on by the Commission itself. So what underlay the cardigan jibe, and how successfully did the new structure usher in a refreshed, modern audit body?

From DAS to District Audit,
1993–97

A memorable aspect of the District Audit Society's annual jamboree in the first years of the Audit Commission had been the guest speaker's toast at dinner. It ran: 'Mr President, Honoured Guests, Miss Gifford, Gentlemen . . .' Seldom can one exception have proved a rule so disarmingly. The senior ranks of the DAS had a lady in their midst – Joan Gifford, a greatly respected senior assistant district auditor based in Reading – but she was the only one. In the mid-1980s the senior ranks of the service still remained virtually closed to women, just as they always had been. There was little doubt among those who worked with her that Joan Gifford had been overtaken by male colleagues who were far less able.

By the time that the first thirteen special project officers for the NHS were appointed in 1989 – one for each of the thirteen DAS districts – a change was clearly in the air. Half a dozen of them were women. Elsewhere, things stayed much the same – as one of the new recruits, Trish Longdon, soon discovered. She arrived (straight from a previous job in the office of the local government ombudsman) just in time to join a couple of hundred male colleagues at that year's DA Society conference on the Warwick University campus. She found herself one of fewer than ten women attending an event with a distinctly laddish flavour. As the beers circulated and her male colleagues joshed their way through sporting quizzes – or drew lots in a sweepstake on the length of the guest speaker's address (a long-standing tradition) – she was left pondering the options for her next career move. 'My jaw just dropped. It was unbelievable.'[1]

She persevered – and saw the number of women project officers growing steadily around her over the next four years. Indeed, by 1994 three women had been appointed as district auditors, no less. (Alas, Joan Gifford was not among them: she had died a few years earlier. The distinction of being the first ever went to Janet Jones, appointed in Wales in 1991.) But beer and sport still largely defined the culture of the service in after-work hours. It was only a slight exaggeration to say that young auditors who could neither bat nor bowl were at a subtle disadvantage.

As with the attitude towards women, so with the general evolution of the service: the DAS had certainly made significant progress by 1994, compared with its situation a decade earlier, but there was a long way still to go. Much of the progress was down to Brian Skinner, the former Met district auditor who had emerged from the non-compliance battles of the 1980s with distinction and become head of the service late in 1988. All of Skinner's predecessors as the chief inspector of audit had been based in Bristol since 1975. This had contributed to a steadily widening gulf between the DAS and its masters in Vincent Square. (Indeed, the last chief inspector, Les Stanford, had begun to see his own office's location in Bristol as grounds for complaint by the end of his term.) By 1988 Howard Davies was keen to see Skinner take over and remain in London. He would have liked him to move into Vincent Square, but there was insufficient space there. So as the new director of audit, Skinner remained in County Hall where he had been located as the Metropolitan DA. He set up shop with a secretary and an assistant, Bill Butler, occupying Room 101.

Through 1989, Skinner led the service's adjustment to seven regions in the reorganization of the DAS that accompanied the transfer of FB4 from the Department of Health. He also laid the groundwork for the audit of NHS bodies and oversaw the redrafting of the audit manual. Then he inaugurated a District Audit Management Board that comprised himself and Bill Butler plus the newly established seven regional directors. They met each month in County Hall, starting in January 1990. Their first job was to create a proper budget for the service, which (remarkably) had never been done before. The total number of audit days for a year had been decided by Cliff Nicholson after consultation with all the district auditors, and they had had to muddle through. Now computerized spreadsheets were prepared, with days allocated to specific regions and detailed projections of costs and revenues for each of them.

Recruitment was another priority. Following the integration of the FB4 staff into the service, hundreds of new appointments had to be made. They were badly needed, as already noted, both to fill the gaps left by defections from FB4 and to take account of the fact that the NHS audit – which was to begin in April 1990 – was expanding to include far more value-for-money work. Over the next three years, this lifted NHS audit days by about 40 per cent. Skinner's assistant, Bill Butler, was well practised at recruitment. After joining the DAS straight from college in 1978, he had spent most of his first two years in the service poring over old GLC records in the windowless sub-basement of County Hall. (He recalled: 'There was no natural light, just a few rats.')[2] After passing his accountancy exams in 1982, Butler had then spent most of the next few years in Bristol interviewing graduates and qualified accountants to meet the rapidly rising staffing needs of the service under John Banham. Now, after working for a while in the interim as the Commission secretary and assistant to Howard Davies, he was at the centre of the service's second big expansion, which would take staff numbers from about 800 to more than 1,200 over the three years to the end of 1993. Many of the senior interviewees, especially for district auditor positions, were interviewed in a meeting room with a large 101 on the door. Butler recalled: 'I said to Brian Skinner: "Anybody who comes in and doesn't make an ironic reference to being in Room 101, we shouldn't appoint!" But they were accountants, so most of them didn't get the irony.' Perhaps he should have brought a few rats up from the basement, too.

Significant progress had also been made by 1993 with the staff functions supporting the service. In 1990, these had still been shared with Vincent Square in rather a haphazard fashion. Martin McNeill recalled: 'There wasn't really a proper management structure at all. There weren't even quasi-contractual arrangements between the Commission and the DAS for finance, personnel, IT and so on.'[3] Three years later, the tripartite structure – comprising the Commission, the DAS and Management Services – was in place, and functions had been redefined where appropriate. In IT, for example, Chris Hurford's dual role as head of computer audit in the field and head of computer services for the Commission itself had been sensibly divided. The assessment of IT costs and services was fast becoming one of the most important aspects of every major audit. (A new series of Information Papers had been launched late in 1989, and Nos. 3 and 4 in the autumn of 1990 – respectively entitled *Knowing What IT Costs* and *Acquiring IT* – brought the Commission's standard analytical approach to bear on IT facilities for the first time.) Hurford remained in charge of computer audit, while new people were brought in from outside to run the central staff function. As head of management services, McNeill had also laid out plans for a new management accounting system which was almost ready for implementation by 1993. Gradual changes in the culture of the DAS were similarly evident in attitudes towards management training. It had started to become much more regularly available for senior staff: some of the new regional directors since 1990 had been sent on college courses.

Notwithstanding all these individual initiatives, the DAS remained recognizably the creature it had been for many decades. As he travelled around the country talking to people in 1993, it did not take long for Andrew Foster to size up its weaknesses. It was now responsible for approximately 70 per cent of the audit appointments made to 450 local authorities and 700 NHS bodies. He heard plenty of stories about wild inconsistencies across this huge client base, with auditors pursuing their own pet interests with scant regard for any policy directives from their seniors. Unsurprisingly, there was also a huge variability in performance standards, not just between regions but even between neighbouring districts. And, where standards were low, it was clear that the audit manual was being regarded as advisory, at best.

Ironically, given the problems encountered over the standards within FB4, it was criticism from within the NHS that confirmed the failings of the DAS most damagingly. Foster heard from several NHS trust boards – where judgements were rarely tinged by any political consideration – that the performance of the DAS had fallen well short of the standards previously set by auditors brought in from the private sector. Foster recalled: 'The service was traditional, old-fashioned, hierarchical – and still very much a culture of Buggins' turn, in terms of how people made it through.'[4]

Hence the decision in June 1993 to push the DAS out as an

arm's-length agency of the Commission. When Brian Skinner retired in 1994, his successor would have to be a professional manager from outside the service. Finding a heavyweight for this role was not seen as a problem. The DAS had had an income of £63 million in 1991–92. This was enough to make it the seventh largest of the country's accounting firms, ranked on the basis of their audit fees. The appointee would also have the distinction of being the first 'chief executive' in the history of the service.*

The man they found for the job was David Prince. In 1993 he was working as the chief executive of Leicestershire County Council. Tall, palpably straightforward with a faintly episcopal air, he had worked his way up the local government ladder since graduating with a degree in English from Exeter University in 1969. He was (in the head-hunters' stock phrase) happy in his current job, and he enjoyed the status of being top dog in an interesting and diverse county – but the attractions of the DAS post were clear to him from the start. After a series of interviews and a cordial meeting with David Cooksey, all that remained for Prince was to satisfy himself that the Commission's controller was someone he could comfortably work with.

Prince recalled: 'I met him at a hotel somewhere – it was typical Andrew, driving up late in the evening to meet me, with his diary crammed full of other things.' Prince's main concern was simple. Would he be left to get on with the brief, or would he find himself effectively relegated to the kind of deputy role he had now left behind in his career? The two of them talked at some length. 'And Andrew convinced me that – provided I set out a sensible plan for the service which they were comfortable with, and that I delivered what they had signed up to – it would be a case of "no surprises, please, but you get on with it". That was the deal I did with Andrew, and he stuck to it.'[5] Prince joined in June 1994, reporting directly to a specially created panel of four Commission members, including the chairman. This had been established four months earlier, and would meet every three

---

* He might have had the distinction of being its first private proprietor. It was later rumoured that a senior partner from one of the firms had reached the shortlist on the basis that, after appointment, he would lead a management buy-out of the service. Commission members had only decided against it, or so the story went, after lengthy deliberation. But there is no formal record of such a discussion.

months. He would have a 'dotted-line' report to the controller. He and Andrew Foster, it was agreed, would meet together on a monthly basis.

The DAS panel was actually one of four that were set up at this point in an initiative led by the members, to establish a better interface between themselves and the executives in the post-Davies era. Each comprised three, sometimes four, commissioners. Two of the panels, overseeing the DAS on the one hand and the purchasing of audits on the other, dealt with practical matters that would require more detailed discussion than would usually be appropriate at Commission monthly meetings. A third, the audit panel, would deal with governance matters. And a fourth would deal with the new Citizen's Charter. Jeremy Orme, a member since 1989, recalled:

The panel mechanism served everyone's interests in providing a way for commissioners to get much more involved than was possible via the monthly meetings alone. And panels would allow different members to be vigorous champions of separate Commission responsibilities, like purchasing and leadership of the DAS, that actually had the potential to be in conflict with each other.[6]

With its reporting lines established, it just remained for the new agency's location to be decided. The Commission had opted a few months earlier to take out a lease on the whole of 1 Vincent Square, adding two more floors to its current space there, and it was decided that Prince and his staff should move in (on the first floor) once a major refurbishment was completed. (The regional director for London and the south-east, Peter Day, had already been operating out of Vincent Square's ground floor, prior to the refurbishment.) For the three remaining months of the refurbishment, Prince joined his new colleagues in their temporary home on two floors of Portland House, a large building near Victoria station.

The irony of the relocation did not go unremarked. When the service had been repackaged by the 1982 legislation as an integral arm of the Commission, some merit had been attached to ensuring at least a physical distance between its boss and Vincent Square. Now that arm's-length arrangements were being put in place, it was paradoxically deemed acceptable – though not without a lively debate in the Commission, with at least one member vigorously dissenting – to have the boss sitting downstairs from the controller and his fellow directors. This was obviously convenient for the Commission, but what the big accountancy firms' partners thought about it can only be supposed. Still, no formal objections ever surfaced – and it would not be long before ways were found to impress the firms with the integrity of the new set-up.

LEAVING THE OLD SERVICE BEHIND

Prince was given a target date of 1 November 1994 for the launch of his arm's-length organization. As three controllers had now done over the years, he set off in his early days to carry out his own personal audit of the service he now headed. For two and a half weeks, he toured the seven regions of England and Wales in numerical order, receiving from each a formal presentation and meeting with scores of audit staff to hear their thoughts on the future. As a chief executive in Leicestershire, and finance director in Cambridgeshire before that, he had already learned a good deal about the ways of the DAS. His travels reminded him of earlier lessons. He recalled:

It had some excellent people and a good ethos built round professional commitment, public service values and all of that. It also had a strong *esprit de corps* and self-image. But like much of the public sector at that time, some excellence upfront brought along too long a tail of indifferent and poor performers behind it.[7]

Perhaps it is a little surprising, given all the effort expended on reorganizations of the service over the previous ten years, that this should have been Prince's first impression of the situation in the field. But it was confirmation in a way of the assessment made by the chairman and his colleagues in the wake of Howard Davies's departure: much less attention had been devoted to the day-to-day management of the DAS than to raising the profile of the Commission at a national level. Probably it had been too easily assumed through the Banham and Davies years that all the excitement of the pioneering culture in Vincent Square would automatically percolate down into the district offices and audit sections scattered across the country. In reality, the very strength of the DAS culture acknowledged by Prince had in some ways been a barrier to this trickle-down effect. The consequence by 1994 was that Vincent Square's ambitions had rather outrun the DAS's ability to deliver on the ground. As will be seen, this was to be the nub of a recurring criticism of the Commission's effectiveness over the years to come.

When Prince returned to his desk in London, he set out on a table the seven presentations he had received. They could almost have come from seven different organizations. In addition to reflecting the inconsistency he had just seen for himself, the presentations also confirmed two other weaknesses that he saw as fundamental. The service was hopelessly under-managed. The Human Resources function, for example, appeared to be limited in effect to the administration of job appointments (though there were plenty of horror stories about these being mismanaged, too, and the service was still severely understaffed). It struck Prince that managing people's careers for its own sake was somehow regarded as rather a sentimental activity. To take it too seriously would run counter to the service's tough macho culture. As in many other professional organizations in which successful practitioners eventually rise to managerial posts for which they have little aptitude, the impact was woeful. 'I had no doubt at all that there were many people [in the service] who lived very miserable lives in small remote teams around the country, under a manager who was probably an excellent auditor but who lived for audit and little else.'[8]

Another flaw lay in the service's attitude to the people it was supposedly serving. At first glance, and at the most senior levels, there was some evidence of the mindset that prevailed in private sector auditing. That is to say, while both sides knew the formal legal responsibilities underlying the role of audit, nonetheless auditors related to business people as their clients. Some district auditors did the same. But many did not, especially within the more junior ranks. Of course it would be an exaggeration to say they handled council employees rather as their Victorian forebears had handled those masters of the workhouse, whose gruel and biscuit budgets needed watching so carefully. But the bloodline was there, and sometimes disconcertingly easy to spot.

One further feature of the DAS took another couple of months to become fully apparent to Prince. He organized a survey of staff attitudes through the early summer – the first ever conducted for the service by an external agency. He thought he knew roughly what to expect. As in every institution with a glamorous centre and a nation-wide network of people toiling in the field, whether in the public or the private sector, there would no doubt be undercurrents of resent-ment and complaints about persistent neglect. What the survey dis-closed, though, was much worse. (Prince recalled: 'It was the most searing document I think I've ever read in my life.')[9] Serious tensions existed between employees of the DAS working in every region of the country and what too many of them appeared to regard as the remote, Oxbridge-educated elite of Vincent Square. Even allowing for the licence offered by an anonymous survey, a worryingly large minority of younger auditors around the country seemed to think they were at the wrong end of a vaguely feudal hierarchy. Nor were their suspicions entirely unjustified. Arriving in Vincent Square a few years earlier, Geoffrey Rendle had encountered a distinctly seigneurial view of the tillers in the field.

I was very surprised when I arrived to see how little attention the studies depart-ment paid to the auditors. I remember saying to one of the associate directors: 'Can you show me one of these VFM reports that the auditors eventually have to write for a council or health authority?' And he said, 'Oh, we hardly ever look at them' – and we had to go down into the basement and dig around amongst audit papers to find one.[10]

More mundanely, a disconcerting number of the auditors were scathing about their own immediate seniors. Plainly, they still felt oppressed by the weight of the DAS layers above them, despite the restructuring of 1989–90 that had seen deputy district auditors swept away and the old ADA and SADA ranks replaced by managers and senior managers. Their disaffection went beyond a natural scepticism about all institutions, which to some extent was a part of any good auditor's make-up. People felt suffocated. 'It seemed as though every-body's perspective was that they could do better if only they were not blocked by the people above them.'[11]

By July 1994, Prince was ready to start his unblocking. He arranged a conference at Henley Management College, to which he invited all of the seven regional directors and – rather to the RDs' chagrin – a district auditor from each of their regions. (The latter included Bill

Butler, who had recently become a district auditor in Birmingham.) They were joined at the college by the half dozen or so individuals whom Prince had already appointed to his staff at the centre. He intended to work with a very small central team. One of them was Trish Longdon, who had survived her baptism of fire at Warwick in 1989 to become one of the leading health specialists in the Commission: she joined Prince's staff as a senior manager. Another was John Sherring, who would give up being the regional director in Birmingham in January 1995 to take on the role of marketing director in London. David Warne, one of the senior FB4 staff who had stayed with the DAS, moved into a financial reporting position, and a newcomer called John Tench was appointed as a kind of roving consultant on organizational change. Prince had also decided to retain the idea of a District Audit Management Board (DAMB). One of the non-DAS people on it was Bill Ogley, the resources director hired into Vincent Square in 1993, who sat on the board as the Commission's representative. Prince already knew Ogley well – they had worked together in the past, at Hertfordshire County Council – and he asked him to watch over the finances of the service in addition to his duties for the Commission. (Clearly the arm's-length arrangement would have a flexible elbow.)

This was the team that met together for the Henley session. As intended, it was quite unlike anything experienced within the DAS before. With help from the resident staff at the college, the party worked its way through a long agenda of management issues. Some important decisions were taken. It was agreed that the thirty or so district auditors could no longer realistically be expected to cover the whole range of institutions included in the Commission's franchise. Prince recalled: 'The culture had been such that, if you were a *proper* auditor, you had to have one of everything – you had a county and a district and an NHS trust and a purchasing body, and so on. And that patently no longer worked.'[12] Some degree of specialization would now be gradually introduced, together with a reduction in the size of each DA's patch. This would entail recruiting an additional twenty or so DAs – some of whom, in a hugely significant break with the past, would be outsiders hired directly into the role.

As the result of a major initiative already undertaken in 1992, every grade within the service – up to and including both DAs and regional directors – had been defined in terms of specific competencies. It was now decided to build on this by ensuring that the recruitment or promotion of any individual would be based on the outcome of an appropriate assessment procedure, grading them against those competencies. The move towards more specialist roles had of course been begun with the creation of the project officers and the rapid rise in their numbers since 1990. This expansion would go on, and the officers would now work as 'added value units' (AVUs) which would put a premium on effective cooperation across regional directorates. As for these directorates themselves, Prince had already decided before arriving at the college to alter their shape, and to reduce them from seven to five. They would be based in future on regional offices in London, Leeds, Solihull, Winchester and Cardiff. (The two offices that disappeared were Chorley and Stevenage.)

The shrinkage in the number of directorates produced a slightly unfortunate moment during one of the conference sessions. The whole group was attending what was supposed to be a general discussion. Confronted at one point with a plainly uncomfortable bunch of regional directors, Prince took the seven of them off for a break-out chat. While they were gone, Bill Butler and another of the DAs, Mike Robinson, took two of the regional directors' seven chairs and lifted them on to one of the tables. When the group returned, Butler mischievously announced that two of their chairs would no longer be required. As a light-hearted way of easing the tension, this was less than ideal – unknown to the DAs, Prince had already opened negotiations with two of the directors to arrange their departures.[13]

Finally, a corporate rebranding exercise was launched, which led – via extensive discussions with some external consultants and a few focus groups at which new colours, shapes and letters were tested out – to the adoption in the autumn of a new name. The service would now be called . . . just plain District Audit, with a 'DA' logo and a purple livery for its stationery. The inclusion of 'Service' in the old title was seen as a little old-fashioned and insufficiently cognizant of the two-way traffic that audit teams would be encouraging in future. At the same time, leaving behind the old name altogether would have meant ditching a label with a strong 'brand equity' accumulated over many decades of working within local government. All this, and much else about the psychology behind the new logo, was carefully relayed from the consultants to the senior auditors by Prince's team – with predictable results. Trish Longdon recalled: 'You have never seen anything so funny in your life as auditors listening to the descriptions of their work by the brand consultants. We soon dropped all the flowery language and just told them: this is how it's going to be.'[14]

All the plans for the new-look service ended up in a District Audit Corporate Plan that was approved by the Commission members in October 1994. And the relaunched DA duly made its appearance, as promised, on 1 November. Prince committed to the Commission that his District Audit would achieve three targets. It would stand on its own feet financially and pay the Commission a decent return (it was called 'the owner's dividend') over and above a contribution to central costs. It would deliver a measurable improvement in the quality of its performance. And it would finally ditch for good the image of the district auditor as a semi-regal figure, best approached via a kneeling mat. In management-speak, DA would embrace 'customer focus'. Over the next twelve months, each of these three targets would end up involving a sort of initiation test for Prince and his central team.

FROM BUDGETS AND MARKET-TESTING TO ASSESSMENTS

By late 1994, the Management Services division in Bristol had been providing the field force with efficient back-office support for three years. No longer, for example, did junior staff in District Audit offices all over the country have to labour over local invoicing, as they had done for generations before the process was centralized at Bristol. Management Services had been set up as an agency arrangement, and this suited the new arm's-length status of DA perfectly. While invoicing and other such matters were now being done Bristol-fashion, however, they were far from ship-shape. The local accounts that underpinned them remained skimpy at best in all too many DA offices. There was little attempt to keep an accurate record of how staff spent their time, nor were costs allocated to audit clients in any systematic way. The paradox of poorly tracked finances in auditors' offices was even more remarkable, given the rapid expansion in the audit business over the decade since the launch of the Commission in 1983. Operating income in that first year had totalled £15 million. By 1989–90, the last financial year before the assumption of the NHS franchise, it had risen to just shy of £34 million. DA's fee income in 1994–95 would come to £37.5 million in local government and £25.9 million in the NHS.

These figures reflected a growth in the range and complexity of the workload that had made better record-keeping a priority by the time David Prince arrived. And he and Bill Ogley, of course, had their own incentive for wanting to keep better track of the finances. DA was contracted now to paying about 8 per cent of its annual revenues to Vincent Square as a contribution to the cost of the central directorates. (This was in addition to the direct payments made to Bristol for its services.) They also had to provide the owner's dividend, which ran along at about 5 per cent of revenues. Unsurprisingly, they were not prepared to go forward with regional-office budgets that did little more than list travel and petty expenses. A comprehensive time-charging system was now rolled out, so that individual offices could keep track of the staff input for each audit, and aim for a better balance between costs and revenues. The latter continued (rather oddly, perhaps) to be based on the traditional 'Audit Days' formula, whereby fees were derived from applying a standard daily rate to a notional number of days devoted to the audit. But overnight, DA offices had anyway to begin keeping proper records of all expenses. Regional directors were required to draw up budgets that balanced these against anticipated revenues. The mechanics of invoicing and collecting those revenues remained with the office in Bristol. (It was not to be until 1998 that full advantage was taken of the time-charging system to move to the 'Fees for Audit' arrangement as used in the private sector, based on actual rather than notional days of work done. But 'full advantage' might not be entirely apt: under the old formulaic approach, it was not unknown for some audited bodies – especially the larger authorities – to be overcharged. In districts suffering from severe staff shortages, the gap between the invoiced time and the reality can't have boosted enthusiasm when the time eventually came for the switch to Fees for Audit.)

Whatever the state of DA's book-keeping, Prince never had any real worries over the buoyancy of DA's finances: he knew a robust income from regularity-audit work in local government and the NHS was being substantially boosted by fees for the certification of claims for central government grants. The test in the financial sphere had less to do with confirming the rude health of DA's finances than with checking that DA's good fortune was merited. Within months of his appointment, and certainly before the new accounting regime had shed any fresh light on the matter, Prince found himself in the middle of a lively debate in Vincent Square over the real calibre of DA's performance. If the service were to be fully exposed to open competition against the private sector firms, would it emerge creditably or find itself priced out of the market? And if there was reason to suspect the latter, ought far more of the audit function to be outsourced to the private sector, in pursuit of a better and cheaper service to the public?

Andrew Foster, always keen to learn from those running public sector services in other countries, had recently visited New Zealand to talk to the Commission's counterpart there, the Office of the Auditor General, about its experience of outsourcing. In this field of social policy, as in many others around this time, New Zealand in the early 1990s appeared to be leading the way. At Foster's behest, David Prince now made the same trip. (It was the start of a close bond with DA's counterpart, Audit New Zealand, both for the Commission and David Prince personally. A few years later, indeed, the post of purchasing director in Vincent Square would be taken up by a secondee from Audit New Zealand, Bruce Anderson.) Both Foster and Prince came back looking for ways to open up the public audit market to more competition. They were not about to open up swathes of the market to private firms, as the New Zealanders seemed to be contemplating, but they were ready to experiment. Amidst all the compulsory competitive tendering that was such a hallmark of the public sector, Foster especially liked the idea of tenders that would allow DA to show it was taking its own medicine. He saw it as a valuable way to strengthen the credibility of the Commission.

The compromise they settled upon was 'market-testing'. Blocks of eight to ten audits would be put up for tender, and DA would be invited to compete against a handful of private firms for the business. (It would not be allowed to price its bids at a loss, to avoid defeat: a little bizarrely, it would be obliged to deposit a model of its underlying costs with a bank prior to any contest.) The director of purchasing in Vincent Square – a post first filled by a secondee from one of the private firms, Mollie Bickerstaff – would coordinate a formal selection procedure, working closely with a panel of Commission members to choose the best auditors on merit alone. (The panel was chaired for most of the 1990s by one member: Jeremy Orme.) The result would reassure the Commission members, if it turned out to vindicate the 70/30 split between DA and the firms (which in value terms was close to 73/27 in 1994). Or it would be a sensible way to prepare for change, if it exposed serious flaws in the competitiveness of DA.

The process was launched in the winter of 1994–95. Three blocks were put up – and one included the audit of Sheffield City Council, which had caused the old DAS so much grief in the 1980s. Foster and Prince were themselves closely involved in the choice of Sheffield as a candidate for the new approach. Once it had been targeted, though, the proprieties of an open competition were scrupulously heeded. Mike Barnes was a member of the interview panel in Sheffield, along with the council's own finance director and Jeremy Orme for the Commission. Barnes recalled:

The firms were very keen to drive home their customer-care message. One of their partners told the panel he would be available any day, at any time – and he would provide his home telephone number to all the councillors. This appalled the city council's own finance director: he said giving councillors his phone number was the last thing he'd ever want to do![15]

In February 1995 – to the astonishment of most people in the service and the dismay of the old guard – a lengthy and meticulous selection process for the award of the Sheffield mandate resulted in it being transferred from the local DA team and handed to one of the private firms, KPMG.

Could this be the start of the upheaval that many had expected back in 1982? Might DA be about to lose many of its mandates in

London, in particular, where the firms might be especially eager to compete? Some feared so – or at least a new preoccupation with pricing in the audit market that would lead to a steady erosion of DA's finances. In the event, the structure of the marketplace emerged little changed. Rather to the surprise of the regional staff on the ground, any DA redundancies in the wake of the loss of Sheffield were vetoed from Vincent Square. Market-testing continued for another four years, but on a scale that never involved more than about 1–2 per cent of the total market's value each year. True, where tenders were held, the audit body generally benefited from a slightly sharper price; but prices in general were little affected. DA won about 25 per cent of the audits it contested, at considerable expense, and this resulted in its share of the market (by value) falling nearer to the 70 per cent level over the four years. Not an insignificant shift, but not the Big Squeeze, either.

Market-testing, though, was far from a washout. As Foster knew would happen, even the marginal losses incurred by DA had an electrifying effect on the way that its auditors viewed their world. (How they viewed Mollie Bickerstaff can well be imagined, given her job, her background and her gender.) The fear of losing audits in open competition delivered a jolt to staff attitudes within both DA *and* the private firms. Prince recalled: 'Market-testing was very clever. At a minimal transaction cost, it achieved massive improvements in both sectors.'[16] Within DA, it handed Prince and his senior colleagues a powerful catalyst for upgrading the quality of their audit teams – and Prince had been left in no doubt, when he started, that a big improvement in quality was urgently required.

It was not exactly the message back from the Commission's own Quality Control Review (QCR). This assessed all of the DA regions and the mandated private firms according to a series of performance bands. One of the old seven regions actually occupied the top slot, and the rest fell (alongside the firms) across the bands in a random fashion, with just one region straggling all the rest. But the QCR, while highly adversarial in its approach and dreaded by most auditors, was beset by all kinds of gamesmanship. Foster and Prince were persuaded by their private soundings that the audit service was rather less professional in many of its activities than its general reputation might suggest. The QCR ratings did nothing to dispel this impression.

Prince sought to raise the DA's quality in two main ways. The first involved persuading auditors to work more faithfully to the service's audit manual. This required the introduction of a much more structured approach to audit, leaving less to local discretion. With an eye to the huge technical departments run by the big private firms, Prince also decided that it would not be appropriate for an independent DA to rely solely on the Audit Support directorate in Vincent Square. Like the firms, it would continue to call on the directorate where it was convenient to do so, but would develop its own in-house unit as the first line of support for DA auditors in the field. This certainly reinforced the message about the DA's new status, but whether it was ever a realistic policy is rather open to doubt. The new unit, like Prince's other direct reports, was set up on the first floor of Vincent Square, under a former regional director called Peter Coombes. But he had only a handful of staff. The top private firms devoted hundreds of people to technical support.

Indeed, by comparison with the firms, even the Audit Support directorate was itself hopelessly under-resourced: it had only about twenty managers in all. These were the audit technicians led for so many years by Harry Wilkinson and now being managed by Mike Barnes, who reported to a new audit support director, Steve Nicklen. Their morale was none too good, even ahead of the shift in the DA's policy. Though Barnes had generally been expected to succeed Harry Wilkinson, he had been passed over in favour of Nicklen, who was an external appointment with a consultancy background. Nicklen had many qualifications – but he was not a professional accountant and had no great interest in audit matters. This struck the technical audit staff as a discouraging signal that neither the senior directors nor the Commission members were really that much interested in their work. Barnes recalled: 'It was a bit of a double-edged sword. As a team we were able to do things with very limited oversight, so could take on broader activities within the profession. But at the same time we did have the feeling that we had just been sidelined and in some ways it didn't stack up.'[17] The new 'proprietary' approach by DA can hardly have lifted their spirits, but they soon adapted to it – and actually went on providing assistance much as they had done before.

Above all else, though, DA's quality would depend on having the best possible people in senior positions, and recruiting accordingly. This applied in particular to the district auditor ranks, which DA soon needed to expand in a hurry. Under Trish Longdon's leadership, 'assessment centres' were set up in the early months of 1995 to interview both internal and external candidates, by testing them against the requisite competencies that had already been identified.

Before they turned to recruitment, though, the assessment centres were instructed by Prince to bestow their blessings (or otherwise) on DA's existing district auditors. This news prompted a sharp intake of breath all around the service. Nothing more alien to its traditional culture could be imagined. If anyone had ever thought to create a Latin motto for the service, its free translation might have been along the lines of 'Always diffident, never blowing one's own trumpet'. Now those who most personified the old, very English ways of the service were going to have to endure US-style two-day ordeals that would include *role-playing sessions* – with obligatory breaks here and there for the odd trumpet voluntary. And the penalty for those who fell short would, appallingly, be early retirement. It so happened that a new-ish district auditor had been stepped down just two years earlier. As was widely noted at the time, however, he was the first to suffer this indignity in living memory. Around the country, district auditors now joked grimly about their Spanish Inquisition. None of them had expected it.

In the event, fewer than half a dozen actually received the *coup de grâce*. And among the rest, as Prince had counted on, assessment centres soon came to be reckoned not such a bad idea after all. District auditors were invited to participate in the work of the centres as they turned to internal promotions. This was a pivotal development for the service. It was the end of the Buggins'-turn culture that had prevailed for generations. The immediate result, though, was problematic. Recruiting for new district auditors, the centres had some success on their first ever trawl of the private sector: several partners or senior managers from the private sector took the controller's shilling. And, internally, a handful of individuals found themselves suddenly promoted to the top rank far earlier than they could possibly have expected just a year or two earlier. One of those who shot up the ranks, for example, was Gareth Davies. He had only joined the service as a graduate trainee in 1987. Emerging from his 1995 assessment as a new district auditor, he had taken eight years to reach the top of a ladder that generations of auditors before him had clambered up for thirty years or more. Of course the top job was different in various respects – but its title was unchanged, as was the aura around it.

Unfortunately, there were still too few like Davies: the number of eligible district auditor candidates fell well below what was expected. Bill Butler, who had succeeded John Sherring as the regional director for the Midlands in January 1995, had worked closely with Trish Longdon setting up the assessment process. He then sat on the leading recruitment team with his chief executive. He recalled: 'We sat in a room late one Friday night, having spent the previous two or three days doing virtually 24-hour assessments, and we realized that the only way that we could fill all the vacancies was to appoint people who weren't actually meeting the standard. We ummed and ahhed for hours.'[18] Discontinuing automatic promotions was one thing; but if promotion on merit was not justified, what then? It was David Prince who supplied the answer.

It was one of the toughest decisions I ever had to take at the Commission. We had to draw a line [on quality] and not be seduced below it by the need to fill vacancies. We said, 'If you're not above that line, you're not getting the post, you'll have to wait, you'll have to have a re-sit.' It was massively unpopular.[19]

DA had to struggle on for much of 1995 with about forty district auditors, rather than the fifty or more it had targeted. This was administratively awkward, and hugely resented by a good many senior managers. But the message that trickled down into the service was unmistakable, as was its impact. DA had adopted a 'gold standard' approach. Butler recalled: 'The district auditors then took ownership of it and it became "the way we do things here". Before long, companies like Marks & Spencer were coming to look at how we were handling our senior management recruitment. It was state-of-the-art stuff.'[20]

COMING TO TERMS WITH CLIENTS

After finance and quality came the customer-focus test. DA's chief executive had trained in local government in the 1970s, and was never in any danger of dismissing customer focus as a trendy business-school nostrum. In David Prince's view, the shift away from delivering services *to* the customer in favour of doing things *with* the customer had been one of the seminal changes in public sector life since those early days of his career, and he welcomed it. The Citizen's Charter was all about treating members of the public with respect. But council and NHS employees could be customers, too. Prince wanted DA to treat them accordingly. He had never believed that local government auditors needed to stand back from constructive relationships, in order to protect the independence of their judgement. He told meetings up and down the country that auditors must of course be independent, but that did not mean they had to work in isolation.

'Independence, not isolation' might have sounded unobjectionable enough to most outsiders, but Prince knew it would mark a momentous shift for DA. Of course there were individual auditors whose attitude and interpersonal skills were exemplary. But this was far from the norm, and Prince was not content to leave DA's image on this score to the vagaries of personal style. He wanted customer focus to be an inherent feature of DA as an organization. And it needed to be entrenched at every level. Indeed, he knew from his own experience that junior auditors were much more likely than their senior colleagues still to be guilty of an old-fashioned regulatory hauteur towards their town-hall counterparts. As he recalled: 'Once you got up to the chief accountant and beyond, it was different. But down in the engine-room where you found Nelly who'd been doing the balance sheet for thirty years, there was still a fair dread of District Audit – it was fading by the 1990s, but it was still around.'[21] Sometimes, it needed to be said, with good reason.

Prince set out to ensure that all ranks of DA would eventually approach their counterparts, from Nelly to her chief executive, as though they were customers to be assisted. No one supposed this would be achievable overnight: it was a policy objective to be pursued consistently over several years. But market-testing proved remarkably helpful in the early stages. For those (relatively few) who actually had to participate in a beauty parade, there was a consultant known to all as Scary Mary. Her task, before any competitive bid, was to cast a sharp eye over the members of the DA team and screen out the beards and brown suede shoes that might look too amateurish up against the suits and polished black brogues of the private sector. The stories about her impact undoubtedly left the service as a whole more responsive to emollient talks from the chief executive and his helpers about the opportunities ahead for those who could rise to them. Trish Longdon recalled: 'Our job was to convince people why they should move on from the way they had always done things. And we didn't just set out to tidy up people's suits. We challenged people to think about how we could develop an audit that would be modern and customer focused.'[22]

This involved new ways of writing reports, interviewing council officers, handling consultation groups, advising on future policy options, and so on. For the younger and more able auditors, it opened new horizons. Prince put a premium on management training accordingly. Over the first year or two, four-week training courses were available at Henley Management College. Then, after Trish Longdon had been appointed to the DA Management Board in 1996 as its director for people development, a programme tailored to DA's needs was pioneered with Ashridge Management Centre. For some of the older and less flexible auditors, there was a different outcome – and Prince needed the Commission to sign off on a stream of redundancies that lasted well into his third year and beyond. There was a full discussion by the Commission members, who took account of advice from external consultants as well as the Commission's internal auditors, Arthur Andersen. As the minutes delicately noted:

DA wished to be able to offer voluntary severance to those employees who find it difficult to adapt to the changed expectations placed upon them ... The Commission was reassured that ... [the packages on offer] were in many cases less generous than those found in both the public and private sectors ... The Commission approved the early retirement scheme on a 'one off' basis ... It was acknowledged that the costs currently under consideration were part of the start up costs of DA as a separate agency.[23]

One departure, though, was linked to the new drive for customer focus in a distinctly singular fashion. From the start of the new DA, it was hard to talk about the changes being sought by David Prince without talking of 'clients'. The word encapsulated the kind of relationship that was now being espoused. By the same token, however, it also let the cat out of the bag. It gave away the fact that DA was intent on a fundamental shift towards the outlook of private sector auditors, who of course had always talked of working with their clients. The DAS had not – and for anyone forgetful of the reason *why* not, there was someone at Vincent Square who was always ready with a reminder: the ever attentive Tony Child.

The Commission's in-house lawyer – whose energies were almost entirely devoted to working for the auditors rather than Vincent Square – was adamant on the point. Professional advisers under the law owed a duty of care to their clients. But auditors were in a different category: they were statutorily appointed persons with a duty of care to the public. *Ergo*, they could not have clients. Indeed, Child had expressly banned all use of the word by any auditors working for the Commission. When invited by Andrew Foster and David Prince to change his mind and issue a fresh edict, he politely declined to do so. Had Child been a backroom boffin, this might not have mattered much. The reality was that he commanded huge respect around DA offices all over the country. He had been vindicated in his stance on rate-capping, the Hammersmith swaps crisis and a host of other, lesser issues since the late 1980s. He was a solicitor whose shrewd judgement on local authority law had been demonstrated so many times that few district auditors would risk a clash with him (and more than a few seemed afraid to act on any delicate issue without his approval). Prince recalled: 'Tony was a sort of shaman to the auditors. He cast strange spells into the ether around judges. People melted before him.'[24]

So when Child stuck to his ruling against any talk of clients, the new managers of DA had a problem. (The Commission members were alive to it, too. When David Cooksey interviewed Prince for his job, one of the first questions he asked him was what he would do with the Commission's legal service.)[25] Prince wanted DA to be seen as a facilitator of better services. His controller was talking publicly about the Commission as 'an enabling regulator'. This was a far cry from local government's general perception of Tony Child's influence. Not for nothing was he widely known in local government as the Abominable No-Man. Superficially, the result of the stand-off was a bizarre nonsense. Formal papers and memoranda started referring after 1994 to 'cl∗∗∗ts' or 'the C-word'. But the underlying issue was real enough, and extended well beyond the precise legal nature of the auditor's relationship with audited bodies. In fact, it went straight to the heart of the familiar dilemma over how far the Commission could act both as a policeman *and* as a consultant to local authorities.

Child was a mainstay of the Commission's work, via DA, as a policeman. But there was no escaping the fact that, partly for this very reason, he was cordially disliked by many authorities. This made him an obvious impediment to the Commission's work as a consultant. Would any management consultancy in the private sector go about marketing itself to clients by harbouring an anti-fraud unit that felt itself entitled to rifle through clients' books without fear or favour? Child was invariably on the auditors' side, not the councils'. As far as many local authorities were concerned, it was as simple as that.

Since Foster and Prince were both determined to build closer links with the councils, a parting of the ways was inevitable. At the first meeting of the members in 1995, the controller drew their attention to 'the present shortfall of resources within the Commission for the provision of legal services'. The Commission required only a modest level of in-house legal advice; but Child could not properly provide this, since he was increasingly busy providing advice to auditors whose interests as independent parties might well differ from the Commission's. After some discussion the members agreed that they would 'favour withdrawal from the provision of direct legal services to appointed auditors on individual cases as a means to stabilize the Commission's workload'.[26] David Cooksey and Jeremy Orme were assigned with a commissioner appointed in May 1991, Clive Thompson, to look into the options – and they reported back in March, with proposals for a settlement to facilitate Child's departure. This duly followed, with Child leaving to take up a partnership in the private sector. He joined the City firm Rowe & Maw – which later became Mayer, Brown, Rowe & Maw – and the Commission began a search for its own exclusively in-house solicitor.

This outcome was generally satisfactory to all parties. The Commission found a perfect external appointee, Rod Ainsworth. Child had a private practice that was the envy of his profession. And DA teams could talk about 'clients' to their hearts' content. (It was not long before chief executives and finance directors were even receiving letters from DA auditors addressing them by their first names – something unheard of, in the past.) But there were many senior auditors who watched Child's departure in the short term with deep misgivings. It was fortunate, perhaps, that he merely decamped to an office off Ludgate Hill in the City. His services remained available to DA and they continued to make heavy use of them.

The immediate rationale for the split might have struck some as curious. After all, the role of the in-house solicitor was a circle that had been squared since 1987. As it happened, though, the Commission's need of a legal adviser other than Tony Child had indeed been growing rather more acute over the past couple of years. It was just one of the consequences of the astonishing tale that John Magill and Tony Child together had uncovered at Westminster since taking the gloves off in 1991.

IN PURSUIT OF SHIRLEY PORTER

Between January 1991 and April 1993, Magill and Child had conducted more than a hundred interviews, in their search for the truth behind what had happened on Westminster City Council that had prompted public objections to its accounts in July 1987.[27] By the spring of 1993, the essentials of the story were broadly clear.

Shirley Porter and her Tory colleagues on the council had received a nasty scare in the local elections of May 1986. Anticipating an electoral triumph, they had only just scraped home with any majority at all. 'Had 54 people voted Labour instead of Conservative in a few streets around Oxford Circus, Westminster City Council would have been lost.'[28] Within four weeks of the election, Porter was plotting ways to safeguard Tory majorities in eight key marginal wards. By November, she and her closest supporters had drawn up a strategy that was announced to the top seventy officers of the council, which would involve the sale of council flats in the key wards as a way of tipping the demographic balance in favour of Conservative voters. The strategy was called 'Building Stable Communities', or the BSC policy. (Officers inside City Hall joked it stood for 'Building Safer Constituencies'.) In subsequent refinements of the strategy, over the first half of 1987, it was agreed that 250 council homes a year would need to be sold in the key wards – but sales of 500 homes a year would be targeted all across the city, to disguise the true motive for the policy.

Westminster had 23,000 council homes *in toto*, with 10,000 people on the waiting list for rented accommodation. Now some 9,800 homes were 'designated for sale': that is to say, if the tenants moved out, the homes would be boarded up to pre-empt squatters and then kept vacant until sold. The impact of this policy on homelessness in the city was potentially dire. It was hardly ameliorated by Porter's plans to ship homeless families out of Westminster into whatever accommodation (including B&B hotels and car-park trailer homes) could be found beyond the council's boundaries, where their votes would be of no consequence.

The policy was launched in 1987. By the time the electoral register closed in 1989 (defining the electorate for the 1990 elections), the cost to ratepayers was so onerous that the whole policy had to be drastically scaled back. The tally had to cover rents (and rates) forgone, the administrative cost of the council's sales drive, discounts for home purchasers that could run to £30,000 or more, the bill for accommodating homeless familes (largely in B&B hotels) who might otherwise have been found a council flat, the expenses of keeping all those empty homes squatter-free – and much else besides. The council, for example, had even paid £15,000 grants to tenants as an incentive to move out and buy property in the private sector. How far the BSC policy ended up influencing the outcome of the 1990 local elections was impossible to say: the Tories triumphed in Westminster, lifting their majority from four seats to thirty-six – but of course the low poll tax seemed to have been an important factor. It was notable, anyway, that the Tories eventually won seven of the eight wards targeted by BSC. Since 1986, the council had completed 618 'designated' home sales and deported 565 families to other London boroughs.[29]

By 1993, with his inquiries fast approaching the end of their fourth year – already the longest investigation of its kind ever mounted by a local government auditor – Magill knew he was dealing with the possibility of some very hefty surcharges indeed. The task that he and Tony Child faced, though, was to find documents showing without doubt that Porter and those immediately around her had launched the BSC policy knowing it to be unlawful. To issue surcharges under Section 20 of the 1982 Act, Magill needed to prove wilful misconduct. As the battles with the Loony Left in the 1980s had made quite clear, the bar for any such proof was set very high. And the task was made no easier by suspicious gaps in the documentary records of the council – particularly for the first half of 1987, when the BSC policy was being finalized in clandestine meetings.

Magill and Child made several visits to City Hall to search for evidence, generally announcing their intentions a day or so previously. Early in the spring of 1993, they turned up some especially important papers. One of the key officers inside City Hall, in the course of perhaps his seventh or eighth interview over two years, suddenly let drop a reference to contemporaneous notes that he had scribbled in a Filofax at all the meetings he had attended during the critical years. Magill and Child were amazed at this casual revelation: neither he nor anyone else had ever mentioned before the existence of any such notes. The loose-leaf contents of the Filofax, refilled many times over, had been deposited by the officer in boxes that he said were still sitting in the basement files belonging to the housing department. Next morning, the team went straight down to the basement. Sure enough, there were the boxes, full of jumbled-up Filofax sheets. When all their jottings were deciphered, they exposed some colourful discrepancies between the formal record of various meetings and what had actually been said. The notes would eventually provide crucial evidence in the courts. More immediately, they made clear to the auditor and his team just how far some of the official's colleagues had been prepared to lie about the events of 1987–89.

Magill and Child now lost patience with the cat-and-mouse game they had had to play for too long, in their quest for papers. Porter had stepped down as leader in February 1991 and had resigned from the council altogether in February 1993. Several of the officers most closely involved with her had also departed, including the council's managing director through the BSC era, Bill Phillips. As Magill recalled: 'We started turning up papers that supposedly didn't exist. That was when we decided we were going to carry out a dawn raid on City Hall.'[30] Having teed up the communications team in Vincent Square with sufficient material to handle press inquiries on the day, Magill and his team manager presented themselves at City Hall with Tony Child and his assistant on the dot of 9 a.m. one April morning. They received the fullest cooperation from Phillips's successor, Bill Roots, and set about a systematic trawl of the filing cabinets, including those in the deepest recesses of the building. Within hours, just as they had expected, they found several crucial documents – including one BSC strategy paper from June 1987 with Shirley Porter's handwriting on it. Several files set out elaborate data from 1987 on the eight key marginal wards. This was material that Magill had asked for in the autumn of 1989. Bill Phillips had denied its existence and rubbished the whole notion of a 'key wards' strategy.[31]

It was now clear to Magill and those immediately around him, including a select few individuals at the Commission, that his investigation was heading to a grim conclusion, with grave implications for Porter and her closest associates. As they continued to dissemble, fudge and prevaricate through further interviews with the auditor, Tony Child and his assistant began the mammoth task of drawing together all of the legal documentation that would have to be included in a provisional report of Magill's findings. And within Vincent Square, David Cooksey and his newly appointed controller needed more than once to reassure the Commission members about the extraordinary way in which the story was unfolding.

It was certainly a most remarkable affair. Here was a woman widely fêted (in Tory circles, anyway) for her political leadership in the 1980s – and ennobled as Dame Shirley, no less, in the 1991 New Year's Honours – being hounded by a Commission-appointed auditor on charges amounting, if proved, to arguably the most egregious case of political corruption in the history of English local government. Porter served as Lord Mayor of Westminster for 1991–92. When Margaret Thatcher was presented with the Freedom of the City of Westminster at a grand ceremony in Whitehall's Banqueting House, it was the Lord

Mayor Dame Shirley in ermine and tricorne hat who presided over events.

It would have been strange, had Magill's investigation *not* prompted misgivings in several quarters. Most obviously, however unmentionably, he seemed likely to cause considerable embarrassment to the party in government. This must have stirred some mixed feelings within his own firm: in 1993 Touche Ross was still the minnow among the Big Eight accountancy firms and the government, thanks to privatization, was actually its *single biggest client.** As for the gist of the case against Porter, it was not just the Tory grandees of St James's clubland who thought the auditor an interfering busybody whose line on the normal cut-and-thrust of political manoeuvring was wholly out of order. It was a common view that Magill was simply naive to suppose local politicians, like any others, did not act in their own electoral interests whenever the opportunity arose.

There were subtler and nobler reasons to feel some disquiet over the investigation, too. If surcharged and not rescued by an appeal through the courts, many of those caught up in the scandal faced financial ruin. This did not apply to Porter herself, the heiress to a huge fortune made by the founder of the Tesco supermarket chain, but the sums at stake were far beyond the personal means of all the other individuals at risk. Were the alleged misdemeanours really so heinous as to justify penalties far more savage than anything ever meted out to erring Westminster politicians? Even Magill had his reservations about this – though, by then a practised commercial litigator, he knew it was his job simply to apply the law as it existed.[32] To many, anyway, the prospective punishment did seem to be out of all proportion to the crime.

Doubts on this score troubled many on the Commission, including

---

* Its propensity for taking on politically delicate briefs was extraordinary. As well as Westminster's Tories, the firm – acting as the liquidator of Freddie Laker's Skytrain business – had crossed swords in the 1980s with ministers struggling to privatize British Airways and, since 1991, later reconfigured as Deloitte & Touche, it had embarked on a lawsuit against the Bank of England, in pursuit of damages for the creditors of the collapsed bank, BCCI. And on behalf of the creditors of a defunct company, Polly Peck, it was even suing the Conservative Party for the recovery of a £400,000 donation made by Polly Peck illegally.

the chairman. David Cooksey recalled: 'I talked extensively to Nicholas Ridley about this [in the early stages, when Ridley was still the environment secretary] and did get a verbal undertaking that, once the case was settled, the government would come back and take a look at the rules again.'[33] And, by the early 1990s, Cooksey was given plenty of opportunities to express his misgivings in public. ('I suddenly became a Very Favourite Person with Shirley Porter – I was invited to everything at Westminster!') The fact remained, of course, that it would have been disastrous for Magill's investigation if the chairman of the Commission had ever hinted publicly at even the slightest equivocation. Nor did he ever do so. Neither Cooksey nor any of his colleagues – nor any of Magill's partners at Touche Ross – ever exerted any influence on Magill or Tony Child in a bid to subvert their investigation. The two of them received unstinting support – which was unaffected by the eventual decision, taken by Foster and Child together, that the latter should work from an independent base outside of the Commission.

In the absence of any startlingly contradictory new evidence, the outcome was never really in doubt after 13 January 1994. That was the day that Magill appeared in front of the media, to issue his interim report. He held a press conference in the International Press Centre, just behind Fleet Street, where he sat demurely beside a mountain of papers, including transcripts of all his interviews alongside copies of his 'Note' of provisional findings and views (236 pages long) and copies of his 'History of Events' (350 pages long). All of these were issued as strictly confidential papers to interested parties, including all the objectors, but of course found their way into journalists' hands within a nanosecond of their release. (Porter later insisted on a police investigation into the leak, but nothing ever came of it.) Most eyes anyway went straight to a single sentence towards the end of the one public document, Magill's press release: 'My provisional view is that the council was engaged in gerrymandering, which I am minded to find is a disgraceful and improper purpose and not a purpose for which a local authority may act.'[34] Ten individuals were given notice by Magill that he provisionally regarded them as guilty of wilful misconduct: they faced the prospect of being issued with a surcharge for just over £21 million. In addition to Porter, they included the Tory deputy leader, David Weeks, and the former managing director Bill Phillips.* Magill absolved of blame a further eighteen individuals named in the 1989 objections.

Press coverage of the whole extraordinary story began at midday, and continued to dominate the news agenda for the next twenty-four hours: Andrew Foster always afterwards described it as the single most dramatic media event of his entire career. 'Savage report embarrasses Major – "Vote-rigging" scandal stuns Tory flagship', ran the front-page headline of *The Times* the next day. And Labour's opposition spokesmen naturally made the most of it. 'It is the stuff of banana republics', said Jack Straw. 'It shows that the Tory Party is rotten and amoral to the core.'[35]

In the weeks immediately after the interim report's release, Labour shadow ministers joined with the Labour councillors on the council in pressing the Commission publicly for the launch of an 'extraordinary audit'. (The 1982 Act gave the Commission all the authority it needed for this, in Section 22 of the statute, and extraordinary audits had been sanctioned for the Lambeth and Liverpool councils in the wake of their failure to set rates for 1985–86.) The shadow environment secretary, Frank Dobson, led the charge 'to clear out corruption in the council'. By now, though, the situation on the council executive under Bill Roots was already far removed from the days of Shirley Porter. As he had already shown, Roots was a man that the auditor and his team could trust – and his dismissive reaction was good enough for the Commission, too. As he recalled it later, 'We were already in tatters when we heard about Labour's demand for an extraordinary audit. The government and the Audit Commission got on to me to ask if staff morale had collapsed because of the [interim] report and were our services failing as a result?'[36] No, said Roots, council staff were coping and services were running as normal – and the Commission responded to Labour's request accordingly.

---

* The full group found provisionally guilty of wilful misconduct comprised six Tory councillors (Shirley Porter, David Weeks, Barry Legg, Michael Dutt, Peter Hartley and Judith Warner) and four council executives (Bill Phillips, Graham England, Paul Hayler and Robert Lewis).

Other fall-out from the interim report took rather longer to settle. Solicitors for Porter and Phillips wrote separately to the Commission in the spring, asking that Magill be disqualified from the case.[37] His provisional findings, they said, clearly showed that his mind was made up and he would therefore be incapable of pursuing the investigation without bias. Certainly legal grounds always existed for the Commission to direct an auditor to step down, where it felt there were appropriate reasons to do so. After taking independent legal advice – and it was around this time that Child had to make absolutely clear that he himself could offer no advice on the case to the Commission since he was acting for the auditor – the Commission rejected both requests within a matter of days. Porter and Phillips asked again a few months later, only to have their request turned down by Magill himself after the arguments had been aired at the start of a Public Hearing in October.

A further two and a half years were needed to deal with interminable oral hearings. They took place in the august Marylebone Road chambers that had once been home to Marylebone Council. These conformed to the classic layout, with a raised dais above the semicircle of councillor's pews, and Magill and Child sat on the dais. (Not to be upstaged, Porter arranged on the first day of the hearings to have an enormous vase of flowers placed on the table in front of her.)[38] But in addition to the hearings, the two of them had to give consideration to copious further legal representations. These came above all from the ten individuals on notice of surcharge, protesting their innocence, but also from others – including the objectors, protesting the guilt of some of those against whom Magill had drawn no adverse findings. All this activity ensured that Westminster was never far from Andrew Foster's attention through these years.

By the spring of 1996, Magill was ready to warn all the interested parties that his final report was imminent. This prompted yet another attempt by Porter and Phillips to have Magill removed from the case, which the Commission rejected as carefully and thoroughly as before. The final report then emerged, early in May. It ran to more than 1,000 pages, in five bound volumes. A simultaneous Public Interest Report constituted, in effect, an executive summary. Of the ten people originally served notices of a surcharge, one had taken his own life.* On three others – councillors Barry Legg and Judith Warner and the council's former deputy solicitor Robert Lewis – Magill decided to change his earlier decisions and not to uphold the objections. This left six individuals – Porter, Weeks, Phillips, Hartley, England and Hayler – facing a surcharge of £31.6 million for which they were joint and severally liable. No one doubted the next stop would be the High Court.

PROGRESS ON REGULARITY AND VALUE-FOR-MONEY

While events at Westminster supplied regular copy for tabloid journalists whose combined knowledge of local government and local audit would scarcely have stretched to a postcard, the rank-and-file auditors of DA had to go on concentrating as ever on the completion of their annual round. This stretched longer by the year. The regularity franchise sometimes appeared especially elastic on the local government front. Compulsory competitive tendering weighed heavily on the auditor, requiring bids to be reviewed and the accounts of (ever more) direct labour organizations to be signed off separately. Then there was the relentless growth of specific grants from Whitehall, for

---

* This was Councillor Michael Dutt, a consultant geriatrician and one of the most ardent of all supporters of the BSC strategy at Westminster. In a curious footnote to a sad story, Dutt had telephoned Vincent Square shortly before the 1992 general election. He had introduced himself to Jonty Boyce simply as a consultant surgeon from St Albans. (Only later did Boyce and the controller together realize it was the Dr Dutt of Westminster Council.) He had viciously harangued Boyce about the poor quality (in his view) of a forthcoming study on bed management in the NHS. Dutt had obtained one of the draft copies of the report sent out for review. He was standing as a candidate in the election for Leicester South. 'I'm going to be elected', he told a rather startled Boyce. 'And once I'm in Parliament, I'm going to make sure that you are out of a job!' Confrontational calls like this might be supposed to have been an occasional feature of life at Vincent Square, given the nature of its special studies, but in fact were very rare. The outcome in this case was soon forgotten: Michael Dutt was not elected. But two years later, in the days immediately following Magill's release of his interim report, he shot himself, leaving a suicide note which Magill's antagonists did not hesitate to use against the auditor in the media over the weeks that followed.

which claims had to be signed off by the auditor. And, since 1993, there had been all those performance indicators to be reviewed and signed off under the Citizen's Charter.

But the Charter applied to the NHS, too, where the DA had to come to terms with a whole range of unfamiliar accounts for bodies ranging from Regional and District Health Authorities and general hospitals to family health service authorities and GP fundholders. And under the Charter legislation of 1992, auditors now had to consider for local government and the NHS alike whether or not the management letter at the conclusion of each audit year should include specific recommendations for future action. Like Public Interest Reports, any such recommendations had to be openly disclosed. And a public response was obligatory. By 1995, the local government and health audit franchises had been neatly and effectively stitched together. At a macro-level, the outcome was impressive. Local government involved 456 authorities that were run by 20,000 councillors in charge of some 2 million employees. The NHS comprised just under 600 principal health service bodies as well as 4,400 GP fundholders, with a total workforce rapidly heading for the million mark. Their combined expenditure under the DA's watchful eye equated to about £100 billion, or roughly 15 per cent of the gross domestic product of England and Wales.

On the ground, the physical arrangements of the DA were often impressive in their own way, too. Within the five regions established by David Prince, large areas of the country had to be administered by a patchwork of head offices, local offices and (for the larger audits) on-the-premises offices made permanently available to DA by the client. Junior and middle-ranking managers often lived reasonably close to their audit charges, and only moved house when promotion took them to a different beat. Many seniors, including all district auditors, were based in local or head offices and had no option but to resort to their cars. Many spent a hundred hours or more each month driving around the clients and audit teams for which they were responsible. (When the rules changed later in the 1990s and auditors could no longer work for more than five years for the same client, it put a huge strain on this network which is still a problem today. Many managers who might previously have worked only in the vicinity of their home now find themselves driving significant distances every day, just as the district auditors have long done.)

To see how all this worked, take the example of Kash Pandya. He was a district auditor in London who in 1993 moved out to the East of England district (District No. 5, until the 1994 restructuring and thereafter part of the London and South-East region) and worked there as a district auditor for the next three years. He lived in Brentwood, worked out of an office with three other district auditors in Stevenage and was responsible for audits across Cambridgeshire, Norfolk, Suffolk and Essex. He reported to a regional director – Jim McWhirr, after Peter Day's retirement in 1994 – who travelled to and fro between Stevenage and the London regional office in Millbank Tower, on the Embankment at Westminster.

Pandya had half a dozen senior managers reporting to him, each leading a unit of three or four more junior managers. With this staff, Pandya had final responsibility for about thirty large audits. Perhaps a third were local authorities, with the rest comprising NHS bodies, including large general hospitals in places like Great Yarmouth, Colchester and Southend. His teams also had to audit hundreds of small parish councils and, up in the fens country, about eighty drainage boards, too. It was a busy life, and for a few months each year the workload was such that the DA units needed to tie up contracts with local accountancy firms that could help them complete all their regularity audits on time.

And then, of course, there was also the value-for-money programme. As of 1995, DA's general approach to VFM work remained essentially as it had been for over a decade. As ever, the model had its shortcomings. Some audit teams were inevitably less sensible or conscientious than others. There was the ever-present danger of a little learning proving a dangerous thing. And where guides were simply applied unintelligently, there was always the risk that the DA would be guilty of adopting a 'one-size-fits-all' approach and wasting people's time. Roy Irwin, who would later join the Commission, was working in the mid-1990s as a director of housing in Bristol. He was an admirer of the national reports published by the Commission, but found many of his dealings with the local District Audit less satisfactory. He recalled:

It was a bit embarrassing when I was quizzed in my role as director [on an issue that had just been made the focus of a management handbook]. You could see that the person engaged on the task had no real knowledge of the subject. It struck me as a waste of resource and opportunity for both sides. And it made the product you thought you were buying in its entirety seem to pale a little between the gloss and the reality. It was as though you'd bought a new colour TV and it's got all these wonderful gadgets that allow you to do lots of marvellous things. But when you actually switch it on, it's just a black and white picture.[39]

But for much of the programme, and in most places, the VFM model was still facilitating a level of engagement with public sector managers that would have been unimaginable twenty years earlier. It was also still prompting the occasional bizarre discovery from time to time. The greatly expanded range of audit work naturally ensured an ever bigger harvest of anecdotes. Endlessly polished in the retelling, they added to the shared memories that were part of DA's culture, as they had been part of the old District Audit Service's culture before 1983. One typical tale sprang from audit work based on a 1993 national report into the use of water by NHS hospitals.

The main findings of *Untapped Savings: Water Services in the NHS* were that water costs to the NHS had been rising rapidly in the late 1980s and early 1990s, and that consumption patterns varied dramatically. In the lower quartile of all acute hospitals, use per patient day was 530 litres or less. In the most profligate quartile it exceeded 1,130 litres per day. Elaborate graphs in the report illustrated the comparative data gathered from around the country – and DA teams in 1994 went their rounds, inquiring as to the relative performance of the hospitals on their patch. An audit team in Hertfordshire was taken aback to discover that their local district general hospital was using more than *three times* as much water as the national average. A long discussion ensued with the hospital managers, which produced no satisfactory explanation. The managers had been completely unaware that their consumption was out of line with the rest of the health service, prior to the auditors' visit, and had no idea what could possibly lie behind it. It was a beautiful day, and during a break over lunchtime the auditors went outside for a stroll around the grounds. Here they came upon a wonderful bog garden, with reeds lining several ponds and the air full of dragonflies. They were soon approached by a proud gardener, happy to talk about the bog plants that were his passion. But where, asked the auditors, did all the water come from? 'No problem', said the gardener, leading them to a corner of the grounds where a channel had been expertly crafted to accommodate the flow from a long crack in the hospital's mains-water pipe.[40]

While they were a fund of good stories, however, the VFM audits were as often as not the main focus of adverse criticism whenever outsiders were invited to appraise the performance of the Audit Commission. Such appraisals were a remarkably common feature of these years. Internal strategy reviews, commissioned reviews from external consultants, Cabinet Office and Treasury reviews, five-yearly reviews for the DoE (which actually appeared in 1992 and 1998), reviews by special bodies like the Nolan Committee on standards in public life – the list went on and on.

An early verdict on the VFM audits was delivered in 1995 by a former senior partner of the accountants KPMG, Jim Butler. He was asked by the Commission itself to review its performance, and was promised in advance that his findings would be published. Fortunately, the general tenor of the Butler review was very favourable to the Commission, judging it to be 'an impressive and professional organization'. (Its findings relied heavily on in-depth interviews with a range of individuals from local government, the NHS and the police – including a London borough's director of finance, Steve Bundred from Camden.) Its main verdict would find an echo in many reports over the next few years:

In achieving its high reputation, the Commission has paid great attention to its national value-for-money (VFM) studies . . . But it is clear that the Commission has paid much less attention to ensuring that effective action is taken at a local level by audited bodies. Without reducing the quality of its national studies, the Commission must now focus on maximizing their practical impact.[41]

Neither David Prince nor anyone else in Vincent Square took exception to this. With full support from the controller and from the four Commission members on the DA's supervisory panel, Prince responded by expanding still further the role of the project officers.

They were now being grouped, as already noted, into working teams known as the added value units, or AVUs. It was a continuation of the trend that had begun when the NHS audit passed to the Commission. Increasingly, AVUs were assigned to the new VFM topics each November – still known, in Banham's parlance, as the 'flavours' for the year ahead – and encouraged to develop an expertise over the following months that took them to levels the auditors themselves would never have time to reach. Many of the new recruits coming into DA after 1995 had also been experts in their own right before they joined: some AVUs in the health sector, for example, included people with medical qualifications.

One consequence was that the DA was increasingly able to devote resources to helping audit bodies with specific problems in a way that belied the simple 'VFM audit' tag. The AVUs proved especially appealing to public sector chief executives: they brought the same integrity and rigour to their work as the auditors, and could be trusted, in a way that private consultancies often could not, to eschew tactics subtly aimed at just securing the next piece of business. Among the senior auditors, most of the initial sensitivities over project officers had now faded. The work of the AVUs was generally seen as a boost to the standing of the DA and to its competitiveness *vis-à-vis* the private firms. It was useful that they could deliver candid assessments in particularly tricky situations, giving auditors at least the option of taking the 'good cop, bad cop' approach to their client body. And AVUs generated a healthy stream of special fees, much appreciated by Prince and his management team.

There was one other significant consequence of the AVUs' expansion. It led inevitably to a rise in the number of VFM projects that were undertaken at the behest of local audit bodies, rather than as the follow-up to a national study. Indeed, conceptually it turned the traditional model designed in the 1980s on its head. Prince recalled: 'We took things that had started locally and worked well in a few specific audits, and we beamed them up so that they could be done nationally.'[42] Probably David Prince would have liked the trend to move further and a little faster than it did. One snag was that district auditors and their senior managers who pursued a local issue in preference to a national flavour could fall foul of the Quality Control

Review, run from Vincent Square. 'The QCR process was slow in coming to accept that if there was a good rationale on file for why you hadn't done every single study, then that should be acceptable.'[43] But by 1997, fewer flavours were regarded as mandatory. Auditors were at last being left with more discretion to pick and choose among them.

This was doubly welcome. As well as leaving more time for local initiatives, it alleviated the need for auditors to go on pushing VFM ideas that had begun, in truth, to encounter some push-back from many audit bodies. In one sense, this reflected how far the management of public sector services had already improved since the fading era of John Banham. The days were over when conspicuous problems still remained to be set right, often with glaringly obvious executive remedies. Management agendas in many large authorities were more sophisticated now, and certainly more crowded. Their chief executives consequently had less time for the Commission's standard VFM product. They respected it – but unless it tackled a topic they were actively pursuing, they were increasingly reluctant to pay for it. It was better by far, where possible, to ask the DA's specialists to look at some pressing issue of direct local relevance. And the DA responded accordingly.

Trish Longdon, now its director for people development, saw this as just another example of the DA enterprisingly making up the script as it went along. She had herself tasted the excitement of working in this kind of environment, as a project officer in the earlier 1990s when the first local VFM projects were just appearing. She recalled:

My whole experience of the Commission was that it was prepared to trust, enable and support its staff to do all sorts of things. It listened and it learned. It didn't say: 'We always do it this way or that way.' What distinguished the Commission was that if you had a great idea, you could usually find someone who would say 'Good idea – go for it.'[44]

One auditor who had had a good idea a few years earlier was Derek Elliott, the impromptu host for John Banham's chat with Jimmy Young from Richmond in the 1980s – and Elliott had certainly gone for it. His enthusiasm for the DA's battle against fraud and corruption had created almost a sub-category of audit work all of its own.

NEW TACTICS AGAINST FRAUD
AND CORRUPTION

Elliott had joined the old District Audit Service in 1970. He was part
of the intake (along with Kash Pandya and a few dozen others) that
followed the service's very first public advertisement for recruits. The
early career planning for Elliott was as meticulously choreographed
as usual:

They said, 'where do you want to work?' and I said 'in London'. Well, they said,
'that's good, we need people in London'. Then a form came through the post and
it said, 'You start in Peterborough on Monday.' So I rang up and resigned. 'But
we don't believe in sending people where they want to go', they said. Anyway,
I insisted, and I eventually got London.[45]

He had been there ever since, progressing up the ranks from audit
examiner (AE) to audit examiner qualified (AEQ) to ADA to SADA
to deputy district auditor and finally, in 1990, to district auditor. He
had had a lively time in the 1980s, working as Brian Skinner's bagman
through the rate-capping crisis in the Labour-controlled London boroughs. The misdemeanours of the Loony Left and some of the wilder
shenanigans in London local government had made a big impression
on him.

By 1993, Elliott was the district auditor responsible for a huge
swathe of audits from London to Lewes – including five Inner London
boroughs, two of the capital's biggest hospitals and a long list of
District Health Authorities across the north of Kent. It struck him
that a shared feature of both local government and the NHS was their
greatly increased vulnerability to fraud and corruption. Compulsory
competitive tendering had led to a proliferation of councils' procurement activities, with a substantial increase in the number of people
responsible for contracts and payments. And the introduction of the
purchaser/provider divide under the NHS Act of 1990 had taken the
health service in the same direction: towards a fragmentation of central
controls and a multiplicity of lightly monitored new financial obligations. (Some media interest in the implications had been prompted
since the legislation by investigations into irregularities at Regional

Health Authorities in Wessex, the West Midlands and Yorkshire – but the coverage had been fairly muted.) Against this background, auditors in the field had virtually no records or comparative data to track the incidence of fraud, and no guides to help them tackle it properly. Elliott began to compile figures for some of his audit bodies in London, and to survey the attitudes to fraud among their middle and senior managers. But it was a big subject, for which he lacked the necessary resources to do much even at a local level.

Elliott and the rest of the London region team were now based a short distance away from Vincent Square on the fourth floor of Millbank Tower, overlooking the Thames. But their regional director, Peter Day, was regularly in Vincent Square and it was not long before Elliott's interest in fraud came to the attention of the newly arrived controller. With a weather eye out for neglected topics that might suitably be targeted with a fresh approach, Andrew Foster conceived the idea of a full-scale report on the fraud problem – but he wanted it done within six months. It was Brian Willmor, the seconded DAS man in Vincent Square, who pointed out that this deadline would need the work to be conducted by a team of field auditors rather than a studies directorate in the traditional way. Foster agreed, and Willmor cleared the way with Peter Day for Derek Elliott to be given the assignment. Never one to hold back, Elliott leapt at the opportunity – provided that he could remain as district auditor and pick his own team. Willmor set up a panel of external advisers and would be the team's link back to Vincent Square.

For six months, Elliott worked early every morning and every evening as a district auditor in Millbank, and put in a nine-to-five day in Vincent Square as a study manager. The result, entitled *Protecting the Public Purse*, survived the Commission members' scrutiny virtually unscathed – a source of much pride to Elliott – and duly appeared shortly before the end of 1993. At one level, the report was a bit of a damp squib. A survey of town-hall finance directors underpinned a first estimate of the yearly incidence of fraud. It turned out to be around 54,000 cases, involving losses of about £25 million. Given annual expenditure by all local authorities of £60 billion – including £8 billion distributed in benefits to around 10 million claimants – this was something short of a sensation. It was fairly pointed out that the modest numbers were a little misleading: any publicized case of fraud was damaging. But the real significance of the report anyway lay elsewhere – and was essentially twofold.

In the first place, it was not so much a one-off report as the start of a process. The report was subtitled *Probity in the Public Sector: Combating Fraud and Corruption in Local Government* and was clearly designed as an agenda for future action. It recommended, for example, the creation of a one-man 'anti-fraud unit': this was accepted, and the unit was placed inside the technical directorate, reporting to Mike Barnes. It was also agreed that only a series of well-conducted annual surveys would deliver a reliable picture of what was happening in future: the responsibility for publishing annual updates was another job for Barnes. And David Prince encouraged Elliott to set up a grapevine around the DA that could be used, informally but effectively, to encourage others to copy his example. Elliott christened it the Good Conduct and Counter Fraud Network.

The ramifications of the first report went further still. Andrew Foster insisted that the Commission had also to produce a parallel *Protecting the Public Purse* on the health service. This idea was not at all well received in Whitehall. DoH officials pointed out that no significant fraud had ever been found within the NHS – which was strictly speaking correct, since none had ever been looked for, prior to 1990 – and health ministers objected on the grounds that any fraud inquiry could only damage the public's confidence in the service. But Foster stuck to his guns, helped by the fact that the Public Accounts Committee in Parliament posed questions very publicly about the levels of probity in the health service. The study went ahead, led by Nick Mapstone with Derek Elliott as part of the advisory group, and a report was published late in 1994. (Within a year, a widespread fraud had been uncovered among opticians, greatly embarrassing the DoH and prompting it to set up its own Counter Fraud Management Services.) Two subsequent updates of the NHS report then appeared, in 1996 and 1998.

The other significant aspect of the original 1993 report was the analysis that it brought to the problem. Defining fraud as essentially any fiddling of the books designed to cover up a theft, it first provided a useful clarification of the auditors' role. All auditors had of course to be alert for any signs of fraud during the course of their work – and they could follow up any hint of it ruthlessly, given their statutory right of access to any information. (The Code of Audit Practice stipulated that auditors had to provide reasonable assurance that financial statements were free from material misstatement, whether caused by fraud or any other irregularity. Under Section 16 of the 1982 Local Government Finance Act, an auditor could ask to see any document he wanted and could require any individual responsible for that document to appear before him in person to provide 'such information and explanation as he thinks necessary'. Failing to turn up at the auditor's bidding was a criminal offence.) But the prevention or detection of fraud at any audited body was *primarily* the responsibility of that body's own management. The best deterrent to fraud was generally the installation by management of conspicuous anti-fraud measures. In practice, auditors could best complement this by checking (in the standard phrase) 'on the adequacy of arrangements' to put these measures in place. The principal insight provided by Elliott and his colleagues, as practising auditors, was that rules and regulations were at best only a minor aspect of such arrangements. Far more important were practical steps, aimed in a hundred different ways at inculcating what their network called an anti-fraud culture.

By the time that David Prince arrived at the DA, Elliott had the bit between his teeth and was hard at work on an Anti-Fraud Manual that was distributed throughout the service at the end of 1994. Fresh from their own experiences of visiting New Zealand, Foster and Prince encouraged him to liaise with his counterparts in other countries – and Foster told him, 'Whichever you think you can learn the most from, you can go to.'[46] Elliott chose Canada. So just as David Henderson-Stewart had once toured the fire-stations of Holland and Steve Evans had travelled round Germany talking to the men who salted the autobahns, Elliott set off as soon as the snows had thawed in 1995, accompanied by Brian Willmor, to meet the Mounties.

They found the Canadians had successfully institutionalized a range of common-sense anti-fraud measures. They used extensive 'data-matching', for example, whereby adjacent authorities compared their computerized records to pick up duplicate applications for the same benefit. Above all, though, Elliott encountered a concept inelegantly labelled Control Self Assessment (CSA) that had been widely adopted in Canada since the late 1980s. Bristling with prescriptions and checklists, much of it boiled down to a sort of office version of Neighbourhood Watch, for employees. All of them, but especially middle-ranking managers, had to be encouraged to attend seminars where the risks of mismanagement or fraud could be properly aired, and safeguards agreed.

As it happened, one of London's most problematic borough councils was keen by the end of 1995 to provide Elliott with a perfect test-pad for the CSA approach. Lambeth Council, for twenty years a byword in local government for gross incompetence and much worse, had finally hit the buffers. The realization that dramatic changes were no longer avoidable had been reached two years earlier with the publication of a celebrated Public Interest Report by its district auditor, Paul Claydon. His was the eighteenth such report since 1979. Over that time, not even the disqualification of the twenty-two Labour councillors surcharged by Brian Skinner in 1986 had been enough to trigger a decisive break with the past. But Claydon's report, which had taken him most of two years to prepare and was published in May 1993, really did mark the end of the line. In ninety-three detailed pages, it chronicled an extraordinary story that had culminated the previous month in the resignation of a reform-minded chief executive, worn out by three years of struggle against the accumulated disasters of the past. Not for eight years had the council managed to file its annual accounts within the statutory time limit.

But that was just a trifle compared with the real story. 'Not only have many areas of the Council's administration fallen lamentably short of minimum acceptable standards but matters have been compounded by an unacceptable incidence of fraud and malpractice' (para. 16). Allegedly homeless people had been accommodated for years at council expense, only for the keys of their emergency accommodation to be sold in an elaborate 'sub-letting' operation. Highway maintenance contracts to a value of just over £20 million had been improperly awarded to in-house DLO teams. And even where rank dishonesty was not suspected, the council's bungling inefficiency was almost as shocking. Since the abolition of the Inner London Education Authority in 1990, some 2,000 teachers had been transferred to Lam-

1. Senior auditors from the District Audit Service, gathered at a dinner for its Staff/Students Society in March 1938. Without doubt most had worked all their lives within the DAS, or anticipated doing so. The gentleman seated centre, John Kendrick, served into the early 1960s and retired as chief inspector of audit.

2. Michael Heseltine, newly installed as secretary of state for the environment in Margaret Thatcher's first cabinet, May 1979. He appears to be writing on the back of an envelope, so this may be the 'To Do' list that Heseltine remembered handing to top officials on his first day – and which included setting up an audit commission as one of his priorities.

3. John Read, the first chairman of the Audit Commission, who was appointed just weeks before the inaugural meeting of the Commission's members in February 1983. He had little prior experience of the public sector, but turned out to be an effective and conscientious chairman.

Local Government Chronicle

31 MARCH 1983
60p

FIRST DAYS
OF THE
AUDIT
COMMISSION

Judgment day

4. By the time the Audit Commission was ready to open its doors for business in April 1983, many in local government had already convinced themselves the end of their world was nigh. The *Local Government Chronicle* caught the mood, even if its headline rather jumped the gun.

5. Immaculately dressed and with all the polish of a successful international management consultant, John Banham swept all before him as the controller of the new Commission. (Note the elegant seascape on the wall, one of a series he purchased to hang around the office.)

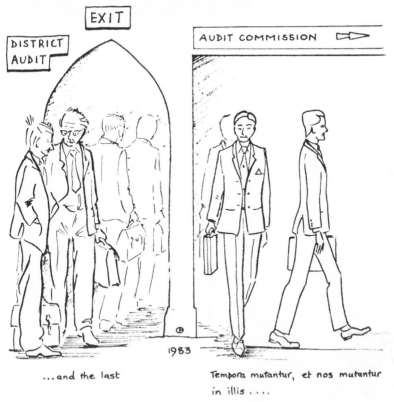

EXIT

DISTRICT AUDIT

AUDIT COMMISSION ⟹

1983

...and the last

Tempora mutantur, et nos mutantur in illis ....

6. Banham's McKinsey background was evident in everything he did, prompting much wry comment on the contrast between its new young consultant-style recruits and the sartorially challenged field auditors of the past. This cartoon ('The times are changing and we are changing with them') was penned by Claire Blackman, one of the few women in the DAS, which she had joined in 1963.

ENVELOPES PURCHASED BY SHIRE DISTRICTS
AUTUMN 1983

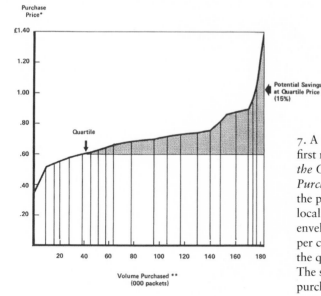

7. A typical chart from one of the first national reports, *Reducing the Cost of Local Government Purchases*. It ingeniously mapped the prices paid by a selection of local authorities for their brown envelopes. The most canny 25 per cent paid prices to the left of the quartile arrow on the slope. The shaded section represented all purchases made at higher prices – and a notional saving of 15 per cent or so, if all could be reined back to the level at the quartile arrow.

* For 100 pocket style DL (100 x 220 mm) buff 90g/m² envelopes gummed across flap with a bursting strength of 175 kpa.

** By groups of ten authorities, each buying in the same price-range; width of the bars represents volume purchased by each group.

Exhibit 1

NORTH AMERICA:
A VIEW OF THE FACTORS CAUSING AN URBAN 'UNDERCLASS'

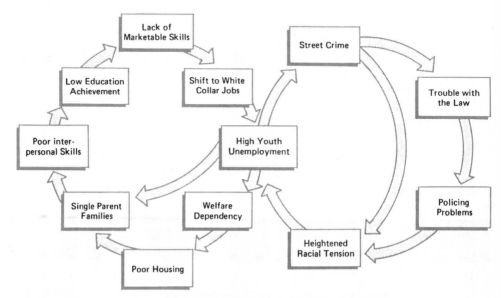

8. Exhibit No.1 from *The Management of London's Authorities: Preventing the Breakdown of Services*, the Occasional Paper penned by Banham towards the end of his term. Many Labour councillors were incensed by its warning that British cities could one day face the same problems as their US counterparts.

9. David Cooksey, taunted by the unions as 'Maggie's Hammer' in his early years, was unquestionably the most successful chairman of the Commission in its first twenty-five years.

10. Howard Davies, the second controller, whose skilful handling of more than one thorny legal issue helped convince ministers that the Commission's audit franchise should be extended to cover the NHS.

11. Liverpool's Loony Left takes to the street in March 1984: left to right at the front are Peter Owen, Derek Hatton, Tony Mulhearn, Eddie Loyden, MP, John Hamilton and Eric Heffer, MP.

12. Cliff Nicholson, the Commission's very own Methuselah, whose long experience in the DAS and shrewdness in Vincent Square ensured a precious link between the 1980s and what had gone before. He is wearing his badge of office as the 1990–91 president of CIPFA.

13. As acting controller through the second half of 1992, Peter Brokenshire bore the brunt of adapting the Commission to the new era of performance indicators and the Citizen's Charter.

14. Andrew Foster, the Commission's longest-serving controller: he answered to five different individuals in the chair in eight years, after David Cooksey's departure in 1995.

15. Few national reports were ever leaked to the media ahead of publication. One exception was *Streetwise*, a study of patrol tactics in the police service: access to an early draft produced a scoop for the *Guardian* in October 1995 and consternation in Vincent Square.

16. The Commission's London head office, until 2004, was tucked into a corner of Westminster's Vincent Square, on the junction of Rutherford Street and Fynes Street, and was no architectural gem. But its grand address was virtually synonymous for twenty-one years with the institution itself.

17. Shirley Porter announces in May 1996 that she will appeal to the High Court against the findings in the final report by the Westminster auditor, John Magill.

18. John Magill outside the Royal Courts of Justice in March 1997, with something (just faintly) to smile about: the Divisional Court had rejected Porter's appeal. It was almost eight years since the allegations of gerrymandering by Westminster City Council had first surfaced ... so Magill had just short of five years still to go, before the final judgment.

19. A third chairman and third controller: Roger Brooke, snappily dressed as ever (*left*), poses with Andrew Foster on the roof of 1 Vincent Square in the summer of 1996.

20. Former county councillor turned Blairite radical: Hilary Armstrong served as the minister for local government and housing in the re-vamped Department of the Environment under John Prescott from 1997 to 2001.

21. Helena Shovelton was the only chairman to have served first as a member of the Commission: she joined in 1995, became an increasingly influential voice after the 1997 election and took over the chair in 1999.

22. Wendy Thomson hit the Commission like an express train in 1999, setting up its inspectorate from scratch in six months. After less than two years she was gone, though, leaving for a job in the Cabinet Office.

23. Nick Raynsford, the minister for local and regional government as part of John Prescott's team at the Office of the Deputy Prime Minister from 2001 to 2005.

24. Adrienne Fresko agreed late in 2001 to step up as acting chairman for a couple of months – then remained in the chair for almost the whole of 2002.

25. Paul Kirby was described by a colleague as 'definitely inspection's representative on earth' by the start of 2002. The *Local Government Chronicle* preferred to see him as Icarus several months later, at least a back-handed tribute to the way he had flown round the country promoting the Comprehensive Performance Assessment (CPA) methodology in the face of much scepticism.

26. The only professional travel photographer to serve as a chairman of the Commission: James Strachan came to the job with an impressive range of previous careers (and some of his own photographs, too).

27. Michael Lyons put his finger on many weaknesses in the Best Value regime, in a notable paper he co-authored in 2001, and as deputy chairman of the Commission from 2003 he continued to point out the need for a radical change of approach towards local government.

28. With a background that encompassed working for the National Union of Mineworkers and digging Camden Borough Council out of a deep hole in the 1990s, Steve Bundred was a resilient chief executive through a period of abrupt changes for the Commission after 2003.

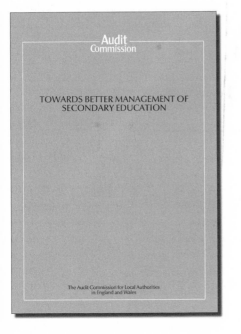

29. The physical appearance of the national reports produced by the Commission evolved steadily over twenty-five years, from the plain Yellow Perils of the mid-1980s to the eye-catching illustrated booklets of the new century.

30. Appointed chairman in 2006, Michael O'Higgins could draw on nearly thirty years of experience as an academic and management consultant in the public sector – plus a fourteen-volume set of induction papers in his new office cupboard.

31. The Commission has been based since 2004 in Millbank Tower, occupying the space rented by the Labour Party for its 1997 general election campaign. The tower itself was built on the site of 40 Millbank, the childhood home of Tony Benn that adjoined the former home of Sidney and Beatrice Webb.

beth's payroll. In three years, they had been overpaid by £1 million – not counting an overpayment of £2.8 million at the end of 1992 (through a systems failure) that had been successfully clawed back.

The elected members in Lambeth responded to the publication of Claydon's report by instructing a QC, Elizabeth Appleby, to conduct a comprehensive investigation into the organization and operations of the council. While she pressed ahead, Claydon became deeply embroiled in the executive officers' attempts to restore some semblance of order to the council's affairs. (No less than six lots of annual accounts were published in December 1993.) In the local elections of May 1994, the old Labour majority was swept away, and a hung council was returned with 16 Conservatives holding the balance between 24 Liberal Democrats and 24 Labour members. The resuscitation efforts continued, but as Claydon noted in his Management Letter of December 1994, 'much time at Council and Committee meetings has been taken up by motions and arguments reflecting personal animosity between Members . . . We remain concerned that councillors are diverted by such matters from their proper duties.'[47]

Elizabeth Appleby's report, when it finally landed on the councillors' desks five months later, was every bit as devastating as had generally been expected. Lambeth was 'an appalling financial and administrative mess with non-existent or incompetent management'. It was spending about £750 million a year on services for a population of roughly 260,000 people, yet in the management of its finances was effectively flying blind. As to the consequences of this for the probity of its affairs, she memorably observed: 'In the past it has been suggested that tackling waste and fraud was so difficult because most people denied its existence and it was so big, so deep and so widespread it was too much for people to comprehend. I think this is true.'[48]

The arrival of the report coincided with the appointment of a brave new chief executive, Heather Rabbatts. Taking her cue from the QC's report, she announced to the council in September 1995 a slew of radical reforms – among them a programme aimed at a wholesale change in the culture of the authority. For this, she said, she had turned for assistance to the Audit Commission and a district auditor newly appointed to Lambeth as Paul Claydon's successor, Derek Elliott. (Paul Claydon had moved on as part of the normal rotation of clients among the district auditors. Popular and widely respected among his colleagues, Claydon continued to handle a number of other Inner London boroughs, including Camden. Tragically, he took his own life just two years later, in 1997.)

When the call came, Elliott was ready with his CSA tool kit from Canada. Given his head by Andrew Foster to help Heather Rabbatts in any way he thought appropriate, Elliott and a colleague drew up a detailed questionnaire for all managers. (This was the basis, compiled in a single afternoon, of the list of concepts and questions that later came to comprise an influential paper called *Changing Organizational Culture.*) It was not clear, though, that anyone would respond. The atmosphere around the council was tense, to say the least. Heather Rabbatts had just launched a series of numeracy and literacy tests for all employees, with startling results that had put everyone on their guard. (It was rumoured that the chief cashier had failed the numeracy test, and that several of the communications staff had failed the literacy test.) But they *did* reply, and the answers people sent back encouraged Elliott to go ahead with a series of workshops based on the content of the questionnaires.

Seven of these were held, each lasting half a day, and more than 250 managers attended them. All were facilitated by Elliott and a small team of colleagues. Elliott recalled: 'The results were really powerful. People were saying, "This is the first time anyone's come and asked us what's wrong with Lambeth. And we've never seen auditors as people you could discuss a problem with!" '[49] Heather Rabbatts was later generous in her acknowledgement of the contribution that Elliott's team had made to the stabilization of Lambeth. 'Having historically been considered one of the poorest boroughs in terms of probity and its capacity to deal with fraud,' she told the councillors, 'Lambeth is now increasingly considered to be ahead of the field. District Audit's involvement was a vital element in this turnaround and I believe the model and approach used here could be applied to other authorities.'[50] But what the episode did for District Audit was also significant. It strengthened a growing confidence within the service that auditors, properly prepared, *could* act as catalysts and facilitators of councils' efforts not only to deter fraud but to improve their governance generally.

And for Elliott personally, of course, it was a hugely encouraging affirmation of the campaign he had been espousing with such enthusiasm since 1993. Whether the work entailed CSA-type seminars, systems reviews or painstaking data-matching trawls through the computer records, his network redoubled its efforts in 1996 across all thirty-three boroughs of the capital. Within a couple of years, he would be ready to circulate to all district auditors and their audit managers a grandly titled new manual: *Preventing and Detecting Fraud and Corruption: Changing Organisational Cultures.* (He submitted the manual to Liverpool John Moores University, too, as part of his research for an MA in Fraud Management.)

All this was timely. The idea suddenly seemed to be taking hold everywhere that fraud in the public sector – like sleaze in high places, indeed – needed tackling more aggressively. Whitehall changed the ground rules on the recovery of benefit-fraud losses, for example, allowing a portion to be retained so that local authorities had some financial incentive to pursue them. The NHS Executive put a new reporting requirement on all trust boards to confirm their anti-fraud arrangements, and it designated CSA as a core component. Across both sectors, anti-fraud units were increasingly being seen as basic prerequisites of good housekeeping.

And within DA itself, there was one other twist in the anti-fraud story around this time that would later yield a huge return. The computer-audit team for London and the south-east, still led by Peter Yetzes as it had been since 1984, had built up an interesting sideline over recent years. On behalf of the London boroughs, it had been using computers to match the data records of neighbouring boroughs in order to track down fraudulent benefit claims. (It was a problem which had been widely known as 'tube fraud' since 1992–93, when Yetzes had first persuaded a couple of London borough treasurers to fund a voluntary audit: one of their biggest fraud problems was the high incidence of multiple grant claims from 'students' who travelled the tube system, extracting payments from borough councils all along the line.) Over three busy years, Yetzes had attracted funding from enough borough treasurers to launch a 'London Fraud Initiative'. Given some free help on the IT front by ICL, a computer company with a flourishing business in the local government sector, he had broadened the range of targets, notably to include fraudulent claims for housing benefit. He had also run some pilot data-matching exercises outside London, mostly in the neighbouring counties of Kent and Sussex.

In 1996, Yetzes extended the exercise to cover the whole of England. It was still open to individual authorities to choose whether or not to participate, but a majority did so and the effectiveness of the work grew exponentially. Corporate support now came from NCR, another computer giant, but the logistics were still daunting. A little bizarrely, all the computerized matching of data records culminated in a printing out by NCR of hard-copy lists of apparent miscreants, all of which had to be duplicated for the participating authorities over a single weekend in Vincent Square. Yetzes led a team of enthusiasts who worked day and night to complete the project. He recalled: 'It was just the most ridiculous set of arrangements, but it was great fun as well – and there was a great deal of camaraderie over things like that.'[51] The lists were copied, hole-punched and filed for despatch by post on the Monday morning to their respective local authorities, for them to pursue. Some London borough councils were sent a list long enough to fill *three* lever-arch files.

It was a mismatch of old and new technology that would last one more year. By 1998, a new system would be based on the despatch of CD-ROM files. The financing would also change. For 1996 and 1997, DA still had some funding from the London treasurers, and received additional help from the Department of Social Security – but more was clearly needed. It was growing easier to justify, as well: the annual savings were starting to add up to millions of pounds. In 1998, the Commission decided to include the anti-fraud data-matching exercise in the statutory audit obligatory for all authorities. It was christened the National Fraud Initiative, and it had a bright future.

TAKING A WIDER VIEW
ON GOVERNANCE

And then there was Doncaster. Never mind an *anti-fraud* culture, Doncaster scarcely deserved to be attributed even a fraud culture. It was a snouts-in-the-trough culture – of such a blatant nature that it prompted another important step in the evolution of District Audit.

Doncaster in the mid-1990s was a tough place. Since the collapse of the miners' strike in 1985, all of the local pits had been closed. Two power stations and an RAF base had also been shut down, and a railway works depot was headed the same way. With the local economy in desperate straits, the city's politics were dominated by vicious squabbling between the residual factions of the National Union of Mineworkers and the strike-defying Union of Democratic Mineworkers. Their feud, and their tactics, set the tone on the Metropolitan Borough Council (which had forty-three Labour members and three Tories). The result – spiced up by the fact that Doncaster was being targeted with some substantial regeneration grants from London and Brussels – was a council run along some unusual lines. And in some unusual places. One of these was Doncaster Racecourse, which was conveniently owned by the council. A Trading Services (Racecourse) Sub-Committee held meetings through the year that happily always coincided with race days. This entitled the committee's members to use a box at the course, with free food and drink laid on throughout the day. They were joined there by other members, all of whom were entitled to two free tickets for every meeting. The drinking sessions that ensued were almost as celebrated among locals as the St Leger itself. (And the equine interests of the councillors and officers extended well beyond the turf. A six-man delegation spent three days in Dublin on one occasion, as an inquiry report would later disclose, meeting with the South Dublin County Council 'to discuss solutions to the problem of management of stray horses'.)[52]

While the council entertained at Doncaster, there were plenty of other sporting venues, from Hillsborough stadium to Trent Bridge, with half-a-dozen racecourses in between, where members and senior officers were lavishly entertained by local developers, construction bosses and service suppliers. Some of these were actually in business with the council itself, as partners in joint-venture companies. Backs were reciprocally scratched as part of the natural order, in a city where almost everyone with any influence or money seemed to live on one or the other of just two streets. (The managing director of one of the council's joint-venture partners lived in the same street as the council's chief executive.)

Nor were junket destinations restricted to the north of England. Fortunately for those who enjoyed foreign climes, Doncaster was twinned with cities in China, France, Germany, Poland and the US. Flying club-class except on important occasions, when only first-class would do, overseas trips typically left council delegations with plenty of time to recover from any jet-lag: a three-day conference in Asia, for example, might easily involve a ten-day schedule, which would allow ample scope for local networking – or just lying around in hotels, watching videos and drinking the mini-bars dry.

It was a culture that the district auditor for Doncaster, Gordon Sutton, had struggled with for years. When he came to contemplate his retirement in 1996, it naturally troubled him that he would be leaving the Augean stables uncleansed – and not just at Doncaster Racecourse. Late that autumn, he telephoned his regional director in Birmingham, Bill Butler, to suggest a meeting. When the two of them sat down together, the Doncaster man produced a set of files full of petty expense claims. It was quickly apparent from a stack of phoney claims for first-class rail fares that something was amiss. Like all experienced auditors, they knew that a pattern of fraudulent expenses was a fair indication of something more serious going on and they were soon sharing their concern with the South Yorkshire police. The serious crime branch, it turned out, had already begun to investigate suspicions of their own about planning corruption.

The Doncaster auditor filed a Management Letter at the end of 1996 that referred to specific shortcomings in relation to ties with local contractors, hospitality arrangements, members' expenses and council travel costs. But after Sutton's retirement in April 1997, the case was taken up by the regional director. Butler's investigations, which were backed up by the work of an internal inquiry team, led to a subtly different kind of process. As word spread about an auditor's inquiry, Butler was inundated with written complaints and allegations. Many of them he followed up himself, interviewing dozens of people through the summer from local builders to the odd wine waiter. These turned up plenty of bizarre incidentals, not least mobile-telephone records that showed the Labour leader of the council making regular late-night calls to the female member who led the Tory group on the council. But they uncovered serious graft, too. One supplier of surveillance installations, for example, had been paid £1 million over five years, with no written quotations, no tender process and no invoice documentation. The company had occupied council premises for three and a half years, rent free.

By the autumn, the council leader and his deputy had resigned and several committee chairmen had been replaced. (The chief executive and finance director followed them out of the door a few months later.) The clear involvement of the police helped to concentrate minds on the need for a fresh start, and the internal inquiry in September 1997 delivered a detailed record of transgressions. The culmination of the disclosure process, though, was a 52-page Public Interest Report that Butler released, with a live briefing for the media, on 19 December 1997.

Butler provided a succinct summary of the year's findings and added some extraordinary details. The management of the council's finances, for example, was virtually non-existent in relation to the largest of the joint ventures set up with local businesses. ('The Council were not able to identify to District Audit anyone amongst the Council's staff who had a clear understanding of the processes and calculations which preceded the declaration of the annual net profit for Doncaster 2000 Ltd.')[53] Above all, however, he made clear that he was concerned not with individual misdemeanours but with 'the overall management arrangements which operated in Doncaster MBC at the most senior levels'. Indeed, Butler actually noted at one point in his report that 'regardless of the difficulties amongst senior officers and members, [public] services in Doncaster MBC have continued to be delivered in an effective manner'.[54] But it was the corrupt culture from which those 'difficulties' stemmed, not the calibre of the services themselves, that was the principal target of his report – and this was something new. 'The effective management of an authority by senior members and officers is critical to good governance,' wrote Butler.

As part of this, there is a balance to be achieved between [them] . . . In Doncaster MBC, a small group of senior members determined the climate and it is my view that at Doncaster, with some exceptions, the balanced relationship did not exist . . . In my view, many of the things that occurred and which are described in this report . . . were patently unacceptable in a public body. (paras. 1, 8 and 15)

It was a break with the style of past reports that Butler had naturally discussed with his seniors in Vincent Square, and they were both supportive and fully aware of its import. David Prince recalled:

It was the first time that a Public Interest Report went beyond being a retrospective forensic account of improper transactions. Here was a report saying there's something rotten in the state of Denmark – for which members and officers should be held accountable. And in so far as it looked at the body politic as a whole, this approach was the seed of the corporate governance inspection that came later.[55]

New senior officers at Doncaster revised many of the council's practices in line with DA recommendations. Other consequences followed in due course. Fully half of the council members were eventually convicted. Most were found guilty only of petty fraud, but a few ended up with short gaol sentences. Butler concluded there was nothing to be gained from serving surcharges on any of the disgraced members. This decision may have strengthened the gathering consensus that surcharges were starting to look like an awkward anachronism. (The auditor's power to impose them would in fact be abolished just a few years later, in the Local Government Act of 2000.)

The decision also exposed Butler and his colleagues to a long litany of complaints through 1998 from members of the public who thought they were showing excessive leniency. One of the most vexing of Butler's assailants was a Scotsman who made angry calls to Butler's office for many months. Getting no satisfaction on the telephone, he finally told Butler that he was taking a coach full of supporters to Vincent Square, where he would play the bagpipes on the pavement to disrupt work inside the Commission's offices. Butler warned his London colleagues to expect this unusual visitation. The Scotsman duly found Vincent Square but failed to locate the correct corner for his lament on the pipes. A secretary, posted as sentry at the Commission, spotted him one afternoon stamping up and down on the opposite side of the square.[56]

I I

Setting the Pace, 1993–97

In succeeding John Banham and Howard Davies as the Audit Commission's third controller, Andrew Foster had two hard acts to follow. He wasted no time aspiring to their kind of bravura. If the one had juggled trays on the high wire and the other had circled the ring at a gallop astride several stallions at once, Foster settled from the outset for a more modest role in tails and top hat. But he would run a first-class show, steadily extending the bill and pulling in the crowds with great skill.

Thus, by the middle of 1994 he had repositioned the District Audit Service as a new body, DA, operating at arm's length from the centre. He had clarified reporting lines within the head office. He had restructured the management board with five directors, adding three newcomers – Bill Ogley, Mollie Bickerstaff and Steve Nicklen – and delegating extensively to all of them. He had made clear his commitment to the work of the two studies directorates, now headed by Bob Chilton and Jonty Boyce, without raising any expectations that he personally would be contributing much to the content of national reports. He had overseen a refurbishment and expansion of the offices in Vincent Square – not least the controller's office on the fifth floor – to which the staff returned in August. And he had knocked into shape a three-year strategy (*Adding Value*), corporate plans and budgets with brisk efficiency. It was all much as David Cooksey and his colleagues had hoped and expected – as the deputy chairman, Murray Stuart, hinted at the March 1994 session of the Commission, when he pointedly 'commended the professional approach taken in drawing up the budget this year'.[1]

As for the external presentation of its work, Foster transformed the Commission's in-house publishing operation within his first six months. Where two people had previously produced documents with not much more than the basic Office software, a team of six was soon at work in Vincent Square equipped with the latest software for professional designers. What followed would have graced an academic institution many times the size of the Commission. National reports, audit manuals, management handbooks and other formal papers streamed out of the head office. (Or at least, computer disks streamed out. Contract printers were used for the final production.) The cycle involving just three or four studies each year had long since given way to rolling programmes of work for local government and for health. Between Foster's appointment as controller and the end of 1997, the Commission would put out over 130 titles – not including Executive Briefings, Executive Summaries, Bulletins to update old reports, a quarterly news-sheet (*Headlines*) on current work and forthcoming reports, occasional guides to the work of the Commission and, of course, regular annual compendia of national performance indicators.

Nor was it just a matter of quantity. The importance attached to good design was evident from the start, even in the changing appearance of the annual report. The year prior to Foster's start had seen a first tentative use of photographs. The cover of the 1992 Annual Report featured a hospital nurse in one corner and three workmen in the other, bent double painting yellow parking lines on a kerbside. Inside were a few small sepia prints of employees, and a curious picture (as if to prove its existence) of the latest Code of Audit Practice. The next report, appearing in mid-1993, had full-page photographs of customer-focus in action – handily illustrating care for the elderly, support for families with children in hospital, and vocational training for teenagers. The pictures contributed to a broader change of tone: it was an annual report intent on making everything about the Commission as transparent as possible. The ingredients of its strategy for the years ahead, the principles governing its appointment of auditors, the aims and principal elements of its quality-control programme – all these and more were set out for the reader as the preamble to a detailed review, through almost fifty pages, of the Commission's work over the year. Even the Commission's members, hitherto simply listed, were now given miniature profiles.

This was the start of a continuous process of embellishment over the years to follow. And the care lavished on the annual reports was just as apparent across the whole range of Commission publications – most especially the national reports. In the years after 1993, these often stretched to about 100 pages in length. Enormous effort went into ensuring their accessibility, not just for the relevant expert but also for the general manager – and, needless to say, those in the media, Whitehall and Westminster at whom all of the reports were indirectly aimed. As this suggested, the new controller saw it as a big part of his job to ensure that the work of the Commission reached as wide an audience as possible – including end-consumers, as well as those responsible for acting on its recommendations. Foster had known before he joined the Commission that it was producing outstanding analysis of a wide range of public services. He wanted to ensure the analysis found its way into real benefits on the ground. He recalled: 'The Commission's output was in a class of its own. I thought the most important thing was always to find ways of engaging with our audiences and ensuring they took ownership of it.'[2]

The heightened regard inside the Commission for what was actually happening on the receiving end of public services did not go unnoticed in Whitehall. Contemplating the next round of appointments to the Commission, officials at the Department of the Environment were by mid-1994 thinking it might be appropriate to recruit at least one person with some direct experience of representing users of one service or another. Someone less concerned with the drive for ever greater *efficiency*, that is to say, and more focused on the *quality* of public services.

THE CHANGING FACE OF
THE COMMISSION

Since early 1991, the Commission had said goodbye to seven members. (This tally does not include the departure of Paul Beresford, the Tory leader of Wandsworth Council who was appointed in May 1991 but left in March 1992 to contest a seat in the 1992 general election. He was successful and became the second former Commission member, after John Gunnell, to enter the Commons.) Two of the three remaining original members, Noel Hepworth and Roy Shaw, had gone. The other five leavers were the former deputy chairman Harry Axton, Andrew Likierman, Eleanor James, John Clout and, in September 1993, Jennifer Hunt, the leading authority on nursing, who had joined in 1991.

They had been replaced over the three years by members with a broad range of backgrounds. In addition to the LSE academic, Tony Travers, there were five others. Lawrence Eilbeck was the leader of Carlisle City Council. Clive Thompson was a businessman and the nominee of the Welsh Office. Peter Kemp had just retired as second permanent secretary at the Treasury. Terence English was a former president of the Royal College of Surgeons, and Kate Jenkins was a former head of the prime minister's Efficiency Unit in Downing Street with various advisory roles and a seat on the NHS Policy Board. By the summer of 1994, the officials in Marsham Street had also lined up for imminent appointment two additional figures from the world of local government: Peter Soulsby, former leader of Leicester City Council, and Iris Tarry, former leader of Hertfordshire County Council (and the current chairman of the county's police authority).

None of these individuals, however, could really be said to have scrutinized public services from the consumer's side of the counter. With the retirement of Lawrence Eilbeck and Bob Wall in April and July 1994 respectively, and four more departures in prospect for January 1995 – of Murray Stuart, Alan Brown, Tony Christopher and, the last of the 1983 intake, Peter Bowness – the officials in Marsham Street were keen to find one or two replacements with just such a background. They turned for help to the Department of Trade and Industry, which after all had a consumer affairs division. One of the bodies with which the DTI worked closely was the National Association of Citizens' Advice Bureaux (NACAB). This dealt with about 7 million users of public services in a typical year, which seemed promising – and it so happened that NACAB was just about to appoint a new chairman. Her name was Helena Shovelton.

The process that culminated in Shovelton's appointment as a member had the merit, it could be said, of being unencumbered by overly formal procedures. But it also suggested a less than obsessive concern in Whitehall for the governance needs of the Commission. For a start, the process took the best part of six months. That July, she was summoned at twelve hours' notice for an interview with the minister for local government and housing, David Curry. This seemed to go satisfactorily enough, after a shaky introduction. She recalled: 'I turned up and was led into his outer office to go into the main one, and in the outer office was a man in a terribly scruffy jersey with holes through the sleeves. He was going through the post box, so I presumed he was the messenger. And that was David Curry, so it was rather an inauspicious start.'[3]

The minister seemed impressed that Shovelton had actually run a Citizens' Advice Bureau, engaging constantly with local government on behalf of people struggling to make sense of welfare payments, housing benefits and so on. (In fact it had been a return to work for her in 1985, after a debilitating illness that had laid her low for ten years. Running a CAB had led to her being co-opted on to the organization's national council, on which she had now been sitting for four years.) 'Well', Curry said to her approvingly at the close of their discussion together, 'I reckon you know the dirty end of local government!'[4] There then followed, for the best part of six months, complete radio silence. Assuming that no job was going to be forthcoming, Shovelton eventually contacted the department for confirmation of this negative outcome early in December. Surprised to hear that, on the contrary, an invitation to join the Commission might be in the offing quite soon, she then caused consternation by asking for a meeting with the Commission's chairman *and* requesting that officials send her some background papers that might help her to prepare for it. Neither had ever been requested before, and a frenzy of telephone calls followed. Fortunately, when eventually they did meet just after Christmas, she and David Cooksey found an immediate rapport. The appointment process lurched on, and on 31 January 1995 Shovelton's formal appointment letter arrived – inviting her to attend her first meeting two days later, on 2 February.

Two other new members were appointed alongside her. Ron Watson was a councillor and former council leader who headed the Tory group within the Association of Metropolitan Authorities. John Foster (who could not attend the February meeting, given the short notice) was chief executive of Middlesbrough Borough Council. Together, they brought the Commission up to fifteen members, including the chairman, leaving room for five more appointments in due course. It would have been sixteen, but for the tragic death in January 1995 of Chris West, the chief executive of Portsmouth and East Hampshire Health Authority, whose work with Vincent Square staff on the NHS franchise had been so valuable in devising basic audit tools in the aftermath of the 1990 legislation.

David Cooksey missed the 2 February meeting through illness. His next meeting turned out to be the last before the announcement of his retirement from the chair. In August, he would finally be stepping down, at the end of what would be his ninth year – and in the wake, rather satisfactorily, of chairing exactly his 100th monthly meeting. Though he did not disclose it immediately, he had agreed to take over the chairmanship of the Local Government Commission for England (LGCE), chaired since 1992 by John Banham. The recommendations of Banham's Commission, finally completed in January 1995, had caused some dismay among government ministers. (As envisaged by the government at the outset, it proposed replacing the existing county/district structure in many shires with so-called unitary authorities, but it also recommended leaving a surprising number of shires unaltered and proposing only a hybrid arrangement for others. Taking their cue from local opinion surveys to an extent that surprised officials in Whitehall, these recommendations fell well short of what ministers were intent on achieving.) Banham had struggled with a difficult brief, to say the least. As he had told a lecture audience in Cambridge a year earlier with his customary frankness, reviewing the structure of local government had turned out to be 'what might charitably be called a political nightmare'.[5] John Gummer, the environment secretary, rejected many of his final recommendations and returned them to the LGCE for further consideration. He announced in March that Banham had resigned.

Cooksey would be greatly missed by the Commission. He had been an effective ambassador for Vincent Square in its dealings with Whitehall. He had been an exemplary chairman to three controllers, offering avuncular guidance on the one hand and a cool decisiveness on the other, as occasion demanded. And he had presided over nine years of discussions among the Commission members with a skill and courtesy acknowledged by all. It was a group that, under his leadership, had grown rather wiser to the ways of the public sector in general and the challenges faced by the Commission in particular. There was a finer appreciation, for example, of the underlying tension between the Commission's roles as a watchdog, as an analytical observer and as an improvement agency. Always implicit in its statutory status, this hybrid calling had become much more of an issue since the advent of the Citizen's Charter and the assumption of responsibility for performance indicators. The members were well aware that a heightened focus on end-users' perceptions of public services was inevitably going to raise expectations of what the Commission could achieve as an improvement agency – even if they had no firm idea yet how best to respond. This was going to pose problems, as Cooksey would shortly acknowledge. In his valedictory Chairman's Foreword to the 1995 Annual Report, he noted that the Commission 'is now moving into much more difficult territory'. Given the growing focus on end-users, 'future work will increasingly be concerned with the quality of outputs and outcomes. To make real impact here, without losing sight of the economy and efficiency with which services are delivered, will be a tough challenge.'

It had always been a part of the Commission's public message that it was there to improve standards in local government. But this had been essentially a *rhetorical* device. The actual improving was to be done by those who noted the Commission's illuminative papers and analyses with sufficient care. Now people would be looking to it for more than a rhetorical commitment to the business of improving how local bodies performed. This was an evolution with which Andrew Foster seemed entirely comfortable, but the members themselves had already anguished over it for hours at regular away-days and half-days, and would continue to do so.

At the same time the Commission had evolved under Cooksey into a body more at ease with the influential role that it now played in the public sector. It was a process easily dismissed as 'going native'. But it could equally be seen as an inevitable concomitant of working effectively over time with local bodies such as councils, police committees and hospital trusts. Tony Travers, a seasoned observer of local government, recalled:

The Commission followed a pattern you could see in other institutions. The London Docklands Development Corporation was a precise parallel. In both cases, the first phase saw business people very much in control, but eventually both bodies migrated to being organizations with a much greater sensitivity towards the public sector. It was partly because that was the only way of surviving. But it was also partly because you can only ever batter the public sector for so long before you just demoralize it, and it gives up.[6]

The Commission's migration was clear enough. In its early years, membership places had been found for businessmen such as Kenneth Bond, David Lees, Ian Hay Davison and Lawrie Barratt – not to mention the men from McKinsey. By March 1995, there was conspicuously just a *single* member left, Clive Thompson, with a purely business background. Six of his peers had built their careers around the local delivery of public services; three had always worked in one guise or another on the formulation of public policy. The businessmen had had their day. Again, it was a remarkable facet of his chairmanship that Cooksey, a venture capitalist to his fingertips, had adapted to this shift with no dent whatever to his authority within the boardroom or his credibility in the world beyond it.

His legacy was a robust team culture. Most newcomers were struck, for example, by the complete absence of any party political allegiances around the table. Past or current council leaders set aside their political differences – not that this required a Herculean effort for moderates like the Tory Peter Bowness from Croydon or Labour's Clive Wilkinson from Birmingham – and pooled their experience of local government in discussions that were genuinely open to all new ideas. The members worked hard, too, and brought to bear a collective experience of the public sector with few parallels. Some brought valuable experience of the workings of Whitehall itself. Kate Jenkins had been a key architect behind sweeping reforms of the civil service during her time inside No. 10 and she had since remained an influential figure as a private consultant: in 1993, for instance, she had chaired a major review of the recent reforms in NHS management. Others

were so distinguished within their own specific fields that their colleagues naturally deferred to them accordingly – and the result was a
de facto allocation of various specialist roles that carried particular
weight. Donald Irvine's career at the top of the medical profession
gave him an unrivalled understanding of the regulation of complicated
institutions within the NHS, and indeed beyond it. Tony Christopher,
a man with an eye for details and a punctilious approach that almost
suggested a military past, brought a huge knowledge of the world of
pay negotiations from his career as a trade union leader. Above all,
perhaps, there was the former City accountant Jeremy Orme, whose
understanding of financial and regulatory matters was much valued
by his colleagues. Orme was especially relied upon as an arbiter of
any issues arising between the Commission and the private firms that
it appointed in the field.

But while the level of each individual's involvement varied, all
contributed in ways that went well beyond a bare monthly attendance.
As a group, they prepared each month for a long and varied agenda.*
And most had additional business to keep them busy, too, between
the monthly meetings: as already noted, four 'panels' had been set up
in 1993 to discuss in detail any issues relating to specific areas, and
every new member was invited to say which panel they wanted to
join. Panel work often obliged members to engage with technical
issues, many of which even involved auditing and accounting – unlike
most of the lively discussions that dominated the formal sessions of
the Commission as a whole.

Indeed, a hostile critic in the mid-1990s could fairly have questioned

* The agenda for the monthly meeting of July 1994, for example, was not untypical.
In addition to discussing points arising from the controller's monthly report, members
had to consider the presentation of a Mental Health Services study, a paper on
proposed NHS studies for 1995–96, a proposal for a study titled 'Care of the Elderly',
a draft bulletin on council tax, the proposed contents for the 1993–94 Annual Report,
a first national summary of Management Letters handed to local authorities for 1992–
93, a paper on proposed audit fees to be charged in 1994–95, a submission from
Westminster City Council *re* the fees being charged for the investigatory work being
undertaken there by John Magill, a proposal for the relaunch of Management Papers,
a proposal for the commissioning of an external review of the Audit Commission
(which would emerge in July 1995 as the *Butler Review*) and – finally – a report on
the state of the Commission's management accounts.

the extent of the members' genuine concern for technical matters – though arguably it had been a standing oddity of the Audit Commission from the start that audit was of little real interest to the commissioners. During his thirteen years as a director at Vincent Square, Harry Wilkinson had single-handedly written large chunks of the canon for public auditing. Yet he had seldom sensed much interest in his work among the members, or indeed the controllers. After an initial chat in 1983, he *never once* spoke to John Banham about it; he was only very rarely asked about it by Howard Davies; and he was consigned by Andrew Foster to a back office for the two years up to his retirement in 1996. As for the members, some had come and gone without his ever meeting them at all. He recalled: 'I had nothing to do with the members, really almost nothing, nor they with me.'[7]

The unavoidable reality was that studies and national reports were the bedrock on which the Commission's reputation was built. No one in David Cooksey's time ever doubted it. They also allowed members to make a meaningful contribution: they could chip in ideas for future studies, meet with team leaders to chew over current drafts and debate for hours the likely future impact of this or that key conclusion. As Tony Travers recalled:

Every now and again, one of the probity and regularity people would be brought into a meeting as if they were some exotic beast that had been captured. We would sit through their presentation – then they would leave, and we could dive into our long deliberations over some new report that was much more fun.[8]

The flow of reports was swelling rapidly by 1994, and most were still discussed in some detail prior to publication. Members were also keen to be more involved in the choice of future subjects, and to have an opportunity to review each report with its senior managers at the half-way stage. On all counts, the work of the Health Studies directorate would almost have been sufficient on its own to fill their agenda. As the minutes of their monthly meetings amply attested, nothing drew the members' avid attention more consistently over the coming few years than the Commission's NHS franchise.

RANGING WIDELY OVER THE NHS

Andrew Foster insisted in 1993 that the views of health authority officials around the country should be widely canvassed in the process of selecting future subjects. The Health Studies directorate went one better in 1994. Boyce recalled: 'We got together some groups of doctors, chief executives, nurses and auditors. We showed them the studies we had done to date, explained the sort of criteria we used for making our choices and asked them to give us their opinions about other areas we might look at.'[9]

The sessions were held at Church House, a beautiful building behind Westminster Abbey (where the House of Lords convened during the second world war). More than forty people attended them. It was agreed from the outset that some criteria were self-evident. Future studies had to focus on issues of material importance to the NHS; there had to be sufficient variation in current practice to suggest genuine scope for improvement; and there had to be grounds for believing that worthwhile recommendations would be welcomed, at least by those with a responsibility for leading the way. Beyond that, the Commission was open to innovative ideas as usual. The discussions went well – prompting a repeat fixture the next year – and a list of ten topics went to the Commission members for their consideration and endorsement in July 1994. They chose four, which eventually emerged at various points of 1996. The choice was primarily driven by the search for reforms that could offer a significant financial return on any successful implementation. No doubt the final pick was also made with an eye to the likely impact of any prospective report on the public standing of the Commission – but that was wholly in keeping with its best traditions. Without doubt, the outcome greatly enhanced that standing. Health-related titles constituted about 45 per cent of the Commission's publications in 1993–97, and covered a remarkably wide range of topics that left scarcely any corner of the NHS untouched.

The directorate had continued to be led until June 1994 by Ross Tristem, who left on secondment that month to run one of the many new bodies that had sprung up in the aftermath of the 1990 NHS

Act: he was to be chief executive of the NHS Trust Federation, the umbrella organization for all NHS trusts. Though he technically left on secondment, it was plain to all his colleagues that Tristem would not be returning. His contribution to the Commission's success since 1983 had been immense. His successor recalled: 'He was great fun to work with, and that's the first thing you always remember about Ross. But he was very sharp and passionately interested in the issues – with no kind of self-aggrandizement whatsoever. The issues were everything.'[10]

Jonty Boyce took over the lead, though he would not be finally confirmed as the full director until 1996. To fill his old position, he promoted someone he himself had hired in 1991, Jocelyn Cornwell. Back then, exploiting the fact that the Commission was not part of the civil service, it had still been possible to pull aboard someone highly recommended by a good contact. Cornwell was introduced to Boyce by Nick Black, a professor at the London School of Hygiene and Tropical Medicine and one of his former colleagues. A Cambridge graduate with a doctorate on patients' views of their own health, she was working at the time in the Islington Community Health Department. Her professor brought her along to meet Boyce for lunch at Bertorelli's in Covent Garden, and he more or less hired her on the spot. She joined the existing two associate directors, David Browning and Ken Sneath. Over the next couple of years, however, Sneath was frequently incapacitated by poor health. He finally took early retirement in 1993 and was in turn replaced by a former management consultant from Boston Consulting Group, Joanne Shaw. (Her recruitment was only problematic in so far as she had an equally brilliant rival for the vacant position, a former hospital manager and social services professional called Andrew Webster.)

Boyce and his three associates headed a team that grew to more than forty people by the late 1990s. More than half worked directly on studies, while others provided back-up services – including the development of an in-house databank of statistics on the NHS and an index of useful research sources. The reputation of the directorate ensured plenty of applicants for every new position. The senior team on several occasions set aside a whole day to put shortlisted candidates through the kind of selection procedures customarily used in picking high-fliers for the civil service. Those who made it to Vincent Square constituted a gifted and eclectic group, with doctorates in various disciplines, from Arabic to ornithology: Ian Seccombe had spent several years in the Middle East, while rooks and crows were the special subject offered by a former DA man, Richard (Dick) Waite. (All showed up in the prefaces to their Commission reports as 'Dr', which probably did no harm.)

The studies they undertook built steadily on the foundations laid by the three inaugural reports of 1990–91; followed in 1992 by the study of bed management in the NHS and the handbooks on nursing. Huge effort had also gone into three reports on community care that had been published under Tristem's lead in 1992. (They were entitled *Community Care: Managing the Cascade of Change*; *Community Revolution: Personal Social Services and Community Care*; and *Homeward Bound: a New Course for Community Health*.) The directorate had a wide remit, covering social services as well as 'community health' – meaning medical services for those still living at home – and hospitals. The directorate generally produced three or four major reports each year, and the Commission itself grouped them by topic under about two dozen different sub-headings. In essence, though, most belonged to one of three categories: they were focused primarily on clinical or management issues, or else they looked specifically at the continuing reorganization of the NHS triggered by the 1990 Act. (Almost all carried a punning title – there was just a single category in that respect.)

Studies in the clinical category either dealt with a single issue – like the inaugural study, into day surgery – or else looked at the implications for the clinicians of broader changes. In 1995, for example, *United They Stand* looked at the treatment of elderly patients with hip fractures (the subject, years before, of Boyce's own D.Phil. thesis) and *Dear to Our Hearts?* dealt with the treatment and prevention of cardiac disease; in 1996, *By Accident or Design* analysed ways of improving accident and emergency (A&E) services; and in 1997, *First Class Delivery* provided an influential study of maternity services (based in part on a series of interviews with 2,350 women). Also in 1997, *Anaesthesia under Examination* had the distinction of being one of the few reports to stump Vincent Square's indefatigable punsters – though the cognoscenti would know it nicely reversed the title of a standard procedure known to doctors as 'examination under anaesthesia'.

The clinical dimension certainly met with the occasional push-back from doctors. The Commission's consistent purpose was straight-forward enough. It sought rigorously to compare what were inel-egantly known as *inputs* and *outcomes*: were the resources being poured into this or that corner of the NHS leading to satisfactory treatment services from the perspective of the patients? But there were always those in the profession who doubted anything so mysterious as medicine could ever be explained to – still less, by – the uninitiated.

A report on radiology services in 1995, called *Improving Your Image*, provoked fury among radiologists in one region of England who castigated one of its recommendations as clinically unsafe. (The report, noting the existence of long waiting times in some departments, argued for a practice known as 'hot reporting' that was being intro-duced in a few departments. One radiologist would be designated 'reader for the day' to report on all the X-rays being taken, regardless of who had supervised them. This made far more reports available, far quicker, for other doctors to refer to.) But serious clinical objections to the directorate's work were rare, especially after the mid-90s. No doubt, after 1993, it helped that the Commission's members included a former president of one of the Royal Colleges. For his part, Terence English soon came to have a high regard for Boyce and his team and was a willing ally.

The media could be a much bigger problem. The 1996 report on A&E departments triggered one of the more unfortunate encounters. Few areas of the NHS could be more newsworthy than A&E: patients make about 15 million visits a year to emergency departments, which for many people therefore represent the face of the health service. Fieldwork across twenty-four hospital trusts underpinned the Com-mission's final report. Its conclusions painted a none too flattering portrait: too few senior doctors, too narrow a role for nurses, too few facilities for children and too much waiting in line for almost everyone – these were just some of the heavily researched findings. Looking to the future, the report noted the considerable variation in departments' workloads. It flagged a widely held view among the experts that smaller departments often struggled to respond properly to serious emergencies. Reviewing the evidence for this, it questioned the need for those with fewer than 50,000 cases a year that were also within 10 miles of an alternative department. There turned out to be sixty-two of these, and the report recommended a full review of each one. Their locations were documented within the back-up papers – but omitted from the published report, for obvious reasons.

On the day before publication, embargoed copies of the report were sent out to the media as usual. That evening, well after most people had left the office, a late media query came through to Vincent Square. One of the younger and more generous-spirited members of the health directorate took the call. It was from a canny journalist at the Press Association, the news agency that reports stories on a continuous basis and makes its copy available to local newspapers all over the country. He had noted the recommendation for reviewing the viability of smaller departments adjacent to others, he said, and was in the process of working out which they were from the publicly available data. He was just wondering, though, whether – simply in the interests of saving time and avoiding silly mistakes, of course – it might be possible to short-circuit the process and just get the names from the Audit Commission directly? Obligingly, the generous spirit faxed over the list. Next morning, local newspapers in many of the affected areas across the country ran front-page stories headlining the PA copy: Top Secret List of NHS Regulator – Local A&E Department to Close. And the national press published the entire list. The story ran for days, and was a brutal reminder of the latent conflict dwelt upon by the *Butler Review* the year before, between the Commission as watchdog and the Commission as consultant or think-tank.

The second category of national reports looked at more purely managerial issues within the NHS. With the Soviet Red Army in meltdown, it was a press cliché that the only human enterprises bigger than the NHS were the Army of the People's Republic of China and the state-owned Indian Railways. How the three organizations might have ranked in a pecking order based on efficiency was thought by some to be a moot point. There was no shortage of experts selling advice on how to change this. While the NHS was spending about £120 million a year on management consultants, however, one of the

Commission's earliest health reports, the optimistically titled *Reaching the Peak?*, showed in 1994 that well over half of all externally sourced recommendations were completely ignored.

This did not deter the Health Studies Directorate itself – nor should it have, since the thrust of its work still complied with that old adage from the Davies era about illuminating choices: the Commission's reports were not there to dictate future policy to local bodies, but rather to help them assess the policy options ahead of them. A new series of NHS Management Papers explored in detail how the best practitioners controlled their senior management costs (*A Price on their Heads*), made the most use of non-executive directors on NHS trust boards (*Taken on Board*) or adapted their NHS trust structures to accommodate managerial reforms (*Form Follows Function*). And there were national reports on the basic management of the NHS, too. An astonishingly detailed study of hospital doctors, *The Doctor's Tale*, provided an overview of their duties, training and working practices.

Inevitably, such work steadily strengthened the impression that piercing analysis of the NHS had been somewhat neglected over the years. This was not always received within the Department of Health as a welcome observation. The fact that the Commission's controller had worked briefly in the department before arriving in Vincent Square – and had been keen, initially at least, to be more accommodating towards it – seemed not to have made much difference either way to a relationship that remained professional but hardly cordial. Foster himself recalled: 'The existence of an independent reporting mechanism, which is what we were, was a source of massive friction over time.'[11]

The relationship cannot have been much improved by two widely noted Commission reports in 1995: they were sharply critical of the development and implementation of information-management systems in many acute hospitals (*For Your Information*) and of the current, shambolic state of their medical records (*Setting the Records Straight*). Whatever the department's views, though, one Commission member responded with particular interest to these titles. Helena Shovelton was at that time chairing one of the independent reviews that were being conducted for District Health Authorities all over the country, to adjudicate between hospitals and social services over the division of responsibilities between them for patient care. (Hospitals were free; residential homes were not. Patients, unsurprisingly, often needed prising out of their hospital beds.) Arguments between the two sides often came down to an inspection of the medical records. Shovelton recalled: 'But what was always interesting, on trawling through them, was how deeply inadequate they were. Often nobody had bothered actually to look through them. Medical records were cited as evidence, where no evidence really existed. They were simply a mess.'[12] The clarity of the health directorate's work in this area impressed her.

The potential for reporting usefully on the NHS's management practices was vast – and within months of Ross Tristem's departure, Andrew Foster was urging the health directorate to look again at the possibility of out-sourcing studies, a practice abandoned in the mid-1980s. (He had already persuaded the local government directorate to do so, resulting in a 1995 report on the fire service, researched by the accountants Ernst & Young and written up by an in-house project team as *In the Line of Fire*.) A topic was chosen – the management of supplies by NHS trusts – and the tender attracted a long list of bidders. The contract went in the end to one of the several large accountancy firms' consultancy arms that dominated the shortlist, Robson Rhodes. Their research (assisted by a secondee from the Commission, Nick Mapstone) was of a high standard – and it so happened that they had an ex-DA auditor on their staff, which made work on the audit guide much easier for them. But it nonetheless proved difficult, and expensive, to translate their early drafts of the report, *Goods for your Health*, into the house style of the Commission. Outsourcing in future would be used to assist with research, but rarely again for whole reports.

A third category of health reports tackled head-on the tumultuous reorganization triggered by the 1990 NHS and Community Care Act. Not without some misgivings among Commission members, the health directorate ventured forth to examine how the reorganization was going. In introducing the concept of purchasers and providers within the NHS, the 1990 Act invited health authorities to become commissioners (or 'purchasers') of health services on the one hand

and invited hospitals on the other to reconstitute themselves as self-governing trusts; together they would constitute a so-called 'internal market'. By 1994, trusts were providing about 90 per cent of all NHS specialist services (and accounting for about two thirds of NHS spending in England and Wales). But these changes were not always conveyed properly to the people working within the NHS. A study team from the Commission surveyed 400 staff working within trusts around the country, and asked them to respond to the statement: 'I am generally well informed about what's happening in the trust.' Fully half of the respondents disagreed with it. The team went on to produce a national report, *Trusting in the Future*, that sought to provide a detailed agenda for those engaged in making the trusts effective. One of the biggest challenges for the trusts involved putting non-medical professionals in charge of new business units and clinical directorates, and the Commission documented plenty of robust comments on that score, from managers and doctors alike.

Reports on the reshaping of the NHS, though, were of course hugely problematic: by their nature, they would encroach on policy territory that was jealously guarded by the officials in Richmond House. It was therefore with some trepidation that the Commission gave the go-ahead for a study into GP fundholders. These were the groups of general practitioners who had taken up an option provided by the 1990 Act, to purchase hospital and community services themselves, rather than remain dependent on contracts arranged by their local District Health Authority. It was arguably the most radical of the Tories' reforms, and it was hated with a passion by most Labour politicians. Whatever the Commission concluded about fundholders was highly likely to offend one party or the other. The eventual report, *What the Doctor Ordered*, ran to 136 pages. It was the longest ever produced in Vincent Square. Its encyclopedic approach suited the complexity of the subject matter – but it also gave the report a Delphic dimension, for both Tories and Labour could be sure to find within it at least something that supported their case.

In so far as the report itself had a conclusion, it was probably that the GP fundholder concept was stronger in theory than in practice. Boyce recalled:

If you could take all of the things that were being done by GP fundholders in different places, and amalgamate them into one ideal that could then be replicated everywhere, the result would have been brilliant. But the reality was that all of them faced an overwhelming agenda that none could really handle. So they used the freedom granted by the 1990 Act to do more of whatever the individual GPs happened to be interested in or good at.[13]

As always, both the health secretary and the shadow spokesman on health were given a preview of the report shortly before its publication. While Andrew Foster spoke to the minister, Stephen Dorrell, it was left to Boyce to brief Labour's Harriet Harman. The health studies director prepared for his meeting with some care – but once it had begun, it was quickly apparent to Boyce's relief that Harman had scarcely opened the report or read any of the papers prepared for her about it.[14] This seemed to sum up the general reaction to the report. It was now late in 1996, and leading figures on both sides of the political divide were too busy preparing for the coming general election to have a row over a report with no especially outspoken conclusions. So the Commission got away with many observations that in other circumstances might have stirred up a hornets' nest. In risking overt criticism of the prevailing model for the NHS, it had strayed a long way into policy-making territory normally regarded as out of bounds.

There was just one area in which the Commission had a de facto licence to stray in this manner – the social services sector. This slight anomaly was a legacy of the powerful contribution made by the Commission to the development of the social services over many years. It went back to the Section 27 report of 1986, *Making a Reality of Community Care*, that had done so much to shape subsequent legislative reforms of the sector. And since then, the Commission had consistently taken a special interest in the welfare of children, the elderly and the mentally handicapped, with a long string of reports, including those of 1992, many of them prepared under the direction of David Browning. Three more substantial publications – two national reports and a management handbook – appeared before the end of 1997. They comprised an update on the progress of the government's reforms, *Balancing the Care Equation*; a report on the adequacy of services for the elderly, *The Coming of Age*; and a management handbook, *Take Your Choice*, to assist social services departments in their commissioning of providers to meet local needs. By this date, however, the Commission's role in the world of social services had undergone a significant extension.

JOINT WORK ON SOCIAL SERVICES AND BOUNDARIES

Responsibility for overseeing local authorities' social services rested in the 1990s with a unit inside the Department of Health called the Social Services Inspectorate (SSI). Theirs was an unenviable lot whenever the tabloids worked themselves into a lather over the latest disclosure of some horrific child-abuse case that an incompetent (or unfortunate) social services worker had failed to pre-empt. But by 1995, a series of mishaps had begun seriously to alarm not just the media, but policy makers inside the government, too. The Policy Unit within 10 Downing Street under Sarah Hogg concluded that the time had come to abolish the SSI and find some more effective oversight body for services that were accounting for annual expenditure of about £7 billion. The prime minister concurred with this, and a meeting was arranged for him to break the news himself to his health secretary, Virginia Bottomley. She was herself a former psychiatric social worker with a more than passing interest in social services, and she objected to the move. It was soon the gossip of the Whitehall village that John Major had made the mistake of tackling his glamorous cabinet colleague over a late-night dinner. To nobody's very great surprise, she had managed to talk him out of abolishing her inspectorate and the hunt was on for a compromise.

Looking around for another supervisory body with a potentially complementary role in social services, Sarah Hogg and her colleagues quickly alighted on the Audit Commission and its famously energetic controller. He was telephoned within days. Would his team be interested, asked Hogg, in a wider mandate on social services? Andrew Foster was not in the business of turning down invitations to expand the Commission's franchise. It was always his instinct to go for growth, and he had no hesitation recommending to David Cooksey that they push ahead with some preparatory papers. When he presented these at a subsequent monthly meeting of the members, however, several of them expressed significant reservations. Taking on direct responsibility, albeit in tandem with another body, for monitoring a corner of the public sector – and being paid fees by the central government for doing so – represented a change of tack for the Commission that triggered considerable unease. Foster recalled:

> They were nervous. But that was the dynamic throughout that time. In the executive we wanted to push on, while the Commission would quite often see lots of political risk. But I thought we were doing excellent work, and I had a vision of an integrated approach to public services that would allow them to be managed much more effectively.[15]

How exactly the Commission's expanded mandate would be reconciled with the continued existence of the SSI was left to a series of long meetings through the autumn between Jonty Boyce and the senior SSI officials. They received little guidance on what was wanted, but Boyce came to a firm view that any joint body that was located organizationally within either Vincent Square or the DoH would simply be unworkable. He recalled: 'I had to persuade the SSI people that the only real way to do it was to create a separate organization that was equally accountable to the SSI and the Audit Commission.'[16]

This was the model adopted for the Joint Reviews of Social Services, to be conducted by a body that would have its own offices (which were rented in Victoria) and its own chief executive, though no very satisfactory name. Its head would report to both the Commission's health studies director and the chief inspector of the SSI. It was given statutory backing in the Audit (Miscellaneous Provisions) Bill, enabling the Commission to 'assist the secretary of state in any study designed to improve the economy, efficiency, effectiveness *and quality of performance* in the discharge of social services functions by local authorities' (italics added). It was introduced that December and enacted in April 1996.

While the Bill was making its way through Parliament, Boyce went after the person he thought ought to run it: this was Andrew Webster, who had so narrowly missed being made an associate director of the health team back in 1993. Webster had a strong background in both social services and health. He accepted the job, and work on the first reviews began under his leadership in July 1996. It was regarded by most observers as a very satisfactory outcome, quickly vindicated by the quality of the joint reviews that began appearing by early 1997 on almost a monthly basis. And the reviews had a mandate for proactive assessment that could be used as a first step towards more innovative work. Within a year, Webster and Boyce together had invented the notion of a twofold inquiry, which would look not just at the current situation within a department but also at that department's capacity to improve in the future. It was an idea with some potential.

For the Audit Commission, meanwhile, the new arrangement marked a watershed of sorts. For the first time, it had accepted direct funding from the government: the Commission would be paid by the Treasury for its contributions to the joint reviews. It also seemed to have been the case that members had been on the receiving end of ministerial pressure to take up the job – though of course no one could be sure of that. Not surprisingly, perhaps, the record of the members' monthly meetings now began to include slightly more frequent references to the sacrosanct importance of the Commission's independence. For it had effectively aligned itself with one of Whitehall's big-spending departments in a manner that had never been envisaged in the 1980s. It was an irony that this was the DoH – given the *froideur* between health officials and Vincent Square – not to say a credit to Boyce's ambassadorial skills in overcoming the *froideur*. (This was hardly improved by the Joint Reviews compromise, once it was realized that the SSI had been left holding the tabloid baby: it would still be responsible for the reactive investigations if things went embarrassingly wrong.) But this made no difference to the principle. The Commission had taken a big step closer to working in partnership with central government, for better or worse.

In the process, a sequence of events had unfolded that would recur in other contexts. In essence, the Commission had established a glowing reputation with its national reports. This had prompted someone in government to think the Commission might add very usefully to the work of an existing supervisory body. Good use had been made of the controller's contacts and assiduous networking within Whitehall. The Commission members – not unreasonably mindful of prospective managerial and operational risks, as well as the incremental political dangers – had reacted a little ambivalently. The controller had enthusiastically embraced the new opportunity as a welcome addition to the Commission's parish – and the distance between Vincent Square and central government had been ever so slightly diminished.

As it happened, the Commission's own chairman prompted something closely resembling this pattern of events, in moving into his new role at the Local Government Commission for England (LGCE) in 1995. David Cooksey certainly had a high opinion of Vincent Square's local government studies. Wearing his new cap as chairman-designate of the local government review body, he realized immediately that harnessing some of his erstwhile colleagues' expertise would be an excellent idea. Within days of his March appointment, he talked to Andrew Foster about the possibility of up to three senior staff moving on secondment to his team. He also co-opted the services of one of his fellow Commission members, Helena Shovelton, as a member of the LGCE. In truth, he needed all the help he could get. In addition to John Banham resigning, the LGCE's chief executive, Martin Easteal, had quit, and the government had dispensed with thirteen of the LGCE's sixteen original commissioners. (Shovelton's experience of the public sector appointment process didn't improve much. Her LGCE seat was offered on the telephone to the first person who took the call, which happened to be her cleaning lady.[17])

The Commission members responded cautiously at their April meeting, setting up a special panel under Clive Thompson – who had succeeded Murray Stuart as deputy chairman in February 1995 – to consider the request. 'The controller would report to the group on the appropriateness of the secondments.'[18] The panel reported back next month that it could see 'no unduly detrimental short term impact' – though they must have given the matter some careful thought, because Cooksey had asked for the services of both the director of the local government studies, Bob Chilton, and one of his most experienced team leaders, Greg Birdseye. The two of them headed off to the LGCE in July – as chief executive and research director, respectively – and ended up being absent for a full year.

Hiring them was a typically shrewd move by Cooksey: there can hardly have been two men in England better qualified than Chilton and Birdseye to advise on local government reorganization. Birdseye recalled:

We had produced a whole series of titles on the topic since 1992. I was leading on it, and we issued half a dozen shorter papers. We looked at how to prepare councils for reorganization, how to prepare for closing down a council or opening up a new one, how to merge authorities, how to look after municipal assets and so on – it was really quite a useful portfolio by the end.[19]

They had even turned out a paper, *Phoenix Rising*, on New Zealand's mixed experience of wholesale reorganization since 1989 'as a reminder of the risks'.

Around the time of their departure in July, members were informed by the LGCE that it intended to tap further into the Commission's expertise. Cooksey's main task was to resolve the uncertainty over the boundaries for twenty-one authorities left over from his predecessor's era. The LGCE had a statutory right to call on the Commission for its opinion on each, and Cooksey intended to exert that right. 'Commissioners expressed some concerns about the extent of the task envisaged for both auditors and the Audit Commission . . .'[20] But of course they acceded.

Several of the Commission's staff were kept busy visiting each of the twenty-one authorities for months thereafter. Many councils had an axe to grind over their treatment at the hands of the LGCE and discussions with them could be a sensitive matter. One of the places that had to be visited was Huntingdon, the prime minister's own constituency. Steve Evans was assigned the job. His evident apprehensions about it prompted some mischief at Vincent Square. Peter Wilkinson produced some notepaper with a House of Commons heading. He and Doug Edmonds concocted an invitation for Evans to join John Major for sherry at the Commons just two days before the date he was due to be in Huntingdon. Edmonds recalled: 'Steve was in turmoil about it. He spent the entire day anguishing over how to turn the PM down. The rest of us deeply sympathized. "Life's full of choices! It's integrity versus your job!" and so on. We eventually came clean about 5.30 p.m. Steve was a bit cross about that.'[21]

Meanwhile, it was no small concession for the Commission to have parted with Chilton's services as head of his directorate (though Peter Wilkinson stepped nimbly into his shoes for the year he was away). While weighing every ounce of their intellectual content as carefully as anyone, Chilton had brought a more disciplined approach and huge energy to all its studies since 1990. If the health franchise had in some respects stolen the limelight, this had diminished the importance of the local government programme not a jot. Two studies in particular had been landmarks. One was a Section 27 report called *Passing the Bucks* published in 1993, which had provided a monumental review of the system by which central government distributed £40 billion a year of funding via the so-called Standard Spending Assessments. (So voluminous were the appendices that they were given a volume of their own, which kicked off with an exemplary historical perspective, 'Never a Golden Age'.)

The other was a study of people, pay and performance in local government. This was one of the most ambitious research projects ever undertaken by the Commission, as befitted a topic of central importance. Between 1987 and 1993, the number of staff in local government's middle and higher management grades had shot up by 60 per cent. Most councils were looking at a steep rise in the wage bill (itself, coincidentally, 60 per cent of their total spending), even though pay rates had not much exceeded inflation. In two national reports published in 1995, *Paying the Piper* and *Calling the Tune*, the study's findings laid into a generally unsatisfactory aspect of town-hall finances with no fudging. 'The study found considerable variation in pay rates, little sharing of information between councils, poor management information, incoherent local pay policies and an absence of the hallmarks of good performance management.'[22]

Most of the other notable reports published in the mid-1990s dealt with one or the other of two sectors that had always been important to the Commission: education and housing. In both, a closer liaison with Whitehall gradually emerged in the usual way. Indeed, the process in both cases made itself apparent even before the 1995 initiative over social service reviews.

FORGING PARTNERSHIPS IN
EDUCATION AND HOUSING

Back in 1990, the introduction of the Local Management of Schools initiative had been seized on by Chilton's directorate as another opportunity to remind schools and local education authorities (LEAs) alike of a message pressed hard in various Commission papers all through the 1980s. A fall in the number of school-age children had still not been properly accommodated: surplus places by 1990 represented a huge drain on the country's educational budget. (In one 1990 report, *Rationalising Primary School Provision*, it was estimated that the primary sector was providing for 22 per cent more pupils than actually existed.) The message made a mark, and reminded Whitehall again of the extent of the Commission's work on schools over recent years. The upshot was an invitation to the Commission, in 1991, to join forces with Her Majesty's Chief Inspector of Schools on an evaluation of educational courses available for 16–19 year olds. The resulting joint report, *Unfinished Business*, was published in 1993. It was the first of a series of joint projects. They included a 1993 report with Ofsted (as the department of Her Majesty's Chief Inspector had become in 1992, coining the acronym from Office for Standards in Education). This was entitled *Keeping Your Balance*, and laid down some standards for good financial management in schools. A Management Paper followed in 1995, called *Lessons in Teamwork*, which offered school governors a primer on how best to fulfil their role.

The man appointed to run Ofsted in 1994 was Chris Woodhead – a former teacher whose views on the importance of traditional classroom values (and rejection of most of the supposedly progressive educational ideas of the 1960s and 1970s) had already made him a controversial figure on the national stage. Woodhead was strongly supported by John Major in his work on raising school standards. Not surprisingly, though, he ran into difficulties in his relations with a number of LEAs run by Labour authorities. At some point, it occurred to officials within the Department for Education and Employment (DfEE) that perhaps the Audit Commission could offer him useful help in tackling inspections of the LEAs.

As ever, Andrew Foster pursued the opportunity with some adroit canvassing behind the scenes. By the summer of 1996, plans were being laid in the education department for legislation that would allow the Commission to participate with Ofsted in joint LEA reviews. On 5 September, at their monthly meeting, Foster broke the news to Commission members – who reacted with their usual misgivings. 'Commissioners expressed their concern that in any joint ventures the independence and integrity of the Commission must be safeguarded and asked to be kept informed of developments.'[23]

It sounded anodyne enough in the minutes – but the true feelings of the members might perhaps be better gauged from the curious sequel. In December, the controller disclosed to them that a report about to be published on LEAs and the operation of school admission policies, *Trading Places*, had been discussed at length with the DfEE – and then *redrafted*. The revised report, he told them, 'had the same shape and outline but differed in tone from the original version'. After the customary remonstrances about the need to safeguard independence and integrity, the members agreed among themselves that two of them, Peter Soulsby and John Foster, should leave the boardroom and trawl through the revisions in detail. 'At a later stage in the meeting these two reported back to the Commission who also received advice on the nature of the Commission's powers from the Commission solicitor.'[24] The report was approved for publication, but it had been a revealing episode. Working closely in cahoots with other Whitehall non-departmental bodies might pose legal difficulties that members were not inclined simply to leave to the controller to resolve at his discretion.

At the start of the new year, 1997, the controller and Bob Chilton received a consultation paper from Ofsted. It outlined Chris Woodhead's views on how the Commission might work alongside his department on LEA reviews. Given the members' wariness in December, it was not hard to predict how they would react. Chilton presented a draft to the next monthly meeting on 9 January, explaining that Woodhead's proposal would involve the Commission 'only on a very selective and intermittent basis'. The members were having none of that, and readily endorsed a sniffy response. Any future requests from Ofsted for help 'would be considered by the Commission on an individual basis'.[25]

Undeterred, though, DfEE officials had meanwhile been pushing ahead with their legislative plans. They remained as keen as ever to secure a role for the Commission. It emerged in the Education Act 1997 that was passed two months later. It cannot have been wholly to the Commission members' liking: 'If requested to do so by the Chief Inspector, the Audit Commission may assist with any [LEA] inspection.'[26] This appeared to leave the ball squarely in Woodhead's court, but Foster did not allow himself to be discouraged. 'We were invited in because it was seen that we had a good methodology, ways of quantifying resources and making an objective assessment of them.'[27] He pressed on until he reached an agreement with Woodhead, and at the July 1997 meeting was able to assure members 'that the working arrangements proposed [with Ofsted] allowed for the Commission to have joint ownership of scheduled inspection reports and to submit specific sections of special inspection reports'. It looked, after all, like another successful expansion of Vincent Square's franchise. True, future relations with the chief inspector were a little difficult to predict. But Foster could at least take comfort by July from the sea-change in the political environment: the New Labour world would be more congenial to him than to his counterpart at Ofsted.

The story in housing was a little less byzantine. Housing was a sector that had figured prominently in the Commission's reports of the 1980s, from the work on council-rent arrears in the earliest days to John Banham's 1986 broadside, *Managing the Crisis in Council Housing*. It was not a subject that the Commission could ever leave for long. Local authorities in England and Wales owned around 3.5 million council houses, and spent about £3 billion a year on managing and maintaining them. The associated problems covered a wide range of topics. Under the leadership of Doug Edmonds – and the keen eye of that other housing specialist, Bob Chilton – housing teams at Vincent Square had carried the torch with a series of major studies, producing especially influential national reports on social deprivation (*Housing the Homeless*, 1989) and the general performance of local government in the sector (*Developing Local Authority Housing*

Strategies, 1992). Within a few weeks of Andrew Foster's arrival in the controller's office, the first national report requiring his sign-off was a study of the national administration of housing benefits (*Remote Control*, 1993).

The principal professional association in public sector housing was the Chartered Institute of Housing, which annually held a conference in Harrogate. It was the Mecca for the sector. By the 1990s, it was a rare conference that did not have Doug Edmonds or one of his colleagues among the guest speakers. As the authority on council housing, the Commission's voice counted. By this time, however, the most interesting development in the sector centred not on council housing but on a different group altogether, the housing associations (HAs, also known as Registered Social Landlords, or RSLs). These were the not-for-profit bodies that had been around for generations. They usually owned just a fraction of the stock levels held by large councils and had long relied on interest-free loans from central government, channelled via a non-departmental public body, the Housing Corporation.

The significance of the HAs had been transformed by the 1988 Housing Act. It had given them permission to borrow money privately using their stock as collateral. It had also given all council-house tenants a legal right to choose whether they wished to rent from their local authority or a housing association. Over the next three years, the stock held by the HAs grew by nearly 30 per cent. They still owned in aggregate well under a million houses, far fewer than local government. But the initiative in the public sector had clearly passed to the HAs – as many councils acknowledged, by arranging for large-scale transfers of their housing stock into HA ownership. This left many of the larger HAs with a challenging task, for which few were at all well prepared. The Housing Corporation had the responsibility for overseeing their activities, and in 1991 it acquired a new chief executive. A former DoE civil servant and member of the Central Policy Review Staff, Anthony Mayer arrived at the Corporation after six years in the City with N. M. Rothschild. He saw immediately an urgent need for some incisive analysis of the HAs' activities.

Late in 1991, a lunch was arranged with Howard Davies. Like John Moore and others before him, Mayer found Davies a persuasive advocate for the charms of the Audit Commission. It was agreed between them that a study team from Vincent Square would work with the Housing Corporation on VFM projects. Roger Jarman was one of the Corporation's senior managers at the time. He recalled: 'If there were any preconditions for the Commission's involvement, we couldn't see them. People were taken aback at the invitation that had been made to the Commission.'[28]

In the wake of Davies's departure, the proposed cooperation seems to have faltered for a while. But what then happened, once Andrew Foster was installed, adhered to the usual pattern. A series of private Whitehall meetings for Cooksey and Foster together led to a chance for the Commission to engage formally with the Corporation and the HA sector. Alerted by the controller in October 1994 to the possibility of a two-year agreement for the secondment of staff from Vincent Square to the Corporation, the Commission responded with its customary caution. Members stressed the need for any agreement to include 'terms which would safeguard its independence and freedom to express in public its opinions'. Whether or not these were included is unclear, but a letter went out the next month from John Gummer's DoE to the Corporation and the Commission, asking them to work together on promoting value for money among the HAs.

Some high-quality analysis followed, on profiles of the larger associations and on a series of six jointly prepared reports. They started with a comparative review of housing activities across all local authorities and HAs that was based upon the performance indicators for 1993–94 (*Homing in on Performance*, 1995). Then followed an assessment of the HAs' substantial new-build programmes (*Within Site*, 1996); a report on the essentials of housing management (*House Styles*, 1996); a report on the rehabilitation of older housing stock (*To Build or Not to Build*, 1998); a report on the selection of new-build sites (*Competing for Attention*, 1998); and a handbook on housing for the vulnerable, including the mentally ill (*A Measure of Support*, 1998). They were liveried in orange and white, with the logos of both bodies on the cover, but there was never much doubting who was the dominant partner. Jarman recalled: 'It was talked about as a joint studies programme, but all the reports were actually written by the Audit Commission and were their responsibility.'[29]

Since the funding for the programme came entirely from the Housing Corporation, the partnership was not without its tensions – but it was plain to ministers and their officials that the Commission had added a critically useful dimension to the Corporation's role. Before the two-year agreement expired, a substantial overhaul of the whole HA sector was enshrined in the 1996 Housing Act. Ministers were careful to ensure that the role of the Commission was consolidated as part of the legislation. In effect, the Commission now had access not only to the whole of the HA sector but to the work of the Housing Corporation, too. It was another signal extension to the Commission's mandate, and work on the sector went forward into 1997 at a brisk pace. Exactly as in health and education, though, the statutory basis of the Commission's engagement with a new partner left considerable discretion to both sides to agree between themselves how best to share their complementary roles.

There was one other partnership embarked upon in these years, where no such discretion was ever going to be available. While its own professional inspectorate would always hold the reins, though, the Commission nonetheless had plenty to contribute towards the management of the police.

PICKING UP THE BATON ON POLICE STUDIES

Andrew Foster's arrival in 1993 more or less coincided with the Commission's publication of its first substantial piece of work on the police since 1991. It was called *Helping with Enquiries*. Here for the first time the Commission was engaging not with peripheral services, like finger-printing, but with core issues of the policing profession. Why were the various categories of crime tackled as they were? Why were the results so varied? What could be done through better management of resources to improve the outcomes? Reactions to it could almost have been scripted before the publication. The Home Office and the HMIC were guarded, as they had been throughout the report's preparation. Senior uniformed officers within the service – far from hostile, thanks to the sensitivity and persistence of

the Commission between 1987 and 1991 – noted the report appreciatively. But they tended to observe that, naturally, its conclusions were
a commonplace among chief constables, who'd been saying this sort of
thing all along. Among rank-and-file detectives, there was a genuinely
warm reception: the report provided hard evidence to justify changes
that the more progressive officers had been urging for a while.

The media showed huge interest in the report. This in turn helped
to encourage more enthusiasm for police studies in Vincent Square. It
was an early pointer for Foster to the huge potential inherent in police
reports for building the media's general awareness of the Commission's work. This was reasonable enough in itself, but his liking
for the subject went deeper. Foster appreciated immediately the way
in which police studies would play to the strengths of the Commission.
Police officers knew the value of hard evidence, but had stuck for
generations with some basic assumptions that had long since parted
company with any evidence at all. This was fertile territory for the
evidence-based analysis the Commission could bring to bear.

The team leader on this report, Kate Flannery, knew all about the
value of challenging basic assumptions. She had been assigned to the
police team by Steve Evans in 1991, within a week of starting work
at the Commission. Her career until then had consisted of twelve
years in local government and management consultancy. She knew
nothing whatever about the police and had certainly never met a chief
constable until the day she and Evans sat with four of them to decide
on the choice of the Commission's next study. This staffing tactic was
of course the Commission's secret weapon: with no prior knowledge,
she was much more likely to ask the naive and therefore truly testing
questions. (One of Flannery's colleagues had worked for years in the
Metropolitan Police Service: he was never allowed near the police
studies.)

Flannery recalled: 'Two study options were put to our panel of
advisers: one was the use of IT in the police service and the other was
the management of criminal investigations. I thought: "If they pick
IT, I'm absolutely done for" and I could see myself not lasting long
at the Audit Commission.'[30] Fortunately for her, they chose the second
topic. But Flannery was still more than slightly dismayed to find herself
pitched straight into leading the initial round of interviews. 'Just get

the police almanac, call half a dozen chief constables and tell them you'd like to talk to them about criminal investigation', said Evans helpfully.[31] Flannery chose the friendliest of the chief constables she'd met and went off to visit him, in Dorset. It was a measure of the Commission's reputation that he received her in his office with half a dozen of his most senior colleagues lined up beside him. Bravely, Flannery took a deep breath and dived in. Why was crime going up? Why were detection rates so low and falling? Why did detectives go to the scene of a burglary after uniformed officers had already been there? Their talk lasted for more than two hours.

After she had left, some of the senior officers sat around with a distinct case of shell-shock. As one of them revealed to Flannery a year or so later, after the two of them had worked together for months, many of her questions had left them completely stumped. She was asking for the rationale behind traditional practices that none of them had ever questioned before. Such questions, of course, were the Commission's real stock-in-trade. The central assumption questioned by *Helping with Enquiries* was that criminal investigations should start at the scene of the crime and work backwards, as it were, towards a list of suspects. This was the standard approach to most burglaries, for example – with a visit to the crime scene by a uniformed policeman customarily leading to a steady procession of other callers from the detective to the crime-prevention officer. Yet detection rates for all reported burglaries were currently dropping to less than 10 per cent. The study team established that, in line with the usual 80/20 rule, a very large percentage of burglaries were accounted for by a relatively small number of prolific villains. It seemed to Flannery and her colleagues, ignorant of all police traditions, that the obvious thing to do was to concentrate on building up as comprehensive a data-bank as possible of the intelligence on those villains. From this hypothesis, much else flowed. Activity at the scene of the crime, for example, might be codified so that one person could handle most of it in a single visit. More importantly, a premium should be set on IT resources so that all nuggets of random information on a crime could be rapidly assimilated and compared with patterns of behaviour recorded for a known group of individuals in the past. There could be more specialization of roles, too, so that new crimes were not handled by fresh officers in a random fashion (taking cases 'off the spike', as it was called) but could be allocated to individual officers with particular expertise.

This 'intelligence-led policing', with its focus on a known group of villains as the starting point of any investigation, was in fact the approach already taken in respect of murders and other serious crime. The Home Office, for example, devoted a computerized enquiry system ('HOLMES') to it that allowed exactly the kind of IT data-management advocated by Flannery and her colleagues. The detection rate for serious crime was very high – almost every murder was solved – and they argued that this was no coincidence. They presented the case for 'intelligence-led policing' in a subtle and persuasive text that was widely admired in the police service. Many of its detailed pro-posals, on the restructuring of investigation procedures and enhance-ment of computer resources, were painstakingly adopted over the next few years. Indeed, so intent were the police on pursuing the report's recommendations that Evans and his colleagues were explicitly asked to put a hold on their next big project until *Helping with Enquiries* had been properly digested.

In the meantime, they produced *Cheques and Balances*, a much more modest study and a tailored response to the 1994 Police and Magistrates Courts Act. This legislation was ostensibly an attempt by Kenneth Clarke as home secretary (and Michael Howard, who succeeded him during the course of the Act's passage) to rejuvenate the tripartite structure comprising the Home Office, the forty-three local police forces and their local police authorities. Political oppon-ents of the 1994 legislation, including many Tory peers, rejected the rejuvenation claims as a sham from the start. The Act was widely attacked as a thinly veiled consolidation of the Home Office's power over the police and a big step down the road towards a nationalized force. But the Commission had itself argued for a genuine revival of the tripartite structure in earlier Police Papers, and now welcomed the 1994 Act a little optimistically as 'the most far-reaching reform of the management of the police service for 30 years'.[32]

The 1994 Act had two main objectives: to revive a sense of local ownership of the police, through local policing plans under the control of the authorities; and to widen the scope of financial delegation from the Home Office to local forces, in the belief that more local responsibility for the money would lead to better local use of resources. The report effectively provided a step-by-step approach to both goals. As its political opponents had been quick to point out, the first was probably always a forlorn hope. (Critics blamed the government for the lack of sufficiently committed laymen to give the authorities any real teeth.) But the Commission's report at least made a big contribution to a successful implementation of the financial reforms. *Cheques and Balances* was a set text for the next few years on management courses at Bramshill Police Staff College (as it was still known at that time) and would be constantly quoted for years as the reference guide by police forces on the ground.

By the start of 1995, the Commission was ready to take on another ambitious study. To pick a suitable topic, the team decided to follow the money. Just a handful of activities accounted for the lion's share of police expenditure. Criminal investigation, for example, represented about 20 per cent of the budget. The largest portion of all, about 30 per cent, went on the activity that was most visible to the general public: patrolling the streets. So Steve Evans assigned the same team that had produced *Cheques and Balances* – led again by Kate Flannery, assisted by a secondee from DA, Steve Jackson – to ask another round of naive questions about police patrols. What, in particular, was the point of them?

Some excellent (and, as usual, scarcely noticed) research within the Home Office had shown very persuasively what patrols were *not* about – catching criminals. It was a blue moon indeed that shone down on a uniformed bobby catching anyone in the act of committing a crime. In this respect, patrols were a massive waste of money. (Indignant critics of the subsequent report usually stopped reading at this point.) On the other hand, of course, it seemed incontrovertible that patrols were highly valued by the public. Asked by a specially commissioned MORI poll whether they found the sight of a patrol officer reassuring, 72 per cent of respondents answered 'always'. The same poll found that three out of five respondents said they would be willing to pay more tax in order to fund more patrols.[33] The challenge, therefore, was to identify ways in which patrolling could be made as effective as possible – and to eliminate those aspects that were essentially random (or, as Flannery recalled it, 'making sure that officers were not just running round like scalded cats').[34] Reviewed in this light, there turned out to be many ways in which patrolling could be systematized and dovetailed into more sophisticated crime-prevention activities. The report, *Streetwise: Effective Police Patrol*, set them out with fifty pages of compelling evidence for its findings.

Unfortunately, the reception for the report was badly compromised by a leak at the draft stage. Almost all good reports were the product of substantial consultation with selected advisers, of course. But for good reason, the Commission (unlike the NAO) had no obligation to expose the draft of any final report to an audited body. Steve Evans, against his better judgement, allowed himself to be persuaded to make an exception for *Streetwise*. The Association of Chief Police Officers had given Flannery and her team a huge amount of help. To acknowledge this, Flannery sent copies of the first draft to a number of ACPO's leading officials. It was the week before the start of the 1995 Conservative Party conference. In the aftermath of the bitter debates over the 1994 Act, interest in the police was as great as ever and ranked high on every party conference's agenda that autumn – and every newspaper editor's, too. Early on the Thursday evening, Flannery got a call from the Commission's PR team to say that a journalist from the *Guardian* had just telephoned. The paper had a copy of the draft report. A story was being prepared for the next day. Would the Commission like to comment? Flannery confirmed the inevitable answer (no) and then rang the president of ACPO, Merseyside's chief constable, Jim Sharples, to warn him. They consoled themselves that it would probably be only a short article. With luck it might be tucked away at the bottom of an inside page where few readers would notice it.

As she often did, Flannery then sat down to watch BBC television's current affairs programme *Newsnight* before heading off for bed. It ended as usual with a review of the next day's press – and the anchorman held up a copy of the *Guardian*. The lead story on the front page was all too plain to see. Its headline was 'Police Chaos Exposed'. And it ran over, viewers were told, to extend across most of page two, as well. The article, which Flannery finally read in the morning after an anxious night, extracted some colourful evidence from *Streetwise* for concluding that police patrols were often stagger-ingly inefficient. With only 5 per cent of all police officers actually available for patrolling at any one time, it was an activity that needed careful direction. Instead, it was too often ill-prepared, random in nature and rarely subject to proper debriefing. Officers sent to inci-dents of domestic violence, for example, commonly set off with no access at all to background information about the family involved. Yet Home Office research showed that '90 per cent of known domestic violence involves systematic, repeated assault'.[35]

All this naturally elicited a fiercely defensive reaction from the police. A deputation of four rather irate chief constables descended on Vincent Square a few weeks later for a discussion with the chairman and controller, who were accompanied to the meeting by Peter Wilkinson (as the director responsible for the team behind the report) and Kate Flannery. It was a delicate occasion, but some plain speaking cleared the air. ACPO and the Police Federation then responded in quite measured terms to the publication of the finished report in March 1996 – as, indeed, did the *Guardian*, too.

Streetwise went on for years being misconstrued by some as an attack on the general competence of the police. This put a dent in the goodwill enjoyed by the Commission with many of the rank and file. It probably also helped explain the cool response to a number of innovative ideas included in the report, which now needed a long gestation. These included, for example, introducing a non-emergency number to complement the 999 system. This would reduce the pres-sure on the 999 system and allow for a more graded response to reflect the fact that fewer than a third of calls concerned genuine emergencies. It would be another nine years before this could be piloted. A second idea was that the service should add to patrol resources by using auxiliary officers without the powers of a fully qualified constable. The Police Federation was implacably opposed to this. But one senior officer, an assistant chief constable of Thames Valley police, worked closely with Flannery's team on the idea. This was Ian Blair, who was instrumental eight years later in the successful introduction of Police Community Support Officers all over the country and who was appointed commissioner of the Metropolitan Police in 2005.

Despite mixed reviews in the months leading up to its publication, though, *Streetwise* did nothing to harm the Commission's relationships with HMIC and the Home Office that by now were growing steadily closer. Both of them actively collaborated with Vincent Square, as did ACPO, on the production in 1996 of two management handbooks. These took the content of *Helping with Enquiries* and *Streetwise* and effectively turned them into detailed operational manuals, copies of which were despatched to all police forces in the country. Flannery recalled: 'Those handbooks were real breakthroughs, in terms of getting us working together and pooling the reports' ideas into more practicable action steps.'[36]

This happy outcome for the Commission had very nearly been aborted at the outset by a clash with the home secretary, Michael Howard. He was sent a final draft of *Streetwise* a few days before its despatch to the printers. The next morning, the Commission's controller was summoned with his team to Queen Anne's Gate. Andrew Foster, Peter Wilkinson and Kate Flannery were received by Howard sitting behind a table, in a chair the size of a throne, obviously angry and flanked by half a dozen of his most senior officials. Here was the downside, of course, of the policy favoured by Foster of disclosing final drafts to government ministers and their shadow counterparts. A fierce objection by a secretary of state would be impossible to ignore without risking a nasty Whitehall battle with unpredictable consequences.

Sure enough, Howard had a problem with an exhibit at the start of the report which he insisted they remove. It showed that the number of police officers available per head of the population in the UK compared unfavourably with the corresponding number in several other EU countries. This was a bogus comparison, insisted Howard, and it drew on a line of academic research that had been completely discredited. Fortunately, the Commission team had anticipated that this point might stick in the ministerial craw. They had agreed among themselves beforehand that it could easily be jettisoned without any damage to the report. The point was therefore quite solemnly conceded – after which, Howard visibly relaxed.

The episode turned out, though, to be the prologue to a bigger drama. One of the Commission members, Tony Christopher, had insisted throughout 1994 that youth justice in England and Wales should be investigated as a priority. He believed with a passion (and quite correctly, as it turned out) that the system was a scandalous mess. A study had been launched in 1995, and assigned to the health directorate as part of its brief to watch over the social services. Under Boyce's overall direction, it was managed by David Browning, whose team included Judy Renshaw and a secondee from the Treasury, Mark Perfect. (David Browning had led the team responsible for an influential report on the criminal justice system that had been published back in 1989, *The Probation Service: Promoting Value for Money*.) Oversight was provided by a steering panel that included Peter Wilkinson (and Bob Chilton after his return from the LGCE) as well as Kate Flannery.

The resulting national report, *Misspent Youth*, was another in the long line of titles from the Commission that seemed to emerge with magical timing: it caught a mounting wave of public concern. This was focused in 1996 on the level of crime against individuals, especially in the inner cities. It was suddenly seen to be rising uncontrollably. (In fact it had risen 73 per cent between 1981 and 1995.) And almost as alarming to the general public was the fact that a quarter of all known offenders were under the age of 18. *Misspent Youth* set out to analyse how this disastrous trend might best be reversed. It looked not only at better ways of dealing with those young people brought before the courts, but at the steps needed to develop a strategy that could reduce the rate of re-offending.

This was in one respect a return to territory already explored by the Commission: it had produced a powerful analysis in 1989 of the improvements that were urgently needed, even then, to the probation service. Ministers had responded positively at the time, but few if any effective improvements had followed for the youth justice system. Above all, it had continued to suffer from a crippling lack of coordination among the many public services that dealt with young offenders – including health, leisure and employment agencies as well as the probation service and the whole gamut of youth justice services. There was a conspicuous absence of what came to be known within the next few years as 'joined-up government'.

To prepare the way for the publication of *Misspent Youth* in

November, the controller decided to invite a number of senior White-hall officials to a briefing on its contents – including the permanent secretary from the Home Office. This lit the end of a very short fuse, and a loud bang followed inside Queen Anne's Gate soon afterwards. Why working drafts of the report had not prompted a stronger response earlier in the usual consultation process was not entirely clear. But there was no mistaking the reaction now. Officials warned Flannery that the home secretary was 'absolutely livid'.[37] Foster was summoned once again, and Howard read him the riot act. The report quite clearly implied that different parts of the Home Office were in effect failing to communicate with each other. This was obviously untrue and a wholly unacceptable allegation. The report, said Howard, would have to be substantially rewritten.

With just days to go before the scheduled publication date, this posed an obvious problem. It might have been a bigger dilemma for Commission members, though, if the home secretary and his officials had chosen to find fault with specific facts in the report. Instead, as the controller now reported back, they had in effect put up nakedly political objections. Foster explained to the members that there was a great deal of disquiet at government level; he pointed out that the home secretary had himself been remarkably exercised about it; he dutifully relayed Howard's demand that the report be significantly redrafted – and the members, with one voice, agreed they would not change a word.[38]

When this was communicated back to Queen Anne's Gate, there followed a memorable row. Once the lines had been drawn on political grounds, though, there was no realistic way that the Commission could possibly accommodate the home secretary's objections. Both sides prepared for a battle royal. The first clash came on BBC Radio 4's *Today* programme on the morning of the report's publication, with a blunt attack on it by one of Howard's junior ministers. It proved, however, to be a short-lived offensive. In the Commons later that day, scenting a potential embarrassment for the government, Paddy Ashdown for the Liberal Democrats laid into John Major at prime minister's questions. 'The Audit Commission said today that we are now less effective on tackling youth crime than we were 10 years ago . . . and that the Government's programmes are ineffective, inefficient and wasteful. Given the fact that the Government have been in power for 17 years, whom do they blame for that?'

The response was unexpected. 'The right honourable gentleman would do well to read the Audit Commission report in full', replied the prime minister. 'He will find that it endorses our strategy . . .'[39] It was a less than Churchillian dismissal of the Liberal Democrats, but the Commission heard no more complaints from Queen Anne's Gate.

While the Tories tripped over themselves, Labour's attitude was unequivocal. The shadow home secretary, Jack Straw, had been invited by Boyce to Vincent Square to talk about the report some weeks earlier. He took a genuine interest in it and came a second time for a further discussion – not just about *Misspent Youth* but *Streetwise*, too, and all of the other reports produced by the Commission on the police since the early 1990s. Straw was already sure in his own mind that police reforms would be a principal theme of Labour's first term in office, assuming that it won the 1997 election. He was impressed with the Commission's work – and its workers, too. Six months later, and newly installed as Howard's successor in Queen Anne's Gate, Straw acted immediately to set up a working group to look at police efficiency and ways of improving it. He personally invited Kate Flannery to join it.

From this moment, Flannery was increasingly to be seen by HMIC and the Home Office as almost an in-house adviser. Back in September, a newly installed chief inspector at HMIC, David O'Dowd, had told her that his ambition was to put the Audit Commission out of business. It was meant as a flattering observation, not a threat: he wanted to re-create, within the Inspectorate, the kind of analytical resources resident in Vincent Square. Inevitably, one step in that direction involved co-opting Flannery herself. She assisted with two further, relatively modest Commission reports on the police over the next couple of years – *The Doctor's Bill* (1998) looked at the provision of forensic medical services to police forces and *Action Stations* (1999) examined the management by police forces of their land and buildings – but she effectively departed for a career with HMIC from August 2000.

It was a neat reversal of the usual process by which talented individuals from Whitehall had been lured away to Vincent Square over the years. Nor was Flannery the only loss to the Commission. Under legislation passed in 1998, the Labour government set up a Youth Justice Board that was quite specifically designed to address many of the issues identified in *Misspent Youth*. To run it, they hired the Commission's Treasury secondee, Mark Perfect. And within months of his installation, he was writing to Jonty Boyce to clear the way for his recruitment of Judy Renshaw.

As such staff moves suggested, the distance between Vincent Square and Whitehall – whether in the context of police work, social services, education or housing – was no longer quite as it had been in the 1980s. Nor, perhaps, did it offer the *cordon sanitaire* it had provided a decade earlier. While its closer involvement with central government had helped to enrich the work of the Commission in many ways by 1997, it had also left it a great deal more vulnerable to whatever passing political initiatives happened to be fashionable at any moment. How problematic this might be in the future would depend, of course, on the new Labour government. Perhaps it would set its face firmly against passing initiatives, only exposing the Commission to the most prudent and carefully prepared extensions of its existing franchise. Anything less measured, though, might spell trouble.

12

Living With New Labour, 1997–99

By 1997, Andrew Foster had spent over three years preparing the Audit Commission for the arrival of its first Labour government. This is not to say he had been directing resources within Vincent Square or DA into a study of detailed Labour proposals for some future reforms of health or local government – there were not too many of those – but nor had he just confined himself to keeping lines of communication open with New Labour, as a simple matter of good housekeeping. Foster had skilfully and very effectively positioned the Commission as a potential ally in any future Labour drive for better public services. And if this required a more assertive approach by the Commission, he was ready to take on the challenge.

It had already been heading in this direction since the mid-1990s, courtesy of John Major's performance indicators (PIs). Since 1993, the collating and analysis of PIs collected from every council in England and Wales had been a huge undertaking for Vincent Square. Individual PIs had had to be agreed with representatives of each tier of local government, and continually revised in a painstaking process overseen by a Commission members' panel under the chairmanship of Clive Thompson. National indicators had then been prepared and published each March in a three-volume compendium, as a guide to local government's overall performance – and to the pecking order of individual authorities.

To some observers, this had all amounted to a subtle break with the past. It was less (to use Howard Davies's phrase) about 'illuminating choices', and more about shining a harsh light on slackers. Others, more sympathetic to the Major government's aims, saw it as not *that* different from what had gone before. This was certainly the stance taken by the Commission members themselves. Discussing the release of the 1994–95 PIs in March 1996, for example, members 'agreed that the Commission should again adopt *a non-judgemental approach* to publication' (italics added).[1] The Commission, they felt, had stopped short of any structured assessment of individual authorities' operations. True, tendering arrangements for CCT contracts had needed rigorous checking – but that was the nearest auditors had come to any hands-on role. Contrary to the wilder claims of the left, the Commission and its field force had kept their non-audit activities within a carefully limited range. John Major and his ministers, like their predecessors in the 1980s, had been content with this. It accorded, perhaps a little ironically, with a Tory sense of local government's basic autonomy.

Labour's instincts were different. Following Tony Blair's election as their party leader in 1994 and the launch of the New Labour project, the parliamentary party had soon begun to hint at a different approach on local government. It seemed likely to be far more interventionist. Labour MPs were determined to rid the party's national image of any lingering contamination by town-hall petty demagoguery. But their ambitions went further. Just as Labour had to be distanced from any suggestion that it might mismanage the national economy, so it had also to slough off any identification with lazy and inept management by Labour-run councils. Above all, no slouching at a local level by councils of any political allegiance could be allowed to impede Labour's drive for a radical improvement in Britain's public services. Several of Labour's front-bench spokesmen were soon in regular dialogue with the Commission. Foster recalled: 'Labour at that time was very hungry to know what we were and who we were.'[2]

With guidance and assistance in the early days from David Cooksey, Foster fed them the briefings they needed. He was the heir to an institution with a glowing reputation in Westminster, and worked hard to exploit this in his dealings with the opposition as well as the government, trying to demonstrate to senior Labour figures that the Commission was politically unaligned, trustworthy and potentially an invaluable ally. Thus, when the first set of national performance indicators was published in March 1995, great care was taken to avoid giving any impression that waste and inefficiency were hallmarks of a Labour majority in the council chamber. More positively, Foster used the growing influence of the national reports to great effect. It had long been the established policy to offer a private briefing on every new national report to the appropriate Labour and Liberal Democrat spokesmen as well as the relevant Tory minister. Jack Straw, David Blunkett, Hilary Armstrong, Margaret Beckett, Harriet Harman, Frank Dobson, David Miliband, even Gordon Brown – all were regularly contacted either by the controller or by one of the other directors with straightforward updates on the work of the Commission. It was a shrewd investment of their time.

And Foster was alert to New Labour's emerging priorities, too – like transparency in government. The *Butler Review*, published in the autumn of 1995, was a rare example of a public body opening itself up to external scrutiny (as its chairman noted in his foreword, confessing he was 'not aware of any comparable precedent'). The following year, the accountants Arthur Andersen were invited into Vincent Square to conduct an Efficiency Review of the workings of the central directorates. Strategies and Plans came thick and fast. Constantly renewing itself, the Commission would always stay more than a step ahead of any significant outside criticism.

As the new controller back in 1993, one of Foster's early decisions had been that the Commission should be well represented at all the autumn party conferences. The Commission henceforth always had a stand at each conference and hosted a fringe meeting for the presentation of recent work. It was certainly no less diligent in paying court to Labour's gatherings than to those of the Tories. In 1995, indeed, it rather bizarrely won a prize from Labour for having 'the best virtual reality stand [*sic*] at the conference . . . [with top marks] received primarily for the interactive computer presentation of the Citizen's Charter performance indicators'.[3] Mike Barnes gave Tony Blair's wife, Cherie, a presentation about PIs on the day that the best-stand prizes were judged – and the Labour leader himself presented them that evening.[4]

In the run-up to the 1995 conference, a feature appeared in *The Times* about Labour's plans for local government. It centred on an interview with one of Labour's prospective future ministers and a one-time leader of Camden Borough Council back in the 1970s, Frank

Dobson. But next to a large photograph of Dobson was a portrait of the Commission's controller. As soon as Labour was returned to power, Dobson was reported as saying, he fully intended to be an activist in the town and county halls. The article reminded readers that some Labour voices had claimed before the 1992 election that the Audit Commission would be scrapped. 'But now Mr Dobson is not only planning to retain the Commission, he also wants to give it additional powers and – if necessary – send it, fangs bared, into recalcitrant councils to rend, tear and generally sort out.'[5]

It was not a mission that could be left to old-fashioned auditors, though. For presentation at the conference itself, Dobson had a paper on Labour plans to set up a group of 'standards inspectors' who would work in cahoots with the Commission. They would together have the power, where necessary, to indict a council, draw up an improvement plan and even draft in 'a team of management trouble-shooters to carry it through'. This public endorsement of the Commission, and talk of extending its powers, went well beyond the private rapprochement of recent years with figures such as Jack Cunningham and Jack Straw – as the author of the article went on to explore. 'The reason for the *volte face* has something to do with the personality of the Commission's controller, Andrew Foster, who has quietly conducted a charm offensive.'

The piece in *The Times* gave the controller and chairman all due credit for their successes with Labour, but it also acknowledged worries in some quarters.

There are, however, people who think Mr Foster may have been too successful in wooing Labour. Labour's plans for the Commission have been criticized by CIPFA on the grounds that its independence would be lessened and it would be turned into a 'creature of government'. Misgivings have been heard from local government, too, where Labour is currently so strong. The Association of Metropolitan Authorities wants the party to make the Commission more accountable – to them. It should not sit in judgment on councils, as they have the electoral mandate.

One other critic mentioned by name in the same article even had some advice for Labour.

Steve Bundred is director of finance for Camden . . . and once was a leading Labour activist on the GLC. 'The [shortly to be published] Butler Report', he predicted, 'will point to confusion between the role of auditors as police – monitoring the probity of councils on behalf of taxpayers – and their conflicting role as consultants, working alongside authorities and seeking to assist them in improving services . . .' Labour, Mr Bundred says, ought to wait for the Butler review of the Commission to be completed before it settles its policy.

Eight years later, Bundred would arrive at the Commission as controller (or chief executive, as the title would by then be renamed).

As these criticisms attested, sailing closer to Labour had drawn the Commission into some tricky waters that would need a deft hand on the tiller. Ironically, though, it was from Labour's ranks at Westminster that the controller came under attack a few months later, over criticisms that had been levelled at management practices within the Yorkshire Regional Health Authority during and after his time as general manager there in 1987–91. Questions raised by the district auditor in 1994 had prompted an internal inquiry by the Department of Health, which in turn led to a report by the National Audit Office, published in March 1996. It singled out for special criticism four managers who were junior to Foster, including his finance director, and cited a number of irregularities mostly arising in the years after Foster's departure.[6] This prompted six Labour MPs, including Ken Livingstone, to sign an early day motion in May 1996, calling for Foster's removal from office. A Commission spokesman pointed out in response that past events had been misrepresented in the motion, and the whole affair was quickly forgotten. But it ensured the controller an uncomfortable few weeks – and even led to some lampooning of the Commission on Channel Four television's *Rory Bremner Show*.

A WIDER ROLE FOR THE CONTROLLER

Prior to arriving in Vincent Square, Foster had spent only a couple of years of his career within the Whitehall village. It was not his natural habitat, as it had been for Treasury insiders such as Howard Davies and Ross Tristem. (Having a hotline to the Treasury, in Tristem's view, had always been especially crucial for the Commission.) Foster had of course had dealings with the Treasury in his capacity as chief operating officer of the NHS, but still needed to build on his relationships there even as he mastered his controller's brief. Hugely valuable was David Cooksey's presence by his side in the first few years. But after August 1995, Cooksey was gone – or at least, he would be bringing his still very considerable influence to bear in rather different ways – and Foster had to make his own way largely unaided.

The search for Cooksey's successor seems hardly to have begun before his departure, and Clive Thompson stepped into the breach as acting chairman. Thompson, a successful industrialist in the chemicals sector, was well liked by his colleagues. He had made a huge personal contribution to the development of performance indicators and was more than ready to assume the chairmanship on a permanent basis. Much to Thompson's evident disappointment, though, officials at the DoE opted to look elsewhere. They appointed a new chairman with a background, like Cooksey's, in venture capital. His name was Roger Brooke. Also like Cooksey, he had founded his own company: he had launched Candover Investments in 1980, and was still its chairman. Prior to running Candover, he had spent eleven years as a diplomat in the Foreign Office and had then been a main board director at Pearson plc for some years, where he ended up as chairman of Longman, the publisher. This breadth of experience had presumably appealed to officials, and it must have weighed in Brooke's favour that he had had at least some involvement in both local government and health. He had been on the council of the London Borough of Kensington and Chelsea for seven years in the 1970s, and was a member of the finance and general purposes board of the Royal College of Physicians. But it was generally assumed in Vincent Square that he had been recommended by the outgoing chairman. Certainly they knew each other well, and any suggestion from Cooksey would have been gratefully received within the DoE, where officials had struggled for months to find appropriate (and politically eligible) candidates.

Brooke kicked off in December 1995 with the usual round of introductory meetings and visits, which prompted congratulations from his colleagues in April when he reported back on his initial findings. He also made a favourable impression on many of the senior managers in Vincent Square, for whom an invitation to a one-on-one lunch with the chairman was as unexpected as it was welcome. It would be misleading, though, to pretend that Brooke filled the chairman's role as Cooksey had done before him. Though personally popular with all of the members, Brooke had arrived in the chair with fewer than four aces in his hand, as quickly became obvious.

To begin with, he lacked any broad knowledge of the public sector, which by 1996 was much more of a disadvantage for him than it had been for John Read in 1983, or even Cooksey in 1986. The difficulty for most of the members was that, when Brooke arrived, it wasn't immediately apparent to any of them why he had been appointed. As already noted, Clive Thompson was now the only other businessman round the boardroom table. Since the arrival of Helena Shovelton, Ron Watson and John Foster early in 1995, three new members had appeared on the Commission – and their backgrounds only reinforced the point. David Heath was a former leader of Somerset County Council, and chairman of his local police authority. Hilary Rowland was the chief executive of a children's hospital in Liverpool, Alder Hey. Rosalynde Lowe was operational director of a hospital trust.

These appointments underlined the anomaly of Brooke's business and City background, which was far more apparent from his general approach to life than had ever been the case with his venture capitalist predecessor. Brooke was especially active in pursuing opportunities under the scheme known as the Private Finance Initiative (PFI) that the Major government had introduced in 1992. (It encouraged the private sector and local government to enter joint ventures together that Labour critics scorned as 'privatization by the back door'.) Brooke had his own company, called Innisfree, which was building a successful PFI portfolio. He had drawn this to the attention of the local government minister, David Curry, in their final discussion together prior to his appointment. Brooke recalled:

I said, 'Do you think this is a conflict of interests?' because no doubt the Audit Commission would be interested in PFI deals from the audit point of view. But they didn't think it was a conflict – in fact, they thought it was quite helpful that I had this interest.[7]

But it was not unknown for the new chairman to flash a business card at meetings where PFI was mentioned. As Brooke saw it, he was carefully flagging up his personal interest in order to avoid any accusation that a conflict of interest had been concealed – but colleagues sometimes construed other motives and the business card did not go down well.

Nor was Brooke as adept as Cooksey at concealing his political pedigree. An outsider, invited to eavesdrop on a Commission monthly meeting, might have struggled to distinguish which other members with local government backgrounds were Conservative and which were Labour. But he would never have had much trouble spotting Brooke's political vantage point. He was every inch a Kensington and Chelsea Tory. From the moment of New Labour's arrival, this effectively left him outside the tent. Brooke had friendly relations with a number of officials, including the head of the NAO, John Bourn, and would meet with permanent secretaries from time to time. But Labour ministers had no interest whatever in his views – especially after Brooke had had the temerity at an early stage to warn the local government minister, Hilary Armstrong, in private that her ideas on reform would only result in a huge bureaucracy. He recalled:

I always had the feeling that [ministers] wished I wasn't the chairman. They would far rather have had one of their own kind as chairman. And they more or less hinted at that. So I said, if you want to sack me, you've got to give me a reason – and they backed off, basically.[8]

Above all, though, he lacked Cooksey's weight in the boardroom. If some are born chairmen, and others achieve success in that role over time, Brooke never quite managed to dispel the impression that he had had chairmanship thrust upon him. As he himself saw it, this was nothing to do with innate ability: he had headed plenty of private sector bodies in his time, after all. But Brooke had clear views of his own on chairmanship.

If you have a good chief executive, you let him get on with it. I decided early on that Andrew was an excellent chief executive and that my job was just to see how he got on, to help him as best I could and not to interfere. From his point of view, I suppose I was quite an easy chairman.

Too easy, believed many of the Commission's members. Brooke was of course aware of their concern.

Some people, I know, thought that I was not assertive enough. But I just felt it was going well and why should I start throwing my weight around, changing everything just for the sake of changing things? So I didn't change anything much. And I think people thought I wasn't much good for that reason.[9]

Unsurprisingly, against this background, he struggled with the difficult task of balancing the views of eighteen members (or more). It did not help that all his colleagues knew that a seasoned campaigner at the table – Clive Thompson – had sought the chair and been denied it. The fact that Thompson remained as deputy chairman until the end of his term in October 1997 was undeniably a source of considerable unease for members on several occasions.

Inevitably, the members looked elsewhere for the real leadership of the Commission. As was bound to happen, it fell increasingly to the controller to provide it – and Andrew Foster unhesitatingly stepped up to the wider role. Within the boardroom, Foster gradually assumed the authority almost of a de facto executive chairman. It was he who led off important discussions with a reminder of the story so far; and, as often as not, it was he who summarized the members' views at the end and pointed out the agreed way forward. The formidable and fastidious Jeremy Orme – who succeeded Thompson as the deputy chairman – was always ready to speak up for the members themselves when the need arose. But for most of their discussions, it was Foster who steered the way.

Externally, too. From around this time onwards, Foster's profile in the media began a steady rise. Not at first a natural performer on TV or the radio, he worked hard (with the help of various private consultants) to acquire the skills and confidence of a practised pundit. His voice began to be heard quite regularly, for example, on BBC Radio 4's *Today* programme. The publication of a new report often meant a breakfast-time interview with Foster. He also pushed communications as an increasingly important item on Vincent Square's agenda. A well-known advertising and PR agency, Lowe Bell, was hired to assist with future strategy. Following a discussion at the June 1996 monthly meeting of the agency's proposals ('. . . a more systematic approach to public speaking, with a model structure for all key speeches . . .'), the controller announced the setting up of a 'communications unit' to draw together all the staff working in this area. Within months, led by an associate controller, Vanessa Couchman, arrangements were going ahead for a programme of focus groups. Huge efforts were made to sound out views of the Commission among managers, councillors and non-executive directors on audited bodies. (The broad response was very favourable – though it was a common grouse that the Commission's recommendations left too little leeway for local variations.) No audience, though, was more important than Westminster's MPs – and especially the Parliamentary Labour Party, which seemed certain by 1996 to be on its way back to power very shortly. The Harris polling organization was asked to track MPs' views of the Commission's work. Foster meanwhile busied himself with constant briefings, policy debates, speeches, lunches, dinners and 'stakeholders' suppers' to prepare for the New Labour dawn.

Foster had huge ambitions for the Commission. He wanted to expand its role in the improvement of public services wherever and whenever opportunities arose. By early 1997, as we have seen, this was fast leading to additional responsibilities in education, housing, the social services and the police. Behind the scenes, Foster also encouraged the best strategic brains in Vincent Square to start thinking about a new stance towards local government itself. (Since returning from the LGCE in June 1996, Bob Chilton had given a lot of time to this. He and his colleagues in the local government directorate were talking to senior Labour advisers about a new concept that was soon being labelled as 'Best Value'.) At last, in May 1997, New Labour arrived. The Commission members in February 1996 had gladly endorsed 'informal discussions with Labour to explore possible initiatives' – and in the fifteen months since then had been generally supportive of the controller's patient wooing of the Labour front bench. Now, with Frank Dobson installed as the secretary of state for health and Hilary Armstrong appointed as minister for local government and housing in a revamped Department of the Environment, Transport and the Regions (DETR), it was finally time to clarify what those 'possible initiatives' might actually be.

SOME SUBTLE REALIGNMENTS

There were many in local government, and not just Labour council-lors, whose first reaction to the New Labour victory was unmitigated relief. There was much rubbing of hands, in anticipation of a great clearing of the municipal decks: it was surely only a matter of time before the whole paraphernalia of Thatcherite constraints on local government could be heaved over the side. True, Labour's election manifesto had included references to the Audit Commission being given 'additional powers to monitor performance and promote effici-ency'. But this was surely just dutiful rhetoric. What had caught the eye of many was Tony Blair's apparent call for a rolling aside, at last, of all the measures by which central government had steadily undermined the powers of the council chamber since 1979. It was one of the reasons, as Blair had put it in his foreword, why New Labour was new. 'Over-centralization of government and lack of accountability was a problem in governments of both left and right. Labour is committed to the democratic renewal of our country through decentralisation . . .'

As the summer months of 1997 wore on, however, the councils' decks remained uncleared. In fact, it began to seem that they might yet become a lot more cluttered. A series of lively policy debates over the future management of the public services ensued. At one level, expectations were focused on specific repeals. Party conference speeches, by Frank Dobson among others, had long promised a quick disposal of, for instance, the hated regime of compulsory competitive tendering (CCT). Opted-out schools and GP fundholders were other examples of specific Tory innovations targeted for the bin. On a more philosophical plane, though, some also pushed the idea that New Labour might jettison the whole approach to government defined by John Major's performance indicators, league tables and ubiquitous targets.

This audacious thought tapped into a growing concern among some commentators on public life in Britain by the later 1990s that the professional classes charged with delivering its public services were being unduly burdened with a box-ticking, target-ridden climate of supervision that risked being profoundly counter-productive. To have the room to exercise the judgements for which their skills and training equipped them, these professionals needed to work within a trusting environment. If too many formal measures of performance were imposed upon them, might that trust not be fatally undermined? An eloquent paper had appeared three years earlier, addressing this broad theme and questioning some of the fundamental assumptions behind 'the audit explosion'.[10] Written by an academic and professional accountant, Michael Power, it had just been republished late in 1996 by Demos, a think-tank with close ties to New Labour.

The paper undoubtedly struck a chord with many readers, especially in discussing the impact of audit on experienced professionals wholly committed to the delivery of a public service but averse to the quantitative bias of too many external assessments. In Power's view, the audit explosion had been 'driven less by an empirically grounded understanding of the productive benefits of audit and more by a pervasive belief, almost ideological in form, in the need for the discipline which it provides'. Some of the tougher questions in his paper seemed to be directed (though not explicitly so) straight at Vincent Square.

Are auditing mechanisms of control themselves out of control? Is there a price to be paid for a logic of auditability? Are there real benefits to service quality and effectiveness which override the local doubts of threatened practitioners? Or is the language of quality and VFM an elaborate rhetoric for cost reduction in the face of a public sector borrowing crisis?[11]

Asking whether audit and quality assurance were really the 'natural' solutions to some of society's most intractable problems, as many supposed, Power was sceptical: 'just as other fashions have come and gone as the basis for management thinking, the audit explosion is also likely to be a passing phase'.

By 1996–97, the reputation enjoyed by the Commission for its national reports and the high standing of its research in government circles were such that no one in Vincent Square saw much need to respond directly to this challenge. Given the evident impact of the Commission's work on so many fundamental tasks in the public sector

– from police patrols to post-surgical care – it was easy enough to dismiss any view of VFM as merely 'elaborate rhetoric for cost reduction'. Nonetheless, Power's paper was on to something of profound importance. Over the next few years, other commentators would elaborate on his theme. A former Commission member, Tony Travers, was one of the authors of the soon-to-appear book, already noted (see p. 296), that traced the growth over the previous two decades of

more routinization and proceduralization [in local government] with recourse to written rules and hierarchy in place of understandings and conventions . . . When central government found it could not get its way with local authorities by the methods of mutuality (informal conversations, appeals, persuasion and advisory circulars) it resorted to heightened forms of oversight, such as the CCT regime, explicit performance indicators, and even proposals for centrally appointed teams to take over not just particular schools or local authority departments but whole local authorities.[12]

Here was an issue that clearly transcended the world of the Audit Commission, and touched on the management of public services not just in Britain but Western society more generally. Just as trust and a gentleman's word were giving way to increasingly elaborate codes of corporate governance in business and finance, so trust and individual judgement in the public sector were being ever more fenced about with rules and audit-ready performance targets. Indeed, the public sector was consciously drawing on the business world as a model. In a more recent assessment of this phenomenon, in a book about the impact of affluence on Britain and the US since the second world war, the economic historian Avner Offer, Chichele Professor at Oxford, has written about the existence of an 'economy of regard' that governs the non-market exchange of goods and services in contexts (like schools and hospitals) where incentives are critically affected by personal relations. Attempts to measure this 'regard' accurately for policy-making purposes, he has suggested, will always be flawed, given the explicit rejection in this arena of price yardsticks. As a result, 'when making policy, there is an inclination to maximise only what is measurable, thus falling short of real optimality. This failure is a feature of public policy.' And he has no doubt that, as Power was warning in 1995 and as Travers and his colleagues observed in 1999, it is a feature that has become more prevalent in recent times. 'In public services, there has been a strong movement towards simulated market forms of provision.'[13]*

The Audit Commission, intent on aligning itself with Labour's reform agenda in the public services, was clearly in the mainstream of this movement, as it manifested itself in Britain. As we have seen, the Commission itself was hardly the instigator: it had fallen into line with the prevailing mood in government since 1991, as it was almost bound to do. And there were few signs in the post-election summer and autumn of 1997 that those newly entrenched in government were ready just yet to rein back on audit and quality assurance as a 'passing fad'. On the contrary: just as senior Labour figures had been on their guard against suggesting any readiness to indulge the antics of left-wing councils ahead of the 1992 election, so now Labour's newly elected ministers were wary of signalling any laxity over standards of performance in the public sector. This is not to say, however, that they – or indeed the Commission itself – were deaf to the entreaties of those like Michael Power who thought auditing had gone too far. They heard and sympathized with this message. The result was a deep-seated tension: Labour wanted to lighten up, without letting go. This would shortly contribute directly to a terrible confusion over audit policy for the public services, with a fresh approach that was initially intended to simplify matters but that ended up as almost an embodiment of the 'audit explosion'.

But that is jumping ahead. In the policy debates of 1997, the optimal extent of auditing in the public sector was only one of several themes under discussion, and by no means the most prominent. What really

---

* Like Travers et al. and Power, Avner Offer also appears deeply sceptical about the consequences of this trend. 'In neglecting the economy of regard, these policies [adopting market forms of measurement and assessment] may fall well short of their objectives, because (a) quantitative measures are often unable to capture quality, which is more easily monitored in face-to-face interaction with peers and clients, (b) quantitative sanctions replace approbation with fear, and informal monitoring with costly evaluation, and lead to neglect of unmeasured but vital tasks, and (c) there are unmeasured losses of regard, goodwill, and trust. Regard is a good in its own right, quite apart from its instrumental value, especially where personal interaction pervades, as in education and medical care' (*The Challenge of Affluence*, pp. 98–9).

focused people's minds was another (though closely entwined) issue: how would New Labour strike the balance between top-down policies from Westminster and the hope among many local authorities that they might now recover some of their long-lost autonomy?

The answer did not take long to emerge. New Labour was just as determined as Margaret Thatcher to dictate the agenda from the centre, if that was the price of ensuring that party objectives were achieved. She had centralized in the fight against inflation and public sector profligacy. New Labour would, if necessary, centralize in the fight for properly administered public services. Numerous surveys since the early 1990s had convinced Labour ministers that the electorate was deeply unhappy over the state of public services. Blair's government now committed itself, on one platform after another, to radical improvements across the board. As ever, these would have to be delivered at a local level. But they were too important to be left to the vagaries of local deliverers. Some demanding ground rules would need to be set from Whitehall. The department in charge of this would be the new DETR, run by John Prescott, and he in turn delegated much of the responsibility for it to Hilary Armstrong.

It was never in doubt that CCT would disappear – but nor was there any question of simply ditching it, and allowing councils to bring tendered services back in-house. The principle of using local government in a *commissioning* role, rather than as a direct deliverer of public services, appealed to Labour ministers and their advisers as much as to their predecessors. The big difference was that the Tories' CCT had focused heavily on minimizing the cost of each service to the commissioner, where Labour's version would focus on optimizing the quality delivered to the end-user. Instead of sweeping away CCT, in other words, Labour would *replace* it – with an approach that was far more concerned with 'outcomes', but just as indifferent as CCT to the politics of public versus private sector delivery. Armstrong recalled: 'I don't think much of local government had understood that from us. Some did – but not a lot.'[14]

And as ministers debated the best way forward, they found in the Commission a ready and helpful ally. A senior civil servant with responsibility at the time for housing regeneration, Mavis McDonald, recalled:

One of the things that really helped, I think, was that Andrew Foster was very keen to get to grips with more [change] and to enable chief executives in local government to do more. He was very much for taking the Commission alongside wherever the Labour government wanted to go, and took the Commission members with him on this.[15]

The government's most immediate challenge was to find a way of making its new approach to local government truly practicable, without the market pricing that had underpinned CCT. A broad concept known as 'Best Value' had been widely aired even prior to the election, drawing on the thoughts of several New Labour policy advisers (notably including Hilary Armstrong's husband, Paul Corrigan). The intention behind Best Value was that it should replace the rigidities of CCT with a simpler regime relying more on the common sense of local authorities. Each would draw up its own plan on how it was going to ensure that all spending on services was optimized. It would conduct its own review of how the plan was progressing. The authority's auditor would assess both the plan and the review with the authority. Together, they would then agree on selected aspects of the council's operations that could usefully be examined by a new force in the local government field: *inspectors with specialist skills*. One great attraction of this for New Labour ministers was that it might allow Whitehall at last to step beyond interminable rounds of auditing and measuring, and actually *implement* changes. They were impatient to see results. For Hilary Armstrong and her advisers – who briefly included one of Chilton's younger colleagues at the Commission, Robert Hill, before he joined the Policy Unit at No. 10 – Best Value looked a robust enough idea to replace CCT because it would make excellent use of inspectors, not just auditors.

In discussions of Best Value, most people envisaged local authorities being given practical guidance on the formulation of their plans by the Commission and its auditors. At the Commission itself, Bob Chilton had explored this idea in some detail with a newly appointed director of audit support, Paul Vevers. But they both saw it as essentially an extension of performance indicators. Chilton had visited New Zealand in 1996 and had written an Occasional Paper for the Commission on the lessons to be learned from that country on *voluntary* benchmarking and *non-compulsory* competitive tendering. (It was published in 1997 as *Kiwi Experience: VFM Messages from New Zealand.*) In line with much of his thinking since the early 1990s, he now saw Best Value as a catalyst for this kind of self-help: it could usefully push more of the onus for improvement down the line. As he recalled: 'You couldn't drive value into the whole of the local-government system from 100 people sitting in Vincent Square. You could do part of the job by just putting in some pressure, but the rest had to be done out there by the authorities themselves.'[16]

Already by the end of the autumn of 1997, though, Chilton's view had in a sense been stood on its head. Far from promoting a greater autonomy at ground level, Best Value was starting to be seen as a vehicle for greater direction from the centre. The notion of councils selecting just a few key targets for external inspectors had gone by the board. Labour wanted to see rigorous inspections of *all* Best Value reviews. It wanted to see every council having *all* of its services inspected every five years. (Ironically, the notion of a five-yearly review seems to have been suggested by the New Zealand model described by Chilton: local authorities there had to put themselves up for re-election every five years, with a detailed business plan and financial model that voters could compare with an alternative published by the opposition.) And to conduct the inspections, in Hilary Armstrong's view, there was no viable alternative to the Audit Commission: 'It was plain it would have to be them – we didn't consider anybody else.'[17]

As the media saw at once, this was potentially a radical innovation. Peter Riddell, the political commentator of *The Times*, swept aside 'a lot of characteristic New Labour guff' to define the essence of what was being proposed.

While unwilling to give local councils the freedom they had before 1979, ministers recognize that the public needs reassurance about the quality and cost of services. But they do not believe this can be achieved by increasing consumer choice directly, so inspectors are being given greater powers to improve local standards.[18]

As for the Audit Commission's prospective role under 'the energetic Mr Foster', Riddell acknowledged that it had 'built up an impressive record over the past decade not just as a watchdog of financial probity but also as a rigorous, and independent, monitor of the effectiveness of local bodies'. There was just one snag, though. 'The dilemma the Commission now faces is how far is it seen as an agent of Whitehall in implementing "Best Value" and how far can it remain an independent auditor, advising local bodies and people.'

Indeed so, and this was putting it lightly. Even leaving aside the (admittedly important) issue of independence, inspecting and auditing were subtly different jobs. What set them apart was now the subject of some impenetrable memoranda. But the nub of the matter could be simply stated. A regularity audit told a council it *had* (or had *not*) acted correctly in the past. A VFM audit told a council how it *could* do things better in the future, if it chose to do so. But an inspection (like a review) told a council where, if at all, it *should* have done things better in the past and how it *should* do them better in the future. Of course, in practice the distinctions were never as simple as this. There was enough common ground between the three jobs that reasonable people could differ over the practicality of asking one institution to handle all three. Some saw their integration as a natural way forward. But others were less sanguine. It had taken years to reconcile traditional auditors with VFM audits and the Added-Value Units (with mixed results, as critics would still maintain). It was perfectly respectable to argue that putting auditors and inspectors under the same roof would be a recipe for confusion and worse. There were many inside DA who took precisely this line. They included its chief executive, David Prince. He recalled:

I took the view that actually inspection required a different skill set and a different kind of client relationship. Audit work lasted through a whole year and was increasingly concerned, in a systems-based approach, with watching trends over time. Inspection was by definition a matter of taking snapshots. It was plotting points on a graph, whereas auditors had to follow the curve between them.[19]

Prince also had his own strategic reasons for thinking that DA should steer clear of Best Value inspections. He was justly proud of what had been achieved with the field force since 1994. Its audit work was generally now of a high technical standard, and the service had steadily earned a reputation for its attention to client concerns without diluting its public sector ethos. Was it really prudent to risk all this on Best Value – a concept that had not even been deemed worthy of capital letters in Labour's election manifesto? ('The basic framework, not every detail, of local service provision must be for central government. Councils should not be forced to put their services out to tender, but will be required to obtain best value.')[20] It was an idea that seemed to have been spirited into existence almost overnight. Might it not drift away as quickly? What would be the impact on DA's reputation a year hence, if it was seen to have recklessly embraced a political will o' the wisp? Just as bad, what if Best Value should emerge as a reincarnation of CCT? Local authorities by the end of 1997 were distinctly suspicious that all the talk of killing off the statutory CCT only concealed plans to bring it back in some other form. Best Value was still little more than a slogan, but had the potential to become extremely unpopular. In short, Prince was in no rush to make DA its champion, and he told Andrew Foster as much.

At the same time, unknown to DA, the controller was being given the same message by Hilary Armstrong and her officials. Of course auditors would be asked to check that councils had sufficient plans in train each year – to check, in the standard jargon of auditing, that there were 'arrangements in place'. But this process would be a mere prelude to the real action. It was the inspectorate that would take forward Labour's agenda. Foster recalled: 'District Audit to them were the people who would chronicle the tale, but were not part of the solution.'[21] Hilary Armstrong was nonetheless explicit from the start that she wanted the Commission to take up the lead on Best Value. She told the members so, during a visit to Vincent Square just a month after the general election. Nor was it just a question of carrying on where Chilton's team had left off before the election. Armstrong made clear the agency role that she envisaged for the Commission, in a forthright style that would have struck a jarring note in the 1980s: it would have, she suggested, 'an enhanced role in monitoring and targeting those authorities not prepared for the required cultural change'.[22]

How exactly all this was to be done, she would leave to the Commission's members. Indeed, as the months passed, it became evident that virtually every aspect of Best Value was being left to the members and officers of the Commission. In a sense, this was flattering. Hugely respectful of its analytical abilities and confident of its readiness to share New Labour's goals for the public sector, Armstrong and her colleagues essentially turned to the Commission for a governance structure that, arguably, should have been designed from the outset in Whitehall. The result would put a heavy strain on the governance of the Commission itself.

SEEKING A BLUEPRINT FOR THE BEST VALUE INSPECTORATE

The members had no illusions about the delicacy of the task they had been assigned. In the same minutes that recorded Armstrong's visit in June 1997 was a tortuous summary of a discussion that preceded her arrival. 'It was acknowledged that there could be tension in pre-scribing something helpful to local authorities which does not stifle nor interpose the judgment of the Commission with [sic] the judgment of the electorate.' The members, no less than David Prince, were uneasy about the proposed extension to their brief. It unsettled them that the concept now seemed so amorphous. What was to happen to performance indicators? Or indeed to local VFM work by auditors, the fees for which effectively underpinned the Commission's finances? At the same time, it was clear that Best Value would demand of the Commission a far more judgemental stance than hitherto. Perhaps, compared with this risky future, it would not be such a bad thing if the Commission simply declined the brief, as DA had done. But in that case, what would be the Commission's longer-term strategic *raison d'être*?

Obviously the Commission had long since outgrown its narrow audit role. But its more extensive modern remit meant that the change in the political landscape since May 1997 inevitably posed tough questions at a fundamental level. Without clear answers, the Com-mission might end up seriously adrift. The members were quick to see this danger. As individuals, all of them had made a heavy com-mitment of their time to the success of the Commission. They had worked hard, especially in guiding its choice of report subjects and usefully amending almost every national report that came before them prior to publication. Setting a basic course for the Commission's development, though, was a challenge of a different magnitude. Months of anguished discussion followed. No meaningful conclusions were reached – or at least, none that set a fresh course. Eventually, probably at some point early in 1998, the members discovered that one of their number had a talent for picking the right moment and asserting a self-evident (but so far disregarded) truth. Cutting through another interminable wrangle over whether or not to grasp the Best Value nettle, Helena Shovelton startled her colleagues round the board table.

I basically said, 'Look folks, if we don't do Best Value, there won't be an Audit Commission. If we settle for just being an audit shop, we shall lose our NHS franchise. And while we focus on regularity, Best Value will go to the National Audit Office. The next thing is that they will get VFM work. Then they will pick up probity audits as well. And that will be the end of the Audit Commission.' And there was a sort of silence and everybody looked at me. Then everyone started shouting at once.[23]

By the time a Green Paper on the future of local government appeared in April 1998, the Commission was committed to making Best Value work. The members set up a 'Best Value and VFM' panel – the chairmanship of which, appropriately, was handed to Helena Shovelton. As for the controller and his management board, there had never been much doubt in their minds that Best Value would have to be embraced. It was Labour's Big Idea in the local government arena – and it offered a marvellous opportunity further to enhance Vincent Square's influence in Whitehall. Yet progress on designing a governance structure and methodology for Best Value moved forward at a glacial pace. It was all very well for ministers and their officials to hand over responsibility for the shaping of a Best Value regime. But in the absence of any firm indication of what they really wanted, Andrew Foster and his colleagues were perhaps understandably reluctant to move ahead with too much detailed planning. This would run the obvious risk of leading the Commission off in one direction, only to find officials headed in the opposite direction a few months later. Hanging back, though, would carry its own risks – as was soon to become all too apparent.

Papers prepared by Bob Chilton for the members discussed issues like the future of VFM audit work and the role of PIs in a Best Value world. And work went ahead on publications for audited bodies, notably a management paper (*Better by Far*) discussing how performance frameworks could be set up to prepare for Best Value. But this was tinkering at the edges, given the scale of the changes in prospect. Some of the bigger, more structural issues were raised in a *Quinquennial Financial Management and Policy Review* published by the DETR in July 1998. As part of the new government's review of all large quangos (or non-departmental public bodies, to give them their formal title), the *FMPR* asked some alarmingly basic questions. Were the Commission's existing functions worth doing? Should some other body be doing them instead of the Commission? Its answers were all broadly favourable to the status quo. It declined, for instance, to back calls for a privatization of DA. But it pulled no punches when it came to Best Value. 'The task of auditing Best Value will be a demanding one, not least in recruiting the skills required within tight resource constraints', noted the *FMPR*.

We propose a centrally driven study, linked with the Best Value project, of the existing pattern of audit, inspection and regulation with the object of putting in place a framework of working arrangements which among other things builds on the strengths of existing arrangements between the Audit Commission and specialist inspectorates.[24]

There is no evidence that this study ever emerged. The Audit Commission Act of June 1998 formally extended the Commission's statutory powers to embrace its steadily rising workload with third-party inspectorates – in education, the police, the fire brigades, the social services, benefits administration and housing. But no 'framework of working arrangements' appeared. Foster pushed ahead with the development of one or other of the Commission's in-house teams wherever opportunities presented themselves. (In the education sector, for example, he appointed a chief inspector of education, Jane Wreford, who built up a notably successful team to work with Ofsted on the inspection of local education authorities.) But as to how any of these teams would relate to Best Value inspectors, no one seemed to have much idea.

Above all, of course, there was the not insignificant matter of who would actually act as the Commission's inspectors, if not the auditors of DA. By the autumn of 1998, resolving this issue was becoming a matter of some urgency. It was undoubtedly an uncomfortable time for Andrew Foster. In effect, he was being challenged to produce a new business model for the day-to-day operations of the Commission. But his talents lay in the art of incremental adjustment rather than inspired invention. Nor, admittedly, was the backdrop very helpful to him. The Commission's business model since 1983 had been drawn up by John Banham in far more propitious circumstances. Back in those early days, the controller had been handed a statute on the books and a clean slate to design his own model with no interference from ministers. Foster's predicament with New Labour through the course of 1998 was very different.

The legislation for Best Value was still far from clear, even by the end of the year. (It would not be enacted, as the 1999 Local Government Act, until the following summer.) So Foster, instinctively cautious in such matters, continued to hold back. Nor was it easy for anyone else to see the answer – especially given the way that Chilton's ideas had effectively been sidelined by ministers. Arguably, the Commission should have gone back to the government at this point, expounding the case – *pace* David Prince – for harnessing DA properly to the implementation of Best Value and asking for more time to think through all the implications. Some of the senior figures in DA, such as Bill Butler and John Sherring, had indeed argued for a fuller debate over this and still remained very uncomfortable over any inspectorate divorced from DA. But Hilary Armstrong's objections to relying on the auditors had been quite firm. So, long and inconclusive discussions continued within Vincent Square, while DA as an independent agency went about preparing itself for the future regime as best it could. The outcome, it must be said, was deeply unsatisfactory – in at least three ways.

First, practical steps to prepare for a *de novo* Best Value inspectorate were conspicuous by their absence. Second, preparations put in place by the auditors effectively became the proxy for the building of the inspectorate – and since auditors always focus on process, the basic idea of Best Value was soon wide open to excessive bureaucracy. And third, coordination between Vincent Square and Hilary Armstrong's officials fell woefully short of what was needed.

Working groups and strategy sessions littered everyone's diary from the late autumn of 1998. There was never any lack of interest among Commission directors. After handing responsibility for the local government directorate back to Bob Chilton in 1996, Peter Wilkinson had become director of resources; he kept a watching brief over the evolution of Best Value, but the main responsibility for it fell to Paul Vevers, the audit support director. David Prince was also keen to remain involved, even though DA itself had been distanced from the process, and Trish Longdon had a natural concern to track the staffing implications. All of them gathered regularly together for meetings, while Chilton continued to refine his own broad ideas on the future of local government in a Best Value world. But there was no shared vision of how an inspectorate might actually function. The Best Value buck was passed from meeting to meeting but stopped at no one's desk.

By February 1999, Chilton and Vevers were ready to present their ideas to the Commission. (Wilkinson had his hands full with other matters, not least leading the Commission's pest-control measures against the Millennium Bug, so took a back seat on Best Value.) They ranged over issues of methodology, early thoughts on implementation and the prospective costs – but their audience was far from persuaded. 'The presentation raised significant questions on the relationship between auditors and inspectors and the relevant skill sets for the different roles', noted the minutes of the monthly meeting. 'The Commission was assured that as far as possible there will be co-ordination between inspectors, and between inspectors and auditors. Commissioners asked for further consideration to be given to the implications of the inspection regime for the audit regime.'[25]

In Whitehall, meanwhile, Armstrong was growing increasingly impatient. Her officials had by now effectively taken back the initiative on designing Best Value, but were soon immersed in the small print of an increasingly elaborate scheme. She had visited New York City and been hugely impressed by the way in which the city managed its public sector contracts. They had found ways, with their procurement process, of cutting through the city's bureaucracy with just three questions to bidders. She thought Best Value ought to be manageable in the same fashion. Certainly it was intended to be a fundamental break with the past. Now she was dismayed by the way that her own department's guidelines for the enactment of Best Value seemed to be growing more complex by the month. Outsiders, glimpsing early plans, shared her dismay.

It was at this late hour that Andrew Foster acknowledged the need to devote resources to Best Value more effectively. He set up a dedicated team to develop an inspection methodology. Leadership of the team was given to a new associate director, Peter Thomas, who had been appointed to the local government directorate just the previous autumn. With a degree in management sciences and a Masters from the LSE in organizational change, Thomas could see the importance of establishing 'buzz points' – how and where the inspectorate would be called upon to help deliver Best Value. But he had already spent twelve years in local government, mostly working at Westminster City Council. He had still been in local government when Best Value had been announced, and what he had heard over his early months in Vincent Square had confirmed his worst fears. Thomas recalled: 'The fact that Best Value was half-baked in scale and focus was obvious. There was a lot of detail that was utterly un-doable. But underneath it was a broad idea that was generally sensible.'[26] To salvage this idea, he assembled more than a dozen external recruits – including some seconded from local government – and some of the Commission's own most able administrators. They included a senior manager with years of experience going back to her days as an assistant to the controller in the late 1980s, Debbie Kirby. The team began work on a Best Value methodology in April 1999.

By then, Bob Chilton had effectively taken his leave of the Commission. There was not much doubt that he had found the Best Value saga to date a deeply frustrating experience. To his mind, the concept opened up tremendous new possibilities. But it also landed the Commission with a raft of new statutory duties, which needed melding into a business model in the way that had happened back in 1983–84. Without such a 'second-generation' model, in his view, the whole organization was struggling. He was happy to accept a secondment from Vincent Square, taking on the post of transitional chief executive of the Greater London Authority that was due to come into being with London's first mayoral election in March 2000. (He had just thirteen months to prepare for its launch.) In the wake of his departure, Foster asked Paul Vevers, with some assistance from Peter Wilkinson, to take up the lead on devising the inspectorate while he himself pushed ahead with a formal recruitment process to find the right person to run whatever they came up with.

Vevers and Wilkinson did their best to make sense of a difficult brief over the next couple of months. Without a compelling vision of Best Value's scope, though, there could be no concrete plan. The two of them set up a meeting for early June, to agree with DETR officials just how far-ranging the future inspectorate should be. Wilkinson recalled:

We had done an analysis of the costs of three levels of inspection regime. We offered them a choice between a substantial regime, a middle regime and a low-cost regime. I remember that as Paul and I got back into the taxi after the meeting, we were both slightly lost for words. The regime they wanted us to implement was *twice the size* of our big regime and at least three times the size of what we'd felt confident of agreeing![27]

It was startling confirmation of what many in Vincent Square (and beyond) had begun to fear by mid-1999: whatever their best intentions, New Labour ministers were presiding over the creation by officials of a hopelessly over-prescriptive regime that would simply be unworkable. Ministers might privately bemoan their predicament. But they seemed determined to spurn the advice of those urging a radical rethink, as the only alternative to a disastrous outcome.

Wilkinson now found himself very briefly in charge of preparing the Commission against this outcome as best he could. Paul Vevers quit in July for a new career in Australia. Wilkinson was left to hold the fort, pending the imminent arrival of the new head of the inspectorate. For him, the whole situation was slightly a case of déjà vu. He had always regarded the competitive tendering element of CCT as a sensible idea, brought low by an excessively bureaucratic process that was introduced to make it compulsory. Now Best Value seemed to be heading in the same direction. Nonetheless, he sat down with David Prince and others to see what kind of organization they could design, that might provide the back-office support for both DA and a team of inspectors. Always keen on diagrammatic representations of any intellectual landscape – mind-maps, as he called them – Wilkinson had an especially large one on a whiteboard in his office within weeks, setting out the Best Value terrain. He recalled:

Everyone who came to talk to me that summer ended up having a discussion with me about that mind-map. It was extremely complicated, but we eventually identified just two issues that dominated everything else: first, the relationship between the auditor and the inspector; and second, all the management arrangements stuff that we later came to call corporate assessment.[28]

Meanwhile, outsiders to the whole process looked on with fingers crossed that Best Value might yet deliver on its potential. The LSE academics whose 1999 book took a rather scathing retrospective view of regulation in the 1980s and 1990s, quoted earlier, were prepared to hope for the best. 'It remains to be seen whether or how Best Value develops, but from a regulatory perspective the initiative could be seen as a reaction against the discredited command and control approach of CCT by instituting what is ostensibly a more "reflexive" regime.'[29]

A NEW CHAIRMAN, WITH SHORTER REINS

Through all the tergiversations over the future of the Best Value concept, it was obvious that the controller lacked the kind of counterpoint relationship with his chairman that, say, Davies had enjoyed with Cooksey. Everyone was conscious of the need for a change at the top. Brooke himself never had any expectation of being reappointed by a Labour government. His private financial activities, and particularly the success of his Innisfree PFI business, made it all but impossible for him to continue in the role. 'If I'd been asked to continue – which I wasn't, because I wasn't part of the New Labour project – I wouldn't have accepted anyway because it was getting too difficult.'[30] He announced he would be stepping down, a few months before doing so in November 1998.

For the search process, DETR officials turned to the head-hunting arm of the accountants PricewaterhouseCoopers. Their short-list quickly picked up the name of the Commission member with a penchant for speaking her mind – Helena Shovelton. By this time, she had been a successful chairman of the National Association of Citizens' Advice Bureaux (NACAB) for well over four years. She had also assembled an impressive portfolio of other positions, including seats on the National Lottery Commission and the Competition Commission. She had risen to prominence on the Audit Commission as it had become clear that she was someone who could speak knowledgeably on behalf of the users of public services. In the discussions over *Misspent Youth*, for example, she had won the respect of all her colleagues. Most importantly, though, she had impressed them with her ability to think strategically and to see the big picture beyond all the minutiae of each monthly meeting. One colleague, Adrienne Fresko, recalled: 'She was becoming very influential. She spent incredible amounts of time on Commission business.'[31]

The head-hunters called her and asked her out of the blue if she might be interested in being considered for the chairman's job. Shovelton was genuinely surprised. She took her time over the next couple of days to think hard about the key issues that the Commission was facing. Of them all, she rated a successful implementation of Best Value and the retention of the NHS mandate as the two most critical. Both seemed to her worthwhile challenges, which she believed she could handle. Her name went forward.

As chair of the NACAB, Shovelton was already leading an organization with almost exactly twice as many people working for it as the Audit Commission. Its democratic structure also meant that she was in close contact with the 1,000 bureaux and 3,000 people throughout the year while running a central office similar in size to Vincent Square. None of this deterred her Whitehall interviewers from cautioning her that the Audit Commission was a big job. But it did give her the confidence to lay out for them her own thoughts about how poorly, in her view, the Commission actually managed some of its own affairs. This she did in a forthright manner that must have dispelled any lingering illusions that the officials were dealing with a woolly-minded consumers' champion. They sent her through anyway to the final interview, which was with the Commission's two sponsoring ministers, Hilary Armstrong and Frank Dobson.

Dobson had just returned from a fact-finding trip to the Caribbean. It so happened that Shovelton's husband, Patrick, had some years previously served as director-general of the Chamber of Shipping, in which role he had been required to spend three weeks in the Caribbean visiting every banana-packing plant and every Geest Line ship in the islands. His wife had accompanied him. Bizarrely, the interview headed off into a long conversation between Shovelton and Dobson about bananas, and the Caribbean's banana economy, while Hilary Armstrong sat by with a slightly glazed look in her eye. There was little time for much else, and the interview closed with Dobson gently inquiring how Shovelton thought he might be able to lift his personal standing among the doctors.[32]

It took several more weeks for Downing Street and the Local Government Association to approve Shovelton's appointment, and the monthly meeting in January 1999 was the first that she attended as chairman of the Commission. That, by chance, was the month in which Andrew Foster's second three-year term expired. There is no record of it in the minutes, but whether or not to reappoint him was certainly discussed at some length by the Commission members. A case could be made, and was, for making a fresh start under a new controller. It was clear, however, that several months might be required to find the right person. Amid the uncertainties surrounding the genesis of Best Value, and given all the other changes to which the Commission was already exposed, it hardly seemed the moment for such an important decision. Shovelton led the way in concluding that the Commission's interests would be better served, on balance, by reappointing Andrew Foster. One of her first steps as chairman was to set the wheels turning on a confirmation of this. An extension of his contract until February 2002 was finally approved at the March monthly meeting.

The two of them developed an effective working relationship, though it was not without its strains. Given Foster's freedom to run things much as he chose under the previous chairmanship – and Shovelton's temperamental aversion to anything *too* part-time – it could hardly have been otherwise. Indeed, colleagues were soon joking that each of them actually coveted the other's job. Certainly it was true that Shovelton took a steadily greater interest in operational details that went far beyond Roger Brooke's involvement and rather beyond the normal remit of a non-executive chairman, too. (Appropriately, she was also the first in the post to make regular use of the chairman's office, a modest room on the first floor of Vincent Square.) Shovelton herself, however, took a less sanguine view of any incursions that she felt obliged to make into the day-to-day running of the Commission. She made them reluctantly – and out of a gradually mounting concern, shared with her colleagues on the Chairman's Advisory Panel, that too many management issues were actually being slightly neglected. An example of this surfaced at the very outset of her chairmanship.

Almost as an aside during her interview for the job, Frank Dobson had remarked that he was giving some thought to the idea of taking its NHS mandate away from the Commission. Shovelton wasted no time in January 1999 before delving a little deeper than her fellow members into what was now afoot in the health sector. She was well aware, from all her time on the Commission, that a series of generally much applauded reports had emerged from the health directorate over the years. Why had this not been more generously acknowledged in Whitehall? In particular, it seemed puzzling that relations between the Commission and the Department of Health seemed almost as poor in 1999 as they had ever been. A few years earlier, when she had participated as an independent chairman in the independent reviews of District Health Authorities, she had had a chance to meet the two senior men in the health service – Alan Langlands, the NHS chief executive, and Graham Hart, the DoH permanent secretary, who had since retired from the department. (The two of them had together been responsible for picking Shovelton's name off a list and involving her in the DHA review programme in the first place.) She resolved to pay Alan Langlands a private visit.

Nothing was said publicly about their discussions, but Shovelton came away satisfied that she had made her point: the two institutions simply had to communicate better with each other in the interests of the NHS. She recalled: 'I never told anyone I was going to do it. I just went off and did it, because it was blindingly obvious that it needed doing.'[33] Her initiative was appreciated and led to a palpable improvement in relations. (Indeed, she was instrumental in bringing Graham Hart on to the Commission, which he joined eleven months later. Around this time Shovelton also prevailed upon Hart to take over the chairmanship of the NACAB, which she was about to give up later in 1999.) It was also timely. Shovelton's gesture towards the DoH – and the active interest she took in the work of Vincent Square's health team – roughly coincided with two significant developments on the health front.

TOWARDS A NEW APPROACH IN THE HEALTH SECTOR

The first was the adoption by the Labour government of a novel interest in the idea of clinical governance. It was clear well before January 1999 that ministers intended to give the lead here to a new body that would be set up under the aegis of the Department of Health. The issue for the Audit Commission's staff was how best to support this initiative substantively – in the interests of building a strong link for the future – without alienating the DoH by seeming to be too pushy with their advice. Clinical governance meant new, systematic ways of assessing the quality (and reducing the risks) of healthcare delivery, as opposed to the administrative governance of the NHS as a huge business. Labour had flagged its intentions in a White Paper at the end of 1997. A new organization would be established, to be called the Commission for Health Improvement (CHI). A new chief medical officer (CMO), Liam Donaldson, was appointed in 1998. Under his energetic lead, the proposed role for CHI was clarified in a 1998 Green Paper called *A First Class Service*. It would begin operations in June 1999.

Hospital doctors collectively would henceforth be held accountable to NHS trust boards for the quality of their work. This was a radical reform. It had never been attempted before, not least because the medical profession had always had proper legal grounds for telling any government with such ambitions to mind its own business. Doctors had historically provided their own insurance cover against litigation for mishaps or malpractice. It had been *their* risk, and they regarded the quality of care as *their* professional preserve accordingly. But this had all been changed by John Major's government, with the introduction of Crown indemnity for doctors' work in the NHS. They no longer had to insure themselves against litigation: the government would pick up any financial consequences of their liability for a clinical lapse, just as it had always done for the hospitals themselves. Doctors welcomed the change to their legal environment. But they no longer had any grounds for rejecting Whitehall's interest in the standards of their clinical services. As CMO, Donaldson was a keen advocate of improved systems in the health service that could reduce the risks of clinical failure and ensure that doctors had the best possible access to continuously improving medical practices. The fact that the boards of NHS trusts now had legal responsibility for the quality of care was just another reason to embrace the same objective.

Unlike Best Value in the environment department, clinical governance was not seen in the health department as a natural extension to the Audit Commission's franchise. It is not entirely clear whether Andrew Foster made a bid for it in 1997. If he did, and was – for once – unsuccessful, he may anyway have sent a useful reminder to the DoH of the Commission's skills. By October 1998, there were different views within Vincent Square on how best to deal with the emergence of CHI. Foster and a majority of the management board, anxious to consolidate the Commission's role, were in favour of seeking a public profile for the Commission as soon as possible – for example, by publishing national guides, rather as the local government directorate was doing for Best Value.

Boyce and his colleagues on the health team were more cautious. They were chary of crossing DoH officials yet again. They thought it better on balance to look for ways of quietly preparing for a future partnership with CHI. It was unlikely in their view that the Commission would be sidelined, given some explicit backing from the government for a CHI-Commission partnership – and private reassurances from the Treasury, too, that it wanted to see the Commission actively involved. (Geoffrey Rendle, one of Boyce's senior managers, kept a private diary through these months. He and Boyce visited the Treasury more than once to keep its officials updated on their talks with the DoH. Rendle noted that their Treasury contacts were 'clearly real allies for us'. The Treasury appeared to have its doubts over how effectively the NHS Executive on its own might be able to implement any CHI initiatives.)[34]

Whichever way the Commission played its hand, though, developing its links with CHI was going to be another case of learning how to handle partnerships effectively in Whitehall. These were fast becoming a crucial aspect of the Commission's operations, as was acknowledged in a paper written around this time by Debbie Kirby, just for internal circulation, setting out some of the lessons to date. Since 1996, the Social Services Joint Review programme had taken off successfully and relations with the Housing Corporation had been developing productively (if a little tetchily, from time to time). And the new education associate director, Jane Wreford, was at this same moment working on her joint LEA inspection plans with Ofsted, which had to be finalized by January 1999. When account was taken of the parallel plans for Best Value, it was plain that the Commission was fast becoming an integral part (whether temporarily or otherwise) of a more dirigiste direction of the public services.

It was a conscious growth strategy on Andrew Foster's part, and he managed it very adroitly. There was always a danger with partnerships, however, that key personnel from Vincent Square might disappear off to work for the partners. It looked likely to happen soon with Kate Flannery, who was spending ever more of her time with the police inspectorate in Queen Anne's Gate. Now, in mid-November, Jonty Boyce told the controller that he intended to apply for the job as chief executive of CHI. This forced a reshuffle of responsibilities on the health team. All of the dealings with the DoH over CHI were delegated to one of the team's associate directors, Jocelyn Cornwell, who would report directly to the controller. Her preferred tactic, like his, was to ensure that Vincent Square was seen to be exploring future opportunities for CHI well in advance of its arrival. (How far CHI would end up as a de facto inspectorate of clinical practices, for example, was still a moot point.) There was an understandable nervousness about this among DoH officials – hence one reason for the timeliness of Helena Shovelton's initiative in January 1999.

Shovelton's intervention seemed at least to help both sides trust each other a little more over the next few months. Indeed, Jocelyn Cornwell was herself seconded to Richmond House some weeks later to assist with the final arrangements for CHI's launch. These went smoothly enough. The position of chief executive was advertised in March. It did not go to Boyce – though the CHI's chairmanship, as it happened, went to one of the Commission members who was a doctor and a former chief medical officer at the Welsh Office, Deirdre Hine. And Boyce was invited to join a group of top advisers to CHI. (One of the other shortlisted candidates for the CHI chairmanship was a second Commission member, Adrienne Fresko. She and Jonty Boyce confided their plans to each other at an early stage and shared a few wry thoughts together when the top appointments were announced. Both would have been keen to nurture a fully collaborative relationship between CHI and the Audit Commission, which was not in the event how things worked out.)[35]

There was a second reason why Shovelton's interest in health was timely, however, and this concerned the personal position of Jonty Boyce. The complications surrounding his declared interest in the CHI job only compounded what had been a difficult relationship between him and the controller for some years. The strain had told heavily on Boyce, and by early 1999 his confidence was at a low ebb. No one, though, doubted his ability and the significance of the contribution he could still make to the influence that Vincent Square had in the wider world. Shovelton made it her business to encourage him and consult regularly with him on the progress of new studies, and their reception among DoH officials. She wanted to see him leading the way again: 'When Jonty was not firing on all cylinders, our health work suffered at the Audit Commission.'[36]

Her confidence in Boyce was soon repaid. Over the next year, he came up with a piece of original thinking that would eventually change the Commission's whole approach to its health mandate. In a sense, he devised the kind of new business model for health that was proving so elusive in the local government arena. Around the start of 1999, part of the health team had stepped back from its day-to-day work to take stock of the directorate's accomplishments to date – and to try to fathom out why local audit work seemed to have made only a modest impact. The verdict was not entirely reassuring. The calibre of the team's research was not in doubt, nor could anyone reasonably dispute that many of the national reports since 1990 had pointed the way to significant improvements in the NHS. Excellent work was still being done. Just months earlier, for example, a seminal report had appeared on value-for-money in the emergency ambulance services (*A Life in the Fast Lane*). As ever, though, a question mark hovered over the steadily lengthening list of 'improvements': they had been signposted, but had they really been achieved? In a few cases, like day surgery, the answer was unequivocally yes. Too often, the outcome was much more ambivalent.

Boyce decided to conduct some research into the local implementation of audits. Two were chosen. For each, auditors were asked to document those instances where their local recommendations had been acted on by the NHS and those where they had effectively sunk without trace. Then the good and the bad were scrutinized in some detail. It all came down, perhaps unsurprisingly, to a matter of trust. Where it existed, auditors could generate a positive spiral of cooperation with their local health body. Where trust was absent, a negative spiral set in: poor data were handed over, local audit reports were therefore likely to be flaky and the ensuing disappointment ensured even less cooperation on the next occasion. But what determined the level of trust? The feedback from the auditors was now beefed up with a survey of NHS senior executives. Pooling all of the findings, three real bugbears emerged. Where they were found in any combination, auditors might be lucky to retain any trust at all.

First, it was deeply resented that each year's 'flavours' were pursued universally without regard to local needs. In some places they might be exactly what the doctor ordered, to coin a phrase. But in others they were regarded as simply a waste of money and everyone's time. Second, if the research pushed too far into professional territory, it ran the risk that auditors in the field would be insufficiently knowledgeable to add real value. There was no concealing the fact that, despite the bespoke audit training courses for each flavour, many auditors were simply mugging up the background as best they could, or lacked the time to cope properly with their workload. And third was the problem of too little continuity from one year to the next. Individual flavours were here today, gone tomorrow. Much of the value in a good audit would derive from the follow-up – but too few auditors had the time for this, because each new year brought them a new agenda.

Boyce recalled:

So we sat and looked at all these findings and asked ourselves, 'what can we do about it?' In theory, we could have switched to offering audited bodies a whole range of topic options and just inviting them to choose which would be of most value. But that would have been to abdicate the audit responsibility. We could never have been sure that we were not being deflected from areas of poor performance on spurious grounds. So we realized what we needed was a system that would allow us to look across a wide range of areas in a cursory fashion. Then, if we found prima facie evidence that further audit work was needed, we could go back and pursue it – using the appropriate specialists.[37]

In effect, a preliminary screening system was needed. But how could this be achieved? The answer, Boyce realized, lay in the sheer range and depth of the national reports that had been prepared over the previous decade. Most of the people behind them were still working for the Commission. It ought to be possible to go back to, say, those responsible for pathology and ask them to identify the critical indicators of quality and performance in pathology work. These would need to be verified again in the field. Once confirmed, the appropriate data-collection forms could then be circulated to all health trusts. They would submit the data from their own records, allowing a central register of national data on pathology indicators to be amassed and analysed. Fresh data would thereafter be submitted by all trusts every year, enabling the Commission and its auditors to discern those trusts where further audit work on pathology was warranted. Over the course of a few years, the same approach would need to be taken across a range of activities. Once completed, though, the aggregate register could be updated each year without imposing much of a burden on health trusts. And the information provided by each year's new data would allow the Commission to screen all of their activities and select the appropriate areas for further investigation.

Boyce christened it the 'Acute Hospital Portfolio'. It was decided to build it around sixteen principal topics and to try to build up to the full portfolio in consecutive tranches of four over four years. The project was duly launched towards the end of 1999, with the collection of data for an initial four topics for publication in 2000–2001. (The first tranche was published in February 2001, providing data on day surgery, A&E, catering and ward nursing.) The following year would see an additional four topics tackled, and so on. From 2003–04 onwards, all sixteen topics would be covered. The beauty of the idea was that it took advantage of so much that had happened in recent years. Computerization was finally instilling sufficient discipline into data collection that no NHS trust could be excused for not having the required information available. The arrival of the internet and e-mails had made the assembly of the data much easier. And ever more elaborate software could allow the central register of data to be interrogated in increasingly sophisticated ways. Above all, though, the Acute Hospital Portfolio distilled the outcome of a decade of painstaking studies by Commission health teams. 'It was based on everything we had learned over all those years. We could never have identified all of the necessary key indicators without the accumulated expertise that we had inside the Commission.'[38]

Once the work on the Portfolio was begun in earnest, there was little capacity left within the health directorate for any other work programmes. The immersion in such an innovative and exciting project was more than welcome by the autumn of 1999, though. It followed a period of upheaval within Vincent Square that put almost everyone in the building under immense strain.

NEW APPOINTMENTS IN VINCENT SQUARE

It began with a survey that had been conducted among all the staff in September 1998, asking a long list of questions about attitudes to their workplace. The survey results came as a shock to the controller and his colleagues, who were startled to discover that many people within the building felt cut off from senior management. Morale was poor and communications within the centre had evidently not kept pace with the rapid growth in the Commission's size and range of activities. This unwelcome news landed at a sensitive moment. The senior management team was none too sure of the way ahead, in the new world of Best Value. It was nervous over the eventual implications of CHI's arrival in the health sector. And it still had no idea at this point who would be succeeding Roger Brooke in the chair. (At this stage, Shovelton's appointment and the reappointment of Foster still lay just around the corner.)

Anticipating any external criticism of the Commission, and moving shrewdly to pre-empt it, was always a hallmark of Andrew Foster's leadership style. Without waiting for the announcement of the new chairman, he characteristically led the way now on a series of initiatives to re-energize the Commission. As ever, changes aimed at longer-term goals brought more disruption in the short term. Both structure and strategy, he decided, needed a full reappraisal. To look into the senior management structure, Foster temporarily reassigned an associate director in the health team, Joanne Shaw, as 'director of performance development'. He asked her to begin by re-examining the basic methodology of the studies directorates. While this project went ahead, the controller injected a new urgency into existing plans to refresh the Commission's future strategy. The whole of the management board was involved in preparing a three-year strategy paper that went to Commission members just three months later. It was titled *Changing Picture, Sharper Focus*, and was broadly aimed at helping local government to make itself more responsive to the needs of those who used public services.

One of those involved in the discussions on the paper was a newly appointed purchasing director. This was Martin Evans, who arrived in October 1998. As technical director at CIPFA, Evans had done much in the earlier 1990s to make Harry Wilkinson's accounting reforms palatable to councillors and their finance officials. He had strong views about the standards of governance to be found in local government. They needed to be improved significantly, he believed, if they were to match the higher standards seen in the corporate sector in the wake of the Cadbury reforms. This accorded with a consensus that had actually been building for some time among the Commission members themselves: they endorsed a job spec stressing regularity issues and looked to Evans's appointment as a way of adjusting the Commission's priorities in that direction.[39] The regularity work of its auditors would need to be given more attention.

Evans thought this work had been neglected for years. Working on the three-year strategy paper and its follow-up gave him the perfect opportunity to remedy this. He had been a little surprised when David Prince had opted to keep DA out of the inspectorate arena, though at the time he judged it a brave decision. (He was now coming round to a different view.) Right or wrong, though, it averted the risk of too many distractions for Evans. He could turn his mind to defining a new model for public audit. He decided that it should entail scrutiny from three angles – looking at an authority's accounts, its governance and its performance. The details would have to be enshrined within a revised Code of Audit Practice, for submission in the spring of 2000. But the general thrust of the whole process was set out in the January paper. (The first draft of the new code took several months to complete.) One other aspect of the new strategy was that Evans himself would become the first 'director of audit policy and appointments'. In other words, Evans would effectively reclaim Harry Wilkinson's old job, that had been scrapped back in 1994.

His was the first of many new appointments in 1999. Two other very important positions were advertised in February. The first was for a director of Best Value inspection (requiring, the members agreed, 'a person of the highest ability').[40] Who would be the answer to everyone's prayers in this role was still anyone's guess, though it was intended that he or she be found before Paul Vevers' departure for Australia at the end of June. The second post, motivated directly by the disappointment over the previous September's survey, was for a 'director of people development'. It was widely (and correctly) assumed that this job would go to Trish Longdon, who had filled the same sort of role for Prince in DA, to much acclaim. Foster had urgent need of her help. Predictably, the mood among senior managers was hardly improved by the work of Joanne Shaw, with all the uncertainties that trailed in its wake. The consequence was acknowledged by the controller himself in the April monthly meeting, when he 'drew commissioners' attention to levels of stress within the organization related to both the uncertainty of the change period and the additional work being absorbed at all levels of the organization'.[41]

Shaw presented some of her main findings at that same meeting.

She had concluded that 'the strength of sectoral expertise was impressive and professionals from many areas hold individuals from the studies directorates in very high esteem'. But individual studies were increasingly going to draw on expertise from both directorates (as had recently been exemplified in a study of housing's role in community care, called *Home Alone*). Shaw pointed to various putative benefits of 'a more homogenous analysis function'. In short, she recommended that the two studies directorates set up in 1989 be merged into one. The controller concurred with this – unsurprisingly, to most of his colleagues, since it was plainly a move he had been contemplating for a long time. But it was deeply unpopular with many of those affected, not least because it was decided that the new department would have to be led by an externally appointed director. Bob Chilton had just departed to start work on the GLA – but Jonty Boyce had to be relegated, in effect, at a time when his leadership of the health work was of some consequence. It was an awkward time.

Foster christened the new department Public Services Research. It was invariably known as PSR from the first, and implementation of the new structure was scheduled for September 1999. To run it, the controller ideally wanted someone with a strategy background and a mix on their CV of top jobs in both the NHS and local government. He was fortunate indeed that the head-hunters came up with someone matching the requirements exactly. Terry Hanafin had been working for six years as the chief executive of Croydon Health Authority (which coincidentally had been chaired since 1992 by the Commission member Adrienne Fresko). Earlier in his career, though, he had worked extensively in local government, ending up as chief executive of Lewisham Council for five years up to 1993. Between Lewisham and Croydon, as it were, he had been a Fellow in Strategic Management at the King's Fund. And his original pedigree was that old stand-by for the Commission, Oxbridge followed by a job in Operational Research with the National Coal Board in the 1970s. He signed up to begin in Vincent Square on 27 September.

This was far from the last new appointment of the summer. A series of advertisements for new associate directors and senior managers appeared over these months. And there were several politically charged topics through which the Commission had to steer a careful course. These included CHI's emergence in the health sector, the creation of the Greater London Authority – and the opening of diplomatic relations with the nascent Welsh National Assembly in Cardiff. Prior to devolution, the Commission had effectively left its presence in the principality in the hands of DA. Wales had its own regional director, Bob Hutchings, who was based in Cardiff and had been steeped for years in all of DA's activities there. But Andrew Foster had realized the need, as devolution became a reality, to build up a presence for the Commission itself. This led to the establishment of the Audit Commission in Wales (ACiW), under Peter Wilkinson's charge. A senior manager from London, Doug Elliott, was posted to ACiW and shared an office with the regional director in Cardiff. It was a delicate situation but it worked out well: Hutchings lent his full support to Elliott in building the Commission's presence with officers of the National Assembly, while Wilkinson made a series of visits to explain the Commission's remit to the local politicians and negotiate a way forward on issues like the wider adoption of the Welsh language.

Housing was another area that kept the appointments panel busy. The chancellor of the exchequer had announced a year earlier, in July 1998, that he wanted to see an inspectorate set up over council housing. It had seemed possible for a short while that the Housing Corporation might be asked to set it up. By the autumn of 1998, John Prescott – who always kept a sharp eye on housing – had made it quite clear that it would be yet another mandate for the Audit Commission. While the housing inspectorate would come under the Commission's roof, though, Prescott was nonetheless adamant that it would have to remain a separate entity. Over the first couple of months of 1999, plans had been drawn up accordingly, with great care being taken to involve local authorities and the professional trade bodies in an 'inclusive approach', as it was described to the Commission members in February. As one of his last significant tasks before heading off to the GLA, Chilton used his deep knowledge of the sector to help design the inspectorate – no doubt with an eye to the possibility that it might one day be able to extend its role in the direction of the housing associations still presided over by the Housing Corporation. (The Commission's monthly meeting minutes for April 1999 were suitably coy about this ambition. 'Officers advised that they were aware of the possible expansion of the regime to other public housing not currently held by local authorities.') Vincent Square staff launched a series of conference speeches, press articles and media briefings to lift the Commission's profile in the housing world generally, while the search went ahead for a director to set up the new in-house inspectorate.

Meanwhile, the legislation for the Best Value project was working its way through to enactment in July as the 1999 Local Government Act. It finally scrapped CCT, with effect from January 2000. And it made unambiguously clear the Commission's responsibility for Best Value's implementation. Weeks earlier at a Best Value panel discussion with the government, as if to parody the process, it had been agreed that Local Authority Performance Indicators (LAPIs) would henceforth be re-labelled as Audit Commission Performance Indicators (ACPIs).

Peter Thomas's methodology group had meanwhile made some substantive progress over three months. Indeed, it had come up with rather a sensible idea: councils could be awarded stars to denote the calibre of their services. A consultation paper seeking local authorities' reactions to it had elicited positive and negative reactions in about equal measure. But it had an instant appeal that any journalist could see. Word of it reached an old hand on the *Financial Times*, Alan Pike. Reporting the publication (in July) of the Annual Report for the year ending October 1998, the *FT* noted recent efforts by the Commission under its new chairman to make all of its findings more user-friendly:

The Commission has, for several years, published annual performance indicators showing how councils compare across a range of activities. It has not proved easy to generate widespread public interest in a mass of competing figures, and the Commission has made a suggestion for Best Value that should certainly guarantee local impact – a hotel-style, five-star scoring system providing an overall summary of a council's performance.[42]

Good ideas were one thing, however; practical logistics were quite another. The Act required the Best Value regime to be launched on 1 April 2000. Where were all the people who were going to carry out the inspections? In his monthly report for June 1999, the controller offered the Commission members an update – but it can hardly have been much comfort. 'We have been considering the longer-term project plan . . . Current thinking is that the first step should be to build a body of experience in-house, alongside letting contracts for parcels of inspection to the private sector.'[43] Fine in principle, perhaps – but how far had the body-building got? Here the statistics looked a little alarming. The controller's report noted that 1,800 'expressions of interest' had been received for inspectors' jobs; but only 400 applications had arrived to date; the head-hunters had interviewed 70 people to the Commission's specifications; of whom 16 had been shortlisted, and just 4 had been offered positions.

The news by early September was not much different. The controller noted the passing of the 1999 Act. 'This means that the Audit Commission can now push ahead with many of the practical aspects of establishing Best Value which were contingent on the legislation formally being in place.'[44] Perhaps there was some nervousness about repeating the experience of 1990, when the Commission had followed up the passing of the NHS Act in June by publishing its first major report (on day surgery) in October – only to be reprimanded by the NAO for spending money prematurely on the new franchise (see p. 298). More likely, there had simply been too many pressures on senior management's time – and, in the wake of losing both Chilton and Vevers, too few senior resources at Foster's disposal. By September, only six modest field trials had been completed – five of them dealing with trading standards and one with libraries. Yet it had been estimated that the Best Value regime due for inauguration in eight months' time would cost the Commission around £55 million. This equated to a 50 per cent increase in the Commission's revenues, if the books were to stay balanced. And these figures took no account of the possibility that the Commission might yet be asked to extend Best Value into the police and the fire service. A paper presented to the members by Kate Flannery in July set out the options in these areas. Her recommendation was that the Commission restrict itself for the moment to examining the 'arrangements in place' rather than tangling with plans and reviews. She suggested, though, that a 'high profile national study . . . will keep the Commission's "place at the table" and could provide a platform for subsequent involvement in inspection'.[45]

The cost of Best Value inspection was of course an issue in itself. Over the summer, the DETR had announced that it would pay fees of up to £20 million directly to the Commission. The remaining £35 million of the prospective total costs would have to be met by local authorities, with appropriate increases in the revenue support grant wherever these were required. An initial sum of £1.89 million was paid to the Commission by the DETR in its 1998–99 financial year, to help meet some of the costs of setting up the Best Value and housing inspectorates. This was the first time since its launch in 1983 that the Commission had received a direct grant from the government. Department officials seemed content that the integrity of the system would be safe with the Commission. How far, if at all, the funding arrangements might one day pose a threat to the statutory independence of the Commission was not a question that prompted much debate outside Whitehall, either. The spring and summer of 1999 saw a plethora of seminars, conferences and forums on Best Value. The Commission's independence rarely featured on the agenda. Perhaps local government was too busy trying to define Best Value to spare much time worrying over how it would be governed.

Not everyone ignored the issue. Helena Shovelton, in the chair since January 1999, had her own thoughts on it. Governance was something she reckoned to know a bit about. She would like to have seen an independent board established for Best Value inspection, with its own chairman. Ideally, this would have been twinned with a similar arrangement for DA – or, indeed, perhaps even involving a separation of DA from the Commission, as a self-standing audit force, which is certainly a possibility that David Prince and his senior colleagues were ready to explore with Vincent Square around this time. Prince recalled: 'It was something that the senior staff and I contemplated towards the end of my time there, and did start to talk to Andrew and people in the Commission about, either as a management buy-out or a hive-off.'[46] While this option made no real headway, the broader governance issue was discussed at the Commission's away-day meeting in May and there was much support for Shovelton's twin-boards idea. It was still formally on the table in July, when a paper entitled *Governance Arrangements* was reviewed by Commission members at their monthly meeting. Referring back to the May discussion, it noted: 'The

Commission broadly accepted the idea of setting up a DA Board with the intention to set up an Inspection Agency Board at the appropriate time.'[47] How officials at the DETR might respond to this proposal was a moot point – but in the event it never needed to be raised. Andrew Foster finally threw himself so energetically into the now desperately urgent task of finding an inspectorate director that there was too little time for any alternative arrangement to emerge.

One of the applicants for the job was David Prince. He was attracted by the challenge of setting up a complex administrative scheme. But he himself was the first to acknowledge that the position really needed somebody from outside DA or Vincent Square.

It was obvious that if the inspectorate was going to work, given that it was going to be operating in some quite hostile territory, it required somebody with current campaign medals – somebody fresh and battle-hardened from the front line. Wendy Thomson was ideal in that respect.[48]

Wendy Thomson had been chief executive of the borough of Newham in London's East End since 1996. Formed from a merger between West Ham and East Ham in 1965, it was a tough place with a highly diverse ethnic mix: it had a higher non-white population, as a percentage of the whole, than any other authority in the country. Through all the years of CCT, its Labour-controlled council had contracted out scarcely a single service. Since 1997, though, Thomson had succeeded in having Newham chosen by Hilary Armstrong as one of a dozen or so authorities that would pilot Best Value schemes. The quality of public services in the borough had soared. Thomson was certainly being mentioned in despatches by 1999. With a glowing reputation within London local government and a powerful network of admirers within Labour circles (not least among them, Hilary Armstrong), Thomson would be a superb catch for the Commission. There were other highly qualified candidates to consider. Indeed, it was rumoured that another prominent chief executive from local government was very close to being offered the job before Thomson's candidacy surfaced. The head of the Joint Reviews staff, the much respected Andrew Webster, was also known to have applied for it. Once alerted to the possibility that Thomson might be willing to take it on, though, Foster was determined to get her.

The chairman and Jeremy Orme joined him on the formal selection panel – and Foster, in recommending Thomson as first choice, made no secret of the fact that she was the government's preferred appointee. Armstrong and her husband, Paul Corrigan, were pushing her hard. Partly because of this, perhaps, Shovelton and Orme only accepted their controller's recommendation with some misgivings – and it was agreed by the panel that the chairman should have a further discussion with Thomson before they reported back on their decision to the Commission members.[49] Meanwhile, Thomson herself – while a keen interviewee – seems to have had her own private reservations. In particular, she was uncertain how she would get along with Andrew Foster and whether she would really have the freedom to do what she thought was needed to implement Best Value. So she happily accepted Helena Shovelton's invitation to a private meeting. The two women sat down for a morning breakfast together at a hotel in Islington, a Jurys Inn on Pentonville Road. Thomson arrived an hour late, but their discussion together was nonetheless amicable and productive.[50] The chairman reported back to her colleagues accordingly, and Thomson decided a few days later to take the plunge. Her appointment was announced in June.

She took up her full-time post as director of inspection three months later, arriving at the Commission on the same morning as Terry Hanafin. And on that first day, 27 September, she was required to chair a conference on the future of Best Value. A diminutive lady with short-cropped hair and a clipped Canadian accent, Thomson took instant charge of the event. It was attended by everyone in the Commission who had any involvement with Best Value at all, plus a number of influential outsiders. The morning was filled with slightly gloomy prognostications of the challenge ahead. Then, in the afternoon, Thomson laid out how she intended to deliver Best Value inspection by the spring of 2000. It was like Joan of Arc presenting her vision of victory to the ranks of dispirited French knights. And, like the Maid of Orleans, Wendy Thomson intended to pursue her vision at a pace that would instantly disarm the sceptics.

COURT ACTION OVER THE
WESTMINSTER AUDIT

There was much about 1999 for the Commission that smacked of a pause to regroup for the future. It was impossible yet to pass judgement on the big ideas that had surfaced over the year, in either health or local government. The same turned out to apply in the battle between John Magill and Shirley Porter and the Tories of Westminster City Council. As anticipated, Porter and the five other individuals facing surcharges had all appealed to the courts. Magill and Child had stood their ground with the tireless support, as ever, of John Howell QC. Unusually, and in deference to its importance, the case had been heard in the Divisional Court by three judges. In December 1997, they had set aside the case against four of the six appellants but upheld it against Shirley Porter and her deputy, David Weeks.*

This had posed a dilemma for Magill, over whether or not to acquiesce in the ruling. There was the obvious danger that the two biggest fish might eventually wriggle through the loopholes opened up by the small fry. There was also a danger that, because neither Porter nor Weeks had been involved in the Committee that made the legal decision on designated property sales, the essential link between *decision* and *loss to the council* might be broken. After much deliberation, Magill decided the risks were outweighed by the benefits of being able to concentrate on the case against Porter and Weeks. To challenge the findings of three such senior judges might strike some as hubris. For two of the four smaller appellants, moreover, he and Child felt considerable sympathy and even some relief over the findings. They accepted the Divisional Court ruling.

Predictably, Porter and Weeks did not. They immediately turned for redress to the Court of Appeal. The case finally came up in April 1999 and was heard by three senior judges – Lord Justice Kennedy, Lord Justice Schiemann and Lord Justice Robert Walker. They announced their ruling on 30 April. To the considerable surprise of

---

* The four cleared by the judges were Bill Phillips, Peter Hartley, Graham England and Paul Hayler.

many within the legal profession, their lordships found in favour of Porter and Weeks by a 2–1 majority. Lord Justice Walker dissented, but his colleagues ruled that neither of them had in fact been guilty of wilful misconduct. The designated sale of council houses, described as gerrymandering by Magill, had in fact been entirely lawful.

The Westminster Supporters' Group had their cannons at the ready. The Appeal Court's ruling was the signal for an instant broadside against Magill and all those behind him – including, of course, the Audit Commission and all its members. A press release from the group issued that afternoon quoted the judges' key findings in Porter's favour. (In essence, they ruled that since she had done nothing in the interests of lining her own pocket but had acted only to further her party's electoral interests, Porter had behaved more or less like any other politician. It was simply unworldly of the auditor to have condemned this. As Lord Justice Schiemann opined: 'Voter-pleasing decisions are lawful in my judgment even if one of the motivating factors in the minds of councillors who vote for them is the desire to be re-elected.') Then the release rounded on the Commission.

Attention now turns to the mounting public costs of this case – which will rise beyond £7 million – if the Auditor and the Audit Commission refuse to accept the judgment of the Court of Appeal . . . Will the Audit Commission accept that as Lord Nolan's Committee on Standards in Public Life has recommended that surcharge should be abolished, and as the Court of Appeal has now found in favour of Dame Shirley, it should refuse to finance the Auditor's case?

Many Tory grandees rallied publicly to Porter's side. A week later, for example, a letter welcoming the ruling appeared in *The Times* from Kenneth Baker and Patrick Jenkin (now both peers of the realm). As former secretaries of state for the environment, their combined assault carried a punch and was brutally dismissive:

The Court of Appeal has restored both the proper role which party political considerations may play in local government, and the value of authoritative legal advice in protecting councillors against charges of wilful misconduct. The judgment is not 'a charter for councillors to pursue improper objects', the accusation levelled by counsel for the auditor. Rather, it restores the *status quo* which was well understood by councillors of all parties prior to the auditor John Magill's intervention . . . The Audit Commission should decline to spend any more public money on allowing Mr Magill to pursue this matter for another year in the House of Lords.[51]

In Parliament, the Conservatives peppered Hilary Armstrong in the Commons and Larry Whitty in the Lords with hostile questions designed to embarrass the Commission. The local government minister had to provide five separate written answers between 10 May and 25 May.[52] While Helena Shovelton could see that this was beginning to unnerve some Commission members, she was also acutely conscious that many senior figures within the Labour Party were watching the Commission's every move. Any whiff of pusillanimity over Westminster was all too likely to be construed as evidence of a political bias. As ever, what had been sauce for the Loony Left goose had to be sauce for the Tory gerrymandering, too.

At their monthly meeting in May, the members were formally notified by Magill that he was reviewing whether or not to appeal to the House of Lords. He had duly asked members to 'inform him early in June of any matters the Commission would like him to take into account when deciding whether to appeal or not'.[53] Item 7 on the agenda for 3 June would be Westminster – and members were later sent a thick wad of papers to prepare for the discussion. In addition to a lengthy briefing from the in-house solicitor, Rod Ainsworth, these included an independent joint opinion from Michael Beloff QC, the distinguished silk and president of Trinity College, Oxford, and a London barrister, Marie Demetriou. On balance, counselled the lawyers, they thought 'an appeal would be likely to succeed'.[54] When the 3 June meeting came around, Helena Shovelton asked each of the members to express a clear view on where they stood. (Only one member, the Tory councillor from Sefton in Lancashire, Ron Watson, was unable to attend.) Carefully avoiding any suggestion that the final decision belonged to anyone other than the auditor, the minutes recorded: 'Commissioners discussed the matter at length and decided that Mr Magill should be informed that the Commission would support a decision to appeal against the decision of the Court of Appeal.'[55] No public statement would be made ahead of his announcing his own decision, and even then only the very briefest of statements would be made.

The Commission knew the risks it was taking and stood its ground on a matter of principle, which needed no small measure of courage. Magill confirmed a couple of weeks later that the case would indeed be taken to the Lords.

13

Stumbling to a Breakthrough,
1999–2001

If it had dawned on Vincent Square's top managers over the summer of 1999 that they had perhaps underestimated the demands of the government's Best Value strategy, it was soon clear over the autumn that nothing whatever had prepared them for the impact of their new director of inspection. For two and a half years, the Best Value campaign had wandered aimlessly in a fog of uncertainty about its true objectives. From the moment of her arrival in September, Wendy Thomson led from the front with assault plans for every rampart in sight.

Her career to date looked almost a parody of New Labour credentials. She had studied social policy as an academic. She had talked herself into a job inside Ken Livingstone's GLC for the last six months of its existence in 1985–86. She had run the policy unit at Islington Borough Council from 1987 to 1993, with a specific brief to work on the rehabilitation of its erstwhile Loony Left leaders. And for three years after that she had led very successfully a Scottish-based charity, Turning Point, running services for the mentally ill and people with serious drug and alcohol problems. When the deputy prime minister, John Prescott, asked the distinguished architect Richard Rogers to set up an Urban Task Force in 1998, to promote the regeneration of Britain's cities, Thomson was an obvious appointee. It confirmed her glowing reputation as the reforming chief executive of the London borough of Newham (soon to be voted Council of the Year).

Like any other New Labour success, she had useful contacts, too. Arriving in England on a Canadian government scholarship from McGill University in 1982, she contacted a London academic who had supervised a close Canadian friend's doctorate. This was Paul

Corrigan, who was teaching applied social studies at North London Polytechnic. Corrigan embarked on a career in local government from 1985 – taking Thomson along under his wing, and introducing her to his politician wife, Hilary Armstrong. The two women became good friends. Above all, in the context of her 1999 appointment, Thomson shared completely the frustration and impatience that Hilary Armstrong and some others in New Labour felt over (as they saw it) the limited impact of the Audit Commission since 1983. It was emphatically not a view of the Commission held by those ministers, such as Jack Straw and David Blunkett, who had taken a closer interest in the Commission's work over the 1990s – but it had its adherents.

Thomson's assessment of the Commission's purpose was superficially the same as Howard Davies's back at the end of the 1980s. She recalled: 'Auditors didn't see it as their role to improve the service [delivered by local government], they just saw it as stating the facts really.' But Davies had drawn this distinction as a way of cautioning people not to overstate the auditor's role; the stating of facts was nonetheless seen as a powerful way of *suggesting* future improvements. Thomson, drawing on her own experience of working with auditors, suspected they were too often the Gradgrinds of local government. They were focused on facts, as though nothing more were needed. But, after sixteen years, 'just stating the facts' had in her view not caused much to happen. Back in 1995, some might have worried that Tony Child's departure from Vincent Square presaged the eclipse of the policeman, as it were, by the consultant. Thomson believed the opposite was true, and that the consultant had never stepped out of the policeman's shadow. 'The worst the Commission would do was produce a Public Interest Report. It never really led to much change.'[1]

It was not a generous verdict on the Commission's past record, nor one that took much account of all the sweeping changes in local government urged on by Vincent Square's output over the years. But Thomson, like many other critics, was less concerned with the lead taken by the Commission at a national level than by the more ambivalent record (as acknowledged in the *Butler Review* and elsewhere) of some of its VFM work at a local level. She was convinced after her experience at Newham that Best Value could do so much better. As its chief executive working with a radical Labour leader, Robin Wales, she had helped to galvanize the Newham's public services. 'We did everything absolutely to the limit. So we were going to do more services, more radically, more quickly . . . We ignored the Audit Commission, really, and [the campaign] was very strategically driven. It was run on a project-managed basis, right at the top of the council with political input.'

She had left all this behind reluctantly, knowing that the job at the Commission would be a big challenge. But she took it on with an almost missionary (and characteristically New Labour) zeal. Trying to build a Utopia in one borough was all very well. But to make a real impact on local government would require a national platform. She never made any bones about her political motivation in joining the Commission. 'I felt I was doing it as a duty. I knew it wasn't going to be fun, but I thought I could help to rehabilitate local government.' In her discussions with Andrew Foster, Thomson believed that she had secured his agreement on two absolutely fundamental points. First, she was explicit that the new operation would bring its own philosophy. It would have nothing to do with regulation, nor was it ever going to be just an extension of existing non-audit work. 'I came in with a clear view that inspection was an opportunity to do something different, and to bring in a more diversified set of professionals to work on performance improvement. The emphasis was going to be on *improvement*.'[2] And second, the Best Value inspectorate would be far from just a bolt-on to the existing organization. It would be a substantial engine of change in its own right. After all, the government had assigned it a £55 million annual budget. This compared with total central costs for the Commission of £12 million in 1998–99 (and was broadly on a par with the £66 million spent by the Commission on DA). And Thomson ruled out any immediate outsourcing to private firms, though the government had made clear it expected this to happen in due course.

In Vincent Square, meanwhile, Peter Wilkinson and his colleagues in the corporate resources department had of course been working on the inspectorate for some months. How it might function had been the subject of extensive discussion and some early plans had been laid out. They envisaged the inspectorate relying quite heavily on the support services of the Commission that were shared with DA. This did not accord at all with Thomson's vision. The unfortunate mismatch caused some dismay on both sides through the autumn of 1999. Andrew Foster's own reaction was hard to read. He had never been inclined to articulate too precise a vision of the Commission's future, preferring (as he would put it) to see its evolution as 'a journey'. This had generally served the Commission well since 1993, under his careful (not to say cunning) orienteering. It had left ample scope to respond pragmatically to ministers' shifting agendas. The problem with no fixed destination, though, was always that some colleagues might one day head in opposite directions. This was what now happened. Those preparing somehow to integrate inspection into the existing infrastructure of the Commission were surprised to find their plans being shelved. Wilkinson recalled:

Wendy didn't like the philosophy we were following at all. Our view was that, while the Commission needed to present different faces externally [for audit and inspection], we still needed to be internally 'joined up' and internally consistent. She took a different line: she wanted to make inspection an entirely separate process.[3]

Alas, his mind-maps cut no ice.

Thomson for her part was shocked to discover how committed Foster's colleagues were to the integration option – and how few practical arrangements had yet been made to prepare for the launch of an inspectorate on any terms at all. Only in one area had anything tangible been achieved: the team under Peter Thomas had almost completed its work on a methodology for the future inspectors. Other than that, as Thomas himself recalled, other colleagues 'may have had some ideas but nothing was really in place'.[4] With just six months to go before Best Value's formal launch date, local authorities across the country were starting to get jumpy. With no systems, no procedures and no organization, the pressure on Thomson was intense. Her response was all the more remarkable, given the turmoil in her private life at this time. She had originally intended to begin at the Commission in July, but her 44-year-old husband had been taken suddenly ill that month. He died five weeks later, leaving her with his two young teenage sons by an earlier marriage. Nonetheless, she now threw herself with demonic energy into building the inspectorate that she wanted.

SETTING UP THE BEST VALUE INSPECTORATE

Thomson's first move was to assemble her own small team at Vincent Square. Peter Thomas brought with him a staff of eight managers. Debbie Kirby, regarded by many inside the Commission as its most talented administrator, joined as a second associate director. And then there were the other inspectors, who would now report to Thomson: Andrew Webster, running the Joint Reviews of social services, and Jane Wreford, in charge of the education inspectorate. In mid-October, they were joined by the just appointed housing inspector, Roy Irwin, who had run the housing department for Bristol City Council since 1991 and was one of the best known names in the sector. Irwin took on the leadership of a small team that included Roger Jarman, fresh from the Housing Corporation, and Gill Green, who had worked in the studies directorate since 1995. (Doug Edmonds had retired a few years earlier, though he still did some consultancy work on housing.)

Irwin's first office was none too grand. 'For the first five weeks, I sat in an overheated storage cupboard on the second floor of Vincent Square. I couldn't turn the lights on until it was dark because the generator was next to an over-efficient radiator and would overheat.'[5] But the discomfort was short-lived. In the middle of November, Thomson and her fledgling department relocated – along with the headquarters staff of DA – to newly leased offices a few minutes' walk away from 1 Vincent Square, at 33 Greycoat Street. Other offices then needed to be set up around the country. Thomson was committed to working as closely as possible with people at the local level. She therefore decided against a policy-oriented structure in favour of setting up five regions, and each needed its own premises and equipment. Above all, though, she had to find five good directors to run them.

Advertisements at the start of November drew more than 200 applications. Thomson made her selection quickly, but time would show that she chose wisely. The regional directors came aboard between early February and mid-May of 2000 – Darra Singh for the north, Paul Kirby for central England including East Anglia, Peter Wylie for the south, Andrew Webster (who transferred to her team from the Joint Reviews staff) for London and Stephen Nott for Wales – and all of them would make their mark on the Commission over the next few years. Even by the high standards of the Commission, they were an exceptional bunch – none more so than Paul Kirby. He had earned his first salary in local government as an English teacher in Liverpool in 1985. (It was earned but actually not received, since the Labour council under Derek Hatton was effectively bankrupt. Kirby was one of those Liverpool council employees in the summer of 1985 whose redundancy notices were distributed around the city by taxi, the *folie des grandeurs* cited by Neil Kinnock in his famous savaging of Militant Tendency that October.) Since then Kirby had worked in the education department at Nottinghamshire County Council and had been a 32-year-old director of the environment at Lincolnshire in 1997 when it was selected (with Newham and a few others) as one of the pilot local authorities for the Best Value idea.

Filling the ranks below the regional directors involved an extraordinary recruitment drive that started well before the directors themselves arrived and ran on beyond the end of 2000. Thomson brought in the head-hunting arm of PricewaterhouseCoopers with a battery of aptitude tests. Several thousand information packs were sent out over the course of the year, and hundreds of written applications flooded back each month. In the field, Thomson needed 'lead inspectors', 'Best Value inspectors' and 'senior housing inspectors'; and in their support, she needed area managers across the five offices, and a substantial support staff at the centre. Each month, the controller's report to the Commission reported back on the bewildering statistics for applications, interviews and appointments. Within a year of her own arrival, Thomson was in charge of nearly 300 people. It would rise eventually to more than 500.

But what exactly were they going to deliver? Even in the months after Thomson's arrival, this was still a mystery to many councillors out in local government, and there were more than a few members of the Commission who might have struggled to give a coherent answer.

As the controller was candid enough to admit in his monthly report for October 1999: 'There is quite a considerable gap in understanding about the role of inspection and the fact that it will exist separately from the audit, and indeed will be expected to cover the full range of Best Value reviews appearing in authorities' Best Value plans.'[6] The uncomfortable truth was that the 'gap in understanding' about the inspectorate's existence as a separate body from DA actually reflected – and gravely compounded – the longstanding ambivalence over how the whole of the studies dimension to the Commission related to the auditors in the field. (Vincent Square's work on purchasing and quality control, of course, was another matter: there was no ambivalence there.) Despite the modernization of DA achieved by David Prince, auditors were still regarded by many within the studies directorates as the humble foot-soldiers of the Commission. In this light, even Prince himself was really only the regimental sergeant major. He did not move in the same circles as the young bloods of Vincent Square who had arrived, as it were, straight from Sandhurst. Despite the restructuring of DA effected in 1994, the consequent underlying tension had never been fully resolved. One result was that much bad blood had been allowed to accumulate on both sides. More critically, the link between the thinkers in Vincent Square and the doers in the field had remained fundamentally flawed. This of course had been the nub of adverse comment on the Commission down the years. Critics had invariably applauded the brilliance of its national reports, while suggesting the need for better implementation on the ground. As the *Butler Review* had put it in 1995: 'Improving the effectiveness of local VFM audit should be a high priority for the Commission.'[7]

This awkward historical legacy meant that Wendy Thomson would have faced a challenging agenda, even had Best Value been designed with all the finesse of an exquisite Swiss watch. Given the clunking Best Value model now handed down from Whitehall – with more moving parts than anyone could count – Thomson's inspectors and Prince's DA auditors alike were saddled with a regime for which they were hopelessly under-resourced. It was scarcely a fair criticism of auditors to say that they focused on the process confronting their council clients: that was what auditors were supposed to do. But the process itself had to track the requirements laid down by ministers and their officials. It was Hilary Armstrong's department that had decreed that every service be reviewed, every review inspected. If the resulting process dumped a 300-step questionnaire on councillors – as happened to Paul Kirby, in his last months as an officer in Lincolnshire before his move to the Commission – it was hardly the auditors who were to blame.

Yet blamed they were – not just by councillors but by Thomson's new inspectors, too, who could only wonder despairingly what had happened to all those clever ideas expounded in the Best Value papers prepared by Chilton and Vevers, and after them Peter Thomas and his team. By November 1999, all the old animosities between the field and Vincent Square were surfacing with a vengeance. The complexity of the situation went far beyond anything Thomson had anticipated, and hugely compounded the pressures of the desperately short time-table that she faced. To have any chance of achieving her goals, she was going to need wholehearted support from the Commission members, and from the controller with all of his top management team. Mere acquiescence would be tantamount to rejection.

She made her pitch to the Commission members at their annual November retreat at a hotel in Hertfordshire, the Harpenden House. Her message was unequivocal. 'Success relies on the leadership of the Commission and intellectual and practical support from people across the organization.'[8] The members were impressed by Thomson's command of her brief and reassured by the trouble she had already taken to build internal support for her plans. (A Best Value Project Board had been set up, comprising Martin Evans, Steve Evans, Terry Hanafin and Andrew Webster. Later in November, an Inspection panel would be inaugurated that would replace the Best Value panel that had been chaired by Helena Shovelton.) But they had their concerns, too. Thomson had circulated in advance the draft copy of a paper explaining the gist of her mission, so they were ready with their questions. Would not inspection be seen as a duplication of the DA? Was the huge effort going into it commensurate with the putative benefits? Could she be confident of finding staff of sufficient quality? In a separate discussion paper for the retreat, one of the three biggest risks for the year ahead was starkly stated as 'inspectomania'. There was never any doubt, though, that Thomson would be given the go-ahead for her inspectorate plans. While the recruitment and office start-ups programme moved into gear, she pushed ahead with her campaign to publicize how Best Value and the inspectorate service would work.

This involved a punishing schedule, both for Thomson and for many of her senior colleagues in Vincent Square. As a starter, local councillors and their officers in cities from Plymouth to Chelmsford were invited to sixteen Best Value breakfasts between October and December 1999. Thereafter, lunches, dinners, conference speeches and seminars followed each other at a hectic pace. Workshops and joint discussions were held with an array of other interested organizations whose acronyms seemed between them to cover most of the alphabet. To assist the communications campaign, the paper that Thomson had presented at Harpenden was published in December under the title *Best Assured*. It explained at last how DA and the inspectors would work together. At the start of each fiscal year, the law required that every authority publish a Best Value Performance Plan setting out how they intended to deliver public services to local people and the standards against which they could be judged. This public document would be subject to audit.

One aspect of each plan that would be critical to a successful audit would be a programme of legally required Best Value Reviews that would look at all of the authority's public services over a five-year span. The reviews would check on the application in each case of the four 'Best Value principles' known as 'the 4 Cs': challenge, comparison, consultation and competition. Auditors would be conducting the usual programme of local VFM work alongside these reviews in the first year, but thereafter 'the Commission foresees a reduction in the amount of local audit work arising from national Audit Commission studies in subsequent years'.[9] And the reviews would be the cue for action by the inspectorate. Each finished review could be examined by a Best Value inspector, who would then look at the actual improvements achieved on the ground. All of the authority's services would be looked at in this way, except those specifically covered by the professional inspectorates (like education, housing, the police and so on). There would also be special arrangements for auditors to call upon the inspectorate to intervene in an authority's affairs where this seemed appropriate – and indeed, a call for 'intervention' could be sent all the way up the line to the secretary of state if this were deemed necessary.

Three months later, in March 2000, the Commission published a much more elaborate paper on the Best Value methodology. Originally to be called *Seeing the Wood through the Trees*, it emerged with the happier title *Seeing is Believing* and it effectively enshrined the work of Peter Thomas's team. A short introduction by Thomson herself articulated the high hopes that many in government and Whitehall had for Best Value:

Local authorities have been given a unique opportunity to show that continuous improvement of local services is best achieved at a local level . . . The Inspection Service will work with authorities to help them to take this opportunity, and to ensure that Best Value makes real improvements to the quality of local services and the quality of local people's lives.[10]

Services would be awarded stars to indicate their current standard to the general public: one star for 'fair', two for 'good' and three for 'excellent', with none at all for 'poor'. (The *Financial Times* back in July 1999 had anticipated five stars, but this had been refined to three in the meantime.) Services would also be appraised on the chances of improvement, a notable second dimension that caught the essence of Best Value – its focus on making things better in the future. Detailed case studies were used to exemplify how the new regime would work. Crucially, inspection styles would vary depending on the performance and attitude of the target authority. Authorities would range from 'Failing' through 'Coasting' and 'Striving' to 'Beacon' status. (The government intended to publish a list of Beacon councils, with the Commission's help.) Inspectors' reports would range accordingly, challenging some and celebrating others.

So much for the theory. The actual outcome was very different.

ANNUS HORRIBILIS

The putative successor to CCT had started off originally as a light shower of new obligations, deliberately kept as non-prescriptive as possible in the 1999 legislation. By the start of 2000 this had given way to a steady drizzle of briefing papers from Whitehall and DA offices on the finer aspects of Best Value plans, Best Value reviews and even Best Value performance indicators. (The government introduced Best Value PIs nationally in December 1999, *in addition* to the Audit Commission PIs. The Commission was informed that it should continue to pursue its own PIs or not, 'as it thinks fit'. The members opted early in 2000 to beat a graceful retreat.[11]) And the drizzle turned to a hard rain, once the government's plans were published for its next Local Government Bill. Every council would soon be required to transform its governance arrangements and to heed a new ethical framework presided over by a body to be called the Standards Board for England.

Local government wilted under the downpour. It seemed to suffer a collective failure of nerve: few officers were inclined to challenge the auditors' reading of Best Value. Even fewer were prepared (like Paul Kirby, in his last few months at Lincolnshire County Council before joining the Commission) to tear up the whole compliance manual and assert their own interpretation of what the new regime intended. The message from Whitehall had been so relentless. Most authorities would follow it to the letter – and in many cases, no doubt, would do so with mischievous pedantry, deliberately to make even heavier weather of a policy initiative they had disliked from the start. Helena Shovelton, looking back later on all the meetings that she had attended with council leaders to discuss Best Value, could not recall a single one where she sensed any appetite for the policy whatever.[12] CCT had only just been jettisoned, after years of misery. Few were ready to embrace its apparent proxy.

There was little doubt by June 2000 of the consequences. The Parliamentary Select Committee on the Environment, Transport and Regional Affairs published a report on the Audit Commission, based on an inquiry held over the turn of the year. Its main findings were unexceptional. The Committee reported that 'the majority of the evidence we received confirmed that the Audit Commission is a well-run organization, produces high quality work and is responsive and relatively open'.[13] (One of those who gave evidence to the committee, 'in a personal capacity', was the chief executive of Camden Borough Council, Steve Bundred.) But the committee members noted ominously: 'We are alarmed at the current and future impact of a developing culture of over-inspection in the public sector. This burden seems to be particularly acute for local authorities. The Government must recognize the potentially dire consequences of failing to minimize and coordinate inspections of local government.'[14]

Councils had been expected to launch on average perhaps three reviews; instead, their plans (some of them up to 700 pages long) had aimed far higher. Thomson and her senior team confronted the outcome at a 'programming workshop' on 1 August. As Andrew Foster reported to the Commission members in his deadpan monthly report a few weeks later: '[they met] to discuss the practicalities of preparing a programme. It needs to cover a workload comprising over 4,000 reviews of diverse services in different combinations, and a number of cross-cutting reviews.'[15] By the autumn, the figure was nearing 4,500. Five months into his role as a regional director, Paul Kirby could see immediately that the first inspectors in the field faced a hopeless situation. He recalled: 'By the time we turned up, Best Value was probably already irretrievable. It was just a shocking mess. People had done endless, minuscule reviews of small things – because that was what they had been asked to do.'

Given the mathematical impossibility of coping with so many reviews, the Best Value inspectorate had no choice but to be severely selective. The Select Committee in June had in fact recommended 'a "managed inspection" approach . . . with only high risk local authorities and a sample of other Best Value reviews being subject to full inspections'. But the Committee's sensible advice was unfortunately only half-heeded. The response sent back to the Select Committee by the Commission argued the case for inspecting all councils, good and bad – 'to identify and disseminate good practice and provide a balanced picture of overall service performance across local government'.[16] The statistics, however, spoke for themselves: over the second half of 2000, the number of completed inspection reports crept slowly up towards the thirty mark. Nor was this de facto about-turn accompanied at any point by a formal acknowledgement – either in Vincent Square or Greycoat Street – that Best Value had gone horribly awry. On the contrary, a paper was published in October called *A Step in the Right Direction*, and Thomson was determined that that they should plough on with a commitment to detailed inspections.

It would have taken huge self-confidence at this point to assert a complete change of tack, but without it most inspectors were simply wasting their time. Some resented this angrily, while others cynically resigned themselves to the nonsense. Tensions ran high among the inspectors, and between them and the auditors. Kirby recalled: 'it was complete and utter warfare, with some of us just saying "this is absolutely stupid" '.[17] Inspectors were now scurrying from city to city – and the more bizarre the assignment, of course, the more ribald the gossip. Pest-control services seemed to feature prominently among many councils' priorities. Auditors in DA marvelled at stories of time spent inspecting a Best Value report on the public conveniences in Scarborough.

In truth, the whole undertaking was beset with problems that might have challenged the most consummate manager on the planet. The director of inspection was not a candidate for this accolade. For one thing, she found it hard to delegate: she insisted on personally approving all inspection reports, so Best Value reviews from local authorities started piling up in their hundreds in Greycoat Street. Worse, she was not a skilful manager of those around her. As a colleague averred in one of the more notable understatements to come out of the Commission's first twenty-five years, 'she did not use an influencing style'. It might have had its comic aspects, had the consequences not been so personally unpleasant for some of the inspectorate's staff. Emotions ran high in the department and there were more than a few departures.

In her relations with DA, meanwhile, Thomson found herself in a hostile situation for which she was wholly unsuited. When she appeared in front of the auditors at their annual conference for 2000, she was cruelly heckled. This was not a fair reflection of the efforts that had been made in many parts of the country to make the DA–inspectorate duopoly workable. In Leeds, for example, the northern region of DA had seen the appointment of a new regional director early in 2000 – Gareth Davies. He and the regional inspector for the north, Darra Singh, had forged a successful alliance that worked well for both of them. (Davies recalled: 'We got on well from the start, and said to each other that we would make something sensible work in the north. It was a classic situation of a new operation starting up within an established organization – but what the inspectorate brought was much needed and very powerful.')[18] But the response of the auditors en masse nonetheless attested to a deep resentment among them over the criticism of DA that was implicit in the inspectorate's approach – and sometimes explicit in its director's quoted observations on the Commission.

Nor was it just a matter of bruised feelings. Many auditors believed that their relations with client authorities were being damaged by the duplication inherent in the new regime. Council officers were bemused, or worse, at being visited separately by auditors and inspectorate staff with little or no coordination of their inquiries. Auditors were quick to spot individual inspectors who did not make the grade – and given the pell-mell speed of their recruitment, there were inevitably some of those. There was also a financial dimension to the rivalry between the two organizations. DA earned substantial fees from conducting local VFM audits. They did not look kindly on an inspectorate that represented a whole new approach with indeterminate consequences for the future of DA's non-audit role.

Few senior colleagues rallied to Thomson's support, which surprised and disappointed her. But she could be a tough operator, as she herself would readily admit – and some colleagues rose to this less well than others. It was also the case by mid-autumn that her relations with both the chairman and the controller had come under severe strain. For this Thomson herself had to take some blame: she had never tried to conceal that she saw her time at the Commission as a means to a bigger end, and was never unduly sentimental about its institutional values. Nor was she especially mindful of the significance to the Commission of its political independence: it was apparent from the start that she regularly met in private with Hilary Armstrong, and that her own political connections were quite as important to her as the Commission's.

The political dimension came to a head over perhaps the most innovative aspect of the new Best Value legislation – the statutory power it provided to the secretary of state to intervene in a local authority's affairs and effectively to usurp control of the council from the elected members. Once all the authorities in the country had submitted their Best Value plans to the auditors in the first three months of 2000–2001, there was just one that had failed to pass muster: Hackney Borough Council. Its public services were a disaster, and its Best Value plan had offered no realistic attempt to improve them. The auditor had referred the council to the inspectorate. Thomson in turn proposed to refer it to the minister. As a matter (in her view) of procedural detail, she approached the Commission members for authorization to do so.

A panel of members was assembled, chaired by Helena Shovelton. The evidence for referral was presented by Thomson personally, accompanied by her London regional director, Andrew Webster. Alas, the Commissioners were not satisfied that the evidence was entirely fair or even accurate. In pointing this out, they also made clear that their role was no mere procedural detail. In fact, they refused to make the referral. This caused a problem. Thomson, it transpired, had already arranged with Hilary Armstrong for the referral to be made that day and for the news to be broken by the minister in a press conference. It was, after all, the first case of its kind. Disclosure of these arrangements not surprisingly prompted an indignant response from the members. There ensued a rather unseemly row. Thomson was very cross indeed, and made no attempt to hide her view that it was yet another case of a dilatory response from the Commission impeding effective action on the ground. Children were at risk in Hackney as a result of dangerous social services. She was going to put that right, and the least she could expect was support from the Commission.

Helena Shovelton for her part had no doubt about the ramifications of the case for the independence of the Commission. She had been making slow but steady headway with efforts to increase its genuine political independence. This was a matter of acute sensitivity to every-one in the Commission at this time. (An academic who interviewed many people in the Commission during 1999 and early 2000, as part of a research project on the Commission, noted in her paper: 'In conversations with Audit Commission staff, the watchword is "inde-pendence", and although this means different things to people at different levels of the organization, it is precious to all of them.')[19] It was simply unacceptable to the chairman that the Commission should be overridden on something so politically charged as a first referral under Best Value. The referral was sidelined, and the press conference was cancelled.*

A few days after the confrontation with Wendy Thomson in Vincent Square, the chairman and her controller were invited over to the environment department to see the local government minister. Arm-strong was angry and dressed them both down for what she regarded as 'the most disgraceful behaviour' in not informing her about the decision *not* to refer Hackney to the department. In response, Shovel-ton simply explained the rationale for the commissioners' decision (which in her view had never necessitated any communication with the minister). It was a stand-off, and the meeting ended abruptly.[20] It must have been acutely uncomfortable for Andrew Foster, whose own social relations with Hilary Armstrong and her husband were by now

---

* The subsequent story of Hackney's woes dragged on for more than a year. An inspectorate team under Andrew Webster proceeded with its own detailed investi-gation into the borough's affairs. It presented its report to the council on 6 November 2000, stating that it had 'found serious problems of political leadership, financial management, culture and management arrangements and service delivery ... In the judgement of the inspectors, the council does not currently have sufficient management capacity to undertake the scale of [sic] speed of action required. It will need to both reduce the management task and secure external assistance to carry out those which remain.' In response, Hackney Borough Council said it accepted the 'broad thrust' of the report and launched a range of remedial initiatives to be closely monitored by the inspectorate. Six months later, though, the finance director had to warn of another crisis. This time the secretary of state, Stephen Byers, intervened immediately: a press release on 22 June 2001 announced that 'front line public services must be put first. We shall take the necessary steps to ensure that this happens.' The council's deficit rose to more than £18 million in July, and the government issued five statutory directions to the council in October – bearing out, in effect, Wendy Thomson's original assessment.

extremely cordial. But it was all of a piece with the general direction of his relationship with Thomson, which was fast deteriorating beyond repair.

Through the autumn of 2000, it disintegrated altogether. The disarray over the progress of Best Value put Foster and Thomson alike under considerable strain: both were very publicly committed to its success, but the prospect of a humiliating retrenchment was clearly looming by the end of the year. No doubt there were other considerations, too. There was no personal accord between them at all: those private reservations that Thomson had harboured ahead of accepting the job had turned out to be all too well founded. And her own high profile on the conference circuit and in Whitehall had obliged Foster to share the media limelight – not something he had needed to do since 1993. (In the summer, Foster had hired a personal media adviser, called Ruth Davison; within weeks, Thomson had hired an adviser of her own.) Both were driven individuals; both were disappointed and frustrated by the failure of a working partnership on which they had set great store only a year or so earlier.

By the end of the year, the two of them were ensconced in their own head offices at either end of the street between the Commission and the inspectorate. Neither was at all comfortable meeting with the other. Both had turned to lawyers for advice on a possible parting of the ways. Helena Shovelton needed to tread with great care in presiding over this troubled situation – which she recalled as 'an absolute cauldron'.[21] True, she was the chairman. But neither Andrew Foster nor Wendy Thomson was simply a paid executive who, *in extremis*, could be dismissed like some wayward corporate minion. ('It was difficult territory.') And Shovelton, meanwhile, had problems of her own.

In addition to her chairmanship of the Commission, Helena Shovelton was now chairman of the National Lottery Commission. Just as the internal difficulties in Vincent Square were assuming serious proportions during the summer, a storm suddenly blew up over the lottery. On her first day as chairman there, a letter had arrived on Shovelton's desk from a whistleblower, alerting the five lottery commissioners to serious technical problems with its current operations. This made the following months extremely difficult. Shovelton and her colleagues had to preside over an auction between competing bidders for a new seven-year licence to operate the lottery. To general surprise, she announced in August that neither of two competing bids was satisfactory – but one would be the subject of further discussions, while the other would not. The rejected bidder was a company called Camelot, the current operator and target of the whistleblower's allegations. (These had already proved to be true and were part of the rationale for going with the other bidder.) Camelot appealed, triggering a judicial review. A High Court judge in mid-September sustained the appeal and reprimanded the chairman – despite the fact that all her meetings had been attended by Treasury solicitors – for showing 'a marked lack of even-handedness'.

It was a lethal phrase. The press hounded Shovelton mercilessly for days on end – plaguing the switchboard at Vincent Square – and on 5 October she resigned from her lottery post. It was a torrid experience for her personally, and its timing could hardly have been worse for the Commission: morale in Vincent Square was at a terrible low. But the question for members, of course, was how far (if at all) her authority as its chairman had been compromised by the episode. Her colleagues reviewed her position, very properly, with a stern Jeremy Orme guiding the proceedings like the senior City regulator he was. Had Shovelton resigned, of course, it would probably have fallen to Orme as her deputy to step up as acting chairman (as Clive Thompson had done in 1995). But it did not come to that. Shovelton herself saw no reason why she could not continue, and no one else ever suggested otherwise. Indeed, it was affirmed by all the Commission members at their private meeting that they wanted her to remain in the chair.

Within weeks of the crisis, Orme had retired from the Commission along with Peter Soulsby and Iris Tarry as part of the cyclical turnover of its members. It was especially a matter of regret to Jeremy Orme that he felt compelled by his position at the newly launched Financial Services Authority to decline an invitation to serve another term. His departure was also a significant loss to the Commission, not least in so far as no other member brought to the table his interest and eagle-eyed expertise in the business of managing its complex procedures for audit appointments, remuneration and quality control. These three were the last to retire of the members appointed during

David Cooksey's chairmanship: since January 1996, the Commission had lost Clive Wilkinson and Peter Wood in 1996, Clive Thompson and Tony Travers in 1997, Terence English in 1998, and Kate Jenkins and Peter Kemp in 1999. One other exit was that of Deirdre Hine, appointed in May 1998, who had left to take up the chairmanship of the Commission for Health Improvement.

In the wake of these various departures and Roger Brooke's retirement, the Commission had acquired nine new members since January 1996 – starting with Adrienne Fresko, an occupational psychologist and human-resources consultant, who now became the deputy chairman. The addition of four new members in December 2000 would bring the Commission up to a complement of seventeen, including the chairman and the three members recruited with her in 1995. The full membership now comprised (in their order of appointment): Helena Shovelton, Ron Watson, John Foster, Rosalynde Lowe, Adrienne Fresko, Richard Arthur, Sue Richards, David Williams, Judy Curson, Julie Baddeley, Brian Wolfe, Elizabeth Filkin, Graham Hart, Gerard Lemos, Pauleen Lane, Nick Skellett and Chris Swinson. Only one was a real businessman – Nick Skellett, the managing director of a firm supplying the furniture industry, as well as leader of Surrey County Council – but several came from accounting, consulting or academic backgrounds. Others had careers in the health sector, local government or the not-for-profit sector.

It was striking that eight of the seventeen members were women, including of course the chairman. Long gone were the 1980s, when the Commission had met for four years before the appointment of its first female member (Elizabeth Anson, the Tory peer, who arrived in February 1987). The gender balance in the boardroom, though, had changed a lot faster than the ethnic mix among the Commission's staff. This was picked up by Ken Livingstone in July 2000, when in his new capacity as mayor of London he met Shovelton and Andrew Foster for the first time. Livingstone was quick to complain to them about the lack of ethnic diversity at the Commission. (The 2000 Annual Report had just been published, disclosing that just 7 per cent of the Commission's staff came from ethnic minorities.)[22] They had a cordial chat, however. And by that stage in 2000, a poor ethnic mix on the staff was the least of the controller's worries.

STRETCHED TO THE LIMIT

As if the travails of Best Value and the crisis in his relationship with the inspectorate's director were not enough to contend with, Andrew Foster had a hundred and one other burdens to bear in 2000 – and all weighed heavily on him in this, the eighth year of his term in office. A lesser man would already have been utterly exhausted by the schedule that he kept, in sustaining his extraordinary network of contacts across Whitehall and beyond. By 2000, perhaps even Foster was beginning to tire. The Commission's remit had grown too broad, too quickly, for the resources at hand. This put huge strain on the controller himself, on the organization and its staff. Arguably the Commission members themselves should have done more to address this. Certainly the crisis might have been more manageable, had the workings of the Commission been reviewed more vigorously in the late 1990s. But by 2000 most of the members had been in post less than half as long as their controller, and his influence over all their activities remained pervasive even after a year of Shovelton's chairmanship. Foster did not make it easy for the Commission members to second-guess his day-to-day management of the organiz-ation. As for the senior executive team, Foster was still supported as loyally as ever by colleagues like Peter Wilkinson, the director of resources. Too many other talented people, though, had drifted away.

Foster himself was left with an astonishingly wide range of activities. For each month of 2000, as in every year, the controller submitted a report to the members, reviewing the Commission's current issues and latest events, the issues confronting DA and the latest news on the inspectorate. In March, not untypically, the report comprised twenty-one pages of commentary on 135 different items, with an extensive diary of events, an appendix on recent studies by the Commission and other bodies, and a scattering of the controller's correspondence with ministers and others.[23] (Naturally, this took no account of his non-Commission business, including membership of the Treasury's Public Services Productivity Panel, on which he sat for all nine years of its existence.) Another constant theme of the monthly reports was the time and effort needed to oil the Commission's interaction with representatives of the many bodies it affected. A regular feature of 2000, as of the years before it, was a dinner with one group or another at the Goring Hotel, a plush establishment just a stone's throw from the gardens of Buckingham Palace. Not all of them were hosted by the controller, but he attended a good many.

Most of the engagements in Foster's diary, though, were far from ambassadorial: he was at the forefront of policy discussions on a whole range of public services. His diary for the month of April, for example, listed eight of them. He attended a Best Value seminar at Worcestershire County Council and a session of the policy board for Labour's newly launched Modernizing Government initiative; he made a presentation to the prime minister on health reforms, and followed this up with one-to-one discussions with the health minister and the chief executive of the fledgling Commission for Health Improvement; and, elsewhere in Whitehall, he met separately with the permanent secretaries of DETR, of the Cabinet Office and of the Treasury. Underpinning Foster's access to all of these powerful individuals, of course, was the importance that they attached to the Commission as the fount of regular, authoritative and widely noted national reports. Studies were in this sense the lifeblood of the Commission – and it was therefore a matter of acute concern in 2000 that the output of the new Public Services Research department was falling short of expectations.

This is not to say the year passed with no notable successes. Some reports struck home with powerful work on highly topical subjects – including two in the summer on the problems posed by the heavy influx of asylum-seekers into Britain around that time: *Another Country* and *New City: Supporting Asylum Seekers and Refugees in London.* (The number of asylum seekers had shot up from about 4,000 a year at the end of the 1980s to more than 70,000 a year by the end of the 1990s.) And an update was produced of a highly influential report first published in 1997, *Retiring Nature: Early Retirement in Local Government,* worth reprising here since the passage of three years had made little difference to its relevance. The report drew attention to a huge problem, until 1997 largely unremarked, over the under-funding of local government pensions. The report began with some sobering numbers. 'Of the 42,000 [council] employees who retired in 1995–96, 32,000 (over three-quarters) went earlier than normal retirement age. Almost 40 per cent of retirements were on grounds of ill-health.'[24] It examined the worrying financial implications of this, given the unfunded nature of some pensions (e.g., for the police and fire service) and the declining funding levels elsewhere – particularly in the wake of the 1997 Budget that had significantly increased the taxation of dividends to pension funds. The study was led by Greg Birdseye, and the ensuing report made a big impact. 'Some chief officers in local government described me as the most hated man in local government at one time. People were retiring in their early or mid-fifties and it was costing a fortune. For many authorities, it was a real eye-opener.'[25]

For the most part, however, publications in 2000 focused on worthy but slightly dull topics such as trading standards and the care of municipal buildings and there were far fewer of them than in previous years. No blame for this attached to PSR's director since September 1999, Terry Hanafin. It was a consequence of the significantly expanded demands that were now being made on his department. In both local government and health, the Commission embarked in 2000 on what were essentially two intensive research efforts: developing the Best Value methodology and amassing the data needed for the Acute Hospital Portfolio (AHP). But no R&D department was available. Instead, PSR lost about half of its local government staff to Best Value and about a third of its health staff to the AHP work. To his own considerable surprise, Hanafin found his nominal staff of about fifty people reduced to fewer than thirty. Since he had also inherited a very much depleted programme of forthcoming studies, the cupboard for 2000 was inevitably a little bare.

This led to some tensions. Over several months of 2000, the PSR director laid plans for the future. He hired more staff; he conducted market research to discover what topics would be of most interest among his target audiences; and he enormously improved the procedures for choosing new subjects and carrying out studies so that they would be completed more quickly, while building in strong quality assurance. But he could do nothing about the immediate dearth of heavy-hitting titles. It clearly frustrated both the controller and the Commission members. This added to a vague sense in Vincent Square that the preoccupation with Best Value through these months had to some extent entailed an eclipse of the studies area. It was no longer the focal activity it had been in earlier times. Certainly no one ever expected the controller to sit down for hours – as his predecessors had often done – to assist a study team in the last throes of drafting a report. Nonetheless, successful studies remained as indispensable as ever to the Commission's public standing in Whitehall. Hanafin found himself struggling for months with a chorus of mixed messages. But he reached the right conclusion in the end. As he recalled:

I didn't realize until I'd been there almost a year that actually the key thing – and it eventually became obvious – was to deliver high-profile studies. Andrew didn't mind having a bit of best-practice stuff to help people out in the field and he wanted PSR to support the development of Best Value inspection – but what he really wanted most of all was high-impact reports.[26]

By his first summer, Hanafin was more than happy to go along with this priority. Not only had he had more chance to appreciate the potency of national reports in Whitehall – he had also learned something most unexpected about attitudes in the field to the work linked with local VFM guides. The lesson came as a bit of a shock. At Andrew Foster's suggestion, between May and July 2000, Hanafin instigated a series of dinners around the country to garner people's impressions of his directorate and of the Commission in general.

I had two or three colleagues with me from different parts of the Commission, and we met a cross-section of chief executives from health and local government in each of the regions. We asked them questions through the dinner. Then after the meal, we had a general discussion. In every case but one, while the local financial audits and the national studies were praised, our local value-for-money work was hammered.[27]

An exception was made for the north-east, where it was acknowledged that a Newcastle-based audit team had earned wide respect for its VFM work. Everywhere else, though, the invariable verdict was that local auditors did not have the skills to conduct the quasi-consultancy work required for effective VFM implementation. Praise ran as high as ever for the national reports and the regularity work of DA. But the great majority of those who spoke up over the coffee and brandies were wholly dismissive of the local VFM audit guides and the work based upon them. It was a view shared by the newer recruits into Vincent Square who had previously worked in local government themselves. Peter Thomas, for example, recalled his attitude while working for Westminster City Council:

From our point of view as council officers, the VFM stuff was churn and a waste of money, whereas we loved the national studies. Frankly, the quality of the people was not good enough to do what a firm like McKinsey could get away with. The Commission was only training its guys for a couple of days. They were too young, and they'd spent all their time as auditors, not local service managers.[28]

Here, in fact, was a second fundamental reason for reappraising the traditional business model of the Commission. Just as New Labour's embrace of Best Value – and the steadily accelerating pace of reform in the public services – had prompted the senior management in Vincent Square to think again about the relevance of the old 'report/audit-guide/local-study' approach, so it was evident now that there were also strong upward pressures from the field to revise it. Too many reports – and some dated this back to *Misspent Youth* in 1996 – were now dealing with complex, national issues that simply were not susceptible to the audit-guide treatment. Their targets were too multifaceted for effective remedies to be regimented into quantitative ('painting-by-number') guides. The author of *Retiring Nature*, Greg Birdseye, was the first to admit that the report on pension deficits in local government had led to a disastrous local audit. One of the great survivors from the Banham era, Birdseye recalled: 'It became so much more difficult to translate the studies into VFM audits. That process was winding down.'[29]

Hanafin fed this conclusion into his preparations for the 2001 studies programme. They would cut the time taken on individual projects, and drop compulsory audit guides. Other changes were introduced, too – some at the behest of the performance development director, Joanne Shaw (though having another director second-guess the fundamental activities of PSR was not much to Hanafin's liking). The team on a prospective new study would be given an initial few weeks to explore the topic, for example, and would then be called upon to submit a formal business case for pursuing it. Critical reviews would be held during and after the research phase 'to confirm the story-lines of each of the products'.[30] None of these changes altered the fundamental team structure underpinning studies, but they certainly strengthened the administrative process.

Then there was another facet of the Commission that had arguably struggled to keep pace with its growth in recent years – and that triggered yet a further crisis in 2000: its own financial housekeeping. While Hanafin could straighten out the studies programme, it began to chafe with him that he was not getting the monthly financial reports showing spend against budget that he had expected to receive as a departmental head. Thomson shared this concern. The two of them believed their operations were being poorly served by the Commission's back-office functions, with consequences that made for some colourful anecdotes. Their frustration led on more than one occasion to a tense stand-off with the director responsible for resources and finance, Peter Wilkinson. One lively exchange embarrassed the controller as well as Wilkinson because it happened at an evening meeting attended by seven Commission members. Terry Hanafin arrived straight from a management retreat with his own team, at which he had been obliged by the hotel to pay the bill with his own personal credit card.

I was very angry. My team had poured out all this stuff about invoices paid by the Commission so late that agencies booking hotels etc. would no longer give us credit. I had known nothing about these concerns previously. So in the evening meeting I spoke up with vehemence. Wendy also joined in but she was much more restrained.[31]

When the full story about the hotel bill later emerged, it did not reflect so badly on the finance department – but by then the damage to its standing in the eyes of the Commission members had been done.

Wilkinson himself felt equally aggrieved. The corporate body was saddled, in his view, with two executive directors who made no allowance for the fact that the Commission's rapid growth had inevitably put a strain on all the staff functions. These were being expanded – a new associate director, Bryn Morris, had been assigned to the Management Services Business Unit (MSBU) in Bristol – and Vincent Square's broader requirements were acknowledged. But it would need a little time for the two to be brought into line. Instead, Hanafin and Thomson took what seemed to him a combative stance towards every aspect of centralized controls – and Thomson even appointed her own finance, IT and HR executives to run a rival operation.

The root of the problem was that the management of the Commission's own central resources had always been a Cinderella function. Ever since DA had become an arm's-length operation with its own finance director, MSBU had been expected to provide it with regular financial reports, as well as taking care of much of DA's housekeeping. But the directors in Vincent Square had typically had much less appetite (or need) for financial information. MSBU's management had therefore increasingly focused on meeting the requirements of DA, and simply did not have the systems in place to meet the new demands from Vincent Square that arose when Thomson launched her inspectorate. No doubt this problem would have been quickly addressed, had the inspectorate been set up at arm's-length, like DA. Once the decision was made to keep the inspectorate in-house, the task of upgrading MSBU no longer seemed so urgent – and it was probably only a matter of time before the finances went awry.

Matters came to a head in the summer, over a plan by the controller to introduce a new position akin to a chief operating officer. It concerned him, he said, that the directors were not working together as a corporate group. He was proposing a new structure to change this. Unfortunately, it would have meant Hanafin and Thomson reporting to the chief operating officer rather than directly to the controller's office – and neither was prepared to accept this. Responding, they pushed hard for the appointment instead of a full-time finance director. This was a step that Helena Shovelton had urged Foster to take when she was first appointed to the chair. He had deemed it unnecessary then, and was reluctant now to change his mind. But the chairman insisted, and a satisfactory resolution was eventually reached. A new post of 'operations director' was created, which David Prince moved into from DA in October 2000. He was to be closely assisted by Jonathan Moor, who had been appointed a few years earlier by Bill Ogley to take charge of budgets and planning – and Moor ended up shortly afterwards being appointed finance director. Peter Wilkinson was assigned the challenge of setting up a new Knowledge and Information directorate. (He also had to take charge of the ever-lengthening agenda for ACiW in Cardiff, or Y Comisiwn Archwilio as it now presented itself there in native guise.)

The episode had added again, though, to an already fraught atmosphere within the Commission. The apparent risk of embarrassing slip-ups on the housekeeping front had certainly unsettled the chairman and her colleagues. Terry Hanafin's relations with the controller had undoubtedly been damaged (perhaps fatally so); and Wendy Thomson's frustration over the operational difficulties facing the inspectorate was a major factor in her growing disaffection with her whole situation. On a more general level, meanwhile, the evident friction among the senior individuals did nothing to help morale among the rest of the staff where a heavy workload was taking its toll. Foster himself noted as much in his monthly report to the members for March. 'At the February [monthly] meeting I raised with you my concerns about the pressures currently faced by staff.'[32] It was agreed in the ensuing discussion to cut back the number of members' panel meetings, for which extensive preparatory papers were often required. (There had been thirty meetings in 1999, up from twenty in 1997.) Some members were distinctly unhappy about this, and worried that they might be kept in the dark over important issues. Whether or not their fears were justified, the supposed benefits of the cutback were not conspicuous. Excessive workloads remained a matter of concern to many staff.

One growing burden was a consequence of the Commission's own success. The greater its reputation, the more its views were sought out by other organizations keen to emulate its influence – and they came from far afield. Within the international context, the Commission had increasingly been seen as a paragon of public sector auditing since the early 1990s. Scarcely a month of 2000 passed without three or four parties beating a path to the doors of 1 Vincent Square. Many came from Asia and Africa; but Poland and the Scandinavian countries also sent regular visitors, as did Russia, China and Japan. Foster had even had occasion, late the year before, to write to the head of the Foreign Office expressing some concern over the amount of time being spent by the Commission on overseas visitors. He'd received a solicitous reply from the permanent under-secretary, John Kerr, who wondered if 'it [might] perhaps be worthwhile thinking of concentrating the effort, for instance, organizing occasional seminars and so killing a number of birds of passage, e.g. from Asia, with a single seminar stone?'[33] Seminars had been duly arranged – but the individual delegations went on unabated. And there were reciprocal overseas trips by members of the Commission's staff, too. One of the more curious followed a visit to Vincent Square in June 2000 by a Mr Woredewold Woldie, who was minister for justice in Ethiopia. He and three colleagues were keen to explore the Commission's work on standards, ethics and performance indicators. Two months later, the head of the Commission's anti-fraud unit found himself being assigned to Ethiopia for a four-week secondment to enlighten his hosts on corruption procedures and anti-fraud training programmes. 'These products have been well received', noted the controller in his September monthly report.[34]

Such exotic assignments, though, were a world away from the mounting pressures on staff of administering the Best Value regime. The resultant disaffection surfaced in the autumn of 2000. After the staff survey of September 1998, it had been agreed that two years would be allowed to elapse before another, leaving time for the new structure built around the PSR, the inspectorate and the audit policy department to bed down. The follow-up survey duly came round now, in September 2000 – and in December 2000, Trish Longdon presented its findings to the members.[35] The external consultants had made a valiant effort to set things in context. 'A change process of the magnitude that we are going through is bound to cause dislocation and uncertainty . . .' But their faint praise for the positive messages that they could discern was a fitting end to a miserable year. 'In all areas we are within the range of other organizations . . . There are no factors where staff feel significantly worse [than in 1998] although in some cases there are small dips in the satisfaction scores.'

Surely, things could only get better in 2001.

TURNING THE CORNER

It began with a knighthood for Andrew Foster in the New Year's honours list. This was no guarantee of sunny uplands ahead, but it was not a bad start. The controller headed off for a tour of Manchester, Sheffield and Nottingham in February, as chairman of the judges for 2001's Council of the Year award sponsored by the *Local Government Chronicle*. Back in Vincent Square, David Prince was soon presenting a strategic review, with plans for a characteristically thorough shake-up of internal procedures. And Helena Shovelton was even able to report back on a 'much friendlier' meeting that she had had with the local government minister.

Behind the scenes, however, the debacle over Best Value had brought the Commission to a perilous point. The paperwork was a disaster, however bravely the controller tried to suggest otherwise to Commission members. 'We will have started 622 inspections', he told them in his report for February, noting only 'some slippage due to local authority delays and lack of inspectors'.[36] Worse, the breakdown in relations between Wendy Thomson and the controller was now a problem that could not be allowed to continue. The monthly meeting papers gave no hint of remedial action, and it might be wondered how much of the real situation was apparent to all of the Commission members. Some of the observations in the same controller's report had a surreal air. 'Wendy has also been interviewed by *Internal Audit* magazine', ran one reference, 'and spent two days inspecting waste management in Bradford.'[37] But Helena Shovelton was showing signs of exasperation at the general management predicament: things were coming to a head.

A way out of the impasse surfaced in the spring. The general election of 2001 loomed. There would be many changes to the senior support staff at the top of government. New blood would be needed. Early in May, Thomson received an approach from the prime minister's staff, inviting her to work for Tony Blair's second administration. The election followed on 7 June. Two weeks later, it was announced that Thomson would be leaving immediately for the Cabinet Office. She had been given a brief to set up a new unit, the Office for Public

Service Reform. The controller commented in his monthly report for June that the appointment was 'a personal compliment for Wendy and can also be seen as an endorsement of the Commission and the regard in which it is held at a national level'.[38] There were of course other reasons to be thankful for the appointment, but these did not need spelling out. Thomson's was a timely and graceful exit.

Hers was not the only innovation at the Cabinet Office that June. A radical reorganization of the department ushered in a bevy of new government units at the apex of the Whitehall machine. (Indeed, so many people were suddenly moving to and fro in the restructured Cabinet Office after the election that confusion reigned for a while over where everybody would sit. Its head, Mavis McDonald, joked with her counterparts from other departments that she was now the permanent secretary for rooms.)[39] One of the most important was boldly christened the Prime Minister's Delivery Unit (PMDU). The product of much agonizing in Downing Street over the meagre progress achieved in the public services since 1997, the PMDU was set up to rescue New Labour's radical plans from exactly the kind of imbroglio in which Best Value was now immersed. Its head would be a former academic turned government adviser called Michael Barber. As he has since written, in a revealing account of the four years he spent in the job called *Instruction to Deliver*, it was the PMDU's premise that 'reforms will only work if they are excellently implemented'.[40]

Barber had himself pulled off several reforms of note at the Department of Education, but he believed he had been fortunate to find himself working with senior civil servants who were not afraid to give a strong operational lead. 'Too much of Whitehall lacked such leadership, and had little grasp of what successful delivery required in practice.'[41] (By the summer of 2002, he would be taking a hard line on the enemies of effective reform: 'Bureaucrats were writing regulations with no thought to what practical implementation would mean on the frontline.')[42] In his own campaign at the PMDU, he would use a boxful of sharp tools in aid of what soon came to be known as his 'deliverology': they included delivery chains, to track the links between ministers' decisions and those ultimately affected by them, delivery reports on departmental performances and stocktakes on the progress of reforms to date – all backed up with a daunting array of targets, planning guides (aka 'delivery trajectories') and assessment frameworks.

Perhaps surprisingly, though, the PMDU never fully engaged with the Audit Commission. It certainly drew upon data (and delivery-chain analysis) from the Commission on many occasions – and was happy to recruit from Commission staff where opportunities arose – but Barber was primarily concerned with the workings of Whitehall and the disciplines imposed (or not) on his delivery chains by government ministers and their top officials. He was also determined to achieve results within four years, which meant his staff would be working at a pace incompatible in his view with the approach taken by the Commission or any of the other existing inspection bodies.* The PMDU's direct impact on the Commission was therefore limited. Nonetheless, its work reflected – and undeniably helped to bring about – a change in the general climate within Whitehall after 2001 that was of huge consequence for those in Vincent Square. There was a fresh determination to secure reforms that had somehow eluded effective implementation since 1997 despite the best intentions – and these included, of course, a reform of many services for which local government was responsible.

The weight of new expectations in this area naturally fell in the first instance not on the Commission but on the new ministerial team charged with local government affairs. In the immediate aftermath of the June election theirs was one of the most politically sensitive and high-profile briefs in Whitehall. Leading the team was Stephen Byers,

---

* Barber was clear on this point from the start. '[Like some other inspectorates] the Audit Commission wrote superb investigative reports but took two years to complete them. Two years! That's an age in this period of extraordinarily rapid change. For the Delivery Unit, I wanted an approach which was much faster and, since we did not plan to produce reports for publication, we did not need to dot every "i" and cross every "t". The conceptual breakthrough for me came in a conversation with someone who had worked on Audit Commission reports. "After how long", I asked him, "did you know 90 per cent of what was in the final report?" "A month," he replied. At that moment I decided we would design a process which took a month, made proposals which were 90 per cent right, and then drove action' (*Instruction to Deliver*, p. 151). Barber always argued, though, for the importance in every policy debate of collecting all the data.

as the secretary of state for transport, local government and the regions. (His department, the DTLR, had lost its environment portfolio to a new ministry, Defra, set up in the wake of the devastating outbreak of foot-and-mouth disease across Britain in previous months.) The minister under him with particular responsibility for local government was Nick Raynsford, who had served a four-year apprenticeship with responsibilities since 1997 for London, the construction industry, housing and planning. Raynsford had extensive experience of dealing with local government, yet had so far had very little to do with the Audit Commission at any point. This was true despite the fact that one of his main tasks since 1997 had been to oversee the creation of the Greater London Authority: like the officials most directly responsible for setting it up, Raynsford regarded the GLA 'as the creation of a new strategic tier of government rather than a type of local authority'.[43] (Indeed, for this reason there had been quite a debate over whether the Audit Commission or the National Audit Office would be better placed to take responsibility for the GLA. The Commission had ended up with it, applying its audit-purchase procedures in the usual way, but not without a scrap.)

Raynsford had already given much thought to local government's future by the time he took up his new post in June 2001. He arrived in office, in fact, with a carefully crafted agenda for the improvement of local public services. Armed with this, Byers almost immediately committed his department to a White Paper on local government before the end of the year. Replacing Best Value was one of its most important objectives. Byers felt no obligation whatever to defend Best Value – or, indeed, the Commission's efforts on its behalf – and he made no effort to disguise his view that it was a bureaucratic mess with no future. Paul Kirby, who was asked by Andrew Foster to step up as acting head of the inspectorate in the wake of Wendy Thomson's departure, heard a very clear message from Byers. 'He said: "We're going to have to do something completely different, and I'm now open for ideas" – but he wasn't looking to the Audit Commission for those ideas.'[44] It was not hard to see what this meant. However unfairly, there was every danger that the Commission might now be made to carry the can for Best Value's failure. Andrew Foster himself had no illusions whatever that he and his colleagues were in a tight spot.

The controller at this point needed a helping hand – and was lucky indeed that he could call on not one but three exceptionally clever young colleagues. In working on the inspectorate, Paul Kirby, Peter Thomas and Andrew Webster had become an unusually close and effective team. They were hugely knowledgeable about local government, of which each had had lengthy personal experience. And they were totally unabashed at any opportunity to put original thinking into practice. Foster's challenge to them could not have been more explicit. Kirby recalled: 'He said to the three of us, this is make or break time. We've got to fight back out of this corner. How should we do it?'[45]

The short answer was reached within a couple of weeks. They would go for what was jokingly tagged 'pre-venge'. The process of Best Value was undoubtedly going to be savaged in December, and the Commission with it – unless, taking a leaf out of the controller's standard manual on pre-empting external criticism, the Commission itself could do a demolition job on Best Value first, and give the politicians something compelling in its place. To this end, work was begun immediately on an appropriate post-mortem for Best Value. It would take an intensive effort that was to last through most of the summer of 2001.

REBUILDING MOMENTUM, AND LOSING SOME

Meanwhile, the business of setting the Commission's miserable millennium year behind it was being pushed ahead on other fronts, too. In respect both of studies and of media communications – always intimately related – progress was being made. In fact, the machinery of report production was now humming quite nicely. In 2000, Hanafin had researched his targets carefully, recruited additional staff and grasped the essential needs of the Commission. The first of several meaty titles appeared in November 2000: *Money Matters: School Funding and Resource Management*. It questioned the prevailing assumption that ever greater delegation of financial management to schools was necessarily desirable, and looked at the contribution that could still be made by local education authorities, if only they were properly run. This was the kind of report that handily enhanced the Commission's reputation for independence. The *Local Government Chronicle* noted approvingly that it 'has the guts to challenge a major strand of government education policy head-on ... Above all, the Audit Commission [has] demonstrated the vacuous nature of the "school good/council bad" sloganizing which has until today been the accepted dogma.'[46]

In the months thereafter, the Public Services Research department published reports across a wide range of topics. *A Uniform Approach* examined huge discrepancies in procurement costs for fire services across the country. *Best Foot Forward* presented a detailed case for more delegation of management decisions in the police service to local stations. A quirky but remarkable report, *The Special School Run*, looked at the obstacles encountered in London by those taking children with special educational needs to school. (Two practical handbooks were published on the same subject in December.) And for the first time since 1987, a major paper was published on the probation system. *A Change of Direction* offered advice and guidance to probation boards still struggling with the aftermath of a huge reorganization in 1999. The National Audit Office had seized on this reorganization as a pretext for arguing that it should be given the audit of the probation service. Andrew Foster had fought off this proposal, which would have deprived the Commission of audit fees worth about £1 million a year. He had instigated work on the 2001 paper soon afterwards, to consolidate the Commission's standing in this arena. (As he explained in his monthly report for December 1999, the home secretary had agreed to retain the Commission's services at a local level, 'although the NAO continues to argue its case "behind the scenes"'.)[47]

In his first months, Hanafin had been careful to salvage a good working relationship with Jonty Boyce, adroitly defusing Boyce's initial anxieties over the implications for him personally of PSR's emergence in 1999. The result in 2001 was the publication not only of some important one-off health studies – notably *Brief Encounters*, on the management of temporary nursing staff – but also of several national reports based on the data-collection exercises devoted to building the Acute Hospital Portfolio. A paper on day surgery led the way. But it was the second report, on the analysis of data relating to A&E departments, which attracted the most attention. The official DoH line was that enormous progress had been made in this area of the NHS, because there were statistics to show that the waiting times between arriving at the department and being seen by a doctor had fallen impressively. The Commission's report, simply entitled *Accident and Emergency*, was dismissive of this analysis. People could be screened in triage within five minutes of arrival – and then find themselves waiting four, five, even six hours for a bed. The meaningful data, it insisted, had to cover the time elapsing between arrival and being given a bed or sent home from A&E. And the score on this count, which the Commission had carefully tallied, looked a lot less rosy. It was a revelation that made a big story in the media. The controller had another day starting on the *Today* programme – and the health secretary, Alan Milburn, had to go around all the morning TV shows, explaining the government's position.

By the time of this episode, Hanafin was wiser to the media aspects of PSR's work. He recalled:

I created a document which set out the likely key messages of each planned publication. It was organized chronologically by publication date. I updated it regularly and shared it with the communications people. In my second year, they used to get very excited. I'd mark the reports that were going to be 'high impact', in media terms – and I made sure that we had one of those coming out at least every couple of months.[48]

Even so, there was a feeling among the Commission members that media relations could perhaps be managed a little more effectively: they wanted to see the message consistently conveyed that the Commission was working for the interests of public-service users. (In the very first Commission board paper of 2001, *A New User Focus*, Trish Longdon had the temerity to suggest that they 'may wish to adopt a media style similar to that of the national charities or the National Consumers Council, where the organizations but not the personalities behind them are well known'.) Here was another chance for the Commission to start afresh in 2001.

For more than ten years, the handling of media relations had been outsourced. In September, the contract of the incumbent agency, Citigate Westminster, was going to expire. Their hold on the account had been rather precarious ever since 1997, when the longstanding account manager (and erstwhile staffer), Mark Oaten, had resigned after being elected the Liberal Democrat MP for Winchester. It was time for a change. As Andrew Foster's personal media adviser, Ruth Davison had come to the Commission the previous summer from the Improvement and Development Agency (IDeA). She had not had a terribly happy time, finding it hard to establish much influence in the shadow of the external agency. Now she saw her chance.

I said 'I'd like to pitch to bring the press office in-house.' Andrew said that was fine, but proper probity would have to be observed. They put Chinese walls round me while I did my bid documents and I had to use external people to validate my figures. I wasn't allowed to talk to the finance team in-house.[49]

But Davison was given the support of a formal team: while she acted as account manager, the bid was formally led by an associate director, Jon Schick, with Peter Wilkinson as its champion on the management board. They won the contract in June, for a formal hand-over in September. Davison was given the go-ahead immediately to start setting up the new unit (which would supposedly report to the head of communications). Within weeks she was interviewing for eight employees at all levels of seniority. She would have an office a short distance away from Vincent Square, supposedly to give her press team more freedom of manoeuvre (a slightly odd arrangement that was abandoned a year or so later). It seemed at least a happy omen for the future when a notably sympathetic article on regulators in general appeared before the end of the month in the *Guardian*. 'Audit has produced genuine progress . . . The Commission is a good example of how monitoring has changed. It began looking at inefficiencies; moved on to measuring performance; progressed to inspection; and is now focusing on users.'[50]

Unfortunately, the view within Stephen Byers's department was a lot less benign. However resurgent the Commission on the studies front, it was its intimate involvement with the Best Value quagmire that seemed to be uppermost in ministers' minds. Byers and Raynsford were determined to be seen to be making a fresh start. Within a month of the election, they decided to seek a new chairman to replace Helena Shovelton when her current term expired at the end of November 2001, and to begin to think about a successor for Andrew Foster in due course. Shovelton was given the news by Nick Raynsford personally at the end of July.

It came as a bitter blow to her, though hardly a surprise. There were those at the Commission who thought her reappointment inconceivable, after the rebuff she had received in the High Court ten months earlier. Shovelton half thought as much herself. But officials insisted the lottery business had nothing to do with it. Ministers wanted a stronger figure in the chair, Raynsford explained to her: someone who would speak out louder and more often on the Commission's behalf. (As a criticism of her record to date, this seemed a less than generous view of the extraordinarily difficult furrow she had had to plough – with two less-than-retiring executives in harness, neither of whom would have been her first choices for their respective roles.) What was apparent, anyway, was that too few people had been prepared to speak up for Shovelton, against those individuals close to Raynsford's ear who preferred to see her gone.

She wasted no time in her July meeting with the minister arguing her corner. Instead, slightly to Raynsford's surprise, she had the presence of mind to ask him how he saw the future of the Commission unfolding. This prompted quite a lengthy and good-natured discussion. As it was ending, Raynsford responded with a surprise of his own, suggesting to Shovelton that it would be most helpful if she could make sure that she had negotiated a firm exit date for Andrew Foster before stepping down. This she did, in an agreed letter to the controller signed on 20 November. (It would be almost the very last thing she did for the Commission – specifying a leaving date for Foster of October 2003 at the latest, to allow for another eighteen months or so in which it was envisaged that he could help both a new chairman and his own successor to find their feet.)

Shovelton declined to pretend in public that the decision was anything but a deep disappointment. She even admitted to the media her conviction that asserting her independence from ministers had hardly helped her cause. This upset officials in the DTLR, and prompted some barbed comments in the press about 'control freaks' in the Blair government. Linking her non-reappointment to that of her counterpart in the prisons service, the respected *Guardian* correspondent Malcolm Dean thought it 'looks like a lack of ministerial guts and gratitude'.[51] While it was a setback for her personally, though, Shovelton could see that her non-reappointment was also a measure of the Commission's severe predicament over Best Value. Accordingly, she wrote to all the members, informing them of her news, and inviting them to a special meeting on 9 August.

It was convened in the Horticultural Halls conference centre, just adjacent to 1 Vincent Square. Seven members were absent on summer holidays, but nine were able to make it, as were the controller and three other directors. It was billed as an informal brainstorming session to develop ideas about Wendy Thomson's successor. In fact, Shovelton and her colleagues were now confronting the full extent of the crisis facing the Commission over Best Value. Shovelton also briefed the members fully on her conversation with Raynsford about the future. She strongly suspected that the Commission might be on the brink of losing its remit in health, and said so. But her colleagues thought this most unlikely, suggesting to her that her pessimism was perhaps understandable in the circumstances – for which they all expressed their 'concern and disappointment'.[52] Then they anguished over the state of the Best Value inspectorate and decided they needed a critical review of its prospects. One of them, Gerard Lemos, was asked to use his expertise as a policy researcher to prepare it over the next two weeks.

His submission back to the controller, on 24 August, was less than reassuring. He could see 'no current case for overturning the fundamentals of the regime', he said.

There is, however, one enormous health warning. The Best Value Inspection Service has no way of guaranteeing that the pace or consistency of improvement or the quality of the improved services will be sufficient to raise levels of public satisfaction (currently only 48%) to a level that the Government or the media regard as acceptable.[53]

He was almost certainly right about that. Fortunately, the controller and the rescue team under Paul Kirby had other ideas.

PUTTING PAID TO BEST VALUE

In practice, Best Value had been stymied by too many prescriptions from the centre and an over-zealous approach to inspection. But it was striking how few local authorities had spoken out against the underlying concept. Mavis McDonald had been the permanent secretary in the Cabinet Office since late 1999. She recalled:

There was no outcry at all. It wasn't a case of 'this is rubbish, we must ditch this'. It was received as a well-founded exercise that had been fairly handled by those on the ground. It was like a very rigorous peer group review – a mixture of hard-edged fact plus an attempt at some degree of sympathetic interpretation.[54]

Perhaps it was a case, now, of not losing the baby with the bathwater. After a deeply flawed implementation – and some prodigious mud-slinging between the auditors and the inspectors – there was no shortage of dirty water. But could a way be found to change it while hanging on to the idea of local initiatives tempered by top–down inspection?

Once again, ironically, Wendy Thomson had actually pointed the way. Back in July 2000, she had written a paper for the Commission, *Corporate Governance Inspection*, which broached the idea of a rather special kind of Best Value inspection.

Corporate governance is often the single most important determinant of success or failure in effective management and an authority's capacity to provide community leadership and service improvement. We need to be able to review the running of the whole authority and tackle corporate issues affecting service quality and improvement. Other [professional] inspectorates often identify corporate issues but tend to limit their inspections to a service perspective.[55]

This approach had effectively been adopted by the team under Andrew Webster that had gone into Hackney, to begin the work of pulling its council back from the abyss in the autumn of 2000. But perhaps the corporate governance paper pointed the way to a methodology with more general application? Perhaps inspectors could recapture some of the boldness envisaged in the original Best Value ideas by focusing on 'the running of the whole authority'? By early 2001, Peter

Thomas had no doubt this was the way to go: 'The more reviews we did, the more obvious it became. A lousy authority's got ten lousy services. Mucking around with them individually was pointless. You needed to address the central problem.'[56]

As a first step, Kirby and the team concentrated on winning themselves more time. Kirby recalled: 'We hadn't fully worked out our game plan [by the summer], but we were clear that we had somehow to keep control of the policy agenda.' They managed this by hijacking a review of Best Value's first year that was just being written by Peter Thomas and one of his colleagues, Michael Carpenter. It was conceived as a straightforward successor to *A Step in the Right Direction* – full of sober judgements and compelling graphics. Indeed, it was going to be called *Stepping up a Gear*. But this might have given DTLR officials the disastrous impression that the Commission was simply pushing ahead with Best Value. So the title was altered to *Changing Gear* – and an ostensibly traditional Commission report was subtly amended. On to a retrospective review was skilfully (not to say, cheekily) grafted a future prospectus. Extensive use was made of excellent market research findings – orchestrated by the team's main man at MORI, Ben Page – to argue the case for a fresh set of rules. And a final section ('Improving Inspection and the National Framework') left no doubt where those rules would come from.

Changing Gear made no attempt at a whitewash of Best Value, or of the Commission's role in its implementation, and it acknowledged 'a number of consistent and fair criticisms over how inspection and audit operate'. But it reserved its most trenchant criticisms for those who had designed the concept in the first place, or failed to apply it sensibly. Government had requested far too much of local government, producing a system of plans that 'is fragmented and bureaucratic, and can hinder councils' capacity to focus on what matters'. And the councils themselves, though generally acknowledging the potential power of Best Value, had not stepped up to the plate as had been hoped: in too many cases, 'they lack the will to ask challenging questions or the vision to tackle difficult choices'. Luckily, though, help was at hand. Best Value had worked well for many councils.

But the world in which audit and inspection operate is considerably more diverse than legislation and guidance anticipated, so they need to be better targeted if they are to add maximum value ... Following its recent strategic review, the Commission is preparing to pilot radical changes ... [and] the forthcoming local government white paper [will] provide a rare opportunity to consolidate (rather than proliferate) initiatives and secure improved performance by councils.[57]

The Commission and the government would be working hand-in-hand to sort out the reforms that were so evidently needed.

Foster and Kirby together sat down with Nick Raynsford to go through the report, line by line, on the afternoon of 11 September. (They broke off for a while to take on board the news from the US about al-Qa'eda's attacks on New York and Washington.) A wily politician, Nick Raynsford no doubt admired the fast footwork implicit in the paper. But he was also struck by the value of the paper as a catalyst for the proposed White Paper, and was greatly impressed by Kirby. Two weeks later, and still in the shadow of the shock news about Helena Shovelton's impending departure, Andrew Foster took the deputy chairman, Adrienne Fresko, along with him to meet the local government minister. *Changing Gear* had just been published, on 19 September. Fresko reported back on their discussion to her colleagues at the October monthly meeting. Raynsford had explained that the White Paper would be about streamlining Best Value – 'but the minister felt that this was in line with our own thinking in any case'.[58] The controller must have been mightily relieved to hear this seemingly bland assurance. There was just a hint of relief, though, in his monthly report for September: 'There are indications that [*Changing Gear*] could be a most important publication, and will be one of the key documents debated over the course of the discussion leading up to the new Local Government White Paper ...'[59]

Meanwhile, Kirby and his colleagues still had much to do. The success with *Changing Gear* had averted disaster. As Kirby recalled: 'At the start of the year, you could say the Commission had been a train out of control. It was heading straight for a big wreck. In effect, we had switched the points just in time.'[60] But ahead lay the real objective: to ensure that the gist of *Changing Gear*, and of the Commission's further thoughts on it, found their way into the finished text of the White Paper itself. Kirby saw that it would not be enough just to address the operational failings of the inspectorate. These were not neglected: the backlog of unfinished reports was cleared within a few months, and new arrangements were soon being made to shake up the staff and raise the general level of competence among inspectors. But Kirby firmly believed the Commission had to seize the initiative in the field. And, by temperament, he was always a man with a strong penchant for seizing initiatives in any situation.

Accordingly, he now launched a series of 'corporate assessments' in selected councils with obvious problems, to pilot the idea of a new inspection approach. They would seek to answer two basic questions. First, and taking account of *all the data* delivered to inspectors and auditors together, how good is the *overall* performance of this council? And second, does it have a grip on what *really* needs doing if performance is to be significantly improved? Best Value's findings had needed a truck loaded with lever-arch files to communicate any verdict on a council. Kirby's approach would deliver a finding that could be sent back to Whitehall on a postcard. He christened the process 'a Comprehensive Performance Assessment' – soon abbreviated everywhere to 'CPA'. And he wheeled it out with astonishing chutzpah. One of the first councils to be targeted was Walsall, where they concluded that there was no option but to sack the whole of the management team and replace the political leadership to boot. Then they moved on to the home city of Labour's deputy prime minister, Hull. In the full glare of the media, not to say of John Prescott, Kirby and his team gave Hull, too, a resounding thumbs-down.

The authorities picked off by the campaign caused little trouble – but the concept *behind* the campaign provoked all kinds of resistance elsewhere. In Whitehall, the other inspectorates (most especially Ofsted) took great exception to the idea of a CPA rating that would boil down their carefully detailed assessments. In the DTLR, department officials had been devising their own assessment methodology, based on using dozens of traditional performance indicators, and were incensed to find themselves being upstaged by the Commission. Within the Commission itself, Kirby's tactics struck many as reckless in the extreme. DA, rather like the professional inspectorates, hated the idea of reducing their separate audit findings to one amalgamated judgement. As for the members, several were aghast at the scope of CPA's ambitions, and frankly appalled to see the future of the Commission being gambled with in this way.

A succession of cabinet committee meetings followed, through November and into December, devoted to the slightly unlikely topic of CPA methodology. At least two secretaries of state were involved – Alan Milburn for health and Estelle Morris for education – as well as the officials from half a dozen departments and Wendy Thomson, from the Cabinet Office, who had been given responsibility for writing much of the forthcoming White Paper. With only a few weeks to go before the launch of the paper, there was still fierce disagreement over the pace of CPA's proposed introduction. Most of those at the meetings – though not Nick Raynsford – favoured running a few pilots a year, perhaps until the next general election. Kirby had a different idea. They should produce CPA ratings for *all the 150 largest councils* in the country by the end of 2002. What was more, a firm commitment to this effect should be included in the White Paper.

And so it turned out. The final version of the paper noted that

The Audit Commission will aim to complete the first comprehensive performance assessments for all upper tier authorities by late 2002 and for district councils by late 2003. The Audit Commission is developing, and will pilot, the methodology for the comprehensive performance assessments with other inspectorates and Departments.[61]

The White Paper was called *Strong Local Leadership – Quality Public Services*. In all essentials, its verdict on Best Value followed the lines laid down in *Changing Gear*. It was a triumph for the Commission. It owed its success above all to the hard work of the team led by Kirby, and to Kirby's boldness in charging ahead while others pored over the map. But the outcome was another tribute, too, to the persuasiveness and perseverance of Vincent Square's greatest salesman, Andrew Foster.

THE DAY OF JUDGMENT FOR
WESTMINSTER

The White Paper was published on Tuesday, 11 December. The same day, John Magill and Tony Child were informed by the House of Lords that the judgment on Shirley Porter's appeal would be handed down at 2 p.m. on the following Thursday. The controller and his colleagues could at least hope that it might prove a good week for drawing long-running sagas to a happy close.

Since announcing their support for the Westminster auditor's decision to turn to the Lords, back in June 1999, the Commission had had to keep a close eye on the technical minutiae of the case. It had been agreed that the council would pursue arrangements for the payment of the surcharge in the event of success in the Lords. But the Commission needed to be ready with its facts in case any objectors should complain over the handling of the surcharge (as, indeed, they later did). Westminster had been a regular fixture on the monthly agenda. With only months to go before the Appeal hearing, scheduled for five days early in November 2001, the members had even sought a fresh opinion from counsel with no previous involvement in the case, David Pannick QC. To John Magill's mind, it was a very puzzling move. 'I remember thinking, what on earth are they going to do if Pannick says, "Don't go ahead"? All the papers had already gone in!'[62] Fortunately, the second opinion that Pannick handed over late in September was entirely supportive: he believed the auditor had 'good prospects of success'. Also encouraging was his view that the Lords would be likely to award costs in favour of whoever won the appeal.[63]

This was of no small consequence to the Commission. The costs of Magill's investigation up to the end of the High Court stage of the battle in May 1996, roughly £3 million, had been paid directly by Westminster County Council, in line with the standard contractual arrangement for all auditors. Since that date, however, the costs of the court action had fallen to the two sides to pay for themselves. The Commission had indemnified Magill and his legal team, again in line with its standard practice. Their costs so far totalled approximately £4.2 million. The Commission had also spent a further £1.3 million on its own costs and just over half as much again on the costs of the four acquitted in the High Court.[64] Porter and her co-appellant, David Weeks, were thought to have spent approximately £6 million or slightly more. In other words, the potential cost to the Commission if Magill lost the case was going to be somewhere in the region of £12 million – roughly equivalent to the value of its total net assets employed at 31 October 2001 of £12.7 million.

Receipt of Pannick's opinion occasioned the last long discussion of the case by the members, at their monthly meeting on 4 October. Those unhappy about it, like the Tory councillor Ron Watson, re-iterated their reservations before acquiescing in the decision to back Magill: Watson 'expressed his view that the Westminster Designated Sales case had caused harm to the reputation of the Commission and the audit regime, but emphasized that he did not oppose the auditor's appeal to the House of Lords'.[65] Otherwise, members largely confined themselves to speculating about the media coverage and reviewing the lavish public relations work that was under way to prepare for it.

On the morning of 13 December, Tony Child and his assistant went directly to the House of Lords, where confidential copies of the judgment were to be handed to the parties at 10 a.m. Magill joined Andrew Foster and a handful of Commission members at Vincent Square, along with the lawyers and PR advisers. Shortly after 10 a.m., the auditor's mobile telephone rang. Everyone in the room watched the colour returning slowly to Magill's face, as he listened to Child relaying the news. They had won the appeal in a unanimous judgment, 5–0.

The decision finally dispelled for good the appalling prospect of the Commission having to write out a cheque to Shirley Porter for several million pounds for her legal costs – and three months later the Lords confirmed, as expected, that she had to reimburse the Commission for its legal costs in preparing for the Court of Appeal and the House of Lords appeal. The surcharge on Porter was finally valued at close to £43 million. She would eventually pay Westminster council £12.3 million under a settlement negotiated with them in April 2004. (A similar surcharge against her deputy, David Weeks, was settled for £48,000.)[66] The Commission received a final sum of just over £1 million, being 10 per cent of the amount recovered, after third-party costs and the council's costs of recovery.[67] The size of the settlement, and the time taken to reach it, provoked one last objection along the way from Westminster's Labour councillors, which had to be dealt with by a subsequent auditor, Les Kidner. His rejection of it came in a Public Interest Report that was published in March 2007 – just a little short of eighteen years after the first approach to Tony Child at the Cemeteries Hearing in County Hall.[68]

But of course the financial aspect of the verdict, however weighty, was a trifle compared with the reputational issues at stake. Public reactions to the Court of Appeal's judgment had left no one in any doubt of the calumny that would have been heaped upon the Commission had it lost. In the event, their lordships vindicated the years of steady endeavour by Magill and Child in every single respect. The essence of their judgment was caught in one magisterial paragraph:

> The passage of time and the familiarity of the accusations made against Dame Shirley Porter and Mr Weeks cannot and should not obscure the unpalatable truth that this was a deliberate, blatant and dishonest misuse of public power. It was a misuse of power by both of them not for the purpose of financial gain but for that of electoral advantage. In that sense it was corrupt . . . and he [the auditor] was right to stigmatise it as disgraceful. (para. 48)

And referring to three of the four individuals whose appeals had been accepted by the Divisional Court, they opined: 'it may very well be that . . . [they] were fortunate to be exonerated to the limited extent that they were exonerated'. As for Magill's conduct of the case, in which the 1982 Act had 'required him to act as investigator, prosecutor and judge', he had never behaved in any way that suggested any bias whatever on his part. It had been a protracted business; but 'having regard to the complexity of the case and the volume of evidence before the Divisional Court, to the immense scope of the auditor's investigations and to his constant activity in the pursuit of information, the proceedings did not exceed the reasonable time requirement' laid down in law for the protection of civil rights.[69]

From all those who had criticized the stand taken by Magill and Child over the years, there came the deafening silence customary on such occasions. But the judgment nonetheless gave Commission members some cause for satisfaction at the end of what had been in many ways a deeply troubling year. After Magill's triumph, and the reaffirmation of the Commission's future status in the December White Paper, perhaps the imminent arrival of a new chairman would at last mark the fresh start for which the members had really been waiting since the dark days of autumn 2000? Alas, the wait was not quite over.

14

A Fresh Start, 2002–03

Who would be the next chairman of the Audit Commission? Or, who would *want* to be its next chairman, as plenty of commentators now wryly observed. To have lost one chairman after a single term might have been regarded as a misfortune, but losing two looked like carelessness. How long might it take Nick Raynsford's officials to find someone with the requisite gravitas and judgement to take on a job that seemed to pose a significantly bigger challenge with each passing year? They were confident by the end of November 2001 that they had found an ideal candidate, but ministers were not yet ready to make an announcement. Raynsford asked the deputy chairman, Adrienne Fresko, to act in the role for a month or two, starting on 1 December.

This was a safe option: Fresko was good at adjusting to abrupt changes of role, as she had proved more than once in her career to date. She had built a career at Citibank before leaving in the late 1980s to start a family – and her first serious appointment in public life was as a board member at the (recently strike-bound) London Ambulance Service, which was assuredly not a pin-striped culture. Nor was she lacking in the courage to take on bigger tasks: in accepting the chairmanship of Croydon District Health Authority in 1992, at the age of 35, she had become the youngest DHA chairman in the country. She had now been on the Commission for almost six years, since February 1996, and had had plenty of opportunity to hone her skills in the public sector as an occupational psychologist and expert on personnel matters. She had worked closely with David Prince on DA's development almost since her arrival, chairing the DA panel and travelling round the organization a good deal more than most

Commission members ever did, and she had served diligently on the advisory panels for several influential reports.

She had been slightly surprised and flattered to be offered the deputy chairmanship when Jeremy Orme stepped down in October 2000. A formal selection process for the deputy chairmanship had ended with two final candidates, Fresko and a senior member of the accountancy profession, Chris Swinson, who had been president of the Institute of Chartered Accountants in 1998–99. Under the circumstances, officials were no doubt anxious to nominate a deputy in whom they would have complete confidence, given the possibility at that point that Helena Shovelton might have been about to stand down. It must have been greatly to Fresko's advantage that she was already known to them. (Swinson went on to join the Commission as a member in December 2000 and subsequently chaired the District Audit panel.) And it was evident that Fresko had always hugely enjoyed her involvement with an organization that she greatly admired. As Orme's successor, she must have looked a good bet as a valuable steadying influence. So it had proved, through some highly charged months. Most recently, for example, it was Fresko who had drafted the final agreement in November 2001 between Helena Shovelton and the controller, setting out the terms for his departure.

It had been agreed that Andrew Foster would stay one more year to provide continuity under the new chairman, and the search for a new controller would start in earnest by early 2003. A few months' hand-over to the new controller might be sensible. At the latest, Foster would leave by October 2003. Within the first weeks of 2002, however, he was already hinting to journalists that it was his intention to leave in the not too distant future. Clearly, the incoming chairman was going to need to hit the road running.

Unfortunately, it was to be more a case of political road-kill: his appointment was run over by events the moment it went public. A former social services director, Norman Warner had been special adviser to Jack Straw from 1997 to 1998. He had been appointed chairman of the Youth Justice Board and made a Labour peer in 1998. He was the unanimous choice of the selection panel for the chairmanship of the Commission, and rumours of his appointment seeped out early in March 2002, when all that remained in the process was formal confirmation of the decision by ministers. On 8 March, Warner's appointment was front-page news in the weekly *Local Government Chronicle*. The same afternoon, as the newspaper had abjectly to report the following Friday, 'the job offer was abruptly withdrawn ... and the government apparently found it prudent to start the search for the new chair of the Audit Commission again'.[1]

It emerged that the Local Government Association had kicked up a huge fuss very late in the process over the prospective appointment as chairman of such an overtly political figure. Stephen Byers was not at that moment a minister who could afford to find himself saddled with another public row. He was already in desperate straits over his decision the previous October to push Network Rail into administration, with no compensation whatever for its outraged shareholders. A rumpus over Norman Warner's appointment was the last thing he needed. Byers decided to can it.

This came as a rude shock to Warner: he had only just quit the Labour benches in the Lords and moved to the cross-benches, precisely to deal with any objections to his political affiliation. He was enraged by Byers's decision, an anger he could scarcely disguise from the media. 'The process is in limbo and [Stephen Byers] has given no indication of what he is going to do next', he told a reporter from the *LGC*. 'I received a unanimous recommendation but if you want an explanation into the mind [*sic*] of Stephen Byers you'll have to ask him.'[2]

Adrienne Fresko soon found herself being asked by ministers if she would mind, please, remaining as the acting chair a while longer. Officials thought her permanent successor ought to be found by September. As for the controller – Andrew Foster found himself once again in a position to which he had become well accustomed in the past. It was no time to be thinking about stepping down. He and Adrienne Fresko would work happily together. (It helped, for example, that she worked as a senior figure in a private sector consultancy called the Office for Public Management, the co-founder and chief executive of which, Greg Parston, had been a private adviser to Foster since the early 1990s.) But there was no one in the Commission who doubted the real significance of what had happened to Warner's appointment. The controller was back in charge.

THE MODEL OF A MODERN
MEDIA ROUTINE

With his self-confidence restored by the evident success of the *Changing Gear* report and strategy since the autumn, Foster enjoyed something of an Indian summer. His power within Vincent Square had never been greater. Around his office on the fifth floor a coterie of 'controller's office' people had emerged over time, and even they wielded considerable authority over the rest of the staff. It was striking that at meetings of the full Commission – which after November 2001 were held only every *other* month – Foster was now accompanied by the Commission solicitor, the head of the controller's office, the Commission administrator and the Commission secretary. Of the other directors, only David Prince was a regular attendee, in his capacity as the director of operations.

Conspicuously, there was no one to represent the Public Services Research directorate. Terry Hanafin resigned in January 2002. His relationship with the controller had never really flourished after the clash in the summer of 2000 over the management of the Commission's finances. But Hanafin had anyway not intended to stay in Vincent Square for too long – and another reorganization of the NHS around this time created a compelling opportunity for him to go back into the top management echelons of the health service. He was regularly contacted through 2001 by Nigel Crisp, a colleague from former days who was now both the permanent secretary of the DoH and the chief executive of the NHS. Crisp wanted Hanafin back inside the NHS – and finally persuaded him to take on the running of one of the new Strategic Health Authorities that were announced in December 2001, replacing the old regional offices and DHAs.

It was not at all clear, in the wake of Hanafin's departure, what would happen to the Commission's studies directorate. In his controller's report for January, Foster noted that recent work on a series entitled *Lessons from Inspection* had been 'a relatively time-consuming process'. It was therefore decided now to outsource to strategy consultants four out of the five new reports that would constitute a second tranche of this series. 'It is anticipated that this will stimulate our own thinking about the future developments of the series', noted the report, 'as well as providing a challenge to current organizational models for delivering research products.'[3] It was not generally interpreted inside Vincent Square as a bright omen.

In the meantime, though, Hanafin had left behind a full pipe-line of national reports. Two of the more notable ones actually appeared just prior to his departure. One was called *A Spoonful of Sugar*, and looked into how medicines were managed by pharmacists, GP practices and hospitals. The other, *NHS Cancer Care in England and Wales*, was the product of a successful joint study between Vincent Square and the Commission for Health Improvement. (The study was directed by Jonty Boyce and managed by his longstanding colleague Dick Waite, the ornithologist, who was appropriately assisted in the work by a senior manager called David Bird.) Boyce had formed a productive partnership with CHI's chief executive, Peter Homa. Their teams delivered a first joint report that attracted an Early Day Motion in the House of Commons: tabled on 13 December, it congratulated both parent bodies on their excellent work, and expressed concern over the striking geographical inconsistencies that the report had revealed.

Under Andrew Webster, Hanafin's successor, there followed a string of notable titles. Their subjects ranged as widely as ever, from the treatment of drug abuse (*Changing Habits*) and competitive services procurement by local authorities, to the treatment of young offenders in the criminal justice system (*Route to Justice*) and the quality of patient-based information in the NHS (*Data Remember*). One report that later became especially influential (*Force for Change*) looked at the efficacy of central government intervention in education and the social services. There were more *Learning from Inspection* papers, on housing repairs and on council library services. And there were four more reviews based on the findings for the second tranche of the Acute Hospital Portfolio.

As of 2002, moreover, the Commission could still boast an impressively efficient press relations machine. In winning the contract to set up an in-house unit the previous summer, Ruth Davison had inherited an area of the Commission's operations that had been refined over many years. The routine adopted for each major national report customarily began with what was called a key-messages meeting in

Foster's office. Here the authors of a new report, having spent eighteen months or more of their lives researching and writing up their analysis of a complex social problem, would have to subject themselves to the usual pre-publication ordeal. How could the message be summed up in a few sentences, for the controller to commit to memory? What two or three facts would be of most interest to the press? Which headline would best capture the gist of the report?

The communications team had two complementary tasks. The first was to work with the authors to prepare a measured press release. This would appear on the Commission's website on the day of the report's publication, and would provide a detailed explanation of the content. Equally important, though, was the job of identifying the 'death-and-destruction' news angle – for this would determine what was said to the press in pre-launch briefings, to capture their attention and drive home the importance of the report. Briefings were given over the telephone some days ahead of a formal press conference. The Commission generally dealt not with news reporters, focused on their daily deadlines, but with health and local government correspondents who could be trusted to sit on a story until an embargo was lifted on its release. For a big report, the briefings would be intense and would typically result in an audience of 30–40 journalists for the eventual press conference in Vincent Square. Davison recalled: 'We did like to see them all lined up there in the boardroom, with the cameras on!'[4]

This would happen on the day before the formal publication date of a report, allowing the television journalists a chance to record their interviews with the controller for broadcast the next day. Release of the news would be embargoed until midnight – and any journalist who broke it knew they would never be invited to the Commission again. Davison would sometimes try to persuade Foster to let them run with a 10 p.m. embargo, so that news of a report could be broken on the late-night news programmes, and especially BBC2's *Newsnight*. Foster invariably turned down the idea. It would look odd, he insisted, to break with precedent. Of course, keeping their powder dry also meant that the news could be broken the following morning by BBC Radio 4's *Today* programme.

Being interviewed on *Today* was always one of Foster's favourite activities: he probably featured on the programme a hundred times or more during his decade at the helm. On publication day, he would arrive at around 6.30 a.m. at BBC Centre in White City, meeting there with one of the Commission's press team (often Davison) so that they could make their way together to the *Today* studio. After the interview, there might be an opportunity to appear on one of the breakfast TV shows with a host such as Eamon Holmes. Then the two of them would typically be driven back across London to the ITN studios on Gray's Inn Road for Foster to do a morning news bulletin there. Returning afterwards to the office, there would be an hour or so to review newspapers not collected during the early morning itinerary, and to check the cuttings collated by an outside agency from all the regional press. These might also include transcripts of any interviews done that morning on local radio stations, or the BBC's General News Service, which Foster was usually happy to leave to the authors of the report. Then, if the story was strong enough and carried real intrinsic interest for a wide audience, he might just make one last excursion – to the BBC at Portland Place, for an interview on the *Jimmy Young Show*.

It was an exhausting routine, yet Foster managed it – or something very like it – on almost a monthly basis. It was the hard graft that underlay the Commission's robust image in the media as a constantly alert and meticulous watchdog of the public sector. The national papers never had that much real interest in the Commission *per se*. (This was the natural territory of the *Local Government Chronicle*, *Public Finance*, *Municipal Journal* and *Health Service Journal*.) But its big reports were often the basis of headline stories that would briefly top the national news agenda. All of the top correspondents were appreciative of the professional way in which the Commission catered for their needs, and in return they gave extensive coverage to its work in ways that were envied by many other non-departmental public bodies (and some government bodies, too). The collateral promotion of the Commission, of course, made a vital contribution to its reputation.

However important on the margin, though, good press-relations work was essentially a matter of tactics. To have any worthwhile influence over policy decisions in Whitehall, the Commission still needed to be seen offering helpful ideas on government strategy – as it had done with great success in the preparation of the December White Paper. New Labour's thinking on the management of public services was now evolving faster than ever. Some decisions in 2002 would bear heavily on the future role of the Commission – and none would wait until a new chairman and controller had been found. In fact, three critical issues were brought to a head during the first nine months.

ROLLING OUT THE CPA CAMPAIGN

Paul Kirby and his team had won a notable battle over that White Paper. Now they needed to win the war. By the end of 2002, they had to deliver sensible verdicts on the performance of the 150 largest authorities in the country. It was a forbidding prospect. As of January, the methodology was far from finalized, and it was unclear how the broad concept of the Comprehensive Performance Assessment would be received by local government – not to mention the Commission's own auditors and inspectors in the field. But at least the initiative lay with the Commission. Its Young Turks were now sufficiently trusted by ministers that they were able to set their own immediate timetable and agenda. (A statutory instrument was passed in February postponing the requirement for councils to have Best Value plans audited and approved until the year-end.) And there was no longer any ambiguity in the stance taken by ministers towards the Commission. As Nick Raynsford acknowledged to the members at their monthly meeting in January, the Commission would have 'a significant role in [not only] providing an independent challenge to audited bodies but also providing guidance and support on how to improve'.[5]

There was no doubt who was leading the way. As Peter Thomas recalled: 'Paul at that point was definitely Inspection's representative on earth.'[6] Kirby made a presentation to the January meeting, explaining how he intended to proceed. He and his team would finalize a CPA methodology that could successfully combine the Commission's statutory obligations under the 1982 Act, as amended in 1998, and the 1999 Act providing for inspection. The proposals laid out in *Changing Gear* would be their starting point – but the critical feature of their work would be a heavy focus on consultation, starting with three months of intense engagement with local authorities.

Kirby recalled: 'My line was: "we don't stop to blink". It was an extraordinary time – but we had to win over hearts and minds, against some huge opposition. We had endless conferences all over the country, plus I would do a dinner three nights a week – week in, week out – with different groups of chief executives and local politicians.'[7] Kirby set up a CPA project team, basing it around members of the inspectorate but crucially recruiting local government officers, too. Rather as he had done the previous year, he charged ahead on the assumption that by the time his opponents rallied to a stand, the essential struggle would be over. The tactic worked, but as in 2001 it made Kirby plenty of enemies – not least within the Commission itself. 'The opposition was bitter – it was really quite savage. But we *were* taking a big risk.'[8] Some Commission directors and senior DA auditors – along with some partners in the private firms – were incensed by what was happening. Having watched Best Value slide into a bureaucratic muddle of epic proportions, they were in no mood for another radical experiment. Letters of protest were written to Commission members, some of whom sounded out legal advice on the prospects of halting the whole business in its tracks.

As this suggests, the legal implications of CPA were no small matter. It was proposing to deliver the kind of verdict on council politicians that had hitherto been treated as the constitutional prerogative of local electors. Kirby had in fact taken extensive legal advice on this himself, and had been assured that the Commission had all the authority required for CPA. But others were not persuaded. Neil Kinghan, a former senior civil servant who had been director of local government finance inside the DoE, was now director of local government finance at the Local Government Association, where he had been since 1997. He recalled of these months in 2002:

Paul was quite young, he was very bright and he knew what the answers were – which of course annoyed senior local government politicians no end. Here was this jumped-up young chap coming along and telling us what we should be doing, declaring such-and-such a council is excellent and such-and-such a council is poor. Well, many just thought 'who the hell does he think he is?'[9]

On one occasion, Kirby was invited to attend a meeting with around sixty local authority leaders at the LGA's offices in London's Smith Square (the former Transport House building). Kinghan recalled: 'He was given a very hard time by people who were very suspicious of the whole idea. He certainly got some very hostile questions.'

Nor were Kirby and his colleagues given much encouragement by the trade press. The *Local Government Chronicle* ran a cartoon of him as Icarus, flying so close to the sun that inspection reports were falling like lost feathers from the molten wax on his CPA wings. In an interview with the paper, Kirby picked a different story and compared the current Best Value environment to the Tower of Babel. There were so many different voices passing judgement on every council that the result was simply incomprehensible to the public. The *LGC*'s comment writers remained sceptical. 'The Audit Commission is being asked to assume omniscience like never before . . . To pull together the inspection and performance management regimes amassed over the last part of the twentieth century is one thing. To distil them into a perfect judgement, a meta-audit, is quite another.'[10]

By April 2002, though, that was exactly what Kirby's team proposed to do. The term 'meta-audit' never really caught on, but was a good description of the CPA objective. It would deliver a definitive label of quality for every council. But this would not just be based on all the available data gathered by auditors and professional inspectorates. It would also incorporate three other crucial (and largely qualitative) assessments. One would be a self-assessment by the council itself. A second would be a corporate assessment by a peer group of council officers and members from other authorities. (Here the CPA would be drawing on the example set by the work of the Improvement and Development Agency, which set great store by the work of peer groups in assisting individual councils to reform themselves.) And third, the CPA would take account of reviews by the Commission inspectors – and by the other professional inspectorates – of councils' key public services. How exactly all of these elements would be weighted for their relative importance, and traded off against each other, the team did not disclose. That would be for a later day. But the broad requirements were identified in time for the start of the 2002–03 financial year. Once all the information was collected, the 'meta-audit' would then constitute a judgement based on the answers to two questions: 'How well is this council doing?' and 'Does this council have the ability to improve itself?'

The consultative process between January and April had been far from cosmetic. It had helped to define the key ingredients of the various assessment procedures. It had also resulted in many detailed changes. For example, the project team abandoned the four categories that had been floated in the White Paper (namely, high-performing, striving, coasting and poor-performing). In their place, it was decided to have five categories with single-word descriptors: councils would be declared Excellent, Good, Fair, Weak or Poor. The months of discussion with local government had also greatly facilitated the task of setting up pilot CPA authorities that could lead the way. Ten were now chosen, and were heralded as the pathfinders.[11] Announcing them to the press in mid-February, Andrew Foster was a happy controller: 'Local authorities have almost bitten my hand off with offers [to join the pathfinders group].'[12] A further forty authorities were chosen as pilots for the appointment by the Audit Commission of 'relationship managers' who would coordinate all of its own dealings with the local authority and ensure no further confusion (or worse) between auditors and inspectors. Over the next six months, the Commission unleashed a force of 800 people in the field to collect all the data. Kirby steered the operation forward quite ruthlessly. 'We just steamrollered on!'[13]

In health, meanwhile, another steamroller was at work – and here the Commission was itself not quite so well placed. By mid-April, in fact, the controller and his colleagues were about to be left feeling distinctly flat.

BACKWARDS ON HEALTH, FORWARDS ON HOUSING

Helena Shovelton had warned her fellow commissioners the previous August that something was afoot in health regulation. She had been alerted to this by remarks made to her by Nick Raynsford, when she met the minister for their conversation about her departure. Raynsford in turn had been prompted by the outcome of what would prove to be an unusually influential official inquiry – the Kennedy Report, published in July 2001. Ian Kennedy, professor of health law, ethics and policy at University College London, and a world authority on the ethics of medical practice, had been appointed in 1998 to look into the management of children receiving complex cardiac surgery at Bristol Royal Infirmary between 1984 and 1995. There had been serious shortcomings at the hospital, resulting in some tragic deaths. The Kennedy Report provided a comprehensive analysis of what exactly had occurred in Bristol – but then went much further. In a second, almost as lengthy section of the report ('The Future'), it reappraised scrutiny arrangements across the whole of the NHS. Its findings, and recommendations, were unequivocal. It was highly critical of the fragmentation and inadequate coordination that it showed to be a prevalent feature of regulation in the health service generally. It urged that the 'various standards and forms of external inspection must be integrated into a single validation process … overseen by a single validating body'. It suggested that the Commission for Health Improvement (CHI), if 'suitably structured', might be well placed to adopt this role.

This in itself carried ominous implications for the Audit Commission – but the report went on to single out the Commission as a specific example of the kind of overlaps in health regulation that urgently needed to be rationalized. It acknowledged a clear role for the Commission in 'ensuring the proper stewardship of public finances' – no problem there. But VFM work and national reports were a different matter.

We recognize that during the 1990s the Audit Commission helped to fill a vacuum in addressing issues to do with clinical effectiveness and comparative performance. Our concern, however, is that notwithstanding the high quality of their work they continue to provide reports on such matters, even though other bodies, in particular NICE and CHI, are now established. In proposing a single validating body and the rationalization of the inspection industry, therefore, we see the need for reappraising the future of this second role of the Audit Commission.[14]

By the time of the report's publication, Peter Wilkinson had already handed over his Knowledge and Information portfolio to another director, Sue Barnes, to take up a new role as director for health strategy. He submitted a paper to the Commission members on the Kennedy Report's implications, which they discussed at their September 2001 meeting. On one point especially the members seemed to be unanimously agreed: the report was mistaken 'in suggesting that auditors' responsibilities for the "3Es" can be easily de-coupled from what it calls "financial stewardship"'.[15] The threat to the Commission's health franchise, though, could hardly have been clearer. As part of their response, members resolved immediately to seek a closer working relationship with CHI. It was worrying that CHI had chosen to submit a response on the report to the Department of Health in August, without even consulting with the controller. But joint-study work with CHI was going ahead smoothly – a second study, on diagnostic practices in the detection of coronary heart disease, was about to be launched in the wake of the cancer services report – and members appeared confident that the two bodies could work together effectively without radical alteration to the role of the Commission. This, anyway, was the gist of the Commission's formal sixteen-page response to the government in October. 'CHI and the Audit Commission should work jointly at national and local levels to address clinical and corporate governance in the round, so that assessments of clinical and resource decision-making are considered together as part of a unified whole.'[16] To drive home the message, Adrienne Fresko and Andrew Foster had meetings with their counterparts at CHI, and a lively exchange of letters followed about future cooperation.

The brutal truth, though, was that the CHI was as powerless as the Commission in determining how the consequences of the Kennedy Report would play out. The decisions would all be made in the Department of Health – where Vincent Square's stock was as low as it had ever been. After years of antipathy, the officials in Richmond House were not about to let slip an opportunity, at last, to clip the Commission's wings. The department published its formal response to the Kennedy Report in January 2002. It was a reply that roamed quite broadly over the government's plans for the future structure of the NHS, already outlined in legislation (in the NHS Reform and Health Care Professions Bill) before Parliament. Yet an executive summary running to thirty-two paragraphs over eight pages contained *not a single reference* to the Audit Commission. Considering the contribution made by the Commission's health studies through the 1990s, it was an eloquent omission. And buried within the response was confirmation of the bad news that Foster and his colleagues must have been dreading.

[The Kennedy Report has called for] a reappraisal of the future role of the Audit Commission in addressing issues to do with clinical effectiveness and the comparative performance of NHS bodies. We accept the logic of this and will take further steps at the earliest opportunity ... to move away from the fragmentation that Professor Kennedy has highlighted.[17]

It was a real blow for the Commission. Jonty Boyce recalled: 'I remember seeing Andrew after he heard the news that day. He looked absolutely devastated.' What exactly the government's 'further steps' would entail, no one could be quite sure. But they seemed certain to make a significant dent in the Commission's overall remit, which had hitherto grown steadily through almost twenty years. The full implications would hang over the health directorate for three long months.

By an unfortunate chance, a parallel turn of events was meanwhile unfolding on the social services front. The murder in horrific circumstances of a little girl called Victoria Climbiè in Haringey in 2000 had prompted an inquiry into the failure of the social services to prevent her death. Chaired by Lord Laming, the inquiry would not present its final report until January 2003. But an independent report had in the meantime been commissioned by the Social Services Inspectorate into the future of the Joint Reviews staff set up by the SSI and the Commission back in 1996. Early in 2002 this report urged the setting up of a new and separate commission for social care inspection. The controller told members about the report's existence in March 2002, though he felt constrained to hold back the full content. (The March minutes recorded: 'The controller had received a copy of the report under strict confidential cover and was not at liberty to share the report with the Commission. The controller had written to the ministers concerned asking for permission to share the report.'[18]) So by April, it was not just the Commission's NHS work that was suddenly under threat.

The government's decisions finally emerged in Gordon Brown's budget, on 16 April. He announced the government's intention to set up two new 'super' inspectorates. One, a Commission for Social Care Inspection (CSCI), would replace the Joint Reviews staff in social services. The other, a successor body to CHI, would take over VFM studies and inspection in the NHS. Both would be given statutory powers in fresh legislation to be drafted in the coming months. The chancellor, though, provided few further details about the latter body. The board of CHI seemed to believe for some months that it would effectively be a son-of-CHI, with many of the same people in charge. But it was evident from the government's plans for new legislation that a clean break was intended. Unfortunately, the budget disclosure took the health secretary, Alan Milburn, by surprise. He had not quite finalized his thinking on the new commission – indeed, as of the afternoon of Budget Day, he had still not decided what to call it.

Andrew Foster had been in constant dialogue with the minister and his advisers for some time on the implications of the new NHS inspectorate for the Audit Commission. He met that evening with Milburn to hear about the minister's proposal to announce further details in the Commons the next day. Stories would soon be circulating in Whitehall about how Foster, Milburn and the minister's advisers had sat late into the night trying desperately to think of a name for the putative body. Since it would be taking on some of the audit function of the Commission, it was resolved finally to add 'A' for audit to the acronym for Commission for Healthcare Inspection. This produced CHAI (Commission for Healthcare Audit and Inspection) – sadly a homonym for CHI and a guarantee of confusion for months to come.

The next day, Foster and his chairman were summoned to a meeting with Stephen Byers. Arriving at the DTLR, they were hardly surprised to find the health secretary, Alan Milburn, sitting with Byers in his office. There was not much time for any discussion of the agenda, which obviously related to Milburn's planned statement to the House that afternoon: the four of them had to leave the DTLR immediately and walk across Parliament Square to see the prime minister in Downing Street. They were shown into Blair's study, and found him flanked by the chief secretary to the Treasury, Andrew Smith, and Alastair Campbell. It was a remarkable turnout. Adrienne Fresko recalled:

They were at great pains to tell us how respected the Audit Commission was – how important and influential it was as a model, which they would now like to replicate in the health service. They were extremely complimentary and Tony Blair had clearly been very well briefed. But the message was simple: they felt they needed to have just one regulator in healthcare.

And that was not going to be the Commission. Or at least, not for the kind of VFM and clinical governance issues that had been part of its health franchise since 1990. The audit of NHS bodies' finances would remain the Commission's responsibility. Other aspects of audit work would be handled by the Commission only in so far as it was undertaken at the behest of CHAI. Milburn duly made his announcement later in the day. A document setting out the proposed changes, *Delivering the NHS Plan*, made clear that it would probably be another two years before the two new bodies – CSCI and CHAI – were actually up and running with the necessary statutory backing. In the meantime, the Audit Commission and other affected parties would be working for a smooth hand-over.

The extraordinary care taken by ministers to avoid a row with the Commission was undeniably a tribute to its stature in Whitehall. But it was also a shrewd bid for the Commission's active support over the next couple of years. As the *Guardian* noted a week later: 'Labour could . . . be going into a general election campaign in 2005 with very little, if any, hard evidence from the new inspectorates. It badly needs to keep the current regulators on side.'[19] Foster responded as positively as he could and took pains to ensure that the press noted his determination to assist with the implementation of the new regime. 'Foster says his preferred solution would have been partnership working through joint teams', reported the *Guardian* in the same article, 'but he accepts that ministers have chosen to go another route towards a goal he had argued for.' Blair had assured him and Adrienne Fresko that the Commission would have an active role in developing the two new inspectorates. They would try to make the very most of this assurance. The controller was also careful to point out to the media that losing the remit for national reports and VFM work would directly affect less than half of the research staff – but this in itself amounted to a huge disruption for the Commission, with the loss of about thirty-five studies personnel and thereby most of the Commission's accumulated expertise in the health sector. Foster was on stronger ground when he reminded journalists that the new era would make little difference to the Commission's income from the health sector, which overwhelmingly consisted of fees for the local work done by auditors.

Indeed, Foster and his health director – Wilkinson had been promoted from 'health strategy' to 'health' now that he was immersed in the real world of health tactics – went to great trouble over the following months to explain that the Commission's audit remit at a local level necessarily entailed a continuing involvement in VFM work, since this was an integral part of the Code of Audit Practice. Wilkinson worked hard over the summer to win acceptance on this point, which prompted much wrangling over the demarcation line between the future CHAI's mandate and the Commission's. Objections were raised both by CHI and by health department officials, who plainly construed the code argument as a disingenuous attempt to claw back the VFM franchise. Regular progress reports from Wilkinson to Commission members spelt out the tiresome details. The minutes of their July meeting noted that the Treasury and the Office of the Deputy Prime Minister were being supportive of the Commission – but 'the Department of Health are driving the process and are not sharing ministerial drafts with AC staff'.[20] In short, it seemed to be business-as-usual in dealings with Richmond House. Adrienne Fresko was soon writing to the health secretary, Alan Milburn, to complain that Tony Blair's assurances about a continuing involvement in the work on the new inspectorates had not been worth much: 'Whilst there have been constructive meetings between officials, we do not feel that the process so far has lived up to the spirit of the Prime Minister's promise.'[21] But Wilkinson pressed doggedly on, even making presentations to policy staff in Downing Street, and the VFM point was eventually taken aboard.

Such complicated turf squabbles were hardly unusual around this time, as the post-2001 Blair government grappled with its agenda for the management of public services. In one area, though, the Commission emerged as a clear winner. Its housing inspectorate under Roy Irwin had begun operations in July 2000. By March 2002, it had published no fewer than 192 reports and enjoyed a good reputation within the sector for the general quality of its work. It was gearing up by the spring of 2002 to take on reviews of another government initiative. Local authorities were to be given the option of outsourcing the management of their housing stock without taking the ultimate step of transferring it (as many did) to an independent housing association. The half-way house, as it were, was known as an arm's-length management organization (ALMO). Reviewing the performance of the ALMOs would be another job for the Commission. But a bigger opportunity lay around the corner.

In the same budget speech that caught Alan Milburn on the hop, the chancellor announced the government's intention to have a single housing inspectorate, in place of the two that currently existed. One of these belonged to the Commission, the other to the Housing Corporation, which was responsible for the governance of housing associations (HAs). (In fact, the second had only just been set up. The Housing Corporation had been urged in a civil service review back in 2000 to introduce inspections along the lines adopted by the Commission in local government, but had been very slow to comply.) So which of the two existing bodies would take on the combined housing brief – or might both lose out to a freshly minted institution? The chancellor offered no clues to this decision. It was ostensibly left to the relevant department, the DTLR. At the end of May 2002, however, Stephen Byers resigned and the DTLR was broken up. Transport went its own way, while the local government and regional affairs portfolio passed to a new department, the Office of the Deputy Prime Minister (ODPM), under John Prescott. Its first permanent secretary, transferring from the Cabinet Office, was Mavis McDonald. With her long experience of the public housing sector, she was soon presiding over the inspectorates decision.

Given its tardy introduction of HA inspections, there was no question of the brief passing automatically to the Housing Corporation. But the Corporation's chairman, Brenda Dean, was a tough former trade unionist who wasted no time putting her case to Prescott. How far he committed himself in private is not clear, but officials at the Corporation were soon confident that their chairman had won him over. As Prescott's local government minister, Raynsford was strongly opposed to giving the combined role to the Corporation. He thought it would be damaging to the CPA process. Coming so soon after the announcement of CHAI, it would also be a blow to the credibility of the Commission. He urged Prescott to reconsider.[22] And he had broad support from officials, who respected what Roy Irwin's inspectorate had already achieved since being set up in April 1999. Raynsford also had support from the Treasury.

As a member of Gordon Brown's public productivity panel over the years, Andrew Foster had missed no opportunity to remind Treasury officials of the greater rigour that the Commission would bring to the task. Foster recalled: 'The Housing Corporation was both the funder and the regulator of the HAs, which was crazy. I had been putting the argument to Treasury people that if they ever wanted to sort this out, they had to split the roles – and we would be available to do the regulation.'[23] The Treasury publicly ruled out a new body in June, but no further decisions surfaced before August. Roy Irwin took his family off to Portugal for their summer holiday at the beginning of the month. They came home on Sunday, 18 August, and Irwin was looking forward to another week off in Scotland. Switching on his home voicemail recorder, he found an urgent message awaiting him from the controller's office. John Prescott would be visiting Vincent Square on the coming Wednesday, to hear from the Commission why it ought to be given the combined housing inspectorate. Irwin was in charge of the presentation.

It was one of the more important ministerial visits to Vincent Square. A slightly grumpy Prescott arrived at 2.30 p.m., straight from a lunch with the Chinese ambassador which he had not enjoyed. Accompanying him were seven officials from his department. Irwin was supported by one of his lead housing inspectors, Jo Killian, and had beside him Andrew Foster, Adrienne Fresko and Gerard Lemos, who was certainly the most knowledgeable Commission member on housing matters. The meeting lasted an hour and a half. It seemed to go well. Irwin put this down to his team's readiness to explain how they would deal with the unfamiliar world of HAs. (The Housing Corporation scored poorly on this count, saying nothing about councils at its presentation the next day.) But Prescott also enjoyed hearing a little about the Commission's work with local authorities – and especially its audacity in ticking off the councillors of Sedgefield – Tony Blair's constituency – for their sub-standard housing policies. Foster also felt the presentation had gone well: 'Frankly, Roy couldn't have been more ideal: gritty, northern, down to earth and practical.'[24]

The deputy prime minister announced his decision at the Labour Party conference in Blackpool at the start of October. From April 2003, the Commission would be responsible for a combined housing inspectorate. It was a significant victory for the Commission, which in due course would add about forty people to its staff and around £2.5 million to its revenues for 2003–04. It also helped to strengthen a close relationship between Vincent Square and Raynsford: Foster and Irwin knew the minister had batted on their behalf, in persuading Prescott to throw open the contest. At Blackpool, though, there was really only one question that every Labour politician had for the Commission. Was Comprehensive Performance Assessment going to work?

DELIVERING CPA, AND THE AFTERMATH

As local government minister, Nick Raynsford had already decided the answer by July. The pilot schemes had delivered everything that could have been expected of them. He came to the Commissioners' monthly meeting in July and offered his congratulations to the controller and his CPA team on the work completed so far. He thought it was important that the outcome was 'not seen as a crude process of naming and shaming'. But the impact of the self-assessment and peer-group procedures had already taken them beyond that point. Raynsford was confident of success, and told members 'the full support of the Government and close working relationship with the Audit Commission was [sic] a key aspect in this'.[25] The beauty of the CPA framework, as Raynsford was effectively acknowledging, was that it allowed for a degree of iterative consultation between the councils and those in charge of the assessment process. Shrewdly handled, this could facilitate an outcome that would be politically acceptable without compromising the integrity of the whole process. And Raynsford had every trust in Kirby to handle it accordingly.

The data assembled by September went into a black box, as far as most people were concerned, and emerged in a series of final ratings that no one outside the process was really in a position to challenge or verify. This left Kirby and his colleagues with scope enough to determine how the broad range of ratings would fall. By weighting the various criteria differently, they could produce either a set of results to show that local government was a basket case, or else a different set illustrating how far it was on the mend. In the end, the dials were tuned in such a way as to ensure that 51 per cent of all the councils received a positive score – mostly 'Good', but with some deemed 'Excellent'. A small group – including Kent, Camden and a born-again Westminster – emerged as flagship authorities, while fewer than ten names were identified as truly calamitous councils that needed urgent help. One of the terrible ten was the deputy prime minister's home city of Hull.

Individual councils were notified of their ratings in November, and the entire CPA table was published in December. The response in local government was broadly positive – for two reasons above all others. With only a few exceptions, Kirby and his colleagues seemed to have called the shots with remarkable accuracy. And they had prepared the ground immaculately. Neil Kinghan recalled:

People's views of CPA changed [over the course of 2002] because the Commission did a good job of involving them, consulting with them and getting them to help shape the way that CPA would work. But the big test came in December – and on the whole, people agreed with its findings. They thought it had got things about right.[26]

The media, too, responded encouragingly. Indeed, the authoritative public policy editor of the *Financial Times*, Nicholas Timmins, delivered what was almost an encomium to CPA by the standards of most local government coverage over the years.[27] His verdict, published in January 2003, is worth quoting at length, for it marked a watershed of sorts:

What was the best thing about the Audit Commission's mighty assessment of the performance of local authorities published just before Christmas? Answer: it was a stunningly slim document which, in a mere 18 pages, allowed not just the local government anoraks but average citizens to see where their council stood, both locally and in relation to others.

For those who have tangled with the mighty weight of performance indicators that the Commission has used in the past to measure service performance – hundreds of pages of the things – this was a distinct form of light among the darkness.

From a mass of data ... came a clear and simple picture ... The results, needless to say, have not avoided controversy ... But what, nonetheless, has made the process sing is that rather than just measure service quality and customer satisfaction, the CPA has included an assessment of each council's capacity to improve. And that judgment has been applied as much to the politicians' ability to run the council as it has to the senior officers.

It might be thought that nothing could be more controversial. The whole point of elections, after all, is that if you don't like this lot you can throw them out and put the other lot in to see if they can do a better job.

But the brute truth of local politics is that there are parts of the country that for decades have been controlled by one party. The real power struggles have been within parties rather than between them, giving the electorate no say in who runs their local services.

And strangely enough – despite the acute nervousness in local government in the run-up to the publication of the results – local politicians appear in the main to have accepted, in a surprisingly grown-up way, that the question of how well they perform is not an unfair one to ask.

Across the country, regional and local newspapers gave huge prominence to the CPA ratings awarded to their authorities. On the day of CPA's publication, Neil Kinghan found himself at a meeting with one of the authorities rated 'Poor' – North East Lincolnshire. Its local Grimsby-based newspaper splashed 'Failure' across its front page. He recalled: 'The council people were upset and they thought it was unfair. But they took it seriously.'[28] Politically, it would inevitably take some time for the impact to become clear, but the early signs suggested CPA had made its mark. A year later, in fact, of all those chief executives who had worked for more than six months in the authorities rated 'Poor', not a single one remained.

As this striking fact attested, it was not just municipal reputations but individuals' careers that were at stake over CPA. In such circumstances, and however lavish the prior consultations, it is perhaps surprising that more of the councils with unflattering scores did not look to the courts for redress. After all, as already noted, the initial work on CPA had prompted plenty of misgivings on legal grounds. Kirby and his team had taken legal advice that CPA did not exceed the Commission's powers. But there was more than enough room, as ever, for different lawyers to take a different view. In the event, only two councils – Ealing ('weak') and Torbay ('poor') – took their scores amiss with sufficient umbrage to seek immediate judicial reviews of the whole process. Indeed, Ealing even sought an emergency injunction at the last minute to stop publication of the CPA results. But the request for an injunction was refused, and both councils quickly abandoned their claims against the Commission in return for promises that their rights to a loftier category would be looked at again. In the meantime, an express power to categorize councils was added to the 2003 Local Government Bill, to put the statutory basis of CPA beyond doubt.

By the beginning of 2003, though, the Commission had been shaken by doubts of another kind about CPA. Or rather, about how to restructure for a CPA-oriented future. Through much of 2002, running along in parallel with the CPA campaign itself, the Commission's senior managers had been struggling with an intractable clash of views over the optimal shape of the organization. The arguments had been simmering almost since the departure of Helena Shovelton late in 2001, and they were brought to a head by an initiative known as the Organizational Development (OD) review. Foster launched it early in 2002, believing that substantial changes were needed. A stream of OD papers and staff conferences followed, with Fresko and many of her colleagues taking an active interest in the process.

There followed months of constant debate about the way that the Commission handled many aspects of its business. Progress on electronic publishing, for example, prompted new ways of distributing national reports. Sue Barnes, as the new knowledge and information director, had inherited a busy programme of work on setting up both an internet website and an intranet for the Commission. She made a presentation to members on her team's work at an Awayday meeting in Beaconsfield in May 2002 and was congratulated by them 'on making the knowledge strategy a reality'.[29] Shortly afterwards, the Commission began to make its national reports available via a download from the website. At the peak of its hard-copy publishing activity, the Commission had been turning out perhaps 7,000 copies of a typical report, for distribution to local government and Whitehall departments. This was soon to be a thing of the past. From the outset, though, it was evident to everyone in the Commission that one issue above all had to be resolved. Would DA and the inspectorate continue to function separately – albeit within a better coordinated framework, over time – or was the day fast approaching when they would finally have to be merged into one field force?

It was equally evident that there were essentially two opposing camps. Leading one camp was Alan Meekings, who had succeeded David Prince in October 2000 as the head of DA. Supported by Prince in his role as director of operations, Meekings wanted to see DA reasserting its leadership of the Commission's field force. He saw this as the only practical way to resolve the confusion that had plagued many of the Commission's field operations and troubled many of DA's clients ever since the launch of Thomson's inspectorate in April 2000. But detaching the inspectorate from the Commission in order to combine it with DA was hardly a practical proposition: unlike the auditors with their statutory independence, the inspectors spoke for the Commission. Subordinating them to an arm's-length DA would also have run directly counter to the political rationale for creating the inspectorate in the first place. Reasserting DA's lead in the field would therefore require a root-and-branch restructuring, merging DA and the inspectorate together as an integral department within the Commission. Most of the members sympathized with this view – as did Trish Longdon, Peter Wilkinson and Martin Evans on the management board.

The opposing camp, of course, was led by Kirby. He was opposed to merging auditors and inspectors, both in principle and in practice. The latter objection certainly was uppermost in his mind through 2002: if the field force allowed itself to be distracted by the debate over integration, then CPA might be derailed. By the same token, he had little time to spare for the debate inside Vincent Square over these months. He deliberately stayed away from it, assuming (rightly) that

Andrew Foster would put no obstacles in his path so long as he was pushing on with CPA's implementation successfully.

Trying hard to find a 'third way' compromise between the two of them was Peter Thomas, who took over from Joanne Shaw as director of performance development in January 2002. This put him on to the management board, along with Kirby and Andrew Webster, now head of Public Services Research (PSR). Thomas suspected that many auditors and inspectors alike were less than convinced of the need for fundamental structural changes. He thought that DA had undergone such a thorough upgrade in recent years, and was proving itself so flexible in adapting to CPA, that a more gradual evolution of the Commission's field presence might be the better option. That said, Thomas could see that the arrival of CPA, the impending change in the health remit and some uncertainty over PSR's future made it imperative that the board should be asking itself tough questions about the strategic goals of the Commission. He wanted to see open discussion on the management board, to reach a shared position on strategy which could then inform a proper debate about the most appropriate structure for the future. It never happened. Too many discussions took place bilaterally between the controller and individual directors, without a proper briefing for the management team as a whole. Too much time was spent on inconsequential technical matters, with ever more elaborate power-point presentations on the management of relationships at a local level. Thomas recalled:

We didn't ask the basic question, 'What is the right size and shape of the Commission?' I completely failed to find a way of working with the team that would allow us to address the real issues. Our failure to do that should have been challenged by the Commission, but it wasn't. I think that it was a basic governance failure by both parties.[30]

It was not how Fresko and her controller saw matters. She felt comfortable that there was a broad commitment all across the Commission to grasp the nettle on reintegrating DA and the inspectorate. Unminuted discussions among the members and the management team at the away-day session in May 2002, at a hotel in Beaconsfield, appear to have persuaded everyone there that big changes were essential. Something Had To Be Done. The outcome, announced by Andrew

Foster to the Commission at its monthly meeting in July, was a radical restructuring that would start with some immediate appointments and continue through to a conclusion in April 2003. At its heart would be the formation of a new operations directorate. It would subsume both the CPA inspectorate and DA. Its first director would be DA's head, Alan Meekings. The existing operations director, David Prince, would take charge of a remodelled strategy and resources department. Peter Wilkinson, as director of health, would continue to coordinate negotiations with the DoH over CHAI's emergence, while supervising some significant studies that were currently well under way. Other important but less controversial moves around this time included a restructuring of the ACiW management team in Cardiff. The Commission's work for Wales had become increasingly specific to the principality, in response to a steadily growing appetite for its output in Welsh local government circles and among National Assembly members. It was also becoming clear by the summer of 2002 that the Welsh Assembly Government was determined to seek a merger between ACiW and the National Audit Office in Cardiff, to produce a new regulatory body tailored to Welsh needs. Whatever the outcome on that front, a more heavyweight presence for the Commission seemed desirable. Andrew Foster appointed as 'director general of the Audit Commission in Wales' a lawyer and former local authority chief executive, Clive Grace.

None of this promised an especially ceremonious ending to 159 years of history for District Audit and the DAS. This, though, was low on the list of objections raised by Paul Kirby when he heard of the proposals. Kirby was amazed by them. In the first place, it had been his understanding that he, Thomas, Webster and Barnes were the core of any future management team. Foster had met with them regularly and assured them that a board restructuring would be aimed in due course at installing a much smaller team, built round the four of them. This notion appeared now to have been shelved. The operations directorate would effectively implement the structure long envisaged by David Prince, Trish Longdon, Martin Evans and Peter Wilkinson. Leaving aside personalities and office politics, Kirby was also hugely disappointed that the new directorate would take the Commission in the opposite direction from the one that he and his immediate colleagues in the inspectorate had in mind.

We all had a passion that the Commission needed to mark that moment in time, which I'd described as a sort of apotheosis of regulation. I said: 'We've graded everybody, we can now see what needs to be done, we need to scale all this down. We should halve the Commission's workforce immediately!' We were all busy talking about what could now make a difference, instead of audit and inspection. If we could get councils to be brilliant at the analytical stuff, we could get our people in the field to work with their top teams so that they would become much better at improving themselves. That was what we should be doing for the next couple of years.[31]

One other aspect of the summer restructuring seriously bothered Kirby: his objection in principle. Was it really right that the controller should pursue such a radical course, just as he was preparing in the months ahead to take his leave from the Commission? Speculation about his departure date was rife within Vincent Square. Commission members had been promised firm news of a new chairman in the autumn. Should not decisions about the basic shape of the Commission not wait at least until his/her arrival?

No compromise was reached. Foster was adamant that big changes were needed, in the face of what had happened to DA. Kirby insisted that the mooted plan would produce turmoil across the organization and a haemorrhage of its most talented people. In the end, he himself was the first to hand in his notice. He resigned in September. Peter Thomas left the same month, accepting a post in the Cabinet Office as deputy director of Michael Barber's Delivery Unit. Andrew Webster would leave early in 2003, joining the London borough of Lambeth as their executive director of social services. The remaining key member of Foster's 'CPA team', Sue Barnes, would depart a few months later for a senior management job with Suffolk County Council.

With no other job in prospect, Kirby himself agreed with the controller that he would stay until the results of CPA were finalized in November. The Commission members were sorry to see him go – and sorrier still, perhaps, on hearing the news within days of his leaving that he had followed Thomas into the Cabinet Office, at the behest of the newly appointed cabinet secretary, Andrew Turnbull. (In a curious twist to the story, Kirby was soon taking over some of the functions there that had been launched in 2001 by Wendy Thomson.) As it happened, Kirby left just days before the new chairman's arrival. The appointment of James Strachan was announced on 5 November and he walked into Vincent Square that same day. He and Kirby met for several private discussions over the following months, though, and there was much on which they were heartily agreed.

ENLARGING THE CHAIRMAN'S OFFICE

After responding positively to a call out of the blue from head-hunters, Strachan had been sent their job specification for the chairmanship in the usual way. When he set it beside his CV, the two documents matched like a pair of gloves. They wanted someone who had managed and led a complex customer-focused organization: he had worked as an investment banker for thirteen years with the US-based Merrill Lynch, heading various operations from London and becoming its youngest ever managing director. They wanted someone with innovative entrepreneurial experience: he had run his own glass wholesaling business. They wanted someone with regulatory experience: he had been on the board of Ofgem, the gas and electricity regulator, for four years up to 2004. And they wanted (finally) someone with a good knowledge of the public sector: for five years Strachan had run one of the more important national charities for disabled people, the Royal National Institute for the Deaf, was well known to ministers for his work on behalf of the disabled and had sat for three years on the board of the National Lottery's community fund. His application must have been a feast for the head-hunter's eye.

Even to the untutored eye, though, there were two features of his career up to that point which stood out as quite remarkable. The first was that Strachan was one of those unusual people who had succeeded in the City, making a lot of money in the process, and then quit while still a relatively young man to pursue a wide range of other interests. Since leaving Merrill Lynch in 1989, aged only 36, he had turned his hand with some considerable success to photography and journalism even while building his impressive portfolio of jobs in the regulatory and charity worlds. The second extraordinary fact took a moment to grasp. Strachan had been born deaf. He could just detect sounds in the lower half of the speech range, but was completely cut off from the rest. If he was not looking at you, he was not listening (which could be disconcerting and made him a hard man to interrupt). But he had mastered lip-reading to an astonishing degree. When the Commission's Ruth Davison heard him mimic her north country accent in jest, she was utterly disbelieving. Strachan was able to lip-read regional accents. Anyone at a board meeting with Strachan who waved fingers in the air at him, by way of pointing out a number, had mistaken their man.

His was a CV that attested at every turn to a man of fierce drive and determination. Unsurprisingly, he made it clear at an early stage of the selection process that the job he envisaged doing might need to be even more than the (unprecedented) three-days-a-week appointment that had been advertised. Ministers and officials in the ODPM were entirely comfortable with the idea of a far more assertive chairman than had existed in the past. They warmed to it further as talks continued. Strachan had some compelling ideas about the job. He had been interested in regulation since reading economics and English at Cambridge, and he had refined his thinking about the future of regulation during his time at Ofgem. He was broadly of the belief that regulatory regimes had gone too far: he had much sympathy for the basic message of Michael Power's 1994 paper, *The Audit Explosion*. There were many contexts, in his view, where less could be better. The ideal outcome he liked to describe as 'strategic regulation'. All of this struck a chord with Nick Raynsford in particular. It seemed to the local government minister exactly what was required as a corrective to procedures at the Audit Commission that he thought had become far too formulaic. He recalled:

I wasn't convinced that the Commission was actually at the cutting edge of major change in local government services. I thought the whole CPA idea was extremely exciting, but we also needed to go down this route of cutting back on regulation. I could see James wanted to make a real impact. He wanted to focus the regulatory function much more on driving up standards – with less frequent inspections, less intrusion, and much better targeting. I found all that very appealing.[32]

There was a slight snag. Officials expressed concern that Strachan's partner was Tessa Blackstone, who had been a minister in the Labour government for six years and was now a Labour life peer. No one wanted to see a repeat of the embarrassment over Norman Warner's last-minute rejection, eight months earlier. But Raynsford stood his ground resolutely. He insisted that Strachan was a uniquely well qualified candidate. John Prescott agreed. The papers went through, with Tony Blair – as well as Prescott, Alan Milburn and Peter Hain, as secretary of state for Wales – approving Strachan's appointment as the new chairman with an extended remit to work up to a maximum of four days a week, until a new chief executive was properly into his stride. This quasi-executive status came as quite a surprise to the Commission members. Some of them had met the new man informally at the Labour Party annual conference in Blackpool a month earlier: Strachan had attended the Commission's fringe party as an interested outsider (though his candidature was known to all). But that was an occasion for charming banter. It was only after his arrival at Vincent Square that his proposed change to the governance structure became apparent.

Strachan ducked the November meeting in favour of introducing himself to each of the members individually through that month. The next members' meeting came round in the last week of January 2003 – by which time, attending the first-floor boardroom as usual, the members could not help observing that the adjacent office belonging to the chairman had grown very much larger and smarter since November. Fresko's colleagues did not need her professional opinion as an occupational psychologist to help them interpret the implications of this. Nor did Andrew Foster. As controller, he had run Vincent Square since David Cooksey's departure in 1995 with remarkably few real constraints on his authority. Playing second fiddle to a powerful chairman was not how he had imagined orchestrating his final months in office. Nonetheless, he did his best to adapt to the situation. It would take months to find a new controller, and Foster remained passionately committed to the institution he had led for so long. A confidential minute was added to the record of January's commissioners' meeting, acknowledging the arrangements made in November 2001 for the controller's departure and noting an agreement now that Foster would stay to facilitate a smooth hand-over of responsibilities to his successor. Accordingly, his leaving date was 'likely to be just before or just after the summer'. As was already apparent to everyone by 23 January, it was not going to be an easy half-year.

It took James Strachan only a couple of months from his appointment to confirm in his own mind what he had long suspected. As a bastion of the regulatory culture that he saw as overblown and poorly targeted, the Commission itself was predictably an institution in urgent need of a radical shake-up. He was disconcerted to find no current strategic plan. He was dismayed to hear people talking about the field force as though it was merely a gloss on the old DA, still as detached as ever from the rest of the organization. He watched as the exodus of impressive young directors continued, with the departure of Webster in January. And he saw Vincent Square as a compartmentalized head office that reflected only too well the rule of fiefdoms within the Commission, which left it fragmented and, to his way of thinking, oddly dysfunctional. Having made this diagnosis by the start of 2003, Strachan powered ahead with a speed and thoroughness that stunned the old guard in Vincent Square. A series of internal changes effectively demolished much of the Commission's twenty-year-old culture, along with the management structure that had already endured so much upheaval since 1999.

The governance of the Commission itself was the first apple-cart to be up-ended. All of the members' sub-committees were scrapped, except the Audit Committee, which Strachan felt urgently needed to be strengthened. This prompted the appointment to the Commission in May of Brian Pomeroy, a former senior partner of the City firm Deloitte Consulting (and the first chairman, as it happened, of the reconstituted National Lottery Commission in 1999, who had handed over the one-year post to Helena Shovelton in 2000 while remaining one of its five members). A strategy board, unsurprisingly regarded as an undesirable 'inner circle' by those not invited to be on it, was also disbanded. At the same time, the new chairman was disarmingly candid with his colleagues about his intention to seek ministerial approval for a substantial change in the membership.

By July, it was clear that some intended changes needed a statutory amendment and would take time to implement. But Strachan pressed ahead quickly with his main objective: and by the end of 2003, he had liaised closely with department officials – and made his own views strongly felt – over the appointment of a further five new commissioners. Nine commissioners stepped down over the course of the year, including Adrienne Fresko, whose prodigious labours since 1996 on behalf of the Commission must have far exceeded her original expectations. The other eight were Richard Arthur (appointed in 1996), Julie Baddeley (1999), Judy Curson (1998), Sue Richards (1997), Nick Skellett (2000), Chris Swinson (2000), David Williams (1997) and Brian Wolfe (1999). The five new recruits plus Brian Pomeroy joined seven existing commissioners: John Bowen, Elizabeth Filkin, Graham Hart, Roger Hoyle, Pauleen Lane, Gerard Lemos and David Moss. So there was some continuity – but the Board had clearly to establish a fresh dynamic.

As a chairman, Strachan was a stickler for detail in all presentational matters and insisted on a meticulous handling of all Commission papers. Nomenclature was also important: now that 'The Audit Commission' was a badge worn by everyone in the organization, the members would be described as sitting on 'The Board'. The controller's monthly report was re-formatted and combined with a performance report. The minutes of monthly meetings were littered for the first time with 'Action' paragraphs. In the same spirit, the Annual Report for the year to October 2002 which appeared in March was briskly businesslike. Each sector of the Commission's activities received the same treatment, with a summary review of targets, impact over the year and priorities for the year ahead. The whole package needed only thirty-two pages.

These were superficial details, perhaps, but they had a cumulative impact on the way that things were done. There was nothing superficial about the chairman's decision to put himself forward as the public face of the Commission, relegating Foster to the bench. Other public bodies and the media were quick to note the change. When the author of the Kennedy Report was appointed as 'shadow' chairman of CHAI in December 2002, for example, it was Strachan rather than Foster that he telephoned to suggest a discussion about CHAI's relationship with the Commission. (Kennedy never met Foster at all.) Journalists were at first simply intrigued by the novelty of Strachan's appointment, but they soon realized that it was he and not the controller who was setting the Commission's real agenda. Strachan was keen to accommodate them – and Ruth Davison now had an awkward dilemma each time she was called by the *Today* programme. (It was resolved once Strachan had made clear that all invitations should be passed to him.) In one public forum after another, Strachan stepped to the fore. When the Parliamentary Public Administration Committee wanted to grill the Commission in January 2003, it was the chairman who went along. And the controller now found himself regularly upstaged at national conferences, such as a Next Steps on CPA conference held in April.

Andrew Foster would have been less than human had none of this irked him. Stepping down in the summer was one thing; being sidelined while still in his office was quite another. He found the situation deeply uncomfortable on several counts. Strachan's views on regulation were completely at odds with the instinctive flair that he himself had shown in expanding the Commission's activities for a decade. Temperamentally, he and the new chairman were streets apart – and so too were their personal styles in the office. Foster abhorred open confrontation; Strachan thrived on it. Most unsettling, perhaps, was the fact that his new chairman obviously intended to take a grip on the Commission's affairs down to a level of detail that had eluded even the controller himself. Since he was leaving in the summer, Foster certainly had no interest in compounding the difficulties inherent in the situation. He recalled: 'I had given myself quite a talking to, that I wanted to leave in a dignified way – so I was prepared to start backing down. I'd had my turn running things and was happy to hand over.'[33] That said, he was under no obligation to make free with his address book and share relationships in Whitehall that he had been nurturing for a decade or more. On many detailed issues, his hold over the Commission's business was unassailable. The atmosphere in Vincent Square grew more charged by the month.

In these circumstances, a less resolute chairman than Strachan might have opted to bide his time on substantive changes to the institution, restricting himself to broad policy speeches and the like. Instead, Strachan drove ahead with characteristic determination. First, he committed the Commission to relocating within London. A report on the available options was presented to the Commission by David Prince in March 2003, and by July the whole project was approved.[34] The premises in Vincent Square and Greycoat Street would be vacated. The operations from both would be transferred to the Embankment's Millbank Tower, where the London regional offices of the Commission had been located since the mid-90s. The entire first floor was available. It had been used for a few years by the Labour Party to house its headquarters (and the centre of operations for its 1997 election campaign) but had been standing empty for three years. Its refurbishment would be completed in time for the Commission to relocate in August 2004. This was not just a bid for more space or lower rental costs (though it did promise savings of around £600,000 a year). The new premises would be substantially given over, at Strachan's express instructions, to an open-floor plan. The sharing of one giant space would make a huge contribution, he believed, to ridding the Commission's culture of all the barriers and secretiveness that had grown up between the different departments over the years. And it would site the Commission in an appropriately austere but distinctive modern building: Millbank Tower was a very different environment from the semi-residential neighbourhood of Vincent Square, with its playing fields and corner pubs. (It was also a famously wind-racked tower – but at least Pevsner's architectural guide could describe it as 'one of the few London office towers to have won affection'.)

Strachan's second, even more fundamental assault on the status quo was a radical redesign of the management structure. Just as Paul Kirby had warned might happen, Foster was confronted with a chairman with strong views of his own on the optimal shape of the Commission. Having committed himself already to the revised (and quite different) structure announced in the summer of 2002, Foster was desperately reluctant to start the process anew. But Strachan insisted, and colleagues watched him wrestling for weeks to tie the controller down. Strachan had a Cambridge blue in judo, so perhaps the result was never in doubt. Apocryphal or not, the story in the office was that the two of them arrived together at Euston station one evening, still locked in dispute over the details of a fresh structure that they had been discussing for hours. As they headed for their train, Strachan took a stand and announced that they weren't going anywhere until they had resolved their argument. Hence the final boxes were defined and linked for the future in the first-class lounge at Euston.

The outcome, announced in July 2003, had much to recommend it. Strachan was clear that they should leave much of the detail, and especially the actual appointments to the key positions, for Foster's successor to decide – but he succeeded in asserting a new overall shape. His concern above all was to forge a single, cohesive organization in which the component parts would work to support and reinforce each other. Six new managing directors at the centre would be given much more clearly defined roles, and they would include one director for local government and one for health. (Candidates for these positions were already being interviewed by July.)[35] Four regional directors would head organizations in the field that would combine health and local government franchises, while allowing more flexibility in the deployment of auditors and inspectors as specialists – though how exactly this would work, the new controller would need to resolve.

In one respect, though, the result of the restructuring was deeply unfortunate. The studies directorate was abolished and those who worked on studies either left the Commission – which they did in droves – or were scattered around the rest of the organization. No doubt the rationale for scrapping the directorate seemed compelling at the time. It was true, for instance, that PSR had been drifting for a while by the spring of 2003. As Peter Wilkinson recalled: 'One of the significant things we lost in the whole process of the restructuring was any sense of where we were on studies – but I would have to say that, by then, our strategy on studies was already floundering.'[36] With CHAI now set to take over the work on national studies of the NHS, and with auditors and inspectors alike preoccupied with CPA and its consequences, PSR was hardly integral to the audit work in the field in the way that the old study directorates had been. The department looked to its detractors more than ever like an ivory tower. James Strachan himself was fond of remarking in speeches that the

Commission would have two patron saints – Adam Smith and Karl Marx. The latter got his incongruous billing because of his alleged contempt for philosophers, who could only *describe* the world rather than also help *change* it.

But of course descriptions – rigorous, analytically driven and always evidentially based – had been at the core of every national report since 1983. Scrapping PSR may have been consistent with the new pragmatism that Strachan was determined to bring to the work of the Commission. It was also a decision, though, that left many people wondering whether the Commission any longer had a genuine commitment to the activity that, more than anything else, had underpinned its success from the start. It led accordingly to the loss of some of the Commission's most experienced and most talented employees. Some of the leavers who retired early – like Steve Evans, Greg Birdseye and David Browning – took with them much of the Commission's shared memory of the work done on reports through the 1980s and 1990s.

The significance of the setback inflicted by the disappearance of so much expertise would take some while to become apparent. In the meantime, the implementation of the summer reorganization left many senior figures in Vincent Square with rather more pressing concerns. Their current jobs had ceased to exist, and they still had no idea whether any of the newly created boxes were going to offer them berths. It had also been disconcerting, to say the least, to work for six months under a chairman and controller who were somewhat short of being a 'dream team'. Presenting his final monthly report to the Commission members in July, Andrew Foster acknowledged as much. There was much unhappiness at the centre, which he wanted members to heed before it was too late. 'He warned that Commissioners must not take for granted the capacity of the organization to cope with substantial and rapid change.'[37] He bowed out two weeks later, setting off soon afterwards for a half-year's restorative travelling in South America.

Arguably, the new chairman had indeed taken on too much, too quickly. On the other hand, he had undoubtedly achieved a dramatic repositioning of the Commission. This was far more apparent to the outside world by the summer of 2003 than problems encountered over the implementation of internal changes.

A BAPTISM OF FIRE

From the outset, Strachan took every opportunity in his meetings and correspondence with ministers and officials to explain his notion of 'strategic regulation'. Under his leadership, the Commission would hack back the vast, tangled apparatus of Best Value inspections. It would focus on selected benchmarks that would track the perform-ance of local bodies and their public services much more meaningfully, with a view at all times to making a practical impact. The days were long gone when it made sense to deliberate over an invisible line between illuminating choices and actually instigating change. As Strachan put it in a letter to the local government minister of the nascent Welsh National Assembly: 'I am very clear that our primary and ultimate purpose [in the Commission] is to contribute to the improvement of public services.'[38]

More dramatically, he had begun to communicate in public his initial thinking on the need for a regulatory watchdog that would put *de*regulation near the top of its agenda. Strachan was hardly a voice in the wilderness, arguing for a need to reverse longstand-ing trends in favour of centralized control over local government by Whitehall. It was a view increasingly being heard around this time. Even the outgoing head of Tony Blair's strategy unit, Geoff Mulgan, had recently signed up to it: 'After several decades of central-isation, the pendulum is now decisively swinging in the opposite direction.'[39] Nonetheless, when the new head of the Audit Com-mission spelt the message out to the Parliamentary Public Adminis-tration Committee in January, the media had a field-day. A paper by Strachan, submitted as prior evidence, gave them due notice of a stance that might rate more news coverage than some of his predecessors' appearances.

On balance, there may be too many national targets. The first step to 'thinning out' would be to pull all the published targets across all service areas together and examine which of them best reflected the Government's stated policy priorities and public concerns . . . Too many targets are ephemeral and are replaced or just lapse because of changing short-term priorities.[40]

Face to face with the MPs on the committee, Strachan gave what the *Guardian*'s political correspondent described as 'a devastating picture' of the misuse of targets across the public services. He was quoted at some length, speaking out with an authority that belied his newness to his job: 'The problem we have faced time and time again is the slavish devotion to targets, many of which have not been set very intelligently. It's a surefire way of not getting improvement in public services.'[41] There was nothing wrong with targets *per se*, if used sensibly. But too often they were being used as sticks rather than carrots. 'Sticks will not promote excellence. They will merely discourage failure, which is not enough.' It was also a serious weakness that many targets were being monitored and validated by government officials themselves. Strachan questioned the sense of using shorter waiting-time targets for hospitals, for example, 'if it means patients feel like widgets on a production line'. He had harsh words, too, for hospital and school league tables.

This was a new philosophy (*pace* Marx) from the Commission, pitched in a new tone of voice. While taking every opportunity to expound on the general shift in thinking, though, Strachan had to lend his weight to the efforts being made by colleagues over these months on a few particular issues of huge consequence to the Commission. First, of course, there was the little matter of CPA. While the great majority of the 150 authorities reviewed in the first round had grudgingly accepted their ratings, most leaders and chief executives alike remained at best sceptical – and in many cases, openly hostile – on the whole package. A MORI poll had been conducted in mid-December 2002. The results amounted to a clear thumbs-down. Strachan campaigned tirelessly to change this, speaking at conferences and handling Q&A sessions with large audiences in a way that often left them deeply impressed. (Strachan handled his disability by having questions relayed to him on a small computer screen by an assistant, technically known as a palantypist.) He recalled:

The single most important thing on the agenda when I arrived was CPA and I spent a huge amount of my first six months on it. In many ways it was the most tangible form, in the early days, of strategic regulation in action. My big challenge was to help get us to the point where, after six months, we could do another MORI poll and find the majority in favour of CPA.

They did in fact complete another poll in June – and it duly delivered the requisite majority. 'That about-face was a remarkable achievement by the Commission, and something I felt was tremendously important.'[42]

A second issue arose in the spring of 2003, when it became clear that council taxes all over the country were being pegged for 2003–04 at levels averaging nearly 13 per cent higher than for 2002–03. An early decision was taken to look carefully into the reasons for this huge increase. Auditors were set the task of gathering data that could be analysed through the autumn.

A third issue involved the future monitoring of the fire service. A radical report on the fire and rescue service (FRS) had just been produced, in December 2002, by an independent inquiry under the chairmanship of the vice-chancellor of Queen's University Belfast, George Bain. One of its key proposals was that a new inspectorate should be established over the FRS. As the report readily acknowledged, many of its conclusions and recommendations closely followed those of the Commission's own 1995 national report, *In the Line of Fire*. It was therefore little surprise that it saw the Commission as the natural home for the putative FRS inspectorate. The government had made clear its support for this idea before the report was even published. Anticipating events, Andrew Foster had turned for help in the autumn of 2002 to Mollie Bickerstaff.

Since resigning after two years as its director of purchasing in 1996, Bickerstaff had hardly been a stranger to the Commission. As head of the public sector practice at accountants KPMG, one of the Commission's suppliers, she had been one of the prime movers behind the setting up in late 1996 of the Auditor Liaison Group. (It was she who had to persuade a sceptical Andrew Foster that it would not be construed by the outside world as a suppliers' cartel. The group brought together representatives of all the private firms working for the Commission, along with DA, and provided a forum for discussions with the Commission on fees, audit practices and any other matters of general interest to the firms.) Bickerstaff had left KPMG in 2001 and had worked for just over a year for the London Assembly. By the time of Foster's approach in the autumn of 2002 she was working as a freelance consultant. Strachan now persuaded her to rejoin the

Commission on a full-time basis. By the spring of 2003, a White Paper on the modernization of the FRS was on its way and it was time to start planning a fire inspectorate in earnest. Bickerstaff took charge of the project.

Above all, though, there was the Commission's health agenda. Reviewing it soon after his arrival, Strachan found an important research programme on the integrity of waiting-list statistics in the NHS was nearing publication. He decided that it would be sensible, before this happened, to clarify the question of the Commission's relations with the new Commission for Healthcare Audit and Inspection. The drafting of the legislation for CHAI, the Health and Social Care Bill, was in its final stages – it would be introduced to Parliament in March – so it seemed a good time finally to clear up any confusion over the nature of Vincent Square's continuing remit in health. Strachan knew this was worth nearly £60 million in total, more than a quarter of the Commission's total income (£213.9 million) in the year to October 2002. Only a sliver of this derived from anything other than financial audit fees, but the ex-banker in him wanted to avoid having any grey areas in the wake of CHAI's emergence. In December, he was happy to receive the call, mentioned earlier, from Ian Kennedy, its newly appointed 'shadow chairman'.

Kennedy was also keen to reach a good rapport between their two institutions. He had watched for months as the Commission and the Department of Health had wrangled over the exact definition of local audit work in the NHS. Sensing a long history of bad blood between them, he was keen to keep his distance on that front. But he was an admirer of the national reports produced by the Commission during the 1990s. Indeed, he had singled out for praise one of the Commission's early health titles, in his own report on the Bristol Royal Infirmary Inquiry. This was *Children First: a Study of Hospital Services*, published in 1993 (and written by John Bailey, who would shortly move to the Healthcare Commission).[43] Kennedy had had little to do with the Commission's financial audit work in the NHS. He recalled: 'Their role in wandering the land, checking the financial data and so on, I wasn't really aware of.'[44] But the national reports had certainly made a big impression on him. 'The quality of those reports persuaded me that in the Audit Commission they had a very good staff and people who could actually *think* – and that commodity is in relatively short supply. So they were an organization that I was anxious to deal with.'

He and Strachan met, and got along well from the start. It was plain to Kennedy that his counterpart had a keen eye on the fee implications of any future arrangement and would be alert to opportunities for the Commission to regain lost ground in health. But at least they seemed agreed on the fundamental point: CHAI would take over all national studies and VFM in the health sector. Some *local* VFM work might be undertaken by the Commission as part of its continuing audit franchise – this, of course, had been the bone of contention between the Commission and the DoH for months past – but the data would be passed to CHAI rather than aggregated in Vincent Square. With goodwill on both sides, it looked a workable arrangement. Kennedy also asked for help from the Commission with his transitional staffing and some early work on the scope of VFM work in the health service. Strachan was very receptive to this idea. It was agreed that Peter Wilkinson would combine his health role at the Commission with a three-days-a-week secondment. (One result of this would later be a short series of jointly branded seminars on the concepts underpinning VFM – though these prompted some reflection on both sides that perhaps VFM did not mean precisely the same thing to each of them.)

Around the same time, but quite separately, Kennedy also began talking to Jonty Boyce about CHAI's plans. The two of them met by chance at a north London school attended by their sons. It was soon clear to Kennedy that the inventor of the Acute Hospital Portfolio had a valuable contribution to make at CHAI. Andrew Foster was loath to part with Boyce, and the evident revenue potential of his work on the AHP, but Strachan agreed to let him be seconded until CHAI was fully established. Boyce never came back. (He first went off to Hong Kong, as a special adviser to an official inquiry into the SARS crisis. He returned to start work with the CHAI transition team in July that year.) After nearly fourteen years at the Commission, Boyce left with no regrets: he had great respect for Kennedy and was impressed by his plans for the future of CHAI. He also knew that the rest of the health studies staff at Vincent Square would anyway be following in his wake within a year or so, as part of CHAI's statutory arrangements.

Wilkinson, meanwhile, still had his hands full as the health director back at Vincent Square. Final discussions on the Health and Social Care Bill had prompted yet another furious row over the Commission's franchise in health. This time, the dispute centred on plans to introduce a new category of hospitals. With certain preconditions, hospitals would be allowed to set themselves up as independent trusts, or 'foundation trusts' as they had been tagged – within, but not directly managed by, the NHS. Strachan was firmly of the view – and quite understandably so – that the Bill should nonetheless require them, as bodies working within the public interest, to go on being subject to auditors appointed by the Commission. On this point, commissioners and Commission staff alike were fully behind their chairman. The Commission had keenly supported the setting up of the Public Audit Forum in 1997 to give weight to its argument that public bodies should be audited in the public interest and that this could *only* be assured if auditors were independently appointed. Allowing foundation trusts (FTs) to choose their own auditors contradicted this principle. The DoH did not accept this, and proposed to leave the choice of auditor to the hospitals themselves. Indeed, it was even mooted by some in the government that the Commission's DA should actually be *barred* from the list of prospective auditors. Strachan campaigned strenuously in favour of retaining the Commission's normal role. He wrote letters of protest in February not only to ministers but to the press as well, pitching arguments in public that inevitably caused considerable irritation to health officials and their secretary of state, Alan Milburn. The press lapped it up. One newspaper quoted Strachan as describing the whole idea of foundation trusts as 'a real red herring' (though he objected that this was a reference to the debate, not the policy).

In the end, the DoH conceded that DA could be included on the list of eligible auditors. There was really little choice, as officials had to acknowledge, since most FTs wanted to retain their existing auditors for at least the first year of the new regime. But the argument in favour of leaving the Commission in charge of appointing all auditors was lost: those fighting to introduce FTs saw them as a way of opening up the NHS to more private sector best practice, and to this end they were willing to set aside the principle (ignored, after all, in the private sector) that audit appointment should not be in the gift of those whose affairs were being audited. The battle cost the Commission's chairman some valuable goodwill in Whitehall.

With unfortunate timing, this was the moment at which the research on hospital waiting-lists produced its report, *Waiting for Elective Admission*. Based on a series of 'spot checks' across forty-one NHS trusts around the country over 2001–02 – instigated originally at the request of the DoH – the report cited various anomalies picked up by the Commission's auditors. Most attested to weak management systems. In just a few cases, though, there was a less innocent explanation. Waiting-list data appeared to have been manipulated, to put the performance of NHS trusts in a better light. Strachan did not shrink from the implication, which journalists were not slow to draw to his attention in interviews. As he acknowledged to the BBC: 'It's not true that this is all about pressure, but it would clearly be rather unbelievable to argue that none of it was due to pressure from above.'[45]

This was exceedingly dangerous territory. Ever since Gordon Brown's announcement of a five-year settlement for the NHS in his April 2002 budget, the waiting-list figures had been imbued with huge importance. From that moment, as the Delivery Unit's Michael Barber saw it, 'the central challenge of the [Blair government's] second term was to ensure that there was powerful evidence that the NHS had significantly improved, especially by massively reducing waiting times'.[46] Hence the pressure Strachan was referring to, of course – but also the reason why his remarks instantly put ministers and their officials in the health department on high alert. Then, opting for a period of diplomatic silence, Strachan returned to the fray early in June with the publication of a follow-up Bulletin, *Assessing the Accuracy of Waiting-List Information*. He accepted an invitation to discuss it on BBC Radio 4's *Today* programme. He had no real choice but to defend references in the Bulletin to the way in which money was being diverted from core programmes in the NHS into ploys aimed at reducing waiting-lists. But Strachan went further, and disastrously coupled the two potent words 'government' and 'spin' in the same sentence. This set the media hounds after the health secretary, Alan

Milburn, who found himself having to spend half a day denouncing any trusts that had deliberately fiddled their numbers. It was not the first time Milburn had been on the wrong end of an Audit Commission report. Back in October 2001, the Acute Hospital Portfolio study of waiting times in A&E units had taken the NHS to task and prompted fierce media criticism of the minister. ('A Good Day to Bury Alan Milburn' ran a cruelly memorable *Daily Mirror* headline.) He had reacted then (more or less) with a stoical shrug. This time, he could scarcely contain his anger.

Six days later, on 11 June, Strachan was summoned to see Milburn and John Prescott together. He took Andrew Foster with him to the meeting. The reception committee comprised the two cabinet ministers, both their permanent secretaries and a posse of other officials. The meeting lasted forty-five minutes, and featured the kind of exchange of views customarily described by diplomats as candid and forthright. Milburn, who was to resign from the government the very next day, was in no mood to mince his words. Prescott was equally combative. Strachan unreservedly apologized for any offence caused by his use of the word 'spin' – but then he insisted that the Commission's report had stopped short of attacking government policy. This ensured a gladiatorial confrontation, with both ministers keen to remind Strachan in the tersest possible manner that a chairman of the Audit Commission was in their view some very considerable way short of the status attached to ministers of the crown. Foster confessed afterwards that he had never witnessed anything like it.[47]

Without doubt, it was by far the sharpest clash between ministers and a head of the Audit Commission since the era of John Banham. The distance between ministers and the Commission had been greater in those far-off days, and Banham had rarely (if ever) locked swords quite so directly with his antagonists in Whitehall. But anyone drawing a parallel might not have been so wide of the mark. Strachan's situation in 2003 and Banham's some twenty years earlier were intriguingly similar in many ways. As big hitters from the private sector, both took on the Commission in the wake of changes (CPA for one, the 1982 Act for the other) that were intended to leave behind an unsatisfactory period of dither and confusion (the Best Value era and the dying days of the unreformed District Audit Service, respectively). Both were determined to use the regularity audit function as the basis of a broader approach. Both were show-stoppers in their different ways, who confronted widespread scepticism in local government by pitching their case persuasively at conferences all over the country. And both could see the importance to their own credibility of a well-researched study into council finances that would signal the Commission's independence from Whitehall: the Block Grant report of 1984 had done this for Banham, and it did not take a clairvoyant in the summer of 2003 to see where the Commission's inquiry into the 2003–04 council-tax rises was heading (though the latter was, as yet, not intended for publication).

As of the summer of 2003, though, there was still one glaringly conspicuous difference between them. Banham had had Cliff Nicholson at his side – someone steeped in the ways of local government, capable of handling the detailed implementation of policy and ready to accept a subordinate position with patience and forbearance. Strachan had no such figure to fall back on. But he knew the man he wanted, and by June was determined to get him.

15

Leading the Way Again, 2003–05

Soon after his appointment, Strachan was invited to dinner by John Prescott so that the two men could get to know each other a little better. They were joined at Shepherd's restaurant in Westminster's Marsham Street by Prescott's permanent secretary, Mavis McDonald. As they talked about their general interests in life, the deputy prime minister asked Strachan what he would regard as his single favourite book. Strachan recalled: 'Without thinking too much, I said *The Outsider* by Albert Camus. Probably it was not the best choice. Anyway, Prescott eyed me with a wry smile. I could see him thinking "well, *that* figures"!'[1]

And it did – in the sense that the public sector was far from being Strachan's natural habitat. Given his work as a regulator and his experience in running the Royal National Institute for the Deaf, he was hardly a stranger to it, but he always viewed it with the mindset of a banker or an entrepreneur. Two aspects of the public sector in particular always irked him: the invariably slow pace of any change, and the general aversion to risk of any kind. His own approach was different – as he had shown in countless ways even within his first several months in the chair of the Audit Commission. He was in a hurry to get things done, and was not afraid to leave some things to chance where he fancied the odds.

He had not been widely known in Whitehall prior to his appointment, but it had not taken ministers and their officials long to spot the passing of the Foster years. Adjusting to the change would take them rather longer – as was obvious, from the celebrated row over NHS waiting-lists in March. There was much about the new man's style that came as a slight surprise to Whitehall, not least the extent of his executive commitment to the job and his early willingness publicly to question government policy on public services. Taken together with his outspokenness on the *Today* programme, there may have been scope here for some to discern the first wobble of a loose cannon. In fact, Strachan was nothing of the kind. On the contrary, he was someone who generally prepared his every move with great care, not least because his disability had always put a premium on forward planning for any meeting. There were two matters of paramount importance in his first half-year, and on both of them he moved with great care and deliberation.

The first concerned the initial message that he wanted to convey about his own strategic priorities. This he did very effectively, with his questioning of the public sector's heavy emphasis by 2003 on targets and league tables. As the year went by, Strachan warmed to this theme. Challenging the apparent urge to measure the performance of public services at every turn, he would refer occasionally to the savant who pointed out that you could not fatten pigs by weighing them. In part, this was an engagingly candid expression of deeply held views about regulation. To be effective, it needed to be selective. Swamping public services with a mass of intrusive checks and measures was almost certain to be detrimental to the performance of those really committed to the services at the point of delivery (and Strachan knew his Wordsworth – 'we murder to dissect'). It would also be a culpable waste of public money. To ignore these facts would be to play into the hands of mindless anti-regulators, opposed to any use of targets and indicators at all. There was of course a need for careful scrutiny, quantified in appropriate ways. The challenge was to retain the essentials while cutting back massively on the demands being made of those in the field. Strachan recalled: 'I had just spent four years on the board of Ofgem, where we had been hell bent on reducing the amount of regulation that we undertook by 80–90 per cent!'[2]

But in giving vent to these views, Strachan was also re-positioning the Commission. He was making a conscious bid to distance it from the excesses of 1997–2002, and to set it at the forefront of a shift in public policy that he believed was coming. It had not yet arrived: ubiquitous targets were still the recipe *du jour* for public services reform in 2003, and 'user choice' had yet to follow, in 2004. But his timing was canny. He knew from his earliest forays on to the local government circuit of conference platforms and dinners that CPA was hardly regarded yet as an alternative to inspection. It was seen as yet another layer of regulation, heaped upon the 'local public service agreements' that had been rolled out since 2001 and were soon due for replenishment. (*Local* public service agreements were a variant of the 'PSAs' first adopted in Whitehall in 1998 and refined in 2000. PSAs were devised to tighten the Treasury's grip on the performance of all the main spending departments. The local variant specified public service targets that local authorities had to agree with the DTLR – or later the ODPM. Councils that met their targets were eligible for a greater degree of local autonomy and some modest financial assistance.) Strachan scented a popular reaction against all this, and was responding accordingly. Mavis McDonald recalled: 'My sense at the time was that he was kite-flying – and events in due course lifted his kite higher.'[3]

Strachan's other great priority in 2003 was to find the next controller – or chief executive, as he re-labelled the position. The appointment process lasted longer than he had hoped at the outset. It happened that his partner, Tessa Blackstone, was a longstanding friend and admirer of one of the best-known figures in London local government: Steve Bundred. They had worked together on the ILEA in the early 1980s. Newly appointed in 1988 as master of Birkbeck College, Blackstone found the place near to bankruptcy and persuaded Bundred to become its finance director. He had done a part-time Master's degree in econometrics at Birkbeck himself, and took up the challenge. He was able to leave two years later, in 1990, having successfully restored its finances. Strachan and Blackstone invited Bundred to dinner at Strachan's flat in Belsize Park, in December 2002 – and before the evening was over, Strachan asked him if he would be interested in applying for the job of executive head of the Commission. He would have the title of 'chief executive', which Strachan intended to introduce in place of 'controller'.

Bundred said he'd love the job. He had enormous respect and admiration for the Commission. Unfortunately, however, he had just signed a contract to become the next chief executive of the Improvement and Development Agency (IDeA), the body set up by the Local Government Association with a remit to help spread best practice within local government, not least through a programme of peer reviews. Neither Strachan's entreaties nor a series of calls from the head-hunter Saxton Bampfylde Hever, could persuade Bundred to change his mind: he had taken one job and felt that applying now for another would simply not be the right thing to do. Six months went by, during which the Commission all but appointed someone else from the private sector. (Terms could not be agreed, and the appointment fell through.) In the meantime, Strachan had begun to see Bundred in his IDeA role quite regularly. Yet more attempts were made to elicit an application from him, all in vain. Finally, one evening early in June, Bundred was invited round to the chairman's office in Vincent Square and pinned against the wall. 'Forget about applying', said Strachan. 'If we offered you the job, would you accept it?'[4]

'Well, I'd think about it', said Bundred impetuously. He had a conversation next day with the LGA's chief executive, Brian Briscoe. Then he called Strachan back and said, 'Okay'. A formal panel interview followed – and he started at the beginning of September.

BRINGING ABOARD A CANDID FRIEND

If the recruitment process had been exasperating for Strachan, it had been far worse for Bundred: privately, he had never doubted that running the Commission was the obvious next move in a career that had positioned him perfectly for the job. Earlier moves had not always been so obvious: he had followed an intriguing path. Born and raised in Liverpool, Bundred had read PPE at Oxford. After graduating, he was contacted by one of his old tutors, Norman Hunt, who had been charged by Harold Wilson in the early 1970s with the job of setting up an independent research unit for the Labour Party. Bundred joined it and made a favourable impression, working on assignments for Tony Crosland and then Eric Varley, the shadow energy minister. After Labour's return to power in 1974, Varley was made secretary of state for energy and Bundred joined him as one of the first of the new breed of 'special advisers' that was to flourish in the years ahead.

(One of the young civil servants whom Bundred worked alongside was Richard Wilson, who ended his career in Whitehall as head of the civil service from 1998 to 2002. He and Bundred looked back on those years in a conversation shortly before Wilson's retirement. Bundred recalled: 'He said I was the first special adviser he'd ever met, and he wished I'd been the last.')[5] But Bundred's stay in the Department of Energy was cut short in 1975 when Varley was replaced by Tony Benn. The young adviser left Whitehall and joined the only institution in the land with more power, as the electorate had reminded Edward Heath, than any mere government department – the National Union of Mineworkers.

Bundred ran the NUM's research department for eight years, reporting directly to the president of the union – Joe Gormley until 1981 and Arthur Scargill thereafter. This naturally identified him as one of the elect in Labour Party circles, and he was soon carving out a career in local politics. He served on Islington Borough Council from 1975 to 1978 and was elected to the Greater London Council as the member for Islington North in the local elections of 1981. (In both places, he crossed paths with Wendy Thomson and the two became friends.) His GLC seat gave him membership of the ILEA and he was elected chairman of its finance committee. This left him working under two political leaders: under Frances Morrell at the ILEA, who had been special adviser to Tony Benn when Bundred was working for Varley, and at the GLC under Ken Livingstone, installed as leader by County Hall's post-election coup of 1981. In 1982, Arthur Scargill transferred the NUM's headquarters from London's Euston Road to Sheffield. Thriving at the GLC and by now embarked on his part-time Master's degree at Birkbeck, Bundred opted to find a new job in London. It was not too difficult. 'The local government finance system has always been a bit like the Schleswig-Holstein question and I was one of the few people at the time who did actually understand it.'[6] Hackney Borough Council gave him a job in its finance department.

A little oddly for someone in this position, he had no accountancy qualifications. Indeed, he was still not a qualified accountant four years later, when he managed to get himself appointed in 1986 as chief accountant at Lewisham Borough Council in south London. But he had embarked on the CIPFA public sector accounting course available at Liverpool University as a programme for serving council officers, and finally qualified in 1988. That was the year he joined Tessa Blackstone's staff for his brief stint at Birkbeck. Thereafter, he made steady progress up to the top echelons of local government, starting as deputy finance director at Hackney (1990–92) and then rising at Camden Borough Council from finance director (1992–95) to chief executive (1995–2002).

The bare details were impressive, but they did not explain why Strachan had been all but ready to offer Bundred the Commission job the first time he met him at that private dinner in December 2002. It was no sudden whim on the new chairman's part. With some input from Tessa Blackstone and the benefit of several lengthy conversations elsewhere, Strachan saw a string of good reasons to rate Bundred very highly for any senior post in the local government world. But there were two credentials in particular that in Strachan's eyes made Bundred the ideal man for the Commission.

First, he had proved himself a chief executive capable of stabilizing organizations in some disarray, and restoring their sense of purpose and direction. Strachan had no doubt within a few months of his own appointment that the Commission was a suitable case for treatment on all counts. Two years after rescuing Birkbeck College's finances, Bundred had landed at Camden in 1992 to find himself in charge of a finance department that had not published annual accounts since 1986–87. He recalled a situation at Camden Council that was close to a financial meltdown:

They weren't collecting their debts; they weren't paying their bills on time; they had no money in the bank; they couldn't produce reliable accounts; they didn't keep within their budgets; and their trading activities made a loss. Otherwise, they were OK – except of course that many of the services they provided were also of poor quality.

Having unwisely assumed for some years that a new Labour government would bail them out, the councillors were all but sunk and desperate for a lifeline. Bundred confronted them with the full ghastliness of the council's predicament – which most of them, even then, had failed to grasp – and effectively handed them an ultimatum. 'They could either sort the council out or be obliterated at the polls. I told them what they needed to do and gave them some confidence that, if they did it, we could have a better council.'[7] They backed him (as too did Camden's long-suffering district auditor, Kash Pandya). Three months after arriving in the job, Bundred presented a budget that cut total spending of £250 million by an immediate 15 per cent. Six months later, assets were sold off with a value of almost £50 million. Within eighteen months, the workforce of 9,500 had been shrunk by a third. And so things continued, through four painful years. By the time that Bundred took over as chief executive, in December 1995, Camden's finances had been restored. Under a leader, Richard Arthur, who happened to sit on the Audit Commission, Camden then started to focus on sorting out the poor quality of its public services. This, too, was achieved according to plan. In 2002, it emerged from the first CPA round as one of the few authorities rated 'excellent' and won the *LGC* Council of the Year award.

And then, from Strachan's perspective, there was Bundred's second great strength. He had been publicly critical for years of the contributions made to local government by the Commission itself – and remained so. He knew Vincent Square was not a place overly burdened with a sense of its own limitations; a little more modesty, in his view, would not come amiss. His professed regard for the Commission was entirely genuine: he had taken a keen interest in it since its creation in 1983. But if given the chance to lead the Commission into a new era, he would be no more awed by its past achievements than Strachan himself.

The principal platform used by Bundred in the past for his cold-eyed commentaries on the Commission had been a column that he had written through most of the 1990s for the *Local Government Chronicle*. It was widely read, and identified its author as one of the Commission's most thoughtful critics – hence, for example, his contributions as a witness to the reviews by Butler in 1995 and by the Parliamentary Select Committee in early 2000. Bundred recalled: 'I thought it was an impressive organization, but one that frequently got things wrong.'[8] On such occasions, he could speak out as a critic with more authority than most. In one of his very first columns, in 1994, Bundred took the Commission to task for the slipshod way in which he felt it had gone about a quality review of its audit work in Camden.

The Commission's director of purchasing, Mollie Bickerstaff, was not someone to be challenged lightly – but she acknowledged the justice of the complaint. ('Mollie rang me up, said "sorry, we got it wrong" and took me out to lunch.')[9] Criticizing the Commission's review in 1996–97 of councils' early pension arrangements, Bundred put a shot over its bows before the report had even been drafted. 'As always with the Audit Commission, there is a sense that it has seized upon half a good idea but has got only one end, and probably the wrong end, of the stick.'[10] And when the Commission produced a leaflet setting out the standards of service that councils should expect from their auditors (*What You Can Expect from Your External Auditors*) in 1996, he greeted it as 'long overdue and hence welcome'. Then he gave it both barrels. 'But instead of addressing the underlying concerns [e.g., a disregard for any council studies already under way, the lack of any appeal process, the cost and inflexible billing arrangements, the absence of any meaningful consultation in advance on audit plans], the new Commission statement and booklet for the most part merely clarify and reiterate the current unsatisfactory situation.'[11]

Above all, he had shown in his *LGC* columns that he understood the big picture. He had a sound appreciation of the broad demands being made of the Commission – and when they made no sense, he said so. Given the obligation on auditors to pursue matters raised by the centrally driven audit guides, for example, were they really going to be able to tackle the agenda envisaged by Best Value? Two years before Wendy Thomson arrived at the Commission, Bundred had put his finger on the critical issue: 'There are doubts about how professionals whose job traditionally requires them to rely on an audit trail of past actions, will approach a new task focusing on how the authority has planned for the future.' Exactly so.[12]

Bundred had remained deeply sceptical of Best Value and the subsequent inspection era. Strachan, to his delight, found in 2003 that the two of them were broadly agreed on the nature of the challenge ahead for the Commission. Here was someone Strachan felt he could rely on to drive through the implementation of the radical agenda he had laid out by September 2003. They would be new brooms together.

TACKLING THE MANAGEMENT
AGENDA

There were many in Vincent Square by that autumn, though, in whose opinion the chairman had laid out an agenda for the Commission rather as Attila had laid one out for Rome. Strachan had posed a huge challenge to the culture of the Commission at every level, and people were struggling to adjust. Another employee survey undertaken in July 2003 had not left much room for doubt. Bundred recalled: 'When I arrived, I was quite shocked. The results of the survey were frankly appalling. It was a very, very unhappy organization – and a less well-run organization than I had expected it to be.'[13] In his early meetings with the staff, Bundred set out his objectives under two headings. He wanted to achieve a better managed Commission, and a better regulated public sector. Between September 2003 and April 2004, with Strachan's active support, he made huge strides on both fronts (and Strachan, as agreed with Raynsford at the outset, reined back his chairmanship to three days a week from early in 2004).

Bundred had his reservations about the new structure that he was inheriting. But he was determined to make no further changes. Vincent Square seemed to have been in a perpetual state of reorganization for the entire twenty-first century to date, and the risks of further restructuring would be too great.* Giving no further thought to the structure, therefore, Bundred set to work on filling the management positions he was given and offering some reassurance for the future to those who were left from Andrew Foster's management team.

They were a dwindling band. The CPA team had gone months ago. Irene Payne, who had taken over running PSR from Andrew Webster, had followed him out of the door within a few months. Trish Longdon

---

* It was perhaps not entirely a self-imposed ordinance: Strachan made it clear many times in the following months that in his view, too, behavioural change was more critical to the Commission's future than structural change. As he told CIPFA's annual conference at Brighton in June 2004: '2,000 years ago, Caius Petronius was more the realist than the cynic when he said: "We tend to meet any new situation by reorganizing and a wonderful method it can be for creating the illusion of progress while producing confusion, inefficiency and demoralization." So no change there, then!'

and Ruth Davison had just departed, and Jonty Boyce was about to leave for CHAI. But among those remaining were three former management board directors – Peter Wilkinson, Martin Evans and Alan Meekings – who had no idea of their future status in the organization. The sole member of the old team to have been assigned one of the new management positions was David Prince: he had been appointed managing director of strategy and resources. Ironically, Prince had just finished his tenth year with the Commission and had made up his mind to look for a chief executive position in another national body. He found it at the Standards Board for England, set up in 2001, and would take up the reins there in March 2004. Bundred in due course would move Peter Wilkinson to replace him. For all of the other positions on the senior management team, Bundred needed to turn to appointments from outside. (In fact he had begun to get involved in the interview process as early as June, following the announcement of his own appointment that month.)

The Human Resources post went to Tracey Dennison, whom he had worked with at Camden. And as the local government managing director, he appointed Frances Done, another former council chief executive. Done had run the organizing committee for the Manchester Commonwealth Games held in August 2002, and had previously worked at the Housing Corporation. For all of her recent career achievements, though, it was her professional background that made her appointment especially noteworthy for most auditors: Done was a KPMG-trained accountant. She had worked as an auditor herself, and been a council finance director. Taken together with the fact that he himself was also a qualified accountant, was it now possible that Bundred intended (as the word went) to 'put the Audit back into Audit Commission'?

Indeed it was. Bundred was acutely conscious that 80 per cent of those working for the Commission were auditors: the business of the Audit Commission was audit. It needed to invest accordingly in its auditors, out in the field. This was essential, to avert the risk of serious error in what Banham, all those years ago, had called 'the errors business'. And to do otherwise would also represent a huge opportunity cost. The breadth and expertise of its field force gave the Commission an unrivalled knowledge of what was going on at the grass roots, which it could put to good use in myriad ways. Bundred had serious doubts that enough was being invested, either to cut the risks or reap the rewards. He recalled: 'Our auditors [in 2003] felt very unloved. All the political attention and all the management focus had been on Best Value, inspection and all that stuff.' He made clear from the start that he would seek to change this. In avowing this intention, of course, Bundred was following in the footsteps of every controller before him. John Banham had initially suggested all studies would be outsourced while the Commission stuck to its audit knitting. Howard Davies had given speeches in 1987 from Whitehall to Washington about the paramount importance of regularity audit over all other activities. Even Andrew Foster, for all the sweeping strategies of *Adding Value*, had put reform of the District Audit Service at the top of his 'To Do' list when it came to making hard decisions. Bundred, though, was different: he reasserted the importance of the auditors' work, and went on reasserting it.

It was a timely corrective. The former audit policy director, Martin Evans, was almost inured by 2003 to the top management's limited fascination with the details of audit activities. He had resigned himself to the fact that a new discussion paper on some aspect of auditing would be lucky to receive a budget of £30,000, while £250,000 was regularly assigned to the production of a new national VFM study (leading to a national report which, in most cases, he privately suspected would be read by very few). He knew his own policy decisions often scarcely registered on the fifth floor of Vincent Square. He would recall the reaction to his decision, taken soon after arriving at the Commission, to stop collecting data from auditors about putative savings from local VFM work. (He thought it a waste of money, since he could see no one using it.) 'We just stopped it – and no one noticed. Much later, Andrew said to me, "Don't we collect information on savings?" And I said, "No, Andrew, I stopped that about three or four years ago." He said, "oh, all right then", and we continued on our way. Nobody questioned it.'[14]

But Evans had been concerned, nonetheless, at some of the press reporting of unguarded comments by the new chairman. Strachan had talked, for example, of the need to break away from the old 'box-ticking culture' of the past – which carried less than flattering connotations for auditors. He had also been quoted describing the audit function (no doubt with more irony than was apparent in cold print) as just adding up the numbers and checking against fraud. Evans knew this had gone down badly in the field. 'Well, when you've got 1,000 auditors in an organization who know the one thing they do *not* do is check if there's any fraud, reports like that suggested a complete misunderstanding and a downgrading of audit.'[15]

Bundred, by contrast, went out of his way to celebrate recent achievements by the auditors. He began to extend their role, for example in the development of one of the important strands of the CPA methodology (the 'use-of-resources' element). And he made sure that Martin Evans had access to his own and Strachan's office whenever he needed it. Early in 2004, Evans had Bundred's full support in commissioning an external report on how to re-energize an audit support directorate. The outsider Evans turned to was the man who had made something of a speciality of advising the Commission since 1983, on everything from its initial start-up, to CCT, to the risks inherent in modern audit work – Michael Dallas. Now retired, Dallas spent most of 2004 talking to all those with a professional interest in the topic. Privately, he was in no doubt that the Commission had lost the primacy it had once enjoyed in this area. He recalled: 'The NAO had come much more to the fore on the technical accounting side, and the Commission wasn't really punching its weight in my view.'[16] The Dallas Report, submitted late in the year, provided a list of recommendations for remedial action.

Evans was not finally reappointed to the management team of the Commission until 2006 – but by then he had long been functioning as a managing director in all but name. His technical advice was generally accorded great respect. And Strachan soon came to be assiduous in correcting any earlier impressions that he took auditing for granted. His more considered view throughout his chairmanship was that the Commission needed a broad range of skills in its field force, though he was keen to nudge it in the direction of the inspectors. He recalled:

The range went roughly from the auditor with a terrier-like determination to pursue forensic examinations at one end of the organization, to the evangelical inspector at the other, hell-bent on spreading best practice around the land. I felt we needed to shift it along a bit in the latter direction – but there was no question of trying to take everyone overnight into the improvement business.[17]

Like Evans, Alan Meekings was another individual who had lost his place on the board of directors and was unsure of his future by the autumn of 2003. The outcome here was less straightforward. The director of operations had been handed the most problematic of jobs, one year earlier. The decision to pool all of the Commission's auditors and inspectors back into one integrated workforce across four regions had been easy to articulate, but was proving just as intractable in practice as everyone had feared. A structure could be changed overnight; but making two cultures into one would take much longer – especially given the quite deep tensions that still existed between auditors and inspectors in some parts of the country. Office signage had been changed, with new Audit Commission logos sprouting up everywhere in place of DA and BVIS (Best Value Inspectorate Service). But the shoots of a new, genuinely integrated organization were still looking very tender indeed.

Bundred felt confident he could nurture them successfully, but patience would be needed. A big step forward had already been taken, with the introduction of client-relationship managers – probably a majority of them from the old ranks of DA, but many coming too from the old BV inspectorate – and other reforms could follow as inspections were scaled back. The idea of a structure built along 'silo' lines, with specialist groups operating independently of each other, had been firmly rejected. All were now agreed on the desirability of a matrix structure, with individual specialists reporting to regional heads as well as to their respective directors at the centre. Meekings was left, in effect, to mediate between the regional heads and the local government and health directors to whom they reported. It was not an ideal arrangement, and Meekings had little to compensate him for the disappearance of his DA directorship. Nor was it clear, in the following months, how the operations directorate at the centre could usefully assist the process of amalgamation in the field. Bundred would eventually decide it was actually holding it back. It was the one exception he would make to the ban on further structural changes: the directorate was scrapped in September 2004, and Meekings left the Commission.

One important appointment had been made by Strachan and Bundred even before the latter's formal arrival as chief executive in September 2003: together, they succeeded in luring across to the Commission a senior figure from the Department of Health, Andy McKeon. A career civil servant with twenty-seven years' service in the DoH – including a stint as Kenneth Clarke's private secretary in 1988–90 when Howard Davies was winning the health franchise for the Commission – McKeon quit as the director of policy and planning, moving to Vincent Square within weeks of Bundred's arrival. News of his appointment came as a considerable surprise to many, not least those busy preparing the formal launch of CHAI. Most of the health directorate, after all, was about to transfer to CHAI. Given the accord that he had struck with James Strachan at the start of the year, Ian Kennedy was slightly mystified by the appointment of such a senior figure – and indeed, someone with whom he had already had discussions at the DoH concerning the work going ahead on CHAI. It certainly put him on his guard, in case it should portend a degree of competitive territoriality from the Commission. (Kennedy recalled: 'I became watchful.')[18] But McKeon for his part had no doubt whatever that he was taking on a real job. He would be responsible for supervising and coordinating the work of some 80 health specialists in the field, along with about 500 auditors who were working within the NHS for a significant part of their time. He agreed with Bundred that this ought to be enough to keep him busy.

While installing his senior management team, Bundred had no shortage of other pressing items on his management agenda. Most immediately, other senior staff positions needed filling. He appointed an associate director, Jo Killian, to lead the CPA process. And to take charge of the Commission's police and community-safety work, Bundred brought in someone who had built a good reputation working within the Cabinet Office, Zoe Billingham. Then there was plenty to do in overhauling the Commission's support services. He was surprised, for example, to find that staff at the Commission were working with a lower level of IT support than had been available in the offices of the much smaller IDeA.

There was one priority, however, that topped Bundred's list:

retrenchment. By the autumn of 2003, James Strachan had been telling conference audiences for months that his version of regulation was going to entail less of it. Whatever credence this message carried in the country, it was taken with a dash of salt within the Commission itself. This, after all, was an institution that had seen strategies come and go in recent times like the seasons of the year. Martin Evans recalled: 'The Commission loved strategic planning. In the past, we had had a year-long process. But it was all completely unconnected with the business. Well, James actually had this novel idea that if you had a strategic plan, you ought to do something about delivering it.'[19] Accordingly, it was agreed between Strachan and Bundred that they would cut the budget for local government work by very nearly 20 per cent, taking £24 million off a total of £125 million. All but £3 million of this would relate to discretionary items. The full list of tasks to be abandoned was published, appropriately, on 5 November. (The remaining £3 million related to fees earned on the audit of Best Value performance plans. Most people in the field regarded this work by 2004 as nugatory in the extreme, but permission to drop it was only finally granted by the ODPM in 2006.)

This was not quite the radical break with the past that they were perfectly content to have it appear. In fact, Martin Evans and David Prince had been preparing a programme of cuts ever since the integration of DA with the inspectorate in 2002. Even before 2002, there had been a clear trend towards less work and lower fees: an exercise in 2001, for example, had reduced audit fees payable by parish councils by almost £1 million. Nonetheless, it was dramatic confirmation of the Commission's retrenchment. And with the curtailment of field activities, inevitably, a loss of jobs would follow. The total workforce at this point stood at almost 2,500 people. Plans were laid for an eventual retreat back below the 2,000 mark. The actual notices for the first compulsory redundancies were not posted until February 2005, but Bundred had to make it clear now that scores of people would be involved, from both support staff and the frontline. Many of the people seconded into the inspection service by Wendy Thomson and Paul Kirby would be returning to their posts in local government. There was no disguising the shock felt, from Vincent Square to the smallest regional office. 'It wasn't a huge redundancy programme', recalled Bundred; 'but the psychological effect was important. It was the first time in the Commission's history that we'd ever been seen in retreat, after years of just expanding.'[20]

No one doubted any longer that Strategic Regulation would be much more than just a clever tagline. The budget cutbacks and redundancies attracted attention in the wider world, too. They certainly intrigued one of the media's most experienced political commentators, who interviewed Strachan early in November. Writing in the *Guardian*, Jackie Ashley confessed to 'finding the whole area of public sector regulation a little dry', but after listening to Strachan 'it is suddenly starting to sound a bit more interesting'. He had persuaded her to take notice of what the Commission was intending to do – and she did, concluding her interview:

We live in a regulators' world . . . [and] few of the bodies that have sprung up to oversee public life have the power and range of the Audit Commission. When its head calls time on excessive regulation, that's significant; if the national mood is turning against the regulatory culture, then here is the moment when the shift began.[21]

As this acknowledged, the Commission's internal management agenda and its external policy agenda were intimately linked. But it was time, now, to focus on the latter.

NEW DIRECTIONS FOR REGULATION

The Commission set out chapter and verse of its new approach to its role in two documents. The first, *Strategic Regulation: Minimising the Burden, Maximising the Impact*, was written by Martin Evans and Steve Bundred together and appeared in November 2003. The chief executive went solo on the second, simply entitled *Strategic Plan 2004-07*.

The main theme of the first was captured in a novel couple of sentences added to the Commission's standard rubric: 'The Audit Commission is firmly committed to providing value for money in its own activities. Through Strategic Regulation we will focus our activity where the need for improvement is greatest.' There then followed, in effect, a list of all the audit and inspection tasks that were *not* deemed value for money and that would now be junked. In spirit, it was the kind of list that many councils might have welcomed in 1997, as part of the demolition job on CCT. Except, of course, for the fact that most of the offending tasks had themselves been introduced since 1997. Thus, service inspections would be reduced 'to the minimum level necessary' to back up CPA. Service inspections of any kind would now be a rarity in councils rated as 'excellent' by CPA. Best Value plans would no longer be audited. VFM work on local services and functions would no longer be mandatory. Probably as welcome in local government as any of these measures was a resolution to abandon the practice of automatically providing an auditor's certificate for every claim sent to Whitehall for a ring-fenced government grant. The number of schemes formally requiring such a certificate had grown from 100 in 1998–99 to 190 in 2002–03. Claims (and returns) in the latter year related to grants totalling £63 billion. *Strategic Regulation* confirmed, as had actually been flagged by the Commission at the start of the year, that claims for any sum below £100,000 would be subject in future to a much more limited audit.

Strategic Plan 2004–07 was a formidable document that emerged in April 2004. Where the earlier publication had explained how the Commission would be cutting back, this one laid out in considerable detail – and conspicuously jargon-free text – the daunting range of tasks it was still intending to tackle. In most respects, it was an eloquent articulation of the thinking behind the CPA. The Plan was focused heavily on the improvement of public services. It was concerned with outcomes, as ordinary citizens would perceive them, rather than managerial processes. It stressed the importance of working with organizations 'at the top level', where all key decisions would be made. It acknowledged the need 'to work better in partnership' with other bodies (most notably CHAI in health, CSCI in social services and Ofsted in education) to minimize the presence of organizational boundaries that were just an irritation to most service-users. And of course, in the spirit of *Strategic Regulation*, it laid a heavy emphasis on ensuring that the game was always worth the candle. All regulatory action would be kept in proportion to the prospective benefits on offer.

But how to define 'regulatory action'? Here the Plan marked a subtle break with CPA. It acknowledged that 'many people have begun to question whether the burden of regulation is now distracting public service managers from their key task of improving the experiences of service users'. It was a return, in effect, to the fundamental debate prompted in the later 1990s by Power's *Audit Explosion*. Indeed, the issues had if anything grown rather more acute since the arrival of the Prime Minister's Delivery Unit in 2001 with its arsenal of targets and trajectories. One of the most eloquent discursions on the import of the whole 'non-financial' audit phenomenon had been aired in 2002 by Onora O'Neill, the philosopher and principal of Newnham College, Cambridge, in that year's *BBC Reith Lectures*.[22] Sceptical that society was really beset by a 'crisis of trust', she had discerned instead a 'culture of suspicion'. And she had fingered a 'revolution in accountability' as one of its primary causes: 'in the last two decades, the quest for greater accountability has penetrated all our lives, like great draughts of Heineken, reaching parts that supposedly less developed forms of accountability did not reach'. While the new regime was ostensibly about enhancing accountability to the public, argued O'Neill, in practice it was too often about imposing ever more forms of central control. The actual outcome for the public, meanwhile, was the opposite of an enhanced level of public services: 'I think that many public sector professionals find that the new demands damage their real work.'

The *Strategic Plan* did not refer explicitly to the admonishments of the Cambridge philosopher, and might have taken issue with her on some points if it had. But it was more than a nod to the reservations she had set out and their implications.* Accordingly, 'we have asked

---

* 'Central planning may have failed in the former Soviet Union but it is alive and well in Britain today. The new accountability culture aims at ever more perfect administrative control of institutional and professional life … But underlying this ostensible aim of accountability *to the public* the real requirements are for accountability *to regulators, to departments of governments, to funders, to legal standards* … Serious and effective accountability, I believe, needs [instead] to concentrate on good governance, on obligations to tell the truth and on intelligent accountability. I think we need to fantasize much less about Herculean micro-management by means of performance indicators or total transparency. If we want a culture of public service, professionals and public servants must in the end be free to serve the public rather than their paymasters.' (*A Question of Trust: the BBC Reith Lectures*, 2002, Cambridge University Press, 2002, pp. 45–59 *passim*.)

ourselves whether some of the approaches to regulation adopted in the past might now be counterproductive'. The long answer was contained in all the paragraphs defining Strategic Regulation. But the short answer was: goodbye to Best Value. As a separate activity, inspection would be massively reduced. Duplicate teams of auditors and inspectors would be a thing of the past. None of this was made too explicit in the Plan. Yet the message could hardly have been clearer: 'auditors', 'inspectors' and 'regulators' were now to be virtually interchangeable terms. The Audit Commission would talk with one voice.

But it would nonetheless talk of many things. The Plan set out the Commission's priorities for each of its five principal regulatory franchises: local government, health ('in partnership with CHAI which has the lead role'), housing, police and criminal justice, and the fire and rescue service. For each of them, the Plan set out an extraordinarily detailed list of objectives and target delivery dates. The document was aimed at many audiences. The Commission sent out consultation copies to all audited bodies, complete with an insert questionnaire. (For weeks afterwards, Strachan and Bundred spent a huge amount of time attending round-table discussions and dinners all over the country. Strachan repeatedly drove home a simple message: 'You improve, we help'.) But Bundred had his own internal audience very much in mind, too. Just as he had once done for Camden's councillors, Bundred was setting out the challenge for the whole of his staff as clearly as he could. Here was what they needed to do, and if they followed the lead that he and the chairman had provided, they could all have a better Commission.

There was much to admire in this head-on approach – but there was one aspect that must have had some experienced colleagues in Vincent Square swallowing hard as they turned the pages of the Plan. Many of the objectives were specifically identified as 'undertaking a national study', 'conducting an analysis' or 'disseminating good practice'. Asterisks marked out no less than twenty-eight such projects, across four of the Commission's five sectors (only health was exempt). It all amounted to a busy agenda for the studies directorate – more or less, unfortunately, on the first anniversary of the studies directorate's abolition. Bundred himself sensed early on that this was going to be a problem. National reports were still being regularly published. 'But every time we published a report, I discovered that the author of the report had got another job and was going off elsewhere. The Commission's reputation had been founded in part on the studies function, and it had suddenly been devalued.'[23]

Devalued or not, studies had to figure prominently on any external agenda. Strachan himself would regularly remind people, 'they are 2 per cent of the budget but account for 80 per cent of our reputation'.[24] Indeed, their central importance had been underlined just a few months prior to the publication of the Plan. *Council Tax Increases 2003–04* had been published in December 2003, with a rigorous examination of the 12.9 per cent average increase in council taxes that had been announced back in the spring of 2003. When auditors had begun collecting the data on the tax increases, there had been no intention of publishing a report. Within a few weeks of joining the Commission, though, Bundred decided that the findings ought to be pulled together as a report. It was a shrewd move: the findings were eminently predictable, but in setting them out clearly with some basic analysis, the ensuing report attracted enormous and understandable interest.

Ministers had been quick to blame councils with 'good' and 'excellent' ratings in the CPA table for taking advantage of an undertaking by the government not to cap their council taxes. (The Treasury would shortly announce that full rate-capping would be reintroduced for 2005–06.) There had certainly been some egregious examples of 'good' and 'excellent' councils grabbing their chance: Wandsworth, for example, had raised its council taxes by a whopping 57 per cent (having cut them by 25 per cent before the last election). But the Commission's study showed there was in fact no significant correlation between councils' tax increases and their CPA scores.[25] And tax increases were certainly not correlated in any meaningful way with party-political allegiances. Its own analysis ranged more widely. The gearing effect of a generally confusing set of financial arrangements was obviously part of the problem. (Little had changed, it seemed, since the Block Grant report of August 1984.) Since 75 per cent of council funding came from Whitehall grants that were fixed, every 1 per cent increase in a council's expenditure prompted a 4 per cent increase in council tax. And expenditure on public services was rising because the public expected more, the government ordained more and regulatory regimes demanded more. 'The conclusion (confirmed by the work of our auditors) is that budget increases were justifiable.'[26]

Strachan and Bundred had a good rapport with Nick Raynsford: he and they saw eye to eye on much of the Commission's agenda, and personal relations were cordial. But for any local government minister, the *Council Tax* report belonged squarely in the Whitehall box marked Very Unhelpful. The three of them had pored over it together, prior to publication. Raynsford asked for twenty-five changes; he was granted just seven. This was indeed a return to the 1980s. Bundred recalled of the outcome: 'Local government loved it. Of course central government hated it – but they were good enough to recognize that it was a legitimate piece of work for the Commission to have done.'[27] On the night of the report's publication, Mike Barnes attended the annual dinner of the Society of County Treasurers. When the time came for Grace before the meal, the usual words were embellished with 'And Lord, we thank the Audit Commission for publishing the *Council Tax* report.'[28]

Echoes of the past, though, could be overstated. The report conspicuously lacked any reference at the front to authorship, or at the back to consultative parties. Both items had been a common feature of national reports published up to 2002. While it was a reminder of the impact that authoritative reports could have, *Council Tax* was the product of a different way of tackling them – drawing author-teams together in a pragmatic fashion, sharing the composition and revision process among senior managers and Commission members, and assigning project leadership to directors with other, more urgent priorities. Alas, it was an approach that was never really to work. Over the next two years, the Commission would certainly go on publishing major reports from time to time. They would be beautifully designed, with powerful covers and excellent photographs. Several would present hard-hitting conclusions that would make a real difference. (Notable subjects included private-finance initiatives in education, the quality of police data, and the treatment of victims and witnesses by the criminal justice system.) None of this would belie the fact that the absence of a dedicated studies directorate was a serious weakness.

Without it, producing reports was a tortuous process. Drafts would invariably be more than just a slick graphic or two short of the finished article when they first reached the Commission members. Basic arguments would need to be reformulated; great slabs of text rewritten. Publication dates would regularly be postponed. More than once, only last-minute changes would save the Commission from serious embarrassment. Above all, perhaps, nothing would change the early impression that Vincent Square's national reports had lost their *flair* – that indefinable ingredient, reflected perhaps in the many punning titles of the past, with which the best reports used evidence and analysis to project compelling insights. The brilliance of so many past publications would prove hard to recapture.

As of the spring of 2004, though, all that lay ahead. For now, *Strategic Regulation* and the *Strategic Plan 2004–07* had undoubtedly conveyed a powerful sense of the Commission's new direction. *Council Tax Increases* had shown the chairman and his new chief executive working together as an effective team, and no one could doubt that they would defend the independence of the Commission as vehemently as any of their predecessors.

REAFFIRMING OLD SKILLS, IN FIRE SERVICES AND HOUSING

Independence never precluded cooperation, of course. The other notable feature of the eighteen months since Strachan's arrival at Vincent Square was that, at last, the Commission and the Labour government seemed to be back in tandem after all the alarums and excursions of 1999–2002. As if to underline the new-found affinity, Steve Bundred wrote a pamphlet for a think-tank in May 2004 that heralded New Labour's promotion of choice as the culmination of a half century of progress. In the 1950s and 1960s, local government had been dominated (as for decades past) by the councils' professional officers. Their power had been usurped in the 1970s and 1980s by local politicians and trade union leaders, protecting jobs and the in-house provision of services. By the end of the 1990s, a long decade and a half of conflict had purged the town halls of party-political squabbling and had switched the focus to lower costs and the better management of services. Since the late 1990s, the councils had increasingly ceded control of the agenda to users of their local services. And users were demanding more choice – which they would be able to exercise on the basis of better information, thanks in part to the Audit Commission.[29]

Here was a thoughtful analysis of the Story So Far that put all the tensions over the ill-starred Best Value project and the reshaping of regulation in health into perspective. For all the difficulties of recent years, past gains had been consolidated. Now New Labour and the Commission could push ahead to the next objectives. In this spirit, the chairman had left behind some of the better jokes from his earliest speeches that took the government to task for its obsession with innovative reform. (He had been fond, for example, of quoting from a press article chiding the government for having 'more visions than Mother Teresa, and more pilots than British Airways'.) CPA, rolled out to a second tier of local authorities in 2003–04 with considerable success, was proving more potent than even its champions had anticipated. The staff transfers to CHAI had just gone smoothly in April, and McKeon had already lifted relations with the DoH to a level unknown since 1989. By the early summer, confidence levels in Vincent Square were palpably rising again.

This was perhaps just as well. For the coming months saw the next seismic shift in New Labour sentiment on regulation and the improvement of public services. And it took the government in exactly the direction that Strachan had been anticipating since his arrival at the Commission. As usual, many different voices could be heard across government at any one time. But it was not quite the cacophony that had accompanied those early years of New Labour policy making, cheekily likened by Paul Kirby in the *LGC* to the Tower of Babel. This time, it was more of a subtly impassioned debate. Indeed, for those in the regulatory world, it was uncomfortably akin to a *balloon* debate. They found themselves caught like those in the proverbial basket, sinking with the weight of too many occupants. Like a nervous pilot, New Labour was quite suddenly intent on turfing out all but a handful, preferably before the general election due in 2005. Only those who could give a compelling account of themselves would be sure of a berth. For the government, in effect, had decided to embrace Strategic Regulation. Strachan and Bundred were summoned to Downing Street early in April 2004 and given the message by the prime minister in person. As the chief executive reported back to the Commission members, 'Whilst the PM was keen to take action, officials were more cautious. Nevertheless, progress on reviewing funding streams [for regulation] was likely as well as rationalization of regulators/inspectorates.'[30]

This confirmed what the Commission members had been told in confidence a couple of months earlier. Neil Kinghan, who had now left the LGA and returned to Whitehall as the director-general of local and regional government inside ODPM, had given them a presentation in February about 'a new strategy for local government'. Areas under consideration included 'greater devolution, less regulation, fewer targets and the funding system'. Fewer indicators, across fewer areas, would be involved.[31] It all very much accorded with the Commission's Strategic Plan – which was gratifying, as Bundred acknowledged in his April report: 'The Commission was seen to be working at the heart of government in shaping the future of regulation.' But he and Strachan were not so naive as to suppose that the Commission could on this account be sure of emerging from rationalization as a clear winner. It was apparent by September 2004 that the government intended a radical change of direction. There was, Bundred noted in his monthly report, 'a genuine recognition that regulation and inspection had become too complex'.[32] The cabinet committee in charge of the policy was talking of a *50 per cent* reduction in regulatory activities. (Even the next round of CPA was not sacrosanct.) One possibility was that all inspectorates would be subsumed within just four, covering local services, education, health and criminal justice.

There would be dangers here for the Commission, as well as opportunities. Piecemeal threats to the Commission's franchise soon surfaced. All spending departments were asked to submit their ideas to a Review of Inspection organized in the Cabinet Office. The DoH suggested (yet again) an end to local VFM work by Commission auditors working in the health service. The Home Office suggested that there should be no role for the Commission in the criminal justice system. The National Audit Office made a play (yet again) for the role undertaken by the Commission in the probation service since the late 1980s.[33] There was certainly plenty for the commissioners to think about, when they assembled at the Hitchin Priory Hotel in Hertfordshire for their November 2004 away-day.

One of the guest speakers invited to join them in Hertfordshire was the former member of the Commission, Tony Travers, and he gave them a cold-eyed assessment of their situation.[34] Travers suggested they see the open season on regulators as part of the government's broader drive to improve efficiency and effectiveness in the public sector. This was going to mean a significantly increased role in public services for private sector suppliers. (Did anyone mention CCT?) Already, a third of the expenditure on social services was going to private contractors. The pursuit of choice was leading inexorably to the creation of quasi-markets in public services. Some local government providers were struggling. There might be a new role for regulators, in assisting them; but there would always be the traditional role, ensuring that users had the information needed to make informed choices. Assuming that there would be no less call for regulators, though, how sure could the Commission be of retaining its position as 'the obvious first choice for [regulating] local services'? Travers did not take its survival for granted. '[It] was susceptible to the burden of mistrust and it would not take much for a negative story to have a major impact on the Commission's reputation. The Commission could also fall victim to regulatory reform itself.' But it had shown in the past its capacity to change with the latest political agenda and now it would have to do the same again. 'The Commission was a facilitator, and helped abstract ideas become tangible.'

If this was the road to survival, then the Commission was on the right track. Under Strachan and Bundred, it was already well on the way to bringing two important new ideas to fruition – in the fire and rescue service (FRS), and in housing.

The FRS idea that had been handed to Mollie Bickerstaff in the spring of 2003 was not entirely abstract. The Bain Report on the FRS had formulated concrete modernization proposals. As already noted, many were closely aligned to the recommendations in the 1995 national report, *In Line of Fire*; but they included the novel element that an independent inspectorate should be established within the Commission. It would apply a methodology along the lines of the Comprehensive Performance Assessment used for local authorities. Devising it was Bickerstaff's assignment. There were two huge obstacles. First, the FRS was a complicated beast. It comprised fifty-four brigades across England and Wales, all part of local government but administered in various ways as part of a complex national framework. Its antediluvian work practices had been the subject of no fewer than seven major reviews between 1970 and 1995 (two of them by the Commission itself, going back to the study by David Henderson-Stewart in 1986). But it was still the case that firemen were paid to fight fires. The fewer the fires, the less they got paid. Astonishingly, fire prevention was low on their list of priorities.

And second, awkwardly enough, the firemen had responded to the Bain Report with industrial action, their first since 1977: by March 2003, it was already the most serious national strike to hit the country through the ten years of Tony Blair's premiership. This involved Bickerstaff directly, because an agreement in March to end the strike rested on a deal: more pay in exchange for the enactment of reforms. While establishing the inspectorate, the Commission was given the additional job of verifying that the reforms were indeed producing the local benefits that had been agreed at national level. The March agreement was repudiated at first, and the strike ran on until June 2003. During its ten months, the country's fire brigades were only actually on strike for fifteen days, but intensive media coverage of all the negotiations and of all the action on the picket lines made the total seem much greater. (There were some memorable stories – including the tale of the fire station at Tooting in south London, where firemen lighting up a brazier for an all-night vigil managed to set fire to their station. Picket lines had to be crossed for the fire to be extinguished.)

Bickerstaff's team fulfilled both of its tasks immaculately. Verification audits were conducted through 2003 and 2004, and the results were published in February and September of 2004 in a low-key fashion that met the political needs of those implementing the original 2003 agreement. (This was not done at the expense of the Commission's independent stance, though. 'Commissioners supported a low key release of the interim result so long as it was hard hitting and did not pull any punches . . .')[35] And the FRS inspectorate was set up late in 2005, with a methodology based on the CPA that had been used through 2003 for district councils. In preparing for it, Bickerstaff had trained many individuals who went back into local brigades and their authorities with a real understanding of how to apply the methodology in future. She recalled: 'We had eight teams of six people working for an intensive period of about three months. On the teams were both elected councillors and people seconded in from the fire service. We trained all of those people: it was a fascinating project and I loved it.'[36]

The new idea in housing was neither more nor less than a re-invigoration of public sector housing through the promotion of local initiatives. What this meant in practice was actually a shower of new ideas, all of them keenly promoted by John Prescott, for whom housing was always a top priority. Putting a single body in charge of all inspections of public sector housing was one of these ideas. The Commission, having won this role in September 2002, carried it through as effectively as anyone could have asked. But it picked up bonus points for the way in which it also accommodated a string of follow-up requests from ODPM, and contributed significantly to the whole debate over housing over the next two years.

Combining the inspection of HAs with its existing inspection of local authority housing was not without its challenges for the Commission. The transfer of data from the Housing Corporation's IT system needed careful handling. It also emerged after the hand-over of responsibilities that the cost of inspecting HAs was appreciably more than the Corporation had disclosed. Since ODPM paid the Commission according to the estimate provided by the Corporation, Roy Irwin and his team were out of pocket from the start. Transitional funding from Whitehall helped them bridge the gap through the first year. Thereafter, the timetable for scheduled inspections had to be significantly extended: a three-year programme launched by the Corporation in 2002–03 would not be completed until probably 2008. Nonetheless, by the summer of 2004 a new inspection methodology was successfully agreed with the Housing Corporation, which remained the overall regulator of the HAs. And no one doubted the quality of the Commission's work.

The inspectorate run by Roy Irwin functioned outside the mainstream of the Commission in a sense. In other spheres, pooling DA and the inspectorate under the Operations Directorate after 2002 meant that auditors and inspectors were drawn together, with relationship managers assigned the task of coordinating their two, rather different messages for each client. (As Irwin put it succinctly: 'Inspection was about challenge, and audit was about assurance. Relationship managers were set up to turn sometimes contradictory messages at a local level into coordinated messages.'[37] It was Irwin's personal view that, in the wake of the merger, auditors were becoming more challenging and inspectors arguably less so.) This did not apply to the housing teams. These remained almost exclusively the preserve of specialized inspectors. They left the auditing of councils' housing to be part of the auditors' local workload in the normal way. The auditing of HAs stayed with external, commercial auditors. This left Irwin's teams to focus on their role as professional inspectors, with a thorough knowledge of all the technical aspects of housing.

Unsurprisingly, perhaps, an ODPM poll of HA chief executives in the autumn of 2004 found that many of them were still thoroughly confused over the respective roles of the Commission and the Housing Corporation. The two bodies were pressed by the department to produce a fresh Memorandum of Understanding to clarify matters and to remind the HAs that the Corporation retained responsibility for 'overall regulation'.[38] And Irwin's team had other demands to cope with, too. As he recalled: 'In housing we had to operate within a more dynamic, fluid political context.'[39] It was prey, in other words, to even more regular initiatives than the rest of local government – and Prescott's ODPM turned to the Commission for help with a succession of new ventures. Two of the most important were launched at the same time as the combined inspectorate itself, in the spring of 2003.

One was called the Sustainable Communities Plan. It entailed having nine 'Housing Market Renewal Pathfinders' in neglected (mostly north country) inner-city areas where the housing market had virtually collapsed. (More than one commentator was quick to criticize the slightly unfortunate name, redolent of RAF pathfinder raids that helped obliterate German cities in the second world war.) Substantial funding was available from the Treasury to back up the pathfinders' business plans – but only if they were signed off by the Commission. The ODPM's permanent secretary, Mavis McDonald, recalled: 'That was a total discretionary activity for the Commission in my view – but I don't think there was ever any question that the plans would be approved.' This kind of assumption had its downside risks for the Commission, reinforcing a mistaken view among some ministers that it was just another non-departmental public body that existed in effect to do the government's bidding – rather like the Housing Corporation, in fact. It was another illustration of the way in which the expanding influence of the Commission could sometimes pose risks for its *reputation* for independence, whatever the underlying reality.

The other was a programme called Supporting People. From April 2003, ODPM looked to each of 150 local authorities to work with a commissioning body in its area, on coordinating a wide range of housing-related services for vulnerable people. Here, again, the Commission's inspectors were asked to keep a sharp eye on proceedings. When Commission members reviewed the range of tasks undertaken in housing, in September 2004, they were quick to acknowledge one of the implications. 'Staff were excellent at service inspections, but needed to be equipped to examine broader issues.'[40] Steve Bundred commented during this discussion that the Commission had three main tools at its disposal in housing. Along with CPA and inspections, it could look to *studies* for a major contribution to the political debate. In fact, its housing titles were among the most distinctive of all the Commission's national reports in these years.

Rent arrears, repairs and maintenance and homelessness were among the subjects in a programme that took the housing inspectorate's output since 1999 to a dozen or more reports. One of the most notable was *Financing Council Housing*, published in June 2005, which included a revealing analysis of the current funding system. Tenants all over the country were in effect making a weekly contribution in their rent of between £2 and £14 a week to a central pot of money, out of which £15 flowed weekly to every council tenant in

London. Here was the kind of insight that would do the Commission's reputation no harm at all. But the title of the report was less beguiling than some would have liked. It hardly suggested the urgency of Banham's *Managing the Crisis in Council Housing*, or the flair of 1990s titles like *Home Alone* and *Stock in Trade*. Reports were now catalogued as part of 'AC Knowledge', a management system devised to help the Commission exploit all its data and research more effectively, and of a programme known as LFAIR ('Learning from Audit, Inspection and Research'). Titles such as *LFAIR on Repairs and Maintenance* hardly had the ring of, say, *To Build or Not to Build*. Still, a good report by any name could make a big impact.

However influential, though, the Commission's labours on housing or the fire service were not going to be enough, on their own, to book Strachan's Commission a safe passage into the putative new world of streamlined inspectorates and light-touch regulation that was beckoning by the end of 2004. For this, the Commission needed to prove its mettle – yet again – in the two principal arenas of health and local government.

ADJUSTING TO CHANGED DEMANDS IN THE NHS

The challenge in the health sector was all too plain. The Commission was handing over to CHAI a sizeable part of its post-1990 franchise – not in terms of revenues, but certainly in terms of staffing and public profile. (Almost thirty of the Commission's directorate staff finally transferred in April 2004.) While studiously avoiding any moves that might compromise its relations with Ian Kennedy and his staff – or, indeed, spoil its new-found amity with Andy McKeon's former colleagues at the DoH – the Commission needed to find ways of consolidating its importance to the governance of the NHS. The good relationship with CHAI had been usefully underwritten in March 2004, with the appointment to CHAI's board of the Commission member with most expertise on health policy, Jennifer Dixon. (One of the five new members appointed in November 2003, she had been policy adviser to the NHS chief executive between 1998 and 2000 and was now the director of health policy at the King's Fund.) No doubt the relationship was further helped, in the immediate weeks after CHAI's formal April launch, by the comforting realization that CHAI had no intention, in the short term anyway, of setting up its own field force. This would surely leave it relying on the Commission for much of its fact-gathering.

Sure enough, in May CHAI asked the Commission to help coordinate the data collection and action plans for the next round of Jonty Boyce's Acute Hospital Portfolio project, which had transferred across to CHAI with a more or less unchanged team in April 2004. The minutes of the Commission meeting for May noted this – the request, that is, *not* the transfer – as 'a small but pleasing precedent'.[41] Later, CHAI similarly asked the Commission to continue with its spot-checks work on NHS waiting-lists.*

From the Commission's perspective, though, the real action lay elsewhere. It had been left with the core task of auditing NHS bodies. A minimalist view of this might have cast the Commission, ironically, as little more than a tougher version of the old FB4 division of the pre-1990 health department. But the radical restructuring of the NHS in the meantime had lifted the role of audit to a higher plane altogether. With the devolvement of many constituent parts of the NHS into autonomous units, only bound to Whitehall by financial and contractual ties, the calibre and integrity of the service's financial management was fast becoming a matter of pressing concern. If audit were interpreted broadly, to cover the monitoring of the whole financial function, then the post-BRI Inquiry reforms had left the Commission with rather more than just a consolation prize. It was sitting on top of one of the hottest issues facing the NHS.

James Strachan had been quick to grasp this, as had Steve Bundred.

---

* Around this time, CHAI was rechristened the Healthcare Commission. Ian Kennedy believed the original name was deeply confusing to many people, and also underplayed the significance of the new body. It seemed to suggest it was simply a re-tread of CHI, rather than the affirmation of a fresh start after the statutory abolition of CHI (and the National Care Standards Commission, too). Kennedy recalled: 'We wrote to the then secretary of state, John Reid, in the very early days and requested permission to re-brand it. The written permission came back, couched in the usual officialese – with a note scribbled at the bottom of the letter from John Reid, "one of the most sensible decisions I've had to deal with this month!" ' (Kennedy, interview).

It was of course the potential of the Commission's supposedly narrower financial brief that they had reviewed with Andy McKeon in 2003, in persuading him to join the Commission. McKeon had wasted no time taking up the challenge. He had found a substantial research project already in the pipeline: it was envisaged as an overview of the current position of financial management in the NHS. McKeon set about sharpening it into a national report. An important late change to the legislation for the Healthcare Commission had cleared the way for the Commission to do this. It had been agreed that national VFM work and national reports would all be the prerogative in future of the new body. But what if local audit work by the Commission's field force revealed issues that needed to be flagged at a national level? Sensibly, the statute had been amended at the committee stage to leave a niche for the Commission to publish national reports provided that they dealt only with *financial* management. The statute had been enacted in November 2003.

Early in 2004, McKeon's team had produced *Achieving First-class Financial Management in the NHS*. Authorizing its publication, the Board members purred over what looked 'a model of what the Commission should be doing – focusing on specifics and hard-edged practicalities'.[42] It went well beyond general recommendations: it set out long lists of questions, which board members responsible for running the new primary care trusts, NHS trusts and hospital foundation trusts could put in front of their managers. While summarizing the current position for officials in Whitehall, it thus laid out a prescription for future action by service managers in the field. The report was also an eloquent statement of the Commission's ambition to fulfil to the hilt its redefined role within the NHS. This it did, over 2004–05, in three principal ways – starting with further national reports that met specific needs with exemplary timing.

Another widely noted title, for example, was *Introducing Payment by Results*, published in July 2004. This explored the implications of a hugely important innovation, which many gave Andy McKeon the credit for designing. Since 1990, hospitals had been paid on an essentially block-contract basis. The purchaser and the hospital management estimated in advance the likely number of operations over a year, and agreed an approximate cost base. Then they agreed an overall payment satisfactory to both sides. In other words, they relied on some old-fashioned horse-trading. In the new world, hospitals would only be paid for what they actually did. Each category of operation would have a price, the number of operations performed within each category would be documented, and the arithmetic would yield a payment due. All this presumed a level of cost accounting and general financial management way above what had previously been required. The Commission's report began the work of upgrading the NHS accordingly.

A second aspect of the Commission's newly oriented NHS role concerned its basic audit work. A few spectacular failures – one of them, by an unhappy chance, located again in Bristol – and mounting evidence of financial difficulties right across the NHS prompted the Commission to reappraise its audit responsibilities. Around sixty in-house auditors and partners from the private firms had been invited to a round-table session held in Greenwich early in December 2003. One outcome was a set of revisions to the Code of Audit Practice, for adoption from April 2005, and a series of national audit guides to help the field force take stock of the rising level of risk within the NHS. Auditors, it was agreed, should not hold back from Public Interest Reports where they were warranted. (PI Reports warning of impending deficits soon began to appear in slightly alarming numbers during 2004.) It was also decided in Greenwich that, as a by-product of their regularity work, auditors should produce an evaluation of each audited body that it could use to compare itself with its peers. This was christened the Auditors' Local Evaluation, or ALE. It was quickly recognized to be a useful step forward, and ALE was adopted by the Healthcare Commission as one of the two main constituent parts in its overall assessment of each NHS body. Whether this led to the formation of a real ALE group is unrecorded.

And third, the Commission showed a willingness to adapt flexibly to the changing NHS landscape by rethinking its stance on the audit of foundation trusts. Having tried and failed to dissuade the government from allowing FTs to choose their own auditors, the Commission pitched itself into the business of winning mandates in open competition against private firms. It was one of the key challenges facing the Commission, according to a paper on its future NHS strategy that was presented by Jennifer Dixon to her colleagues at the November 2004 away-day. (Other challenges included how best to argue for higher fees in line with increased risks, how to get closer to the primary care trusts, and how to prove the efficacy of the Commission's work to a wide audience. She was also careful to remind the Board that 'while excellence in financial management is its mainstay in health, the Audit Commission will need to cultivate sufficient intelligence across a much wider terrain'.)[43] The first half-dozen or so FT tenders came up in the opening months of 2005 – and the Commission failed to win a single one. It was not helped by guidance for the FTs from Monitor, the body given charge of regulating them, that they should use auditors with extensive *commercial* experience. Steve Bundred had secured Monitor's assurance that it 'would make clear that it was not their intention to exclude the Commission', but the guidance had been reaffirmed in December 2004.[44]

In the wake of its early FT setbacks, the Commission dropped talks initiated a year earlier to seek a tie-up with one of the private firms, Ernst & Young. Instead, in the spring of 2005, it began hiring its own auditors with commercial experience. They were assigned to a new 'Trust Practice' department set up by McKeon and dedicated to FT business specifically. Its first FT contracts were picked up later in 2005, and it was soon clear that the Commission could hold its own against the firms. Within a couple of years, just over sixty FTs would commence operations, and the Commission by 2007 had been appointed auditor to half of them.

This was the sort of expedient response to a potential shrinkage of the Commission's income that would have appealed to Andrew Foster. (In time, it was envisaged that all NHS trusts would be transformed into foundation trusts, so this was no mere adjunct to the Commission's NHS franchise.) How far, strictly speaking, it was consistent with the principles of Strategic Regulation – or the new commitment espoused since 2003 to making best use of the private firms, which emphasized partnership and collaboration – was fortunately a question that only occurred to a few alert insiders. Strachan and Bundred by the end of 2005 could be confident that the Commission was well on top of its brief in the health sector, and seen to be so.

A SECOND MODEL OF THE CPA

At all three party conferences in October 2004, Steve Bundred and several of the commissioners were delighted – and perhaps just a little surprised – to find themselves being accosted by councillors and others, wanting to say how pleased they were with various aspects of the work being done by the Commission. As Bundred noted in his report for the month: 'A commissioner commented that there had been a noticeable change in recent years – people were now hugely supportive of CPA, for example.'[45]

There was no doubt that CPA had been the salvation of the Commission since 2002. Initial antipathy had given way on most sides to grudging acceptance, at the very least. It was still seen by some as an added and unwelcome layer of bureaucracy. But the council chief executives, at their own SOLACE annual conference for 2004, had overwhelmingly endorsed it as 'a positive driver for improvement'. The Commission itself was keen by 2004 to instigate a revised version of CPA, and one that would raise the bar for local government. There was a view, shared by Bundred, that without some harder test, the motivational value of CPA would wither away (especially given the game-playing among the councils, inspired by categories defined by a points-based system). Ministers accepted this and agreed to the roll-out of a new version in 2005–06. Inevitably, this quickly became the Commission's biggest test of all. Whatever its progress in other areas such as housing and health, it would be judged by the new CPA. If it could deliver on the sequel, as it had on the original in 2002, Strachan and Bundred could surely be confident of a busy future. But there were two complications. The first was a practical matter: every department in Whitehall had a long list of items for inclusion in the new version. The second was more fundamental. Ideas about regulation had moved on, and the methodology behind CPA 2005 needed to reflect this.

Exhaustive consultations had been taking place with local government since the second half of 2003, and the Commission had been given responsibility for keeping track of the Whitehall consultation papers that had been circulating since January 2004. Here was the thick end of the wedge that had begun with Peter Brokenshire's advisory role on the formulation of the Citizen's Charter in 1993. The Commission was acting almost as a Downing Street taskforce, steering drafts of the CPA methodology through innumerable sub-committees. Jo Killian was the Commission's main coordinator. On one occasion, she took along Martin Evans to an inter-departmental meeting that looked likely to involve critical audit issues. He recalled:

It was the most bizarre meeting I've ever been to. It was in the basement of the Department of Transport on the corner of Horseferry Road. There was a representative there from every department in Whitehall. It was like an assembly of the United Nations. And all of them were saying 'CPA 2005 has got to have this in it from our department.' It was absolutely crazy.

That day's meeting was just a glimpse of the process that saw hundreds of performance indicators argued over for months. Indeed, some departments were still telephoning the Commission to argue over their respective PIs long after the launch of the methodology in April 2004. At that point, there were more than 300 separate streams of work for single-tier and county councils to take aboard. The architects of CPA 2005 were determined to reduce what they called the 'key lines of inquiry' – and to introduce standardized descriptors across all public services – but it was a struggle.

The shift in the *ideas* behind CPA 2005 reflected the thinking of the whole board, including those members currently serving on councils. But the Commission's persuasive articulation of the new approach owed much to someone brought into the Commission by James Strachan in November 2003 – Michael Lyons. Indeed, the desire to move local government away from the agenda of 2002's CPA had been one of the new man's motives in joining the board at all. And he arrived on it packing a bigger punch on local government matters than most new conscripts over the years. Lyons had been a successful chief executive of three local authorities – most recently, Birmingham City Council (1994–2001) and, before that, Nottinghamshire County Council (1990–94) and Wolverhampton Borough Council (1985–90). The head-hunters got to him early in 2003. They were searching for a successor to Andrew Foster, and approached him just as he was starting a second year as owner of a portfolio of distinguished positions that included a chair in public policy at Birmingham University.

It was not Lyons's academic pedigree that the head-hunters thought most likely to appeal to their client, though, nor even his member-ship of the three-man Bain Review into the fire and rescue service (though this had certainly given Lyons himself a special interest in at least one item on the Commission's agenda for 2004–05). At the invitation of Gordon Brown, Lyons had been a contributor since 1999 to the work of the Treasury's Public Services Productivity Panel. What marked Lyons out now as a potentially ideal partner for the Commission chairman was a paper he had written with another member of the Productivity Panel, the former Treasury economist and regulator of Britain's water industry from 1989 to 2000, Ian Byatt. *The Role of External Review in Improving Performance* was pub-lished in late 2001, and set out their views on the effectiveness of regulation in local government.

The paper took what could (at best) be described as a sceptical line. As Steve Bundred would later summarize its message, in a paper of his own (see pp. 622–3) that was published a few years later: 'Their report suggested that inspection can generate perverse outcomes, with the inspected bodies distracted from other key responsibilities, and argued for more systematic appraisal of the costs and benefits of inspection.'[46] In fact, Michael Lyons was privately scathing about the impact of Best Value since 1998 and the paper reflected this. He recalled: 'Best Value got lost in process. It was hideously prescriptive. It took the brightest, most creative leadership individuals in most local authorities and consigned them to the backroom for two years. The result was a disastrous period for local government.'[47] He had not been greatly impressed by CPA 2002, either. He distrusted the use of terms like 'excellent' in relation to local authorities ('completely useless'). He disapproved of its almost exclusive preoccupation with public services ('far too narrow'). And he positively deplored the 'poor' rating assigned by it to Birmingham, where investment in public services had deliberately been held in check since the mid-1980s while the city gave priority to rebuilding its run-down, post-industrialization centre. ('Making decisions like that is what you have local government for!')

Not surprisingly, Lyons had followed Strachan's early progress at the Commission since November 2002 with considerable interest.

He was reaffirming the independence of the Audit Commission, which I think had got eroded a little bit, and he was beginning to shape this concept that he summarized as Strategic Regulation. So after I'd told the head-hunters that I wasn't interested in the chief executive position, I said I would welcome a discussion with James just the same.[48]

A meeting was arranged, and they hit it off immediately, predictably finding much to agree about – though Strachan took a decidedly more benign view of CPA 2002, in deference to the PR value of a simple message. He waved aside the chief executive idea, and asked Lyons at the end of the meeting: would he have any interest, instead, in joining the board, prospectively as deputy chairman in succession to Adrienne Fresko? Yes, said Lyons, he would. Thereafter the appointment wheels turned for months – and Lyons took on the job that November.

He had had a longstanding affection and respect for the Commission, stretching back to its inception in 1983. In fact, he believed that it was arguably the single most important stimulus to the improvement in local government over the intervening years. Its misadventure with Best Value had done little to diminish his enthusiasm for its role, but Lyons was anxious now to help Strachan and Bundred steer CPA 2005 towards a broader remit. As the Commission papers on CPA came and went through 2004, Lyons was instrumental in persuading both his fellow members and ministers that the new version should amount to a more rounded assessment. It would pose a *more sophisticated* test for councils. This was not quite the snappy wording that Strachan and his colleagues had in mind for the formal title – and it emerged eventually as *CPA 2005: the Harder Test*. But the result was just the same. Lyons recalled: 'A council would be judged not only on the extent to which it was meeting nationally prescribed expectations with its services, but also on the simple question: does it have a clear sense of what it is trying to do?'[49]

Ministers responded positively to this approach. They welcomed the additional dimension brought to the CPA discussions by the Commission's deputy chairman, and his stock in Whitehall rose accordingly. When ministers turned that summer to finding someone who could lead a review of local government finance and the management of public sector assets, Lyons was their first choice for the job. His appointment as chairman of the review was announced early in September 2004.

The final six months of preparation for the launch of CPA 2005 saw one last flurry of local consultations. The local government managing director, Frances Done, told the board members at the Hertfordshire away-day in November that it 'would not be the one-off "big bang" approach of CPA 2002'.[50] The new version would be rolled out over a longer timescale, with more staff and the benefit of findings from more pilot councils. The burden on local authorities would be much reduced, it was hoped, by the removal of service inspections. It was true some councils remained apprehensive – not least because the old five categories were now to be replaced by four (with stars in place of adjectival descriptors) and some feared relegation compared with their rating in 2002. But everything possible was being done to ensure that CPA 2005 would slip into place as 'a natural progression'.

And so, in the end, it did – but not before another legal scare for the Commission that briefly posed a much more serious threat than the fleeting complaints of Torbay and Ealing, back in 2002. The strengthening of the statutory basis for CPA in the Local Government Act of 2003 appeared to have successfully deterred most aggrieved councillors from trying their luck in the courts. Legal squabbles over CPA findings had not been avoided altogether, of course. One of the councils originally targeted for a pilot run of CPA 2002, the metropolitan borough of Walsall, had turned to the lawyers in 2004 for help in arguing the toss over its rating. (The findings of the original inspection at Walsall, as already noted, had been so dismal that it was probably lucky to have been classified as 'poor' in CPA 2002. A new chief executive had wrought impressive improvements by 2004 that she deemed worthy of a 'fair' rating – but it was an important feature of CPA that the bar was raised in successive years for each category, and the improvements were thus deemed by the Commission to have fallen just short of the new threshold for 'fair'. Once again, legal action was abandoned in exchange for the promise of second thoughts – which led in due course to a 'fair' rating. Perhaps that should have been 'fair enough'.) And, as ever, a few especially unhappy councils were making belligerent noises in the run-up to the annual publication of CPA results towards the end of 2004. In general, though, all had been reasonably quiet on the legal front.

Until December 2004. Then a letter arrived at the Commission – now fully settled into Millbank Tower, to which it had relocated over an August Bank Holiday six months earlier – announcing another legal action against a much resented category rating. Once again, the complaining council was Ealing ('weak', as in 2002). This time, though, the basis of its challenge was that the Commission had allowed its rating to be dictated, in effect, by the findings of another inspectorate. This amounted, claimed Ealing's solicitors, to an unlawful delegation of the Commission's CPA powers. It seemed a curious argument, given that the Commission had quite explicitly designed the rules of CPA to allow it to draw on other inspectorates' findings in this way. How else, in practice, could it possibly have aspired to being a *comprehensive* assessment? It needed to rely on a wide range of professional bodies. It would simply be unworkable, if any rating could be challenged by a council that disputed the findings of this or that inspectorate on which the CPA was partly based. (Ealing had been undone by scoring very poorly on its social services. Here the CPA rules were especially explicit: if a council's social services fared poorly on the CSCI star-system – and Ealing had scored *zero* – then that council would automatically receive a 'weak' CPA rating, however stellar its performance elsewhere. Education was similarly assigned trumps status.) In short, a victory in the courts for Ealing would fling a huge spanner into the whole machinery of CPA.

This was well understood within Millbank Tower, where a new Commission solicitor had just taken over the post from Tony Child's successor, Rod Ainsworth. The new man was Roger Hamilton, a former borough solicitor at Brent Council. (By an odd coincidence, the chief executive of Ealing had been Roger Hamilton's boss when they worked together at Brent in the 1980s. A third solicitor in Brent's legal department in those days was – Rod Ainsworth. It was another reminder of what a small world English local government could be.) Steve Bundred and the Commission readily accepted Hamilton's advice that they had no choice but to reject Ealing's argument. 'We should win', Hamilton told them – though he chose his tense carefully.[51]

Which was just as well, because the High Court in February 2005 found in Ealing's favour. The Commission would have to look again, said the judge, and decide Ealing's CPA category afresh. Fortunately, this judgment was short-lived. Two months later, the Court of Appeal reversed it and emphatically reaffirmed the legal basis of the CPA approach – much to the relief of everyone at the Commission, not least its new in-house solicitor. The court also obliged Ealing to pay the Commission's legal costs, which added further to the value of the case as a deterrent for other councils contemplating a similar challenge. (The episode had one final twist for the Commission: within months of the Appeal hearing, Ealing's chief executive moved on and was succeeded by the former regional director for the Best Value inspectorate in the North, Darra Singh.)

Most local authorities, though, seemed already to have decided on a more positive response to CPA. Within weeks of the general election of May 2005, the smooth launch of the new round was being acknowledged in government. Touring the offices of the freshly appointed ministers, Strachan and Bundred were both thanked sincerely for the work done by Frances Done and her team. (Jo Killian had just left the Commission, moving to Essex County Council, where in due course she would rise to be chief executive.) At the June meeting of the board, the chairman 'highlighted the praise ministers had given to the development of the new framework.'[52]

By common consent, CPA 2005 was successfully engaging the attention and commitment of people throughout local government. Many went on objecting to CPA, as they had done after 2002, as a bureaucratic nuisance. But this made little difference to its impact. The ratings it later produced would be given credence and treated as a sensible measure of the quality of individual councils. They would also bring pressure to bear constructively on those councils that fared least well. The scores for *CPA 2005: the Harder Test* were published in December 2005. Out of 150 authorities, 29 were granted four stars; 65 collected three stars, 49 two stars and six scraped home with one. The only authority awarded no star at all was North East Lincolnshire, where Neil Kinghan had seen the council savaged by the local press in 2002. To little effect, apparently.

Meanwhile, discussions had resumed across Whitehall early in the summer of 2005, over the future consolidation of inspectorates. There was no longer any real doubt that the local services inspectorate would be the Audit Commission. By September, a different debate was starting on the prospective role of the Commission as a *gatekeeper* for all of the inspectorates. When the chairman and chief executive of the Local Government Association made a presentation to the board in November, they told members that the LGA 'would welcome a strong role for a local services gatekeeper . . . [to promote the work of] coordinating all inspection and assessment in an area'.[53] It hardly needed to be added that this would be a job for the Commission.

MAKING FRIENDS AND MAKING WAVES

The plausibility of a gatekeeper role for the Commission was not just an affirmation of its competence in taking on new assignments in recent years. It was also a fair reflection of the extent to which, by year end, Strachan and Bundred together had successfully built up the Commission's working relationships with its sister bodies in the regulatory universe. This in itself marked quite an achievement. Back in March, an earlier verdict on those relationships had been less encouraging. In a presentation to the board based on a recently completed 'Perceptions Survey' for the Commission, Ben Page of MORI broached the issue with his usual professional caution. On the whole, the results of the survey were 'highly creditable'. It was apparent, though, that 'some other regulators were not positive about relationships with the Commission and felt it to be predatory'. In the discussion that followed, board members professed to be 'not unduly concerned that other regulators felt the Commission to be predatory: this was to be expected in a competitive environment'. But they acknowledged a real enough issue: 'Comments about poor working relationships [with other regulators] should be examined.'[54]

In fact, considerable thought had already gone into addressing the issue. The agendas for seven out of the ten board meetings in 2005 included time for a presentation by one or another of the Commission's various partners. A good start had been made in January, when the DoH's finance director, Richard Douglas, confirmed the significant improvement in relations between his department and the Commission. ('Mature debates were now the norm...'[55]) Other speakers included Ian Kennedy and his chief executive from the Healthcare Commission; the chairman and chief executive of the National Housing Federation; and the chairman, Denise Platt, and her chief inspector from the Commission for Social Care Inspection.

Strachan and Bundred reciprocated these visits by themselves devoting huge time and effort throughout the year to representing the Commission on public platforms and in private round-table discussions. Significant contributions were made by the Commission to government initiatives such as the Gershon Review of efficiency in the public sector, conducted in 2004–05. And relations with the National Audit Office were, as ever, treated with special care.

The Commission and the NAO were closer by 2005 than they had ever been in the past. Combined studies, of both local government and NHS topics – though not without their difficulties – had undoubtedly been a success. A merger of the NAO in Wales with ACiW to form a combined Wales Audit Office WAO had been effected without any rancour, though the top job had gone to a former NAO official in London rather than the Commission's own Clive Grace, who lost out in an open competition. The WAO continued to work closely with the Commission after its formal launch in April 2005. The NAO and the Commission were also involved closely together in the government's work on 'delivery-chain analysis', looking hard at the ways in which initiatives from the centre were actually translated into action on the ground. (The Commission's chairman liked to refer here to the Humpty Dumpty effect: top-down initiatives were broken into pieces by having to make their way down via insufficiently coordinated agencies, leaving people at a local level struggling to put them together again in a form recognizably akin to the original idea.) It helped, too, that James Strachan got along well with John Bourn, the NAO's comptroller and auditor-general.

When the most senior 100 staff of the NAO met for an internal conference in May 2005, Strachan was invited to address them as one of very few guest speakers. Reporting back to the Board on the event, and on a recent meeting between the senior management teams of the two bodies, Strachan spoke about their relationship more broadly. He acknowledged that ministers 'had previously contemplated a merger'. In the aftermath of the May 2005 general election, though, there appeared to be 'little appetite for it at present'. Strachan privately thought merging the Commission and the NAO would be a perfectly logical step, which would never happen because Westminster's politicians would baulk at the creation of such a powerful beast. Many of his colleagues on the Commission, mindful of the fact that Parliament would always insist on the NAO controlling any such combination, unhesitatingly rejected arguments for a merger as tantamount to the death of the Commission.

Personal relationships at the top always counted for a great deal across the whole range of the Commission's dealings with other bodies – and it helped that Strachan had many fervent admirers. But he was always a man who provoked strong feelings in both directions, and there was little doubt that some reacted badly to his hard-hitting style. He could be witheringly dismissive of those in charge of other non-departmental public bodies – and his finger-prodding with senior ministers could sometimes leave department officials at a loss over whether to admire his chutzpah or despair at the difficulties it left in its wake. And attitudes to the chairman within the Commission itself were not so different. By 2005, many admired the way in which he had led from the front and positioned the organization so adroitly in the national debate over regulation. But there were those, at every level, who took exception to the unusually high demands that he made of those around him. Their concerns reverberated beyond Millbank Tower.

The chief smoother of feathers internally, and mender of fences in the wider world, was inevitably Steve Bundred. The strain weighed on his own relationship with Strachan, though it did not stop the two of them working together very effectively as partners with complementary strengths – especially as time wore on, and the chairman felt increasingly comfortable stepping back to leave the quietly authoritative Bundred in charge. Many times during Strachan's chairmanship,

Bundred was asked how it felt to be working for a chairman who really wanted to be the chief executive. But he recalled: 'I never saw it like that. James always understood the difference between the two roles. Sometimes it caused me a little difficulty that I had a chairman who wanted to be the secretary of state, but that was a different matter.'[56]

Morale within the Commission had generally improved steadily since the dark days of 2001–03. In September 2004, the chief executive handed the board his own assessment of progress: he saw 'an organization increasingly in good shape, although some weaknesses remained'.[57] But none could doubt there was room for improvement. The head of the Board's audit committee, Brian Pomeroy, reported the following month that the Commission was still faced with a staff turnover of just over 10 per cent a year; and 40 per cent of the leavers were departing for lower-paid jobs, which carried its own message about the stress levels that had travelled from Vincent Square to Millbank Tower. Nor was everything perfect at the top of the organization. Adding to the busy agenda for the November 2004 away-day, Strachan invited a senior partner from the accountants PricewaterhouseCoopers, Tony Allen, to review the effectiveness of the Board itself. He found much to praise – 'high scores on performance, trust and decision-making' – but it must have been disconcerting to hear that the senior executives of the Commission took a much less generous view of the Board's work than did the commissioners themselves.[58]

By the spring of 2005, however, the mood inside the Commission was brightening perceptibly. Despite the shock over the compulsory redundancies finally announced in February, an employee survey reported back to the Board that 84 per cent of staff considered the Commission to be a good place to work. Given that the outcome of the last survey, in April 2003, had never subsequently been disclosed to employees, it was perhaps unsurprising that many were now sceptical about the value of the whole exercise. But changes did follow, helping especially to open up the office culture within Millbank Tower – and this time, the survey results *were* published. Much to the Board's delight, Bundred was also able to report that the Commission's accreditation by the Investors in People organization had been renewed.

Externally, the spring of 2005 marked a less happy milestone. Following the general election, the knowledgeable Nick Raynsford was perversely replaced as the local government minister within the ODPM. His presence was missed by the Commission on several counts over the following months – not least because he had been a valuable intermediary between Strachan and the deputy prime minister. Those close to John Prescott were painfully aware that he regarded the Commission chairman as less than a kindred spirit. He had respect for him, but their personal dealings could be difficult. The need to mediate between them was rarely far from the mind of either the ODPM's permanent secretary or the Commission's chief executive. Once they had lost the services of Nick Raynsford in this context, the prospect of an unfortunate clash was never far away.

And the deputy prime minister was well aware of how polarized were others' views of the Commission's chairman, too. Strachan had made some powerful enemies in Whitehall. As the time neared for a reappointment decision, due by early November, Prescott had his reservations and they appeared to be causing a problem. At almost the last moment, Strachan found himself being offered a second term of less than the traditional three years. Before any contract could be signed, a press release went out, announcing his reappointment. But no formal contractual papers had yet been made available, nor was Strachan happy with an abbreviated tenure. It was not what he had expected.

He himself, meanwhile, had begun to reconsider his future options. Much had been accomplished over his three years as chairman. Speaking in September, at the launch of a think-tank report into government targets, he noted that the latest CPA proposals implied that the amount of inspecting by the Commission could fall by 70 per cent over the coming three years. This represented the fulfilment of his own personal agenda to a considerable extent. There were many other private and voluntary activities that he was keen to pursue. Strachan decided in November that he would tackle the deputy prime minister over the unsatisfactory nature of the reappointment decision to date. As ever, he was not afraid to take a few risks.

Unfortunately, Prescott also had some strong views of his own that he wished to impart. Discussions followed in November that remained strictly private between the two of them. But the outcome, announced just before Christmas, came as a shock to almost everyone: Strachan announced that he would not be accepting the offer of reappointment and would stand down in January 2006. The news coincided with a spat between the Commission and the Local Government Association over a press release about the results of CPA 2005. Strachan had been typically outspoken in some remarks that were not shown to the LGA before their release to the press. It had no connection whatever with his departure, as some in the media wrongly assumed; but it did ensure that Strachan went on making waves, right to the end.

16

An Even Keel, 2006–08

While James Strachan spent Christmas of 2005 holidaying in the jungles of Cambodia, officials in the ODPM were left with a sudden need to find an acting chairman in his place. Michael Lyons was the obvious candidate. This was a little unfortunate for him, in two respects. He had just informed the board in November that he would not be seeking reappointment as deputy chairman because of the pressure of other commitments on his time. On the other hand, under different circumstances, he might well have been open to an offer of the full position. Now both considerations had to be set aside. Approached about taking on the acting role, Lyons knew immediately that it was something he would have to do: Strachan's unexpected departure had rocked the boat, and Lyons could see that he was uniquely placed to steady it again. But he could only accept on one condition, as he explained to the ODPM's permanent secretary, Peter Housden. As Lyons recalled: 'In my view, the only way I could take on the role in the short term was by saying unequivocally that I would not be a candidate for the permanent post.'[1]

Housden, who had just succeeded Mavis McDonald in October, had himself worked briefly at the Commission, in 2000–01. (On secondment from local government – he had been chief executive of Nottinghamshire County Council for seven years – he had preceded Peter Wilkinson as health strategy director, working on a new approach to the health sector for the Commission in light of the government's NHS National Plan.) So he well understood the demands of the Commission chairmanship. His own concern in approaching Lyons had been that it might pose too heavy a burden for someone already charged by the chancellor with delivering a review of local government finance. On this score, though, Lyons was ready to accommodate the new situation. His deadline was December 2006. Provided that a new chairman was in place by September, there was no insuperable obstacle to him being the Commission's third acting chairman. Housden was relieved; Lyons accepted the job; and the brief went out to begin the search for the sixth chairman proper.

The acting chairman's first task, inevitably, was to calm some frayed nerves within the Commission, and especially Millbank Tower. The abruptness of Strachan's exit prompted plenty of wild stories in the early months of 2006 – fuelled, of course, by colourful stories about his clashes with government ministers over the years. (The same had happened in 1986 when the news broke of John Banham's resignation, though Banham had stayed on for nearly six months to hand over to his successor.) He laid on the balm with finesse. As deputy chairman since 2004, Lyons had been accustomed to sitting down privately with Strachan once a month to talk over in some detail the latest issues facing the Commission. So he was able to step into an effective working relationship with Steve Bundred without a blip. It also helped that he and Bundred enjoyed each other's company. Like Strachan, the two of them were fascinated by the intellectual challenges ahead of the Commission and took a similarly cerebral view of the business agenda. A good relationship between the two people at the head of the Commission always improved the whole working atmosphere of the centre, no less than poor relations harmed it. But the impact of the changes at the top early in 2006 did more than lift the mood among the senior staff: Lyons and Bundred also acted quickly to adjust the structure of the Commission in ways that were welcomed at every level of the organization.

It was an easy decision to reshape the technical support and audit-appointments function: most senior managers already treated Martin Evans as though he was on the management team. Bundred effectively re-created the old role of audit director, held for so many years by Harry Wilkinson. Once installed, Evans assembled his own team to raise the profile of the Commission's core audit work – and to take over the work already begun on the next tender round for the private firms, which was due in the summer of 2006. The process at first produced a surprising outcome, with just four firms awarded 22 per cent of the total audit market (with in-house auditors retaining 72 per cent). One of those excluded was the hitherto easily dominant market leader among the private firms, PricewaterhouseCoopers; but PwC were given the opportunity to bid again early in 2007, and did so successfully. The outcome of the two tender rounds was a significant reshuffle of the firms, with three – PwC, Robson Rhodes and KPMG – emerging with most of the tendered market shared equally between them. (See Appendix 6.)

More dramatic, though, was another decision, taken in March 2006 and implemented by May, to restore a separate studies directorate. For most of the past two years, members had debated on almost a monthly basis how best to restore studies to their former glory. Many changes had been tried. Most obviously, the number of published reports had been severely curtailed: twenty-two appeared in 2004, but only eight in 2005. (The reduced number of reports was part of a general contraction in the Commission's publishing. The tally of all non-report titles – covering briefings, bulletins, consultation papers, corporate documents, guidance papers and management handbooks – came to twenty-four in 2004 and thirteen in 2005.) Procedures had been amended to allow commissioners to become more involved in each report at a much earlier stage, rather as had been the case in the 1990s. In 2005, the budget for studies had been almost doubled. All this, Strachan had felt, would surely be enough to set matters right. 'Following recent improvements and several detailed examinations of the issue', as he told commissioners in July 2005, 'he was content for staff to get on and deliver a robust, quality programme.'[2]

Without a resurrection of the formal department, though, the extra money had made no real difference. The Commission had a head of policy and a head of studies – but in both cases the brief was more concerned with process and coordination than with content. Quality reports required dedicated researchers and writers. Most had left the Commission. People of the same calibre would not be found to replace them until the Commission once again had a department commanding the respect that had once been accorded, say, the teams led by Ross Tristem or Jonty Boyce. Bundred had come to see this many months ago. It was simply unrealistic to expect line-managers in other areas to take on the supervision of studies in addition to their operational roles. He recalled: 'Studies would never command the attention of any local government managing director, because other things would always be more urgent.'

So a new unit was set up, and christened the Policy, Research and Studies directorate: the old PSR was thus reborn as PRS. Those already working on studies elsewhere in the Commission were all transferred into PRS – with the exception of those working under Andy McKeon on NHS financial work, who remained separate – and plans were made to expand staff numbers and bring in new blood. It would be headed by Peter Wilkinson, who had been working since 2003 as managing director of strategy and resources. The great survivor on the Commission's executive team, Wilkinson had had years to reflect on the studies process. He had briefly run the old Local Government Studies directorate in 1995 during Bob Chilton's secondment to the LGCE, and had later set up the Knowledge and Information directorate. He was clear in his own mind where studies had gone wrong since the end of the old regime in 2003, as he recalled:

We stopped paying attention to the value of a scientific methodology, based on the formulation of hypotheses and the gathering of hard evidence. We started paying too much heed instead to what the eventual sound-bite and headline would be – which of course gave the initiative to those who were more interested in broad policy than detailed research. So the studies lost all their depth.[3]

He was determined now to recapture what had been lost.

And he wanted to go further. The Commission had a statutory duty to undertake studies – but Wilkinson had come to appreciate also the huge importance of managing the Commission's intellectual property in a disciplined way, and of marshalling research from time to time that might have great value even though it was not destined for publication. The new PRS would do both, in addition to studies. Its policy arm would embrace the knowledge-management function; and the research arm would be able to undertake quick research projects, aimed for example at quantifying the impact of CPA in specific localities. It was a wide brief, and Wilkinson would tackle it with the support of four directors. The initial four were Marcial Boo (policy), John Kirkpatrick (studies), Michael Hughes (studies) and

David Caplan (research). The last three all came aboard during 2006.

It was also decided to divide the study teams of PRS between two locations – one of them outside London, to widen the pool of new recruits. John Prescott had chivvied Strachan almost since 2003 to push more of the Commission's staff away from the capital. Strachan had been reluctant to do so, arguing that the Commission was already a geographically diffuse organization by its very nature. (He had had to make a gesture in this direction, though, and late in his term had transferred some London-based back-office functions to Nicholson House in Bristol. When Strachan reported this decision in person to Prescott, the deputy prime minister could not hide his exasperation. 'But James, Bristol is not *in the North*!')[4] With Lyons in the chair, it would have to be a different story: the acting chairman, after all, had himself authored an independent review into the scope for relocating more public sector activities away from London and the south-east. A heated debate was soon under way in Millbank Tower over which staff departments would go where. Since PRS was a new department, agreeing a second main location proved straightforward enough and it was sited in Solihull. This, it was hoped, would allow staff to benefit from the proximity not just of Birmingham University's INLOGOV and other related faculties, but also of the universities at Warwick, Aston and Leicester. Aptly enough, the first director of the Solihull office would be Michael Hughes, a former head of INLOGOV, who had succeeded Michael Lyons in that post. Some other PRS staff were based in Bristol and in Leeds.

This physical change in the layout of the Commission, coming just eighteen months after the move into Millbank Tower, seemed usefully to reinforce a sense within the organization that the entrenched fiefdoms of the past were at last being left behind. Bundred himself had no doubts on this score: he recalled that the cooperation between disparate parts of the Commission was 'massively improved' by the middle of 2006. It made a big contribution to rising morale among all employees. Most managers, though, were inevitably reserving judgement on the outcome of Strachan's departure until a new permanent chairman had made his presence felt.

THE COMMISSION'S SIXTH CHAIRMAN

The search for a new chairman got off to a slow start. Perhaps the immediate availability of Michael Lyons punctured any sense of urgency. Whatever the explanation, the job did not surface, as an advertisement in the appointments section of the *Sunday Times*, until the end of April. One man who saw it there was reading the first copy of the *Sunday Times* that he had bought in fifteen years. Michael O'Higgins was curious to see what kind of positions were carried in the supplement. This had never been of any interest to him in the past. As a successful academic-turned-management consultant, he had enjoyed a seamless career with no job-hunting for almost thirty years – until that weekend. But on the Friday, he had just formally announced to all his colleagues at PA Consulting, a leading management consultancy, that he would be leaving in the late autumn. At 50, and with plenty of money in the bank, he had decided it was time to make a break from the corporate treadmill and start out on a portfolio career.

When his eye fell on the Audit Commission advertisement ('Chairman: two days a week . . .' – the non-executive status was carefully emphasized), O'Higgins was intrigued immediately. His past dealings with the Commission were hardly extensive, but they went back quite a way. As a Dubliner with degrees in economics and social policy from Trinity College, Dublin and the London School of Economics, O'Higgins had taken a first job in academia in 1978, as a lecturer in social policy at the University of Bath. His faculty head there was the influential teacher and writer on public policy matters, Rudolf Klein. By the time that the Audit Commission was set up five years later, he and Klein were again working together in Whitehall as advisers to the Commons Select Committee that monitored the DHSS. They thought it would be interesting to talk to John Banham about his ambitions for the Commission. O'Higgins recalled: 'Rudolf's definition of a semi-structured interview was lunch, so we had a splendid one with John at a beautiful place just outside Bath.'[5] Both took an active interest thereafter in the achievements of Banham and his successors in Vincent Square.

By the mid-90s, O'Higgins had exchanged the sackcloth of academia for a lucrative post in the public sector consultancy practice of Price Waterhouse. He had been made a partner, largely on the back of winning for his firm two big contracts on community care from CIPFA, where the client was Martin Evans. And in 1995, O'Higgins was hired by the Commission to help it 'formulate a strategy for the development of databases of comparative performance in local government and the NHS'.[6] Working closely with the Commission over five months of that year, O'Higgins had formed a high opinion of many of the individuals working within it – but had also gained an impression of a place shaped around fierce competing baronies. It was an image that stayed with him.

In more recent years, O'Higgins had heard much less of the Commission. To an extent, this was a reflection of his own career path: very early in a ten-year stint at PA Consulting, he had closed down the local government section of the public sector practice. (The modest fees available for fragments of work around the country made its economics unappealing.) But there was another, more contentious explanation for the Commission's lower visibility that intrigued him. In the weeks after spotting the advert in the *Sunday Times*, O'Higgins quizzed colleagues in the consulting world about the current standing of the Commission. There seemed to be a general consensus that it had been many years since its national reports were genuinely required reading for anyone at work on policy in the public sector. This struck O'Higgins as more of a challenge than a deterrent, though. In many ways, the chairmanship of the Commission looked to O'Higgins like a perfect start to his post-consultancy career. He applied, and set about four testing interview sessions.

To Peter Housden and his fellow officials, at least three aspects of O'Higgins' candidacy must have shone out from the start. His consulting background pointed to a sharp mind. This he confirmed in the interviews with an incisive agenda of priorities that he listed with eloquence. (They could be summarized as emphasizing 'place', 'user-choice', 'outcomes' and 'real-time data' – and they would crop up in a variety of guises over the year ahead.) His list of contacts within Whitehall was exemplary: he had worked as a consultant to almost every single department of government, at some point in his career –

Andy McKeon had been a client at the DoH – and he had been especially closely involved with Defra, the Foreign Office and the Cabinet Office in more recent years. And his easy-going Irish affability suggested that, as chairman, O'Higgins would deal with others in a relaxed, straightforward fashion that Steve Bundred and his executive colleagues would especially appreciate. O'Higgins would not be averse to sharing a drink or two with junior auditors on the conference circuit and swapping football stories. The Commission's sponsoring department after May 2006 was the newly formed Department for Communities and Local Government (CLG). Its secretary of state, Ruth Kelly, offered O'Higgins the job late in July. Over the following months of the summer, he worked his way into it by reading a survey of the Commission's work that Steve Bundred had instigated to help with the induction process. It ran to a mere fourteen volumes.

A friend and senior colleague at Price Waterhouse had once complimented O'Higgins on the flawless progression of his career, while hinting at his good fortune. He himself recalled: 'He described me as the best strategist he knew, provided you defined strategy as an *ex post* rationale!' In taking up the chairmanship of the Commission in 2006, O'Higgins had demonstrated this happy knack once again: rather fortuitously, he had taken up the helm at an institution poised to fulfil its considerable potential in ways that had too often eluded it in the years since the late 1990s. To the big questions over its future, James Strachan had brought essentially the right answers; and Steve Bundred had steadily emerged since 2003 as a purposeful chief executive with a strong grasp of the Commission's long-term objectives. There was still much to be done. But O'Higgins arrived in time to lead the Commission to a more than satisfactory conclusion of its first quarter-century. Over the next couple of years, it would be apparent that the Commission had at least four reasons to feel confident about its future.

Internally, morale was steadily improving. Externally, relations with Whitehall departments and other non-departmental public bodies appeared to be as healthy as they had ever been: the Commission's franchise was expanding once again. In its positioning *vis-à-vis* the outside world, the Commission seemed at last to have settled on a modus operandi that suited it well, while meeting with broad support from its main stakeholders. And, finally, political debate over the governance of councils, the NHS and other public bodies outside central government appeared to be shifting in a direction that could hardly fail to underscore the continuing importance of the role played by the Commission in this context.

A STEADY IMPROVEMENT IN MORALE

Michael Lyons stepped down and retired from the Board in September 2006 to finish work on his Review of Local Government Finance. (There was no need for him to worry about a December deadline, though: Gordon Brown postponed the review's publication date until 21 March, the day of the 2007 budget. If Lyons was dismayed at the consequent lack of immediate coverage for his report, he concealed it well. But then, his appointment as the chairman of the BBC Trust was announced just fifteen days later.) Michael O'Higgins stepped into the chair that month and had his first chance to make an impact on the Commission at a conference of 600 managers that was convened at a Birmingham hotel a few weeks later.

The October conference was the first of its kind in the history of the Commission, bringing together managers from all levels and all across the organization. It turned out to be a big success – plans soon followed to make it an annual event – and it featured a perfect debut for the new chairman. O'Higgins came across as eminently approachable and keen to hear the views of those working in the front line. At the same time, though, he was extremely well briefed and had some trenchant observations to make of the Commission in his main speech. Considering its formidable reputation and the hard work invested by so many hundreds of highly skilled professionals, he suggested, it was punching well below its weight. It needed to assert itself with more confidence. Reports from the centre, for example, could be targeted at specific audiences much more effectively. (Perhaps he might have said *even* more effectively, given how hard Strachan had tried to push reports in this direction already.) And the views and contacts of those working in the field could be tapped more often and more systematically, not least as an invaluable sounding-board for central government. Candid views like these, of course, did the self-esteem of his listeners no harm at all.

At the same conference, it struck many that their chief executive already seemed to have taken on board the chairman's message about confidence, in his own platform style. Steve Bundred had never been renowned as a speaker and was not about to become suddenly the Cicero of the conference circuit. But his had too often been an unenviable billing in the past, in the shadow of James Strachan – a speaker who left most audiences as impressed by his rhetoric as they were amazed by his handling of his deafness. By the autumn of 2006, Bundred was generally being seen as a more assertive speaker, and a more visible leader, too.

Another leader, just below him, also made a useful impact around this time. Immediately prior to the Birmingham conference, the local government director, Frances Done, had stepped down after her much-praised handling of CPA 2005's implementation. The person chosen to succeed her was Gareth Davies, the northern regional director. Initially an interim appointee, he beat off some strong external competition for the permanent job. A popular figure, his appointment had a special significance for many: Davies had joined the Commission in 1987 straight from Cambridge as a graduate trainee. His rise to the top was a timely reminder, after the heavy influx of external appointees since the mid-1990s, that experience within the Commission could still be highly prized and rewarded. Since emerging as a district auditor from one of David Prince's assessment centres, Davies had worked for two years in Vincent Square under Mollie Bickerstaff as part of her Quality Control Review team. He had worked as an auditor in Yorkshire since 1997 and had helped steer the northern region through all the vicissitudes of Best Value and its aftermath. His promotion, though not finally confirmed until March 2007, added a welcome note of continuity to the top team.

Other new arrivals around this time included a new director of corporate services, Dave Stewart, and a new director of 'communications and public reporting', Jenny Grey, who joined in July 2006. If corporate services had once been the Commission's Cinderella function, this tag was in danger of being attached now to communications. Morale among the forty or so people working in communications was very low by 2006, after two of Jenny Grey's predecessors had struggled in vain to win the confidence of the Board. Internally, staff had been bombarded with a plethora of poorly coordinated messages, of the kind that only invite a weary cynicism in any office environment. Above all, hard-hitting and image-boosting reports had been thin on the ground since 2003, impoverishing the Commission's media relations. The risk in all this was clear. The Treasury under Gordon Brown had been pushing since the 2005 election for a consolidation of the regulatory sector. With a Brown premiership impending, it was no time for the Commission to risk appearing stale and bureaucratic by comparison with a host of other regulatory bodies.

The chairman's words at the October conference about the need for the Commission to assert itself with more confidence captured the gist of the challenge facing the new communications head. Grey launched an immediate reorganization of the department, though this inevitably added at the outset to stress levels already pumped up by arguments over which jobs might go to Bristol. (Around half ended up being relocated, though few if any of the incumbent staff moved with them.) Then, with a grasp of broad strategic objectives that was welcomed on the Board, she instigated a re-vamp of the Commission's brand image, last reviewed back in 2002. She also acted quickly to improve internal communications – just in time, perhaps, to have a positive impact on an employees' opinion survey conducted early in 2007, the first for two years.

The complete survey was not available until May, but its headlines were presented to the Board in March 2007. Steve Bundred had reported his own perceptions, back in January 2006. His view then was that, while there was much to be positive about, 'the organization was fragile, overstretched and reliant on a small number of key people'.[7] The new survey found high workloads still a problem for many staff. But in the main, the news was far better. 'While in 2005 nearly half the Commission's employees felt its standing as an employer had declined over the previous year, there has been a major shift of opinion so that now three quarters believe it is as good or better now than it was a year ago.'[8] The minutes in March 2007 recorded the commissioners' view that 'the overall figures were positive and encouraging'.[9] Across the country, the matrix organization and use of relationship managers had bedded down as smoothly as could reasonably have been expected. Traces remained, of course, of the split culture that had grown up in the years after 1999. Given the different professional backgrounds of auditors and inspectors, though, the post-2004 commitment to a 'one-organization' culture had begun to pay off surprisingly quickly. Peter Wilkinson recalled: 'There were residual differences, but it was no longer the cacophony it once had been.'[10]

And what of the commissioners themselves? It was no secret that some of them had found the Strachan years rather bracing from time to time. On the other hand, all of them knew in the wake of his departure that the quality of the board owed much to Strachan's own personal efforts in attracting high-calibre individuals to serve on it. The commissioners who welcomed O'Higgins to the chair comprised as thoughtful and experienced a group as any that had occupied the boardroom in twenty-five years. Its expertise in the health sector alone was remarkable: members included Peter Smith, an economics professor from York University and director of its highly respected Centre for Health Economics, Jennifer Dixon, who was still director of policy at the King's Fund, and David Moss, a long-serving general manager within the NHS. Another of the 2003 intake was Peter Jones, a former City banker and Tory leader of East Sussex County Council since 2001. New additions since the start of 2004 included Tom Legg, who had served as permanent secretary in the Lord Chancellor's department for ten years up to 1998, and Jim Coulter, who had been chief executive of the National Housing Federation for seventeen years until 2005. (The full list comprised seven new names since 2004, including the chairman's. There had been eleven departures over the same period – reducing the Commission's membership from fifteen to eleven at the end of its 2006–07 financial year. (See Appendix 3.))[11]

And it was probably fair to say that the resident expertise on the board in 2007 was matched by a renewed confidence that the Commission itself was building steadily on the strong intellectual foundations that had been re-laid in the Strachan era. Peter Smith had regular contact as a health economist with many prominent public policy institutions all over the world. It gratified him to see the Commission enjoying a high reputation among them, and he had no doubt it was deserved: 'I think the Commission had regained its intellectual edge.'[12]

Towards the end of O'Higgins's first year as chairman, in July 2007, fresh appointments to the Board brought a novel element of ethnic diversity and restored a little of the old 1980s balance between public sector and private sector backgrounds. Bharat Shah (a certified accountant, arriving as deputy chairman) and Raj Rajagopal were both successful chief executives from the business world. Victor Adebowale and Jenny Watson were notable figures in the public sector as head of Turning Point (the charity led by Wendy Thomson for three years in the 1990s) and chair of the Equal Opportunities Commission, respectively. A fifth new arrival, Denise Platt, was already well known to many of her new colleagues at the Commission, having been chief inspector of social care inside the DoH between 1998 and 2004.

The July appointments marked the biggest shake-up of the Board's membership since November 2003. The changes on that occasion had done nothing to dilute a generally convivial culture that was greatly valued by all of the commissioners, and it looked set to continue. Monthly meetings, for example, would go on being preceded by dinners the previous evening. These provided for regular informal discussions between Board members, and they opened up additional opportunities for discussion between Board members and Steve Bundred's executive team. And the dinners, like the annual away-days and the monthly meetings themselves, were invariably genial occasions.

Chris White, as well as being a chartered accountant and a lecturer on audit matters, was one of three serving councillors who occupied seats on the Board. (It had for years been accepted in Whitehall, at the instigation of the Local Government Association, that the three main political parties should be represented in this way.) White had joined in June 2005, as the leader of the Liberal Democrats on Hertfordshire County Council. He took a keen interest in how the deliberations of the Commission were translated into action on the ground: he and Peter Smith led a work group that kept track of the external impact of the Commission. But he was also appreciative of the not unduly formal way in which much of the board's business was conducted. 'It is a friendly culture, and that is a thread that I think runs through all Board activities, whatever the difficulties.'[13]

AN EXPANDING FRANCHISE

By any measure of the Commission's external impact by 2006–08, its remit was fast expanding. And no aspect of these years was more encouraging for the Commission – nor indeed more startling in its novelty – than the about-turn in its relations with the Department of Health. A concerted campaign by Andy McKeon to build a constructive rapport with his old department led to a breakthrough in 2006. There was no doubt by the start of the year that the NHS was facing a mounting crisis over the inadequacy of financial management throughout the organization. Introducing foundation trusts and Payment by Results (PbR) was effectively going to require NHS managers to line up their numbers as neatly as accountants in a commercial business. But many, perhaps most of them, were in no fit shape to do this.

Prior to the 2005 election, most advisers to No. 10 had been adamant that rigorous auditing had no place in a future reform programme for the NHS. The problem had been set out starkly since then, in a first joint report issued by the Audit Commission and the National Audit Office together in June 2005. *Financial Management in the NHS* examined the books of 600 local NHS bodies in 2003–04. It found that, while the service *as a whole* was broadly balancing its accounts, an alarming number of individual bodies were not: almost one in five of them ended the year seriously out of pocket. Since any NHS trust with a deficit at the year-end automatically saw its funding cut for the following year, under the prevailing Whitehall budgeting regime, it did not take a financial wizard to spot the trap. Officials at the DoH seemed appreciative of the work put into the report, but in 2005 were still transparently wary of the Commission. Nigel Crisp, the permanent secretary and chief executive of the NHS since 2000, cannot have read the press release that accompanied the *Financial Management* report without a twinge of irritation. 'The Department's welcome policy of greater transparency on financial matters means that many of the old practices which obscured the year-end financial position are no longer possible', announced James Strachan. 'We can now see where the real financial problems lie, which is the first important step on the way to addressing them . . . We will help in that process.' In a world with generally polarized views of Strachan, Nigel Crisp was not at the friendly end of the spectrum.

But changes were on their way and were encouraged by Patricia Hewitt, appointed health secretary after the 2005 election. Those tasked inside the DoH with implementing PbR asked the Commission around the start of 2006 for help on the project. Perhaps emboldened by this, Michael Lyons wrote to Hewitt, alerting her to the Commission's concerns over a sequel to *Financial Management* just being finalized. A second joint study with the NAO had looked at the figures for 2004–05. Even more NHS bodies were now in deficit – including twelve out of the twenty-eight Strategic Health Authorities.

Meanwhile, a separate report was being prepared within Millbank Tower. This one put under the microscope the twenty-five NHS bodies that, by February 2006, had been subjected to Public Interest Reports issued by their auditors. It was going to be called *Learning the Lessons from Financial Failure in the NHS*. During February, Andy McKeon sent a draft copy of the so-far-completed chapters to Richard Douglas, the DoH finance director. It seems reasonable to suppose that they were seen by his minister. The next development, anyway, was ground-breaking – and prompted an unusual entry in the minutes of the March monthly meeting.

A letter was tabled from the secretary of state for health . . . The department welcomed our offer to support and work with it to secure the delivery of improved financial management . . . [Secretary's note: Following a subsequent telephone conversation with the secretary of state, the acting chairman announced that the Commission had been asked to review the NHS' financial management and accountancy framework. This offer would be accepted . . .][14]

Work on the review began immediately that March (a month also marked by the retirement of Nigel Crisp). The executive team led by McKeon was assisted by a 'Financial Management Advisory Group' that included Richard Douglas from the DoH, Bill Moyes, the chairman of Monitor, one of the leading healthcare economists from the Healthcare Commission, a director from the NAO and several senior figures from NHS trusts around the country – not to mention several commissioners, Martin Evans and Steve Bundred himself. Their report

(*Audit Commission Review of the NHS Financial Management and Accounting Regime: a Report to the Secretary of State for Health*) landed on Hewitt's desk as scheduled, in July 2006. It ran to ninety-one pages, and made twenty-nine detailed recommendations. All but two were accepted, and implementation of them was begun by the department within a few months.

The commissioners themselves were at least as pleased with the report as was the department. As they noted in a discussion at their July monthly meeting: 'This was a very impressive document. It was potentially a seminal report and could help re-establish our reputation.'[15] An effusively positive response to the report from Hewitt herself did nothing to discourage this assessment. The minister then encouraged the Commission during the autumn to launch into new projects on the use of real-time data by the health service, and the mechanics of commissioning by the primary care trusts in the NHS. The Commission in September won its first new audit mandate from a foundation trust (that is, from a trust to whom it had not previously been the auditor). And it was hard at work by 2007 on two joint reports with the Healthcare Commission into topical public health issues.

It all amounted to a promising platform indeed for the Commission's future work in the health sector – and a backdrop that might at least be conducive to finding imaginative solutions on another challenging front. Tony Blair's third administration had moved quickly since 2005 to refine its proposals for a consolidation of Whitehall's many inspectorates into just four, accompanied by yet another set of fundamental reforms for local government (and the assessment of it). Here again, the results for the Commission seemed broadly auspicious. By the time that formal consultations were over, Steve Bundred had been assured not only that the Audit Commission would be the body responsible after April 2008 for fulfilling the 'Local Services Inspectorate' role – but also that it would be spared the need to change its name. (A firm stand against it by Bundred led to the LSI tag being quietly dropped.) The creation of the new Communities and Local Government department slowed work on a consequent White Paper by a few months. But *Strong and Prosperous Communities* finally appeared in October 2006.

Central to the government's new thinking was that the CPA regime should give way in 2009 to a fresh approach based on what it labelled a 'Comprehensive Area Assessment' – or CAA. In essence, the state of any locality's public services would not be measured by examining the performance of its local authority alone, or even the individual records of separate service-delivery bodies within the locality. Rather, all would need to be assessed in one seamless impression – yielding an overall rating that might equate, in fact, to the broad impression of the locality available to citizens living within it.

The new performance framework will . . . improve the arrangements for external assessment and inspection so that they are better coordinated between the various inspectorates and related more proportionately to risk by reforming the current performance assessment arrangements for local government, putting in place the following key elements: an annual risk assessment, . . . an annual scored Use of Resources judgement for local public sector bodies, drawn from the annual audit; an annual scored Direction of Travel judgement . . . [and] inspection activity by relevant inspectorates targeted primarily on the basis of risk assessment.[16]

Some of the implications for the Commission were clear enough. Its field force would need to leave behind the old world of retrospective performance assessments and focus instead on identifying *risk* and the potential for public service failures before they happened. The Commission's officers would be faced with new audit obligations. Above all, though, they would have to formulate ways of fulfilling effectively the duty that would now be placed on the Commission to act as *gatekeeper* in every locality. There was much to welcome in all this. It did not go as far in rolling back the burden of CPA as some, notably the Local Government Association, had urged. But the government intended that CAA would mark a radical reduction in the bureaucracy of local assessment. It was to be another step forward for the Lighter Touch. Councils, for example, would in future have a maximum of 35 local targets to meet, and a maximum of 200 or so performance indicators in place of the 1,200 or so that still existed as of 2006. At their first discussion of the White Paper, in October 2006, the commissioners concluded optimistically that CAA might be an opportunity for auditors in general 'to adopt a more mature [sic] relationship with local government'.[17]

The Local Government and Public Involvement in Health Bill that followed from the White Paper, though, left a huge amount to be resolved by the putative four inspectorates themselves. It had its first reading in the Commons in December 2006. During its subsequent passage through Parliament, the proposal to amalgamate the existing five criminal justice inspectorates into one was defeated in the House of Lords. This left the five of them still in place, plus the Audit Commission and Ofsted – with plans still in place for a combined health and social services inspectorate, Ofcare, absorbing the Healthcare Commission and CSCI, to be established at a later date. The Board of the Commission received a draft report and presentation from Gareth Davies in February 2007, setting out his thoughts on how best the Commission might approach early consultations with the other inspectorates about the future implementation of Labour's latest ideas.

If the ghost of Best Value hung over the discussion that followed, the minutes made no reference to it. But the parallel was surely there: the Bill enshrined a bold concept, but like Best Value in 1999 was sketchy on the practicalities and dauntingly vague on how today's circle would be squared tomorrow. Bundred and his colleagues would need to proceed with great caution. The Board members appear to have had no illusions on this score, as the minutes recorded:

The landscape was likely to change a great deal and not necessarily in the way the government thought it would . . . It would be a challenge to make an outline framework into a reality. It was a tough timetable and the report [from Gareth Davies] raised some philosophical and strategic issues . . . There was not a clear definition [in the Bill] of what CAA would actually report on and how risks would be measured and reported. [The Commission] had to be cautious of being too prescriptive before the government and other inspectorates had fully got to grips with CAA . . . For that reason, the consultation document would have to be frustratingly general.[18]

On one point, though, the Bill was still disappointingly precise. Objections from Bundred and his colleagues during the drafting stage had failed to derail a proposal that the Commission should be deprived of its statutory ('Section 35') right to conduct local VFM studies at the request of local authorities. This appeared too basic an assault on the Commission's historical role to be left unamended for long. In the event, the government ended up amending the Bill to replace the Commission's Section 35 powers with a wider remit. This not only restored the right to work for local authorities but also clarified a right, long sought by the Commission, to undertake modest projects in other jurisdictions. The Commission had of course been actively engaged for years in giving out support and advice to counterpart bodies all over the world. But its overseas work to date had generally been *pro bono*, while staff secondments had been structured as training projects. Now the Commission would be able, if the opportunities arose, to charge fees for project work – including audit assignments – that it had hitherto been obliged to turn down.

Nor would new projects have to be restricted to foreign governments. If Whitehall departments cared to approach the Commission for help, it would be at liberty to take them on. The notion of setting the Commission loose in Whitehall had brought a glint to the eye of its founder, all the way back in 1982 (see p. 38). As Michael Heseltine himself recalled a quarter of a century later: 'I wanted the Audit Commission to do central government as well. As you can imagine, that went over with cabinet colleagues like a lead balloon. I was keen on the notion of subjecting central government to the same disciplines that we were going to impose on local government. But I never got away with it.'[19] The 2007 statute – it was enacted at the end of October – did not envisage anything as sweeping as Heseltine had had in mind. The Commission would be given statutory power to work in Whitehall, if invited, but no duty to do so. Nor was any of this likely to add much to its revenues. Still, it was a significant step in that direction – and the extension to its remit was a welcome sign of the renewed confidence in the Commission within government circles.

Broader remits in health and local (or even central) government accounted for the lion's share of the new work in prospect for the Commission in the post-Blair years, but there were other, smaller extensions to its franchise, too. The functions of the Benefits Fraud Inspectorate, for example, were brought into the Commission. A more notable change involved the National Fraud Initiative. Since its inauguration in 1998, the NFI team led by Peter Yetzes had completed five audits, each consisting of a two-year cycle beginning with a trawl of local authorities' data files and ending with a national report on the outcome of the resulting investigations by the authorities. The financial yield on this project broke every record in the book: for a total investment by 2007 of just £5 million, the NFI had led to recouped losses of well over £300 million. A complex operation that had only been made possible in the first place by computers was greatly facilitated in 2006–07 by the creation of a secure Audit Commission website, for the exchange of information between the central team and local authorities. The NFI, with strong backing from Steve Bundred, was now a far cry from its London Fraud Initiative forebear: its remit covered, for example, tenancy fraud, payroll fraud, council-tax fraud and 'NHS tourism', as well as the staples of student-grant and housing-benefit fraud. Its potential value was clear – but the project was still constrained by limitations on the powers of the NFI. As of 2006, it could not match data *across* all the audit regimes within the UK – though it did work within Scotland and Northern Ireland for the local audit bodies – nor could it obtain data from bodies outside the Commission's audit regime such as banks, building societies and insurance companies. Following a wide-ranging presentation by the Commission to a Fraud Review conducted by the government in 2005–06, legislation was introduced in 2007 (as part of a much wider Serious Crime Bill) to broaden the NFI's remit and beef up its statutory powers.

In housing, it was difficult to be sure by late 2007 how the Commission's role would finally emerge from a long-running reappraisal of all regulation in the sector (the *Cave Review*). The outcome was anything but ambiguous for the Housing Corporation: from 2009 its investment function would pass to a freshly minted body to be called the Homes and Communities Agency; and its regulatory responsibility for HAs would go to yet another new watchdog, the Office for Tenants and Social Landlords. But the Commission in the meantime retained its broad inspection duties across the sector and seemed assured of a significant housing role under the future CAA regime.

The Commission's lengthening agenda was an acknowledgement by Whitehall that the executive team built up by Steve Bundred had much to offer. It was a fair reflection of the trust that ministers were now prepared to place in Michael O'Higgins and his colleagues on the Board. It also looked encouraging for the Commission when

Gordon Brown's first cabinet emerged at the end of June 2007 with a secretary of state for communities and local government who had actually worked in local government: Hazel Blears was a former councillor and local government officer, as well as a politician with past Whitehall responsibilities for the police and for public health.

Relations between the government and the Commission were already close on many levels. This was facilitating, by 2007–08, a degree of cooperation with Whitehall that went beyond anything seen in earlier years. But how did the proper desire to be an effective player in Whitehall sit with the Commission's need to guard its own independence? Here was just one of several delicate balances that the Commission had struggled with, over many years. How they were struck determined, in effect, the Commission's modus operandi. And arguably, they were now being struck as satisfactorily as at any time past.

STRIKING THE RIGHT BALANCE

When serious work began on the *Strong and Prosperous Communities* White Paper early in 2006, Steve Bundred agreed to second Peter Wilkinson for half a day a week to ODPM to assist officials on the project. As this suggests, the Commission had indeed moved closer to central government even since the early years of New Labour, never mind the distant days of the 1980s. Nor could there really be much doubt that its new relationship with the DoH effectively precluded the kind of bruising verdicts on NHS management that had appeared in the past, from the work on GP fundholders in 1995, to the study of A&E waiting times in 2001 and the critique of waiting-lists in 2003. Whether friendly relations with the health department were compatible with the Commission's watchdog status had of course been a bone of contention in years past. When Andrew Foster had set out to explore ways of improving the relationship, during his early days, one senior civil servant took the opportunity of a lunch in Vincent Square to caution the chairman and his new controller that it was not their job to be nice to the health department: the Commission was there to keep a sharp eye on the NHS.[20]

The nature of the Commission's 'independence', in other words, had changed profoundly over the years – but this was no cause for a crisis of identity. It was simply a reminder of the fact that, in the words of the Healthcare Commission's chairman, Ian Kennedy, 'independence in the context of politics is a commodity that you have to negotiate every day: there are no lines drawn in the sand'.[21] Since the early 1990s, the government had steadily shifted the centre ground of this negotiation. The Commission had had to choose between accepting more of a cooperative relationship with Whitehall, or being excluded from the policy-making process. The Commission had no kind of constitutional status, unlike the NAO, whose head was formally an officer of Parliament. It was a creature of statute – and whatever powers the government had given, the government could take away. The loss of the national VFM franchise in health left no room for illusions on that score. In short, as one former permanent secretary put it, it was a case of accepting 'independence up to a point, Lord Copper – which is basically all that any public body appointed by government ever manages to achieve'.[22]

The Commission had opted accordingly for a degree of complicity, shrewdly handled by Foster, in the belief (generally vindicated) that this would add powerfully to the value of its 'independence' ticket. To stop selective complicity merging into chronic compliance, the Commission needed to keep a tight hold on the skills and values it had honed from the first – supporting its arguments with hard evidence and standing by them with integrity; consulting widely with audited bodies and sister organizations as well as Whitehall departments; and adopting open and stimulating positions on regulatory matters that might usefully stir the media's interest. The Commission's record under James Strachan had been generally impressive on these counts, though this had sometimes been forgotten in the excitement over occasional personality clashes.

It seemed unlikely that the Commission under O'Higgins and Bundred would attach any less importance to all of this. Indeed, there was plenty of evidence that the two of them would guard the Commission's independence quite as carefully as any of their predecessors. Anyone doubting it could turn, for example, to *The Future of Regulation in the Public Sector*, an Audit Commission discussion paper written by Steve Bundred himself and published in March 2006.

In a meticulously considered review of the ways in which public regulation would need to be reappraised in unison with the changing nature of public services themselves, Bundred underscored the importance of independence to any worthwhile regulatory activity: '[regulation] must be delivered with unimpeachable integrity and authority, by a wholly disinterested party'. Government, he wrote, had a legitimate role to play in deciding how far regulation should focus on democratic *accountability* on the one hand or *improvement* on the other (another recurring theme, of course, of many past debates among the auditors). But if government were to stretch this role 'to deciding which specific public bodies should be assessed and when, perceptions of the independence of the regulator could be fatally undermined'. It was also the case that regulators had now to act as advisers to the government, as well as agents of government. Whitehall had coercive powers, for example, to step into any council's affairs and take over the running of public services. In such an event, 'government relies on the regulator to direct it to take action but reserves the right to differ from the regulator's view, which requires the separation of government from regulation'.[23]

Readers of *The Future of Regulation* could reflect that here was a level of intellectual leadership for the Commission fully on a par with Strachan's thinking – and not seen from a chief executive since the days of Howard Davies. In the context of striking the right balance on independence, it certainly suggested the Commission was in safe hands. Perhaps it was also possible, without taking too Panglossian a stance, to discern in many other areas the same kind of balance as had been achieved in relations with the government. With the private firms, for example, the Commission now enjoyed a better structured and more stable arrangement. Its role as purchaser of audits remained as central as ever to the Commission's whole *raison d'être*, and Strachan had taken a keen interest in it. At his behest, for example, the tender rounds in 2005-07 had invited the private firms to compete much more aggressively on pricing as well as the prospective quality of their work. The result had allowed the Commission to make substantial cost savings without losing any goodwill among the firms with which it went on working.

Again, the perennial debate over the tensions between its role as a policeman and its role as a consultant had lost its resonance by 2006–08. The heightened attention to audit matters, since Martin Evans's appointment to the management team, had certainly reaffirmed their importance. (Bundred and Evans persuaded the nascent Financial Reporting Council to bring the Commission and its in-house auditors within the scope of its Audit Inspection Unit, so that there would now be a regular independent assessment of the Commission's audit quality.) At the same time, much of the Commission's studies agenda – not least its work for the DoH on financial management inside the NHS – carried a clear consultative dimension. By convention, every-one had now spoken for years about 'audited and inspected bodies' ('AIBs') rather than 'clients' – but the huge significance once vested in such labels was now all but forgotten. The issue no longer seemed meaningful: AIBs and clients were as one. And whether they operated in the health sector or any other sphere, all alike would be targeted with reports that combined descriptive analysis with *pre*scriptive recommendations.

One of the first national reports to be published by the new PRS was *Crossing Borders*, which appeared in January 2007. It looked at the challenges posed for local authorities by the massive influx of migrant workers into the UK, mostly from the new member states of the European Union, since 2004. (Foreign nationals comprised 6 per cent of the workforce by 2006, up from 3.5 per cent ten years earlier, and migration had become the country's main driver of demographic change.) The report provided a wide-ranging, and often graphic, account of the impact of this development, with colourful case studies based on individual council responses in Cornwall, Cheshire and east Lancashire.* The report then concluded with almost five pages of specific recommendations for future action by both local *and* central

---

* One of the case studies in the report, for example, described a crisis for the County Council and Hyndburn Borough Council in Lancashire, after an employment agency had recruited 200 Polish workers for a factory in Accrington. They were promised twelve months' work and given private rented accommodation. 'After 13 weeks the factory terminated contracts, leaving 200 people unemployed and threatened with homelessness, but no eligibility for benefits. Many still owed the agency for travel to Britain. Scare stories circulated claiming that the police would evict tenants who did not leave. Some Polish workers were found sleeping rough' (*Crossing Borders*, opposite p. 25).

government. *Crossing Borders* was followed in December by *Staying Afloat*, an 86-page report on Whitehall's cash aid for councils in the wake of 2007's disastrous summer floods. Both titles must have pleased members of the Board, too: they had noted a couple of months earlier, at the first monthly meeting chaired by Michael O'Higgins, that 'the whimsical titles of former reports were much more effective in raising awareness and keeping reports in people's minds'.[24]

That meeting of the members in October 2006 was the occasion of the members' first discussion of the White Paper introducing CAA. The minutes made clear the Commission's stance on two other questions, where balance was all. First, on whose behalf was the Commission primarily acting – the taxpayer or the citizen as a user of public services? For ten years, most of the rhetoric had emphasized the importance of the citizen-user. Until the early 1990s, though, the taxpayer had featured far more prominently in the Commission's thinking. Now, members seemed content that they were at least clear in their own minds where the balance lay. 'Although we need to have regard to both perspectives, our primary focus must be on the taxpayer and ensuring the efficient use of public money.'

The biggest 'balance issue' of all, of course, had been at the heart of the Commission's history for the past quarter-century. What was the optimal half-way point between excessive 'top–down' meddling in the management of local public bodies on the one hand, and an excessively 'hands-off' approach on the other that might leave them stewing in a state deeply unsatisfactory to the local people dependent on them? Here, the Commission had to strike a balance that it could sustain in the context of whatever was happening between central and local government in the wider political context. This had been a source of considerable tension in the 1980s, when Margaret Thatcher's ministers had often pressed the Commission to play a more interventionist role than it thought advisable. It had caused few problems for a decade after the early 1990s, because the Commission under Andrew Foster had generally shared the government's aspirations to use steadily heavier intervention in the pursuit of better public services. In recent years, the relationship between the government and the Commission had again been more troubled – not least, of course, because the government itself had grown increasingly ambivalent over the efficacy of its whole top–down approach to public service reforms.

The doubts had begun with academic and think-tank pieces around the time of the 2001 election. Goaded by Tory criticism of the more egregious failures of centrally ordained reforms, Labour ministers had then increasingly adopted the rhetoric of what was called 'the new localism' – but it sat awkwardly with the still prevailing Labour consensus. While the government's broad strategic approach remained essentially unaltered, the political climate was unquestionably chang-ing. As Simon Jenkins later observed: 'There was little doubt that the political establishment craved a new approach to public service reform and even sensed where it might lie – witness speeches and writings advocating decentralization by almost all the players in British politics in the new decade.'[25]

It could fairly be said that the Commission had played its part since 2003 in trying to add substance to the rhetoric. Strachan's Strategic Regulation had led the Commission in the direction of a new balance, entailing much less meddling from the centre. This had become part of a wider debate over decentralization by 2006–08 – in which the Commission was well placed on several counts. It could take some credit for leading the way. It could speak with some authority, given its presence on the ground and daily involvement with public bodies in every sector. And it was led for the best part of 2006 by the individual whose ideas were doing much to define the debate, Michael Lyons.

AT THE FOREFRONT OF A GENERAL RETHINK

By the time that his final report appeared, in March 2007, Lyons had been gone six months from the Commission. But as a member of it for almost three years (and acting chairman for nine months), he had been at the centre of its deliberations while at the same time chairing his inquiry. (Originally requested to look into its financing, he had been asked in the course of his work to form a much broader appraisal of the sector.) Unsurprisingly, the views that he set out in his final report – entitled *Place-shaping: a Shared Ambition for the Future of Local Government* – carried some intriguing implications for the Commission.[26]

For Lyons, the great bugbear of the CPA approach (of whatever vintage) – and of much that preceded it in the regulation of councils – was the preoccupation with public services, to the virtual exclusion of all other aspects of local government. In his report, he set out to paint a much wider canvas. What was local government in the twenty-first century *for*, and how could it be reinvigorated? A substantial part of the technical answer came down (as ever) to a root-and-branch reform of the funding system. But Lyons had a more philosophical answer, too. Different localities should be allowed, indeed encouraged, to develop their own identities, with their own political and financial priorities. A modest threshold of parity on public services would clearly be required across the country. Above that level, though, variation should be welcomed.

This was a profound rejection of the consensus that had prevailed for many years, which typically castigated local variation as a source of unfairness to those in any way disadvantaged by it. Their standard battle-cry was that people should not be left as hapless victims of 'a postcode lottery'. Wherever you lived, your blessings should be the same. To ensure this outcome, any degree of standardization was warranted in the regulation of the nation's public services. And it was precisely in order to press home this standardization that performance indicators had been piled up in numbers fit to wallpaper a fair-sized room. (The Local Government Association once did exactly that, for a press conference in 2006. It took the 1,200 forms addressed to the typical municipal borough, requesting performance indicators, and papered the walls of a room at its headquarters in London's Smith Square.)

Arguing the case in favour of variation, Lyons proposed a wide-ranging role for local government which he labelled 'place-shaping' and defined as 'the creative use of powers and influence to promote the general well-being of a community and its citizens'. Much flowed from this. There would need to be a greater degree of political accountability at a local level, since councils would be left to make more choices. (These would extend, for example, to deciding on the contribution of the private market to the delivery of public services.) There would be a marked reduction in 'the levels of guidance, reporting requirements and central pronouncements [by inspectorates] on areas which are of local concern and responsibility'.[27] Above all, there would need to be a halt to the increasing centralization of public services that had been evident since 1979 – and an incremental reversal of the whole process.

There were three things to say about this radical agenda, from the Commission's perspective. First, it contained some intriguing additional jobs for the Commission itself. Given his close identification with the Commission, Lyons was careful not to push them to the fore too explicitly. Nonetheless, several stood out. It could be asked to monitor the government's progress in slashing back performance indicators, and conversely to report on the cost of any fresh regulatory burdens (recommendation 4.8). It could audit progress on the promised reduction in the volume of ring-fenced and conditional grants flowing from central to local government (recommendation 4.11). It could be asked to ensure that its 'Use of Resources' judgement should include consideration of the spending priorities adopted by councils in the future (recommendation 4.14). Most intriguing of all, it could perhaps take up the gauntlet thrown down by Lyons, with his proposal that an independent authority be mandated by Parliament to watch over Whitehall's funding of local government *in toto* and provide, in effect, a running commentary on it (para. 4.56).

Second, the Lyons Report usefully reaffirmed the wider relevance of the Commission's own strategic thinking, as set down in Steve Bundred's March 2006 paper *The Future of Regulation* and as laid out in a *Strategic Plan 2006*, published the same month and also largely authored by Bundred. (The implicit endorsement was hardly surprising, of course, given that Lyons as acting chairman was a co-signatory to the foreword of the Plan.) The Plan had made no assumptions about the nature of the regime that would replace CPA after 2008. But its strategic objectives had taken careful heed of the dynamic changes in prospect for 2006–10, acknowledging in particular the concept of local area assessments that lay just around the corner: 'We will increasingly consider performance on an area-wide basis, for example to provide a rounded picture of how well councils and their partners work together to promote the social, economic and environmental well-being of their communities.'[28]

The Lyons Report looked forward to a world in which the Commission might take exactly this kind of area-wide approach. It left plenty of scope, too, for the Commission to develop its role as a catalyst for change – acting, in effect, as a proxy for the competitive market that spurred change in the private sector. (This was a theme to which Michael O'Higgins returned in various speeches through 2007. As the Commission chairman put it to the annual conference of CIPFA in June, all good regulators in the modern era needed to heed this market-proxy function: their job was 'to stimulate and animate' public services by finding 'ways to mimic' the attributes of the marketplace – including the market's encouragement of *innovation*.)[29]

And third, of course, the Lyons Report greatly added to the momentum of the debate over decentralization that had been gathering pace now for a few years – over the possibility, that is to say, of a significant devolvement of political power from central government *back* to local government. There was a sense in 2007–08 that the flow of power from town halls up to Whitehall, running hard as a tidal river since the earliest days of Thatcherism, was at last on the turn. The waters were hardly ebbing yet. But there were eddies swirling stronger by the month, several of them centred around ideas to which the Lyons Report gave extra credence.

The Local Government Association, for example, produced two reports in the months immediately after the *Strong and Prosperous Communities* White Paper, identifying in great detail some fifty 'subregional' economies of England and proposing a range of governance models based on a substantial devolvement of Whitehall controls down to local decision-makers.[30] The LGA could also take much of the credit for the drastic reduction in targets and performance indicators enshrined in the 2007 Local Government Act. Its chairman, Sandy Bruce-Lockhart, was the former Tory leader of Kent County Council. He was one of those most committed to turning back the centralization tide: 'It is blindingly obvious that the extraordinary burden of central controls – in funding and guidance to councils, in the plans that have to be submitted, in the targets and inspections that come back – has been very, very damaging.'[31] As a part of the remedy, he wanted to see a substantial change in the governance of central funding for local government – and had urged the Lyons Inquiry to recommend a real devolution of funding as well as a central role for the Audit Commission as an independent commentator on the process.

His predecessor at the LGA from 1997 to 2005, Jeremy Beecham, was a former Labour leader from the opposite end of the country, Newcastle. He, too, had no doubt there was scope for the Commission to widen its future brief. He wanted to see it taking more of an initiative in the future as a gatekeeper, facilitating effective decision-making between different public services at a regional level. Beecham saw an urgent need for such 'cross-cutting' projects – to tackle the impact of immigration, for example, or the enormous impact of reoffending on the criminal justice system.

In an ideal world, the large local authorities would sit down with the Commission and with ministers in a central–local partnership structure. We would identify, say, four big issues over a couple of years on which the Commission could report with the full cooperation of the authorities and all of the relevant public service agencies. That way, we could get a better understanding of the big picture as well as some detailed recommendations for action on the ground.[32]

What the former Tory county leader and the former Labour city leader had in common was a conviction that a new era beckoned in local–central relations. No doubt, for both the wish was to an extent father to the thought. And there remained plenty of scope for deep scepticism that Labour intended anything truly devolutionary. How could it be otherwise, once the hitherto arch-centralizer had moved from the Treasury across the road to No. 10? (By the time Gordon Brown made the move, in June 2007, it was already a widespread view at Westminster that he had rejected the core proposals of the Lyons Report while the ink on it was still drying.) Nonetheless, Bruce-Lockhart and Beecham had been shrewd observers of central–local relations for decades (four of them, in Beecham's case). Both sensed a fundamental change. If they were right, then the implications for the Commission might be far-reaching.

Those pressing for reform included the Westminster grandee responsible for creating the Commission in the first place. Now in his mid-70s, Michael Heseltine chaired a 'cities taskforce' that delivered its report to David Cameron's Tory shadow cabinet in June 2007. He proposed a rejuvenation of local government in English cities, led by the democratic election of executive mayors and 'freed from the suffocating regime of central targets'.[33] It was Heseltine who saw the latent potential of the District Audit Service in the early 1980s and set loose John Banham to shape a new and powerful catalyst for change all those years ago. His 2007 report called for more of the same radicalism, to salvage a local leadership in the cities 'emasculated and hollowed out by successive over-centralizing governments'. And David Cameron himself appeared to endorse this thinking, in a well-received leader's speech to the Tory faithful at Blackpool four months later.[34]

It could be argued that the hollowing out had always been well intentioned. Tory and Labour governments alike had insisted since 1979 that their treatment of local bodies was just the first half of a two-stage process. The Thatcher governments had had to purge the town halls of a profligacy that imperilled the health of the national economy and would (if unchecked) have made a nonsense of local democracy. The Major and Blair governments had had to take a firm grip on the dreary delivery of public services that were far too important to be left to the vagaries of inadequate and inconsistent local management. The outcome in both cases, anyway, had been much the same: an inexorable shift in policy-making to Whitehall. But this had never been rationalized on the basis that government from London was best, though no doubt many privately believed it to be so – or at least, to be inevitable. Rather, it was all about putting councils and public services on a sound footing for the future. One day, with this accomplished, it would be time to hand power over their own affairs back to the local bodies. That would be the second instalment of the two-stage process.

Things had worked out less neatly, of course. By the end of the Blair era, a state of perfection among England's public bodies was less conspicuous than the astounding sums of money that had been poured into local services, with often disappointingly modest gains to show for it. Spending on the health service by Labour alone had *trebled* in current terms. Here as elsewhere, the bigger the cash outlay, the more glaring were the limitations of command-and-control from the centre.

Nonetheless, enormous progress *had* been made. The late 1970s, when central government had handed £20 billion a year over to local authorities with next to no way of tracking its expenditure, seemed almost as distant as the days of those Victorian municipal corporations watched over by the very first district auditors. As for the financial black hole that had been the NHS in the 1970s, its culture, unreformed, would simply have been irreconcilable with the expansion of the modern health service. Those along the way who had poured scorn on audit and inspection, targets and regulation dismissed too lightly the appalling standards that had characterized much of the public sector before the onset of Thatcherism. The *mechanics* of government at a local level had been improved almost (were it not for all those auditors and inspectors) immeasurably.

On both counts – with limits reached on the one hand, and foundations laid on the other – there was a gathering consensus by 2008 that it was time for the remorseless centralization of 1979–2007 to give way to an incipient devolvement of power away from the centre to the regions, the sub-regions and the great cities of England. Through its initial twenty-five years, the Audit Commission had played a pivotal part in the first half of the two-stage process. If it could replicate this in the second, it would have an eventful next quarter-century ahead of it.

Appendix 1
Selected bibliography of Audit Commission publications

Listed below are most of the Audit Commission's national reports and other publications since 1983, many of which have been at least referred to in the main text. Omitted are some corporate publications – mostly consultation documents and feedback reports – which are available in a complete bibliography on the Commission's website at www.audit-commission.gov.uk.

The publications have been grouped under the following categories and are listed in chronological order within each sub-category (national reports, updates, etc.):

(a) Local government
(b) Health: health-service management
(c) Health: hospital services
(d) Education
(e) Housing
(f) Police, fire, community safety and criminal justice
(g) Social services
(h) Cross-sectoral
(i) Citizen's Charter performance indicators
(j) Anti-fraud
(k) Environment
(l) Culture and leisure
(m) The role and work of the Audit Commission

See also the Index of Audit Commission Publications (pp. 711–14), where those publications mentioned in the main text have been listed alphabetically.

(A) LOCAL GOVERNMENT
National Reports

Impact on Local Authorities' Economy, Efficiency and Effectiveness of the Block Grant Distribution System, 1984
Improving Vehicle Fleet Management in Local Government, 1984
Reducing the Costs of Local Government Purchases, 1984
Capital Expenditure Controls in Local Government in England, 1985
Computer Fraud Survey, 1985
Saving Energy in Local Government Buildings, 1985
Improving Cash Flow Management in Local Government, 1986
Improving Supply Management in Local Authorities, 1987
Vehicle Availability Bonus Schemes, 1988
Rough Guide to Europe: Local Authorities and the EC, 1991
Passing the Bucks: the Impact of Standard Spending Assessments on Economy, Efficiency and Effectiveness: Volume 1, 1993
Passing the Bucks: the Impact of Standard Spending Assessments on Economy, Efficiency and Effectiveness: Volume 2: Appendices, 1993
Realising the Benefits of Competition: the Client Role for Contracted Services, 1993
Behind Closed Doors: the Revolution in Central Support Services, 1994
Is Anybody There? Improving Performance in Answering Letters and Telephones, 1994
Calling the Tune: Performance Management in Local Government, 1995
Improving Value for Money in Local Government: A Compendium of Good Practice from Audit Commission Value for Money Reports, 1995
Paying the Piper: People and Pay Management in Local Government, 1995
Talk Back: Local Authority Communication with Citizens, 1995
Capital Gains: Improving the Local Government Capital Expenditure System, 1997
Retiring Nature: Early Retirement in Local Government, 1997

Promising Beginnings: a Compendium of Initiatives to Improve Joint Working in Local Government, 1998

Measure for Measure: the Best Value Agenda for Trading-Standards Services, 1999

Price is Right? Charges for Council Services, 1999

Hot Property: Getting the Best from Local Authority Assets, 2000

Improving Value for Money in Local Government: a Compendium of Good Practice from Audit Commission Reports, 2000

Step in the Right Direction: Lessons from Best Value Performance Plans, 2000

Changing Gear: Best Value Annual Statement 2001

Competitive Procurement: Learning from Audit, Inspection and Research, 2002

Councils and E-government: Research So Far . . ., 2002

Equality and Diversity: Learning from Audit, Inspection and Research, 2002

Force for Change: Central Government Intervention in Failing Local Government Services, 2002

Message Beyond the Medium: Improving Local Government Services through E-government, 2002

Comprehensive Performance Assessment: Scores and Analysis of Performance for Single Tier and County Councils in England, 2003

Patterns for Improvement: Learning from Comprehensive Performance Assessment to Achieve Better Public Services, 2003

Council Tax Increases 2003/04: Why Were They So High?, 2003

Comprehensive Performance Assessment: Scores and Analysis of Performance for Single Tier and County Councils in England, 2004

Comprehensive Performance Assessment: Scores and Analysis of Performance for District Councils in England, 2003/04, 2005

CPA – The Harder Test: Scores and Analysis of Performance in Single Tier and County Councils, 2005

The Efficiency Challenge: the Administration Costs of Revenues and Benefits, 2005

Efficiency Challenge: Costs of Administering Local Government Pension Funds in London, 2006

Learning from CPA in 2005/06: Findings from Assessments, 2006

CPA – *The Harder Test: Scores and Analysis of Performance in Single Tier and County Councils 2006, 2007*

Updates

The Melody Lingers On . . .: a Review of the Audits of People, Pay and Performance, 1997
On Merit: a Review of Progress on Local Authority Recruitment Training, 1999
Retiring Nature: Early Retirement in Local Government, 2000
Halfway Home: an Analysis of the Variation in the Cost of Supporting Asylum Seekers, 2001

Briefings and Bulletins

Sooner the Better: Progress Report on the Council Tax, 1993
Now, the Good News: the First Year of Council Tax, 1994
Paving The Way: Helping Councils Prepare for the Future, 1994
From Administration to Management: the Management of the Finance Function in Local Government, 1995
Making Markets: a Review of the Audits of the Client Role for Contracted Services, 1995
On Merit: Recruitment in Local Government, 1995
Opening the Doors: a Review of the Audits of Central Support Services, 1995
All Change: Managing Local Government Reorganisation and Beyond, 1996
Councils 'Through the Looking Glass': Briefing for Councillors, 2001
Modernisation Through the Prism: Key Decisions to Implement the Choice of New Political Structures, 2001
Picture of Performance: Early Lessons from Comprehensive Performance Assessment, 2002
Workforce Development Confederations: Findings from the 'Fitness for Purpose' Audits, 2004

Guidance and Management Handbooks

Economy, Efficiency and Effectiveness in Local Government in England and Wales, Vol. 1, 1983

Economy Efficiency and Effectiveness in Local Government, Vols 2 and 3, 1985

Managing the Implementation of Community Charge, 1988

High Risk/High Potential: a Management Handbook on Information Technology in Local Government, 1994

Collecting Local Taxes: a Management Handbook, 1995

Counting Down to Competition: a Management Handbook on Financial Support Services, 1995

Paying the Piper . . . Calling the Tune: People, Pay and Performance in Local Government, 1995

Seize the Day! Guidance for Incoming Unitary Councils, 1995

Rome Wasn't Built in a Day: a Management Handbook on Getting Value for Money from Capital Programmes and Construction Projects, 1997

Taken for Granted: Local Authorities' Arrangements for Grant Claims, 1997

Retiring Nature: a Management Handbook on Early Retirement in Local Government, 1998

Quality of Life: Using Quality of Life Indicators, 2002

Quality of Life: a Good Practice Guide to Communicating Quality of Life Indicators, 2003

Management Papers and Occasional Papers

Competitiveness and Contracting out of Local Authorities' Services, 1987

The Management of London's Authorities: Preventing the Breakdown of Services, 1987

The Competitive Council, 1988

Better Financial Management, 1989

Managing Services Effectively: Performance Review, 1989

More Equal than Others: the Chief Executive in Local Government, 1989

People Management: Retaining and Recruiting Professionals, 1989

Cutting Energy Consumption in Local Government, 1990

Management Buy-outs: Public Interest or Private Gain?, 1990

Managing Sickness Absence in London, 1990

Preparing Information Technology Strategy: Making IT Happen, 1990

We Can't Go on Meeting Like This: the Changing Role of Local Authority Members, 1990

Competitive Counsel: Using Lawyers in Local Government, 1991

People Management: Human Resources in Tomorrow's Public Services, 1991

Benefits Administration: a Management Handbook, 1993

Phoenix Rising: a Study of New Zealand Local Government Following Reorganisation, 1993

Putting Quality on the Map: Measuring and Appraising Quality in the Public Service, 1993

Regular as Clockwork: Raising the Standards of Local Government Financial Accounting, 1993

Called to Account: the Role of Audit Committees in Local Government, 1996

Form Follows Function: Changing Management Structures in the NHS and Local Government, 1996

Kiwi Experience: VFM Messages from New Zealand, 1997

Learning Experience: Service Delivery Planning in Local Government, 1997

Representing the People: the Role of Councillors, 1997

Better by Far: Preparing for Best Value, 1998

Fruitful Partnership: Effective Partnership Working: Management Paper, 1998

Stitch in Time: Facing the Challenge of the Year 2000 Date Change, 1998

Taking the Initiative: a Framework for Purchasing under the Private Finance Initiative, 1998

Worth More than Money: the Role of the Local Government Finance Director, 1998

Listen Up! Effective Community Consultation: Management Paper,
1999

Planning to Succeed: Service and Financial Planning in Local Govern-
ment, 1999

An Inside Job? Internal Audit and Best Value: Management Paper,
2000

Getting the Groundwork Right: Financial Health for Local Authority
Trading Units, 2000

May You Live in Interesting Times: the Consequences of Political
Restructuring for Officers, 2001

To Whom Much is Given: New Ways of Working for Councillors
Following Political Restructuring, 2001

We Hold These Truths to be Self-evident: Essential Principles to Guide
Political Restructuring, 2001

Worth the Risk: Improving Risk Management in Local Government,
2001

Acting on Facts: Using Performance Measurements to Improve Local
Authority Services, 2002

Learning from Comprehensive Performance Assessment of District
Councils: Improvement Breakthroughs, 2005

(B) HEALTH: HEALTH-SERVICE
MANAGEMENT
National Reports

Improving the Supplies Service in the NHS: a Report for the NHS
Management Executive, 1991

NHS Estate Management and Property Maintenance, 1991

Practices Make Perfect: the Role of the Family Health Services
Authority, 1993

Their Health, Your Business: the New Role of the District Health
Authority, 1993

Untapped Savings: Water Services in the NHS, 1993

Prescription for Improvement: Towards More Rational Prescribing
in General Practice, 1994

Protecting the Public Purse 2: Ensuring Probity in the NHS, 1994

Trusting in the Future: Towards an Audit Agenda for NHS Providers, 1994

What the Doctor Ordered: a Study of GP Fundholders in England and Wales, 1996

Comparing Notes: a Study of Information Management in Community Trusts, 1997

Higher Purchase: Commissioning Specialised Services in the NHS, 1997

Cover Story: the Use of Locum Doctors in NHS Trusts, 1999

First Assessment: a Review of District Nursing Services in England and Wales, 1999

Improving Value for Money in the NHS: a Compendium of Good Practice from Audit Commission Reports, 1999

PCG Agenda: Early Progress of Primary Care Groups in 'The New NHS', 2000

Testing Times: a Review of Diabetes Services in England and Wales, 2000

A Picture of Health? A Summary of Findings from Local Value-for-Money Studies Undertaken During 1999 and 2000 in the NHS in Wales, 2001

Dentistry: Primary Dental Care Services in England and Wales, 2002

General Practice in England: a Focus on General Practice in England, 2002

The Performance of the NHS in England: Developing an Independent Commentary, 2002

Achieving the NHS Plan: Assessment of Current Performance, Likely Future Progress and Capacity to Improve, 2003

Achieving First-class Financial Management in the NHS: a Sound Basis for Better Healthcare, 2004

Introducing Payment by Results: Getting the Balance Right for the NHS and Taxpayers, 2004

Quicker Treatment Closer to Home: Primary Care Trusts' Success in Redesigning Care Pathways, 2004

Transforming Primary Care: the Role of Primary Care Trusts in Shaping and Supporting General Practice, 2004

Early Lessons from Payment by Results, 2005

Managing the Financial Implications of NICE Guidance, 2005

Audit Commission Review of the NHS Financial Management and Accounting Regime: a Report to the Secretary of State for Health, 2006

Financial Management in the NHS: NHS (England) Summarised Accounts 2004–05, 2006

Learning the Lessons from Financial Failure in the NHS, 2006

Better Safe than Sorry: Preventing Unintentional Injury to Children, 2007

Update

Setting the Records Straight: a Review of Progress in Health Records Services, 1999

Briefings and Bulletins

Briefing on GP Fundholding, 1995

Fundholding Facts: a Digest of Information about Practices within the Scheme During the First Five Years, 1996

PCGs: an Early View of Primary Care Groups in England, 1999

Local Health Groups in Wales: the First Year, 2000

Developing the Roles of Non-Executive Directors: a Bulletin for Primary Care Trusts, 2002

NHS Plan Implementation Review: National Briefing, 2002

Primary Care Prescribing: a Bulletin for Primary Care Trusts, 2003

Strategic Health Authorities: Key Issues and Notable Practice from the 'Fitness for Purpose' Audits, 2003

Information and Data Quality in the NHS: Key Messages from Three Years of Independent Review, 2004

Auditors' Local Evaluation 2005/06: Summary Results, 2006

Management Papers and Occasional Papers

Saving Energy in the NHS, 1991

Value for Money in the NHS Sterile Services, 1991

Taken on Board: Corporate Governance in the NHS: Developing the Role of Non-Executive Directors, 1995

Healthy Balance: Financial Management in the NHS, 1999
Data Remember: Improving the Quality of Patient-based Information in the NHS, 2002

(C) HEALTH: HOSPITAL SERVICES
National Reports

Short Cut to Better Services: Day Surgery in England and Wales, 1990
The Pathology Services: a Management Review, 1991
The Virtue of Patients: Making the Best Use of Ward Nursing Resources, 1991
Lying in Wait: the Use of Medical Beds in Acute Hospitals, 1992
Children First: a Study of Hospital Services, 1993
Critical Path: an Analysis of Pathology Services, 1993
What Seems to be the Matter?: Communication Between Hospitals and Patients, 1993
Dear to Our Hearts? Commissioning Services for the Treatment and Prevention of Coronary Heart Disease, 1995
Doctors' Tale: the Work of Hospital Doctors in England and Wales, 1995
For Your Information: a Study of Information Management and Systems in the Acute Hospital, 1995
Improving Your Image: How to Manage Radiology Services More Effectively, 1995
Setting the Records Straight: a Study of Hospital Medical Records, 1995
United They Stand: Co-ordinating Care for Elderly Patients with Hip Fractures, 1995
By Accident or Design: Improving A&E Services in England and Wales, 1996
Goods for Your Health: Improving Supplies Management in NHS Trusts, 1996
Anaesthesia under Examination: the Efficiency and Effectiveness of Anaesthesia and Pain Relief Services in England and Wales, 1997
First Class Delivery: Improving Maternity Services in England and Wales, 1997

Getting Sorted: the Safe and Economic Management of Hospital Waste, 1997

First Class Delivery: a National Survey of Women's Views of Maternity Care, 1998

Life in the Fast Lane: Value for Money in Emergency Ambulance Services, 1998

Critical to Success: the Place of Efficient and Effective Critical Care Services within the Acute Hospital, 1999

Accident and Emergency: Review of National Findings – Acute Hospital Portfolio, 2001

Brief Encounters: Getting the Best from Temporary Nursing Staff, 2001

Catering: Review of National Findings – Acute Hospital Portfolio, 2001

Day Surgery: Review of National Findings – Acute Hospital Portfolio, 2001

Hidden Talents: Education, Training and Development for Healthcare Staff in NHS Trusts, 2001

Spoonful of Sugar: Medicines Management in NHS Hospitals, 2001

Ward Staffing: Review of National Findings – Acute Hospital Portfolio, 2001

Access to Care: Ear, Nose and Throat and Audiology Services, 2002

Data Quality Reviews and Spot Checks for 2001/02, 2002

Medical Staffing: Review of National Findings – Acute Hospital Portfolio, 2002

Medicines Management: Review of National Findings – Acute Hospital Portfolio, 2002

Procurement and Supply: Review of National Findings – Acute Hospital Portfolio, 2002

Radiology: Review of National Findings – Acute Hospital Portfolio, 2002

Bed Management: Review of National Findings – Acute Hospital Portfolio, 2003

Operating Theatres: Review of National Findings – Acute Hospital Portfolio, 2003

Outpatients: Review of National Findings – Acute Hospital Portfolio, 2003

Waiting for Elective Admission: Review of National Findings – Acute Hospital Portfolio, 2003

Updates

Finders, Keepers: the Management of Staff Turnover in NHS Trusts, 1997

Accident and Emergency Services Follow-up: Progress against Indicators from By Accident or Design, 1998

Day Surgery Follow-up: Progress against Indicators from A Short Cut to Better Services, 1998

Bulletins

A Price on their Heads: Measuring Management Costs in NHS Trusts, 1995

Doctors' Tale Continued: the Audits of Hospital Medical Staffing, 1996

Waiting-List Accuracy: Assessing the Accuracy of Waiting-List Information in NHS Hospitals in England, 2003

Management Handbooks

Caring Systems: Effective Implementation of Ward-Nursing Management Systems: a Handbook for Managers of Nursing and Project Managers, 1992

Making Time for Patients: a Handbook for Ward Sisters, 1992

Managing Pain after Surgery: a Booklet for Nurses, 1998

Occasional Papers

Measuring Quality: the Patient's View of Day Surgery, 1991

All in a Day's Work: an Audit of Day Surgery in England and Wales, 1992

(D) EDUCATION
National Reports

Obtaining Better Value in Education: Aspects of Non-teaching Costs in Secondary Schools, 1984
Obtaining Better Value from Further Education, 1985
Towards Better Management of Secondary Education, 1986
Assuring Quality in Education: the Role of Local Education Authority Inspectors and Advisers, 1989
Rationalising Primary School Provision, 1990
Home-to-School Transport: a System at the Cross Roads, 1991
Management within Primary Schools, 1991
Two Bs or Not . . . ? Schools' and Colleges' A-Level Performance, 1991
Getting in on the Act: Provision for Pupils with Special Educational Needs – the National Picture, 1992
Adding up the Sums: Schools' Management of Their Finances, 1993
Adding up the Sums 2: Comparative Information for Schools, 1993
Unfinished Business: Full-time Educational Courses for 16–19-year-olds, 1993
Adding up the Sums 3: Comparative Information for Schools – 1994
Adding up the Sums 4: Comparative Information for Schools – 1995/96
Counting to Five: Education of Children Under Five, 1996
Trading Places: the Supply and Allocation of School Places, 1996
Held in Trust: the LEA of the Future, 1999
Missing Out: LEA Management of School Attendance and Exclusion, 1999
Getting the Best from Your Budget: a Guide to the Effective Management of School Resources, 2000
Keeping Your Balance: Standards for Financial Management in Schools, 2000
Money Matters: School Funding and Resource Management, 2000
Schools' Views of their LEA: Learning from Inspection, 2001
Special School Run: Reviewing Special Educational Needs Transport in London, 2001

PFI in Schools: the Quality and Cost of Buildings and Services Provided by Early Private Finance Initiative Schemes, 2002

Special Educational Needs: a Mainstream Issue, 2002

Statutory Assessment and Statements of SEN: In Need of Review?, 2002

Improving School Buildings: Asset Management Planning in LEAs and Schools, 2003

Education Funding: the Impact and Effectiveness of Measures to Stabilise School Funding, 2004

Out-of-Authority Placements for Special Educational Needs, 2007

Updates

Counting to Five: a Review of Audits of Education for Under-Fives, 1997

Getting in on the Act: a Review of Progress on Special Educational Needs, 1998

Trading Places: a Review of Progress on the Supply and Allocation of School Places, 2002

Bulletins

The Act Moves on: Progress in Special Educational Needs, 1994

Guidance and Management Handbooks

The Local Management of Schools: a Guide to Local Education Authorities, 1988

Getting the Act Together: Provision for Pupils with Special Educational Needs, 1992

Keeping Your Balance: Standards for Financial Administration in Schools, 1993

Under-Fives Count: a Management Handbook on the Education of Children Under Five, 1996

Trading Places: a Management Handbook on the Supply and Allocation of School Places, 1997

Improving Home-to-School Transport for Children with Special Educational Needs, 2001
Improving Mainstream Home-to-School Transport, 2001
Managing Special Educational Needs: a Self-review Handbook for Local Education Authorities, 2002

Management Papers and Occasional Papers

Delegation of Management Authority to Schools: June 1988
Surplus Capacity in Secondary Schools: a Progress Report 1988
Losing an Empire, Finding a Role: the LEA of the Future, 1989
Lessons in Teamwork: How School Governing Bodies Can Become More Effective, 1995
Changing Partners: a Discussion Paper on the Role of the Local Education Authority, 1998

(E) HOUSING
National Reports

Bringing Council Tenants' Arrears Under Control, 1984
Improving Council House Maintenance, 1986
Managing the Crisis in Council Housing, 1986
Housing the Homeless: the Local Authority Role, 1989
Healthy Housing: the Role of Environmental Health Services, 1991
Developing Local Authority Housing Strategies, 1992
Remote Control: the National Administration of Housing Benefit, 1993
Homing in on Performance: Social Housing Performance in 1994 Compared, 1995
House Styles: Performance and Practice in Housing Management, 1996
Fraud and Lodging: Tackling Fraud and Error in Housing Benefit, 1997
Competing for Attention: Identifying and Selecting Sites for Housing Associations New-Build Development, 1998

To Build or Not to Build: Assessing Value for Money in Housing Association Rehabilitation Programmes, 1998
Balanced Account: the Audit Arrangements for Registered Social Landlords, 1999
Stock in Trade: Good Practice in Business Planning for Stock Transfers, 1999
Group Dynamics: Group Structures and Registered Social Landlords, 2001
Housing Benefit Administration: Learning from Inspection, 2001
Housing After Transfer: the Local Authority Role, 2002
Housing Benefit: the National Perspective, 2002
Housing Repairs and Maintenance: Learning from Inspection, 2002
Rent Arrears: Rent Arrears and Housing Benefit in the Welsh Social Rented Sector, 2002
Homelessness: Responding to the New Agenda, 2003
Housing Association Rent Income: Rent Collection and Arrears Management by Housing Associations in England, 2003
Learning from the First Housing ALMOs, 2003
Local Authority Housing Rent Income: Rent Collection and Arrears Management by Local Authorities in England and Wales, 2003
Housing: Improving Services through Resident Involvement, 2004
Improvement Drivers in Local Authority Housing: Evidence from Inspection, 2004
Supporting People, 2005
Financing Council Housing, 2005

Updates

Building in Quality: a Review of Progress on Development Control, 1998
Developing Local Authority Housing Strategies: a Review of Progress in Housing Management, 1998
Fraud and Lodging: Progress in Tackling Fraud and Error in Housing Benefit, 1999

Housing Reviews

Housing Inspection Service Annual Review: in Pursuit of Excellence,
2001
Audit Commission Housing Review 2002: Part 1, 2003
*Promoting Positive Practice: Audit Commission Housing Review:
Part II, 2003*

Guidance and Management Handbooks

Local Authority Property, 1988
Building Maintenance Direct Labour Organisations, 1989
Countering Housing Benefit Fraud: a Management Handbook, 1997
*Measure of Support: Good Practice in Managing Supported Housing,
1998*
Closing the Gap: Working Together to Reduce Rent Arrears, 2002
Housing Repairs: the Strategic Challenge, 2002
Housing: Improving Services through Resident Involvement, 2004

Management Papers and Occasional Papers

Local Authority Property, 1988
Building Maintenance DLOs in London, 1990
Who Wins? Voluntary Housing Transfers, 1993

(F) POLICE, FIRE, COMMUNITY SAFETY AND CRIMINAL JUSTICE

Police Papers

Administrative Support for Operational Police Officers, 1988
Improving the Performance of the Fingerprint Service, 1988
Improving Vehicle Fleet Management in the Police Service, May 1989
Management of Police Training, 1989
Calling all Forces: Improving Police Communications Rooms, 1990
Effective Policing: Performance Review in Police Forces, 1990

Footing the Bill: Financing Provincial Police Forces, 1990
Taking Care of the Coppers: Income Generation by Provincial Police Forces, 1990
Pounds and Coppers: Financial Delegation in Provincial Police Forces, 1991
Reviewing the Organisation of Provincial Police Forces, 1991
Fine Lines: Improving the Traffic Warden Service, 1992

National Reports

Probation Service: Promoting Value for Money, 1989
Helping with Enquiries: Tackling Crime Effectively, 1993
In the Line of Fire: Value for Money in the Fire Service – the National Picture, 1995
Misspent Youth: Young People and Crime, 1996
Streetwise: Effective Police Patrol, 1996
Doctor's Bill: the Provision of Forensic Medical Services to the Police, 1998
Action Stations: Improving the Management of the Police Estate, 1999
Safety in Numbers: Promoting Community Safety, 1999
Uniform Approach: a Study of Fire Service Procurement, 2001
Community Safety Partnerships: Learning from Audit, Inspection and Research, 2002
Route to Justice: Improving the Pathway of Offenders through the Criminal Justice System, 2002
Victims and Witnesses: Providing Better Support, 2003
Crime Recording: Improving the Quality of Crime Records in Police Forces in England and Wales, 2004
Verification of the Progress of Modernisation: Fire and Rescue Service in England and Wales, 2004
Second Verification Report on the Progress of Modernisation: Fire and Rescue Service in England and Wales, 2004
Comprehensive Performance Assessment: Learning from CPA for the Fire and Rescue Service in England 2005, 2006
Crime Recording 2005: Improving the Quality of Crime Records in Police Authorities and Forces in England and Wales, 2006

Neighbourhood Crime and Anti-social Behaviour: Making Places Safer through Improved Local Working, 2006
Fire and Rescue Performance Assessment: Scores and Analysis of Performance in Fire and Rescue Authorities 2006, 2007

Updates

Misspent Youth '98: the Challenge for Youth Justice, 1998
Misspent Youth '99: the Challenge for Youth Justice, 1999
Misspent Youth in Wales '99: the Challenge for Youth Justice, 1999

Briefings and Bulletins

Detecting a Change: Progress in Tackling Crime, 1996
Youth Justice 2004: a Review of the Reformed Youth Justice System, 2004

Guidance and Management Handbooks

Cheques and Balances: a Management Handbook on Police Planning and Financial Delegation, 1994
Tackling Crime Effectively, 1994
In the Line of Fire: a Management Handbook on Value for Money in the Fire Service, 1995
Tackling Patrol Effectively, 1995
Tackling Crime Effectively: Management Handbook, Vol. 2, 1996
Action Stations: a Management Handbook on Improving the Management of the Police Estate, 1999
Uniform Approach: a Good Practice Guide on Fire Service Procurement, 2001

Management Papers and Occasional Papers

Value for Money in the Fire Service: Some Strategic Issues to be Resolved, 1986
Going Straight: Developing Good Practice in the Probation Service, 1991

Best Foot Forward: Headquarters' Support for Police Basic Command Units, 2001

Change of Direction: Managing Changes in Local Probation Areas, 2001

Local Criminal Justice Boards: Supporting Change Management, 2003

(G) SOCIAL SERVICES
National Reports

Managing Social Services for the Elderly More Effectively, 1985

Making a Reality of Community Care, 1986

Community Care: Managing the Cascade of Change, 1992

Community Revolution: Personal Social Services and Community Care, 1992

Homeward Bound: a New Course for Community Health, 1992

Finding a Place: a Review of Mental Health Services for Adults, 1994

Seen But Not Heard: Co-ordinating Community Child Health and Social Services for Children in Need, 1994

Coming of Age: Improving Care Services for Older People, 1997

Home Alone: the Role of Housing in Community Care, 1998

Children in Mind: Child and Adolescent Mental Health Services, 1999

Making Connections: Learning the Lessons from Joint Reviews, 1998/ 99, 1999

Charging with Care: How Councils Charge for Home Care, 2000

Forget Me Not: Mental Health Services for Older People, 2000

Fully Equipped: the Provision of Equipment to Older or Disabled People by the NHS and Social Services in England and Wales, 2000

People Need People: Releasing the Potential of People Working in Social Services, 2000

Way to Go Home: Rehabilitation and Remedial Services for Older People, 2000

Integrated Services for Older People: Building a Whole-System Approach in England, 2002

*Services for Disabled Children: a Review of Services for Disabled
Children and Their Families*, 2003
*Older People – Independence and Well-Being: the Challenge for
Public Services*, 2004
*Older People – a Changing Approach: Independence and Well-Being
1*, 2004
*Older People – Building a Strategic Approach: Independence and
Well-Being 2*, 2004
Supporting Frail Older People: Independence and Well-Being 3, 2004
*Older People – Assistive Technology: Independence and Well-Being
4*, 2004
Support for Carers of Older People: Independence and Well-Being 5,
2004
*Living Well in Later Life: a Review of Progress Against the National
Service Framework for Older People*, 2006
*Managing Finances in Mental Health: a Review to Support Improve-
ment and Best Practice*, 2006

Updates

*United They Stand: Co-ordinating Care for Elderly Patients with Hip
Fractures*, 2000
*Forget Me Not 2002: Developing Mental Health Services for Older
People in England*, 2002
Fully Equipped 2002: Assisting Independence, 2002
*Losing Time: Developing Mental Health Service for Older People in
Wales*, 2002

Annual Reports

Joint Review Team annual reports, annual series 1997–2003
*Old Virtues, New Virtues: an Overview of the Changes in Social Care
Services over the Seven Years of Joint Reviews in England 1996–
2003*, 2004

Bulletins

Taking Care: Progress with Care in the Community, 1993
Taking Stock: Progress with Community Care, 1994
Balancing the Care Equation: Progress with Community Care, 1996

Management Handbooks

Take Your Choice: a Commissioning Framework for Community Care, 1997
Messages for Managers: Learning the Lessons from Joint Reviews of Social Services, 1998
Improving Non-Emergency Patient Transport Services, 2001
Improving Transport for Social Services Users, 2001
Let Me Be Me: a Handbook for Managers and Staff Working with Disabled Children and Their Families, 2003

Occasional Papers

Community Care: Developing Services for People with a Mental Handicap, 1987
Developing Community Care for Adults with a Mental Handicap, 1989

(H) CROSS-SECTORAL
National Reports

Get Well Soon: a Reappraisal of Sickness Absence in London, 1993
Reaching the Peak? Getting Value for Money from Management Consultants, 1994
Another Country: Implementing Dispersal under the Immigration and Asylum Act 1999, 2000
New City: Supporting Asylum Seekers and Refugees in London, 2000
Going Places: Taking People to and from Education, Social Services and Healthcare, 2001

Changing Habits: the Commissioning and Management of Community Drug Treatment Services for Adults, 2002

Recruitment and Retention: a Public Service Workforce for the Twenty-first Century, 2002

Human Rights: Improving Public Service Delivery, 2003

Choice in Public Services, 2004

Drug Misuse 2004: Reducing the Local Impact, 2004

Journey to Race Equality: Delivering Improved Services to Local Communities, 2004

Governing Partnerships: Bridging the Accountability Gap, 2005

Choosing Well: Analysing the Costs and Benefits of Choice in Local Public Services, 2006

Delivering Efficiently: Strengthening the Links in Public Service Delivery Chains, 2006

Changing Lanes: Evolving Roles in Road Safety, 2007

Crossing Borders: Responding to the Local Challenges of Migrant Workers, 2007

Staying Afloat: Financing Emergencies, 2007

Updates

A Stitch in Time, 1998

Time Marches On: Facing the Challenge of the Year 2000 Date Change, 1998

No Time Like the Present: Facing the Challenge of the Year 2000 Date Change, 1999

Time Waits for No One: Facing the Challenge of the Year 2000 Date Change, 1999

Briefings

Acquiring IT, 1990

Knowing What IT Costs, 1990

Targets in the Public Sector, 2003

The Evolution of Regulation: Comprehensive Area Assessment and the Changing Face of Public Service Improvement, 2007

Guidance

Numbers that Count: Making Good Use of the 1991 Census, 1991
Acquisition of IT: a Good Practice Guide, 1992

Management Papers and Occasional Papers

Less Dangerous Liaisons: Early Considerations for Making Mergers Work: Management Paper, 1995
Measure of Success: Setting and Monitoring Local Performance Targets, 1999
Aiming to Improve: the Principles of Performance Measurement, 2000
Getting Better All the Time: Making Benchmarking Work, 2000
On Target: the Practice of Performance Indicators, 2000
Building for the Future: the Management of Procurement under the Private Finance Initiative, 2001
Change Here! Managing Change to Improve Local Services, 2001
Healthy Outlook: Local Authority Overview and Scrutiny of Health, 2001
Directions in Diversity: Current Opinion and Good Practice, 2002
Performance Breakthroughs: Improving Performance in Public Sector Organisations, 2002
Connecting with Users and Citizens, 2003
Corporate Governance: Improvement and Trust in Local Public Services, 2003
World Class Financial Management, 2005
The Future of Regulation in the Public Sector, 2006

(I) CITIZEN'S CHARTER
PERFORMANCE INDICATORS

Corporate

Citizen's Charter Indicators: Charting a Course, 1992

National Publication of the Citizen's Charter Indicators: a Consultation Paper from the Audit Commission, 1992

Staying on Course: the Second Year of the Citizen's Charter Indicators, 1993

Citizen's Charter Indicators: Consultation on the Audit Commission's Proposals for 1995/96, 1994

How is Your Council Performing? An Introduction to the Citizen's Charter Indicators, 1994

Watching Their Figures: a Guide to the Citizen's Charter Indicators, 1994

Guidance

Read All About It: Guidance on the Publication by Local Authorities of Citizen's Charter Indicators, 1994

Have We Got News for You: a Guide to Good Practice in Publishing the Local Authority Performance Indicators, 1995

Performance Indicator Reports

Quality Counts: a Standard Consumer Survey of Aspects of Local Council Services, 1994

Local Authority Performance Indicators [1993/94]: Volume 1: Education Services, Social Services and Total Expenditure, 1995

Local Authority Performance Indicators [1993/94]: Volume 2: Council Housing, Housing Benefit, Recycling, Planning, Council Tax Collection and Total Expenditure, 1995

Local Authority Performance Indicators [1993/94]: Volume 3: Police and Fire Services, 1995

Local Authority Performance Indicators 1994/95: Volume 1: Education, Social Services, Libraries, and Expenditure, 1996

Local Authority Performance Indicators 1994/95: Volume 2: Council Housing, Recycling, Planning, Benefits, Council Tax Collection, Inspecting Food Premises, Complaints Systems and Expenditure, 1996

Local Authority Performance Indicators 1994/95: Volume 3: Police and Fire Services, 1996

Local Authority Performance Indicators 1995/96: Police Services, 1997

Local Authority Performance Indicators 1996/97: Police Services, 1998

Local Authority Performance Indicators 1995/96: Volume 1: Education, Social Services, Libraries, Trading Standards, Fire and Total Expenditure, 1997

Local Authority Performance Indicators 1995/96: Volume 2: Council Housing, Recycling, Planning, Land Searches, Benefits, Council Tax Collection, Inspecting Food Premises and Total Expenditure, 1997

Local Authority Performance Indicators 1996/97: Council Services in Wales, 1998

Local Authority Performance Indicators 1996/97: Education Services, 1998

Local Authority Performance Indicators 1996/97: Volume 1: Social Services, Libraries, Trading Standards, Pedestrian Crossings, Fire and Overall Spending, 1998

Local Authority Performance Indicators 1996/97: Volume 2: Housing and Homelessness, Recycling, Land Searches, Council Tax Benefit, Council Tax Collection, Inspecting Food Premises and Overall Spending, 1998

Best Value and Audit Commission Performance Indicators for 2000/ 2001: Volume 1: The Performance Indicators, 1999

Local Authority Performance Indicators 1997/98: Council Services in London, 1999

Local Authority Performance Indicators 1997/98: Council Services in Wales, 1999

Local Authority Performance Indicators 1997/98: Education Services, 1999

Local Authority Performance Indicators 1997/98: Police and Fire Services, 1999

Local Authority Performance Indicators 1997/98: Services for People with Special Needs in England, 1999

Local Authority Performance Indicators 1998/99: Council Services in Wales, 2000

Local Authority Performance Indicators 1998/99: Housing Services in England, 2000

Local Authority Performance Indicators 1998/99: Police and Fire Services, 2000

Local Authority Performance Indicators 1999/2000: Environmental Services in England, 2001

(J) ANTI-FRAUD
National Reports

Survey of Computer Fraud and Abuse, 1987
Survey of Computer Fraud and Abuse 1990, 1991
Protecting the Public Purse: Probity in the Public Sector: Combating Fraud and Corruption in Local Government, 1993
Opportunity Makes a Thief: an Analysis of Computer Abuse, 1994
National Fraud Initiative 2002/03, 2004
National Duplicate Registration Initiative, 2006
National Fraud Initiative 2004/05, 2006

Updates

Protecting the Public Purse: Ensuring Probity in Local Government, annual paper published for the six years 1994–99
Ghost in the Machine: an Analysis of IT Fraud and Abuse, 1998
Protecting the Public Purse: Ensuring Probity in the NHS, 1998
Protecting the Public Purse: Ensuring Probity in the NHS, 1999
Perfect Match: Report of the 1998 National Fraud Initiative, 2000
Protecting the Public Purse: Ensuring Financial Probity in Local Government, 2001
Yourbusiness@risk: an Update on IT Abuse 2001
Match Winner: Report of the 2000 National Fraud Initiative, 2002
ICT Fraud and Abuse 2004: an Update to yourbusiness@risk, 2005

Guidance

Audit Commission/Metropolitan Police: How Should you React to Suspected Fraud? 1997

Audit Commission: What Should You Do if You Suspect a Fraud? (leaflet), 1997

Code of Data Matching Practice, 1997

National Fraud Initiative 2002 Handbook, 2002

National Fraud Initiative 2002 NHS Handbook, 2002

National Fraud Initiative 2002 Pensions Handbook, 2002

National Fraud Initiative 2004/05 Handbook: Local Government, 2004

National Fraud Initiative 2004/05 Handbook: NHS, 2004

National Fraud Initiative 2004/05 Handbook: Pensions, 2004

(K) ENVIRONMENT
National Reports

Securing Further Improvements in Refuse Collection, 1984

Improving Highways Agency Arrangements Between Counties and Districts, 1987

Competitive Management of Parks and Green Spaces, 1988

Improving the Condition of Local Authority Roads: the National Picture, 1988

Urban Regeneration and Economic Development: the Local Government Dimension, 1989

Impact of Competitive Tendering on Highways Maintenance, 1991

The Competitive Grounds Maintenance DSO, 1991

Towards a Healthier Environment: Managing Environmental Health Services, 1991

Building in Quality: a Study of Development Control, 1992

Just Capital: Local Authority Management of Capital Projects, 1996

It's a Small World: Local Government's Role as a Steward of the Environment, 1997

All Aboard: a Review of Local Transport and Travel in Urban Areas Outside London, 1999

Life's Work: Local Authorities, Economic Development and Economic Regeneration, 1999

Waste Management: Guidance for Improving Services: Learning from Inspection, 2001

Development Control and Planning: Learning from Audit, Inspection and Research, 2002

Neighbourhood Renewal: Policy Focus, 2002

Street Scene: Learning from Audit, Inspection and Research, 2002

Economic and Community Regeneration: Learning from Inspection, 2003

People, Places and Prosperity: Delivering Government Programmes at the Local Level, 2004

Planning System: Matching Expectations and Capacity, 2006

Securing Community Benefits through the Planning Process: Improving Performance on Section 106 Agreements, 2006

Briefings

Environmental Health Survey of Food Premises, 1990

Working Capital: Sustainable Communities, 2002

Management Handbooks

Improving Highways Maintenance, 1988

Waste Matters: Good Practice in Waste Management, 1997

Management Papers and Occasional Papers

Managing Cemeteries and Crematoria in a Competitive Environment, 1989

Safer Food: Local Authorities and the Food Safety Act 1990, 1990

Urban Regeneration and Economic Development: the European Community Dimension, 1991

Urban Regeneration Experience: Observations from Local Value for Money Audits, 1991

Waste Management: the Strategic Challenge, 2001

(L) CULTURE AND LEISURE
National reports

Sport for Whom? Clarifying the Local Authority Role in Sport and Recreation, 1989
Local Authorities: Entertainment and the Arts, 1991
Road to Wigan Pier? Managing Local Authority Museums and Art Galleries, 1991
Due for Renewal: a Report on the Library Service, 1997
Building Better Library Services: Learning from Audit, Inspection and Research, 2002
Sport and Recreation: Learning from Audit, Inspection and Research, 2002
Public Sports and Recreation Services: Making them Fit for the Future, 2006

Management handbook

Local Authority Support for Sport, 1990

(M) THE ROLE AND WORK OF THE AUDIT COMMISSION

Audit Commission: Report and Accounts, annual series 1985–2007
Auditing Local Government: a Guide to the Work of the Audit Commission, 1993
How Effective is the Audit Commission? Promoting Value for Money in the Local Public Services, 1993
An Inspector Calls: Quality Control Review Programme for Auditors, 1994
Code of Audit Practice for Local Authorities and the National Health Service in England and Wales, 1995
Best Assured: the Role of the Audit Commission in Best Value, 1999
Best Value and the Audit Commission in England, 1999
Best Value and the Audit Commission in Wales, 1999

Changing Picture, Sharper Focus: Audit Commission Strategy 1999–2002, 1999

How Your External Auditors are Appointed: and How You Can Influence the Choice, 1999

Audit Commission Corporate Plan 2000 to 2003, 2000

Best Value Inspection in Wales, 2000

Code of Audit Practice, 2000

Seeing is Believing: How the Audit Commission Will Carry out Best Value Inspections in England, 2000

Health Strategy 2000–2003, 2000

Statement of Responsibilities of Auditors and of Audited Bodies, 2000

Another Step Forward, 2001

Appointing Auditors: the Audit Commission's Approach, 2001

Councils' Accounts: Your Rights, 2001

Delivering Improvement Together: Audit Commission Strategy 2001–2004, 2001

Managed Audit, 2001

Who Audits the Auditors?, 2001

Statement of Responsibilities of Local Councils and Their Auditors, 2002

Auditing the Auditors: Quality Review Process 2001/02, 2003

Celebrating the Achievements of District Audit, 2003

CPA – The Way Forward: Single Tier and County Councils, 2003

CPA for Districts: Final Assessment Framework, 2003

Strategic Regulation: Minimising the Burden, Maximising the Impact: Audit, Inspection, Analysis, Improvement Tools, Minimising Bureaucracy, Maximising Impact on Public Services, 2003

Councils' Accounts: Your Rights: England, 2004

CPA 2005 – The New Approach: Single Tier and County Council and District Council Comprehensive Performance Assessment from 2005, 2004

Something to Complain About?: What to Do if You Want to Complain about the Audit Commission or its Appointed Auditors, 2004

Strategic Plan 2004–07: Minimising Bureaucracy, Maximising Impact on Public Services, 2004

Code of Audit Practice 2005: for Local Government Bodies, 2005

Code of Audit Practice 2005: for Local NHS Bodies, 2005

Comprehensive Performance Assessment of District Councils, 2005

CPA – The Harder Test: Single Tier and County Councils' Framework for 2005

CPA – The Harder Test: The New Framework for Comprehensive Performance Assessment of Single Tier and County Councils from 2005 to 2008, 2005

Statement of Responsibilities of Auditors and of Audited Bodies, 2005

Assessment of Local Services Beyond 2008, 2006

Code of Audit Practice 2005: for Local Government Bodies (Revised January 2006), 2006

Councils' Accounts: Your Rights: England, 2006

CPA – The District Council Framework for 2006

CPA – The Harder Test Framework for 2006

Strategic Plan 2006

Making Equality and Diversity a Reality: Our Diversity Scheme 2006–2009, 2007

Appendix 2

CHAIRMEN OF
THE AUDIT COMMISSION

(In chronological order; italics denote acting chairman status)

John Read	January 1983 – August 1986
David Cooksey	September 1986 – August 1995
Clive Thompson	September 1995 – November 1995
Roger Brooke	December 1995 – November 1998
Helena Shovelton	December 1998 – November 2001
Adrienne Fresko	December 2001 – October 2002
James Strachan	November 2002 – January 2006
Michael Lyons	January 2006 – September 2006
Michael O'Higgins	Since September 2006

CONTROLLERS/CHIEF EXECUTIVES OF
THE AUDIT COMMISSION

(In chronological order; italics denote acting controller)

John Banham	January 1983 – March 1987
Howard Davies	March 1987 – June 1992
Peter Brokenshire	July 1992 – December 1992
Andrew Foster	January 1993 – August 2003
Steve Bundred	Since September 2003

Appendix 3

MEMBERS OF THE AUDIT COMMISSION

(In alphabetical order)

Start	Finish	Surname	First name(s)	Brief background
2007	current member	Adebowale	Victor	Chief executive of the Turning Point charity
1987	1990	Anson	Elizabeth	Conservative peer
1996	2003	Arthur	Richard	Councillor and leader of the London Borough of Camden. Vice-chairman of the Association of London Government
1986	1991	Axton	Henry Stuart (Harry)	Businessman
1999	2003	Baddeley	Julie	Associate fellow of Templeton College, Oxford and executive director of Woolwich plc
1986	1989	Barratt	John	Chief executive of Cambridgeshire County Council

Start	Finish	Surname	First name(s)	Brief background
1983	1986	Barratt	Lawrie	Founder and chairman of Barratt Homes
1991	1992	Beresford	Paul	Leader of the London Borough of Wandsworth
1983	1986	Bond	Kenneth	Deputy managing director of GEC plc
2001	2005	Bowen	John	Retired solicitor and chairman of the Employment Tribunal
1983	1995	Bowness	Peter	Leader of the London Borough of Croydon and chairman of the London Boroughs Association
1983	1986	Bridge	Keith	Chief executive of Humberside County Council
1995	1998	Brooke	Roger	Founder and chairman of Candover Investments, executive director of Pearson plc and Kensington and Chelsea councillor
1989	1995	Brown	Alan	Chief executive of Oxfordshire County Council
2003	current member	Bundred*	Steve	Executive director of the Improvement and Development Agency and chief executive of Camden Borough Council

* Steve Bundred, the current chief executive, is the first head of its executive to have also been appointed a member of the Commission.

Start	Finish	Surname	First name(s)	Brief background
1989	1995	Christopher	Tony	General secretary of the Inland Revenue Staff Federation
1990	1993	Clout	John	Leader of North Yorkshire County Council
1986	1995	Cooksey	David	Founder and chairman of Advent Venture Partners
2005	current member	Coulter	Jim	Chief executive of the National Housing Federation
1983	1990	Coutts	Ian	Member of Norfolk County Council and chairman of the Association of County Councils' Finance Committee
1998	2003	Curson	Judy	Director of public health and acute care in North and Mid-Hampshire Health Authority
2003	current member	Dixon	Jennifer	Director of health policy at the King's Fund and policy adviser to the chief executive of the NHS
1983	1988	Drain	Geoffrey	General secretary of the National Association of Local Government Officers '
2004	current member	Drew Smith	Sheila	Board member of the Housing Corporation and the South-East Regional Housing Board

Start	Finish	Surname	First name(s)	Brief background
1991	1994	Eilbeck	Lawrence	Leader of Carlisle City Council
1993	1998	English	Terence	President of the Royal College of Surgeons
1999	2004	Filkin	Elizabeth	Parliamentary commissioner for standards and chief executive of the National Association of Citizens' Advice Bureaux
1983	1988	Fisher	Dudley	Chairman of the pre-privatized British Gas in Wales
1983	1988	Foster	Christopher	Partner of Coopers & Lybrand, London School of Economics professor and special adviser to the government
1995	2001	Foster	John	Chief executive of Middlesbrough Council
1996	2003	Fresko	Adrienne	Occupational psychologist and human resources consultant, chairman of Croydon Health Authority
1983	1990	Gunnell	John	Leader of West Yorkshire Metropolitan County Council
1999	2004	Hart	Graham	Permanent secretary of the Department of Health and chairman of the King's Fund

Start	Finish	Surname	First name(s)	Brief background
1983	1986	Hay Davison	Ian	Senior partner of accountants Arthur Andersen and chairman of the Accounting Standards Committee
1995	1997	Heath	David	Chairman of Avon and Somerset Police Authority
1983	1991	Hepworth	Noel	Head of the Chartered Institute of Public Finance and Accountancy
1998	1999	Hine	Deirdre	Chief medical officer for Wales
2006	current member	Houghton	Stephen	Leader of Barnsley Metropolitan Borough Council
2002	2005	Hoyle	Roger	Chief executive of Liverpool Health Authority
1991	1993	Hunt	Jennifer	Chief nurse and member of the Clinical Standards Advisory Group
1990	1995	Irvine	Donald	Chairman of the General Medical Council's Standards Committee
1988	1991	James	Eleanor	Academic at Aberystwyth University
1993	1999	Jenkins	Kate	Head of the prime minister's Efficiency Unit and member of the NHS Policy Board

Start	Finish	Surname	First name(s)	Brief background
2003	current member	Jones	Peter	Leader of East Sussex County Council, and investment banker
1993	1999	Kemp	Peter	Second permanent secretary at the Treasury
1983	1987	Kimmance	Peter	Head of the District Audit Service
2000	2006	Lane	Pauleen	Deputy leader of Trafford Metropolitan Borough Council and member of the North-West Regional Assembly
1983	1990	Lees	David	Finance director of GKN plc
2005	current member	Legg	Thomas	Permanent secretary in the Lord Chancellor's Department
2000	2004	Lemos	Gerard	Partner in Lemos & Crane, specializing in social research
1988	1991	Likierman	Andrew	Professor of management accounting at the London Business School
1995	2001	Lowe	Rosalynde	Chief executive of Hounslow and Spelthorne Community and Mental Health NHS Trust
2003	2006	Lyons	Michael	Chief executive of Birmingham City Council, Nottinghamshire County Council and Wolverhampton Borough Council

Start	Finish	Surname	First name(s)	Brief background
1983	1986	McCallum	Ian	Member of Woking Borough Council and chairman of the Association of District Councils
1986	1989	Meade	Eric	Accountant
2001	2007	Moss	David	Chief executive of Southampton University Hospitals NHS Trust
2006	current member	O'Higgins	Michael	Managing partner of PA Consulting
1989	2000	Orme	Jeremy	Managing partner of accountants Robson Rhodes and member of the Securities and Investments Board
2006	2006	Parker	Tim	Chief executive of the Automobile Association
2007	current member	Platt	Denise	Chairman of the Commission for Social Care Inspection
2003	current member	Pomeroy	Brian	Senior partner of Deloitte Consulting
2007	current member	Rajagopal	Raj	Businessman
1983	1986	Read	John	Chairman of LEP Group plc and partner of accountants Price Waterhouse
1997	2003	Richards	Sue	Professor of public management at the University of Birmingham

Start	Finish	Surname	First name(s)	Brief background
1995	2000	Rowland	Hilary	Chief executive of the Royal Liverpool Children's Trust at Alder Hey Hospital, Liverpool
2003	2004	Scott	Rosalind	Liberal Democrat peer
2007	current member	Shah	Bharat	Businessman
1983	1991	Shaw	Roy	Leader of the London Borough of Camden and vice-chairman of the Association of Metropolitan Authorities
1995	2001	Shovelton	Helena	Chairman of the National Association of Citizens' Advice Bureaux
2000	2003	Skellett	Nick	Leader of Surrey County Council
2003	current member	Smith	Peter	Professor of economics at York University and director of its Centre for Health Economics
1994	2000	Soulsby	Peter	Leader of Leicester City Council
2002	2006	Strachan	James	Chief executive of the Royal National Institute for the Deaf, board member at Ofgem and investment banker
1986	1995	Stuart	Murray	Scottish businessman

Start	Finish	Surname	First name(s)	Brief background
2000	2003	Swinson	Chris	Senior partner of accountants BDO Stoy Hayward and president of the Institute of Chartered Accountants
1994	2000	Tarry	Iris	Leader of Hertfordshire County Council
1991	1997	Thompson	Clive	Businessman
1992	1997	Travers	Tony	Academic at the London School of Economics
1986	1994	Wall	Robert	Member of Bristol City Council and pro-chancellor of Bristol University
2007	current member	Watson	Jenny	Chairman of the Equal Opportunities Commission
1995	2001	Watson	Ron	Sefton councillor and leader of Conservative Group within Association of Metropolitan Authorities
1990	1995	West	Chris	General manager of Portsmouth and East Hampshire Health Authority
2005	current member	White	Chris	Leader of the Liberal Democrats on Hertfordshire County Council
1987	1996	Wilkinson	Clive	Leader of Birmingham City Council

Start	Finish	Surname	First name(s)	Brief background
1997	2003	Williams	David	Leader of the London Borough of Richmond upon Thames
1999	2003	Wolfe	Brian	Director of IT at Marconi
1990	1996	Wood	Peter	Chairman of Huddersfield Health Authority

Appendix 4

Name	Post held	Year of joining senior management	Year of leaving Commission
Bruce Anderson	Director of purchasing	1996	1998
Sue Barnes	Director of knowledge and information	2002	2003
Mollie Bickerstaff	Director of purchasing	1994	1996
Jonathan Boyce	Director of health studies	1994	2004
Peter Brokenshire	Director of management practice	1983	1992
Tony Child	Director of legal services	1987	1995
Bob Chilton	Director of local government studies	1989	2001

* That is, those individuals who have served on the Commission's senior management team during the period 1983–2008, as directors or managing directors. The list does not include those who held acting director posts. Where individuals have held more than one post on the top management team, the table shows only their current or final post, but shows all the years for which they were members of the team. Where individuals went on secondment to another organization and did not subsequently return to the Commission, the 'Year of leaving Commission' column shows the year in which they started their secondment.

Name	Post held	Year of joining senior management	Year of leaving Commission
Gareth Davies	Managing director local government and housing	2006	Present
Tracey Dennison	Managing director human resources	2003	Present
Frances Done	Managing director local government and housing	2003	2006
Colin Douglas	Director of communications	2002	2004
Martin Evans	Managing director audit	1998	Present
Clive Grace	Director general, Audit Commission in Wales	2003	2005
Jenny Grey	Managing director communications and public reporting	2006	Present
Terry Hanafin	Director of public services research	1999	2002
Paul Kirby	Director of inspection	2001	2002
Trish Longdon	Director of people development	1999	2003
Andy McKeon	Managing director health	2003	Present
Alan Meekings	Director of operations	2002	2004
Cliff Nicholson	Deputy controller	1983	1991
Steve Nicklen	Director of audit support	1993	1997
Bill Ogley	Director of corporate resources	1993	1996

Name	Post held	Year of joining senior management	Year of leaving Commission
Richard Peel	Managing director communications and public reporting	2004	2006
David Prince	Managing director of strategy and resources	1994	2004
Bert Pyke	Chief inspector of audit	1983	1984
Joanne Shaw	Director of performance development	1998	2002
Brian Skinner	Director of audit	1989	1994
Les Stanford	Chief inspector of audit	1985	1989
David Stewart	Managing director corporate services	2007	Present
Peter Thomas	Director of performance development	2002	2002
Wendy Thomson	Director of inspection	1999	2001
Ross Tristem	Director of health studies	1983	1994
John Vaughan	Director of finance and administration	1983	1987
Paul Vevers	Director of audit support	1997	1999
Bob Walding	Director of knowledge and information	2003	2006
Andrew Webster	Director of public services research	2002	2003
Harry Wilkinson	Director of accounting practice	1983	1996
Peter Wilkinson	Managing director policy, research and studies	1995	Present

Appendix 5

STAFF NUMBERS AND OPERATING INCOME

Year ending	Staff	Operating income (£000s)
March 1984	524	14,991
March 1985	596	20,062
March 1986	600	21,545
March 1987	610	23,754
March 1988	643	25,558
March 1989	669	28,263
March 1990	748	33,793
March 1991	1,043 (incl. FB4 staff since 10/90)	46,623 (incl. NHS fees since 10/90)
March 1992	1,154	63,765
March 1993	1,265	77,479
March 1994	1,299	82,864
March 1995	1,354	88,881
March 1996	1,324	92,395
March 1997	1,280	91,945

Year ending	Staff	Operating income (£000s)
October 1997	1,306	57,574 (7-month period)
October 1998	1,403	105,156
October 1999	1,600	111,956
October 2000	1,885	144,345
October 2001	2,271	178,524
October 2002	2,437	213,917
October 2003	n/a	n/a
March 2004	2,356	331,291 (17-month period)
March 2005	2,307	233,202
March 2006	2,023	195,756

Appendix 6

THE PRIVATE FIRMS AND THEIR SHARE (BY VALUE) OF THE MARKET FOR PRINCIPAL AUDITS *

Fiscal year	Fee income (£m)	As % of total market value	No. of firms	List of firms employed and subsequent changes
1983	2.2	15	13	Price Waterhouse; Armitage & Norton; Coopers & Lybrand; Deloitte, Haskins & Sells; Arthur Young; Arthur Andersen; Ernst & Whinney; Robson Rhodes; Thomson McLintock; Touche Ross; Binder, Hamlyn; Peat, Marwick, Mitchell; Thornton Baker – all taken on after previous selection by local authorities concerned.

* Principal audits are those relating for all or part of the period 1983–2008 to local authority bodies (down to the level of District Councils); Town Councils designated as Best Value Authorities; Fire, Police and Probation Authorities; Passenger Transport Authorities and Executives, National Park Authorities and Waste Disposal Authorities; NHS Trusts and Primary Care Trusts, District Health Authorities, Regional Health Authorities, Family Health Service Authorities and Strategic Health Authorities. Excluded are the audits of Internal Drainage Boards, non-Best Value Town Councils, Parish Councils and other miscellaneous bodies, for which total fees in the year to

Fiscal year	Fee income (£m)	As % of total market value	No. of firms	List of firms employed and subsequent changes
1984	5.6	28	13	No changes.
1985	6.7	31	13	No changes.
1986	6.9	29	11	Arthur Andersen withdraws; Armitage & Norton merges into Peat, Marwick, Mitchell.
1987	7.1	28	9	Thornton Baker is reconfigured as Grant Thornton and withdraws; Peat Marwick merges with Thomson McLintock as part of KPMG (finally adopting KPMG name in 1995).
1988	8.1	29	9	No changes.
1989	8.0	25	8	Ernst & Whinney merges with Arthur Young to form Ernst & Young.
1990	11.2	25	7	UK partnership of Deloitte, Haskins & Sells merges with Coopers & Lybrand to become Coopers & Lybrand Deloitte.
1991	15.9	25	8	Kidsons Impey (later part of Baker Tilly) taken on as established NHS auditor.

March 2007 amounted to approximately £1.5 million. As of 2007, around 70 per cent of this smaller market (by value) was awarded to six private firms: Mazars, BDO Stoy Hayward, Clement Keys, Lubbock Fine, Moore Stephens and UHY Hacker Young.

Fiscal year	Fee income (£m)	As % of total market value	No. of firms	List of firms employed and subsequent changes
1992	20.1	26	8	Coopers & Lybrand drops the Deloitte name.
1993	22.0	27	8	No changes.
1994	23.5	27	8	No changes.
1995	25.3	28	8	No changes.
1996	26.2	29	8	Touche Ross becomes Deloitte & Touche.
1997	28.5	30	8	No changes.
1998	30.8	30	5	Ernst & Young and Binder, Hamlyn withdraw; Coopers & Lybrand merges with PW as PricewaterhouseCoopers.
1999	28.6	27	6	Pannell Kerr Forster (PKF) taken on.
2000	35.1	28	6	No changes.
2001	39.3	29	7	Mazars taken on.
2002	46.1	29	7	No changes.
2003	n/a	n/a	n/a	n/a
2004*	83.3	32	7	No changes.
2005	59.7	32	7	No changes.
2006	43.1	28	7	No changes.

* 17-month period from November 2002 until March 2004.

Fiscal year	Fee income (£m)	As % of total market value	No. of firms	List of firms employed and subsequent changes
2007	65.5	36	7	Robson Rhodes merges with Grant Thornton.
				List of firms now comprises: Baker Tilly, Deloitte & Touche, Grant Thornton, KPMG, Mazars, PKF, PricewaterhouseCoopers.

Source: *Outsourcing Audit and Inspection Services*, research paper prepared for the Commission by Martin McNeill, 2007

Notes

INTRODUCTION

1. Local Government Finance Act 1982, Section 27, para. 1.
2. Local Government Finance Act 1982, Section 15, para. 1(c).
3. Derek Matthews, *A History of Auditing*, Routledge, 2006. Admittedly, it is a book focused narrowly on the techniques of audit used for companies in the private sector since the nineteenth century.
4. Christopher Foster, *British Government in Crisis*, Oxford University Press, 2005; Simon Jenkins, *Accountable to None: the Tory Nationalisation of Britain*, Penguin, 1996, and *Thatcher & Sons*, Penguin/Allen Lane, 2006. See also Christopher Hood, Colin Scott, Oliver James, George Jones and Tony Travers, *Regulation Inside Government – Waste-Watchers, Quality Police and Sleaze-Busters*, OUP, 1999.

CHAPTER 1 THE AUDIT TRAIL TO 1982

1. Reginald Jones, *Local Government Audit Law*, HMSO, 2nd edition, 1985, p. 3.
2. R. U. Davies (ed.), *Watchdogs' Tales*, HMSO, 1986, p. 40. This excellent collection of reminiscences by senior and retired members of the DAS has been drawn on heavily for the pre-history of the Commission.
3. Ibid., p. 22.
4. Ibid., p. 141.
5. Ibid., p. 46.
6. Ibid., p. 239, from an account written by Cliff Nicholson, later a long-serving deputy controller and director of operations at the Audit Commission. He added: 'So far as I have been able to establish, that was the first expression of the proposition and the title.'

7. Ibid., p. 157.

8. Michael Heseltine, *Where There's a Will*, Hutchinson, 1987, p. 37.

9. As deputy chief inspector in 1977–79, Peter Kimmance was the DAS official responsible for liaising with the Advisory Committee – 'and oh, how we tried! But it wasn't the answer because it was a completely non-statutory, floating body. It had no teeth . . . [The chairman, Brian Maynard] tried very hard, but since he had no powers and local government didn't think much of the Advisory Committee anyway, we were struggling.' (Interview.)

10. *Layfield Report*, HMSO, 1976, p. 98.

11. Michael Heseltine, interview.

12. Heseltine, *Where There's a Will*, p. 206.

13. Peter Kimmance, interview.

14. Michael Heseltine, *Life in the Jungle*, Hodder & Stoughton, 2000, p. 206.

15. Cliff Nicholson, interview.

16. Davies Papers, No. 107. These papers are the file notes kept by Howard Davies between 1987 and 1991.

17. Heseltine, *Where There's a Will*, p. 39.

18. *The Times*, 7 May 1980.

19. Heseltine, *Where There's a Will*, p. 43.

20. Margaret Thatcher, *The Downing Street Years*, HarperCollins, 1993, p. 643.

21. Davies Papers, No. 18.

22. Terry Heiser, interview.

23. Simon Jenkins, *Accountable to None*, Penguin Books, 1996, pp. 231–3.

24. Introduction to the *Report of the Chief Inspector of Audit for the Year Ended 31st March 1982*.

25. Nicholson, interview. On the action in the courts, see Jones, op. cit., p. 18. In *Derby City Council v. Secretary of State (1982)*, the government actually won the first round.

26. Nicholson, interview. He added: 'I'm not quite sure what their motivation was, but they were trying to put us in another straitjacket. We had bitter meetings.' In his contribution to *Watchdogs' Tales*, he wrote more guardedly: 'where they attempted to provide ready-made answers for the Commission, those answers were too much the product of the Departmental approach to meet the Commission's needs. I cannot think of any of those ready-made answers which were actually adopted' (p. 244).

CHAPTER 2 GETTING STARTED, 1982–83

1. Roy Shaw, interview.
2. Noel Hepworth, interview.
3. Peter Kimmance, interview.
4. John Banham, interview.
5. Cliff Nicholson, interview.
6. Banham, interview.
7. Commission Paper 83/3, on *Top Management Organization for the Audit Commission*, 14/2/83.
8. Davies Papers, No. 14.
9. Commission Paper 83/2, *Launching the Audit Commission Successfully: Proposed Start-up Strategy*, 14/2/83, and CP 83/3, see note 7.
10. Chris Hurford, interview.
11. Nicholson, Kimmance interviews. The DoE was clear it wanted an auditor in the deputy job, but couldn't persuade Kimmance to take it. 'I thought that actually I was too past it at 60. I was fairly worn out because I'd been holding the whole thing together – and Cliff Nicholson was ideal, because he'd dealt with all the papers relating to the Audit Commission.'
12. Nicholson, interview.
13. Ibid.
14. Banham, interview.
15. Ross Tristem, interview.
16. Ibid.
17. Ibid.
18. Ibid.
19. Ibid.
20. *Audit News* newsletter, October 1983.
21. Minutes of the 28 April 1983 commissioners' meeting.
22. It had been prepared for the Audit Inspectorate by the Local Authority Management Services Advisory Committee (LAMSAC). The other three came from Ernst & Whinney, Coopers & Lybrand, and Price Waterhouse.
23. Tristem, interview.
24. Commission Paper 83/15, *Controller's Report – June 1983*, 15/6/83.
25. Commission Paper 83/3, *Top Management Organization for the Audit Commission*.
26. Letter from John Banham to Harry Wilkinson, 22 June 1983.
27. Hepworth, interview.

28. Commission Paper 83/11, *Proposed Assignments of Auditors and Audit Commission Staffing – FY84*, 18/4/83.
29. Minutes of the 6 April 1983 commissioners' meeting.
30. Jeremy Orme, interview.
31. The 13 firms (with their assignment of the 456 principal authorities) were: Price Waterhouse (24), Armitage & Norton (19), Coopers & Lybrand (17), Deloitte, Haskins & Sells (16), Arthur Young (6), Arthur Andersen (5), Ernst & Whinney (5), Robson Rhodes (4), Thomson McLintock (5), Touche Ross (5), Binder, Hamlyn (3), Peat, Marwick, Mitchell (5), and Thornton Baker (4). The total of 118 assignments marked a switch of 77 from the DAS.
32. Michael Dallas, interview.
33. Commission Paper 83/18, *Revised Operating Budget for FY84*, 15/6/83.
34. Commission Paper 83/7, *Conflicts of Interest: a Possible Commission Response*, 28/3/83.
35. Banham, interview.
36. Letter to Harry Wilkinson, 22 June 1983.
37. Harry Wilkinson, interview.
38. Ibid.
39. Ibid.
40. Nicholson, interview.
41. *Audit News*, February 1984, p. 4. The in-house newsletter quoted Jenkin's fulsome praise at some length.

CHAPTER 3 DECLARATIONS OF INDEPENDENCE, 1983–85

1. Doug Edmonds, interview. One of Tristem's former colleagues from the DHSS was close to joining the Commission as an associate director in Special Studies but had a last-minute change of heart because it all seemed too precarious.
2. David Butler, Andrew Adonis and Tony Travers, *Failure in British Government: the Politics of the Poll Tax*, OUP, 1994, p. 267.
3. Quoted in Simon Jenkins, *Accountable to None*, Penguin, 1996, p. 49.
4. All were published, as were Audit Commission titles to be for many years ahead, by HMSO (or its successor, the Stationery Office).
5. Published by Dow Jones-Irwin, 1985.
6. From the introduction to Zelazny's internal McKinsey training document, *Choosing & Using Charts*.

7. Cliff Nicholson, interview.

8. Minutes of the 14 February 1984 commissioners' meeting.

9. Minutes of the 3 August 1983 commissioners' meeting.

10. Minutes of the 3 November 1983 commissioners' meeting.

11. John Banham, interview.

12. *The Impact on Local Authorities' Economy, Efficiency and Effectiveness of the Block Grant System*, para. 36.

13. *The Times*, 31 August 1984, p. 11. The editorial ended with a magisterial rebuke to the government – intriguingly, just months before the earliest talk in Whitehall of a poll tax – for ignoring arguments for both financial and political reforms to local government. 'It is the failure of the Government to address itself to those matters, even while if necessary forging temporary fetters, that forms the burden of the charge that constitutionalists and administrators combine to lay against it.'

14. *Audit Commission Policy Review (ACPR)*, DoE, January 1987, para. 3.31.

15. Thatcher, *The Downing Street Years*, HarperCollins, 1993, p. 646.

16. David Butler et al., op. cit., p. 42.

17. Ibid., p. 83.

18. *ACPR*, op. cit., para. 3.31.

19. Banham, interview.

20. Ibid.

21. Ross Tristem, interview.

22. David Butler et al., op. cit., p. 219.

23. *ACPR*, op. cit., para. 3.32.

24. Minutes of the 5 April 1984 commissioners' meeting, para. 9.

25. Banham, interview.

26. Derek Elliott, interview.

27. See, for example, the *Guardian*, 28 June 1985.

28. Nicholson, interview.

29. Banham, interview.

30. The full list of sixteen comprised (within Inner London) Greenwich, Camden, Hackney, Islington, Lambeth, Lewisham and Southwark; and (outside Inner London) Haringey, Brent, Basildon, Leicester, Merseyside, Sheffield, South Yorkshire, Thamesdown and Tory-controlled Portsmouth.

31. Minutes of the 4 October 1984 commissioners' meeting.

32. Peter Jenkins, *Mrs Thatcher's Revolution*, Jonathan Cape, 1987, p. 239.

33. Brian Skinner, interview.

34. Ibid.

35. Nicholson, interview.

36. *Capital Expenditure Controls in Local Government in England*, HMSO, April 1985.

37. Nicholson, interview.

38. Skinner, interview.

39. See Peter Jenkins, op. cit., pp. 238–53 for a fuller account of the background.

40. Nicholson, interview.

41. Peter Yetzes, interview.

42. Skinner, interview, from which this account of the Islington visit is extracted.

43. Elliott, interview.

44. Roy Shaw, interview.

45. Minutes of the 7 November 1985 commissioners' meeting.

46. Minutes of the 5 February 1987 commissioners' meeting.

47. Minutes of the 2 October 1986 commissioners' meeting.

48. Banham, interview.

49. Nicholson, interview.

50. Banham, interview.

51. *New Society*, 28 March 1986.

52. Banham, interview.

53. Davies Papers, No. 14. Davies recorded: 'I later [on 24 March 1987] had a slightly alarming conversation with Alex Smith of Sheffield who said he had drafted two papers about the Sheffield situation, one justifying the issue of a certificate [relating to losses or deficiencies caused by wilful misconduct] and the other not. He maintained that he had taken counsel's opinion on the basis of the information in the first paper and was told to go ahead but was now quite firmly inclined to not take action. He, however, had no intention of taking any further legal advice. This seems likely to be a problem.'

CHAPTER 4 UNDER THE BANHAM BANNER, 1985–87

1. Ross Tristem, interview.

2. Doug Edmonds, interview.

3. Steve Evans, interview.

4. Commission Paper 83/2.

5. Tristem, interview.

6. Minutes of the 4 July 1985 commissioners' meeting.

7. *Sunday Times*, 7 July 1985.

8. Michael Heseltine, interview. He had no specific recollection of the Banham presentation, however.

9. Tristem, interview.

10. John Banham, interview.

11. *Audit News*, May 1987.

12. Chris Hurford, interview.

13. Cliff Nicholson, interview.

14. Copy of speech provided by HW to the author.

15. 'Who Audits the Auditor?', *Public Finance and Accountancy*, 19 July 1985.

16. Commission Paper 85/17, *Quality Reviews: 1983–84 Audits*, April 1985.

17. For Noel Hepworth, 'it showed that a lot of the claims by the firms appeared to be overstated and could be construed as marketing hype' (interview).

18. Harry Wilkinson, interview.

19. Minutes of the 3 July 1986 commissioners' meeting.

20. Minutes of the 12 December 1985 commissioners' meeting.

21. Wilkinson, interview.

22. Minutes of the 6 March 1986 commissioners' meeting.

23. Minutes of Commission Meeting, 7 March 1985.

24. Greg Birdseye, interview.

25. John Banham, *Managing the Crisis in Council Housing*, p. 72.

26. Ibid., p. 3.

27. Davies Papers, No. 8.

28. Minutes of the 10 May 1984 commissioners' meeting.

29. Noel Hepworth, interview.

30. Birdseye, interview.

31. Minutes of the 1 May 1986 commissioners' meeting.

32. Hepworth, interview.

33. Banham, interview.

34. David Cooksey, interview.

35. Banham, interview.

36. Minutes of the 2 October 1986 commissioners' meeting.

37. Commission Paper 86/26.

38. Minutes of the 1 May 1986 commissioners' meeting.

39. *Making a Reality of Community Care*, published by HMSO, December 1986.

40. *Audit Commission Policy Review*, DoE, March 1987, para. 3.33.

41. Banham, interview.

42. David Henderson-Stewart, interview.

43. Cooksey, interview, and Davies Papers, No. 2.
44. Minutes of the 5 September 1985 commissioners' meeting.
45. Cooksey, interview.
46. Occasional Paper No. 3, para. 14.
47. Ibid., p. 11.
48. Ibid., para. 61.
49. Howard Davies, interview. Davies's recollection was that the conversation happened in the aisle of the plane en route to London. Banham recalled it taking place after they had arrived back at Heathrow and were waiting for their luggage.
50. Tristem, interview.

CHAPTER 5 STRAIGHT DOWN THE LINE, 1987–89

1. David Cooksey, interview.
2. Davies Papers, No. 1.
3. Noel Hepworth, interview.
4. *Audit Commission Policy Review*, DoE, March 1987, para. 3.4.
5. Ibid., para. 0.4.
6. Davies Papers, No. 17.
7. Ibid., No. 18.
8. Ibid., Nos 14 and 16.
9. Ibid., No. 12.
10. *Audit Commission Review*, March 1987, para. 3.24.
11. Audit Commission 1986 Annual Report, p. 11.
12. Report and Accounts for the Year Ended March 31 1987, p. 33.
13. Howard Davies, interview.
14. Cliff Nicholson, interview.
15. Davies, interview.
16. Davies Papers, No. 60.
17. Ibid., No. 81.
18. Ibid., No. 55.
19. Chris Hurford, interview.
20. Davies Papers, No. 61. The same point had been made by a leading Inner London councillor, Margaret Hodge, at a local government seminar that Davies had attended back in February 1987. She reported seeing auditors at a recent DAS meeting who had crossed the words Audit Commission off their identity badges.

21. Hurford, interview.

22. Davies, interview.

23. Ibid.

24. Greg Birdseye, interview.

25. Davies Papers, No. 1.

26. Ibid., No. 66. The formal minutes of the afternoon meeting made only a brief reference to a paper on VFM achievements and the fact that a strategy session had been held.

27. *Audit Commission Policy Review*, March 1987, para. 0.5.

28. Davies Papers, No. 47.

29. Davies, interview.

30. Ibid.

31. One of the earliest national reports put out by Vincent Square had made the point quite bluntly. *Capital Expenditure Controls in Local Government in England* was the 1985 follow-up to the 1984 Block Grant Report. As its executive summary noted, 'Revenue and capital are obviously inter-related and authorities face a choice between them ... This calls into question any system that seeks to control the two forms of expenditure separately. The present arrangements are a recipe for unproductive creative accounting.'

32. Davies Papers, No. 41.

33. Minutes of the 3 September 1987 commissioners' meeting.

34. By amendment this became Section 25D of the 1982 Act underpinning the Audit Commission.

35. Tony Child, interview. The assistant was Judy Libovitch, who worked with him throughout his time at the Commission.

36. *Central Management and Administration at Coventry*, June 1987.

37. David Henderson-Stewart, interview.

38. Davies, interview.

39. Davies Papers, No. 25.

40. Ibid., No. 40.

41. Commission Annual Report 1989, p. 27.

42. Davies, interview.

43. Davies Papers, No. 94.

44. Ibid., No. 103.

45. Henderson-Stewart, interview.

46. *The Times*, 29 March 1988, pp. 20–21.

47. Adam Tickell, 'Creative finance and the local state: the Hammersmith and Fulham swaps affair', *Political Geography*, 17 (7), 1998, p. 875.

CHAPTER 6 CLOSING THE SWAP SHOP, 1988–91

1. The following account draws on interviews by the author with Mike Barnes, Howard Davies and Tony Child.
2. Davies Papers, No. 76b.
3. Quoted in Adam Tickell, 'Creative finance and the local state', *Political Geography*, 17 (7), 1998, p. 869.
4. High Court affidavit of Tony Hazell, 30 May 1989, para. 82.
5. Ibid., para. 83.
6. Ibid., para. 84.
7. Ibid., para. 62.
8. Tony Child, interview.
9. Tickell, op. cit., p. 869.
10. Ibid., quoted on p. 871.
11. Child, interview.
12. Davies Papers, No. 117.
13. Tickell, op. cit., pp. 871–2.
14. Davies Papers, No. 119.
15. Child, interview.
16. *Financial Times*, 23 February 1990, p. 26. Also quoted in Tickell, op. cit., p. 872.
17. David Cooksey, interview.
18. Ibid.
19. Minutes of the 13 March 1990 extraordinary meeting, para. 4.
20. Minutes of the 5 July 1990 commissioners' meeting, para. 12.
21. Child, interview.
22. Tickell, op. cit., p. 873.

CHAPTER 7 A CREDIBLE AUTHORITY, 1988–91

1. Steve Evans, interview.
2. Davies Papers, No. 26.
3. David Cooksey, interview.
4. Ross Tristem, interview.
5. Ibid. The following account is Tristem's recollection, as corroborated by Nicholson.
6. Minutes of the 2 April 1987 commissioners' meeting, para. 19.

7. Minutes of the 4 June 1987 commissioners' meeting, para. 11.

8. Davies Papers, No. 58. Davies's account of the conversation continued: 'On cleaning [reported John Potts] there were cleaning standards which often meant offices being cleaned twice in every 24 hours and sometimes cleaned at 7pm and 7am when there was nobody in the office in the meantime. I said that clearly they needed to clean those rooms where there was blood on the walls. He said that contrary to public impression there were parts of police stations where there was not very much blood at any time.'

9. Police Paper No. 2, para. 21.

10. Howard Davies, interview.

11. Police Paper No. 8, para. 96.

12. Kenneth Baker, *The Turbulent Years: My Life in Politics*, Faber & Faber, 1993, p. 449.

13. Davies Papers, No. 126.

14. Ibid., No. 119.

15. Evans, interview.

16. Michael Dallas, interview.

17. *Competitiveness and Contracting Out of Local Authorities' Services*, February 1987.

18. Occasional Paper No. 7, January 1989, para. 62.

19. *School Meals Audit Guide*, September 1983, para. 2.6.

20. Occasional Paper No. 10, para. 65.

21. Davies, interview.

22. David Butler, Andrew Adonis and Tony Travers, *Failure in British Government: the Politics of the Poll Tax*, OUP, 1994, p. 127.

23. Davies Papers, No. 10.

24. Ibid., Nos 5 and 12.

25. Ibid., No. 16.

26. Ibid., No. 20.

27. Ibid., No. 72.

28. Ibid., No. 97.

29. Davies, interview.

30. Thatcher, *The Downing Street Years*, HarperCollins, 1993, p. 663.

31. David Butler et al., op. cit., p. 159.

32. Ibid., p. 160. But its subsequent account of how the prime minister's thinking developed makes no reference to the 6 May lunch or the paper from the Commission's controller.

33. Thatcher, op. cit., p. 664.

34. Davies Papers, No. 121, from which comes this whole account of the 6 May session at Chequers.

35. Thatcher, op. cit., pp. 664–5.
36. David Butler et al., op. cit., p. 164.
37. Harry Wilkinson, interview.
38. John Magill, interview.
39. Andrew Hosken, *Nothing Like a Dame: the Scandals of Shirley Porter*, Granta Books, 2006, pp. 47–8.
40. Magill, interview.
41. Hosken, op. cit., p. 86.
42. Ibid., p. 98.
43. Ibid., p. 105.
44. Magill, interview.
45. Quoted by Hosken, op. cit., p. 267.
46. Public Interest Report, May 1996, para. 20.
47. Magill, interview.
48. Davies, interview.
49. *Minutes of Evidence*, PAC, 8 December 1986, para. 306.
50. *Capital Accounting by Local Authorities*, published by CIPFA, January 1993, para. 3.3.
51. Ibid., para. 4.7.
52. Ibid., para. 5.2.
53. Martin Evans, interview.
54. *Capital Accounting by Local Authorities*, CIPFA, para. 3.14.
55. Ibid.
56. Ibid.

CHAPTER 8 AT THE CUTTING EDGE, 1989–91

1. Davies Papers, No. 68.
2. Ibid., No. 56.
3. Ibid., No. 65.
4. *The Times*, Tuesday, 26 January 1988, p. 1.
5. Nigel Lawson, *The View From No. 11*, Bantam Press, 1992, p. 614.
6. Davies Papers, No. 94. His source was Mark Call, a McKinsey consultant who had followed in Davies's wake as a special adviser to the chancellor.
7. Ross Tristem, interview.
8. Howard Davies, interview.
9. Lawson, op. cit., p. 619.
10. Tristem, interview. Ironically, the official heading up the Treasury team,

Hayden Phillips, was on secondment from the Home Office – where he, also, had worked with Tristem.

11. Davies Papers, No. 101.

12. Ibid., No. 103.

13. Lawson, op. cit., p. 619.

14. Ibid.

15. Davies Papers, No. 106.

16. Ibid., No. 112.

17. See *How Effective is the Audit Commission?* para. 38.

18. Davies Papers, No. 111.

19. *Organizing for the 1990s* was written by the present author as part of a brief consultancy project that he undertook for the controller over the first few months of 1989.

20. Cliff Nicholson, interview.

21. David Cooksey, interview.

22. Tristem, interview.

23. Lawson, op. cit., p. 613.

24. From a speech quoted in *The Hospital*, June 1950.

25. Davies Papers, No. 111.

26. Ibid.

27. Ibid., No. 114.

28. Jonathan Boyce, interview.

29. Davies Papers, No. 120.

30. Nicholson, interview.

31. Tristem, interview.

32. Boyce, interview.

33. Ibid.

34. Davies Papers, No. 122.

35. Davies, interview.

36. Geoffrey Rendle, interview.

37. Boyce, interview.

38. Davies Papers, No. 125.

39. Ibid.

40. Boyce, interview.

41. Commission Away Day Strategy Review, 24 November 1992, Paper 2, para. 21.

42. *Urban Regeneration and Economic Development*, p. 1.

43. Tristem, interview.

CHAPTER 9 MATTERS OF SUCCESSION, 1991–93

1. *The Times*, 3 July 1990.

2. Minutes of the 5 July 1990 commissioners' meeting, para. 28.

3. Minutes of the 4 July 1991 commissioners' meeting.

4. Davies Papers, No. 128.

5. Ibid.

6. Ross Tristem, interview.

7. Howard Davies, interview.

8. Ibid.

9. John Major, *The Autobiography*, HarperCollins, 1999, p. 248.

10. Anne Barron and Colin Scott, 'The Citizen's Charter Programme', in *Modern Law Review*, 55, July 1992, p. 541. The Cabinet Office paper prefigured the Citizen's Charter itself, in all essential details.

11. Minutes of the 2 July 1992 commissioners' meeting.

12. Christopher Hood, Colin Scott, Oliver James, George Jones and Tony Travers, *Regulation Inside Government – Waste-Watchers, Quality Police and Sleaze-Busters*, Oxford University Press, 1999, p. 98.

13. Minutes of the 7 November 1991 commissioners' meeting.

14. Local Government Act 1992, Part I, section 1.

15. Minutes of the 6 February 1992 commissioners' meeting.

16. *The Times*, 1 April 1993.

17. David Cooksey, interview.

18. Jonathan Boyce, interview.

19. Geoffrey Rendle, interview.

20. Tristem, interview.

21. Peter Brokenshire, interview.

22. Ibid.

23. Cooksey, interview.

24. Ibid.

25. Brokenshire, interview.

26. Tony Travers, interview.

27. Peter Wilkinson, interview.

28. Travers, interview.

29. Commission Awayday Strategy Review, 24 November 1992, Paper 1, paras 9 and 11.

30. Steve Evans, interview.

31. Peter Wilkinson, interview.

32. Bevan made the remark during his address to the centenary dinner of the District Auditors' Society at the Connaught Rooms in London on 14 November 1946 – the society's first post-war gathering.
33. Harry Wilkinson, interview.
34. *LGC*, 18 June 1993.
35. Harry Wilkinson, interview.
36. Peter Wilkinson, interview.
37. Andrew Foster, interview.

CHAPTER 10 FROM DAS TO DISTRICT AUDIT, 1993–97

1. Trish Longdon, interview.
2. Bill Butler, interview.
3. Martin McNeill, interview.
4. Andrew Foster, interview with the author.
5. David Prince, interview.
6. Jeremy Orme, interview.
7. Prince, interview.
8. Ibid.
9. Ibid.
10. Geoffrey Rendle, interview.
11. Prince, interview.
12. Ibid.
13. Butler, interview.
14. Longdon, interview.
15. Mike Barnes, interview.
16. Prince, interview.
17. Barnes, interview.
18. Butler, interview.
19. Prince, interview.
20. Butler, interview.
21. Prince, interview.
22. Longdon, interview.
23. Minutes of the 1 August 1996 commissioners' meeting.
24. Prince, interview.
25. Ibid.
26. Minutes of the 5 January 1995 commissioners' meeting, para. 17.
27. Public Interest Report, May 1996, paras, 24–5.

28. Andrew Hosken, *Nothing Like a Dame: the Scandals of Shirley Porter*, Granta Books, 2006, p. 124.

29. Ibid., p. 281.

30. John Magill, interview.

31. Hosken, op. cit., p. 300.

32. Magill, interview.

33. David Cooksey, interview.

34. Magill's press release, 13 January 1994.

35. *The Times*, 14 January 1994, p. 1.

36. Hosken, op. cit., p. 316.

37. Phillips's lawyers wrote on 29 March and Porter's on 19 April.

38. Magill, interview.

39. Roy Irwin, interview.

40. Jonathan Boyce, interview.

41. *Review of the Audit Commission, February–July 1995*, conducted by P. J. Butler, assisted by Bain & Company, paras 17 and 20.

42. Prince, interview.

43. Ibid.

44. Longdon, interview.

45. Derek Elliott, interview.

46. Ibid.

47. Lambeth BC 1993–94 Management Letter, 30 December 1994, para. 13.

48. Quoted in Derek Elliott, *Preventing Fraud and Corruption in the Public Sector*, Volume 1, *Changing Managerial Cultures*, MA dissertation, January 2000, p. 54.

49. Elliott, interview.

50. Rabbatts' statement to Lambeth Council, 1997, quoted in Elliott's MA dissertation, op. cit., p. 67.

51. Peter Yetzes, interview.

52. Doncaster MBC Public Interest Report, December 1997, para. 86.

53. Ibid., para. 51.

54. Ibid., para. 14.

55. Prince, interview.

56. Butler, interview.

CHAPTER 11 SETTING THE PACE, 1993–97

1. Minutes of the 3 March 1994 commissioners' meeting (held at Nicholson House in Bristol, as was the normal practice for one meeting each year).

2. Andrew Foster, interview.

3. Helena Shovelton, interview.

4. Ibid.

5. The 16th Denman Lecture, 17 February 1994.

6. Tony Travers, interview.

7. Harry Wilkinson, interview.

8. Travers, interview.

9. Jonty Boyce, interview.

10. Ibid.

11. Foster, interview.

12. Shovelton, interview.

13. Boyce, interview.

14. Ibid.

15. Foster, interview.

16. Boyce, interview.

17. Shovelton, interview.

18. Minutes of the 6 April 1995 commissioners' meeting, para. 28.

19. Greg Birdseye, interview.

20. Minutes of the 12 July 1995 commissioners' meeting, para. 23.

21. Edmonds, interview.

22. Annual Report and Accounts 1995, p. 38.

23. Minutes of the 5 September 1996 commissioners' meeting.

24. Minutes of the 5 December 1996 commissioners' meeting, para. 9.

25. Minutes of the 9 January 1997 commissioners' meeting, para. 33.

26. Education Act 1997, Section 41.

27. Foster, interview.

28. Roger Jarman, interview.

29. Ibid.

30. Kate Flannery, interview.

31. Ibid.

32. *Cheques and Balances*, p. 7.

33. *Streetwise*, pp. 14–15.

34. Flannery, interview.

35. *Streetwise*, para. 52.

36. Flannery, interview.

37. Ibid.

38. This account is based on the recollections of the members. The minutes of the 7 November 1996 commissioners' meeting oddly make no reference to the discussion at all. When the final version of the report had been introduced at the October monthly meeting, the members had anyway made their

backing for the report clear enough: 'Commissioners were concerned that the impact of the study should not be lessened, as failure to address this problem effectively would be extremely costly to society', Minutes of 3 October 1996, para. 9,

39. *Hansard*, 21 November 1996, column 1099.

CHAPTER 12 LIVING WITH NEW LABOUR, 1997–99

1. Minutes of the 7 March 1996 commissioners' meeting.
2. Andrew Foster, interview.
3. Minutes of the 5 October 1995 commissioners' meeting, para. 4.
4. Mike Barnes, interview.
5. *The Times*, 21 September 1995.
6. *Health Service Journal*, 2 and 23 May 1996.
7. Roger Brooke, interview.
8. Ibid.
9. Ibid.
10. Michael Power, *The Audit Explosion*, Demos, 1994. The paper was republished in 1996, and Power elaborated on his thesis in *The Audit Society: Rituals of Verification*, Oxford University Press, 1997.
11. *The Audit Explosion*, 1994, p. 30.
12. Christopher Hood, Colin Scott, Oliver James, George Jones and Tony Travers, *Regulation Inside Government – Waste-Watchers, Quality Police and Sleaze-Busters*, Oxford University Press, 1999, p. 104.
13. Avner Offer, *The Challenge of Affluence: Self-control and Well-being in the United States and Britain since 1950*, Oxford University Press, 2006, p. 98.
14. Hilary Armstrong, interview.
15. Mavis McDonald, interview.
16. Bob Chilton, interview.
17. Armstrong, interview.
18. *The Times*, 15 December 1997.
19. David Prince, interview.
20. Labour Party Manifesto, 1997.
21. Foster, interview.
22. Minutes of the 5 June 1997 commissioners' meeting.
23. Helena Shovelton, interview.
24. *Quinquennial Financial Management and Policy Review of the Audit Commission*, Part 1, July 1998, p. 60. Part II appeared in 2000.

25. Minutes of the 4 February 1999 commissioners' meeting, paras 18–21.
26. Peter Thomas, interview.
27. Peter Wilkinson, interview.
28. Ibid.
29. Christopher Hood et al., op. cit., p. 104.
30. Brooke, interview.
31. Adrienne Fresko, interview.
32. Shovelton, interview.
33. Ibid.
34. Geoffrey Rendle, diary.
35. Fresko, interview.
36. Shovelton, interview.
37. Jonty Boyce, interview.
38. Ibid.
39. Jeremy Orme, interview.
40. Minutes of the 4 March 1999 commissioners' meeting.
41. Minutes of the 15 April 1999 commissioners' meeting.
42. *Financial Times*, 20 July 1999, p. 9.
43. Commission Paper 99/56.
44. Commission Paper 99/72.
45. Commission Paper 99/64.
46. Prince, interview.
47. Commission Paper 99/62.
48. Prince, interview.
49. Orme, interview.
50. Shovelton, interview.
51. *The Times*, 8 May 1999, p. x.
52. *Hansard*, 10, 14, 18, 21 and 25 May 1999.
53. Commission Paper 99/52.
54. Ibid.
55. Minutes of the 3 June 1999 commissioners' meeting, para. 35.

CHAPTER 13 STUMBLING TO A BREAKTHROUGH, 1999–2001

1. Wendy Thomson, interview.
2. Ibid.
3. Peter Wilkinson, interview.
4. Peter Thomas, interview.

5. Roy Irwin, interview.

6. Commission Paper 99/90, para. 48.

7. *Review of the Audit Commission*, conducted by P. J. Butler, assisted by Bain & Company, para. 20.

8. Commission Paper 99/95, *The Future of the Best Value Inspection Service*.

9. *Best Assured*, para. 88.

10. *Seeing is Believing*, p. 1.

11. *Strategy for ACPIs*, Commission Paper 99/101.

12. Helena Shovelton, interview.

13. Commission Paper 2000/60.

14. Report of the Environment, Transport and Regions Select Committee, 22 June 2000, para. 48.

15. Commission Paper 2000/76, para. 100.

16. Ibid.

17. Paul Kirby, interview.

18. Gareth Davies, interview.

19. Jill Humphrey, *A Scientific Approach to Politics? On the Trail of the Audit Commission*, published in *Critical Perspectives on Accounting*, volume 13, Elsevier Science Ltd, 2002.

20. Shovelton, interview.

21. Ibid.

22. Commission Paper 2000/76.

23. Commission Paper 2000/19.

24. *Retiring Nature*, 1997, p. 5.

25. Greg Birdseye, interview.

26. Terry Hanafin, interview.

27. Ibid.

28. Thomas, interview.

29. Birdseye, interview.

30. Commission Paper 2000/60, para. 57.

31. Hanafin, interview.

32. Commission Paper 2000/32.

33. Letter to Andrew Foster, 30 September 1999, Commission Paper 99/90.

34. Commission Paper 99/72.

35. Commission Paper 2000/106.

36. Commission Paper 2001/25.

37. Ibid., para. 86.

38. Commission Paper 2001/68, para. 7.

39. Mavis McDonald, interview.

40. Michael Barber, *Instruction to Deliver – Tony Blair, Public Services and the Challenge of Achieving Targets*, Politico's Publishing, 2007, p. 128.

41. Ibid., p. 45.

42. Ibid., p. 143.

43. Nick Raynsford, interview.

44. Kirby, interview.

45. Ibid.

46. Commission Paper 2000/112, Appendix F.

47. Commission Paper 2000/1, para. 11.

48. Hanafin, interview.

49. Ruth Davison, interview.

50. Malcolm Dean, 'Regulation: going soft at the centre', *Guardian*, 20 June 2001.

51. *Guardian*, 22 August 2001.

52. Shovelton, interview and *Best Value Update*, Commission Paper 2001/87, Appendix 1.

53. Ibid., Appendix 2.

54. McDonald, interview.

55. Commission Paper 2000/69, para 4.1.

56. Thomas, interview.

57. *Changing Gear*, pp. 2–3 and paras. 77 and 123.

58. Minutes of the 4 October 2001 commissioners' meeting.

59. Commission Paper 2001/101, para. 9.

60. Kirby, interview.

61. *Strong Local Leadership – Quality Public Services*, CM 5237, December 2001, paras 3.16–3.23, 'Performance assessment'.

62. John Magill, interview.

63. Commission Paper 2001/95.

64. The figures for the Commission's spending were provided in a written parliamentary answer, *Hansard*, 16 November 2001.

65. Minutes of the 4 October 2001 commissioners' meeting.

66. Andrew Hosken, *Nothing Like a Dame: the Scandals of Shirley Porter*, Granta Books, 2006, p. 361.

67. On the financial settlement with Porter and how it was reached, see ibid., pp. 326–58.

68. For the story of the Labour councillors' objection and of a bitter dispute that sprang from it, see Paul Dimoldenberg, *The Westminster Whistleblowers*, Politico's Publishing, 2006.

69. *The Weekly Law Reports*, 25 January 2002, *Porter v. Magill*, pp. 37–9.

CHAPTER 14 A FRESH START, 2002–03

1. *LGC*, 15 March 2002, p. 11.
2. Ibid., p. 1.
3. Controller's Report, January 2002, para. 46.
4. Ruth Davison, interview.
5. Minutes of the 24 January 2002 commissioners' meeting.
6. Peter Thomas, interview.
7. Paul Kirby, interview.
8. Ibid.
9. Neil Kinghan, interview.
10. *LGC*, 15 February 2002, p. 11.
11. The pathfinders were Bolton MBC, Camden LBC, Havering LBC, Hertfordshire CC (where the chief executive was still the Commission's former finance director, Bill Ogley), Kent CC, Leeds City Council, Telford and Wrekin Council, Wiltshire CC, Wigan MBC, and Windsor and Maidenhead Council.
12. *Municipal Journal*, 15 February 2002.
13. Kirby, interview.
14. Quoted in Commission Paper 2001/81 – *The BRI Inquiry: Findings, Recommendations and Possible Implications*, p. 3.
15. Minutes of the 6 September 2001 commissioners' meeting, para. 9.
16. Commission Paper 2001/100 – *Comments by the Audit Commission on the BRI Inquiry*.
17. Department of Health Response to the Kennedy Report, quoted in the Controller's Report for February 2002, para. 71.
18. Minutes of the 7 March 2002 commissioners' meeting, para. 35.
19. *Guardian Society*, 24 April 2002.
20. Minutes of the 4 July 2002 commissioners' meeting.
21. Fresko to Alan Milburn, 9 July 2002, Fresko Papers.
22. Nick Raynsford, interview.
23. Andrew Foster, interview.
24. Ibid.
25. Minutes of the 4 July 2002 commissioners' meeting.
26. Kinghan, interview.
27. *Financial Times*, 9 January 2003.
28. Kinghan, interview.
29. Minutes of the 9 May 2002 commissioners' meeting.
30. Thomas, interview.

31. Kirby, interview.
32. Raynsford, interview.
33. Foster, interview.
34. Minutes of the 17 July 2003 commissioners' meeting, para. 8.
35. Ibid., para. 16.
36. Peter Wilkinson, interview.
37. Minutes of the 17 July 2003 commissioners' meeting, para. 9.
38. James Strachan to Edwina Hart, 10 January 2003.
39. Quoted in Simon Jenkins, *Thatcher & Sons: Revolution in Three Acts*, Penguin/Allen Lane, 2006, p. 317.
40. Quoted in the *Independent*, 10 January 2003, p. 8.
41. *Guardian*, 10 January 2003, p. 12.
42. Strachan, interview.
43. The Kennedy Report commented on the Commission's *Children First* report: 'The principles set down by the Audit Commission in 1993 strike us as robust and we endorse them ... Indeed, had the principles set out in the DoH's 1991 guidelines and the Audit Commission's report been implemented in Bristol, a good number of the shortcomings in care [at the BRI] would have been addressed much earlier.' Quoted in Commission Paper 2001/81.
44. Ian Kennedy, interview.
45. Interview on BBC News Online, 5 March 2003.
46. Michael Barber, *Instruction to Deliver – Tony Blair, Public Services and the Challenge of Achieving Targets*, Politico's Publishing, 2007, p. 131.
47. Strachan, interview; Foster, interview.

CHAPTER 15 LEADING THE WAY AGAIN, 2003–05

1. James Strachan, interview.
2. Ibid.
3. Mavis McDonald, interview.
4. Steve Bundred, interview.
5. Ibid.
6. Ibid.
7. Ibid.
8. Ibid.
9. Ibid.
10. *LGC*, April 1996.
11. Ibid., July 1996.

12. Ibid., October 1997.

13. Bundred, interview.

14. Martin Evans, interview.

15. Ibid.

16. Michael Dallas, interview.

17. Strachan, interview.

18. Ian Kennedy, interview.

19. Evans, interview.

20. Bundred, interview.

21. *Guardian*, 10 November 2003, p. 13.

22. Onora O'Neill, *A Question of Trust: the BBC Reith Lectures 2002*, Cambridge University Press, 2002.

23. Bundred, interview.

24. Strachan, interview.

25. *Council Tax Increases 2003–04*, paras 73–5.

26. Ibid., para. 34.

27. Bundred, interview.

28. Mike Barnes, interview.

29. *Promoting Choice in Public Services*, published by New Local Government Network, May 2004.

30. Commission Paper 46/04.

31. Minutes of the 11 February 2004 commissioners' meeting, para. 3.

32. Commission Paper 101/04.

33. Commission Paper 117/04.

34. Minutes of the 11 November 2004 commissioners' meeting, para. 9.

35. Minutes of the 11 February 2004 commissioners' meeting, para. 25.

36. Mollie Bickerstaff, interview.

37. Roy Irwin, interview.

38. Commission Paper 122/04.

39. Irwin, interview.

40. Minutes of the 9 September 2004 commissioners' meeting, para. 7.

41. Minutes of the 13 May 2004 commissioners' meeting, para. 17.

42. Minutes of the 11 February 2004 commissioners' meeting, para. 19.

43. *Refreshing Our Corporate Strategy: Health*, Appendix to Minutes for the 11 November 2004 commissioners' meeting.

44. Commission Paper 147/04, para. 5.

45. Commission Paper 117/04, para. 12.

46. Steve Bundred, *The Future of Regulation in the Public Sector*, March 2006, para. 29.

47. Michael Lyons, interview.

48. Ibid.
49. Ibid.
50. Commission Paper 137/04.
51. Roger Hamilton, interview.
52. Minutes of the 9 June 2005 commissioners' meeting, para. 8.
53. Minutes of the 17 November 2005 commissioners' meeting, para. 3.
54. Minutes of the 10 March 2005 commissioners' meeting; Commission Paper 26/05.
55. Minutes of the 13 January 2005 commissioners' meeting, paras. 3–4.
56. Bundred, interview.
57. *Taking Stock and Moving Forward*, Commission Paper 111/04.
58. Commission Paper 129/04.

CHAPTER 16 AN EVEN KEEL, 2006–08

1. Michael Lyons, interview.
2. Minutes of the 14 July 2005 commissioners' meeting, para. 27.
3. Peter Wilkinson, interview.
4. James Strachan, interview.
5. Michael O'Higgins, interview.
6. Minutes of the 2 March 1995 commissioners' meeting, para. 9.
7. Minutes of the 24–25 January 2006 commissioners' away-day conference, para. 9.
8. *Employees' Opinion Survey*, May 2007, Executive Summary.
9. Minutes of the 22 March 2007 commissioners' meeting, para. 3(d).
10. Wilkinson, interview.
11. The new arrivals were Sheila Drew Smith (June 2004), Thomas Legg and Jim Coulter (both in April 2005), Chris White (June 2005), Tim Parker (January 2006) and Steve Houghton (June 2006). The departures, in addition to James Strachan, were Graham Hart and Elizabeth Filkin (both in April 2004), Gerard Lemos and Rosalind Scott (both in November 2004), John Bowen (April 2005), Roger Hoyle (June 2005), Pauleen Lane (April 2006), Michael Lyons (September 2006), Tim Parker (October 2006) and David Moss (March 2007).
12. Peter Smith, interview.
13. Chris White, interview.
14. Minutes of the 9 March 2006 commissioners' meeting.
15. Minutes of the 20 July 2006 commissioners' meeting, para. 67.
16. *Strong and Prosperous Communities*, para. 6.7.

17. Minutes of the 26 October 2006 commissioners' meeting, para. 3(h).

18. Minutes of the 1 February 2007 commissioners' meeting, para. 31.

19. Michael Heseltine, interview.

20. Ross Tristem, interview.

21. Ian Kennedy, interview.

22. Mavis McDonald, interview.

23. Steve Bundred, *The Future of Regulation in the Public Sector*, March 2006, paras 21–2.

24. Minutes of the 26 October 2006 commissioners' meeting, para. 31.

25. Simon Jenkins, *Thatcher & Sons: Revolution in Three Acts*, Penguin/Allen Lane, 2006, p.321.

26. The final report was preceded by two earlier publications. His *Interim Report and Consultation Paper* was published in December 2005 and concentrated on the financial dimensions of his brief. A second paper, published in May 2006, was titled *National Prosperity, Local Choice and Civic Engagement: a New Partnership between Central and Local Government for the 21st Century*.

27. *Lyons Inquiry into Local Government*, para. 64.

28. *Strategic Plan 2006*, para. 22.

29. Speech entitled 'Modern Regulation' at the CIPFA annual conference, 14 June 2007.

30. *Prosperous Communities – Beyond the White Paper*, November 2006, and *Prosperous Communities II, Vive la Dévolution!*, February 2007.

31. Sandy Bruce-Lockhart, interview.

32. Jeremy Beecham, interview.

33. *Cities Renaissance: Creating Local Leadership*, para. 4.

34. Cameron's conference speech on 3 October 2007 included this passage: 'I believe it's time in our big cities for elected mayors, so people have one person to blame if it goes wrong and to praise if it goes right . . . I think it's time with local government to tear up rules and all the ring-fencing and the auditing and actually say to our local councils: "It's your money, spend it as you choose and get judged in the ballot box by people that you serve." ' The speech was unscripted, and what Cameron meant by his reference to auditing was none too precise – but the general drift of his remarks was clear enough.

Index of Audit Commission Publications

Listed alphabetically within categories. See Appendix 1 for chronological lists.

General Index

heightened role in 1996–9 420, 547

and predicament over Best Value 434, 436, 453–4, 468, 473, 490, 493–4

review of structure and strategy 449–53

reappointed for third term 440, 449

and Helena Shovelton 440–41, 477–8, 487, 498

and Wendy Thomson 456–7, 464–5, 477–8, 487, 490–91

ascendancy and workload 481–2

knighted 490

and success of *Changing Gear* 502–4

and punishing media routine 513–15

and CPA 2002 519

and setback on health 521–5, 541, 549

and 'Organizational Development' review 531, 533–5, 542

relations with James Strachan 538–9, 541–3, 552

retirement from AC 498, 510, 535, 544

Foster, Christopher 18, 44, 167, 208, 226–7, 271

Foster, John 374, 396, 418, 480

foundation hospital trusts *see* NHS

fraud-prevention work by AC 356–64 *passim*

Fraud Review 620

French, J. 199

Fresko, Adrienne 439, 445, 451, 480, 538, 540

 as deputy chairman 480, 502, 509–11, 521–8 *passim*, 531–3, plate 24

Froggatt, Clive 260, 260*n*

Future of Regulation in the Public Sector, The 622–3, 628

Gaughan, John 115

gender bias

 in local government 185

 in the DAS 318–19

 absent from AC 480

general elections

 of 1983 79

 of 1987 172, 209, 250

 of 1992 298, 301, 425

 of 1997 388, 410, 421, 425, 542

 of 2001 490, 492, 626

 of 2005 524, 594, 597, 599

General Medical Council 272

George, Eddie 197

Gershon Review 596

Gifford, Joan 318–19

Goldman Sachs 188–9, 203

Good Conduct and Counter Fraud Network 358

Goring Hotel dinners 482

Gould, Bryan 287–8

GP fundholders 387–8, 422

Grace, Clive 534, 596

grant claims 331. 349–50, 570, 628

Greater London Authority 437, 452, 493

Greater London Council (GLC) 95–6, 101–3, 127, 462, 558

Green, Gill 466

Greenwich Borough Council 105, 107, 175, 184, 309–10

Greenwich conference on NHS audit work 586

Grey, Jenny 610–11

Griffiths, Brian 228, 233–4

Griffiths, Roy 182, 251–2, 258, 260, 273

Special Studies directorate – *cont.*
  use of external advisers 220, 225, 279
  divided, reunited and abolished 268, 451, 543–4
  conspicuous by its absence 572–5, 603–4
  restored as PRS in 2006 603–5
Spencer Stuart 46–7, 306, 309, 311
Sprigg, Jack 64
staff recruitment by AC 16
  via personal contacts 53–4, 64, 79, 269–70, 270n, 381–2, 410–11
  via formal hiring process 293, 296, 451–2, 466–7, 497
staff surveys
  within DAS/DA 325–6
  within AC 448, 489, 562, 598, 611–12
Standards Board for England 472, 563
Stanford, Les 162, 262, 319
Statswomped District Council 308
Stewart, Dave 610
Stowe, Kenneth 147
Strachan, James 14, 536–53 *passim*
  background and appointment 536–8, plate 26
  espousal of 'strategic regulation' 537, 545–6, 568–9, 587, 626
  and governance of AC 538–40, 542–3
  as public face of AC 540–41, 546, 596, 610
  and special studies 543–4
  and AC's NHS remit 548–52, 614–15
  row over waiting lists 551–2, 554
  parallel with early Banham years 552–3

  repositioning AC's role 554–6, 572, 576, 608
  working partnership with Steve Bundred 556–7, 559–61, 595, 597–8
  challenges to AC culture 539–40, 542, 562, 564–6
  relations with NAO 596–7
  personal style 537, 554, 597, 622
  unexpected departure 599–601
  strategy/marketing papers *see Index of AC Publications*
Straw, Jack 287, 347, 410, 414–15, 463, 510
Stuart, Murray 136, 207, 270n, 305, 309, 370, 373, 392
Suffolk County Council 535
Sunday Times 119, 606–7
surcharge
  origins and impact 24, 40–41, 102
  on Lambeth and Liverpool councillors 106
  averted, for non-compliance councils 110–11
  on Westminster CC members and officers 346–7, 349, 505–6
  abolished 368, 459
Surrey County Council 480
Sutton, Gordon 366
swaps crisis *see* Hammersmith and Fulham swaps crisis
Swinson, Chris 480, 510, 540

Tarry, Iris 373, 479
Tench, John 327
ten-day rule at AC 138
tenth anniversary conference of AC 313
Thatcher, Margaret 89, 241–2, 250n, 344